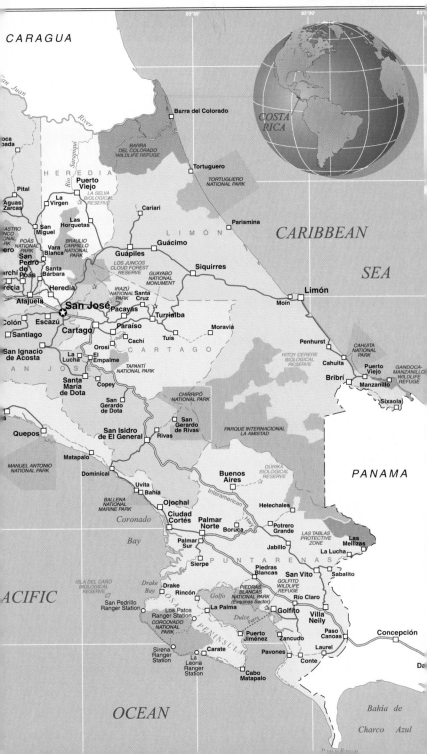

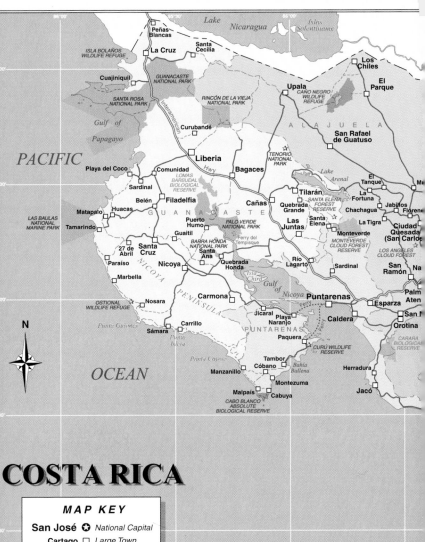

PACIFIC

Lake Nicaragua

Islas Solentiname

Peñas Blancas
Santa Cecilia
La Cruz

ISLA BOLAÑOS WILDLIFE REFUGE

Los Chiles
El Parque

Cuajiniquil

GUANACASTE NATIONAL PARK

SANTA ROSA NATIONAL PARK

Upala
CAÑO NEGRO WILDLIFE REFUGE

Gulf of Papagayo

RINCÓN DE LA VIEJA NATIONAL PARK

A L A J U E L A

San Rafael de Guatuso

Curubandé

Playa del Coco

Liberia

TENORIO NATIONAL PARK

Lake Arenal

El Tanque
Me

Comunidad
Bagaces

LOMAS BARBUDAL BIOLOGICAL RESERVE

Tilarán

SANTA ELENA FOREST RESERVE

La Fortuna

Sardinal

Belén
Filadelfia

Hwy

Cañas

Quebrada Grande
Santa Elena

Chachagua
Jabillos
Florencia

La Tigra

Matapalo
Huacas

Puerto Humo

Las Juntas

Monteverde

Ciudad Quesada (San Carlos)

LAS BAULAS NATIONAL MARINE PARK

Tamarindo

PALO VERDE NATIONAL PARK

MONTEVERDE CLOUD FOREST RESERVE

LOS ÁNGELES CLOUD FOREST

Guaitíl

BARRA HONDA NATIONAL PARK

Ferry del Tempisque

27 de Abril

Santa Cruz

Santa Ana

Río Lagarto
Sardinal

San Ramón
Na

Paraíso

Nicoya
Quebrada Honda

Isla Chira

Gulf of Nicoya

Palm Aten

Marbella

P E N I N S U L A

Carmona

Puntarenas

Esparza

San

OSTIONAL WILDLIFE REFUGE

Nosara

Jicaral
Playa Naranjo

Caldera

Orotina

N

Punta Guiones

Carrillo

P U N T A R E N A S

CARARA BIOLOGICAL RESERVE

Sámara

Punta Islita

Paquera

CURU WILDLIFE RESERVE

OCEAN

Punta Coyote

Tambor
Cóbano

Bahía Ballena

Herradura

Manzanillo

Montezuma

Jacó

Malpaís
Cabuya

CABO BLANCO ABSOLUTE BIOLOGICAL RESERVE

COSTA RICA

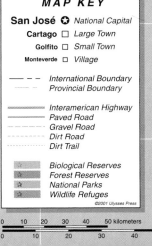

MAP KEY

San José ✪	*National Capital*
Cartago □	*Large Town*
Golfito □	*Small Town*
Monteverde □	*Village*

— — — *International Boundary*
— · — · *Provincial Boundary*

▨▨▨▨ *Interamerican Highway*
———— *Paved Road*
———— *Gravel Road*
- - - - *Dirt Road*
········· *Dirt Trail*

✫ *Biological Reserves*
✫ *Forest Reserves*
✫ *National Parks*
✫ *Wildlife Refuges*

©2001 Ulysses Press

0 10 20 30 40 50 kilometers
0 10 20 30 40 50 miles

ISLA DEL COCO

PACIFIC

Bahía Chatham

Bahía Wafer

ISLA DEL COCO NATIONAL PARK

OCEAN

Bahía Yglesias

0 1 2 3 kilometers
0 1 2 3 miles

THE NEW KEY
TO COSTA RICA

THE NEW KEY TO COSTA RICA

Fifteenth Edition

BEATRICE BLAKE
ANNE BECHER

DEIDRE HYDE
Illustrator

NIK WHEELER
Photographer

Ulysses Press

Published by: Ulysses Press
           3286 Adeline Street, Suite 1
           Berkeley, CA 94703
           www.ulyssespress.com

ISSN 1098-7398
ISBN 1-56975-219-2

Printed in Canada by Transcontinental Printing

20 19 18 17 16 15 14 13 12 11 10

Publishers: Ray Riegert, Leslie Henriques
Managing Editor: Claire Chun
Project Director: Lynette Ubois
Copy Editor: Steven Zah Schwartz
Editorial Associates: Marin Van Young, Lily Chou, Ryan Gowland, Melissa Millar
Typesetters: Lisa Kester, Lindsay Mugglestone, David Wells
Interior maps: XNR Productions
Color maps: Stellar Cartography
Indexer: Sayre Van Young
Cover photography:
    Front: Kevin Shafer (Monkeys)
    Back: Kevin Shafer (Corcovado National Park)
    Back: Markham Johnson (Horseback riding)

Illustrations on pages 84 and 85 by Anabel Maffioli
"Fishing" section in Chapter Five written by Jerry Ruhlow
"Notes for Gay and Lesbian Travelers" and "Gay Nightlife" sections written by John Brown
Part of Chapter Two was compiled by Sorrel Downer and J. Patrick O'Marr, and originally published by *Costa Rica Today*

Distributed in the United States by Publishers Group West, in Canada by Raincoast Books, and in Great Britain and Europe by World Leisure Marketing

For peace with justice in harmony with nature

Table of Contents

Maps

Acknowledgments

During my travels to update this edition of *The New Key to Costa Rica*, I was pleased to meet so many people involved in tourism who were also committed to the environment. That was not always the case. Foreigners who had tourism projects often carved out their little pieces of paradise, not really taking note of the people or the environmental struggles around them. Ticos who had tourism projects were often so intent on trying to please tourists that they lost sight of their own culture and values and were embarrassed by the simplicity of their surroundings. This has changed, as a new generation of inspired foreign and local business owners have taken up the challenge of making the environment a major priority of tourism. I salute their dedication in the midst of frustrating bureaucracy and heartbreaking environmental defeats, such as the government's refusal to ban logging in the Osa Peninsula.

I was very lucky on this trip to have wonderful companions who made my travels a lot of fun. Old friends Barry Biesanz and Sarah Blanchet took me on a jaunt through the Northern Zone. I learned a lot from their fascination with trees and seeds, and was amazed at how harmoniously they worked as a team to change several flat tires (and let me type in the shade while they were sweating in the dust!). Don Hernan Barquero Zamora of the Instituto Costarricense de Turismo took me through the Central Valley, Guanacaste, the Nicoya Peninsula, and Talamanca. I cannot appreciate enough his patience, good humor, dedication to service and the little prayers he would say each time we set out on a new leg of our journey. I am also grateful to his wife, Doña Coca, for packing with an eye to absolutely every possible eventuality, so that there was never a situation in which Don Hernan could not pull whatever we needed from the back of the car (electric teapot, tortilla warmer, oranges from their farm, rope, tiny can opener. . . . Many thanks to Pedro Melendez and Emilia Gonzales of the ICT for arranging my trips with Don Hernan. During my trip to the Southern Zone, I was accompanied by Walter Odio of Selvamar Tours in San Isidro, who never once got stuck on roads so rutted and muddy that his Toyota jeep would tilt and sway like a boat on the high seas. Besides his Olympian driving skill, Don Walter is a witty and knowledgeable teacher and community leader whose personal experience with local environmental struggles was inspiring to me and to others we met along the way. He even tried to improve my vocabulary of *dicharachos* (slang)!

Many other wonderful people assisted me in the information-gathering process, including Phillip, Marilyn, and Simon Edwardes of Club de Mar, Regis Fillon of Zuma Rentacar, and Zach McDuffie of Escuela del Mundo in Playa Jaco; Jennifer Rice of El Mono Azul in Manuel Antonio and Ana and Richard Sutton of Quepolandia in Quepos; Eugenio Gonzalez of the OET in Palo Verde; the Montealto Community in Hojancha; Richard Moffatt of Casa Tucán in Nosara; the Roots of Hotel Fenix-on-the-Beach in Sámara; the Iaconos of El Sano Banano in Montezuma; and Luis Mena of ASEPALECO.

In the Southern Zone, Noel Ureña, who leads Selvamar's tours up Mount Chirripó, helped greatly with his knowledge of current conditions there. Thanks also go to the Dúrika Community; to Sierra, Shawn, Vanessa, Star, and Jerry of Delfín Amor in Drake Bay; to Nancy Aitken and her volunteers at Proyecto Campanario; to the folks at the Zancudo Beach Club; and to Andrew and Susan Robertson of Zancudo Tours.

Dale Dagger of Surf Nicaragua and Donna Tabor of Another Night in Paradise in Granada helped with the Nicaragua update, and I also learned a lot from Heather Guidi of La Veranda in Bocas del Toro, Panama. Haymo Heyder of the Arco Iris in Santa Elena and Lynne Rosselli of the Monteverde Reserve helped with the Monteverde section. Leona Wellington of Rancho Leona helped me update the Sarapiquí region, and Modesto and Fran Watson helped with Tortuguero. I am also grateful to Max and Sylvia of Samasati Nature Retreat, and to Mel Baker of ATEC in Puerto Viejo de Talamanca.

Gary Benton and Kate Unkel made many phone calls and did internet research, respectively, for which I am very grateful.

I really value letters from readers with feedback from their own experiences. Thanks to the following people whose responses contributed to this edition: Kevin Beck, Barbara Best, Sonia and Kevin Connors, W. R. Fahey,

Emily Fintel, Anne Galbreath Fisher, Edwin S. Friendly, Terry Gardner, Hazel Georgetti, Pete Harwood, Lara Jacobson, Gail Leonard, Travis Lloyd, Catherine Mingo, Mr. and Mrs. William E. Mullins, Dan Stendahl, Dr. John W. Travis, Maya Van Putten, and Ben J. White.

I also want to give heartfelt thanks to Celina, Mac, Raquel, and Alex of the Fundación CEPPA in San José, who helped me in innumerable ways when I really needed it; to Robert Lee and Robert Wells for their continuing friendship, laughter and sharing of their talents; to John, Marc, Jorge, Isaias, and Mr. Grey of Seventh Street Books and Zona Tropical for getting me out of a pinch; and to Deedee Hyde for yet another memorable evening in her plant-filled patio. Thanks too to Alexis Fournier of Hotel Le Bergerac for stimulating conversation over wine and excellent French cuisine.

Thanks to my family: Dennis, Danny, Elizabeth, and Bootsie for accepting my absences and being there for me during the arduous process of putting together another edition. Group hug! And thanks to all my focusing partners in Boston for helping me gain insight into the process.

Even though Anne Becher was not involved in this edition, her words, spirit, and values still pervade the book, and we wish her well in her busy life as mother, professor, and freelance writer.

Thanks to Jerry Ruhlow for authoring the "Fishing" section. We have cited information from the following sources throughout the book: Richard Garrigues' "Nature's Way" columns in *Costa Rica Today*; Daniel Jantzen's *Costa Rican Natural History*; Don Moser's *Central American Jungles*; Don Perry's *Life Above the Jungle Floor*; Skutch and Stiles' *A Guide to the Birds of Costa Rica*; and "Tis the Season: Olive Ridley Turtle Nesting is in Full Swing," David Norman, *The Tico Times*, September 22, 1995.

Thanks to the Ulysses Press staff for their patience, for their skill and eye for detail, and for their ability to pound out yet another edition of the manuscript into a user-friendly guide: Ray Riegert, Leslie Henriques, Claire Chun, Bryce Willett, Lily Chou, Steven Schwartz, Marin Van Young, and Lynette Ubois.

Beatrice Blake
October 2000

Costa Rica: Disarmed Democracy

Costa Rica once produced more bananas than any other country in the world, but it is far from being a "banana republic." Armyless, democratic, conservation-minded—people in many other developing countries are fighting for what Costa Rica has had for years. How did this come about?

Costa Rica acted progressively long before it became the general trend. The establishment of free, obligatory tax-financed education in the constitution of 1869, the elimination of the death penalty in 1882, and the abolition of the army in 1948 all testify to Costa Rica's unique character and vision, and all helped lay the groundwork for the present social order.

Historically, Costa Rica has almost always remained aloof from the conflicts that have shaken her sister republics. John L. Stephens, a North American archaeologist who visited in 1840, mentioned even then that Costa Rica was an island of tranquility compared to the rest of Central America. Although the national character tends to ignore or imagine itself above the problems of its neighbors, former president Oscar Arias (1986–1990) took a decisive and responsible role in waging peace, especially where Nicaragua was concerned. His unflagging efforts to bring warring parties to the conference table won him the 1987 Nobel Peace Prize. At the same time, many Costa Ricans resented his concentration on international issues and wished he would pay more attention to the economic problems at home.

Costa Rican family trees show that 75 percent of the leading figures in her history were descended from only four *conquistadores* and, of course, their indigenous consorts. The native people of Costa Rica were never completely dominated by the Spanish colonizers, so the class divisions that exist to this day in other Latin American countries did not develop to the same degree here. The few indigenous groups not decimated by war and disease moved away to isolated mountain regions, where they still live. Costa Rica's poverty and isolation led colonial families to fend for themselves, resulting in the establishment of more egalitarian values than in other Latin American countries.

When it was discovered in the 1830s that coffee grew well in the highlands of Central America and fetched a high price in European markets, the powerful elites of most of the newly independent nations on the isthmus forced *campesinos* off the land in order to create large coffee plantations. Not so in Costa Rica. Small farmers were encouraged to grow coffee and sell the beans to central *beneficios* or processing plants owned by wealthier farmers, who would prepare the beans for export. Thus rich and poor participated together in the coffee-growing process, each small farmer caring for his bushes in a personal way. (Coffee plants demand a lot of attention, and Costa Rican coffee has always been known as one of the finest on the international market.) The *beneficio* policy gave stability and importance to the small farmer, and allowed him to grow subsistence crops for his family.

The development of the educational and electoral systems during the late 1800s provided the basis for a participatory democracy. By the end of the 19th century, political violence was on the decline and the budget of the police force exceeded that of the army. When the victorious forces of the 1948 civil war decided to constitutionally abolish the army, a *de facto* situation that had been evolving since the beginning of the century was legally ratified.

Costa Ricans, by nature, seek to avoid conflict, so being armyless fits in with the national character. Abolishing the army has had several functions: it inhibits the formation of a military group capable of gaining autonomy; it frees public funds for development; it makes elections the only route to power; it establishes Costa Rica's neutrality in the region—a militarily weak country cannot be attacked without provoking international condemnation of the aggressor; and it shows the illegitimacy of armed opposition toward a state that has renounced the use of force.

The pragmatic thinkers who brought about the abolition of the army recognized the United States as the dominant superpower of the region, and as their ally and friend. Implied in the army's abolishment is the belief that the U.S. would come to Costa Rica's rescue if it were attacked. During the years of Sandinista arms build-up in Nicaragua, many Costa Ricans longed for the United States to invade and put an end to that regime. Then-president Arias faced as much internal opposition to his peace plan as he did external. In fact, it was not until he won the Nobel Prize that his critics started to let up a bit. Similarly, the vast majority of Costa Ricans lauded the U.S. invasion of Panama. Disarmament does not necessarily imply pacifism.

Costa Ricans view the military as an encumbrance to their political and social life as well as to the public budget. They prefer to channel their national resources into health and education. Because of their nationalized medical and social security systems, Costa Rican health care is on par with that of industrialized nations. And, in an attempt to ensure the well-being of future generations, 26 percent of Costa Rica's territory is legally set aside for national parks, biological reserves, forest reserves and buffer zones, wildlife refuges, and Indian reserves. Having enough money to patrol and protect these areas is another story.

Even without an army, finding the money to pursue goals of social justice and ecological balance has become well-nigh impossible for Costa Rica as she fights an uphill battle against her tremendous deficit. The International Monetary Fund demands austerity from a government whose bureaucracy employs seven percent of the workforce. The largest chunk of the country's budget—almost one-third—goes to service the same foreign debt!

Costa Rican currency has suffered regular devaluations over the last two decades. The annual per capita income is only $6,650, and the gap between rich and poor is growing. The richest 20% of the population earns 12.6 times more than the poorest 20%.

Despite all this, Ticos, rich and poor, actively support their democracy. On election day they honk horns, wave party flags, dress up in party colors, and proudly display their index fingers dipped in purple indelible ink to show they have voted. Usually 90 percent of the electorate turns out to vote, as compared to 20 to 50 percent in the United States. Voters in the February 1998 presidential election were called "apathetic" because only 70 percent showed up at the polls. This was cause for concern because the margin of victory of Unidad Nacional over Liberación was only 1.5 percent, less than 6000 votes!

Even with the enthusiasm that turns their election day into a national fiesta, Costa Ricans are skeptical about politics and politicians. Their roots are still in the soil and in the unity of their families. Babies are the acknowledged rulers of the household. Mother's Day is one of the biggest national holidays. Foreigners complain that it is hard to make deep friendships here because family ties are so strong. The united family that made it possible for early poverty-stricken farmers to survive is perhaps still the real basis of Costa Rican stability.

At the same time, women are a solid 50 percent of the workforce, and are rapidly increasing their numbers in such traditionally male-dominated fields as medicine, law, and government service. Both of the Vice Presidents of Costa Rica are women—Elizabeth Odio and Astrid Fischel—and a high percentage of women hold cabinet posts. A major contender in the 1994 presidential election primary was former First Lady Margarita Penón.

Costa Ricans' love for the beauty and freedom of their country is almost palpable. At 6 p.m. each September 14, the eve of their Independence Day, everyone drops what they are doing to sing the national anthem. In corner stores and homes across the country, everyone joins in. It's a rousing hymn in tribute to peace, hard work, and the generosity of the earth, but it's also a warning that if these things are threatened, Costa Ricans will "convert their rough farming tools into arms," as they did when William Walker tried to invade in the 19th century.

Now Costa Rica faces another kind of invasion. The increasing popularity of "eco-tourism" has opened the country to a huge influx of visitors, attracted by her incredible ecological diversity. Convinced that the "clean industry" of tourism will be a source of much-needed foreign exchange, the government has offered incentives for large tourism projects that provide hotel rooms to keep up with the demand. No one is listening to the *campesinos* who still have not been paid for their land, which was made part of a biological reserve, or to the dairy workers who cannot afford to buy more pasture for their animals because the price of land has gone up due to foreign and local speculation, or to the coastal dwellers who suddenly find there's no room on the bus to town because it's filled with surfboards. A more serious threat is the kind of tourist development that regards local people merely as a pool of potential maids, waiters, gardeners, laundresses, and nothing more. The traditional values of the small independent farmers who are the backbone of Costa Rican democracy could be lost in the process.

On the other hand, most Costa Ricans are proud to share the beauty of their land with visitors and know how to make foreigners feel at home. Some programs are trying to incorporate native skills into tourism and ecology: young men who were raised hunting turtles have been trained to help visitors understand the ancient ritual of turtle nesting; sharp-eyed *campesinos* are learning to be taxonomists in the national parks; men and women from the dry Guanacaste region are reviving the ancient pottery-making techniques of their ancestors; indigenous women from Talamanca have written a book to explain their beliefs about conserving the forest and its wildlife.

Even though the *campesino* and the ox cart are powerful symbols in Costa Rican life, over half the population of the country now lives in urban areas. Cramped housing developments cover the fertile soil of the Central Valley. As happens everywhere, the city dwellers quickly forget their roots. Hopefully, visitors like you will take time to meet Costa Rica's rural inhabitants and learn to value their knowledge, cultures, and lifestyles, as well as support the small businesses they have created.

Beatrice Blake
October 2000

Sustainable Eco-tourism Rating

The New Key to Costa Rica has been developing its Sustainable Eco-tourism Rating for the last ten years. With it, we aim to give special recognition to nature lodges that actively protect the environment, and foster rural economies and culture. Our rating has gone through many changes since it first appeared in our 1992 edition. From 1993–1996 we tried to make the survey as "scientific" as possible. Ing. Elias Rosales and Ing. Liliana Abarca from the Instituto Tecnológico de Costa Rica helped us understand sewage and garbage treatment, respectively. Experienced hotel owners Amos Bien and Michael Kaye, and tourism researcher Ana Baez looked over our questions with a magnifying glass and pointed out important omissions. The creation of the survey was the source material for Jane Segleau Earle's master's thesis at the Latin American University of Science and Technology (ULACIT). Her committee (Professors José Carlos Chinchilla, Emilio Vargas, and Carlos Quesada) also offered invaluable comments. Deans of the Tourism School at ULACIT, Sebastian Salazar, Mercedes Corrales, and Eduardo Leitón also lent their expertise.

In April 1996, we were invited to a conference at the Yale University School of Forestry and the Environment titled "Eco-tourism, Measuring the Impacts." During a talk in which we were explaining our methodology and what we felt were the positive effects of the rating, a representative of the Costa Rican Tourism Board (ICT) stood up and announced that the government of Costa Rica was going to be the first government in the world to rate the sustainability of its tourism industry. The ICT's Certification of Sustainable Tourism is now up and running. The program has been adopted by the World Tourism Organization's Sustainable Tourism Commission as the standard to be implemented by nations worldwide. To learn more, see their website at www.turismo-sostenible.co.cr.

The 150-question ICT survey is much more "scientific" than we ever could have been. But the Tourism Board differs from our rating system in that they lump city, suburban and wilderness lodges together. A large suburban hotel like the Marriott gains points by recycling and using local products, which balances out its overuse of electricity and water. It is ranked at the same level as one of Costa Rica's pioneer wilderness eco-tourism projects, Rara Avis. Travelers who expect that the ICT rating will lead them to responsible eco-tourism businesses will be grossly misled.

In contrast, here are the latest criteria for the *New Key to Costa Rica* Sustainable Tourism Rating.

1.   We support lodgings that offer a true experience of nature.

2.   We support lodgings that strive to use sustainable practices in their construction, operations and waste disposal systems.

3.   We support lodgings that are actively involved in protecting the natural wonders that attract tourists to them.

4.   We support lodgings that benefit local communities.

5.   We support lodgings that do all of the above and are also warm, attractive places where we ourselves would like to spend our vacations.

While most of the lodgings we mention in the book are not on our sustainability list, there are quite a few places that we deliberately do not mention at all. This is either because we have gotten complaints from readers about them, have had negative impressions of them ourselves, or find them just too boring and commercial to draw attention to. We also do not mention any hotels owned by the Spanish hotel chain Barceló, which has been fined several times by the Costa Rican Environmental Crimes Court and continues to buy up other hotels and build megaprojects.

The hotels on our sustainable tourism list are marked with a ✪ in the book, and are listed below. They were inspirational to visit; their owners are all engaged in creative, heart-felt work. The lodgings vary in levels of comfort and luxury, as well as price, but all are carefully designed places run by people who care about the effect they are having on the environment and their neighbors.

As a last note, we want to appeal to you, as travelers, to help us in the difficult task of evaluating hotels for their sustainability. Many of the hotels that didn't make it onto our list were too new to have ironed out the wrinkles, or were just learning about better practices. At the end of this book is a form for you to send us your comments and observations. You can also e-mail us at info@keytocostarica.com. Your input about what you see and hear during your visit will help us continue to improve our sustainable eco-tourism rating.

CENTRAL VALLEY

ATLANTIC COAST

NORTHERN ZONE

GUANACASTE

Palo Verde: Rancho Humo *(page 316)*
Playa del Coco: Rancho Armadillo Estate *(page 322)*
Hojancha: Monte Alto Forest Reserve *(pages 343–44)*
Nosara: Lagarta Lodge *(page 348)*
Rincón de la Vieja National Park: Santa María Volcano Lodge *(pages 360–61)*

CENTRAL PACIFIC ZONE

Montezuma: The Nature Lodge Finca Los Caballos *(page 388)*; Hotel La Aurora *(page 389)*; El Sano Banano *(page 389)*
Quepos: Hotel Rancho Casa Grande *(pages 414–15)*
Manuel Antonio: Hotel Plinio *(page 418);* Si Como No *(page 422)*
Cerro de la Muerte: Albergue Mirador de Quetzales *(page 428)*

SOUTHERN ZONE

San Gerardo de Dota: Albergue de Montaña Río Savegre *(page 430)*
San Isidro de El General: Albergue de Montaña Talari *(page 433)*
Chirripó National Park: Posada del Descanso *(pages 434–35)*
Dominical: Hacienda Barú National Wildlife Refuge *(page 441)*; Bella Vista Lodge *(page 444)*; Pacific Edge *(page 445)*
Ballena National Marine Park: Rancho La Merced *(page 446)*
Drake Bay: La Paloma Lodge *(page 452)*; Cocalito Lodge *(pages 452–53)*; Delfin Amor Eco-Lodge *(page 453)*; Punta Marenco Lodge *(page 453)*; Poor Man's Paradise *(page 454)*; Proyecto Campanario *(page 454)*; Casa Corcovado *(pages 454–55)*; Cabinas Jade Mar *(page 455)*; Mirador Lodge *(page 455)*; Río Sierpe Lodge *(page 456)*
Osa Peninsula: Playa PreciOsa Nature Lodge *(page 461)*; Lapa Ríos *(page 462)*; Bosque del Cabo *(pages 462–63)*; El Remanso *(page 463)*; Corcovado Lodge and Tent Camp *(pages 463–64)*; Bosque del Río Tigre Sanctuary and Lodge *(page 464)*; Coope Unioro *(page 470)*
Piedras Blancas National Park–Esquinas Sector: Esquinas Rainforest Lodge *(page 474)*
Golfe Dulce: Golfe Dulce Lodge *(page 475)*; Caña Blanca *(page 476)*
Pavones: Cabinas La Ponderosa *(page 480)*; Tiskita Lodge *(page 480)*
San Vito: Las Cruces Biological Station and Wilson Botanical Gardens *(pages 481–82)*
Parque Internacional La Amistad: Albergue Monte Amuo *(page 484)*; Dúrika Biological Reserve *(pages 484–85)*

ONE

Costa Rica: A Brief History

To understand the unique character of the Costa Rican people today, it helps to know something of their history. Over the centuries, Costa Rica has taken some decidedly different turns from her Central American sister states.

PRE-COLUMBIAN COSTA RICA

The largest and most developed pre-Columbian population in Costa Rica was that of the Chorotegas, whose ancestors had migrated from Southern Mexico to the Nicoya Peninsula, probably in the 13th century. They were running away from enemies who wanted to enslave them—their name translates as "fleeing people."

Much of the information we have about the Chorotegas was collected by Gonzalo Fernández de Oviedo, a Spanish explorer who lived with them for a short period in 1529.

Outstanding farmers, the Chorotegas managed three harvests of corn per year. They also grew cotton, beans, fruits, and cacao, which they introduced to Costa Rica and whose seeds they used as currency. Land was communally owned and the harvest was divided according to need, so that old people and widows with children could be cared for.

The Chorotegas lived in cities of as many as 20,000 people, which had central plazas with a marketplace and a religious center. Only women could enter the market. Women wore skirts, the length of which depended upon their social level. Men could go naked, but often wore a large cloth or a woven and dyed sleeveless cotton shirt.

Women worked in ceramics, producing vessels painted in black and red, decorated with plumed serpents (the symbol for unity of matter and spirit), jaguars, monkeys, and crocodiles. They carved stylized jade figures in human and animal shapes. The figures may have been used in fertility ceremonies or to bring good luck in the hunt. They wrote books on deerskin parchment and used a ritual calendar.

War was institutionalized. A permanent military organization fought to obtain land and slaves, who were used as human sacrifices. Eating someone who had been sacrificed to the gods was a purification rite. The Chorotegas also sacrificed virgins by throwing them into volcano craters.

The Chibcha people from Colombia migrated to the South Pacific region of Costa Rica, where they lived in permanent, well-fortified towns. Their concern with security could have arisen from their possession of gold—which they fashioned into human and animal figures (especially turtles, armadillos, and sharks). Both women and men fought for the best lands and for prisoners, who were used as slaves or as human sacrifices. They believed in life after death; vultures performed a vital role in transporting people to the other world by eating their corpses.

These people probably made the granite spheres that lie in linear formations in the valley of the Río Térraba and on the Isla del Caño off the coast of the Osa Peninsula. These spheres range in diameter from 7.5 centimeters (the size of an orange) to 2.5 meters. Their almost perfect roundness and careful placement make them one of Costa Rica's pre-Columbian mysteries.

Peoples from the jungles of Brazil and Ecuador migrated to the lowland jungles of the Costa Rican Atlantic Coast. They lived semi-nomadically, hunting, fishing, and cultivating *yuca* (manioc), *pejibaye* (small cousin to the coconut), pumpkin, and squash. Their chief's nobility was hereditary, passed down through the female line of the family.

Social prestige was gained by good warriors. Apparently, decapitated heads of enemies were war trophies. Their stone figurines represent warriors with a knife in one hand and a head in the other.

They worshiped the sun, the moon, and the bones of their ancestors and believed that all things had souls. During religious festivals there was a ritual inebriation with a fermented *chicha* made from *yuca* or *pejibaye*. The burial mounds of these people have yielded the greatest number of pre-Columbian artifacts in the country.

COLONIAL COSTA RICA

On September 18, 1502, during his fourth and last voyage to the New World, Christopher Columbus anchored in the Bay of Cariari (now Limón) after a violent tempest wrecked his ships. During the 17 days that he and his crew were resting and making repairs, they visited a few coastal villages. The native people treated them well, and they left with the impression that Veragua (a name that Columbus used for the Caribbean Coast between Honduras and Panama) was a land rich in gold, whose gentle and friendly inhabitants could be easily conquered.

A few years later, in 1506, King Ferdinand of Spain sent a governor to colonize Veragua. Governor Diego de Nicuesa and his colonizers received a different welcome. First, their ship went aground on the coast of Panama, and they had to walk up the Atlantic shore. Food shortages and tropical diseases reduced the group by half. Then they met the native people, who burned their crops rather than feed the invaders. The Spanish realized that their task was not going to be easy. There was no centralized empire to conquer and sack, and the scattered tribes were at home in a climate and terrain that the explorers found devastating. This first attempt at colonization was a miserable failure.

After Vásco Núñez de Balboa discovered the Pacific Ocean in 1513, the Spaniards started exploring the west coast of Veragua. In 1522, an exploratory land expedition set out from northern Panama. Despite sickness, starvation, and tropical weather, the survivors of the long, hazardous trip called it a success: they had obtained gold and pearls, and their priest claimed he had converted more than 30,000 of the native people to Catholicism between Panama and Nicaragua.

More explorers and would-be colonizers arrived. There were attempted settlements on both coasts, but they ended in tragedy for the settlers, who died of hunger, were driven out by the native people, or fought among themselves and dissolved their communities.

Juan Vásquez de Coronado arrived as governor in 1562. He found a group of Spaniards and Spanish *mestizos* living inland from the Pacific Coast. Coronado explored Costa Rica, treating the Indians he met more humanely than had his predecessors. He decided that the highlands were more suitable for settlement, so he moved the settlers to the Cartago Valley, where the climate was pleasant and the soils were rich from the lava deposited by Volcán Irazú. In 1563, Cartago was established as the capital of Costa Rica.

In contrast to most other Spanish colonies, there was no large exploitable workforce in Costa Rica. The indigenous population had been decimated early on by war and disease. Because it had no riches and was difficult to reach from Guatemala, the seat of Spain's Central American empire, Costa Rica was left free from foreign intrusion. Forgotten by its "mother country," Costa Rica was almost self-sufficient in its poverty. At one point, even the governor was forced to work his own small plot of land to survive.

While some Costa Ricans were slaveholders, they owned few compared to other countries. Most slaves tended cacao plantations in the Atlantic Coast town of Matina, or served in Central Valley homes. The Calvo Chinchilla household held 27 slaves, more than any other family in colonial Costa Rica. Their case illustrates a tendency that was common in colonial times. Son Miguel had five children with his parents' slave Ana Cardoso. He acknowledged them, and his parents eventually freed her and their grandchildren. The tendency of slaveowners to have children with their slaves—mostly by force, though not in this case—contributed to the "bleaching" of African roots in the Central Valley population. Historian and genealogist Mauricio Meléndez Obando identified several causes for African slaves' not maintaining a strong identity: 1) forced and accelerated racial mixing; 2) a relatively small black population; 3) the heterogeneous nature of the slave population, since they were from various parts of Africa; and 4) their integration with other constituents of the population, including poor Spaniards, *mulatos*, *mestizos* (one parent Spanish and the other indigenous), and Zambos (one parent indigenous, the other black).

Costa Rica's Spanish population remained small and its lifestyle humble through the 17th century. In 1709, Spanish money became so scarce that settlers used cacao beans as currency, just like the Chorotegas. Women wore goat-hair skirts; soldiers had no uniforms. Volcán Irazú erupted in 1723, almost destroying Cartago. Nevertheless, the Spanish survived, and the area settled by Spaniards actually increased during the 1700s. Three new cities were founded in the Meseta Central (Central Valley): Cubujuquí (Heredia) in 1706, Villanueva de la Boca del Monte (San José) in 1737, and Villa Hermosa (Alajuela) in 1782.

INDEPENDENCE

In October 1821, word arrived from Guatemala that Spain had granted independence to its American colonies on September 15th. It had taken the news one month to travel through the mountains and valleys to Costa Rica. After a period of internal strife between conservative elements in Cartago who wanted to continue the monarchy, and a more liberal faction in San José who wanted to join South America's liberation movement, Costa Rica declared itself a state in the short-lived Federal Republic of Central America, and the capital was moved from Cartago to San José.

The first president of free Costa Rica, Juan Mora Fernández, built roads and schools and gave land grants to anyone who would plant coffee, the most profitable export crop at the time. This epoch was one of the most influential in the evolution of Costa Rican democracy, because small farmers were encouraged to grow coffee and sell the beans to wealthier farmers, who would prepare the beans for export. Thus, rich and poor each had an important place in the coffee-growing process, and mutual respect was developed.

By the mid-1800s, coffee was Costa Rica's principal export, and coffee growers were a powerful and wealthy elite. They built a road to transport coffee from the Meseta Central to Costa Rica's port, Puntarenas. They exported first to Chile, then later to Germany and England. By mid-century, European money was entering the pockets of Costa Rican coffee growers, and Europeans were arriving en masse at this tropical frontier. Costa Rica was becoming cosmopolitan. A university was founded in 1844 to disseminate European thinking, and Costa Rican politicians sported European liberal ideologies.

By 1848, the coffee elite was influential enough to elect its own representative for president, Juan Rafael Mora. He was a self-made man who had become one of the most powerful coffee growers in the country. He was charismatic, astute, and respected by the coffee elite and the campesinos alike. He became a veritable national hero by leading an "army" of Costa Ricans to defend his country when it was invaded by one of the most detested figures in Central American history, the North American William Walker.

THE SAGA OF WILLIAM WALKER

A study of William Walker's early life gives one little indication of how he would later come to be the scourge of Central America. Walker was graduated from the University of Nashville at the age of 14. By the time he was 19, he held both a law and a medical degree from the University of Pennsylvania. He followed this memorable academic record with two years of postgraduate study in Paris and Heidelberg.

His success stopped there. Returning from Europe, Walker quickly failed as a doctor, lawyer, and journalist. He had an ill-fated courtship with a beautiful deaf-mute New Orleans socialite, then in 1849 turned up as a gold miner in California. He didn't fare well in this occupation either, and soon started working as a hack writer in several California cities.

At this point, something happened in the mind of William Walker, and he launched himself on a career as a soldier of fortune. From then on, he succeeded in creating chaos wherever he took his five-foot, three-inch, one-hundred-pound frame.

In the early 1850s, Walker sailed with several hundred men on a "liberating expedition" to the Baja California Peninsula and Mexico. The expedition was financed by the Knights of the Golden Circle, a movement bent on promoting the "benefits" of slavery. Walker spent a year in Mexico, during which time he awarded himself the military title of colonel and proclaimed himself "President of Sonora and Baja California."

Back in the United States after several encounters with the Mexican army, he was arrested for breaking the Neutrality Act of 1818. His acquittal of the charge gained him fame and followers. His next expedition was to Nicaragua.

Walker went with two main goals. One was to convert Central America into slave territory and annex it to the southern United States; the other was to conquer Nicaragua and ready it for the construction of a transisthmic canal. The new riches that were being discovered in California attracted many Easterners, but crossing the United States by land was slow and difficult. Walker had made contacts with a group of economically powerful North Americans who thought that a sea route could be more efficient and profitable. Southern Nicaragua would be a perfect site for the isthmus crossing; ships could sail up the San Juan River, which formed the Nicaragua–Costa Rica border, cross Lake Nicaragua, then pass through a to-be-built 18-mile canal from the lake to the Pacific Ocean.

Walker's contacts arranged for an invitation from the Liberal Party of Nicaragua, which at the time was embattled with the Conservatives. In June 1855, he landed in Nicaragua with 58 men. After losing his first encounter with the Conservatives, Walker managed to hold out until several hundred reinforcements arrived from California, bringing new model carbines and six-shooters. They soon overpowered the Conservatives, and, after an "open" election, Walker became "President of the Republic of Nicaragua."

Central Americans from throughout the isthmus rose to fight Walker and his band of *filibusteros*. In February 1856, President Juan Rafael Mora of Costa Rica declared war on Walker, but not on Nicaragua. Mora raised an army of 9000 in less than a week. This "army," led by Mora and his brother-in-law José María Cañas, was composed of campesinos, merchants, and government bureaucrats ill-dressed for combat and armed only with farm tools, machetes, and old rifles. They marched for two weeks to Guanacaste, where they found 300 *filibusteros* resting at the Santa Rosa hacienda (now a national monument in Santa Rosa National Park). Having invaded Costa Rica, the *filibusteros* were preparing to conquer San José. The Costa Rican army, by then diminished to 2500 men, attacked the *filibusteros*, who fled back to Nicaragua after only 14 minutes of battle.

Two thousand Costa Ricans followed Walker up to Nicaragua and, in a generally masterful campaign, fought him to a standstill. The turning point came in Rivas, Nicaragua. Walker and his band were barricaded in a large wooden building from which they could not be dislodged. Juan Santamaría, a drummer boy, volunteered to set fire to the building and succeeded in forcing Walker's retreat. In his action, Santamaría lost his life, and became Costa Rica's national hero.

Walker's attempt to convert Nicaragua and the rest of Central America into slave territory was backed by U.S. President James Buchanan, and his failure angered the president. When Walker confiscated the transisthmic transportation concession that U.S. financier Cornelius Vanderbilt had already started installing, Vanderbilt began to finance some of Walker's enemies. This was the beginning of the end of Walker's career.

After another engagement in late 1856 on Lake Nicaragua, where the Costa Rican army brilliantly cut Walker off from his support troops, the ragtag *filibustero* forces were near defeat. On May 1, 1857, Walker surrendered to a U.S. warship.

The adventurer traveled to Nicaragua again in late 1857, but this time he was taken prisoner before he could wreak any havoc. When he was released in 1860, he sailed to Honduras, where, upon landing, he seized the custom house. This brought a British warship to the scene, upon which Walker, pursued by the Hondurans, eventually took refuge. Offered safe conduct into U.S. hands by the British commander, Walker insisted he was the rightful president of Honduras. The British therefore put Walker ashore again, where he was taken by the Hondurans and promptly shot.

The net result of Walker's Central American marauding was the death of some 20,000 men. The inscription on William Walker's tombstone reads, "Glory to the patriots who freed Central America of such a bloody pirate! Curses to those who brought him and to those who helped him."

Juan Rafael Mora is now acclaimed for having saved Central America from Walker and the interests he represented, but he wasn't that popular

La Casona,
scene of Walker's defeat

when he returned from battle. People accused Mora of having been too ambitious and blamed him for an epidemic of cholera that infected Costa Rican soldiers in Nicaragua and spread to kill almost ten percent of the population.

Mora manipulated the 1859 election to win despite massive opposition. In August 1859, his enemies overthrew him. A year later, Mora led a coup d'etat against the new president, also a member of the coffee elite. His attempt failed, and he was shot by a firing squad in 1860—an inglorious end for a man who is now a national hero. All through the 1860s, quarrels among the coffee growers helped to put presidents in power and later depose them. Nevertheless, most presidents during these years were liberal and intellectual civilians. Despite the political instability of the decade, the country managed to establish a well-based educational system. This was a time when new schools were founded, European professors were brought over to design academic programs, and the first bookstores in San José opened their doors.

THE ATLANTIC RAILROAD AND UNITED FRUIT

By the mid-1800s, Costa Rica realized it needed an Atlantic port to facilitate coffee export to Europe. When Tomás Guardia declared himself Chief of State in 1871, he decided to build a railway to Limón. He contracted Henry Meiggs, a North American who had built railways in Chile and Peru. Meiggs went to England to secure loans for the project. He obtained 3.4 million sterling pounds, of which only 1 million actually arrived. These loans created the first foreign debt in Costa Rica's history.

Costa Rica's population wasn't large enough to provide the project with the necessary labor force, so thousands of Jamaican, Italian, and Chinese workers were recruited. After an optimistic start, it soon became evident that it was going to be a slow, dangerous, and costly process. Construction of the railroad claimed some 4000 workers' lives, cost the equivalent of $8 million and lasted 19 years. The jungle proved itself a formidable and deadly barrier.

Meiggs' nephew, Minor C. Keith, became the director a few years after the project started. The railroad he inherited was constantly beleaguered by severe shortages of funds, so he started experimenting with banana production and exportation as a way to help finance the project. When he realized that the banana business could yield very profitable results, Keith made a deal with the new president, Bernardo Soto, in 1884. In return for a grant from the Costa Rican government of 323,887 hectares of untilled land along the tracks, tax-free for 20 years, and a 99-year lease on the railroad, Keith would renegotiate the project's pending debts to England, and complete construction at his own expense.

By 1886, Keith had settled the financial problems with England. He spent the next four years laying the last 52 miles of track that climbed through the steep, treacherous valley of the Reventazón River. Relations between Keith and the labor force weren't good. In 1888, Italian workers organized the first strike in Costa Rica's history, demanding prompt payments and sanitary working and living conditions.

The railroad was completed in 1890. Until 1970, it was the only route from the Meseta Central to Limón. And, until the line was closed in late 1990, it was still the major means of transportation for many of the people who lived in the tiny towns it passed. Children took the train to school; it served as an ambulance for the sick and as a hearse for the dead.

After they finished the railway, many Italian workers settled in Costa Rica's highlands. Chinese workers settled in various parts of the country. The Jamaicans stayed on the Atlantic Coast and started working on the banana plantations that Keith established on his free acres. The development of banana plantations where there had once been jungles forced the native peoples to move up into the mountains.

In 1899, Keith and a partner founded the United Fruit Company. La Yunai, as it was called, quickly became a legendary social, economic, political, and agricultural force in many Latin American countries. Costa Rican author Carlos Luis Fallas describes work conditions on the steamy plantations in his book *Mamita Yunai*, and Gabriel García Márquez tells what it did to the imaginary town of Macondo in *One Hundred Years of Solitude*. Although Costa Rica was the smallest country where it operated, United possessed more land here than anywhere else. Costa Rica became the world's leading banana producer.

Keith ended up a very wealthy man and married the daughter of one of the presidents of Costa Rica. Most profits from the banana industry went to the foreign owners of the production, shipping, and distribution networks that made export possible.

United's peak year in Costa Rica was in 1907. By 1913 the company was facing serious problems. Panama disease had infected banana trees, and United's employees were protesting unfair working conditions. A 1913 strike was broken by the Costa Rican government—two strike leaders were chased into the plantations and killed.

United initiated a new policy: it would lease company land to independent growers and buy bananas from them. Tensions with workers grew; a 1934 strike led by two young San José communists, Manuel Mora and Jaime Cerdas, finally brought better working and living conditions. They maintained the original demands of 1913 and added to the list regular payment of salaries, free housing, medical clinics on plantations, and accident insurance. United wouldn't talk with the strikers, but the planters leasing land from United did, and convinced United to sign an agreement.

In the late 1930s, a new disease, *Sigatoka*, infected banana trees up and down the coast. In 1938, United decided to pick up and move west to the Pacific lowlands around Golfito, where banana remained king until violent labor conflicts and dwindling Pacific markets compelled the company to abandon its installations in 1985. Now bananas are again becoming big business on the Atlantic lowlands, as huge projects buy up land, cutting down whatever forest remains in their way and forcing small farmers out of the area.

LIBERALISM ARRIVES IN COSTA RICA

The 1880s saw an increasing split between a traditional, conservative church and a liberalizing state. The bishop of Costa Rica criticized the European ideas that were becoming popular with the elite and the politicians. The bishop was summarily expelled from the country in 1884, and in 1885 there was an official denouncement of an earlier church-state concord that had declared Catholicism the state religion. Public outcry at the government's treatment of the church was minimal.

The first truly democratic election, characterized by real public participation (male only), took place in 1889. Liberals saw it as the result of their efforts to educate and raise democratic consciousness in the people. In fact, their efforts worked so well that the public gave their overwhelming support to the liberals' opposition. Supporters of the liberals threatened not to recognize the new president, so 10,000 armed opposition members flooded the streets of San José. The liberals then demonstrated their firm commitment to democracy by recognizing the new, rightfully elected president.

Costa Rica's democratic tradition has endured until today, with only a few exceptions. One was in 1917, when the Minister of War and the Navy, Federico Tinoco, overthrew an unpopular president. Tinoco's brutal and repressive dictatorship lasted through 30 months of widespread opposition. Finally, Tinoco fled the country. A provisional president held office for a year until normalcy was reached, and Costa Rica resumed its democratic tradition with a fair presidential election.

ROOTS OF THE 1948 CIVIL WAR

Rafael Angel Calderón Guardia was the legally elected president between 1940 and 1944. A profoundly religious Catholic, Calderón's political ideology was Social Christian. One of his first actions was to reinstate religious education in public schools. Another was to found the University of Costa Rica. He initiated many social reforms that still exist today, including social security, workers' rights to organize, land reform, guaranteed minimum wage, and collective bargaining. These reforms earned Calderón the adoration of the poor and the opposition of the upper classes.

Calderón ran a puppet candidate, Teodoro Picado, in the 1944 election. Picado won, but the election was widely criticized as being fraudulent. Young, middle-class intellectuals, as well as traditionally anticommunist Costa Ricans distrustful of church-state involvement, resented Calderón's grasping for power and criticized the odd alliance he had made with Catholic Archbishop Monseñor Víctor Sanabria and Manuel Mora of the Communist Party.

Farmers, businesspeople, campesinos, liberal labor unions, and young intellectuals organized against Calderón. Calderón's allies were the government, the church, the communist labor unions, and the army.

In the 1948 election, Calderón ran against Otilio Ulate, who represented the unified opposition. Ulate won the election by a small margin, but the government demanded a recount. Disagreement was complicated by a fire that destroyed half the ballots the day after the election. Government forces refused to yield to Ulate, and Teodoro Picado remained in power.

José María (Pepe) Figueres, a coffee grower and outspoken opponent of Calderón who had been exiled in Mexico, had returned to Costa Rica before the elections. On March 12, 1948, he and his men captured the airport at San Isidro de El General. Foreign arms were airlifted in quickly, due to Figueres' advance planning. Armed groups, trained by Guatemalan military advisors, were formed throughout the country. President Picado declared a state of siege, using borrowed Nicaraguan soldiers and mobilized banana workers from the communist unions. Unaccustomed to the cool climate of San José, they wore blankets over their shoulders, Mexican style, to keep warm. For this reason, Calderón supporters were called *mariachis*. After 40 days of civil war, during which more than 2000 people died, a negotiated treaty was signed. Picado stepped down and Figueres took over as provisional president.

Figueres governed for 18 months, long enough to draft a new constitution. Prohibition of presidential reelection, banning of communist labor unions and parties, abolition of the army, the right to vote for women and blacks, and the establishment of a neutral body that would oversee elections were some of the new constitutional laws. Banks and insurance companies were nationalized, and ten percent of all bank funds were seized for reconstruction. All of Calderón's social reforms were maintained. In 1949, Figueres turned the country over to Ulate, the rightful president.

Thanks to a constitutional amendment permitting presidential reelection if not for consecutive terms, Costa Rica elected Figueres president twice, once in 1953 and then again in 1970. "Don Pepe" died June 8, 1990, and was mourned by people of all political persuasions as the defender of Costa Rican democracy and development.

The 1948 revolutionaries formed the National Liberation Party (PLN). Almost without fail, Costa Ricans have alternated their presidents—one from the PLN, the next from the opposition. The opposition is an odd coalition of wealthy business owners, who see the PLN's social democratic direction as harmful to their interests, and poor people, who generally side with the party that is out of power. There have been only two exceptions to this pattern in the 13 peaceful national elections that have been held since 1948. Costa Rican voters have a deep distrust of power being concentrated in one party's hands for too long.

SINCE 1948

Costa Rica fortified its progressive social policies during the three decades following 1948, and enjoyed a gradual upward economic trend. The policy of the 1960s and 1970s was to try to become more self-sufficient agriculturally and industrially, which actually led to a heavier dependence on imported pesticides, fertilizers, raw materials, machinery, and oil. Costa Rica and many other Third World countries accepted large First World loans for infrastructure projects like bridges, hydroelectric dams, and roads. When the price of oil rose in the early 1970s, the economy could no longer do without it. Then coffee, banana, and sugar prices went down on the world market, the loans came due, and Costa Rica found itself entering the 1980s with its economy in shambles.

The instability of neighboring countries like Nicaragua and El Salvador impeded cooperation in the Central American Common Market and made Costa Ricans feel insecure. From 1978 to 1979, under President Rodrigo Carazo, northern Costa Rica served as a virtual base for Sandinista operations. Costa Ricans had no sympathy for the Somoza dynasty and were hopeful that the Nicaraguans could make a go of democracy. But after Somoza was deposed, the Sandinista arms build-up and Marxist-Leninist doctrine disillusioned many Costa Ricans. Although the government had an official policy of neutrality, PLN President Luis Alberto Monge (1982–1986) lent tacit support to the Contras, who were operating out of the northern jungles of Costa Rica.

Costa Rica elected a president in February 1986 from the younger generation of the PLN. Oscar Arias, an economist, lawyer, and author of several books on the Costa Rican economy and power structure, campaigned on the promise to work for peace in Central America. The first part of his task was to enforce Costa Rica's declared neutrality policy, and to stand up to the United States and the politicians within his own party who were supporting Contra activity in Costa Rica (such as the secret airstrip that figured in the Iran-Contra scandal).

As the world knows by now, Arias' untiring efforts to fulfill his promise won him the 1987 Nobel Peace Prize. While the peace process met with skepticism and even ennui in the First World press, for many Central Americans it signified a coming of age—a chance to unite and shape their future in a new way. The first democratic elections in Nicaragua's history, held February 25, 1990, were largely a result of the peace plan and saw the Sandinistas defeated. Progress toward democracy in El Salvador and Guatemala can also be traced to Oscar Arias' efforts for peace.

Rafael Angel Calderón Fournier, son of Rafael Angel Calderón Guardia, succeeded Arias in 1990. Calderón Fournier was inaugurated as president 50 years to the day after his father assumed power. In 1994, José María Figueres, son of Don Pepe, took over from "Junior" Calderón, becoming one of the youngest presidents in history. Following in his father's footsteps, he initiated some truly novel policies, like the sale of "carbon-sequestering" bonds. He built on Costa Rica's reputation for having a well-educated populace to attract software giant Intel, which opened a 400,000-square-foot plant in April 1998. He also enforced a restrictive fiscal policy to try to gain control of the economy, which made him unpopular, but seems to have had positive results. However, service on Costa Rica's combined internal and external debt continues to eat up one third of its gross domestic product.

All three administrations have implemented the "structural adjustment programs" recommended by international lending institutions for Latin America's developing nations. This has resulted in a strengthened macroeconomy and a relatively low level of unemployment. Another thrust of the international bankers is to privatize much of Costa Rica's large public sector, until recently Costa Rica's sacred cow. Government offices have had to slash their payrolls, with some ministries having to lay off one-quarter to one-third of their employees. While this cuts costs, it has caused some bitter strikes in Costa Rica (and throughout Latin America). The country was virtually shut down in April 2000 by student, union, and environmental protesters who opposed the privatization of ICE, the national electronics and telecommunications company. Three weeks of protests were ended when the government appointed a commission with representatives from the protesting sectors to figure out how to resolve the issue.

Rural and urban poor feel that their interests are being ignored, as public infrastructure, which they rely on heavily for health care and schooling, deteriorates. According to a 1998 United Nations study, 20 percent of Costa Ricans live in poverty. New nontraditional agro-industries promoted by the IMF and World Bank demand high startup and input costs, and are not labor-intensive; this shuts the small farmer out. As they become islands in an ocean of monocrop plantations owned by wealthy corporations, small farmers are being forced off land once granted them by government agrarian development institutions. Since traditional crops and sustenance farming are no longer encouraged, Costa Rica must import some of its most basic food staples.

The 1998 election was won by a wealthy and well-educated economist and businessman, Miguel Angel Rodriguez. Although the Rodriguez administration started out with promises to put a ban on logging in the Osa Peninsula, in 1999 it awarded permits to cut 10,000 forest giants in that biologically rich area. A peaceful demonstration to block lumber trucks leaving the Osa was crushed by police, who dragged protesters away. Later that year, a study conducted by biologists, forestry engineers, and geographers found significant anomalies in the logging permits that had been granted, and concluded that current lumber-harvesting laws have serious loopholes that threaten the few remaining unprotected forests. Eight months later, the government still had not responded to the findings of the study. The Rodriguez government's commitment to the environment also came into question when he abolished the vehicle emissions testing program and made it one of the duties of normal police. The government then announced plans to deregulate environmental building controls, and to abolish laws that halted building permits when archaeological sites were unearthed during construction projects. Under the Rodriguez administration, oil exploration and exploitation rights were granted to a U.S. company, which is now setting off intense sonar probes in the oceans off the beautiful Talamanca coast, posing a threat to marine animals that use sonar to survive and endangering pristine coral reefs.

Costa Rica has been a world-leader in fostering the notion that forested areas perform a service for the planet, and that the owners of these areas (public or private) should be compensated for this service. In Costa Rica, 87 percent of the water for hydroelectric generation comes from protected forests. Replacing it with fossil fuel generation would cost $104 million. With money from a 15 percent fuel tax, the Figueres administration initiated the National Fund for Forest Financing, which pays landowners for the environmental services provided by their forests. Under the Rodriguez administration, this program is languishing, with only 40 percent of the fuel tax funds going to forest owners, the rest being taken up by other government needs. It is sadly obvious that Costa Rica's current government no longer supports the far-sighted environmental policies that have made it famous.

Former President Oscar Arias would like to run again, but the Costa Rican constitution prohibits the re-election of presidents. A movement is underway to change this for the 2002 election.

TWO

The Ecological Picture

Costa Rica measures only 185 miles across at her widest point, but four mountain ranges divide her like a backbone. Mount Chirripó, at 12,000 feet, is the highest point in southern Central America. It is part of Costa Rica's oldest and southernmost mountain range, the Cordillera de Talamanca, which extends into Panama. The Central Volcanic Range is made up of volcanoes Turrialba, Irazú, Barva, and Poás. More than half of Costa Rica's 3.5 million inhabitants live in the Central Valley, whose fertile soil was created by the activity of these volcanoes over the last two million years. To the northwest is the Tilarán range, which reaches 5500 feet at Monteverde and includes the active Volcano Arenal. Farthest northwest, toward the Nicaraguan border, is the Guanacaste Range, which boasts five active volcanoes, including Rincón de la Vieja and Miravalles (now being used to generate geothermal energy). The most ancient rocks in the area are more than 100 million years old and occur in the "Nicoya complex," low mountains that crop up here and there along the Pacific.

Costa Rica may be one of the smaller countries in the Americas, but it boasts the most diverse selection of flora and fauna in the hemisphere. There are several reasons for this diversity: Costa Rica's topography ranges from the bleak, treeless paramo, 12,000 feet above sea level, to rainforests on the coasts only 50 miles away, with countless microclimates in between. Costa Rica's latitude contributes steady temperatures year-round, and abundant precipitation creates hospitable conditions for many forms of life. Perhaps most important is Costa Rica's position between the Americas: a land bridge between North and South, where migrating animals and plants meet. North American white-tailed deer sniff at South American brocket deer and northern rattlesnakes slide by southern bushmasters. There are animals here that have evolved nowhere else in the world: pacas and agoutis (cousins of guinea pigs), dantas (huge tapirs), and prehensile-tailed porcupines, to name a few. The ecology of Costa Rica is so complex and fascinating, that this brief chapter should only be considered a very elementary and anecdotal survey.

ECOSYSTEMS

From high, dry mountains to verdant rainforests, Costa Rica is home to a wide range of ecosystems, a term used to describe a community of living organisms and their complex interactions with their environment. Following are descriptions of some of Costa Rica's more common ecosystems.

The **paramo**, related to the Andean ecosystem of the same name, covers the summits of Costa Rica's southern Talamanca mountain range. Just as the foliage is tough and small, which protects it from the elements and conserves energy, the animals that live here are mostly small rodents and tiny lizards activated by strong sun. Paramos originally were limited to the highest peaks of Costa Rica, but due to deforestation, this bleak zone is extending downward. There is paramo at Cerro de la Muerte, Chirripó, and the high mountain peaks in Parque Internacional La Amistad (visit through Dúrika Biological Reserve above Buenos Aires).

The highest rainforests, blanketing the slopes of the Continental Divide, are called **cloud forests** because they are nearly always veiled in clouds. Clouds pause momentarily at the Divide after ascending the Atlantic slope, and the forest soaks up their moisture. Scientists postulate that global warming is making the clouds rise higher over the divide, depriving cloud forests of their mist. They think that this subtle drying effect might be responsible for the disappearance of moisture-sensitive frogs and toads. These forests provide a crucial watershed for areas below. Monteverde is Costa Rica's most famous cloud forest. There are many others, as well, some of which are easier to reach from San José: Los Angeles Cloud Forest, Bosque de Paz, Braulio Carrillo National Park, and the ancient oak forests on Cerro de la Muerte.

The Atlantic Coast and the Corcovado Peninsula are home to what most of us think of when we hear the word "**rainforest**": tremendously tall trees with vines twisting up their girth, hanging roots of philodendrons whose leaves are high above. Rainforest pilgrims may also visit the many reserves in the Sarapiquí and Gúapiles areas. Carara and Manuel Antonio national parks are the most (over)visited rainforests in the country, due to their easy accessibility.

The characteristic that most differentiates tropical rainforests from their temperate counterparts is their diversity. Year-round warm temperatures and abundant rain have produced a plethora of species, each with a high degree of specialization. There are insects that blend in perfectly with the type of leaves they eat. Some of the most fragrant flowers only release their scent at night, to attract nocturnal, nearly blind bats.

The forest has several levels, from ground-covering ferns and mosses, to short bushes and tree ferns, to canopy species stunted by a lack of light, to shade-loving trees that reach a certain height and provide a mid-canopy, to the canopy trees, which, depending upon the life zone (determined by altitude and precipitation), can reach up to 180 feet in height. Seeds are eaten or unwittingly carried by birds or monkeys who travel through the forest and drop them along the way, often far from the mother tree. Many seedlings flourish in the shade at ground level. Species that demand much light will flounder in the relatively dark forest floor until an old tree dies or falls, and leaves a "light gap." At that point, the light-demanding species will shoot up until one reaches the canopy and fills the hole.

A true rainforest is evergreen: trees will never all lose their leaves at once. The **dry pacific forest** is deciduous, shedding its leaves during the severe dry season to conserve water. The canopy is significantly lower than in the rainforest. When the trees are bare, it is often easier to see wildlife here. Many of the animals that frequent the dry pacific forest are seasonal visitors from other ecosystems. Tropical dry forests occur only in Guanacaste. Santa Rosa protects a large tract, and Lomas Barbudal and Palo Verde are home to others.

Mangroves are found in intertidal zones at river mouths and estuaries where fresh water and saltwater meet. Comprising the various species of tree that are virtually the only flora that can live half the time submerged in salty water, the other half in nearly airless mud, the different types of mangroves (red, black, white, tea, and buttonwood) are actually from four unrelated families, each having developed ways of coping with these challenging conditions. They resist osmosis by maintaining a higher concentration of salt in their tissues than in the seawater, and secrete excess salt from their leaves or roots. To aerate, as well as to survive in a natural flood zone, mangroves have aerial roots with multiple buttresses. By preventing large predators from entering, their tangle of roots provides a habitat for many species of marine life at their most vulnerable stages of development. Baby oysters and sponges attach to the roots. Algae generated in the nutrient-rich mud is abundant food for young crabs, lobsters, shrimp, and barnacles.

Some types of mangroves gradually turn a wet intertidal zone into dry land. As their leaves drop onto silt collected in the roots, a layer of soil slowly develops. Eventually, the mangroves, which can't live outside their tidal habitat, are stranded on dry land and die. At the same time that this curious suicidal behavior occurs, however, unique floating seedlings with weighted bottoms are carried in the water until they can lodge in the mud. Because seeds germinate while still on the tree, they quickly take root, in a never-ending quest for new territory.

Some of the best areas to observe mangroves include the estuaries of the Pacific Coast, the Río Sierpe boat trip to Drake Bay, the Atrocha route between Golfito and Zancudo, and the canals just north of Moín on the way to Tortuguero.

Mangroves filter sediment-rich river water so that much clearer water flows into the ocean. In some areas off the coast, where the water is very clear, **coral reefs** develop. Coral reefs are animals, plants, and geologic formations all in one. They create habitats of rich biological gardens populated by life forms as diverse as those found in the rainforest, from unicellular organisms such as algae to fish like the damselfish. (The damselfish actually tends her garden, plucking undesirable sea grasses from her seascape.)

The coral structure is formed by unique plantlike animals that live within it, filtering water to obtain nutrients then excreting calcium carbonate, which becomes the coral skeleton. The coral reef itself breaks waves, creating a calm interior thick with sea grasses, and important nutrients for turtles, manatees, and other marine animals.

Manuel Antonio's third beach has calm waters and a lovely reef. The point at Cahuita has too, although sediment carried downriver from banana plantations is diminishing its growth. The Manzanillo Reef south of Puerto Viejo has only recently been mapped, and we hear it is spectacular. We have had mixed reports about the reef in Bahía Ballena National Marine Park south of Dominical.

FLORA

Costa Rica is home to an incredibly diverse selection of flora, each type adapted for life in a particular ecosystem. At forest floors, the predominant color is green, but at eye level there are brightly colored and fragrant flowers. Especially common in rainforests are species of the heliconia flower—large red, yellow, or orange bursts of tropical exuberance. Fragrant orchids, too, are common here, as are a spectacular array of ferns. From the lowliest lichen to the towering ceiba tree, the Costa Rican landscape offers a rich display of plant life.

EPIPHYTES   Whether in the ghostly, fog-draped cloud forests or the towering lowland rainforests, branches and treetops look impossibly top-heavy, covered as they are with orchids, mosses, ferns, lichens, bromeliads, and other families of epiphytes (plants whose roots grasp tree branches and absorb their nutrients from leaf matter and water dripping off the canopy).

Among the tiniest epiphytes are the mosses found growing on leaf surfaces and the lichens clinging to tree bark. They are restricted to areas that are moist year-round. Because they can hinder a plant's ability to photosynthesize, many plants have developed a variety of techniques for getting rid of these pesky hangers-on. "Drip tip" leaves will drain water collected on them so that their surface is dry, making it difficult for mosses to colonize. Some trees slough off their bark regularly, shedding lichens as well.

Ferns are a diverse category of flowerless epiphyte. Notable species among the 800 types found in Costa Rica include the primordial-looking tree fern (an upright fern with prickly spines) and the resurrection fern, which dries and curls up during periods of drought, only to spring back to life with the return of the rains.

The 1500 species of orchids that are found in Costa Rica are the showiest epiphytes, with intricate and spectacular flowers. Orchids appear on every continent except Antarctica, but are most diverse in the tropics, where they range in size from half an inch to twenty-five and one-half feet. Because they do not have edible pollen to offer their pollinators, orchids rely either on an alluring strong scent or mimicry to deceive insects into believing they are something they are not.

Bromeliads are epiphytes that collect and store water in their tightly joined leaf bases, or trap tiny droplets in their hairlike trichomes. This water is rendered nutrient-rich when particles fall into it or when mosquitos and other insects that breed in it die and decompose there. The 170 species of bromeliads found in Costa Rica provide niches for up to 250 forms of life.

FLOWERS   Costa Rica offers a variety of flowering plants, many of which have developed very specific traits for survival. For instance, the angel's trumpet tree produces pendulous white flowers that open only at night and are just the right shape for a bat snout. They exude an almost dizzying smell. The aristolchia flower, which attracts one particular bat as its pollinator, mimics the genitalia of the female of that species of bat to attract the males. The dracontium flower depends on feces-loving flies as pollinators and has a distinct stench almost everyone recognizes.

TREES   The diversity of the tropical forest is evident in the trees that make it up. In just two and a half acres, there can be over 90 species of trees. Following are descriptions of just a few of the many unusual types of trees you may encounter during your visit to Costa Rica.

Coconut trees lean out over the beach to reach more sunlight and to drop their nuts where the waves will pick them up. Coconuts can float in the ocean for several months and land on another beach thousands of leagues away before they sprout. The infant plant is nourished by the rich coconut milk and meat, and once leaves emerge and photosynthesis begins, thousands of roots emerge from the nut and anchor the young tree to the beach. Biologists have observed this colonization process on new volcanic islands. Coconuts are what have made human habitation possible on otherwise inhospitable islands. New leaves grow and old ones are shed about once a month. So, in order to calculate the age of a coconut tree in years, count the number of leaves and leaf scars on a coconut tree trunk, and divide by twelve.

Recognizable by its prominent orange-red roots, the milk or cow tree is common in the rainforest of Corcovado National Park. Its Latin name is *Brosimum utile*, and useful it is. Through the trunk flows a drinkable white latex. The tree's sweet fruit is edible, and its wood is useful for construction. The indigenous people of the area used its bark to stay warm: they would cut a portion of bark from the tree, soak it, then dry it and beat it to make a warm, soft blanket.

Indio desnudo (naked Indian, also known as the "sunburned gringo"), with bright orange bark, is another easily recognizable tree found mostly in dry Pacific forests. The leaves fall off during the dry season, but chloroplasts under the bark's surface allow photosynthesis to continue. Each tree produces a bounty of between 600 and 6000 fruits, which are savored by white-faced monkeys. When the monkeys accidentally drop fruit-laden branches onto the forest floor, collared peccaries eat them too.

Considered sacred by Costa Rica's indigenous people, the ceiba or kapok tree is one of the fastest-growing trees known, climbing as much as 13 feet a year to a maximum recorded height of 198 feet. This makes it a prime pioneer, quickly colonizing fields allowed to regenerate. Its seed pods contain envelopes of cottony fibers that enclose the seeds. The envelopes are carried by the wind and eventually the seed falls out. Kapok fiber has long been used as stuffing for pillows, saddles, and clothing. The wood is too light for construction, but is used for canoes and coffins.

Strangler figs are parasitic tree-like plants that begin as epiphytes on a tree limb when a seed from a bird dropping takes root in a hospitable nook. Once the seedling is established, it sends roots that surround the host tree trunk in a close embrace, and branches reach to cover the upper branches of the host tree. The host tree eventually dies, probably not because of strangulation, but because the fig's branches block the host tree's light source.

FAUNA

As rich and varied as is Costa Rica's flora, you'll find the fauna that use it as a habitat equally diverse.

REPTILES AND AMPHIBIANS   Rainforest amphibians generally have toxins in their skin. The mildest poisons just taste bad, while the strongest can kill predators (including humans) by causing vasoconstriction, respiratory paralysis, hypertension, and other mortal conditions. The toxin may be ingested through the mucous membranes of the mouth or throat, or through the pores in the skin. The message: don't touch these guys. (Ironically, they may be the source of lifesaving antibacterial and antiviral compounds that scientists are still researching.) Big bullfrogs that are common near beaches can even shoot toxin a distance of up to six and one half feet, so be wary of them, too.

So named because indigenous warriors poisoned their arrow tips with its venom, the vermilion-colored poison dart frog spends its entire life high above the rainforest floor. Bromeliad water vessels serve as the frog's breeding grounds, protecting the developing tadpoles from predators. At the end of the two-month gestation period, an adult dart frog emerges from the plant shelter with a fully developed defense system: Its skin glands exude a poison that rolls off its back like drops of sweat. Any animal taking a poison dart frog into its mouth is poisoned. The frog's brilliant red color serves as warning.

Other toxic amphibians warn predators with "flash colors"—brightly colored legs or groin areas, which are revealed only when the animal jumps. This startles the predator, and might dissuade it from attacking.

Three kinds of sea turtles nest on Costa Rica's shores: the Pacific or olive ridley at Playa Nancite in Santa Rosa National Park and at Ostional near Playa Nosara; the green turtle at Tortuguero; and the leatherback at Playa Grande near Tamarindo, Tortuguero, and the Gandoca Manzanillo Wildlife Refuge in Talamanca. We provide descriptions of these giant sea creatures and their nesting habits in the geographic chapters that cover their nesting grounds.

Two kinds of crocodiles are found in Costa Rica. The smaller ones, called caymans, which grow no longer than three feet, live in creeks, ponds, mangrove swamps, and beach lowlands. They are most common in the Corcovado area. What are commonly called crocodiles are the larger animals, reaching up to 13 feet in length. We have seen them lounging in the muddy banks of rivers in the Northern Zone, and on the boat trip to Tortuguero.

SNAKES   Due to their camouflage and wariness of humans, you are not likely to see snakes in a brief visit to the forest, but it is worth knowing which ones are dangerous. Boa constrictors are long (reaching 18 feet in length), fat snakes with dark squares on a light brown or gray background. They sit and wait until a likely prey appears (they have been known to eat lizards, tanagers, opossums, young porcupines, deer, and even ocelots), and then they strike, impale the animal on their fangs, lift it, strangle it, then swallow it head first. Because they have few recorded predators, boas are believed to be at or near the top of the food chain. When a boa feels threatened, its body fills with air along its entire length, and it emits a deep, ghostly roar.

Of the 136 species of snakes in Costa Rica, 18 are lethal. Fer-de-lance *(terciopelo)* snakes are venomous residents of rainy jungles, large rivers, and overgrown fields. They are brown and black with a white "X" pattern running down their back, which make them almost impossible to see among the twigs and leaves. When disturbed, this aggressive six-and-a-half-foot snake bites anything that moves, and its bite can be fatal to humans. Its usual diet consists of mammals and birds. At Parque Viborana in Turrialba, we observed snake expert Minor Camacho walking in a cage of angry *terciopelos*. When they prepared to strike, he stood completely still until they calmed down. Then he would take a step, they would rear their heads again, he would stand still again and they would relax. He did this several times, demonstrating how knowledge of this snake's behavior can keep people from getting bitten, and also keep snakes from being killed by fearful humans.

The dreaded eyelash vipers are so named for a visor-like scale that extends beyond their eyes. These snakes are small, less than three feet in length, and come in green, brown, rust, gray, or light blue, with a darker diamond pattern on the back, although some are gold, without the pattern. They hang in trees. Three to six people per year in Costa Rica die after being bitten by this highly venomous snake.

Costa Rica has its own species of rattlesnake, as well, with stripes on its neck and diamonds on its back. They are mostly found in Guanacaste. Their venom can cause blindness, paralysis, and suffocation.

These are the poisonous snakes. You can look them in the eye at one of the country's serpentaria: in San José (see Chapter Six), in Grecia (see Chapter Seven), and the one we feel is the best designed—the above-mentioned Parque Viborana near Turrialba (see Chapter Seven). Hopefully, those will be the only snakes you will encounter on your trip.

BIRDS   Costa Rica's most famous cloud-forest bird is the resplendent quetzal, a large, brilliant green bird whose males sport a two-foot-long wispy tail. Despite their size and bright colors, they are not easy to spot because they remain very still, high up in the trees while tracking insects or small arboreal frogs and lizards. During their mating season in March, they are more visible. Quetzales cannot live in captivity, a poetic quality that has made them a symbol of freedom for the people of Central America. Quetzales migrate during the year to follow ripening fruits of trees in the avocado family.

Other birds that follow ripening fruits up and down the mountains include the three-wattled bellbird, which gets its name from its bell-like voice and the three wattles or wormlike pieces of skin that flop over its beak. This bird eats the same avocado-like fruits as the quetzal, and also migrates to much lower elevations after breeding in the cloud forest.

There is also the bare-necked umbrella bird, whose males are large and black with big fluffy pompadour headdresses and bright red featherless throats that they inflate to attract the much less ornate females. Male birds are generally considerably more spectacular than their female counterparts, perhaps to attract their mates. Females are usually much less conspicuous and camouflage their young while nesting.

Other, more notable birds include the liquid-voiced *oropéndolas*. These large, dull-colored birds with yellow tails weave long, sac-like nests on dead tree branches. Visitors from temperate climes enjoy sighting parrots, abundant in the tropics. Sixteen species of this raucous family inhabit Costa Rica, from tiny parakeets and parrotlets, to the giant scarlet macaws. Scarlet macaws, who are monogamous and mate for life, used to live throughout the lowlands of Costa Rica, but massive deforestation and poaching have restricted the few remaining birds to Carara Biological Reserve and the Osa Peninsula. Our sharp-eyed guide, Modesto Watson, spotted a pair in Tortuguero in 1988, an encouraging sight.

Green macaws used to range through the entire Atlantic lowland region of Costa Rica, nesting in giant *almendro* trees. Until recently, these trees were left by lumbermen because their wood was too hard to process as lumber. However, new technology has been developed and the trees are being cut at an alarming rate. The habitat for green macaws has been reduced by 95 percent, and biologist George Powell estimates that only 25 to 35 nesting pairs remain on the northeastern plains. The International Union for the Conservation of Nature has been working to save the remaining birds and their habitat.

Of the 330 species of hummingbirds known to exist in the world, almost one-fifth are found in Costa Rica. These tiny nectar-eaters have unusual wings that can rotate at the shoulders, allowing them to fly in any direction or hover over a flower while they fit their beak into the floral tube and suck out the nectar. Almost any pink, red, or orange flower attracts hummingbirds.

Among the many waterbirds frequenting Costa Rica are the frigate bird (pterodactyl-like with a six-and-a-half-foot wingspan, whose primitive body type makes landing and taking off difficult) and the six species of kingfishers (short-necked, large-headed, and sharp-billed divers who dwell at rivers and coasts).

About a quarter of Costa Rica's 850 species of birds are seasonal visitors from North or South America. They fly to the tropics to escape scarcity during harsh winters, making long, arduous journeys over land and sea. Among the most amazing feats is the first leg of the ruby-throated hummingbird's annual trip south: a nonstop 500-mile flight over the Gulf of Mexico. The raptors (hawks, falcons, and eagles) fly over Costa Rica on their way south every October. Traditionally, they have sought temporary shelter in the Atlantic Zone, but this is becoming less common as the rainforests of that area are cut down and replaced with banana plantations. Birds that summer in North America and winter in Costa Rica include warblers, swallows, thrushes, finches, orioles, flycatchers, and tanagers.

Ornithologist Carmen Hidalgo offers these suggestions for birdwatchers: The best hours of the day to see most birds are before 8 a.m. and for an hour or two before sundown; use lightweight binoculars; in general, the best time of the year to see birds is in May, the beginning of the rainy season and nesting season for many species, but for aquatic varieties the end of the rainy season (November–December) is best.

Serious birders will want to bring *A Guide to the Birds of Costa Rica* (Gary F. Stiles and Alexander Skutch, Cornell University Press). They will also want to hear the companion CD to that book, as well as the other bird-call CDs that we mention under "Audio Field Guides" at the end of the book. Rainforest Publications (P.O. Box 1306, Stanwood, WA 98292; phone/fax: 360-382-6436) publishes a series of laminated cards with bird species for various areas of the country. Order them ahead of time for about $5 apiece, or look for them in their respective areas of the country.

MAMMALS   Even though you must have a lot of patience and be accompanied by an experienced guide to see birds in the forest, they are still easier to observe than most other animals. Mammals such as the jaguar and the tapir are part of the hype that is attracting so many ecotourists to the rainforest. However, they are rarely seen by visitors because they flee from humans and are nocturnal.

Jaguars, the largest Costa Rican carnivores, are most common in areas where there has been little human penetration. Each jaguar adult requires a forest-covered hunting ground one hundred miles in size. As humans colonize their territories, the jaguars recede, crowding into areas too small for them. A reduced gene pool leads to weakened animals and mutations; this might eventually lead to their extinction. One interesting conservation plan is the "Paseo la Pantera" project to link protected areas internationally through Central America in order to create one unbroken reserve the length of the isthmus for large cats and other animals who need vast amounts of space to roam.

Huge vegetarian tapirs have long been considered one of the finest delicacies a Costa Rican hunter can bring home, so these mammals are also in danger of extinction. Currently, they can be found only where hunting has been prohibited. Their immense size does not prevent them from being swift runners. Their feet have an interesting adaptation that aids them when running through the muddy forest floor. Their feet spread out as they step down, then their toes draw together to make pulling out of the mud easier.

With a keen eye, you might see a sloth hanging from a tree limb. This animal's name is no coincidence—a sloth hardly moves. Most vegetarian animals must eat berries or nuts to generate the energy they need to survive. Sloths just eat leaves, so they need to carry out a low-maintenance lifestyle. They have little muscle tissue, compared to other animals. As much as they annoyed energetic explorers of the colonial period (Captain William Dampier whipped a sloth to make it move—it wouldn't), they do have a perfect system worked out: their upside-down position hanging from tree limbs is ideal for scooping hanging leaves into their mouths. Algae-shrouded fur camouflages them in the treetops, and their meat does not taste good. When attacked by one of their few predators, their slow metabolism allows them to survive wounds that would kill other animals.

Monkeys are the most sociable forest dwellers. Intensely attached to their family group or troupe, they are among the most intelligent animals. There are four types of monkeys in Costa Rica. The diminutive, insect-eating white-faced monkey inhabits the Caribbean lowland rainforest, Manuel Antonio Park, Monteverde premontane forest, the Osa Peninsula, and the dry forests of Guanacaste. Large howler monkeys, audible if not always visible throughout Costa Rica, are so named because their bellows resonate through the forest, making them sound like a much more terrifying animal than the vegetarians they are. Blond-chested spider monkeys have long, prehensile tails with a fingerprint-like imprint at the end, adapted for gripping. Their increased agility allows them to leap up to 30 feet. These monkeys love physical contact so much that they sleep in a big heap. Tiny squirrel monkeys live in the Pacific lowland area and are highly social, living in bands up to 30 strong. Often the first indication that monkeys are near is the sight or sound of branches bouncing as they jump from tree to tree.

Coatis (*pizotes*), who look like jungle raccoons with long, slightly bushy, monkeylike tails, are diurnal and easily seen in open areas. Agile in trees, they are competent ground dwellers as well. They live in every habitat in Costa Rica, and eat everything from fruit and mice to tarantulas and lizards. Females and young live in bands that can number 30 (this contributes to their being easy to spot); adult males are solitary.

Another community-oriented mammal is the pig-like collared peccary. Living in groups of 3 to 30, they greet one another by rubbing their heads to the scent glands near their tails, and sleep together to conserve heat. They have long hair covering their gray-black skin; a band of white rings their neck.

INTERACTIONS

Even more fascinating than the individual species in the forest is how they interact. Nature's most intimate and complex relationships involve what biologists call "mutualisms." In mutual relationships, each actor provides a necessary service for the other, and often neither could survive alone. Following are a few intriguing examples of nature's interdependencies.

Tiny tree frogs, who never touch ground, have one of the most intimate relationships with bromeliads. The female vermilion poison dart frog lays a few eggs in damp humus, but when they hatch she carries them on her back to her "nursery": bromeliad water vessels. In this secluded habitat, they develop virtually unthreatened. The mother visits daily, locating them easily because they wiggle their tails to make ripples in the water. She lays unfertilized, protein-rich eggs, which the tadpoles perforate and suck. Two months after birth, they are fully developed, two-centimeter-long adult frogs. The frogs' waste products decompose in the bromelaid's stored water, making absorbable nutrients for the plant.

Ants participate in some of the most complex and perfect mutualisms. One example is the azteca ant/cecropia tree relationship. Cecropias are medium-sized, weak-limbed rainforest trees. Azteca ants live in the hollow trunk and stems of the cecropia, and obsessively scour the limbs for epiphyte seeds and seedlings, which they dump off the side. This act is crucial for the cecropia, because the weight of epiphytes would break its limbs. Cecropias produce fat and protein-packed capsules at their leaf tips, which nourish the ants. Azteca ants appreciate sweet nectar, too, but since the cecropia doesn't produce flowers, the ants tend masses of aphids inside the tree. The aphids do not harm the cecropia, but produce a sweet honeydew, which the ants eat.

Sometimes a mutual relationship can appear quite exploitative. Cowbirds and *oropéndolas* have a very intricate relationship that puzzled scientists for many years until biologist Neal Smith, working at his research site in Panama, discovered what was really happening. *Oropéndolas* are bird artisans who craft long, sacklike nests that hang from bare-limbed trees in the forest. Cowbirds are parasitical, laying their eggs in *oropéndolas'* nests and then leaving the *oropéndola* to incubate and raise the cowbird hatchling. Although cowbird chicks do preen *oropéndola* chicks, cowbird chicks are aggressive and develop faster than *oropéndola* chicks, and can deprive *oropéndolas* of food. Sometimes *oropéndolas* tolerate this, sometimes they don't. It wasn't until another threat to *oropéndolas* was discovered that the *oropéndolas'* decision-making process was revealed. *Oropéndola* chicks are born without a protective downy coat of feathers, and are particularly vulnerable to botflies burrowing into them and killing them. When wasps and bees are present in the area, they prevent a botfly population from developing. *Oropéndola* mothers allow the cowbirds to lay their eggs only if the nest is located in an area with no wasp or bee populations to control the botflies. If there are wasps or bees around, the *oropéndola* will chase away the cowbird mother or dump her egg out of the nest.

The Biodiversity of Costa Rica (by Zaidett Barrientos & J. Monge Nájera) is available in San José bookstores, or contact INBio (244-4730; www. inbio.ac.cr). Its entertaining vignettes describe some of the more unusual species of flora and fauna, and explain their complex interactions.

DEFORESTATION

The interactions of species that are so fascinating to observe in Costa Rica forests are a lesson for humans in how to live cooperatively with nature, rather than exploiting, exterminating, and controlling it. Despite the steps that the country has taken to conserve nature, about 7000 hectares of land are deforested annually. Current estimates are that only a quarter of Costa Rica's original forest cover is still standing. About half of this is protected by national parks and biological reserves; the rest is in indigenous reserves, forest reserves, and wildlife refuges, or is privately owned. Laws still do not adequately protect this second half from deforestation, and recent changes in the forestry law make it easier to get logging permits.

A traveler in Costa Rica sees evidence of deforestation all over. Huge trucks piled with massive tree trunks rumble along the highways from Talamanca, Osa, and Sarapiquí, all areas recently opened to roads. A flight to Tortuguero will show you the real story—a thin border of rich, tropical forest lines the seashore, and inland, where few tourists see, the land is naked except for a few reserves and national parks. Only a few tall trees remain from the majestic forests that once covered the country.

The causes of deforestation are many. Lumbering activities destroy large areas of forest to extract certain profitable (and often endangered) species of trees, leaving the rest to rot. The roads these companies build into virgin areas allow civilization to encroach farther. The past half-century has seen a spontaneous expansion of agricultural frontiers, often in response to foreign credit possibilities. In the 1960s, millions of dollars in loans were given to Costa Rican ranchers by the U.S. to stimulate beef production. Cattle ranching has ruined about 60 percent of the land, yet has produced very few jobs and has contributed little to the national economy. Banana plantations, which displace lowland rainforests—one of the most diverse ecosystems—have expanded since 1994 in response to growing markets; they now cover 123,000 acres of formerly forested land, mostly in the Northern and Atlantic zones.

The plantations expose workers to high levels of dangerous pesticides, which may cause serious health problems and, in the 1970s, even left thousands of workers throughout Central America sterile. The pesticides also contaminate streams with pesticides, sediment, and lots of trash (especially the pesticide-impregnated plastic that wraps the bananas as they grow). Plantations of citrus or mango trees, usually owned by multinational companies or wealthy Costa Ricans, are buying out small farming families in the Northern Plains too, converting the region into a quilt of monocrops and attracting hordes of wage workers.

Contributing to the problem of deforestation is an inequity of land distribution. With the best agricultural land concentrated in the hands of a few wealthy landowners and multinational companies, poor farmers must clear and work lands on steep hillsides and other inappropriate areas. The number of these campesinos is sure to grow. Costa Rica's population is expanding at an alarming rate—optimists believe that the population's size will double in 25 years; pessimists think it will happen in 20. It is not hard to imagine that the small amount of land still covered with forest will be threatened by this population boom. Costa Rican laws are very progressive in their protection of nature, but unfortunately the government lacks the resources to enforce them.

Deforestation has serious consequences. Costa Rica faces not only erosion and desertification, but flooding, long-term hydroelectric shortages, sedimentation in canals and rivers, destruction of beautiful coral reefs from silt, climactic destabilization, loss of forest wildlife and valuable wood resources, loss of genetic reserves of incalculable value, scarcity of drinking water in some areas during the dry season, and, of course, loss of natural beauty. The legacy of Hurricanes César (July 1996) and Mitch (November 1998)—loss of life due to floods, mudslides, and whole towns being washed away—is attributed in large part to vast deforestation in watersheds.

Efforts are being made to protect what forest still exists. The Ministry of the Environment and Energy (MINAE) encourages private citizens to take responsibility for conservation by offering farmers financial incentives for protecting primary or secondary forest on their own land or for reforesting. So far there is no incentive to plant native species (including precious hardwoods, which take years to mature) rather than exotic species like pine or eucalyptus trees. These trees grow fast but do not re-create native ecosystems —it takes hundreds of years to make a rainforest or cloud forest. In many national parks, the administrators encourage neighbors to develop their own private reserves, which will take pressure off the parks. Most of the forests located outside of the parks are now harbored in privately owned nature reserves. Many of the Park officials also support development of small, tourism-oriented businesses near park entrances so that local people can benefit economically (and, MINAE hopes, will help see to each park's protection).

In this way, ecotourists are helping Costa Ricans make a living from protected areas. Countless nongovernmental conservation organizations are at work throughout the country too (you can read about their activities below). A green seal for bananas (ECO-O.K., known as "Better Bananas" in Europe) has been developed by the New York–based Rainforest Alliance and the Costa Rican Fundación Ambío, in collaboration with scientists, environmentalists, and banana growers. It gives a marketing incentive to growers who make the effort to protect workers and produce bananas away from rivers and with less dangerous pesticides. Twenty-five percent of the banana-cultivated land in Costa Rica has passed the test so far, including all of Chiquita's Costa Rica–based operations, and Chiquita has resolved to bring all of its Latin America plantations up to ECO-O.K. standards.

There is still a long way to go before Costa Rica can be considered a true model for harmony between humans and nature, but many people are dedicating their lives toward this end. The struggle is especially worthwhile in a country with the immense biodiversity of Costa Rica.

HOW TO HELP

Fortunately, many Costa Ricans and international conservationists have good ideas about how to turn the tide away from deforestation toward restoration and preservation of the country's natural resources. Below, you can read about their efforts, as well as their suggestions for how you as a tourist can help.

Note: If you observe any activity you suspect is illegal and harmful to the environment, report it in detail to FECON, the Costa Rican Federation of Environmental Groups (283-6128, fax: 283-6046; www.virilla.net, e-mail: feconcr@racsa.co.cr) or APREFLOFAS (240-6087, fax: 236-3210; www. preserveplanet.org, e-mail: preserve@racsa.co.cr).

FOLLOW A CODE OF ENVIRONMENTAL ETHICS

The Institute for Central American Studies' Department of Responsible Travel has outlined a code of ethics for sustainable tourism. Most responsible ecotourism agencies try to follow the code as closely as possible. If you experience violations of this environmental code, please contact us via e-mail at info@keytocostarica.com.

1. **Tourism should be culturally sensitive.** Visitors should be given the opportunity to enjoy and learn from Costa Rica's mix of cultures. Tourism should serve as a bridge between cultures, allowing people to interact and enrich their understanding of how other people live. Tours should be designed to provide participation in and enhance appreciation of local cultural traditions.

2. **Tourism should be a positive influence on local communities.** Tourism and tour operators should make every reasonable effort to allow communities near natural areas to benefit from tourism. By hiring local guides, patronizing locally owned restaurants and lodges, and buying

local handicrafts, tourists can help convince residents that wild and historical places are worth saving.

3. **Tourism should be managed and sustainable.** Tour operators and visitors should encourage managers of parks, preserves, archaeological sites, and recreational areas to develop and implement long-term management plans. These plans should prevent deterioration of ecosystems, prevent overcrowding, distribute visitors to underutilized areas, and consider all present and future environmental impacts.

4. **Waste should be disposed of properly.** Service providers should set a good example for visitors by making sure that all garbage is confined to the proper receptacles. Boats and buses must have trash cans. Special care should be taken with plastic that is not biodegradable. No littering of any kind should be tolerated. When possible, travelers should use returnable or reusable containers.

5. **Wildlife and natural habitats must not be needlessly disturbed.** Visitors should stay on the trails, remain within designated areas, and not collect anything (except litter). Some ecosystems, such as coral reefs and caves, are particularly sensitive, and special care should be taken to avoid damaging them.

Visitors should keep their distance from wildlife so it is not compelled to take flight. Animal courtship, nesting, or feeding of young must not be interrupted. Birds and their nests should be observed from a safe distance through binoculars. Nesting sea turtles should be observed only with the assistance of a trained guide. Photographers should keep their distance: foliage should not be removed from around nests, and animals should not be molested for the sake of a picture.

Monkeys and other wild animals should not be fed, because this alters their diet and behavior.

6. **There must be no commerce in wildlife, wildlife products, native plants or archaeological artifacts.** Strict international laws prohibit the purchase or transport of endangered wildlife and archaeological artifacts. Tourists should not buy or collect ANY wildlife, and should make sure that the natural products they wish to purchase are commercially grown. Wood crafts generally constitute a viable economic option for local artisans, and tourists should encourage local production from sustainable timber sources.

7. **Tourists should leave with a greater understanding and appreciation of nature, conservation, and the environment.** Visits to parks, preserves, archaeological sites and recreational areas should be led by experienced, well-trained, and responsible naturalists and guides. Guides

should be able to provide proper supervision of the visitors; prevent disturbances to the area; answer questions of the visitors regarding flora and fauna, history and culture; and describe the conservation issues relevant to the area.

8. **Ecotourism should strengthen conservation efforts and enhance the natural integrity of places visited.** Companies offering "ecotourism" must show even greater concern for the natural areas visited, involving tourists in conservation efforts. Tour operators should collaborate with conservation organizations and government agencies to find ways to improve Costa Rica's environmental programs.

Visitors should be made aware of Costa Rica's great achievements as well as the problems. The best tour operators will find ways for interested tourists to voice their support of conservation programs: by writing letters of support, planting a tree, contributing money, volunteering to work in a park, or other creative outlets for concerned activism.

If tour operators, tourists, government agencies, conservation and development organizations work together, ecotourism in Costa Rica can continue to grow, visitors will leave this country satisfied and enriched, and local efforts to conserve our natural heritage will be stronger and more diverse.

Formed in 1990, the **Ecotourism Society** (P.O. Box 755, North Bennington, VT 05257; 802-447-2121, fax: 802-447-2122; www.ecotourism.org, e-mail: ecomail@ecotourism.org) is an international organization promoting a type of tourism that is more responsible to host communities (be they human or plant and animal). They recommend that before they go, travelers become as informed as possible about their destination and the impact they will have; that they bring along conservation and environmental information to share with locals; that travelers act as guests, not consumers; that they see their trip as an opportunity to learn about local ecology; and that they follow up their trip by sharing the information they gained. Giving slide shows, buying guest memberships in international conservation organizations for local conservationists they met, and creating organizational links between conservationists at home and abroad are just a few ways travelers can help. Members of the Ecotourism Society receive the society's newsletter and have access to a large collection of ecotourism-oriented papers.

ASK QUESTIONS

When you want to buy hardwood souvenirs or stay in a hotel built with precious woods, ask about the materials, and how the business has contributed to conservation and reforestation efforts. Most beautiful hardwoods are not "sustainably harvested" but are mined right from the rainforest. Conservationists prefer to see them used for high-value products like handicrafts, rather than for banana crates or pallets. One rainforest tree can be used to make dozens of coffee tables or hundreds of bowls. Since the wood is much more valuable when used in this way, the hope is that its value will generate more respect. While it is not necessarily unconscientious to use endangered woods, those who use them should recognize their endangered status and contribute to efforts to reforest with these types of trees. If nothing else, your questions might sensitize the handicraft dealer or hotelier.

WRITE LETTERS

Tourism is Costa Rica's largest industry, and officials need to maintain the country's image as a tourist's eco-paradise. Letters from travelers worried about environmental destruction, unbridled growth of mega-tourism projects, and abuses by police or bureaucrats all serve to inform and pressure the government about these problems. Your experience in Costa Rica is of interest to policymakers. Write to the president of Costa Rica (Hon. Miguel Angel Rodriguez, Presidente de Costa Rica, Apdo. 520, Zapote, San José; fax: 253-9078) or to the minister of tourism (Walter Niehaus, Ministro de Turismo, Apdo. 777-1000, San José; fax: 223-5107). It's a good idea to send a copy of your letter to the media as well (*The Tico Times*: Apdo. 4632, San José, e-mail: ttimes@racsa.co.cr; or in Spanish, *La Nación*: Apdo. 10138-1000, San José; www.nacion.co.cr).

CONTRIBUTE MONEY

Visitors are important financial collaborators in the efforts of Costa Rican conservationists. Following is a list of some of the most active conservation groups at work here. If you are especially interested in a particular region of Costa Rica, and would like to help conservation or social projects in that area, ask around for local grassroots organizations. These groups, because they often don't have a San José office or contacts with international aid organizations, need even more help. Also, because they usually depend on volunteers, their overhead costs are lower and more of your money will reach its destination. However, check out the reputation of the group and its leaders in the community before writing out your check.

AECO (Asociación Ecologista de Costa Rica; 233-3012, phone/fax: 223-3925; e-mail: aecoced@sol.racsa.co.cr) approaches environmental destruction from two angles. One is to work with local grassroots groups against threats to their areas. The other is to help small-scale campesinos find economic alternatives to environmental destruction.

APREFLOFAS (Asociación Preservacionista de Flora y Fauna Silvestre; phone/fax: 240-6087, cell phone for emergency reports: 381-6315; www. preserveplanet.org, e-mail: preserve@racsa.co.cr) organizes volunteers on weekend patrols of wilderness areas to report illegal hunting, fishing, and logging to the appropriate authorities. They urgently need funds to maintain their vehicles in order to continue this work.

Arbofilia (phone/fax: 240-7145; www.sustainablefutures.com, e-mail: arbofilia@hotmail.com) is an organization of 460 campesino families who design restoration plans for their own watersheds, raise native species tree seedlings in communal greenhouses, and raise cacao (chocolate) and honey. They accept hardy volunteers willing to work on environmental, social, or health projects, and are willing to share the simple lifestyle of El Sur de Turrubares, the remote community that borders Carara Biological Reserve, and site of Arbofilia's field station.

CEDARENA (Centro de Derecho Ambiental y de los Recursos Naturales; 225-1019, 224-8239, fax: 225-5111; www.cedarena.org, e-mail: ceda rena@racsa.co.cr) seeks to make the environment a fundamental element within the legislative and judicial order. Their projects range from promoting biological corridors (unbroken strings of protected land the length of Mesoamerica), to better demarcating indigenous reserves, to legal regulation of hazardous materials. Thanks to their example and outreach, centers similar to CEDARENA have opened throughout Central America. Researchers will be interested in CEDARENA's publications on Costa Rica's environmental laws.

FECON (Costa Rican Federation of Environmental Groups; 283-6128, fax: 283-6046; www.virilla.net, e-mail: feconcr@racsa.co.cr) is a network formed to unify the forces in the Costa Rican environmental movement. They are the main environmental lobby in the legislative assembly. They also help grassroots organizations throughout the country channel reports of environmental abuse to the proper authority for legal action, and try to follow through on these cases to assure positive results.

Fundación Iriria Tsochok (234-1512, 225-5091, fax: 253-6446; e-mail: firiria@sol.racsa.co.cr) is a defense team made up of indigenous people and campesinos living in the Parque Internacional La Amistad. Their main concerns are to protect the people and the forests of La Amistad from agro-industrial expansion, mining, deforestation, and fires. So far they have been able to stall the creation of a coast-to-coast road crossing the Talamanca Mountains in the south of the country, and to halt a proposed oil pipeline; they're now working on community development projects.

Fundación Neotrópica (253-9462, fax: 253-4210; www.neotropica.org, e-mail: fneotrop@sol.racsa.co.cr) promotes conservation and sustainable development in communities near national parks and other protected areas. Their *Editorial Heliconia* sells a wall-sized map of Costa Rica showing locations of all national parks, refuges, and reserves; Deidre Hyde's beautiful posters of the flora and fauna of each life zone; and photo-illustrated books on the national parks.

Grupo YISKI (297-0970, 236-3823, fax: 235-8425) is a student-parent group that has done much to persuade Costa Ricans to recycle. They publish an informative booklet about garbage management, maintain a library, and travel to communities throughout the country to give workshops. Every two years they organize a Youth Conservationist Meeting for high school students.

VOLUNTEER

Volunteering opportunities exist all over Costa Rica. They are outlined in the regional sections of the book, complete with websites and e-mail addresses.

For instance, there are three different turtle protection projects on the Atlantic Coast: **ANAI** in the Gandoca/Manzanillo Wildlife Refuge, the **CCC** in Tortuguero, and the **Reserva Pacuare** in Parismina. ANAI also takes volunteers at its experimental farm in Gandoca. You can live at the beautiful **Samasati Retreat** outside Puerto Viejo in exchange for work, too.

Caño Palma Biological Station (in Canada: 905-831-8809, fax: 905-831-4203; cell phone at station: 381-4116; e-mail: coterc@interhop.net), near Tortuguero, welcomes volunteers who are at least 18, fit, and able to adapt to remote field station conditions. Minimum stay is two weeks ($100/week, meals included). Volunteers assist researchers and help run the station, contributing to kitchen and yard work as well as research projects. During their free time, volunteers can enjoy the station's kayaks and hammocks.

In the Northern Zone, **Monteverde Institute** coordinates a number of volunteer projects ranging from trail maintenance to working in health clinics to organizing women's groups. Also in Monteverde, the **Centro Panamericano de Idiomas** includes volunteer work with its Spanish classes. At **Ecolodge San Luis**, people with a strong background in biology and ecology can receive room and board for helping with research and acting as nature guides.

In Guanacaste, volunteers can work protecting turtles at Playa Grande, Playa Langosta, or Santa Rosa (see ASVO, below).

In the Central Pacific, volunteers are needed at the **Karen Mogenson Reserve** and **ASEPALECO** on the Nicoya Peninsula. In Manuel Antonio,

Jardín Gaia and **Coope El Silencio** need help with their macaw release and endangered orchid-raising projects.

In the Southern Zone, **Proyecto Campanario** and **Delfin Amor** are exciting projects in the Drake Bay area, working in rainforest ecology and cetaean research, respectively. In Puerto Jimenez, the **Fundación Cecropia** needs helps in its work to protect the last remaining forests of the Osa Peninsula.

Volunteers almost always have to pay their own room and board, usually $10-$15 per day, and usually have to make a definite time-commitment to the project they work on.

Through **ASVO** (Association of Volunteers for Service in Protected Areas; MINAE Building, Calle 25, Avenida 8-10; 233-4533, ext. 182 or 135, fax: 233-4989; www.minae.go.cr/asvo, e-mail: asvo89@racsa.co.cr), visitors at least 18 years old can donate support services to the severely understaffed national parks and reserves. Volunteers must adapt themselves to work in all kinds of weather, and they should be willing to do everything that a normal park ranger would do. Initiative and willingness to learn are more important than previous experience. Volunteers pay $10 per day to cover coordination from the central office, lodging, and food. Volunteers must also pay for their own transportation, but especially remote parks will provide rides from a nearby point. Volunteers should speak basic Spanish and provide two letters of reference from organizations abroad or from individuals in Costa Rica, a photo, and a copy of their passport. They must fill out an application form and have a personal interview before being formally accepted. You can choose from a list of parks that have requested volunteers.

NOTE: Sometimes it is possible to just walk up to a national park or reserve and volunteer without going through an organization. Try it!

THREE

Planning Your Trip

SURFING THE WEB

Our website, **keytocostarica.com**, has links to the webpages and projects we think are the most helpful for travelers. If you would like our help with your travel plans, contact us at info@keytocostarica.com (fee).

There is a lot of information on the internet about Costa Rica, but nothing truly comprehensive, and not a lot about low-cost accommodations, so your trusty guidebook is not yet obsolete. Most websites charge the hotels that appear on them, so you will only see the hotels that have paid to be on that site. No website (so far) has as complete a rundown on hotels in an area in all price categories as we do in our book, so you only get a partial view of what is available. We have tried to list websites in the text whenever we could, so with the combination of our recommendations and the websites, you should be able to make very good choices. New websites are springing up every day, so if you want to find out more about a hotel that has no website in the book, type its name and "costa rica" after it, and you might well find it on the web. Here are some of the websites we think can be the most helpful in planning your trip:

www.costarica.com has good information on weather (with satellite images updated hourly), visas, what documents you need to get married in Costa Rica, how to bring your car with you, and much more.

www.cocori.co.cr has a good overview of websites, called Completely Costa Rica.

www.yellowweb.co.cr/crbuses has an online listing of bus schedules and bus stop locations.

www.centralamerica.com gives flight, car rental, and reservation information and tells you about some of the best places in Costa Rica, but they're all pretty pricey.

Some of the best sites are created by community-minded groups of tourism people from the areas you are interested in visiting, like **nosara.com**, **samarabeach.com**, **tamarindo.com**, **greencoast.com** (an excellent site about the Talamanca region on the Atlantic coast), **maqbeach.com** (Manuel Antonio and Quepos) and **costaricasur.com** (Southern Zone). These websites usually put you in direct contact with the hotels. It is best to look for such sites rather than going through a third party website; you are more likely to get lower rates that way.

WHEN TO GO

In Costa Rica, the tourist season is Christmas through Easter, which corresponds to the dry season. You can almost depend on clear, sunny weather, but there are occasional unseasonal storms from the north, which can last for several days. The rainy season usually takes a while to get started in May, and often diminishes for a couple of weeks in July. The rains dwindle in November.

There are certain advantages to coming during the off-season: The mornings are almost always clear and warm. The scenery is fresher and greener. The days are cooled by the rains, which can be a blessing, especially at the beach. The clouds usually clear in time for a magnificent sunset. Many hotels offer substantial discounts during the off-season, sometimes as much as 50 percent. All places are less crowded, more peaceful. Less harm is done to the ecosystems in the parks when fewer people come trooping through at one time.

The only time you really need to plan ahead for nowadays is Christmas week and the week before Easter. Hotel rooms are booked months in advance. But during the rest of the year you can take a "let's just explore and see what happens" vacation, and you'll almost always find a place to stay. Airlines are usually booked far in advance from about December 10 to January 10, so make your plane reservations early if you want to come during that time. The same goes for the weeks on either side of Easter.

CLIMATE

Given Costa Rica's latitude—between 8 and 12 degrees north of the Equator —day length and temperature do not change drastically with the seasons. The sun rises around 5 a.m. and sets around 6 p.m. year-round. Temperature differences are experienced by changing altitude. The misty highlands are in the 10°–13°C (50°–55°F) range, while the Central Valley, at 3800 feet, averages 26°C (78°F). At sea level, the temperature is 30°–35°C (85°–95°F), tempered by sea breezes on the coast. Slight variations occur in December, January, and February, due to cold winds from the North American winter. These cooler temperatures bring on the dry season or "summer," as Central Americans call it, which lasts from December through April. Temperatures start to rise as the sun approaches a perpendicular position over Costa Rica. This causes increased evaporation and brings on the rainy season, or "winter," which lasts from May through November, except for a two-week dry season, a time called *el veranillo de San Juan* (the "little summer"), which occurs sometime in July.

Costa Rica's weather pattern is changing and is not as predictable as it used to be. Now there are many dry days during the "winter" and a few storms during the "summer." Here's a new rule of thumb: the more gloriously sun-drenched the morning during the rainy season, the harder it will rain in the afternoon. Conversely, on a cloudy morning there will be less evaporation, and thus a generally drier day.

The Atlantic Coast has always been an exception to the rule. Trade winds laden with moisture from the Caribbean approach Costa Rica from the northeast. As the moisture rises to the chilly heights of the Cordillera, it condenses into rain on their eastern slopes. For this reason, there is no definite dry season in the Atlantic zone, but the beaches tend to be sunnier than the mountains. In a similar phenomenon, trade winds from the southeast discharge their moisture against the mountains that separate the Osa Peninsula from the rest of the country. The Atlantic plains and the Osa both receive 150 to 300 inches of rain a year, compared to an average of 100 inches in the Central Valley.

One of the most surprising things for newcomers to the Central Valley is that it's not as warm as they expected. The truly hot months are at the end of the dry season, March and April. December, January, and February are usually rain-free, but the weather can be downright chilly, especially at night or if a wind is blowing. During the rainy season, May to November, the days tend to start out warm and sunny and cloud over by noon. The downpour usually starts around 2 or 3 p.m. and it can get pretty cold then, too. Usually a sweater and long pants are enough to keep you warm. When it rains, it *really rains*, but afternoon downpours are usually short-lived. If you go down in altitude from San José's 3800 feet, you'll be able to wear the kind of clothes you hoped you could wear in the tropics.

HOLIDAYS

Costa Rica has 11 official *feriados* (holidays) per year, and they are taken quite seriously. Do not expect to find government offices, banks, professional offices, or many stores open on *feriados*. Twice during the year, the whole country shuts down completely. These are *Semana Santa* (the week before Easter) and the week between Christmas and New Year's Day. Transportation stops totally on Holy Thursday and Good Friday, making Wednesday's buses very crowded. Good Friday is the most important day of Holy Week in Costa Rica and is a day of mourning throughout the country.

Easter week is the time to see picturesque religious processions in the countryside. There are large nonreligious parades in San José on Labor Day, Independence Day, and during Christmas week. *The Tico Times* will tell you where the most interesting events are. It's best to avoid visiting the beach during Easter week because it's often the last holiday young Ticos have before school starts, and they're all there with their radios.

Following is a list of Costa Rica's *feriados*:

January 1   New Year's Day
April 11   Anniversary of the Battle of Rivas
Holy Thursday through Easter Sunday
May 1   Labor Day
July 25   Annexation of Guanacaste Province
August 2   Our Lady of the Angels (Costa Rica's patron saint)
August 15   Assumption Day, Mother's Day
September 15   Independence Day
October 12   Día de la Raza (Columbus Day, Carnival in Limón)
December 24 and 25   Christmas Eve and Christmas Day

CALENDAR OF EVENTS

JANUARY

Santa Cruz: Tico-style bullfights and lively regional folk dancing are the main attractions at the **Santa Cruz Fiestas**.

San José: Top junior tennis players from around the world compete in the week-long **Copa del Café**.

FEBRUARY

San Isidro de El General: A cattle show, agricultural and industrial fair, and orchid show highlight this town's **fiestas**.

Rey Curré: See a re-creation of the struggle between the Indians and the Spaniards at the time of the conquest during the **Fiesta of the Diablitos** held in this small Indian village near Buenos Aires in the Southern Zone.

MARCH

San Antonio de Escazú: A parade of brightly colored carts and the blessing of the animals and crops mark **Día del Boyero** (Ox-Cart Driver's Day).

San José: March is a busy month in San José. You'll find the **National Orchid Show**, featuring more than 500 species, as well as the **Bonanza Cattle Show**, the year's biggest event for cattlemen (but many visitors come for the Wild West fun of the rodeos and horseraces). An **International Arts Festival** brings musicians and theater groups from all over the world to perform. There's also a **Craft Fair**, offering the wares of more than 200 local artisans. The **Carrera de la Paz** marathon attracts as many as a thousand runners.

Ujarrás: The ruins of the first colonial church in Costa Rica, in Ujarrás, is the destination of a **religious procession**.

APRIL

Alajuela: Fiestas are held in honor of Costa Rica's national hero in this, his hometown, on **Juan Santamaría Day**.

Countrywide: **Holy Week** processions throughout the country.

MAY

Limón: May 1, celebrated as **International Labor Day** all over Costa Rica, is a day for picnics, dances, and cricket matches.

San Isidro: Any town of this name—and there are several—is likely to be celebrating **San Isidro Labrador** on May 15 (this saint's day) with festivities that include a blessing of the animals.

San José: The University of Costa Rica marks **University Week** with parades, dances, and cultural events. San Juan Day sees the running of the **Carrera de San Juan**, the year's biggest marathon.

JUNE

Countrywide: On June 29, **Saint Peter and Saint Paul's Day** is celebrated throughout the country.

JULY

Liberia: Fiestas and rodeos are the highlight of the celebration commemorating the **Annexation of Guanacaste** to Costa Rica in 1824.

Puntarenas: Don't miss the regatta of beautifully decorated fishing boats and yachts celebrating the **Fiesta of the Virgin of the Sea**.

San José, mountain and beach hotels: The **International Music Festival.**

AUGUST

Cartago: The old capital is the destination of an annual national pilgrimage honoring Costa Rica's patron saint, the **Virgin of Los Angeles**, known for her miracles.

Countrywide: **Mother's Day** is August 15 in Costa Rica.

San José: **International Black Peoples' Day** is the focal point of **Semana Cultural Afro-Costarricense** (Afro–Costa Rican Culture Week), and features lectures, panels, and displays on black culture.

San Ramón: All the saints from neighboring towns are brought on a pilgrimage for **Día De San Ramón** in the town named for this saint. Fiestas follow the parade.

SEPTEMBER

Guanacaste: Playa Hermosa is the site of **Festival Marino**, featuring such outdoor events as sandcastle-making and jet- and waterskiing.

San José: **Independence Day** is celebrated with parades in the capital and the rest of the country. The Freedom Torch is passed across the Nicaraguan border to relay runners who deliver it to the President in the old colonial capitol of Cartago at 6 p.m. on September 15.

OCTOBER

Puntarenas: The annual **Regatta** is an international event held at the Costa Rica Yacht Club.

Limón: The **Columbus Day Carnival** resembles Mardi Gras in Rio, with brightly costumed dancers parading through the streets all night, concerts, and general merrymaking.

NOVEMBER

Countrywide: From an **International Surf Tourney** to special services in honor of **All Soul's Day**, events take place all across the country this month.

Central Valley: Harvest time for one of Costa Rica's major crops is marked by a **Coffee-Picking Tournament**.

DECEMBER

Countrywide: Christmas celebrations begin early in the month everywhere in Costa Rica, with music, special foods, *rompope* (eggnog), *chicha* (homemade corn liquor), and tamales. There are three annual **Christmas Bird Counts**, each in a different part of the country. Call La Selva (710-1515) for information, or watch for announcements in *The Tico Times*.

Boruca: This indigenous village hosts **Fiesta de Los Negritos**, honoring the village's patron saint with ancient rituals.

Guanacaste: Nicoya is the site of **Fiesta de la Yegüita**, with a procession, foods made from corn, music, bullfights, and fireworks.

San José: December 15 is the start of **Las Posadas**, a Christmas tradition in which children, musicians, and carolers go door-to-door re-creating Mary and Joseph's search for lodging. The week between Christmas and New Year's Day offers San José's biggest celebration of the year. There are Tico-style bullfights, a giant parade with floats, and *El Tope*, a huge equestrian parade in the Sevillian tradition in which elegantly clad riders show off their purebred steeds. The fairground in Zapote turns into an amusement park. On New Year's Eve, a dance to welcome the new year is held in San José's Central Park.

COMING AND GOING

ENTRY REQUIREMENTS

When traveling with a passport, citizens of the United States, Canada, and most Latin American and European countries are entitled to stay in Costa Rica for 90 days. They must enter the country with at least $300 and a departure ticket. Citizens of some Latin American, Asian, African, and East European countries must obtain a visa from a Costa Rican consulate and pay a deposit upon entering the country, refundable when they leave. Check with the consulate nearest you for the latest information.

Always carry your ID: While in Costa Rica, if you don't want to carry your passport with you, get a copy of it made. Don't go anywhere without identification. You can have your passport copy *emplasticado* (laminated) at various street stands in San José. You *will* need your passport to change money at banks.

EXIT AND EXTENDED VISAS

All tourists must pay an airport tax of about $17 when they leave.

If you overstay your 30- or 90-day visa, you will need an exit visa in order to leave the country. These cost about $44; they're paid instead of the airport tax. An exit visa must be used within ten working days (two calendar weeks) of the date it was issued. Almost any local travel agent can obtain an exit visa for you, but be sure to request it at least a week before you are scheduled to depart. They charge a small fee for this service, well worth it compared to the hassle of getting the visa yourself. If you try to get your exit visa yourself, know that it will involve at least half a day of waiting in various lines. They cannot be processed on weekends or holidays. In addition to the cost of the exit visa, you will be charged $1.50 for each month or part of a month that you stayed without a valid tourist card.

You can stay legally by leaving the country for a few days every three months and coming back in with a new tourist visa. If you leave the country while your tourist visa is still valid, you don't need an exit visa. *Be sure that your passport is stamped as you re-enter Costa Rica.* If your passport is not stamped correctly on re-entry, your efforts to renew your visa will have been in vain, and you will have to pay a higher fee for your exit visa. Longer stays are granted only to those applying for student visas or residency. (See Chapter Ten for getaways to Southern Nicaragua, and Chapter Eight for trips to Bocas del Toro, Panama.)

After you've gotten your exit visa and are ready to leave, be sure to confirm your departure flight 72 hours in advance.

Get to the airport at least two hours ahead of flight time. Flights are often overbooked.

TRANSPORTATION

AIRLINES SERVING COSTA RICA

Costa Rica's new international airport terminal opened in August 2000, with 58 additional check-in counters to alleviate the long lines that plagued the old terminal. **LACSA** is Costa Rica's only international airline. It is known for its almost accident-free record—and for jolly Costa Rica–bound flights where everyone gets tipsy on free wine or wired on Costa Rican coffee, and returning Ticos applaud as the plane touches down. We have also heard some complaints about their cavalier attitude when baggage is lost and about chronic overbooking. The toll-free number in the U.S. is 800-225-2272; in Canada, 800-663-2344; England, 553-330; Japan, 81-03770; Taiwan, 551-8866. LACSA is now part of Grupo TACA, the alliance of Central America's airlines.

American Airlines, **Delta**, **United**, **Continental**, and **Canadian Airlines** have flights to Costa Rica with package connections to all major American cities. Discounted rates are offered several times a year, especially in the off-season. **British Airways**, the German airline **Condor**, Spain's **Iberia**, and the Dutch **Martinair** connect Costa Rica with Europe. Try to get a travel agent who is experienced in sending people to Costa Rica because there are many alternatives.

Exito (800-655-4053, fax: 510-655-4566; www.exitotravel.com, e-mail: exito@wonderlink.com), a California-based travel agency, has some of the best rates we've found. Because they send a lot of people to Costa Rica, they get sizeable discounts from the major airlines, and offer attractive group and student rates. Recommended.

Whatever airline you take, make reservations several months ahead if you are going during the dry season, and confirm your reservation 72 hours in advance, because schedules sometimes change. Get to the gateway airport at least two hours before flight time or allow two hours between connecting flights, unless you're going all the way with the same airline. Check-in lines are lengthy and documentation checks and payment of airport taxes may take time. You are required to pay a $29.95 airport tax in Miami. (If you have some time to spare, the **Hotel Mia** in the Miami airport has a health spa on the eighth floor with a swimming pool, sauna, jacuzzi, and running track.) If you are traveling with small children, there is a special nursery room with a changing table and stove in the airport near the LACSA desk.

CHARTER FLIGHTS   Any travel agent can give you glossy catalogues about charter flights to Costa Rica with all-inclusive stays at big fancy beach hotels. Charter flights usually only operate between December and May. Packages including airfare, room, and meals run from $920 to $1600 per week.

Canadians have been flocking to Costa Rica because of the availability of charter flights. Travel agencies throughout Canada book charter flights from Toronto (on **Canada 3000**, 416-674-0257; www.canada3000tickets. com) and Montreal (on **Transat**, 514-476-1011; www.airtransat.com) to San José from November to April. Canada 3000 takes charters from Toronto to Liberia as well. You can also call **World of Vacations**, an affiliate of Canadian Airlines, at 800-661-8881. Tourists have the option of staying one, two, or three weeks.

DRIVING TO COSTA RICA

If you're driving, allow about three weeks from the time you enter Mexico to the time you reach Costa Rica, ten days if you don't want to sightsee on the way. Avoid the highlands of Guatemala and El Salvador, drive only during the day, do not plan to camp in any country except Costa Rica. *Driving the Interamerican Highway to Mexico and Central America* supplies helpful tips, an in-depth account of one such journey, and addresses of hotels en route (6th edition, 160 pages, $21.95 from Costa Rica Books, Suite 1, SJO

981, P.O. Box 02516, Miami, FL 33102-5216; 800-365-2342, fax: 619-421-6002; www.bookzone.com/costarica). You may drive your car tax-free for up to six months as a tourist. You pay $40 when you enter the country and another $40 to renew your visa after three months. After that you have to pay taxes or pay to have the car stored. Chapter Four has information about shipping your car to Costa Rica.

SAMPLE ITINERARIES

Costa Rica offers thousands of places to visit during your vacation. These few sample itineraries are designed to accommodate particular interests, with as much efficiency in routing as possible. We've tried to include off-the-beaten track destinations in these suggestions. Combine several circuits for a longer vacation. These itineraries work best if you have your own car.

If you design your own vacation, travel in slow motion. For example: if you take the Braulio Carrillo highway to the Atlantic coast, spend some time at the forest reserves in Guápiles. If you travel to the Southern Zone, stop at the high-altitude lodges along Cerro de la Muerte for brisk hikes and quetzal searches.

OLD ROUTE TO LIMÓN, WITH RAINFOREST

Day 1	San José
Day 2	Drive to Turrialba
Day 3	Drive from Turrialba to Talamanca
Day 4	Talamanca
Day 5	Talamanca
Day 6	Rainforest visit in Guápiles or Sarapiquí or tour Tortuguero
Day 7	Back to San José

NORTHERN ZONE AND CENTRAL HIGHLANDS

Day 1	Central Valley hotel
Day 2	Early-morning visit to Poás; drive via Vara Blanca to Sarapiquí
Day 3	Rainforest visit in Sarapiquí
Day 4	Drive to Arenal Volcano
Day 5	Visit volcano and hot springs
Day 6	Return by way of San Ramón, visiting Los Angeles Cloud Forest
Day 7	Drive from San Ramón to Zarcero to Bajo del Toro. Stay at Bosque de Paz or Catarata Bajo del Toro
Day 8	Return to Central Valley via Sarchí

GUANACASTE

A one-week indirect trip to the beach.

Day 1	San José or Central Valley
Day 2	Drive north to visit Rincón de la Vieja, Montealto Reserve, Barra Honda, or Palo Verde National Park
Day 3	Drive to Carrillo, Samara, or Nosara
Days 4 to 6	Stay at beach
Day 7	Back to Central Valley via Tempisque ferry

GUANACASTE AND ARENAL

Ten days with volcano, national park, and beach visits.

Day 1	From Central Valley, drive to Rincón de la Vieja; camp or lodge nearby
Day 2	Rincón de la Vieja
Day 3	Santa Rosa National Park; camp or lodge in La Cruz or Liberia
Day 4	Visit beaches of northern Guanacaste, near La Cruz or Liberia
Day 5	Stay at beach
Day 6	Drive south through the Nicoya Peninsula, and stay at Montealto, Barra Honda, or Rancho Humo
Day 7	Spend day in Montealto, Barra Honda, or Palo Verde
Day 8	Drive back through Cañas, Tilarán, and around Lake Arenal. Stay on the lake or near Volcán Arenal
Day 9	Visit volcano and Tabacón Hot Springs
Day 10	Back to Central Valley or San José

SOUTHERN ZONE

This area is still off the beaten track for most visitors, but tourism is definitely increasing.

Day 1	San José; leave early afternoon for Copey, Mirador de Quetzales, San Gerardo de Dota, or Avalon
Day 2	Drive south to San Isidro after a morning birding hike, drive east to San Gerardo de Rivas, or go west to visit the beaches of Dominical or Uvita
Day 3	Explore previous day's destination
Day 4	Continue south to Sierpe, take boat to Drake Bay
Days 5 to 7	Tour Isla del Caño, Corcovado, watch dolphins or whales
Day 8	Head back to San José

CLASSIC COSTA RICAN TOUR

This route passes through some of Costa Rica's most spectacular and best-known destinations. The itinerary includes what most visitors come to see, so expect lots of company.

Day 1	San José or Central Valley
Days 2 & 3	La Fortuna
Day 4	Around Lake Arenal to Monteverde (you can make this a more pleasant trip by spending a night on the lake)
Days 5 & 6	Monteverde
Days 7 & 8	Stay at the beach: Nicoya or Santa Cruz area, or Central Pacific
Day 9	Return to San José

PACKING

Tourists are permitted to bring binoculars, two cameras, and electrical items that are for personal use only, like a small radio, a hairdryer, a personal computer or electric typewriter, a video camera, etc. The most important thing to remember is that the items should not be in their original boxes and not look too new. The government doesn't want tourists to "import" electronic items for resale.

In San José during the rainy season, people usually carry umbrellas—brightly colored *sombrillas* for women and black *paraguas* for men. In the mountains, a lightweight rain poncho is usually more convenient. You'll be glad to have high rubber boots if you go hiking in the rainforest, especially in Corcovado or Sarapiquí. You can buy good ones in Costa Rica for under $7 at San José's Mercado Central and at provincial supply stores, and many places, like Monteverde, rent them to visitors for around $1. Bring boots from home only if you wear an especially large size. Along with your rubber boots, you must have a couple of pairs of fairly thick socks that extend up your calf beyond the top of the boots. If you don't, the boots rub and irritate your skin.

When you go to the beach or rainforest, bring at least one shirt for each day. You're bound to get sweaty. Lightweight cotton or cotton-mix clothing is best, protected inside a plastic bag in case of sudden downpours. Even if you are going to the steamy lowlands, you often have to pass through high mountains to get there—Cerro de la Muerte on the way to the Osa, Braulio Carrillo or Vara Blanca on the way to Sarapiquí. You'll be happier if you have a windbreaker, long pants, and socks that can be peeled off as you get to lower altitudes.

Most hotels will let you store excess luggage while you venture off. You can usually fit everything needed for a trip to the country in a day pack. Start out in a bathing suit, lightweight pants, a cotton overshirt, socks, and running shoes. In addition, bring two bathing suits, two pairs of lightweight pants or shorts, extra socks, and shirts for each day. Bring something to sleep in, sandals, and a scarf, as well as insect repellent, a flashlight, a book, an umbrella or rain poncho, a towel, and toilet paper. Highly recommended: a lightweight, one-layer, hooded nylon windbreaker, especially the kind that folds up into a handy little pouch made out of the front pocket. This handy jacket takes up almost no room and can even be used as a pillow on the bus! If you are traveling during the dry season and not planning to spend a lot of time on top of volcanoes, it's all you'll need to keep warm and to ward off occasional raindrops. If you are going to Irazú, Poás, Chirripó, or other high-altitude areas, you'll need a jacket and warm socks.

Things that are not made in Costa Rica are sold with a 100 percent import-port tax, and therefore are much more expensive here than elsewhere. Following is a list of items that are imported or impossible to find. Bring them with you.

Film and camera equipment
Cassette tapes
Binoculars
Pocket alarm clock or watch
Pocket calculator
Swiss army knife
Good walking shoes
Insect repellent
Sulfur powder (sprinkle on
    socks to deter chiggers)
Anti-itch ointment

Water purifying device
Small first-aid kit
Contact lens solution
Tampons
Birth control items
Vitamins
Earplugs
A universal plug for bathroom
    sinks
Beach towel
Washcloth

If you are traveling on a tight budget, you will also find the following items handy:

Your own cup
Flashlight
Toilet paper
A cotton sheet or two (some
    hotels have nylon or poly-
    ester covers, which are
    uncomfortable in the humid
    heat at the beach)

String and clothespins for hang-
    ing wash
Towel and soap (most places,
    even cheap ones, supply
    towels and soap, but there
    are exceptions)
Battery-operated reading lamp
    for late-night readers

ELECTRICITY

The electrical current used in Costa Rica is 110 volts, AC. The sockets are American-style, but budget places usually don't have a place for a grounding prong. American and Canadian appliances whose plugs don't have grounding prongs should work, but it's always a good idea to check with your hotel about the voltage *before* you plug anything in.

TRAVELING EXPENSES

Costa Rica is not as inexpensive for travelers as other Central American countries. Although public transportation is cheap, restaurant and hotel prices are relatively high. If you are determined to spend as little money as possible, bring a tent and go during the dry season, or visit during the rainy season and take advantage of the off-season rates. You can also find clean and decent rooms with shared baths for under $12 almost anywhere, but nicer rooms range from $25 to $100 and higher. Meals cost between $2 and $15, depending on the "atmosphere." Groceries cost about two-thirds as much as in the United States. According to Tourism Institute statistics, most visitors spend between $75 and $116 per day. However, two people can travel for about $25 a day each, including bus transportation, comfortable lodging (double occupancy), and restaurant meals. If you go to the least expensive places, you can get by for $20 each. Camping out is cheaper still, but you have the inconvenience of hauling around equipment and making sure your tent is guarded at all times.

CURRENCY AND BANKING

The currency unit is the *colón* (¢). Bills come in denominations of ¢50 to ¢10,000, and coins from 1 to 20 *colones* in the silver-colored coins, and 1 to 100 *colones* in the newer gold-colored coins. The exchange rate (check www.costarica.com for up-to-date rates) is around ¢310 per US$1. The *colón* "floats" against the dollar, so rates change all the time.

CHANGING MONEY

Use U.S. dollars or dollar traveler's checks: Costa Ricans are usually happy to be paid in dollars because their currency is constantly being devaluated in comparison to the dollar. But the dollar is not the official currency. So while it is good to carry *colones,* don't worry if you run out. Just carry a calculator with you to make sure the person changing your dollars or traveler's checks is giving you the right amount. Everyone knows the *tipo de cambio*, the rate at which dollars are being bought and sold on a particular day. The rate appears in the newspaper. If you are from a country other than

CREDIT CARDS

Most, though not all, tourism businesses accept major credit cards. Visa seems to be the most widely accepted. There is often a 6% surcharge for credit card transactions.

American Express has two travelers' assistance offices in San José, one downtown in the Credomatic/Banco de San José building (open Monday through Friday, 8 a.m. to 7 p.m.; Saturday, 9 a.m. to 1 p.m.; Calle Central, Avenidas 3/5; 257-0155 ext. 351) and the other in Sabana Sur (Oficentro La Sabana, behind the Contraloría, Edificio 1, Oficina 1; 220-0400). They will cash personal checks if you have an American Express card and valid identification, and you may withdraw up to $500 from your bank account at home (for a commission) if you have the account information, a passport, and an American Express card. Europeans can obtain "cash on the card," similar to a cash advance. In case of a lost or stolen credit card, call 001-800-528-2121. They will authorize the San José offices to make you a new one. Call 0-800-011-0080 to have lost or stolen traveler's checks replaced.

The downtown Credomatic office (location and hours above; 257-0155 ext. 476) also helps **Visa** and **MasterCard** clients in emergency situations and can negotiate emergency cash advances. For lost or stolen Visa cards, call 0-800-011-0030; for Master-Cards, 0-800-011-0184.

The office for **Diners Club** cardholders is in **ScotiaBank of Costa Rica** (Avenida 1, Calles Central/2; 257-2351, weekdays; 257-7878, weekends).

the U.S., you will probably find it easier to buy U.S. dollars before leaving home than to try to exchange your currency for *colones* in Costa Rica. (Airport taxis will accept dollars, but small bills only so they don't have to make change.)

Before your get there: There is no advantage to trying to change dollars to *colones* before you get to Costa Rica.

At the airport: You can change money at the airport banks until 5 p.m. There are two ATMs there as well. Ask for the *cajera automática.*

At your hotel: Hotels are authorized to change money and traveler's checks for their guests; sometimes their rates are less favorable than the bank rate, but only by a few cents on the dollar. Smaller hotels might not have enough money on hand to cash your checks; it's wise to carry $20 traveler's checks if you're planning to spend time in the countryside.

ATMs: There are quite a few ATMs in Costa Rica, but they are more often found in urban areas, and you don't want to spend your vacation in urban areas. For a complete list of ATM locations, see www.incostarica.net.

In the provinces: It is possible to change money in towns other than San José. Often the provincial banks' process is faster. Even if you are not near a bank, certain hotels, tourist information centers, and *pulperías* (corner stores) usually provide this service for travelers. In fact, most places are glad to be paid in dollars, but you'll have better luck with cash than with traveler's checks.

Bring your passport: To change money or traveler's checks at banks, you must have your passport with you. They won't accept photocopies.

At San José banks: Banks are open from 9 a.m. to 3 p.m., and some branches stay open until 5 p.m. State-owned banks (Banco de Costa Rica, Banco Nacional de Costa Rica, Banco Popular, Banco de Crédito Agrícola) are more crowded. The many private banks such as Banex and Banco de San José are quicker, and the money-changing process is simpler. One exception is the *Operaciones Internacionales* Department at the central offices of Banco de Costa Rica on Avenida Central, Calle 4. This second-floor office is devoted only to changing currency and is pretty efficient (open weekdays, 8:30 a.m. to 3 p.m.). On Monday, Friday, and any day following a holiday, the lines will be longer than usual.

On the street: Don't risk changing money with the guys who saunter around on the streets near Radio Monumental (Avenida Central, Calle 2). Their scam is to pretend to panic and run because "the police are coming" —before you have time to count the *colones* they give you. They're experts in folding bills so that the stack appears larger.

Special note for Canadians: **ScotiaBank of Costa Rica** (Avenida 1, Calles Central/2; branches also in Curridabat, Sabana, and Multiplaza; 257-6868) buys Canadian dollars. The central offices of two state banks buy them as well: **Banco de Costa Rica** (Avenidas 2/Central, Calles 4/6; 287-9000) buys Canadian dollar traveler's checks, and **Banco Nacional de Costa Rica** (Calles 2/4, Avenidas 1/3; 223-2166) accepts cash or traveler's checks, but again, you have to waste your time standing in line.

HEALTH PRECAUTIONS

INOCULATIONS

See your doctor before taking any foreign journey to be sure you're up to date on your regular vaccinations (tetanus, polio, measles, and so on). You probably won't need to get any special vaccinations or inoculations before traveling to Costa Rica, but it's a good idea to check for current recommendations by calling the **Centers for Disease Control** hotline in Atlanta at 888-394-8747, or visit www.cdc.gov on the web.

WATER

Water is safe to drink in most of Costa Rica. However, bottled water is recommended in the San José suburbs of Escazú and Santa Ana, and in Puntarenas and Limón. *Soda* is the term to use when asking for carbonated mineral water. Several brands of non-carbonated bottled water are sold in most supermarkets throughout the country. Responsible beach hotels usually provide bottled water for guests in their rooms.

AMOEBAS AND PARASITES

Even though Costa Rica's water is good in most places, visitors traveling in the provinces sometimes have intestinal problems. If symptoms are persistent, they might be due to *amibas* or *giardia*. If you get a strong attack of diarrhea, it's wise to take a stool sample to a local lab to have it analyzed. Put it in a clean glass jar, and deliver it immediately, or just appear at the lab and they will give you the appropriate receptacles to take a sample then and there. Amoebas can't be found in samples that are a few hours old. The **Clínica Bíblica** (257-5252) lab is open weekends and holidays. **Clínica Americana** (222-1010) has a good lab, and **Dr. Gil Grunhaus** (221-3423), across from Hospital San Juan de Dios on Paseo Colón, gives the most complete reports. Your results will be ready the same day, especially if you bring your sample before noon ($6-$8 in advance). If results are negative, take up to three samples. Sometimes the offending organisms are not found the first time. The most dangerous one is *entamoeba histolytica*. This can migrate to your liver and cause damage later.

It is not necessary to go to a doctor unless you want to. A pharmacist can give you the needed drug based on your lab results. We have not found that natural methods cure amoebas. Even if you get over your diarrhea, the organisms can still be doing damage to your system unless you've taken the proper medicine. Symptoms often show up as a tendency toward constipation and a feeling of depression and low energy. It's best to take the chemicals and be done with the bugs. Be sure to ask for the literature that goes with the medicine so you'll know about possible side effects.

To avoid bugs when traveling outside San José, stay away from drinks made with local water or ice, and fruits and vegetables that cannot be peeled.

DEHYDRATION

Dehydration can be a problem at the beach and other steamy lowland areas where you sweat a lot, and equally problematic if you suffer excessive diarrhea or vomiting. Bring a drinking bottle of good water if you hike. The water in green coconuts (*agua de pipa*) is both pure and full of the very same minerals that you lose when you sweat or vomit. *Caldo*, a clear soup with vegetables and chicken or meat, can also help you regain lost liquid and salt, and it is one of the easier foods to get down when you're not feeling well.

DENGUE FEVER

The disease that has caused the most trouble in the last few years is dengue fever, a virus carried by mosquitoes. It begins with a sudden fever of 102° or higher that can last for as long as seven days. Acute pain in the head, muscles, joints, and eyes, and a rash on the chest and back can accompany the fever. You should seek medical treatment as soon as symptoms appear. Government efforts to fumigate and destroy the puddles where mosquitoes breed have proved successful in the communities where dengue has been a problem. People usually recover from dengue, but if you catch the disease twice it can be life-threatening.

MALARIA

Malaria is not a danger for most travelers to Costa Rica. According to the Ministry of Health, it only occurs in very isolated areas of the country, principally at the banana plantations in the Valle de la Estrella in inland Talamanca. If you are going to this area, or just want to take precautions, you can pick up chloroquine at the Dispensary of the hospital San Juan de Dios in San José (Calle 14, Avenida Central/6).

CHOLERA

The cholera epidemic that has taken so many lives in Latin America has so far been held at bay in Costa Rica because of a strong public education campaign and a concerted effort on the part of health officials to identify and treat any cases imported from other countries.

Cholera causes an extremely strong attack of watery diarrhea, sometimes accompanied by vomiting. Its victims die from dehydration. The treatment is a simple oral rehydration solution, called *suero*, available for a few cents in any drugstore. If you have frequent, copious, watery diarrhea without fever, don't wait to take a sample to a laboratory—get medical help right away. You can be sure that if there is an epidemic of cholera in Costa Rica, it will be all over the media, and the areas where it is occurring will be clearly defined. After observing the determination with which Costa Ricans have confronted this danger, we doubt the disease will reach epidemic proportions here.

SWIMMING POOLS AND RIVERS

Look for any visible signs of pollution before you jump into a river or pool, and always be sure to wash well with soap and water after you come out. To avoid fungus infections in the ears, clean them with rubbing alcohol and a swab after swimming.

INSECTS

Mosquitos can be a problem, even in breezy San José at night during the dry season. Anti-mosquito spirals can be bought at supermarkets and *pulperías* for about 40 cents a box. Smaller stores will often sell you just a pair for about 12 cents. Be sure to ask for the little metal stand (*soporte*) that goes with them. Light up the spiral and circle it several times over your bed, then put it as far away from your bed as possible, or even outside the window or door. They usually work pretty well, though some people can't stand the smell.

Mosquito nets (*mosquiteros*) can be purchased at La Gloría (Avenida Central, Calles 4/6) in San José. Be sure to bring strings and hooks to screw into the ceiling in case there is no place to hang a net.

On the Atlantic Coast, beware of **sandfly** bites that seem to become infected and grow instead of disappearing. This could be a sign of *papalomoyo* (Leishmaniasis), a disease that can be life-threatening if untreated. See a tropical disease specialist immediately.

Purrujas (no-see-ums) are perhaps the most aggravating of Costa Rican insects. They bite you without your even seeing or feeling them, then the bite itches for days. *Purrujas* like to hang out at the edge of the beach where the sand meets the trees. They seem to be more active at dusk. You can buy sulfur powder at Farmacia Fischel (Calle 2, Avenida 3) by the quarter kilo for very little money. Sprinkle it on your socks to discourage sandflies. That means you should wear shoes and socks on the beach for your sunset walk. Dusk is generally the time to apply insect repellent, too.

Eating lots of garlic and brewer's yeast tablets purportedly makes your blood unpalatable to mosquitoes, flies, and no-see-ums.

Some people have serious allergic reactions to **ant** bites. A person having an allergic reaction might begin to itch all over, then turn red and swell up. If that happens, get to a hospital as soon as possible. In the worst scenario, a person's throat swells up, causing asphyxiation. To avoid ant bites, wear closed shoes whenever you're in the jungle or on the beach.

Africanized bees have worked their way north from Brazil, and can attack humans with fatal results if the bees' nests are disturbed. Bee colonies are ten times denser in hot, dry areas than in rainforests. If attacked, run as fast as you can in a zigzag direction, or jump into water. Bees don't see well over distances. Never try to take cover; don't crawl or climb into a precarious position from which you cannot make a quick exit. Throw something light-colored over your head to protect your eyes and nose; keep your mouth closed. For more detailed information, contact the OTS (240-6696). If you know you are allergic to bee stings, talk with your doctor before you come to Costa Rica and carry the proper medication with you. You might want to buy a self-injector kit for bee stings, available in pharmacies in the U.S. with a prescription or in Costa Rica without one. This could save you if you can't get to a hospital fast enough.

SNAKES

Although not all snakes in Costa Rica are dangerous, a few are potentially deadly: fer-de-lance, eyelash vipers, bushmasters, and rattlesnakes. To recognize these snakes should you run across one in the wild, visit the Serpentarium in San José (see Chapter Six), El Mundo de los Serpientes in Grecia, or Parque Viborana in Turrialba (see Chapter Seven). If you are bitten, stay calm and head to the nearest health post for a shot of antivenin. According to *The Tico Times*, you shouldn't waste time trying to suck the venom out cowboy-style; experts say it doesn't help. And definitely don't use a knife or razor to enlarge an opening in your skin: bleeding and risk of infection will only make matters worse.

ACCOMMODATIONS IN COSTA RICA

How we list hotel rates: Our hotel rates are based on *double* occupancy (un-less otherwise indicated), and include a 16.4 percent tax. Most hotels give their rates without the taxes, so amounts in this book might appear to be more than those stated in hotel advertising or on their websites. Prices change; although we try to be as accurate as possible, don't take it on faith that a hotel still charges what we said it charges—always ask. Rates will vary if you are alone or in a group, or if meals are included. In theory, the Tourism Institute (ICT) each year determines the rates hotels can charge. These rates are given in *colones*, and must be posted in each room. In prac-tice, many hotels charge in dollars and maintain the dollar price even if it no longer matches the price in *colones*. You have a right to demand to pay the official price that is posted in your room.

Reservations: Make reservations three months ahead at Christmas or Easter. Most hotels have fax or e-mail numbers, which we have tried to in-clude, as it's often easier to correspond this way. Some hotels require a deposit. Travel agents have told us that even if you have confirmed your reservation, you can still get bumped if you haven't sent a deposit.

Rates to expect: You can find clean, fairly comfortable rooms almost anywhere for $10 to $30 for two. Atmosphere costs more, getting you into the $50-$100 range. If you can afford them, there are plenty of places with great atmosphere, equipment, and service. We have tried to draw your atten-tion to the few hotels in the $30-$50 range that provide "atmosphere."

Noise pollution: Our main complaint about many hotels, even some ex-pensive ones, is that you're often subjected to noise pollution from some-body's high-powered sound system. The usual source is a nearby dance hall or neighbors with a loud radio. A place can seem perfectly *tranquilo* when you arrive during the day; the thumping disco across the river only comes on at night. The best solution is to get up and dance. Places owned by for-eigners are often quieter than places owned by Ticos, who regard loud music as *alegre*. The sounds of trucks and motorcycles rumbling by during the day might not be a problem, but it can keep you awake at night, so be aware of your hotel's distance from the road.

How many words for hotel are there in Spanish? We should clarify the meaning of various terms referring to lodging.

Hotels usually have more than one story, though not always. *Cabinas* are the most common form of lodging at the beach or in the mountains. They may be separate, or connected in rows or duplexes, roughly corresponding to what a North American would call a "motel." However, here *motel* refers to a small number of establishments, mostly on the southeastern side of San

José, that couples use for clandestine romantic trysts. Motels rent by the hour. *Villas, bungalows,* and *chalets* are fancy cabinas, usually separate from one another. *Pensiones* and *hospedajes* are usually converted houses, and often serve family-style meals. A *posada* is an inn. An *albergue* is a lodge, usually in the forest or the mountains, and most often oriented toward eco-tourism.

Youth hostels are also called *albergues* or, less commonly, *hostales.* Most of them are simply hotels and lodges that give substantial discounts to International Youth Hostel Federation members. If you are already a member, your card will be honored; otherwise, purchase one at **Toruma Hostel** (Avenida Central, Calles 29/31; 224-4085) in San José. Bring a photo. There are affiliated hostels in San José, Puerto Viejo de Talamanca, Liberia, Rincón de la Vieja and Guanacaste National Park, Monteverde, Jacó, and Puntarenas. The hosteling desk at Toruma can also arrange tours and transportation throughout the country. Often a cheap hotel is less expensive than a hostel.

Homestays offer the opportunity of a more authentic Tico experience. If you study Spanish in San José or at schools in beach or mountain locations, you can choose to live with a Tico family fairly inexpensively. See the listings for Spanish schools near the end of this chapter. **Bell's Home Hospitality** (225-4752; www.homestay.thebells.org, e-mail: homestay@racsa.co.cr) is another great way to hook up with Tico families and get comfortable accommodations in the $40-$50 price range. See their listing near the end of the San José Chapter. If you have young children, homestays might be a good alternative, as many Tico homes have children of their own.

Discounts: Beach and mountain hotels often give discounts in the green season (May to November). Weekly and monthly rates are common as well. If you are staying in one place for a while, consider renting a house. See *The Tico Times* for listings, or ask at a local *pulpería*; www.greencoast.com lists inexpensive house rentals on the Caribbean coast.

Shower temperature: We have four categories for telling you about water temperature in the shower when we describe a hotel.

Cold water means just that—no hot water. However, showers at places near the beach are often "solar-heated" naturally, and it sometimes feels good to take a cool shower instead of a hot one.

Heated water refers to an electric device that warms the shower water as it comes out of the showerhead. *Note:* These contraptions are usually set to come on when the water is turned on, but in some places you have to turn them on yourself. Check how yours works while you are dry and have your shoes on. You don't want to be fooling around with it while you are wet and barefoot in the shower. If there is too little water pressure, the little buggers become too hot and can burn out, so be careful. Usually they make for a pretty limp, lukewarm shower.

Hot water refers to water heated by a hot water tank.

Solar-heated water indicates the use of solar-heating devices, often something as simple as black tubing on the roof.

Natural ventilation refers to places at the beach that, because of their location or construction, take advantage of ocean breezes and thus don't need fans.

NOTES FOR SENIOR TRAVELERS

Older travelers will certainly be able to find good company, comfortable traveling conditions and lodging, with the assurance that excellent health care is available if they should need it.

Note: The bad condition of the sidewalks is a real problem in many places, and much care must be taken by pedestrians.

Elderhostel, which sponsors inexpensive and interesting trips for people 60 years of age or over, includes Costa Rica in its itinerary. For more information contact Elderhostel (877-426-8056; www.elderhostel.org).

A tour company oriented toward travelers over 50 is Boston-based **Grand Circle** (800-597-3644; www.gct.com). Their Costa Rica trip includes visits with University for Peace visionaries. A foundation arm of the company makes significant donations to nonprofit organizations in Costa Rica.

NOTES FOR TRAVELERS WITH DISABILITIES

In 1996, activists for disabled rights won a victory when legislation was enacted that guarantees education, social services, and jobs for all disabled people in Costa Rica. Public transportation is to be accessible to all people as is any new public construction. However, great laws aren't always implemented in Costa Rica.

Unfortunately, very little has been done to make access easier for people with disabilities and parents pushing strollers. Streets and sidewalks are often in deplorable condition, some curbs are more than a foot high, and many roads do not have sidewalks at all, forcing everyone into the street. Despite all this, several people with disabilities have told us that they felt conditions were better for them here than in the U.S. because of the climate, the relatively low cost of quality health care and hospitalization, and the low cost of maids and other helpers. Many neighborhoods do have sidewalks and downtown San José has some sidewalk ramps at intersections, but they are often too high to be helpful.

FAUNA (Fundación Acceso Universal a la Naturaleza; 771-7482; e-mail: chabote@racsa.co.cr), a non-profit organization dedicated to promoting tourism for people with disabilities, prepares personalized itineraries to answer the needs and interests of physically challenged persons visiting Costa Rica. The Montreal-based **Instituto Internacional de Desarrollo Creativo** (514-481-2835; www.consult-iidc.com) organizes easy-access tours in conjunction with FAUNA.

FAUNA classifies the following hotels as adapted or accessible: Hampton Inn near the airport, Aurola Holiday Inn in downtown San José, Vista del Valle Plantation Inn in Rosario de Naranjo, Villa de Alegre in Tamarindo, Wilson Gardens in Puntarenas, Oasis del Pacífico in Playa Naranjo, Aubergue du Pelican in Esterillos Este, and Hotel del Sur in San Isidro de El General. Classified as "accessible with help" are Hotel Don Carlos in San José, Cabinas Playa Hermosa in northern Guanacaste, Hotel Playa Nosara in southern Guanacaste, Tilajari Resort in the San Carlos area, Hotel Fonda Vela in Monteverde, and Cabinas Espadilla in Manuel Antonio. You can look these up in the lodging index at the back of the book.

Some of the most accessible tours in the Central Valley are those to Poás Volcano, the Café Britt Coffee Tour, the Zoo Ave in La Garita de Alajuela. and the Calypso boat tour in Puntarenas. In the Northern Zone, the Aerial Tram makes special arrangements for travelers with disabilities if you let them know in advance.

Vaya con Silla de Ruedas (391-5045, fax: 454-2810; www.ourworld. compuserve.com/homepages/eshzk, e-mail: vayacon@racsa.co.cr) is a new transportation and tour company with an ADA-approved van with elevator, three wheelchair stations, front and back air conditioners, and room for friends and companions. They custom-design trips to accessible places starting at $150 per person for a half day, $270 for a full day.

Otherwise it is best to get around by taxi. Taxi service is fairly reasonable, but you'll have better luck if you summon a taxi by phone instead of trying to hail one on the street. Taxi drivers seem to ignore the disabled if they have the opportunity to pick up others.

For further information in Costa Rica contact **CENARE** (Centro Nacional de Rehabilitación, office behind Hospital México in San José's La Uruca district; 232-8233). The best person to talk to is Dr. Federico Montero. They also sponsor weekly wheelchair sports events such as basketball games, Ping Pong, races, and archery.

The most wheelchair-accessible bathrooms in San José are at the **Hotel Aurola** Holiday Inn and other modern, upscale hotels. American fast-food restaurants are also likely to have accessible bathrooms.

Many shopping malls in San José suburbs are wheelchair accessible. The **Mas x Menos** in Novacentro, Moravia, has motorized shopping vehicles for the handicapped.

For information in the U.S., contact the **Society for the Advancement of Travel for the Handicapped** (212-447-0027, fax: 212-725-8253; www. sath.org, e-mail: sathtravel@aol.com); **Travelin' Talk** (931-552-6670, fax: 931-552-1182; www.infinitec.org, e-mail: trvlntlk@aol.com), a networking organization, also provides information. In Canada, contact **Keroul** (514-252-3104, fax: 514-254-0766; www.keroul.qc.ca), which specializes in tourism for people with restricted physical ability.

NOTES FOR TRAVELING WITH CHILDREN

Ticos love children. You won't get dirty looks for bringing them along—only smiles and a helping hand when needed. Both men and women seem to be naturally sensitive to the needs of children, whether it is to spontaneously help you lift them on or off the bus, or to include the kids in conversation. If you have a baby (especially a fair-haired one), be prepared to be stopped in the street while people admire your little treasure.

Exit visas: If you are planning an extended stay (more than 30 days) in Costa Rica with a child, one or both of whose parents will not be in the country, you have to get a letter from the absent parent(s) giving you permission to take the child out of Costa Rica again. (Even if you are one of the parents, you need a letter from the other if he or she is absent.) To check on these regulations, call the Costa Rican embassy nearest you. See www.costa rica.com/embassy for a list.

What to bring: When preparing for your trip here, you should pack a junior first-aid kit with baby aspirin, thermometer, vitamins, diarrhea medicine, oral rehydration solution in case of serious dehydration, sunblock, bug repellent, tissues, wipes, and cold medicine.

Pack extra plastic bags for dirty diapers, cloth diapers for emergencies, baby sunscreen, a portable stroller and papoose-style backpack, a car seat if you plan to use a car, easy-to-wash clothes, swimsuits, a floppy hat to wear in the water, a life jacket, beach toys, and picture books relating to Costa Rica.

Travel tips: Try to plan a flight during your child's nap time, but feed a baby during take-off and landing to relieve pressure in the ears. If you are pregnant or breast-feeding, be sure to stay well hydrated during the flight. Bring everything you need on board—diapers, food, toys, books, and extra clothing for kids and parents alike. It's also helpful to carry a few new toys, snacks, and books as treats if boredom sets in.

Pace your trip so your child can adapt to all the changes in routine. Don't plan exhausting whirlwind tours, and keep travel time to a minimum. You'll be a lot more comfortable if you splurge on a rental car rather than taking buses, at least until your kids are over seven. Our seven- and nine-year-olds did great on bus trips. The thing that really bothered them was getting too hot, so we'd try to take early-morning or late-afternoon rides. Seek out zoos, parks, plazas, outdoor entertainment, and short excursions to amuse your child. Costa Rica's marketplaces are more fascinating to some children than museums. On the other hand, our kids didn't like the crowds, noise, hustle and bustle of San José at all.

Bathrooms are hard to find sometimes, and it is perfectly acceptable for little ones to pee in the bushes or even against a building if you are in the city. Disposable diapers are readily available for trips, but you won't find many places with changing tables. A portable changing pad comes in handy. People will help you find the best place to do what has to be done.

Activities: During the Costa Rican summer (January to March), the Ministry of Culture, Youth, and Sports (257-1433, 256-4139) sponsors many interesting courses for kids age seven to 15, ranging from art to dance to archaeology to astronomy. There are children's theater performances on Sundays and some arts-and-crafts stuff in the parks. Playgrounds, like Central American plumbing, seem to get trashed and ruined overnight. The Friday and Sunday editions of the daily *La Nación*'s *"Viva"* section and the "Weekend" section of *The Tico Times* list whatever is happening for children over the weekend.

One place most kids will enjoy is the **Parque Nacional de Diversiones** (open daily December through March, Monday through Thursday, 9 a.m. to 5 p.m., and until 9 p.m. on Friday, Saturday, and Sunday; Wednesday to Sunday the rest of the year; 231-2001), a large, clean, and well-run amusement park with all kinds of mechanical rides in La Uruca, west of San José. About $7 will entitle your kid to all the rides he or she can take in a day, as well as admittance to **Pueblo Antiguo**, a model of old-time Costa Rican life, where dance and theater performances are often held. All proceeds go to support the Children's Hospital. There are plenty of places to eat there, but they are all of the greasy fast-food variety, so bring your own snacks and juices.

The park is located a few kilometers west of Hospital Mexico, the large building you see on the left as you leave the western suburbs of San José heading for Puntarenas. To find it, you must get off the main highway at the Juan Pablo II rotunda and take the access road that runs parallel to the highway directly in front of the hospital. Or take the "Hospital Mexico" bus that leaves from Calle 8, Avenidas Central/2 hourly during the week and every half-hour on weekends.

San José converted its castle-like penitentiary into a well-designed **Children's Museum** (admission: adults, $2; children under 18, $1.50; open weekdays, 8 a.m. to 3 p.m.; weekends, 10 a.m. to 5 p.m.; at the extreme north end of Calle 4; 222-7485). It is fairly well maintained and has lots of exciting interactive exhibits. (You have to cross a pretty bad neighborhood to get there, so spring for a cab.)

Our favorite beaches for kids—those that are shady and have gentle waters—include: Bahía Junquillal Recreation Area, Playa Hermosa, Playas del Coco, Sámara and Carrillo in Guanacaste, and the third beach at Manuel Antonio (though it's a 20-minute walk through the park to get there). The beaches are beautiful and lined with palms in Talamanca, but the currents can be so strong that nothing more than wading or playing in knee-deep water is suggested. At low tide in Playa Chiquita (south of Puerto Viejo), Drake Bay, Dominical, Playa Santa Teresa, and Montezuma, there are tide-pools that are fun for kids to play in.

David Norman's inexpensive and informative wildlife coloring books are a good way to prepare your children; look for them at bookstores and gift-shops in San José, or order through www.amerisol.com.

To prepare your six- to twelve-year-olds, order *Let's Discover Costa Rica*, a bilingual, 64-page book full of activities like cut-out-and-assemble mobiles, mazes, and paint-by-number pictures, all woven into a story of intercultural friendship. Order from A. Gingold, Apdo. 1-6100 Mora, Ciudad Colón, Costa Rica; 249-1179, fax: 249-1107; e-mail: agingold@racsa.co.cr.

NOTES FOR WOMEN

Costa Rica is one of the safest countries for women travelers in Latin America, given its peaceful nature and well-developed tourism industry. Although domestic violence is, unfortunately, all too common, the sexual assault rate is much lower than in the United States. However, as in any area, women traveling alone must use caution, especially at night. Be aware of which neighborhoods have a reputation for trouble.

This is a country where machismo is still considered normal male behavior. An unaccompanied woman should disregard the flirtatious comments many Tico men will call out, such as *mi amor* (my love), *machita* (if you are a blond), or *guapa* (pretty). If they are farther away, they hiss as a woman passes by. It's annoying, but not dangerous. The best policy is to ignore them and keep walking.

Ticos can be compelling in their professions of eternal devotion. Whether they are married or single does not seem to have much to do with it. Take anything that is said with a grain of salt. Ticos often regard foreign women as easy conquests. But, as in most other Latin countries, they look for *la Virgen Purísima* when making a lasting commitment.

NOTES FOR MEN

Prostitution is legal in Costa Rica, and prostitutes are given medical tests on a regular basis. Some prostitutes have been found to be carrying AIDS. Prostitutes have been known to gang up on men in the street and rob them. There have also been cases of men being drugged and robbed after having invited women to their apartment or room—or just for a drink. Be careful, guys.

Costa Rican women are known for their loveliness and intelligence. Ticas are also good at being *chineadoras*, i.e., taking care of men as if they were babies. Many foreign men have sought out Costa Rican women for relationships. Although we know of many successful intercultural marriages, we urge our readers to pay close attention to deeply ingrained cultural differences that can cause major communication problems when the idyllic glow wears off.

NOTES FOR TRAVELING WITH PETS

Dogs are not regarded with the same affection as they are in North America and Europe, and are used as guards rather than as pets. Most Costa Ricans are scared to death of dogs. If there is a rabies epidemic, government agents go around feeding poisoned meat to dogs, especially in the countryside. Several friends have lost pets in this way.

Another problem might be finding a temporary place to stay with your pet. In general, bed and breakfasts are more willing to take animals.

To learn the current requirements for bringing pets to Costa Rica, go to www.costarica.com/travel/plan/pet.

NOTES FOR STUDENT TRAVELERS

See "Accommodations in Costa Rica" section earlier in this chapter for details on youth hostels and Chapter Two for volunteer opportunities.

An International Student Identification card entitles you to discounted flights to Costa Rica and many discounted tours. They are $20 at any Council Travel office, a chain of U.S. student travel agencies. If there is no office near you, request a *Student Travel Magazine* from the **Council on International Educational Exchange** (CIEE, 212-822-2700, fax: 212-822-2719;

www.ciee.org, e-mail: info@ciee.org). The catalog has an application form. With card in hand, you can purchase the discounted ticket only through a student travel agency.

NOTES FOR GAY AND LESBIAN TRAVELERS

Costa Rica continues to enjoy a steady increase in gay and lesbian visitors. This is in part due to the social tolerance exhibited here, at least when compared to other Latin American countries. But keep in mind, this is a small and deeply religious country and the gay lifestyle is primarily discreet in nature. This may be an extension of a cultural dislike for conflict rather than overt homophobia.

Gay rights have only recently been allowed out of the closet. After a 1995 police raid on the popular gay disco Deja Vu, the owners filed suit and, with a legal victory, opened the door for a more public gay rights movement. Costa Rica's government sanctioned a gay and lesbian rights organization, **La Asociación Triángulo Rosa** (Spanish, 442-7375; English, 234-2411). The nation's first exclusively gay and lesbian news magazine, *Gente 10*, began. In 1999, protesters blocked the arrival of a bus of gay tourists who were headed for a festival in Manuel Antonio. After a lot of press coverage and apologies by key officials, the controversy seems to have blown over.

Gay and lesbian businesses are springing up throughout the Central Valley. (See Chapter Six for gay and lesbian bars and discos in San José.)

You shouldn't have any trouble in other areas of the country. When checking in to your hotel as a couple, you should both be at the desk so they know you're staying together. Managers get nervous when they see unknown people in their hotel. Once again, the best policy is to be discreet but not deceive. You might be more comfortable in the hotels or cabinas that offer a greater sense of privacy.

For hotels, **Colours** in the western suburb of Rohrmosher remains the city's most established exclusively gay hotel. They have a similar hotel in Florida, and their U.S.-based travel agency (800-277-4825, fax: 305-534-0362), can make reservations at Colours and throughout Costa Rica. **Hotel Kekoldi** is a midrange alternative in San José. They coordinate with Holbrook Travel in Gainesville, Florida, which provides quality natural-history travel to the gay and lesbian community (800-858-0999; e-mail: travel@holbrooktravel.com). They also have a branch at Manuel Antonio.

Most gay and lesbian travelers head for the Pacific beach of Manuel Antonio, where **Casa Blanca Hotel** (an exclusively gay and lesbian facility) is a favorite spot. La Playita, the tiny private beach just past the northern point of Manuel Antonio, is a gay and lesbian scene, especially during Christmas and Easter holidays.

For up-to-date gay and lesbian information in English or Spanish, go to www.gaycostarica.com. You can also contact them by phone at 506-276-8197 or 506-388-4109. ILPES (Instituto Latinoamericano de Prevención y Educación en Salud) runs the "Con Voz" hotline (280-4832, 280-4835). They use a holistic approach to AIDS prevention, and sponsor support group therapy, public information, and pride events. Volunteers are accepted.

Uno en Diez (open Monday through Saturday, 9 a.m. to 9 p.m.; Sunday, 3 to 9 p.m.; 258-4561; www.1en10.com) is an internet café, gallery and gay information center on Calle 1, Avenidas 9/11, 200 meters north of Radiográfica.

There is also excellent orientation for gay travelers at www.members. aol.com/gaycrica/guide.

SPECIAL WAYS TO VISIT COSTA RICA

NATURE TOURS

The following companies specialize in setting up nature tour packages, including round-trip transportation from your home country. But you can easily arrange nature tours when you get here, through your hotel or through tour companies listed in this book. Setting up tours when you get here allows you to go with the flow and take time to relax if you need it. We have noticed that many package tours, though they go to great places and have excellent guides, often keep a pretty hectic pace. However, they are a good way to see everything you wanted to see in a week and not have to drive.

Costa Rica Expeditions
San José, CR
222-0333, fax: 257-1665
e-mail: ecotour@expeditions.co.cr
www.costaricaexpeditions.com
Natural-history and adventure travel, especially in Monteverde, Tortuguero, and Corcovado; rafting.

Cultourica
249-1761, 249-1271
www.cultourica.com
e-mail: cultourica@expreso.co.cr
Low-cost nature tours that visit cooperatives and other community-based tourism projects, emphasizing community development and inter-actions with local people.

Costa Rican Sun Tours
phone/fax: 233-6890, 257-3418
www.crsuntours.com
Specializing in Pavones and Arenal.

Ecole Travel
223-2240, fax: 223-4128
e-mail: ecolecr@racsa.co.cr
Low-cost tours to Tortuguero, Corcovado, Monteverde-Arenal, Manuel Antonio.

Horizontes
San José, CR
222-2022, fax: 255-4513
e-mail: horizont@racsa.co.cr
www.horizontes.com
Natural, cultural, and educational
tours to all locations; hiking tours.
Can arrange conventions, seminars.

Serendipity Adventures
556-2592, 800-635-2325, fax: 556-
2593
www.serendipityadventures.com
e-mail: serendip@ix.netcom.com
High-end, customized adventure and
nature tours for couples, families,
and work or affinity groups.

Temptress Cruises
In the U.S.: 305-871-2663, fax:
305-871-2657
220-1679, fax: 220-2103
www.temptresscruises.com
Week or half-week cruises to
national parks on the Pacific
with a naturalist guide.

U.S.–BASED NATURE TOUR
COMPANIES
Costa Rica Connection
San Luis Obispo, CA
800-345-7422, 805-543-8823
fax: 805-543-3626
www.crconnect.com
e-mail: tours@crconnect.com

Forum Travel
Pleasant Hill, CA
925-671-2900
fax: 925-671-2993
e-mail: forum@ix.netcom.com

Geo Expeditions
Sonora, CA
800-351-5041, 209-532-0152
fax: 209-532-1979
www.geoexpeditions.com
e-mail: sales@geoexpeditions.com

Halintours
Austin, TX
800-786-8207

Journeys
Ann Arbor, MI 48103
800-255-8735, 734-665-4407
fax: 734-665-2945
www.journeys-intl.com
e-mail: info@journeys-intl.com

Overseas Adventure Travel
Cambridge, MA
800-955-1925, 617-876-0533
fax: 617-876-0455

Preferred Adventures
St. Paul, MN
800-840-8687, 651-222-8131
fax: 651-222-4221
www.preferredadventures.com
e-mail: paltours@aol.com

Tread Lightly Limited
Washington Depot, CT
800-643-0060, 203-868-1710
www.treadlightly.com
e-mail: info@treadlightly.com

Voyagers International
Ithaca, NY
800-633-0299, 607-273-4321
fax: 607-273-3873
www.voyagers.com
e-mail: explore@voyagers.com

Wildland Adventures
Seattle, WA
800-345-4453, 206-365-0686
fax: 206-363-6615
www.wildland.com
e-mail: info@wildland.com

Costa Rican Tourist Board
800-343-6332

LANGUAGE-LEARNING VACATIONS

Many people like the idea of learning Spanish on their Costa Rican vacation. The excellent language schools listed here offer a variety of experiences. **www.studyabroad.com** has a linked list of language-learning opportunities.

Most schools arrange for students to live with Costa Rican families to immerse themselves in the language, but some, like ICAI, have guest houses where students can stay if they want more privacy. Most schools set up weekend sightseeing trips for participants. Intensive conversational methods are used for four to six hours a day in programs lasting from one week to several months. Students are placed according to ability. All language schools assist their students in extending their tourist visas.

Centro Lingüístico Conversa (see below) is located on a lovely six-acre campus overlooking the beautiful Santa Ana Valley, and also has a center in San José. Students and staff eat breakfast and lunch together, and can socialize at the pool and on the volleyball court. Satisfied students recommend **COSI** for well-structured intermediate and advanced programs. The **Centro Cultural** teaches Spanish and English (maximum ten students per class), and sponsors plays and concerts by Costa Rican and U.S. performers. They also have a large English-language library and a TV room for viewing CNN. Students must pass through security as they enter. **Escuela del Mundo** includes classes on ecology and many other subjects, including surfing. They can accommodate families. **Forester Institute** also has classes for teens and children. The **ICADS** Spanish Immersion Program includes lectures and activities emphasizing environmental issues, women's studies, economic development, and human rights, with optional afternoon internships in grassroots organizations. **ICADS**, **CPI**, **Comunicare**, and **SEPA** students also participate in a wide variety of volunteer projects, giving them a chance to practice their Spanish in the real world. **ILISA** has an online Spanish course. **IPEE** teaches standard and business Spanish, and accommodates businesspeople who must stay in contact with their companies at home. They also teach a two-week course for Spanish language teachers. **Montaña Linda** has some of the least expensive courses we've encountered, including meals and lodging in their backpacker's hostel in the village of Orosi. In addition to affordable, conversation-oriented classes, **Mesoamérica** has a one-day class on "Survival Spanish for Tourists," which includes lunch and tips about travel and local customs ($60). **Instituto de Cultura, Intercultura**, and **El Marañon** emphasize Costa Rican culture. Many institutes spice up their curricula by teaching Latin American dancing!

Although San José's cooler climate and city vibes might be better for your concentration, it makes sense to combine language learning with a beach or mountain vacation. The following schools let you study near some of Costa Rica's favorite destinations, or at least in a rural setting in the Central Valley:

CENTRAL VALLEY

Alajuela:

Instituto de Cultura y Lengua Costarricense
458-3157, fax: 458-3214
www.institutodecultura.com
e-mail: info@institutodecultura.com

La Guácima de Alajuela:

Rancho de Español
438-0071
www.ranchodeespanol.com
e-mail: ranchesp@racsa.co.cr

La Trinidad de Ciudad Colón:

El Marañon
249-1271, fax: 249-1761
www.cultourica.com
e-mail: cultourica@expreso.co.cr

Heredia:

Intercultura Costa Rica
260-8480, fax: 260-9243
www.spanish-intercultura.com

Instituto de Lenguaje Pura Vida
phone/fax: 237-0387
www.costaricaspanish.com
e-mail: puravida@amerisol.com

Orosi:

Montaña Linda
phone/fax: 533-3640
e-mail: mtnlinda@racsa.co.cr

Santa Ana:
Centro Lingüístico Conversa
221-7649, 256-3069, 800-354-5036, fax: 233-2418
e-mail: conversa@conversa.co.cr

CPH Spanish and Cross-Cultural School
282-6556
www.spanishincostarica.com
e-mail: info@spanishincostarica.com

BEACHES AND MOUNTAINS

Ballena National Marine Park and San José:
Costa Rican Spanish Institute (COSI)
253-9272, 800-771-5184
www.cosi.co.cr
e-mail: office@cosi.co.cr

Jacó:
Escuela del Mundo
643-1064
www.speakcostarica.com
e-mail: info@speakcostarica.com

Manuel Antonio:
Escuela de Idiomas D'Amore
777-1143, 777-0233
www.amerisol.com/costarica/edu/damore
e-mail: damore@racsa.co.cr

Monteverde, San Joaquín de Flores de Heredia, and Playa Flamingo:
Centro Panamericano de Idiomas
265-6866, phone/fax: 265-6213, 888-694-0452
www.cpi-edu.com
e-mail: info@cpi-edu.com

Nicoya:
Instituto Guanacasteco de Idiomas
686-6948
www.spanishcostarica.com
e-mail: info@spanishcostarica.com

San Isidro de El General:
SEPA
771-4582, fax: 771-8841
www.online.co.cr/sepa
e-mail: sabalo@racsa.co.cr

Tamarindo:

WAYRA Institute
phone/fax: 653-0359
www.spanish-wayra.co.cr,
e-mail: spanishw@sol.racsa.co.cr

The famous **Green Tortoise** has a **Language School on Wheels** that tours the whole country by bus (415-956-7500, 800-867-8647; www.green tortoise.com).

SAN JOSÉ

Centro Cultural Costarricense-Norteamericano
225-9433, fax: 224-1480
e-mail: acccnort@sol.racsa.co.cr

Comunicare
phone/fax: 224-4473
www.comunicare.co.cr
e-mail: comunica@sol.racsa.co.cr

Forester Instituto Internacional
225-3155, 225-1649, 225-0135, 800-444-5522, fax: 225-9236,
www.fores.com
e-mail: forester@sol.racsa.co.cr

ICADS, Institute for Central American Development Studies
234-1381, fax: 234-1337
www.icadscr.com
e-mail: icads@netbox.com

ICAI, Central American Institute for International Affairs
233-8571, fax: 221-5238
In the U.S.: 916-432-7690, fax: 916-432-7615
www.educaturs.com
e-mail: icai@expreso.co.cr

ILISA, Instituto Latinoamericano de Idiomas
225-3155, fax: 225-4665
In the U.S. and Canada: 800-343-7248
www.ilisa.com
e-mail: spanish@ilisa.com

Instituto Costa Rica
phone/fax: 283-4733
www.intensivespanish.com
e-mail: iespcr@racsa.co.cr

Intensa
225-5009, 224-6353, fax: 253-4337
www.intensa.com
e-mail: intensa@sol.racsa.co.cr

IPEE, Instituto Profesional de Español para Extranjeros
283-7731, fax: 225-7860
In the U.S.: phone/fax: 813-988-3916
www.ipee.com
e-mail: ipee@gate.net

Mesoamérica
fax: 253-3195, phone/fax: 234-7682
www.amerisol.com/costarica/edu/mesoamer
e-mail: mesoamer@sol.racsa.co.cr

STUDY PROGRAMS

Spanish, architecture and planning, women's studies, Latin American culture, politics, economics, literature, tropical biology, ecology, international relations, international business—you can study nearly anything in Costa Rica. There are several options for university-level students who want to spend a semester or a year here, as well as shorter seminars for nonstudents. All programs require advance planning, so start thinking about it early. Also, since there are two decidedly different seasons, choose your months according to your preferred weather.

Many of the projects listed here, as well as some of the Spanish courses above, provide opportunities for volunteering. This is a great and inexpensive way to see the real Costa Rica. There are other volunteer opportunities listed at the end of Chapter Two.

Associated Colleges of the Midwest, **Friends World College**, **University of California**, **University of Kansas**, and **State University of New York** are among the many universities that send students to Costa Rica. Your college probably does, too, or can coordinate with an existing program. Check out **www.studyabroad.com** for a complete list of options with handy links to each program's Web page.

People who would like to enroll directly in the **University of Costa Rica** do so as "special students." All foreigners fall into this category for the first two years of their studies at the university. Admission fees are about double those for Costa Rican students, but the price is still quite low by U.S. standards. There is also the option of being an *oyente* (auditing a class). The first semester runs March through June, the second July to December.

In February, *cursos libres* on many subjects are open to the public for a nominal registration fee. "Exploring Language and Culture Abroad" is the University's four-week summer Spanish intensive, which includes seven field trips to historic, cultural, and ecological sites. For more information, contact:

> Oficina de Asuntos Internacionales
> 24-3660, fax: 225-5822
> www.elcacr.com
> e-mail: info@elcacr.com

The **University for Peace**, located on a beautiful tract of forested farmland in Villa Colón, southwest of San José, is the world's only truly international university. It offers degrees in Communications, Human Rights and Education, and Environmental Resources, all with an emphasis on how the subjects relate to the search for peace.

> University for Peace
> 249-1072, 249-1511, fax: 249-1929
> www.upeace.org
> e-mail: info@upeace.org

Lisle Intercultural Programs welcome students, families, and elders to explore what it means to be a global citizen. Their tour ranges from rainforest reserves and beaches to agricultural cooperatives, and participants volunteer to help the communities they visit. Basic Spanish is helpful but not required. Academic credit is available through the University of Toledo.

> Lisle Intercultural Programs
> 800-477-1538, fax: (512) 259-0392
> e-mail: lisle@utnet.utoledo.edu

The **Monteverde Institute** offers unique courses in which architects and planners, biologists, ecologists and those interested in women's studies can use the Monteverde forests and communities as laboratories for practical, hands-on learning experiences. Professors can collaborate with the institute to create courses, or individuals can sign up on their own. The institute also coordinates volunteer work in the zone.

Monteverde Institute
phone/fax: 645-5053, fax: 645-5219
www.mvi.cea.edu, www.ciee.org
e-mail: mviimv@racsa.co.cr

Proyecto Campanario runs 10- to 14-day courses in Tropical Ecology for secondary students and teachers from its rainforest reserve on a beautiful cove in the Osa Peninsula. Students also participate in a service or conservation project in one of the nearby communities or at the reserve. It is hoped that by meeting and working together with the people of the area, students will gain an appreciation for the problems that face the tropics in general. Campanario also accepts volunteers.

Proyecto Campanario
282-5898, fax: 282-8750
www.campanario.org
e-mail: campanar@racsa.co.cr

The **Organization for Tropical Studies** is a consortium of universities and research institutions dedicated to education, investigation, and conservation in the tropics. They offer "Tropical Biology: An Ecological Approach," a two-month lecture/field experience course, twice a year at their research stations in La Selva, Palo Verde, and Wilson Gardens, as well as undergraduate semester-abroad programs in Tropical Biology and Spanish Language and Culture, and shorter courses for Elderhostel groups and the general public. They also provide logistical support for dissertation research.

OTS
919-684-5774, fax: 919-684-5661
In C.R.: 240-6696, fax: 240-6783
www.ots.duke.edu
e-mail: nao@acpub.duke.edu

The **Institute for Central American Development Studies** was formed to educate first-worlders about Central America through hands-on experience, in order to gain insight into current social and economic realities and their effect on women, the poor and the environment. ICADS has a semester-abroad study program, including coursework and structured internship opportunities in Costa Rica, Nicaragua, and Belize. Subjects include Women's Studies, Environmental Studies, Public Health, Economic Development, Education, Human Rights, and Wildlife Conservation. One program is devoted solely to resource management and sustainable development. The internships allow students to give something back to the host society through service projects. There are fall and spring terms with credit. Noncredit summer internship placement is also available.

> ICADS
> 225-0508, fax: 234-1337
> www.icadscr.com
> e-mail: icads@netbox.com

Mesoamérica (The Institute for Central American Studies) publishes an excellent newsletter on Central American politics, with the help of volunteer interns. People who are fluent in Spanish and willing to volunteer for at least 20 hours a week for six months will read newspapers and journals, and write articles for the monthly magazine. Internships must be confirmed in advance. College credit can be arranged.

High school and college students can sign up for month-long summer "service-learning" trips with **Colibrí Adventures**, an affiliate of Mesoamérica. The program includes Spanish instruction, a homestay, and volunteer work on environmental projects. A major focus is on watershed monitoring and protection. (Despite Costa Rica's high amount of rainfall, water resources are threatened by deforestation and erosion.)

> Mesoamérica, The Institute for Central American Studies
> 253-3195, phone/fax: 234-7682
> www.igc.apc.org/colibri, www.amerisol.com/costarica/
>   edu/mesoamer
> e-mail: mesoamer@sol.racsa.co.cr

Opportunities Abroad offers an eight-day tour for those interested in living here, with trips to the Arenal Volcano and Tabacón Resort as well as residential areas in the Central Valley. Longtime residents share their experiences. Tours are led by Chris Howard, author of *The Golden Door to Retirement and Living in Costa Rica* (see Recommended Reading).

> Opportunities Abroad
> In the U.S.: 888-535-5289, fax: 618-659-0283
> www.opportunitiesabroad.com
> e-mail: info@opportunitiesabroad.com

DENTAL VACATIONS

You'd love to go to Costa Rica but you've got too many dental bills? Why not get your dental work done here? The money you save could pay for your ticket. Costa Rican dentists are well-trained and professional, and charge a fraction of what you'd pay at home. For instance, a root canal costs about $75, fillings cost about $20. **Dental Vacation International** (289-9618, 289-4670; www.goldnet.co.cr/dentavac, e-mail: dentavac@ns.goldnet.co.cr) specializes in porcelain laminated crowns, bridges, fillings, inlays, onlays, root canals, bleaching, and implants. Other dentists advertise in *The Tico Times*, or you can get referrals once you get arrive.

HEALTH VACATIONS

Costa Rica has finally developed some great places to go for relaxation and healing. They are listed in the various geographical sections of the book. **Scarlett's Fountain of Youth** at the Tara Resort in Escazú (www.tararesort. com; see San José deluxe hotels section) offers a gym, spa, facials, and massages in an antebellum atmosphere. **Tabacón Resort and Spa**, at the base of Arenal Volcano (www.tabacon.com; see Northern Zone chapter), offers thermal springs, massages and mud packs in a garden setting. The elegant **El Tucano**, near San Carlos (www.centralamerica.com/cr; also in the Northern Zone) has saunas and jacuzzis, and thermal and mud baths administered by Romanian spa physiotherapists. In La Garita de Alajuela, **Hotel Martino** (433-8382, 433-9052; www.orbitcostarica.com) offers Mediterranean-style steam baths and massages.

More affordable alternatives are **Cabañas Escondidas Retreat**, south of Dominical (282-9816, 391-1428; www.crdirect.com/retreats; Southern Zone chapter), for vegetarian food, massage, tai chi, yoga and group meditation, and **Dolphin Quest** (www.dolphinquest.com), near Golfito, where you can practice simple living and swim with the dolphins. **Samasati Nature Center** (www.samasati.com), in the hills of Talamanca between Cahuita and Puerto Viejo (see Atlantic Coast chapter), has a beautiful forest meditation and yoga space, serves delicious vegetarian food, and has experienced bodyworkers and yoga teachers. **Pura Vida Spa** (888-767-7375; www.puravidaspa.com) in the mountains above Alajuela brings yoga and growth workshops to Costa Rica and has week-long wellness packages.

Clinica de la Paz (234-7659), 20 meters north of the Iglesia de Fátima in the upscale Los Yoses section of San José, offers acupuncture, homeopathy, aromatherapy, massage, and clinical psychology.

An increasing number of people are coming here for face-lifts, liposuctions and other cosmetic surgeries that are not covered by regular health insurance. Experienced doctors, low prices, and luxurious post-op recovery facilities make for a truly transformational experience. For more information, see **www.cocori.com/healthtourcr** on the Web.

FOUR

Once You Arrive:
Getting Around in Costa Rica

STREET ADDRESS SYSTEM

As you can see from the Downtown San José map in Chapter Six, San José's streets are laid out in a very logical system. Odd-numbered streets (*calles*) are east of Calle Central, even-numbered streets are west. Odd-numbered *avenidas* are north of Avenida Central and even-numbered avenues are south. So if an address is on Calle 17, Avenidas 5/7, it is in the northeastern part of the city.

However, most Ticos completely ignore the street numbering system. *Calles* and *avenidas* appear in the phone book, and that's about it. The accepted way to give directions is from *puntos cardinales* or landmarks. If you call for a taxi, you have to give the name of a church or a *pulpería* (corner store) or a well-known business (like Pollos Kentucky). Then you state how many *metros* you are from there and in what direction. *Cien* (100) *metros* roughly corresponds to one city block. These are some examples of typical ways of giving directions: *"De la pulpería La Luz, cien metros al norte y cincuenta al oeste."* ("From the La Luz grocery store, one block north and half a block west.") *"De la Iglesia La Soledad, doscientos al sur y trescientos al este."* ("From the Soledad Church, two blocks south and three blocks east.")

The absence of street signs complicates the issue, but the post office has ambitious plans to put signs on all streets and numbers on all houses by the year 2003. We will see if the Costa Ricans adopt the program or if they ignore it the way they ignore the already logical and efficient street numbering system.

"TIQUISMOS"—
HAVING FUN WITH COSTA RICAN SPANISH

Ticos are amused and delighted when foreigners try to speak Spanish, especially when they include *tiquismos*, expressions that are peculiar to Costa Rican or Central American culture.

Not only the vocabulary, but the way you use words is important. Spanish speakers use a lot of *muletillas* (fillers, literally "crutches") in their speech. They directly address the person with whom they are speaking more often than is done in English, and they do it in a way that English speakers might consider slightly offensive. It is common for women to be called *mamita*, *madre*, *mi hijita* (little mother, mother, my little daughter, all roughly corresponding to "honey"). Latins love to use salient physical characteristics as nicknames. Common ones are *gordo* (fatty), *flaco* (skinny), *macho* (Costa Rican for fair-skinned or fair-haired), *negro* (dark-skinned), *chino* (it doesn't matter if you're Asian or just have slightly slanting eyes, your name is Chino), *gato* (blue or green eyes). You need only be slightly *gordo* or *flaco* to merit those names. If you're really *gordo* or *flaco*, and people really like you, you get a special name like *repollito* (little cabbage) or *palito* (little stick). *Gordo* and *negro* are commonly used as terms of endearment, regardless of appearance. The feminine of all the above nicknames ends in -a instead of -o.

Any male under 30 is usually called *maje* by his friends. This literally means "dummy," but figuratively is more like pal or buddy. It is used widely as a *muletilla*. *Majes* have various expressions of approval—such as the famous *pura vida* (great, terrific), *tuanis* (cool), and *buena nota* (groovy). *Mala nota* is ungroovy, *furris* is uncool, and *salado* means "too bad for you." Expressions of extreme approval are *qué bruto*, *qué bárbaro*, and disapproval, *qué horror*, or *fatal, maje*.

The above expressions are the slang of urban youth. However, all Ticos are aware of polite, courteous, and respectful forms of speech. They make their world more pleasant by using little expressions of appreciation. For example, if someone helps you in a store or on the street, you say *"Muchas gracias, muy amable."* ("Thank you very much, you are very kind."), and they will say *"Con mucho gusto."* ("With much pleasure.")

It is customary in the morning to ask, *"¿Cómo amaneció?"* ("How did you wake up?") *"Muy bien, por dicha, ¿y usted?"* ("Very well, luckily, and you?") *"Muy bien, gracias a Dios."* ("Very well, thank God.")

When talking about a future event or plan, Ticos will often include *si Dios quiere* ("if God wants" or "God willing"): *"Nos vemos el martes, si Dios quiere."* ("We'll see each other Tuesday, God willing.")

If you are in the city and see someone on the other side of the street whom you know, you call *"¡Adiós!"* In the countryside, when you pass someone on the road, it is customary to say *adiós* even if you don't know them. In these situations, *adiós* means hello. It is only used to mean good-bye when you're going away for good. Everyday good-byes are *hasta luego* (until then, until later), and the other person might add *"Que Dios le acompañe."* ("May God accompany you.")

Giving a coin to a beggar in the street often earns you a special blessing: he or she will say *"Dios se lo pague."* ("May God repay you.")

Although "now" and "in a little while" have very different meanings in English, here they can be expressed with the same word: *ahora*. Perhaps this is the linguistic root of the *mañana* attitude that so frustrates gringos. If you want to express the idea of "right away," you can emphatically use the word *¡ya!* keeping in mind that *ya* can also be used to mean already, later, and soon. Eskimos have 26 different words for snow. Latin Americans have the same words for many different time concepts, perhaps because time is not of such vital importance to their existence. It's what people love and hate about the tropics. Keep that in mind when dealing with the bureaucracy, or when deciding whether or not you have enough time to buy a cold drink when you've been told the bus is coming *ahorititica*.

Vos is a form of second-person-singular address used throughout Central America instead of *tú*. The verb form used with *vos* is made by changing the *r* on the end of an infinitive to *s* and accenting the last syllable. Thus with the verb *poder*, *"tú puedes"* becomes *"vos podés,"* and with *sentirse*, *"tú te sientes"* becomes *"vos te sentís."* Much to the consternation of their Spanish and South American friends, more and more Ticos use the formal *usted* for everyone, probably because it's easier and safer.

Other common Spanish fillers are terms like *fíjate*, *imagínate*, and *vieras que*, for which there are no real equivalents in English. Roughly, they could be translated as "would you believe" or "just think!" These expressions are used to give emphasis to what the speaker is saying. For example: *"¡Fíjate vos que no me dejaron entrar!"* ("Would you believe it—they wouldn't let me in!") Or you might say, *"Imagínese cómo me dió pena verla así."* ("Imagine how bad I felt to see her like that.")

Vieras is often used the same way we use "sure" in English: *"¡Vieras qué susto me dió!"* ("I sure was scared!" or, "You should have seen how it scared me!")

Achará is another particularly Tico expression and indicates regret at a loss: *"Fíjese que el perro comió mis begonias. Achará mis florecitas."* ("Would you believe it—the dog ate my begonias. My poor little flowers!")

When you come to someone's house, especially in the country, it is customary to stand on the ground near the porch and say *"¡Upe!"* as a way of letting them know you're there. When they ask you to come in, as you enter the house you say *"Con permiso."* ("With your permission.") If they offer you something to eat, it is polite to accept. Giving makes people happy; if you don't let them give to you, it hurts their feelings. People will ask you about your family, whether you're married, how many children you have. Most can't quite grasp the idea of people not being married or not having children. When you're sitting and talking and finally no one can think of anything else to say, you say, *"Pues, sí."* ("Well, yes.")

Learn some of these expressions and practice them until you don't make any *metidas de pata* (literally, "putting your foot in it," or mistakes). Ticos will be glad to help you. If you do make a mistake, there is a word which is instant absolution: just say, *"¿Diay?"* That means, "Well, what can you expect?" or "What can be done about it?" As you get to know the Ticos, you'll find that this little word comes in very handy.

FRUITS AND VEGETABLES

Costa Rica produces an amazing abundance of fruits and vegetables. To get an idea of their beauty and variety, elbow your way through the **Mercado Borbón** (Calle 8, Avenidas 3/5), a two-level vendors' circus in a tough part of San José. Or go to any of the Saturday- or Sunday-morning neighborhood *ferias del agricultor,* where streets are closed to automobiles and farmers sell their fresh produce. At San José's Saturday-morning market, west of Plaza Víquez (Calles 7/9, Avenidas 16/20), you'll find fresh homemade whole-wheat bread and pastries, eggs, chickens, fish, cheese, and honey, as well as every imaginable fruit and vegetable. Bring your own shopping bags. Many suburbs of San José also have weekend street markets—Escazú, Guadalupe, Tres Ríos, and Zapote, to name a few.

You can buy organic fruits, vegetables, grains, and coffee at the **Féria Orgánica** in Rohrmoser, 100 meters west and 500 meters north of the U.S. Embassy, on Saturday morning and Tuesday and Friday afternoons, and in San Pedro 150 meters north of the church on Saturday morning. Call 232-2643.

Here are some tips on how to identify and choose the best produce:

A ripe **papaya** will always be slightly soft, but still firm. A too-soft papaya should be avoided. To find the perfect papaya, shoppers will surrep-

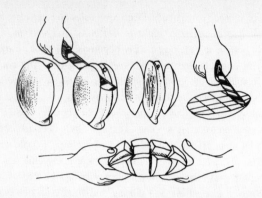

titiously stick their thumbnail into the skin to see if it is thin enough to be easily pierced. That also lets them see if the color is of an intensity that indicates ripeness. It is customary for papaya vendors to cut a triangular piece out of the papaya to show you its color. Some people are fans of the rounder *amarilla* or yellow-orange papaya. Others will swear that only the more elongated, red-orange *cacho* papaya is worthy of the name. You don't have to buy a papaya just because the vendor cut a piece out of it for you—at least Ticos don't.

Mangos should be slightly soft but still very firm, and red and yellow in color, although it's okay for part of them to be green. Reject any that have mushy spots. By far the most delicious are the large *mangas*, given feminine gender because of their voluptuous size. The neatest way to eat *mangas* is to slice them close around the flat oval seed to get two meaty halves. With the skin side down, score each piece into one-inch divisions without cutting through the skin (use a butter knife for this part). Now gently turn each half inside out, and you will have a bunch of delicious bite-sized pieces offering themselves to you. Ticos also love to eat green mangos sliced and sprinkled with lemon and salt. (Some people get a rash or irritation around their lips from eating mangos. This can be avoided by cutting off the part of the fruit nearest the stem, as the irritation is caused by the sap.)

Ticos judge the ripeness of a **piña** (pineapple) by giving it a slap. A good *piña* should sound firm and compact. The yellow pineapple is best for eating. The white pineapple is more acidic and is used in cooking and to tenderize meats. It produces a hollow sound when thumped. A green color on the outside does not necessarily mean the fruit is unripe. You should be able to pluck a leaf easily from the top of a ripe *piña*.

Sandías (watermelons) are considered sweeter if they produce a firm rather than a hollow sound. The best watermelons come from the hot coastal zones. One of the nicest parts of driving to Puntarenas is stopping at a fruit stand in Esparza for a delicious *sandía*.

Don't make the mistake of a friend of ours who, on a hot San José afternoon, came home with what he thought was a delicious, red, juicy watermelon. "And what a bargain!" he said as he thirstily cut into the **chiverre**, only to find a mass of whitish spaghetti-like pulp. *Chiverre* (spaghetti squash) looks just like a watermelon from the outside. You'll see them sold on the roadsides during Semana Santa. Their pulp is candied with *tapa dulce* to make special Easter treats.

Melón (cantaloupe) is judged for sweetness by its firm sound, but a fragrant smell is the best indication of a fully ripe *melón*.

Moras (blackberries) are used in *refrescos* and ice cream. You have to liquefy *moras* in a blender, strain, and add sugar and water to the sour juice.

Four types of **limones ácidos** (sour lemons) grow here. The seedless *verdelio* is rare. The *criollo* is small, juicy, and greener. The *bencino* is more the size of a North American lemon but is green and has much less juice than the criollo. The *limón mandarina* looks like a bumpy tangerine, and is very sour and juicy; it's good for making lemonade. The **limón dulce** (sweet lemon) has a mild, slightly sweet flavor, and is said to be an appetite stimulant and general cure-all.

Guayabas (guavas) are plentiful in Costa Rica from September through November. Their pink fruit is used for jam or guava paste.

Similar to the *guayaba*, **cas** is a little round fruit whose tart tropical flavor is popular in *refrescos* and sherbets. Try the *nieve de cas* at Pop's, a local ice cream chain.

Tamarindo is a tart and sweet *refresco* made from the seed pod of the tamarind tree. You will see the orange-sized balls of brown tamarindo seeds and pulp at the markets. The seeds are put in hot water so the sticky tamarindo dissolves. Then sugar and cold water are added. The resulting light brown *refresco* is somewhat similar in flavor to apple juice. Add grated ginger and lemon juice for a fine alcohol-free cocktail.

Granadillas (passion fruit) are yellowish-red and slightly larger than an egg. They have a crisp but easily broken shell. Inside are little edible seeds surrounded by a delicious, delicately flavored fruit, which is first slurped and then chewed. **Maracuyá** is a larger, yellower cousin of the *granadilla*, too tart to slurp, but delicious in a *refresco*. Its taste has been described as a mix between pineapple and tangerine.

Marañón is an unusual fruit. Its seed, the cashew nut, grows on top of it in a thick, rubbery shell. Don't try to bite open the shell; it's very bitter. Cashews must be roasted before they can be eaten; they are poisonous when raw. The ripe fruit can be eaten or made into a *refresco* or fermented into wine. The dried fruit is like a cross between a prune and a fig and is sold in supermarkets. You can make a quick and elegant dessert with half a dried *marañón* topped with a dollop of cream cheese and a cashew.

When you travel to Limón, you'll see several highway stands near Siquirres selling large, green, bumpy **guanábanas**. Inside these football-sized fruits, you'll find a sensuous surprise. Some spoon out the fibrous white flesh and eat it as is, but most people prefer it in *refrescos*, *en leche*, or *en agua*. Its English name, significantly less melodious, is soursop.

Avocados are called **aguacates**. They are usually a little less buttery and flavorful than their North American counterparts. They are soft when ripe, but if bought green can be left inside a paper bag to ripen.

Zapotes look like big brown avocados, and their texture is avocado-like, but their pulp is bright red-orange and sweet. Some places make *zapote* ice cream.

Fresh **coco** (coconut meat) can be found at fruit stands downtown. **Pipas** or green coconuts are popular with Ticos on hot days at the beach. They are sold whole, with a straw stuck through a hole in the outer shell so that the coconut water can be drunk.

The best way to get coconut meat out of its shell is to hack it open with a machete or a hammer, then heat the shells on the stove in a pan. This makes the meat shrink a little so it's easier to remove.

Pejibaye, a relative of the coconut, is one of Costa Rica's most unusual treats. *Pejibayes* grow in clusters on palm trees, like miniature coconuts. The part that you eat corresponds to the fibrous husk, while the hard *pejibaye* seed, when cracked open, reveals a thin layer of bitter white meat around a hollow core. The bright orange or red *pejibayes* are delicious boiled in salted water, then peeled, halved, and pitted and eaten alone or with mayonnaise. You'll see them sold on San José streets year-round. Their flavor is difficult to describe. They are not sweet, but more a combination of chestnut and pumpkin with a thick, fibrous texture. You can buy a *racimo* (bunch) of raw *pejibayes* at the Mercado Borbón and boil them up for parties, or

Pejibayes

Mamón chino and carambola

you can buy them peeled and canned in the supermarkets to take home as souvenirs.

Palmito (palm heart) is another delicacy worth trying. It is sold raw at the *ferias* or tenderly pickled in jars or bags in the supermarkets. It is the succulent inner core of small palm trees. Even though whole trees must be cut so that you can savor *palmito*, the trees are cultivated as a crop, so are replaced.

As human nature would have it, the most highly prized fruits in Costa Rica are imported apples, grapes, and pears. They signify the advent of the Christmas season, and Ticos pay big prices for them. Recently though, highland Ticos have started to grow a good, sweet-tart variety of apple. You also might enjoy the native **manzana de agua**, a dark-red, pear-shaped fruit that is light and refreshing.

Mamones are little green spheres, which you can break open with your fingers or teeth to expose a large seed covered with a layer of fruit that tastes like a peeled grape. Be careful when small children eat *mamones* or *mamones chinos*. Because of their size and shape they can get stuck in their throats.

Mamón chino is the *mamón*'s exotic cousin, sporting a red shell with soft spines growing all over it. It resembles a fat, round, red caterpillar and has a larger grapelike fruit inside its outrageous shell.

When you slice a yellow **carambola**, the pieces look like five-pointed stars. It makes a delicious *refresco*.

COMIDA TÍPICA (NATIVE FOOD)

Those who expect to find spicy food anywhere south of the border will be disappointed in Costa Rican cuisine. It is quite bland for the most part and doesn't have a whole lot of variety. But, except for being a little heavy-handed with the grease, Ticos have a wholesome high-fiber diet, with rice and beans included in every menu. Lunch is the big meal of the day, and many businesses still give two hours off at lunchtime so that people can take the bus back to mama's for a substantial *casado*. People often content themselves with soup and toast in the evening. Those who stay in Costa Rica develop a certain affection for the noble bean, and a good *gallo pinto* is a real delight. Ticos who want to spice up their food usually have a jar of tiny pickled red and yellow chilies on the table. Be wary of these. They are pure fire!

Sodas are small restaurants where you can get inexpensive snacks and light meals. They line San José's streets and fill the Mercado Central. Following are some of the foods you'll run across at *sodas* countrywide.

arreglados—sandwiches, usually made of meat, on a tasty but greasy bun

arroz con pollo—rice with chicken and vegetables

cajeta de coco—delicious fudge made of coconut, *tapa dulce*, and orange peel

casado—a plate of rice, black beans, cabbage and tomato salad, meat or egg, *picadillo*, and sometimes fried plantains

ceviche—raw seabass cured in lemon juice with *culantro* (chinese parsley) and onions—delicious

chicharrones—pork rinds fried crisp and dripping with grease, sometimes with wiry hairs still sticking out

chorreados—corn pancakes, sometimes served with *natilla*

cono capuchino—an ice cream cone dipped in chocolate

dulce de leche—a thick syrup made of milk and sugar

elote asado—roasted corn on the cob

elote cocinado—boiled corn on the cob

empanadas—corn turnovers filled with beans, cheese, or potatoes and meat

gallo pinto—the national breakfast dish of rice and beans fried together

gallos—meat, beans, or cheese between two tortillas

guiso de maíz—fresh corn stew

horchata—a sweet drink made of roasted ground rice and cinnamon

masamorra—corn pudding

melcochas—candies made from raw sugar

milanes and tapitas—small, foil-wrapped, pure chocolate candies, available in corner stores and restaurants all over the country. Beware: these delicious little things are addictive

natilla—sour cream, often more liquid than North American sour cream

olla de carne—literally "pot of meat," but actually a meat soup featuring large pieces of *chayote* (a green, pear-shaped vegetable that grows on vines), *ayote* (a pumpkin-like squash), *elote*, *yuca*, *plátano*, and other vegetables

palomitas de maíz—"little doves," or popcorn

pan bon—a dark, sweet bread with batter designs on top—a Limón
specialty

pan de maíz—a thick, sweet bread made with fresh corn

patacones—fried, mashed green plantains, served like french fries with
meals on the Atlantic Coast

patí—flour-based *empanadas* filled with fruit or spicy meat, sold on the
Atlantic Coast

picadillo—a side dish of sautéed vegetables, often containing meat

plátanos—plantains. They look like large bananas, but cannot be eaten
raw. Sweet and delicious when fried or baked. Also sold in a form
similar to potato chips. A Central American staple

queque seco—pound cake

refrescos—cold fruit drinks. Most *refrescos* are made with a lot of sugar.
If you order a *refresco* that is not made in advance, like *papaya en
agua, papaya en leche*, or *jugo de zanahoria* (carrot juice), you can
ask for it *sin azúcar* (without sugar) and add your own to taste. Similarly, an *ensalada de frutas* (fruit salad) might come smothered in
jello and ice cream. You can ask for it *sin gelatina, sin helados*

sopa de mondongo—tripe soup

sopa negra—soup made from bean gravy, with hard-boiled egg and vegetables added

tacos—a bit of meat topped with cabbage salad in a tortilla

tamal asado—a sweet cornmeal cake

tamal de elote—sweet corn tamales, wrapped in cornhusks

tamales—cornmeal, usually stuffed with pork or chicken, wrapped in
banana leaves and boiled—a Christmas tradition

tapa dulce—native brown sugar, sold in a solid form that looks like an
inverted flower pot. It's grated with a knife or boiled into a syrup
from which is made *agua dulce*, a popular campesino drink

torta chilena—a many-layered pastry filled with *dulce de leche*

tortas—sandwiches on bread rolls

tortilla—may mean the Costa Rican thin, small, corn tortilla, but also
another name for an omelette

tortilla de queso—a large, thick tortilla with cheese mixed into the dough

yuca—manioc, a thick tuber, another staple of the Central American
diet. *Enyucados* are *empanadas* made from a yuca-based dough

If you want to try your own hand at Costa Rican cuisine, pick up *A Bite
of Costa Rica* by Oscar Chavarría (San José: Gallo Pinto Press, 1994). The
recipes for *comida típica* are creative and flavorful. Also look for *My Kitchen*
(Nelly Urbina Castro, 1993), a no-nonsense collection of Tico recipes.

SOUVENIRS

Tiny *huacas*, copies of pre-Columbian jewelry representing frogs, lizards, turtles, and humanesque deities, are relatively inexpensive and make lovely necklaces, earrings, and tiepins. Authentic pre-Columbian artifacts cannot be taken out of the country, so don't believe anyone who tells you something is original. If it is original, the item has been stolen from an archaeological site.

The creative, bilingual coloring and activity book, *Let's Discover Costa Rica*, is the answer for the kids on your souvenir list. It is sold almost everywhere, or you can order it from A. Gingold, Apdo. 1-6100 Mora, Ciudad Colón, CR; fax: 249-1107; e-mail: agingold@racsa.co.cr.

David Norman's inexpensive Costa Rican **wildlife coloring books** are also good for kidshopping. Intelligently written, they tell about some of the animals you might encounter on a trip to Costa Rica. The drawings are so accurate that they can be used as guides to the animals. Norman also produces a series of pamphlets that give detailed descriptions of particular species, such as crocodiles, quetzales, and leatherback and green turtles. Look for the coloring books and pamphlets in gift shops or see www.amerisol.com.

If you're staying for a while, avail yourself of the low prices and excellent work of local tailors and seamstresses. They make fine formal clothes, or can copy your favorite designs. The best way to find one is to ask well-dressed Ticos whom they would recommend.

You can buy freshly ground **coffee** or coffee beans at the Central Market, or at the airport in souvenir shops. It is usually ground fine for use in the *chorreador*, a filter bag that hangs from a wooden stand. Percolator grinds are available in supermarkets, where you'll find *Caferica*, a coffee liqueur, as well as dried bananas, coconut twirls, macadamia nuts, cashews, yummy Angel jams, fruit leathers, and pastes. *Tapa dulce*, the native hard brown sugar, can be grated to add a rich flavor to baked goods or used on cereal and in coffee. We've heard of tourists who take home cases of **Salsa Lizano**, a tasty bottled sauce that Ticos love to sprinkle on their *gallo pinto*.

Souvenir shops all over the country carry souvenirs made from renewable resources by rural artisans. These include seed jewelry, carvings and boxes of plantation-grown wood, pencils made from coffee branches, and recycled paper notebooks and stationery.

The capital of Costa Rican **woodcraft** is Sarchí, about an hour northwest of San José (see the Central Valley chapter). Everything from salad bowls to rocking chairs to miniature ox carts (the rocking chairs fold, and the ox carts come apart for easy transport) can be purchased there. **Artesanía Napoleon** (454-4118), across from Fábrica de Carretas Joaquín Chaverri,

One of the places to view the eruptions on Volcán Arenal is from the thermal waters at Tabacón Hot Springs. You can easily spend half a day soaking in the hot-water pools, enjoying the waterslides, or strolling through the lush gardens.

Above: Cowboys on the Nicoya Peninsula drive cattle back to the ranch. Ranching is one of the main industries here.

Below: Playa Espadilla, one of the most scenic beaches in Manuel Antonio National Park, is also a refuge for sailboats.

will take care of mailing your purchases home for you. The capital of Costa Rican **leathercrafts** is Moravia, a suburb of San José, where there are a couple of blocks filled with souvenir shops near the main square. **Artesanía la Rueda** (235-8357), 100 meters south and 100 meters east of the Municipalidad in Moravia, will mail all your gifts for you.

If you are going to Monteverde, save some of your souvenir budget for **CASEM**, the women's crafts cooperative there, which specializes in embroidered and hand-painted clothing depicting cloud-forest wildlife. You'll see it on the right as you enter Monteverde. There is also a **crafts cooperative** on the main square in Ciudad Quesada, and tons of souvenir shops in La Fortuna.

Leona of **Rancho Leona** in La Virgen de Sarapiquí makes beautiful earrings from rainforest seeds. She also designs intricate, colorful jungle scenes for stained-glass windows and lamps, which her husband Ken crafts.

Wicker, raffia, and woven palm-leaf items should be spray varnished when you get home. Don't be tempted to buy tortoise shell or alligator-skin goods—they are made from endangered animals that are internationally protected. Customs officials at your home-country airport will confiscate those items.

See the "Souvenirs" section in the San José chapter for more on where to shop in the capital.

TIPPING

A 10 percent service charge and a 13 percent tax are included in your restaurant bill, so it's not customary to tip unless you really feel like it. It is not customary to tip taxi drivers either. A nice thing about Costa Rica is that people aren't always standing around with their hands out—partly because tourism is so new, partly because of a tradition of equality and pride. We hope that these qualities survive the influx of massive tourism. You would be surprised to know how little the staff at most hotels, including luxury hotels, earns (usually less than $200/month), so a little gratuity here and there for the maids who clean your room is certainly helpful, especially if you have appreciated the service received.

Many times when you park your car a man will appear, point to his eyes, and point to your car. That means he will watch your car for you, and it's worth it, for the 200-300 *colones* you will give him when you return (more at night or for long periods of time). Even though it might appear that he is hired by the restaurant, nightclub or other facility he is in front of, he is probably only working for tips.

Anyone who helps take your groceries from a supermarket check-out expects a tip as well, usually 100-200 *colones* per bag.

When you pay with a credit card at restaurants, the waiter will often leave the "tip" and "total" spaces blank, even though a 10 percent gratuity has already been included. Beware: Unless the "total" space is filled in by the customer, any amount could be written in later.

BUSINESS HOURS

Costa Ricans tend to start the day early. You'll find that stores are generally open from 8 or 9 a.m. until 6 or 7 p.m., six days a week (most businesses are closed Sunday). Core banking hours are 9 a.m. to 3 p.m.; government offices are open from 8 a.m. to 4 or 5 p.m.

THE METRIC SYSTEM

Whether you're getting gas, checking the thermometer or looking at road signs, you'll notice the difference: everything is metric. Costa Rica is on the metric system, which measures temperature in degrees Celsius, distances in meters, and most substances in liters, kilos, and grams.

To convert from Celsius to Fahrenheit, multiply times 9, divide by 5 and add 32. For example, 23°C equals [(23 x 9)/5] + 32, or (207/5) + 32, or 41.4 + 32, or about 73°F. If you don't have a pocket calculator along (but you probably should), just remember that 0°C is 32°F and that each Celsius degree is roughly two Fahrenheit degrees. Here are some other useful conversion equations:

- 1 mile = 1.6 kilometers. 1 kilometer = 3/5 mile
- 1 foot = 0.3 meter. 1 meter = 3-1/3 feet
- 1 pound *(libra)* = 0.45 kilo. 1 kilo = 2-1/5 pounds
- 1 gallon = 3.8 liters. 1 liter = about 1/4 gallon, or about one quart

TIME ZONE

All of Costa Rica is on Central Standard time, which is six hours behind Greenwich mean time. During daylight savings time in the U.S. (early April to late October) Costa Rica is on Mountain time.

COMMUNICATIONS

While Costa Rica boasts more phones per capita than any other Latin American country, patience and perseverance are still key when dealing with the communications bureaucracies.

COUNTRY CODES

Throughout the text, Costa Rica phone numbers are listed without the country code, which is 506. Other country codes you may need are 505 for Nicaragua and 507 for Panama.

TELEPHONES

Most public phones now require that you use a telephone card with a tiny computer chip. You can usually buy them for 500, 1000, or 3000 *colones* at a store located near the public phone. Ask for *tarjetas telefónicas chip*. You can also buy them at the airport when you arrive. They are handy to have in an emergency. Public phones have a little screen that tells you how many *colones* you have left on the card. Sometimes the screen will say "tarjeta inadecuada" (inadequate card) when you insert it. Just jiggle it around a bit or insert it differently, and it will usually work again.

If you can't find a number in the directory, try dialing 113, the directory assistance line.

In rural areas, like Puerto Viejo or Monteverde, hotels and *pulperías* have phones to call out on, called *teléfonos administrados*. The staff does the dialing and charges you for the length of time you speak. Communications centers in most rural areas will send and receive faxes and e-mail for you. We mention the ones we know about in each area.

If your hotel room has a telephone, you can usually use it to call out on; charges will be billed to you when you leave, unless you have made the calls on a 197 or 199 card (see below). Some hotels, like the Aranjuez and the Best Westerns, offer free local calls.

Since calls to cell phones are charged to the caller, public and hotel phones often do not access cell phones. We have tried to indicate if numbers are cellular whenever possible.

If you bring your digital cell phone from home, you can have it re-programmed by ICE, but we don't know how long that would take. Cell phone service also requires a very high deposit it Costa Rica. If you are going to remote areas you will probably be out of range anyway.

INTERNATIONAL CALLS

The access numbers for credit-card calls are:

United States:

   AT&T 0800 011 4114

   MCI 0800 012 2222

   SPRINT 0800 013 0123

Canada: 0800 015 1161

England: 0800 044 1044

Japan: 0800 081 1081

The complete list of numbers is also in the White Pages under "Costa Rica Directo, País Directo"; or dial 175.

Keep in mind that the calling cards you use at home have very expensive rates when calling from Costa Rica. You can purchase a "Servicio 199" calling card for $10 or $20 at ICE that will allow you to make international calls from any touch-tone phone at the normal rates. You key in the number on the card, dial your number, and the amount of your call is deducted from the value of the card. International call rates are cheaper evenings and weekends. The exact times are found in any telephone directory. You can also buy "Servicio 197" calling cards, which allow you to make calls within Costa Rica from private phones.

If you have access to a private phone, direct dialing is easy from Costa Rica. The telephone directory has a list of codes for various countries. To dial the U.S. or Canada direct, for example, dial 001 first, then the area code and number.

To call person-to-person or collect, dial 175 and an operator will then come on the line. For international information, dial 124.

If you don't have access to a phone in San José, go to **Radiográfica** (open daily, 7 a.m to 7 p.m.; Calle 1, Avenida 5).

FAX AND E-MAIL SERVICES

If your hotel lists a fax or e-mail number, they will usually accept a fax or e-mail for you. Several downtown hotels, like Don Carlos and Aranjuez (see the San José chapter), make a point of offering free e-mail access to guests. Internet cafés are listed with the restaurants in the San José chapter.

MAIL

In San José, the Main Post Office (Correo Central, open Monday through Friday, 7 a.m. to 6:45 p.m.; Saturday, 8 a.m. to noon; 223-9766) is located on Calle 2, Avenidas 1/3. Mail letters from a post office. There are hardly any mailboxes on the streets, and they are seldom used.

Beware of having anything other than letters and magazines sent to you in Costa Rica. A high duty is charged on all items arriving by mail in an attempt to keep foreign merchandise from entering illegally. Receiving packages can mean two trips to the *Aduana* (customs office) in Zapote, a suburb of San José. The first trip is to unwrap and declare what you have received. The second one, that day or the following day, is to pay a customs charge on every item in the package before you can take it home. If the package contains food, medicine, or cosmetics, it must be examined by the Ministry of Health—a process that takes even longer.

Photographs can be received duty-free if just a few are sent at a time. Individually sent cassette tapes can also make it through. Usually anything that fits in a regular-sized or magazine-sized envelope will arrive duty-free. But you will have to pay outrageous fees for a box of blank checkbooks, or the cookies Grandma sends to remind you she cares—in short, beg your loved ones not to send you anything. Once the duty has been assessed, you can't even have the package sent back. It will be confiscated by the *Aduana*.

You can send most things from Costa Rica to North America or Europe with no problem, although postal rates for packages are pretty high. Mail packages from the entrance to the far left of the main entrance as you face the downtown San José Post Office. Surface mail (*marítimo*) is somewhat cheaper than *correo aéreo* (airmail), and takes four to six weeks to arrive.

There is a general delivery service (*Lista de Correos*). If you are planning to stay in Costa Rica for a while, you can rent a post office box (*apartado—Apdo.* for short), or have your mail sent to a friend's box, which is safer than having it sent to a street address. Many foreign residents are turning to private mail services. You can sign up with **Interlink** (296-4980, fax: 232-3979; www.interlink.co.cr, e-mail: sales@interlink.co.cr), which, for $15/month, gives you a post office box in Miami from which mail is delivered to you twice a week in Costa Rica. Subscribers have access to all U.S. mail services for their outbound mail—registered, express, certified, etc. Interlink also allows you to send or receive up to four pounds of mail per month, lets you subscribe to periodicals at U.S. resident prices, gives you access to catalog and toll-free ordering, and offers you a ten percent discount on courier service. **Aerocasillas** (255-4567, fax: 257-1187; aerocasillas.racsa.co.cr, e-mail: aerosjo@racsa.co.cr), a similar service, charges $12 for their "mini-account," which allows you to send or receive one-and-a-half kilos of mail per month. **Mail Boxes Etc** (232-2950, fax: 231-7325; e-mail: mbeetc@racsa.co.cr) has just opened a branch in Pavas, 300 meters east of the U.S. Embassy with similar services, plus internet access, copying, printing and binding, office supplies, etc.

Courier services DHL, UPS, and JETEX are all available in Costa Rica.

LAUNDRY

Laundromats are uncommon in Costa Rica because most people have maids or relatives who do their laundry for them. Many hotels have laundry services. Most cheaper hotels have large sinks (*pilas*), where you can wash your own clothes, or they can connect you with a woman who will wash them for you for about $1 an hour.

There are many *lavanderías* (non-self-service laundries) in San José, but they are quite expensive. Beware of hotel laundry services that charge by the piece. We once spent over $10 on one load of laundry.

Recently, some self-service laundromats have opened up—**Lava Más** (225-1645) in Los Yoses next to Spoon, **Burbujas** (224-9822) 50 meters west and 25 south of the Mas x Menos in San Pedro, and **Betamatic** (234-0993) 125 meters north of Muñoz and Nanne in San Pedro—where it costs about $4 to wash and dry a load of clothes.

LOCAL TRANSPORTATION

FROM THE AIRPORT

Taxi service into San José is about $13 per taxi. A bus (45 cents) goes into San José, but you can't take much baggage on it. A taxi to Alajuela from the airport should only cost $3-$7.

TAXIS

Taxis are relatively inexpensive by northern standards. Drivers are supposed to use computerized meters, called *marías*, in the San José metropolitan area or for trips of 12 kilometers or less. As soon as you get in the cab they should press a button and the number 195 should appear on the meter. If they don't put the *maría* on, ask them how much they will charge you to get to your destination. Prepare yourself by asking beforehand at your hotel how much it should cost to get to where you're going. Also check the official rates, because they might have changed. Official rates in May 2000 were ¢195 (65 cents) for the first kilometer and ¢100 for each additional kilometer, with a 20 percent increase after 10 p.m. Each hour a *taxista* waits for you costs ¢1500. It is not customary to tip taxi drivers here.

A few taxi drivers do not use their meters or claim that they are broken. Legally, they must have a letter from the Ministerio de Obras Públicas y Transporte certifying that their *maría* does not work. Passengers can take down their license plate number (*número de placa*) and report it to the MOPT if they refuse to use their meters within a ten-kilometer radius of San José. If you are going more than ten kilometers, agree on a rate with the driver before you get into a taxi. Keep your eye on the *maría* when you reach your destination. Some taxi drivers turn it off just before you get there and then charge you whatever they want.

There are many honest taxi drivers and many dishonest ones. Even if they overcharge you, their rates are very reasonable compared to other places. However, it's good to know your rights. If you are on a budget, watch out for taxis that are called for you by hotels. They charge more because they are on call for the hotel. They also justify charging more because many of them provide "special service," i.e., they speak English.

If you have a serious altercation with a taxi driver, and are burned up enough to want to take legal action, note down the license number and the driver's code number, which should be on the card displayed on the windshield. Write or visit the Transport Ministry's Unidad de Información y Denuncias (Information and Report Unit; Avenida 18, Calle 7; 257-7798 ext. 2512 or 2535, fax: 222-2918; atención: Jefe del Departamento de Denuncias). Give them the license and code number, a physical description of the *taxista*, and describe the problem. All this should be done in Spanish, of course. Include your address, so they can write and tell you what transpired.

Most taxis are very well maintained. Taxi drivers cringe when passengers slam the doors shut, because they feel it damages the car. One driver told us that he no longer stopped for foreign tourists because they usually slam doors. Ease the door closed, or let the driver do it for you.

Taxis can come in handy if you want to visit hard-to-get-to places but do not want the expense of renting a car. You can take an inexpensive bus trip to the town nearest your destination and hire a jeep-taxi to take you the rest of the way. Usually taxis hang out around the main square of any small town. It's best to ask several drivers how much they charge to make sure you are getting the going rate.

Taxis can be a lot cheaper than renting a car or taking a tour, especially if there are several of you. For instance, a tour to Volcán Poás with a travel agency usually costs $40-$50 per person. You can hire a taxi in Alajuela to take you to Poás for $40 per *carload*—including the time spent waiting for you at the top.

CARS FOR HIRE

As an alternative to a taxi, your hotel can probably recommend a bilingual driver you can hire to show you around. Sometimes these drivers have vans that can hold up to seven people. In Monteverde, for instance, you can hire a van to take you to San José or Liberia for $100. You can divide the fee between the number of people in the van. Sometimes your hotel will find other guests who need the same service, and you can split the cost with them. Adobe Rentacar (www.adobecar.com) includes bilingual chauffeurs with their cars for $174/day.

HITCHHIKING

Because bus service is widely available, most people prefer to take buses. Hitchhiking is rare. In the countryside, where bus service is infrequent or nonexistent, cars often stop to offer rides to people on foot.

BUSES

Since most Costa Ricans don't have cars, buses go almost everywhere. Most buses that travel between San José and the provinces have well-padded seats and curtains on the windows to shade you from the sun. Fares rarely run more than $7 to go anywhere in the country. Some provincial buses are a bit rickety, but you won't find pigs and chickens tied to the roof, and most buses are fairly punctual. Buses from San José to the provinces are crowded on Friday and Saturday and the day preceding a holiday or three-day weekend. Likewise, it is difficult to get buses back to San José on Sunday, Monday, and the day following a holiday. This is especially true when trying to make connections to beach or mountain tourist destinations.

Some buses don't have buzzers or bells to tell the driver when you want to get off. When the bus gets close to your stop, shout *"¡La parada!"* or whistle loudly. If you are not sure where you should get off, ask the driver to let you know when he reaches your stop. Most drivers are very accommodating about letting people off right where they need to go. If you are traveling cheaply by bus, it's a good idea to bring as little with you as possible and leave most of your luggage at your hotel. Big suitcases are very inconvenient for bus travel. We have traveled for up to two weeks with just what we could fit in a day pack.

The second half of this book gives detailed information on transportation, including locations of bus stops and numbers to call to check schedules. English is usually not spoken.

The **ICT** (Tourism Institute) (underneath the Plaza de la Cultura, Calle 5, Avenidas Central/2; 222-1090, 223-1733) keeps an updated, computerized list of bus stops and related information. **Kitcom** (Calle 3, Avenida 3; 258-0303) publishes a great folder called *Hop on the Bus!* It has all the bus schedules and a map of the bus stops. It's widely available at hotels and tourist information centers, and is distributed free of charge. You can access it from their website, www.yellowweb.co.cr/crbuses.

For those of you who are shy about taking public buses, **Fantasy Tours** (220-2126; www.fantasy.co.cr/fantasy_bus) runs daily air-conditioned buses from San José or Playa Jacó to Tamarindo, Liberia, Arenal, Puerto Viejo de Talamanca, and Manuel Antonio for $19/person. They also connect the Guanacaste beaches with Volcán Arenal. Check their schedules on their website. **Interbus** (283-5573; www.costaricapass.com) has buses to even more destinations (including Monteverde), but costs more.

A Safe Passage is a new service designed to save tourists the trouble (and danger) of going to San José's bus terminals to buy tickets in advance. They will supply you with tickets at a safe Alaguela bus stop. They also orient travelers, have a bulletin board, and sell tourist supplies such as money belts. Find out more at rchoice@racsa.co.cr.

SAN JOSÉ AND SUBURBAN BUSES   The Sabana–Cementerio bus will take you through the area between downtown and the Sabana. The San Pedro buses (Avenida 2, Calles 5/7) cover the eastern side of the city, through Los Yoses to San Pedro. The northern and southern boundaries of downtown are only an eight- or nine-block walk from Avenida Central. Most urban buses cost about 20 cents. Suburban buses cost 20 to 60 cents and run from 5 a.m. to 10 or 11 p.m.

If you are returning to San José by bus from the north or west, and want to get all the way downtown, get off early on Paseo Colón and hop on the Sabana–Cementerio or take a taxi. That way you avoid going to the Coca Cola bus terminal or some other bad neighborhood terminal.

The City of San José plans to move the suburban bus stops out of downtown to cut down on congestion and pollution, and to build an electric streetcar system.

BUSES TO PANAMA AND NICARAGUA   Since both Panama and Nicaragua are somewhat unstable, it is essential to talk to people who have been there recently before going. Be sure to get an exit visa if you have been in Costa Rica more than 90 days (see Chapter Three).

People who have only read about **Nicaragua** in the headlines are usually surprised by the friendliness of the Nicaraguan people and their willingness to talk about their lives. You do have to watch out for contaminated water carrying amoebas or hepatitis. Because of the desperate economic situation there, it is good to bring simple things that people might need, like toilet paper, pens, toothpaste, clothes, and canned or dried food. You do not need a visa to enter, but your passport must be valid for at least six months from the date you enter. For the latest rules, check with the Nicaraguan Consulate (Avenida Central, Calles 25/27; 222-2373, 233-3479). Most car rental agencies will not allow you to rent a car to go to Nicaragua. Airfare from Costa Rica costs about $108 one way. See the Guanacaste chapter for travel tips on Rivas, San Juan del Sur, Granada, and Isla de Ometepe and schedules for buses to the Costa Rica–Nicaragua border.

The **SIRCA** bus leaves San José (Avenida 8, Calles 7/9; 222-5541; $7.50 one way) for **Managua** at 5:45 a.m. Sunday, Monday, Wednesday, and Friday.

Tica Bus (Calle 9, Avenida 4; 221-8954; $8 one way) has better buses than SIRCA and goes to Managua daily at 6 a.m. and 7:30 a.m., arriving around 5 p.m. and 7 p.m. Make reservations three days in advance. The Tica buses continue all the way to **Guatemala** (a three-day trip with overnight stops in Managua and San Salvador; $35 one way).

The deluxe **Transnica** bus (Calle 22, Avenidas 3/5; 256-9072; $9 including movies and snacks) leaves San José for Managua at 5:30 a.m.

People used to go to **Panama** to change dollars and buy film before continuing to South America, but the economic situation is precarious there now. Between the police and the robbers, personal safety is not assured. That does not seem to be the case in peaceful Bocas del Toro, on the Caribbean in Northwestern Panama (see the Atlantic Coast chapter for how to get there). You can find out if a **tarjeta de turismo** (tourist card; $10) is required for your nationality by visiting or calling the Panamanian Consulate near Paseo Colón (Calle 38, 350 meters north of the Centro Colón; 221-4784). If you do need one, buy it at the airport or once you get to your Panamanian destination.

Tica Bus (Calle 9, Avenida 4; 221-8954; $18 one way) leaves for Panama City daily at 10 p.m., arriving at 4 p.m. Buy tickets three days early.

Panaline (Calle 16, Avenidas 3/5; 255-1205; $21 one way) leaves at 2 p.m., arriving at the Hotel Internacional in Panama City between 4 a.m. and 5 a.m. Bus passengers can rent a double room at the hotel for a discounted price of $22.

TRACOPA buses (Avenida 5, Calle 14; 222-2160, 222-2666, 223-7685; $8) leave San José daily at 7:30 a.m. and arrive in David, Panama, nine hours later. From David, you can get hourly buses to Panama City (seven hours), or an express bus twice daily (five and a half hours).

You can avoid at least seven hours on the bus by flying with **SANSA** to Coto 47 (daily at 6 a.m.; $61 one way; see below) and taking a taxi to Paso Canoas on the border, then catching a bus from there. The border closes for lunch from 12 noon to 2 p.m. It's very hot and muggy in Paso Canoas.

Airfare from San José to Panama City is $157 one way on **Copa** (Avenida 5, Calle 1; 222-6640).

PLANES

Because of Costa Rica's mountainous terrain, small aircraft are frequently used. A 20-minute flight can get you to Quepos and Manuel Antonio on the Pacific Coast, as opposed to three-and-a-half-hour bus ride. **SANSA**, a government-subsidized airline, flies fairly inexpensively to all corners of the country. **Travelair** their flights cost more than SANSA's but it's worth it for their increased reliability and convenience. If you buy roundtrip tickets from Travelair, there's a 15 to 26 percent discount. This discount decreases the difference between SANSA and Travelair.

Children between ages two and eleven fly half price on Travelair, but only get a 25 percent discount on SANSA. Travelair has a maximum luggage allowance of 25 kilos per passenger, SANSA has a 12 kilo allowance. Travelair charges $15 each way for surfboards, bikes, and other oversize pieces, SANSA charges $7.

In our "Getting There" sections for each area we give flight schedules for SANSA and Travelair. But schedules change frequently, so check their websites.

SANSA (221-9414, fax: 255-2176; www.grupotaca.com): Flights leave from a small terminal just west of the Juan Santamaría Airport. Passengers can take a free airport shuttle from their new office in the Grupo TACA building, near the Sabana, 50 meters south of Yaohan's. Ask what time it leaves in order to meet your flight. Some destinations, like Quepos, Tamarindo, Tambor, and Carrillo have a shuttle ($2.50) to take you to your hotel and pick you up for the return. At others, ask your hotel to arrange for ground transportation. Request this information when making flight and hotel reservations.

You can purchase SANSA tickets from your local travel agent or through American airlines. SANSA is now part of Grupo TACA, the alliance of Central American airlines, along with LACSA. It is best to make reservations a few weeks in advance in the dry season.

Travelair (220-3054, fax: 220-0413; www.travelair-costarica.com, e-mail: information@travelair-costarica.com) uses the Pavas airport west of La Sabana. They do not provide ground transportation to San José or at their destinations, so you should arrange for pick-ups through your hotel. You will need to take a taxi to the airport and arrive 45 minutes before departure. **Adobe Rentacar** offers to meet you at any of SANSA or Travelair's destinations if you are renting for three days or more (www.adobecar.com).

For the purpose of planning your itinerary we have included the routes that were in effect in 2000. Some of these are condensed or combined in the green season.

DAILY ROUTES FOR SANSA (HIGH SEASON):

San José–Coto 47–San José

San José–Golfito–San José

San José–Quepos–San José

San José–La Fortuna–San José

San José–Liberia–San José

San José–Palmar Sur–San José

San José–Puerto Jimenez–San José

San José–Punta Islita–Sámara–Nosara–San José

San José–Tamarindo–San José

San José–Tambor–San José

San José–Barra del Colorado–Tortuguero–San José

DAILY ROUTES FOR TRAVELAIR (HIGH SEASON):

San José–Tortuguero–San José

San José–Carrillo–San José

San José–Puerto Jiménez–Golfito–San José

San José–Tambor–San José

San José–Tamarindo–Liberia–San José

San José–La Fortuna–San José

San José–Quepos–Palmar Sur–Quepos–San José

San José–Puerto Jimenez–Quepos–San José

Alfa Romeo Aero Taxi (phone/fax: 735-5112) is one of several companies that has small planes available for charter. For a single-engine plane with room for three passengers you will pay about $275 per hour, plus $30 for landing and $40 for each hour the pilot waits for you at your destination. A double-engine plane with room for five costs about $385 per hour of flight time. Check the Yellow Pages under "*Aviación*" for additional companies.

DRIVING IN COSTA RICA

CAR RENTALS

A car rental costs around $55 per day, $250-$300 per week, including insurance and mileage (four-wheel drives are about $75-$100/day, $350-$400/week). The insurance has a $750 deductible, which you can waive by paying $10 more. All major rental agencies have branches in Costa Rica. You're more likely to get a special rate if you book a rental car in your country of origin. Local companies are fairly uniform in their rates, though you can often get a discount of up to 30 percent in the off-season. If you don't have an American Express, Visa, Diners Club, or MasterCard, you must leave a deposit of about $1000. Some agencies (National, Budget, Toyota, and Dollar, for example) allow you to decline their insurance if you have a gold credit card; Visa's gold card is the most commonly accepted one. Valid foreign driver's licenses are good in Costa Rica for three months. If you are already here, reserve a car as far in advance as possible, especially in high season. Look under *"alquiler de automóviles"* in the phone book, or in the classifieds of *The Tico Times* for less expensive rentals.

Note: A reader has written us that car rental companies do not rent to people under 21 or over 70. We are not sure if this is true for all companies, but it certainly would be good to ask before making plans.

An alternative to renting a car is **Siesta Campers** (289-3898; www. edenia.com/campers, e-mail: siesta@racsa.co.cr), which rents VW camper vans with fully equipped kitchen, bedding, and a hammock. Two-person campers rent for $540 per week, four-person campers for $650, including taxes, insurance, and mileage. You have to put down a deposit of $750. These vans have a high clearance, and can make it down roads that are inaccessible for the Suzuki Sidekicks that most tourists rent. Siesta will meet you at the airport and advise you on the best places to go.

A high clearance is more important than four-wheel drive, especially in the dry season. Regular cars can take you most of the places you want to go in Costa Rica, but you'll feel less paranoid if your chassis isn't scraping on the occasional cantaloupe-sized rock that juts up from the surface. Some rental companies won't even rent you a regular car if they know you plan to go to Monteverde, for instance. Some of the worst roads are the paved ones that have gone to potholes: they are more uneven and less predictable than a well-graded gravel road.

Note that all repairs must be okayed first with the main office, or you will not be reimbursed. According to Jim Corven's "Consumer Almanac" column in *The Tico Times*, "Since most rental cars are compacts with small engines and the terrain is rarely level, stick shift is the norm. Coupled with the lethal potholes and winding roads, these cars must endure conditions unseen elsewhere. Reduce your chances of a breakdown by checking the

PROVINCIAL RENT-A-CAR AGENCIES

Some car-rental agencies have branch offices in the provinces. You could take a bus and rent a car when you get there. Branch offices are in: Liberia (Toyota: 666-0016, Dollar: 668-1061, National: 666-5594), Flamingo (Economy: 654-4152), Jacó (Economy: 643-3280; Zuma: 643-3207, Elegante: 643-3224), Quepos (Elegante: 777-0115), Tamarindo (Elegante: 653-0115). Adobe Rentacar offers free drop-off or pick-up at any SANSA or Travelair destination (www.adobecar.com). Drop-off fees at other offices range from about $40 to over $100.

car out thoroughly before heading out. Do not assume the agency did it for you. Check the oil, water, brake fluid, tire pressure, air conditioner, lights, belts, and hoses while still in San José. Make certain there is a spare tire and jack. Also report any small nicks or dents on the surface. If you have any concern whatsoever, contact the agency for service. You will have far less chance of getting their understanding after you've driven the car for a couple of days and develop problems." He also points out that the insurance you pay covers damage to vehicles, but not your possessions within the vehicle. Make sure you return the car with a full tank of gas. The agency's rate may be four times as much as the gas would cost at a service station.

Renting a car makes exploring easier and is less time-consuming than taking the bus. However, if you get impatient driving roads riddled with potholes, washboards, or farm animals, or if crazy traffic makes you nervous, think twice about driving yourself. It is said that the more polite people are in person, the ruder they are behind the wheel. The impeccably courteous Costa Ricans are no exception. Passing on blind curves is common. Getting stuck behind an ancient truck overloaded with green bananas and climbing a two-lane highway at 5 mph is to be expected. Parking in the middle of the driving lane on a highway (often there is no shoulder) for repairs is the norm. Buses pull into traffic lanes without looking or signaling. Dividing lines and other road markings are ignored. And if you happen upon a pile of branches in your lane while feeling your way through the fog at night, *watch out*. Someone has broken down just ahead.

If you decide you want your own wheels, try to arrange to rent the car on the day you will leaving San José for the provinces, because driving in San José is more hassle than it's worth. The car must be left in parking lots at all times to avoid theft. Driving in the city is like driving through a beehive, requiring a mix of finesse and aggressiveness. In San José and many other cities, most streets are one-way but are totally unmarked, so you have to guess if a street is one-way or not—and if it is, which way? Particularly tricky are streets that are two-way for a few blocks, then suddenly become one-way without any signs. Taxis or buses are much cheaper and easier for city travel.

If you do decide to rent a car, do not leave anything in it, even for a minute, unless it is in a well-guarded place. Rent-a-car plates are an open invitation to thieves.

You should be aware that Costa Rica recently passed a set of strict new traffic laws with high fines for a variety of new infractions. Booklets with all the points are available in the car rental offices, but if you always wear your seatbelt, go the speed limit (100 kilometers per hour on multi-lane highways, 40 to 80 elsewhere), pay special attention to school zones (where the speed limit drops to 25 kph), and watch for occasional signs or numbers painted on the road surface, you will probably be okay. Policemen usually station themselves in the shade at the side of the road and flag down drivers. In the past, tourist plates on rent-a-cars were an open invitation to certain policemen who stop tourists for "speeding," tell them they must appear in court at an inconvenient time in an inconvenient place, then offer to let them "pay on the spot" to avoid ruining their vacation. But now the Transportation Ministry has cracked down on this practice and boosted the meager salaries of traffic cops. If you attempt to bribe a policeman, you can be arrested. So if you get a ticket, just take it and drive away. You can pay at any state-owned bank (Banco de Costa Rica, Banco Nacional de Costa Rica, Banco Popular, or Banco de Crédito Agrícola), or the car rental agency will make sure your payment gets into the right hands upon your return. Officers are legally required to show their *carné* (ID card) on request, so if you feel you are being harassed or unduly pressured, get the ID number or at least the license plate number and report the officer to the Ministerio de Transporte, Operaciones Policiales (257-7798 ext. 2376 or 2862; fax: 222-7479).

SHIP YOUR OWN CAR

Shipping used cars from the U.S. is big business nowadays, and you can do it for about $400 to $700 depending on where you ship from. **Cartainer Ocean Line** (in the U.S.: 800-227-8096, in CR: 258-3062; www.penbroke cartainer.com) picks up cars in New Jersey, Delaware, Texas, and Florida and ships them to Puerto Limón. As a tourist, you have to buy a permit for $32, plus an $8 insurance policy when your car enters the country. That covers it for three months. To extend your car's visa for another three months, you go to the National Insurance Institute (INS) to renew your insurance, then get a new permit at a customs post (another $40). You must have the original title in the car at all times. After six months, your permit expires and you must pay taxes on the car equal to 60 to 100 percent of its *Costa Rican* market value, which is usually more than it would be worth at home. If you don't pay the taxes, you have to pay to have the car stored. Find out more at www.costarica.com/embassy/travel/vehicles.html.

MAPS

Small yellow posts mark the distance in kilometers from San José on Costa Rica's highways, but these aren't enough to find your way around. If you're going to be traveling on your own by car or by bus, *The Essential Road Guide for Costa Rica* is a must. The book breaks any trip down into maps accompanied by charts showing landmarks along the way, mileage, travel time, and notes on photo opportunities. Spiral-bound so that it can lay flat on your car seat, the 125-page guide is full of handy information about bus routes, driving customs and hazards, and regional notes. It can be used to plan a customized itinerary and lets you evaluate your progress en route. Available for $19.80 (including postage) from 104 Halfmoon Circle H3, Hypoluxo, FL 33462-5480, or call 800-881-8607 in the U.S. and Canada.

The ICT (Tourism Institute) has put out a new road map that includes the locations of most national parks, reserves, and wildlife refuges. Order it through the ICT offices, or pick one up at the ICT office under the Plaza de la Cultura. ITMB Publishing also puts out an excellent map that's available throughout Costa Rica. You can order it from amazon.com.

Even with a map, it's best to call a hotel at or near your destination and ask about current road conditions and travel times. A heavy afternoon rain can cause landslides, changing road conditions in a short time. Because of the unreliability of many roads, try to limit your driving to daylight hours. Hotels will also have current bus schedules.

Topographical maps can be purchased at **Librería Lehmann** (Calle 3, Avenidas Central/1), **Librería Universal** (Avenida Central, Calles Central/1), or the **Instituto Geográfico Nacional** (Avenida 20, Calles 5/7). Ask for *mapas cartográficos*. You'll be shown a little map of Costa Rica divided up into 20 x 30 kilometer sections. Indicate which sections you want. Maps show roads, trails, water sources including rapids, and contours at every 20 meters. They cost about $1.50 a section.

GAS

Fill up before leaving San José going west—there are no gas stations on the highway between San José and the airport. There are several gas stations on Avenida Central going east from downtown. Gas costs about $2 per gallon, but is sold here by the liter, roughly equivalent to a quart. There are no self-service stations in Costa Rica.

ACCIDENTS

Costa Rica now has the second highest auto-accident mortality rate in the world, surpassed only by the United States. Thanks to long-time insurance agent Dave Garrett and *The Tico Times* for this updated information.

1. Do not move vehicles until you are authorized to do so by an official. This is very important. Let people honk their horns. Offer paper and pencils to witnesses to write their names and *cédula* numbers (legal identification).

2. Find out your location according to *puntos cardinales* or *señas,* i.e., *"300 metros al sur del antiguo higueron en San Pedro."* Call 911, 222-9330, 222-9245, or 800-012-3456 for a traffic official if one doesn't immediately appear. If it appears that the other driver has been drinking, ask the officer to give him or her an *alcoholemia* test.

3. Do not remove badly injured people from the scene. Wait for the Red Cross ambulance (call 911 or 128). Make no statements on the cause of the accident except to the official or a representative of the National Insurance Institute (INS), whom you can summon by calling 800-800-8000. If an inspector cannot come, they will give you a code number, and you will have *three working days* to fill out an accident report at the nearest INS office (in Curridabat, Heredia, Alajuela, Cartago, Ciudad Neilly, Ciudad Quesada, Golfito, Guápiles, Liberia, Nicoya, Puntarenas, San Isidro, San Ramón, or Turrialba). Keep track of the code number, because it assures them that you called right after the accident. The insurance inspector often gets there sooner than the police. Pay attention to what he says about how to proceed with your claim. Do not make any deals with other people involved in the accident. If the INS finds out that a deal has been make, it will not pay a claim.

4. A tow truck is likely to appear on the scene, even if you haven't called for one, as towing services routinely monitor the police radio. You may even have more than one to choose from. Make sure your car gets to one of the 270 body shops authorized by the INS. Do not allow a tow truck operator to take your vehicle to an unauthorized body shop, because they do not do the paperwork that the INS requires.

5. Make a sketch of the area and the positions of the vehicles before and after the accident. Make note of the principal characteristics of the other vehicles involved, as well as the damage to your car and others. Avoid further damage by staying with your car.

6. You should report the accident to the police, even if it is insignificant, in every case. If you don't report it and get witnesses' names, things can get changed around and you may be accused of doing terrible damage and then driving away.

7. You will be given a citation by the police, telling you when and where to appear at the traffic court. Make sure you understand what it says before the police official leaves. It usually gives you ten working days to appear. A copy of this report must be presented to the INS (Avenida 7, Calles 9/11; 223-5800), along with your driver's license, insurance policy, police report, and information about injuries and witnesses.

Foreign insurance policies are not effective in court and only the INS can provide local service for defense or adjustment of claims. Insurance is included in car rental fees unless you have declined and are using a gold-card policy.

ROAD TROUBLE

If you have a rented car, call the rental agency first in all cases, and they will tell you what to do.

If you are driving your own car, by law you should have fluorescent triangles to place on the road in case of a breakdown or accident as a warning to other vehicles. Probably the best service to call in case of trouble with your car in San José is **Coopetaxi Garage** (235-9966). Some operators understand English. Or you might want to consider a temporary membership in the Costa Rican Automobile Club (256-6557; www.fia.com/tourisme/infoclub/accrgb) that will cover you for off-road recovery.

Do not abandon your car, if you can avoid it. If you don't speak Spanish well, have someone explain your location in Spanish when you make the phone call. If a wrecker is needed, it can be called by Coopetaxi radios.

SAFETY AND THEFT

THEFT

Take precautions to avoid theft. So far, San José is much safer than most other cities, except for theft. The whole downtown area of San José has become a mecca for pickpockets and chain-snatchers. Other places to watch out for are Limón and Quepos. The zippered compartments of backpacks are excellent targets. It's best not to wear them downtown. Don't carry a lot of packages at once. Purses should be zippered and have short shoulder straps so that you can protect them with your upper arm. If you wear a waistpack, keep it under your shirt or jacket, or rest your hand on it when walking. Wallets and passports shouldn't be carried in your back pocket, and expensive watches, chains, and jewelry should not be worn. Unless you will need the original for banking, just carry a photocopy of your passport, specifically the pages with your photo and personal information and the

TOURISTS BEWARE!

Though San José is generally a safe city, it's not crime-free. Following are two scams to watch out for:

THE FLAT TIRE SCAM   Recently there are more and more reports of tourists picking up rental cars and finding after a few minutes that they have a flat tire. They stop by the side of the road to repair the tire. Friendly passers-by offer help and end up robbing them, or robbers just swoop down on them without trying to be friendly. If you get a flat tire, just keep going until you get to a gas station or a place where there are a lot of people. Some agencies will deliver rental cars to your hotel, but in general the Suzuki Sidekick four-wheel drive is a dead giveaway that you are a tourist—Ticos rarely drive Sidekicks.

THE SLIMY GOO SCAM   Tourists are walking down the street and someone squirts their clothes with slimy goo. Helpful onlookers appear with tissues and before they know it, the tourist's purses and wallets are gone.

Costa Rican entry stamp. Most hotels will keep your passport in their safety deposit box, and many now have safety boxes in each room. Before setting out for your destination downtown, check your route.

If, while on a bus or in a crowd, you feel yourself being jostled or pinched between several people at once, don't just be polite. Protect your purse or wallet and elbow your way out of the situation immediately. If you are driving downtown, keep your window rolled up high enough so that a thief can't reach in and grab your necklace, glasses, or watch. Don't leave tents or cars unguarded anywhere. Don't leave cameras or binoculars in sight of an open window, even a louvered one. A pole can be stuck in and they can be fished out. If you follow these precautions, you probably won't have any trouble. We've never been robbed on the street in 14 years of living in Costa Rica. However, if you do have the misfortune of getting robbed, you might want to file a *denuncia* at the OIJ (Organismo de Investigación Judicial). There is one in most major towns and in San José at Avenidas 6/8, Calle 21. It is unlikely that they will investigate your robbery, but the document they type up and give to you can be presented to your insurance company. Take a Spanish-speaker with you.

EARTHQUAKES

These little surprises can make you question the very ground you walk on and remind you of the transience of being. The frequency of minor *temblores* (tremors) depends on the state of the tectonic plates Costa Rica sits on and can range from 40+ times a month to only once or twice. Most of them register less than 4.5 on the Richter scale and are barely perceptible. Those that register 4.5 to 6 can rock you but cause little damage.

If you happen to be caught in a big *terremoto* (earthquake), this is the official advice: Stay calm. Turn off electric appliances and extinguish cigarettes. Move away from windows or other breakables, or places where something could fall on you. Look for refuge under a desk or in a doorway. Don't lean against walls. Don't use stairs or elevators during the quake. Afterward, use the stairs, not the elevator. Leave the building you're in through the closest exit, as soon as possible.

BOMBETAS

If you hear two very loud explosions in rapid succession, don't run for cover —that's just the Tico way of celebrating momentous occasions. Usually the fireworks are from the neighborhood church, which is celebrating a Saint's Day, or are to announce events at a *turno* (town fiesta). In the case of a *turno*, the *bombetas* often begin at dawn and are fired off at regular intervals during the day, usually ending around 9 or 10 p.m. Sounding all the sirens in town is another way of expressing joy, as when the Pope or Tico astronaut Franklin Chang Diaz arrived in San José.

EMBASSIES AND CONSULATES

Many consulates are only open in the mornings. Following is a list of phone numbers for embassies and consulates in San José:

Austrian Consulate: Avenida 4, Calles 36/38; 255-3007, fax: 255-0767

British Embassy: Centro Colón; 221-5816, fax: 233-9938

Canadian Embassy: Sabana Sur; 296-4149, fax: 296-4270

Dutch Embassy: Sabana Sur; 296-1490, fax: 296-2933

German Embassy: Rohrmoser; 232-5533, fax: 231-6403

Guatemalan Embassy: Curridabat; 283-2555, fax: 283-2556

Japanese Embassy: Rohrmoser; 232-1255, 231-0357, fax: 231-3140

Mexican Embassy: Los Yoses; 280-5690, 280-5701, fax: 234-9613

Nicaraguan Embassy: Barrio California; 222-2373, fax: 221-5481

Panamanian Consulate: Paseo Colón; 221-4784, fax: 257-4940

Swedish Consulate: La Uruca; 232-8549, fax: 220-1854

Swiss Embassy: Centro Colón; 233-0052, 221-4829, fax: 255-2831

United States Embassy: Pavas; 220-3939, fax: 232-7944

United States Consulate: Pavas; 220-3050

HEALTH CARE

The following hospitals have emergency medical, x-ray, laboratory, and pharmacy services available to foreigners: **Clínica Bíblica** (Avenida 14, Calles Central/1; 257-5252, emergencies: 257-0466), **Clínica Católica** (Guadalupe; 283-6616), **Clínica Santa Rita** (specializes in maternity care, Avenida 8, Calles 15/17; 221-6433). The new, $40-million **Hospital CIMA San José** (208-1000), located on the highway to the western Central Valley town of Santa Ana, is more like a five-star hotel than a hospital. Its "suites" have separate living rooms with TV and minibar. It enjoys an interhospital agreement with Baylor Medical University in Dallas that allows its doctors to go there for training, and has the latest CAT scan equipment as well as neonatal and trauma units.

According to a United Nations study, Costa Rica holds first place in Latin America for development of preventive and curative medicine. It is ranked near the United States and Canada among the 20 best health systems in the world. Many Costa Rican doctors have been trained in Europe and the United States, and the University of Costa Rica Medical School is considered one of the best in Latin America. A full seven percent of visitors to Costa Rica come here specifically for medical or alternative treatments. See "Health Vacations" at the end of Chapter Three.

Many dentists are fluent in English. Services, such as crowns, fillings, and root canals, cost about half of what they would in the United States. Ask the United States Consulate or foreign residents for recommendations.

FIVE

The Outdoors

Costa Rica is an outdoor adventurer's paradise. From volcanoes and cloud forests to pristine beaches, this tropical wonder boasts breathtaking beauty. You'll find every imaginable activity—from birdwatching to bungee jumping. This is definitely the place to come to take that walk on the "wild side."

NATIONAL PARKS, RESERVES, AND WILDLIFE REFUGES

Costa Rica's 39 national parks, reserves, and wildlife refuges occupy approximately 12.5 percent of national territory and protect jewels of the country's rich but diminishing wilderness. They are organized into nine mosaic-like "Conservation Areas." Each of these has as its nucleus one or more totally protected national parks or absolute reserves. These are buffered by forest reserves and "protected zones" where sustainable land use is supposed to take place. In these buffer zones, reforestation, forest management, ecotourism, and private conservation projects are promoted.

National parkland acquisition has been supported primarily by international conservation organizations. But, in recent years, international funding has diminished. As a result park entrance fees have been adjusted; foreign visitors to the national parks pay $6 per person per day. Ticos pay $1 per day. The park service justifies the lower rate for nationals because Ticos pay taxes to support the parks.

In some areas surrounding the national parks there are private reserves. Visitors to these wild areas can stay at small private lodges and tour the privately held land, seeing flora and fauna similar to that in the national parks; their money helps preserve these important buffer zones.

Where private reserves are few, local guides and some tour-package hotels send tourists to unregulated (i.e., free) scenic areas outside the parks. Tourists crowd these areas and impinge on the parks' edge ecology.

For information about national parks and reserves, call SINAC's English/Spanish phone line: dial 192 (7:30 a.m. to 5:30 p.m.) or 257-2239 and tell them which park you want to visit. They give information about camping facilities, availability of meals, nearby lodging, and transportation. Both phone numbers can be used from outside Costa Rica by dialing 011 and the country code 506 first. You can also get information by e-mail: azucena@ns.minae.go.cr.

Most parks have camping facilities; most refuges and reserves don't. Detailed information can be obtained by calling specific conservation area offices, whose numbers are listed in park descriptions throughout this book. The best source for current weather and road conditions, they will also take reservations if required.

All national parks, reserves, and refuges are indicated on the National Parks map of Costa Rica, published by Editorial Heliconia (253-9462, fax: 253-4210; www.neotropica.org) and available throughout the country. We describe each park, reserve, and refuge in our chapters on the various regions.

For specialized information on biodiversity in the protected areas, contact MINAE's Departamento de Mercadeo at 283-8004, or the Instituto Nacional de Biodiversidad (INBio, 244-0690, fax: 244-2816; www.inbio.ac.cr), located in Santo Domingo de Heredia, 15 minutes northwest of San José.

INBioparque (open daily, 7:30 a.m. to 4 p.m.; 244-4730; www.inbio.ac.cr, e-mail: inbioparque@inbio.ac.cr; entrance fee $18; children under 12, $9; students $15), is a new project that showcases the work of INBio and its parataxonomists, who are trying to identify all the plant, insect and animal species in Costa Rica. At INBioparque you can learn about the National Park System and see examples of three native ecosystems, plus gardens of ornamental, medicinal, and aromatic plants and fruit trees. Guided tours last from two and a half to four hours, depending on visitors' interests and needs. A delicious typical breakfast or lunch (also emphasizing biodiversity) can be enjoyed in their attractive cafeteria for $6 to $10. Family rates and transportation from San José are also available.

Safety guidelines for the parks: Although Costa Rica has been described as a Disneyland of ecological wonders, you must be aware that here you are dealing with Mother Nature in all her harsh reality. Every year several overconfident hikers get lost in Costa Rica's dense forests. For example, hikers were lost in unseasonal fog and rain for 11 days on Barva Volcano on the west side of Braulio Carrillo National Park. Their goal was a simple day hike around the crater lake, but landslides blocking the trails threw them off course. Two hikers became lost and died in the mountains of Talamanca in 1999, and in April 2000 a Canadian hiker ignored signs telling him to keep on the trail and ended up sliding into the crater of Volcán Rincón de La Vieja, where he was stranded for four days with only a water bottle and a camera. Luckily, the volcano was in an inactive phase, and he was rescued. Costa Rica's famous parks are victims of the country's budget deficit, and trails are not maintained with the same rigor foreigners are used to. Tropical weather itself makes trail maintenance a full-time job.

The Red Cross gives the following recommendations for hikers:

- prepare for the worst
- tell someone where you're going and when you'll be back
- wear boots and layer your clothing
- carry a canteen, knife, flashlight with extra batteries, candy, dried fruit or granola bars, a compass, a map, a poncho or plastic in case you need to make a shelter, a first-aid kit, matches, a small piece of rubber and a candle (for lighting fires), and if possible a machete and light sleeping bag
- pack everything in plastic bags
- don't touch anything without looking
- bring medications
- if you get lost, stay calm and work with other people in your group as a team

Always stay on the trail when hiking in mountainous areas. The hikers who have gotten lost for several days—and survived—have done so by drinking river water, eating palmito (the edible core of certain palm trees), and hunting wild animals. Rescuers recommend building a primitive shelter and tying a brightly colored cloth to it, if you think anyone will come looking for you. If no one knows you are lost, following a river downstream is probably the best way to reach civilization.

CAMPING

Don't expect to find many well-organized campgrounds in Costa Rica. It's possible to camp in many places, but you often have to carry in your own water or make arrangements with local people to use their facilities. The national parks that allow camping are mentioned throughout the book. The main problems with camping are rain (it's better to come during the dry season if you plan to camp) and not being able to leave things in your tent unless there is someone around to watch it.

A good place to buy camping equipment in San José is **La Tienda de Camping** (Avenida 8, Calles 11/13; 221-9070). They sell Swiss Army knives, compasses, binoculars, first aid kits, and battery-powered lanterns.

BEACH SAFETY

Each year, hundreds of ocean bathers suffer serious near-drownings or death due to their ignorance about rip currents, a phenomenon found on wave-swept beaches all over the world—including Costa Rica. Ironically, these currents can be fun if properly understood—yet they are responsible for 80 percent of ocean drownings, or four out of every five.

What is a rip current? A rip current is a surplus of water, put ashore by waves, that finds a channel to drain and reach equilibrium. All rip currents have three parts: the feeder current, the neck, and the head. The feeder current is made up of water moving parallel to the beach. You know you're in one when, after a few minutes, you notice that your friends on the beach have moved down 30 to 50 yards, yet you thought you were standing still.

At a depression in the ocean floor, the current turns out to sea. This can occur in knee- to waist-deep water, and is where the "neck" begins. The current in the neck is very swift, like a river. It can carry a swimmer out to sea at three to six miles per hour, faster than a strong swimmer's rate of two to four miles per hour, and can move a person 100 yards in just a moment. It's typical for an inexperienced swimmer to panic when caught in the neck, and it is here that most drownings occur.

What to do if you get caught in a rip current: If you're a weak swimmer, you should call for help as soon as you notice a current is moving you and making it difficult to get in toward land. Most drowning victims are caught in water just above waist level.

If you realize that you can't walk directly in, you should turn and walk sideways, leaping toward the beach with every wave, to let the water "push" you toward shore.

A crashing surf can throw you off balance, so it's dangerous to turn your back to it. Once off balance, a swimmer is unable to get traction on the ocean floor and can be dragged out five feet into deeper water with each swell. After a few swells you may be in over your head, and it becomes extremely important to float—by arching your back, head back, nose pointing in the air.

Floating conserves energy. The human body is buoyant, even more so in saltwater. Everyone should learn to float, because every minute you can salvage gives someone the opportunity to make a rescue.

Once you are no longer touching bottom and are in a rip, you should not fight against the current in a vain effort to get back to shore, for this is like "swimming up a river" and will sap your strength.

The rip current loses its strength just beyond the breakers, dissipating its energy and eventually delivering you to relatively calm waters. This area, known as the "head," may appear to have a mushroom shape when seen from the air, as debris picked up by the current is dispersed.

Here, the water is deep but calm. You can get back to shore by moving parallel to the beach in the direction of the bend of the current, and then heading toward shore at a 45-degree angle rather than straight in, to avoid getting caught in the feeder current again.

Where do rip currents occur? There are four types of rip currents: permanent, fixed, flash, and traveling:

Permanent rips occur at river mouths, estuaries, or by small streams, and can be quite wide. They also occur at finger jetties designed to prevent beach erosion, where the water's lateral drift is forced to turn seaward.

Fixed, flash, and traveling rips are caused by wind-generated waves.

Fixed currents, which appear only on long, sandy, surf-swept beaches, can move up or down the beach depending on shifts in the ocean floor, but they are generally stable, staying in one spot for several hours or even an entire day.

Flash, or *temporary*, *rips* are created when an increased volume of water is brought to shore from sudden wave build-ups. These currents can occur on a warm, sunny day, generated by distant storms whose waves do not lose their energy until they crash on a shore. The excess water build-up has no opportunity to drain and reach equilibrium while the unusually large and fast waves are coming in; a flash rip current therefore forms during a lull in wave action.

A *traveling rip current* is just what the name implies. You'll see it in front of you; then, five minutes later, it may have moved 15 yards up or down the beach. Traveling rips can move 30 yards in a minute. They occur on long, sandy beaches where there are no fixed depressions on the ocean floor.

How to spot a rip current: Some beaches, such as **Espadilla** at Manuel Antonio, or **Jacó**, are known to have rip currents and *always* must be approached with caution. The currents can be spotted by the trained eye by a brownish discoloration on the water's surface, caused by sand and debris;

or there can be a flattening effect as the water rushes out to sea, making the surface appear deceptively smooth.

As a safety precaution, before you enter the ocean, throw a buoyant object like a coconut or a stick into the water and watch where the current carries it, for this is the direction you will have to go before you can get back to shore. There is definitely one direction that is better than the other.

Rip currents aren't dangerous to people who understand them. The more you know about the ocean, the more fun it can be. Surfers use rip currents as an energy saver, since they provide "a free ride" out to sea just beyond the breakers. Good swimmers are encouraged to seek out rip currents under controlled conditions—and with experienced trainers. As long as you swim in the ocean, you might get caught in a rip current, so it's critical that you know how to get out of one. Following are some rip current rules of thumb:

- Weak swimmers should avoid surf-swept beaches.

- The safest beaches include Playas Rajada and Jobo near La Cruz, Bahía Junquillal Wildlife Refuge, Playa Hermosa in northern Guanacaste, Playas del Coco, Sámara, Carrillo, Bahía Ballena/Tambor, any beach on the Golfo Dulce between Puerto Jimenez and Golfito, and the third beach at Manuel Antonio.

- Be sure to ask at your hotel where it is safe to swim, and observe other swimmers. At certain beaches, playing in knee-deep water is the only water play recommended.

- Never swim alone.

- Always be prepared to signal for help at the earliest sign of trouble.

- After a long period in the sun, rest in the shade before swimming to avoid hypertension.

FISHING

With two oceans, beautiful freshwater lakes, and endless miles of magnificent rivers—all only a few hours' drive or minutes by air from the capital city of San José—Costa Rica offers anglers some of the most fantastic and diverse sportfishing in the world.

For the freshwater angler, Lake Arenal and many of the rivers that flow to the Caribbean provide outstanding action on rainbow bass (*guapote*). There are trout in the mountain rivers, and a range of such exotic species as the *machaca*, *bobo*, *mojarra*, and *vieja* to be found in lower elevation waters.

But Costa Rica's greatest claim to fame is the incredible deep-sea fishing for sailfish, marlin, tuna, wahoo, and more than a dozen other species on the Pacific Coast, and what is without doubt the world's finest tarpon and snook angling on the Caribbean.

PACIFIC COAST

There's action year-round, but fishing will vary in different areas depending on the time of year and prevailing conditions.

In northern Guanacaste, where the country's largest concentration of charter boats fish out of **Flamingo Beach Marina**, **Tamarindo**, and the **Coco Beach area** (including **Ocotal**), action peaks on sailfish and marlin from about May through August, but often continues well into December, when northerly winds kick up in that area. January, August, and September are also good marlin months, but the warm waters that come with El Niño seem to send the marlin away.

Boats usually run from 7 to 15 miles outside Cabos Velas looking for marlin and sails, but also take advantage of the structure and fast drop-off at the Murciélago and the nearby Catalina Islands. Big tuna, roosterfish, giant cubera, jacks, wahoo, and more are available.

The only problem in that area is the heavy northerly winds that whip through beginning in late December and continuing through March. The fish are there, but customers are sparse and boats generally have a longer run as they move around the corner of Cabo Velas and head south toward Punta Guiones and calmer seas, or fish locally inshore.

Below Guiones there are boats at **Nosara**, **Sámara**, and **Playa Carrillo** that enjoy a year- round season, with billfish outside and a selection of tuna, wahoo, snapper, etc., inside. The Playa Carrillo charters have a good shot at the fish as they move north from the central coastal area beginning in April, and a few boats move there from Flamingo during the early spring.

A handful of boats fish out of **Puntarenas** and across the Gulf of Nicoya below Playa Naranjo, but it's a long run to the blue water outside Cabo Blanco or off Herradura to the south, so most concentrate more on the inshore fishing for jacks, *sierra*, snapper, *corvina*, and tuna.

The central coast at **Quepos** has soared in popularity over the past two or three years as the billfish have diverged from their traditional migratory pattern and started moving into those waters in December. Fishing is little short of sensational into April and May, when they begin moving north.

In 1996, Costa Rica's venerable International Sailfish Tournament moved from Flamingo to Quepos and had one of its highest release counts in many years, averaging 2.2 sails per day per angler.

You will find some billfish in that area all year, along with tuna, wahoo, jacks, and roosterfish.

Local anglers have long known that the river mouths from **Jacó** south to **Golfito** are loaded with snook, but it has only been since about 1991 that a couple of operators began targeting that species. While most of the snook fishing is done from shore, an all-tackle International Game Fish Association boat caught a Pacific black snook while trolling a Rapala lure just off the mouth of the Naranjo River a few years ago.

Boats from Quepos also run multi-day trips to **Drake Bay** and **Caño Island**, overnighting at one of the wilderness camps or lodges to be found there. Drake Bay Wilderness Camp and Aguila de Osa Lodge also offer quality boats and special fishing packages. That region has its share of sails and marlin, but is best known for its big tuna, record-challenging Pacific cubera, snapper, wahoo, and roosterfish.

On the extreme southern coast, the **Golfito** region offers charters out of Golfito Sailfish Rancho, at the upper end of Golfo Dulce, and at Playa Zancudo, where Roy's Zancudo Lodge and Golfito Sportfishing provide exceptional fishing packages at moderate prices. Here again, you can find plenty of sailfish, with the heavy concentrations moving in a bit earlier than at Quepos to the north, along with the previously mentioned species.

CARIBBEAN COAST

Here you will fish quiet jungle rivers and lagoons where you're likely to see bands of monkeys in the trees overhead, crocodiles basking along the shoreline, and a host of brilliantly plumed birds flitting through orchid-draped tropical growth.

But when the surf is down at the river mouths, allowing the boats to get outside to the open water, the fishing is often spectacular. That's when you may see tarpon spreading for acres in every direction, and each cast is a hook-up.

If you have never battled a tarpon, you have a surprise and perhaps a shock in store. When those silver rockets, weighing an average of 80 pounds each, take to the air, jumping and twisting and turning and tumbling, and then running halfway to hell and back, only to start jumping again . . . well, all we can say is, "Try it."

While we have caught tarpon every month of the year in Costa Rica, the peak season is from January through May, probably because that's when there is the least rain and the most fishermen. However, the fishing will vary more from one day to the next than it will from month to month, and if we had our choice we would opt for late July, August or September, when you are more likely to get through the river mouths.

Like tarpon, snook can be taken throughout the year, with 12 to 20 pounders common and much larger fish not unusual. They are caught trolling along the banks of the lagoons and at the river outlets, but the most productive method is surf fishing from the beaches near the river mouths.

Best fishing is usually late August through November or December. And from about October through early January, the area also enjoys a run of the smaller Fat Snook (known locally as *calba*) that average about five pounds. When the run is in full swing, you can boat 20 or more a day.

Most lodges in the area now run center-console boats, up to 23 feet, with powerful motors that allow them to get through the mouths of rivers more often and provide greater safety in the outside ocean.

The equipment has provided a new dimension to the Caribbean coast fishery, with anglers supplementing the traditional tarpon and snook with tuna, jacks, kingfish, *sierra*, and even an occasional wahoo or Atlantic sailfish. In 1996, a boat out of one of the tarpon lodges caught the first Atlantic blue marlin ever reported, on a hook and line, in the Caribbean of Costa Rica.

For a change of pace, the rivers and backwaters of the area also provide an assortment that includes drum, catfish, gar, rainbow bass, *machaca*, and *mojarra*. And all are dynamite on light tackle.

There are six or seven lodges in the northern Caribbean area. Most are centered around the **Río Colorado**, where fishing is most consistent, with others at **Tortuguero** and **Parismina**. All provide full fishing packages, including air transportation from San José, lodging, meals, guide, fishing license, and loaner tackle if required.

FRESHWATER FISHING

Lake Arenal, nestled at the base of a spectacular volcano in the San Carlos Valley, is the favorite freshwater fishing spot for Costa Rica residents. The lodges and hotels on or near the lake and guides operating out of nearby La Fortuna are making it increasingly available to visitors.

If you are a bass fisherman, you'll love the rainbow bass that abound there; five-pounders or better are considered keepers and seven to ten pounds a legitimate bragging size. A member of the *cichlid* family and first cousin to the peacock bass, these beautiful fish are hard to beat on the dinner table or the end of a line, and are fished just as you would for largemouth bass.

They can also be found in the rivers of the eastern seaboard, in **Caño Negro Lagoon** and its tributary rivers near the border with Nicaragua and in **Lago Hule**, near Cariblanco. But the nine-kilometer road into Hule is one of the worst in the country and shouldn't be attempted without at least two four-wheel-drive vehicles going together.

The immense Caño Negro Lagoon is known for the huge tarpon that have migrated up from the Caribbean along the San Juan, as well as for snook, *guapote*, drum, *machaca*, and other species.

Rainbow trout abound in the **Río Chirripó Pacífico** in San Gerardo de Rivas at the entrance to Chirripó National Park. The **Savegre River** at the Chacón Ranch just below San Gerardo de Dota has small rainbows, introduced here many years ago when eggs were brought in from Oregon. There are private ponds off the road to **Tapantí** in the Orosi Valley only an hour from San José, in **Copey de Dota,** and on the **Cerro de la Muerte**, and some rent gear. They charge about $7 per kilo for whatever you pull out. Many other rivers also offer great fishing for a variety of species, and a few guides are now available, some of them specializing in fly fishing and float trips. For more information on inland fishing, see www.fishcr.com.

PERMITS

Fishing permits ($30) can be obtained in any agency of the **Banco Credito Agricola** (open Monday through Friday, 9 a.m. to 3 p.m.; San José: Avenida 4, Calles Central/1; 223-8855); they're valid for one month. Deep-sea fishing permits are usually taken care of by your fishing guide. If you encounter wildlife rangers at your fishing site, you must present the permit and your passport.

CHARTERS AND LODGES

Information and reservations for charter boats and fishing lodges on both coasts, and some freshwater guides, are generally available through the resort hotels in the area or from the many tour agencies located in Costa Rica. Some specialize exclusively in fishing. Hotels in La Fortuna will arrange trips to Arenal and some of the nearby rivers. A freshwater fishing license is required (see above) and most species have seasons and limits that are subject to change from year to year, so check in advance.

Costa Rica Outdoors is a monthly on-line and print magazine devoted to fishing and outdoor adventure in the country (800-308-3394; www.costa ricaoutdoors.com, e-mail: jruhlow@racsa.co.cr). See their website for up-to-date fishing reports. Jerry Ruhlow, the magazine's editor, probably knows more about fishing in Costa Rica than anyone else. He also operates **Costa Rica Outdoors Travel Service** (e-mail: jruhlow@racsa.co.cr), which arranges sportfishing and outdoors trips with most of Costa Rica's operators.

We mention the sportfishing operations in each area in the chapters on each region.

OTHER OUTDOOR SPORTS

SURFING

Costa Rica has become famous for its great waves. The Pacific, with its long point breaks, river mouths, and beach breaks, keeps surfers busy all year. Guanacaste and the Central Pacific are better in the windy season from December through March. From April through November, the whole coast has swells from the south and southwest. If they want to get serious, surfers go to the Atlantic from December through March, where waves from deep water break over the shallow reef, creating the perfect imitation of Hawaiian surf. The Atlantic Coast also has a "winter" season from June through August. You can find out how the waves are in Jacó, Hermosa, and Dominical at www.crsurf.com.

The nearest surfing beach to San José is **Boca Barranca**, between Puntarenas and Puerto Caldera, known for long waves at high and low tide. It's good for beginners. About a half-hour to the south are **Playa Jacó** and **Playa Hermosa** (not to be confused with Playa Hermosa in Guanacaste), where an international surfing contest is held each year. These beaches have a large expatriate and Tico surfing community that provides services like board repairs, wave reports, surfing tours, and cabinas with surfers' discounts. The whole area between Jacó and **Playa Dominical** to the south has many excellent surfing spots. Parents of teens might want to check out the Wild Waters Surf Camp in Dominical (www.wildwaters.com).

Playa Pavones, south of Golfito on the Golfo Dulce is said to have a left "so long you can take a nap on it." Across the Golfo Dulce, **Playa Matapalo** near the tip of the Osa Peninsula attracts surfers.

Playas Carrillo, **Nosara**, **Negra**, **Junquillal**, and **Tamarindo** in Guanacaste have areas for surfing, as well as swimming and snorkeling spots. **Playas Malpaís**, **Santa Teresa** and **Coyote** on the west side of the Nicoya Peninsula are becoming known for their waves, and **Playa Cedros** on the east side of the Peninsula below Montezuma is good for beginners (see Central Pacific chapter). **Playa Naranjo**, in Santa Rosa National Park, is known for **Witch Rock**, where there are perfect tubular waves. The road to Playa Naranjo is very rough; rented Suzuki Sidekicks get stuck there regularly; we have heard that the high-clearance VW vans rented by Siesta Campers (289-3898; www.edenia.com/campers, e-mail: siesta@racsa.co.cr) fare better. You can camp right on the beach. Or you can charter a boat from Playas del Coco or Playa Ocotal.

On the Atlantic Coast, **Playa Bonita**, just north of Limón, offers waves that are very thick, powerful, and dangerous. **Puerto Viejo**, south of Limón, is famous for "La Salsa Brava," a challenging ride responsible for many a broken surfboard. Most surfers say they can't decide which coast they like best.

There are board-rental shops in Puntarenas, Jacó, Manuel Antonio, Limón, Puerto Viejo, and Cahuita. Many car-rental agencies and hotels give discounts to surfers, especially May through November.

SCUBA DIVING

The incredible underwater seascape of Costa Rica used to be available only to PADI-certified scuba divers, and there are many PADI-certified operations and instructors throughout Costa Rica. In Playa Jaco, **Ocean Adventures** (phone/fax: 643-1885, 643-1305; e-mail: fishjaco@racsa.co.cr) has a state-of-the-art surface-supplied air system—a 150-foot hose that connects you to the boat so you can dive in 15- to 20-foot water where decompression is not a problem and PADI certification is not necessary ($250 for four people).

Inexpensive scuba-diving excursions and courses are available through **Aquamor** (www.greencoast.com) in Manzanillo on the Talamanca coast. In our Guanacaste chapter you'll find diving operations mentioned in Playa del Coco, Ocotal, Playa Hermosa, Brasilito, Flamingo, and Tamarindo. In our Central Pacific chapter look for divemasters in Punta Leona and Playa Jacó. Drake Bay on the Osa Peninsula in the Southern Zone is a mecca for divers because of the clear waters found off Isla del Caño. Six or seven hotels offer diving there, and some go to Isla del Coco, 500 kilometers southwest of Costa Rica, which offers some of the best diving there is.

SEA KAYAKING

Various companies and hotels along both coasts rent kayaks and offer sea kayaking trips. We mention them in the regional chapters. Kayaks are quite stable, and first-timers can feel safe and get a rush when exploring with a good guide. The gentle waters of the Golfo Dulce on the east side of the Osa Peninsula lend themselves to peaceful sea kayaking. **La Llanta Picante** (www.members.aol.com/spicytire) specializes in customizing kayak and bike trips for families. If you need an adrenaline rush, contact **Kayak Joe** (787-0121) who can lead you through the natural tunnels in **Ballena National Park** south of Dominical. He also knows how to train beginners. The dolphins of the Caribbean know well the kayaks and guides of **Aquamor Adventures** (391-3417; www.greencoast.com) in the Manzanillo Wildlife refuge south of Puerto Viejo de Talamanca.

RIVER CANOEING/KAYAKING

Rancho Leona (761-1019; www.rancholeona.com) takes beginners on kayaking trips down the Río Puerto Viejo in Sarapiquí. Halfway between Orosi and Turrialba, in El Duan de Tucurrique, Mike and Sally Swanson's **Kayak Costa Rica** (cell phone: 380-8934) plans trips for families, active adults, and seniors that include kayak instruction, hiking, biking, camping and horseback riding. Members of the Costa Rican **Canoe and Kayak Club** take weekend jaunts to all the best places. Call Jay Morrison at 282-6053 for more information.

Vermont-based **Battenkill Canoe Ltd.** (802-362-2800, fax: 802-362-0159, 800-421-5268; www.battenkill.com) leads canoe tours down Costa Rica's slower jungle rivers, in Talamanca near the Bri Bri Reservation, on the Sarapiquí, and at Caño Negro Reserve. **Laughing Heart Adventures** of Willow Creek, CA (phone/fax: 530-629-3516; e-mail: tecwaves@laugh ingheart.com) also does canoe trips. See Tortuguero section in the Atlantic Coast chapter for info on *cayucas*. Florida-based **Canoe Costa Rica** (732-350- 3963; www.canoecostarica.com) leads customized five- to ten-day trips all over Costa Rica from December to April.

WHITEWATER SPORTS

Rafters, canoers, and kayakers flock to Costa Rica for its exciting rivers. The Río Pacuare, considered world-class by sportspeople and ranked #10 on the list of wild and scenic rivers worldwide, is threatened with being dammed for a huge hydroelectric project. **Ríos Tropicales** (233-6455), **Costa Rica Expeditions** (222-0333, 257-0766), and **Aventuras Naturales** (225-3939) will take you on one- to three-day rafting trips on the Pacuare or the Río Reventazón, with challenges graded to your level of skill and experience. The one-day trip is $69-$89, including transportation, breakfast, lunch, and expert guides.

In Turrialba, **Serendipity Adventures** (556-2592, fax: 556-2593, in the U.S.: 800-635- 2325; www.serendipityadventures.com) specializes in rafting trips for families and other groups. **Loco's Tropical Tours** (556-6035; www. whiteh2o.com) has been recommended by readers. **Rios Aventuras** (556-9617, in the U.S.: 888-434-0776; www.costaricarios.com) offers canoe and kayak instruction and certification, as does **Miti's Kayak School** (556-6828).

In Manuel Antonio, **Iguana Tours** (777-1262, fax: 777-0574) offers trips down the Savegre River; in the Northern Zone, **Aventuras de Sarapiquí** (766-6768; www.sarapiqui.com) rafts the Río Sarapiquí, as does **Aguas Bravas** (761-1123, 292- 2072, 296-2626, fax: 229-4837). You can usually book whitewater rafting tours through your hotel.

GOLF

In the Central Valley, guests at the Hotel Cariari near the airport in Alajuela, may use the 18-hole, par-71 championship golf course at the **Cariari**

Country Club (239-0022). Cariari hosts the Friendship Golf Tourney and the American Professional Golf Tourney, which attract PGA professionals. Cariari rents equipment and provides pros for golf lessons.

Tango Mar Surf and Saddle Club (683-0001), on the Gulf of Nicoya near Tambor, has a tough par-31, nine-hole golf course, for guests only. In Guanacaste, **Rancho Las Colinas** (654-4089), near Playa Grande, and the **Melia Conchal Golf Club and Resort** (654-4123, 654-4501) at Playa Conchal have public 18-hole, par-72 championship courses. Marriott is creating an 18-hole course for its **Los Sueños** complex, which opened at Playa Herradura in December 1999. The above courses all have websites where you can get prices and package deals.

Several other golf resorts are scheduled to open near Playa Jacó, Playa Hermosa, Liberia, and La Cruz in Guanacaste. We have no idea where all these developments are going to get the water needed to maintain golf courses in this brutally hot, bone-dry region, and we wonder about the effects of the pesticides they will surely have to use to maintain their greens. We salute the Marriott for pledging to use only organic fertilizers and pesticides on its Los Sueños golf course. Golfers tell us that starting at dawn is the only way to beat the heat, with maybe another round in the late afternoon. Be sure to take plenty of water and sunblock with you on the course.

TENNIS

Among the most important international tennis matches here is the World Friendship Tournament at the **Cariari Country Club** in March and April. In the Central Valley, the **Costa Rica Country Club** in Escazú hosts the Coffee Cup Tournament. **Los Reyes Country Club** (La Guácima), the **Costa Rica Tennis Club Hotel** (Sabana Sur), Cariari, and **La Sabana** courts offer programs for learning and practicing tennis. Many upscale beach and mountain hotels have tennis courts.

HORSEBACK RIDING

Most beach and mountain resorts rent horses, and we mention them throughout the book. Most noteworthy in the Northern Zone are the famous horseback ride between Monteverde and Lake Arenal (we recommend that you don't do it in the rainy season) and the trip to Río Celeste. Brasilito-based **Costa Rica Riding** (654-4106; www.brasilito.com) leads a five-day horseback tour for experienced riders that covers 42 beaches in Guanacaste, staying in four beachside resorts ($1200 including meals); **Río Nosara Tours** (www.nosara.com) delights guests with sunset horseback rides on the beach. In Montezuma, **Finca Los Caballos** specializes in high-quality equine experiences. **Brisas del Nara** (www.maqbeach.com) takes you to mountain waterfall inland from Manuel Antonio, as does **Don Lulo's,** inland from Dominical. For a beautiful down-home Costa Rican experience, rent a horse from Don Concho of **Poor Man's Paradise** to explore the beaches south of Drake Bay in the Osa Peninsula.

Make sure that the horses you rent are not tired and do not have sores or swollen places. Give them plenty of opportunity to drink water during the trip and don't leave them standing in the sun. If you feel horses or any other animals are being mistreated, you can report it to the Asociación Humanitaria para la Protección Animal de Costa Rica (Apdo. 73-3000 Heredia, CR; 267-7158, fax: 267-7296) in Los Angeles de San Rafael de Heredia.

SOCCER

Costa Ricans are very sports-minded. There isn't a district, town, or city where *fútbol* (soccer) isn't played. It's said that Costa Ricans learn to kick a ball before they learn to walk! There are teams all over the country in every imaginable category, including all ages and both sexes, although only men play on the major teams. If you want to experience the Ticos' love for this sport firsthand, attend a Sunday soccer match. Be aware that Ticos can get pretty crazy at these games. During the final games of the 1993 national championship at the Cartago stadium, a bad call was made. Fans cut through the chain-link fence and streamed onto the field in the middle of the game. A riot ensued. The referees fled, the national guard was called to the scene, and the game was terminated. In the next week, the Cartago team went to the Supreme Court to demand retribution for this "violation of their human rights" (no joke). After tempers cooled, the teams had a private game with no spectators, and Heredia was declared the national champion. The whole episode gave Tico men something to discuss in the back of buses for months.

RUNNING

There are many marathons throughout the year, including the one sponsored each April by the **University for Peace**. The **Hash House Harriers** (www. costaricasjhhh.com), a world-wide organization devoted to running and beer-drinking, also meets here once a week. Call their hotline (222-3043) for information.

BIKING

Mountain-biking is one of the fastest-growing sports among Costa Ricans. International biking superstars come each November to participate in the annual **Ruta de los Conquistadores Race** which starts in Puntarenas, climbs 10,000-foot Volcán Irazú, and ends up on the Caribbean coast. You can take a tour along the same route at a more relaxed pace (225-8186; www.adven turerace.com). **BiCosta Rica** (380-3844, 446-7585, fax: 258-0606; www.yel lowweb.co.cr/bicostarica) organizes mountain-bike tours lasting from one day to one week. **La Llanta Picante** (phone/fax: 735-5414; members.aol. com/spicytire) offers bike tours for everyone in the family based on the Osa Peninsula. **Coast to Coast Adventures** (652-0552) does touring and sponsors the Soledad Adventure Race in Playa Sámara in Guanacaste. There are rental places in Puerto Viejo de Talamanca, La Fortuna, Sámara, and Jacó.

BUNGEE JUMPING

Bungee jumping has come to Costa Rica. Thrill-seekers jump from a 265-foot abandoned bridge near the Grecia exit on the highway to Puntarenas. **Tropical Bungee** (232-3956; www.bungee.co.cr) offers this ultimate adrenaline rush at $45 for the first jump, $25 for subsequent jumps. They give students discounts.

HOT-AIR BALLOON RIDES AND ULTRALIGHTS

Floating in a hot-air balloon will give you a hawk's view of the Costa Rican countryside. The one-and-a-half-hour tours begin at daybreak and depart from Naranjo, San Carlos, and Turrialba. **Serendipity Adventures** (556-2592, fax: 556-2593, 800-635-2325; www.serendipityadventures.com, e-mail: serendip@ ix.netcom.com) specializes in custom adventures for families, couples, and groups of friends or co-workers. Trips include breakfast and transportation from your hotel.

The Flying Crocodile (656-0413; www.samarabeach.com), specializing in ultralight flying trips, is run by a German pilot just north of Playa Samara.

TREETOP EXPLORATIONS

Inspired by biologist Donald Perry's explorations of the rainforest canopy and his subsequent Rainforest Aerial Tram (Chapter Nine), there are now many opportunities for visitors (who don't suffer from vertigo) to ascend into the treetops, either to sit on an observation platform, or to zoom from tree to tree using a cable-and-pulley system.

The Canopy Tour (phone/fax: 257-5149; www.canopytour.com) has sites at Termales del Bosque hotsprings near San Carlos in the Northern Zone, at Monteverde (645-5243), and at Hacienda Guachipelín, near Rincón de la Vieja. **Albergue de Montaña Rincón de la Vieja** (695-5553) has a similar cable-and-pulley system on its property. Near Lake Arenal, **Lago Coter Eco Lodge** (257-5075) offers its own version of the canopy tour, along with **Hotel Villablanca** (228-4603), near San Ramón in the Central Valley. The Manuel Antonio version is called **Canopy Safari**. Prices for these tours range between $40 and $80.

Monteverde Preserve, the **Skywalk** (also in Monteverde), the **Rainmaker Reserve** north of Manuel Antonio, and **Centro Neotrópico Sarapiquis** in the Northern Zone all have bridge systems suspended above the canopy, so that you can walk instead of zip.

Rara Avis's Treehouse (www.raraavis.com), constructed by Don Perry, lets guests spend a night 100 feet above the ground on a double-occupancy treetop platform. Visitors can spend one night here and the rest of their stay at Rara Avis in the less expensive accommodations. **Corcovado Lodge and Tent Camp** (222-0333, fax: 257-1665) has a platform 120 feet off the ground in an *ajo* tree an hour's hike from the Lodge. Also in the Osa, **Bosque del Cabo** (www.bosquedelcabo.com) has an observation platform you get to on a zip-line. In Dominical, **Hacienda Barú** (787-0003) has a tree platform easily accessible from the road. In the Guápiles area, **Casa Río Blanco** (382-0957) can help you ascend, and stay suspended, 125 feet up a *pulsinia armada*. **La Isla Botanical Gardens** in Puerto Viejo de Talamanca (www.greencoast.com) also has an observation platform in a tree.

SIX

Getting to Know San José

In 1821, after learning that Guatemala had declared its independence from Spain, Costa Rica began creating its own form of self-government. During this process, General Agustín de Iturbide, self-proclaimed emperor of Mexico, sent word urging immediate annexation to his empire. The citizens of the older cities of Heredia and Cartago were in favor of annexation, but the more liberal residents of Alajuela and San José saw de Iturbide's demand as imperialist and chose independence. A short civil war ensued, which was won in 1823 by the *independistas*, who moved the capital city from Cartago to San José.

Today San José is a noisy, bustling city—the economic, political, and cultural center of the country. If you have come to Costa Rica to get close to nature, you will probably want to get out of San José as fast as possible. Set in the middle of the Central Valley, surrounded by high mountains, it is battling the demons of its rapid growth: congested one-way streets filled with too many cars, buses, and taxis belching black diesel smoke into the mountain air; a lack of jobs for all the country people who haveing the land and are trying their luck in the city; increasing petty theft.

On the upside, San José still ranks as one of the safer cities in the Western Hemisphere and has much less violent crime than most U.S. cities. Foreigners enjoy the city's springlike climate, the availability of high-quality cultural events like National Symphony concerts and international music, dance, theater, and film festivals, and the relaxed life in suburban areas like balmy Rohrmoser, Escazú, and Santa Ana to the west, and Moravia, Curridabat, and brisk San Ramón de Trés Ríos to the east. Great places to dine are also plentiful in San José, as you'll see in this chapter. Modern supermarkets and shopping malls have largely taken the place of the Mercado Central, but Saturday morning farmers markets held in the streets of different neighborhoods still provide a folksy tone and a fairlike atmosphere. And Costa Ricans are almost always friendly and polite, ready to take a moment off for a joke or to help you find where you're going.

Here are some tips for while you're in the city:

- When crossing streets in downtown San José, always look over your shoulder at the cars coming from behind you. In practice, the pedestrian does not have the right of way. Drivers love to whip around corners whether or not people are trying to cross.

- When a traffic light for oncoming cars changes from green to yellow or red, do not take it to mean that the cars will stop. Look at the cars, not the light. When you see that the cars have stopped, run across real quick. This habit is easily developed because another characteristic of San José is that traffic lights are hung so that pedestrians cannot see them. *Buena suerte*.

- Street numbers are attached to the sides of buildings near intersections. Not all corners have them, but keep looking and you're bound to find one.

- To ask directions, you don't have to use a lot of fancy Spanish. It is acceptable to say "¿Para (name of your destination)?", like "¿Para Heredia?" or "¿Para la Coca Cola?", and the person you ask will point you in the general direction. We've found it's best to ask people who look like they drive, and it's best not to ask people standing in front of bars.

- If you're driving downtown, keep your window rolled up high enough so that a thief can't reach in and grab your purse, necklace, or watch. Better yet, don't even try to drive downtown unless you think of driving as a competitive sport.

See a description of the street address system in Chapter Four.

A WALKING TOUR

The following tour can take several hours to a full day, depending on how involved you get.

We will start out at the **Correo Central**, or Central Post Office (223-9766) on Calle 2 between Avenidas 1 and 3. The entrance is in the middle of the block. Stop by for an espresso, a latte, or a coffee milkshake at **Cafe Tostadora La Meseta**, a charming coffee shop hidden behind the post office boxes in the former guards' headquarters (open Monday through Saturday;

View with sombrilla del pobre.

9 a.m. to 7 p.m.). Philatelists will be interested in the commemorative stamp department on the second floor. Also on the second floor is a museum of old telephone and telegraph equipment as well as historic stamps and photos.

Walk two blocks west on Avenida 1, and you're at the **Mercado Central**, entering through the flower section. The market is a crowded, bustling maze of shops, restaurants, and produce stands covering the whole block between Avenidas Central/1 and Calles 6/8. Although there are quite a few more sedate places to buy souvenirs, at the Central Market you can get a glimpse of the lives of everyday Costa Ricans. Everything from hammocks to leather goods to fresh fish to mangoes is sold there. Of special interest are the stands where herbs are sold, labeled with their medicinal uses. It's easy to get quite disoriented in the market, but try to come out at the southeast entrance on Avenida Central and start walking east again. (If you don't like crowds, skip the market.)

Between Calles 6 and 4 on Avenida Central, you'll pass **La Gloria**, Costa Rica's largest department store. Across from that is the huge black marble **Banco de Costa Rica**. Their second floor has a special department for efficiently changing traveler's checks. They exhibit local artists' work on the ground floor. You can also take an elevator to the eighth floor to get a bird's-eye view of the city.

Continuing on Avenida 1, turning left on Calle 4, you'll see one of San José's monuments to its democracy: a group of bronze campesinos stands humbly but solidly looking up at some unseen authority, waiting to be heard. In keeping with the Tico tradition of avoiding conflict, they are staring south. If they had been placed looking east, it would be more to the point—the large building beside them is Costa Rica's **Banco Central**. On the south side of the Banco Central on weekday afternoons, you might be lucky enough to see San José's version of the Buena Vista Social Club—*La Nueva Marimba de San José,* a group of retired musicians who play just for the fun of it. Passersby stop to dance, and you can too.

East of Calle 4, Avenida Central has been made into a pedestrian mall, so you'll have a little more room to walk. This is San José's busiest commercial section, with shops and restaurants vying for your attention on either side of the street.

In two blocks, look to the left on Calle Central and you will see **La Casona**, a two-story wonderland of souvenirs. Half a block ahead on Avenida Central is **Librería Universal**, where you can buy anything from electronic appliances to art supplies, as well as books and stationery. It sells large-scale maps, which are helpful for hiking.

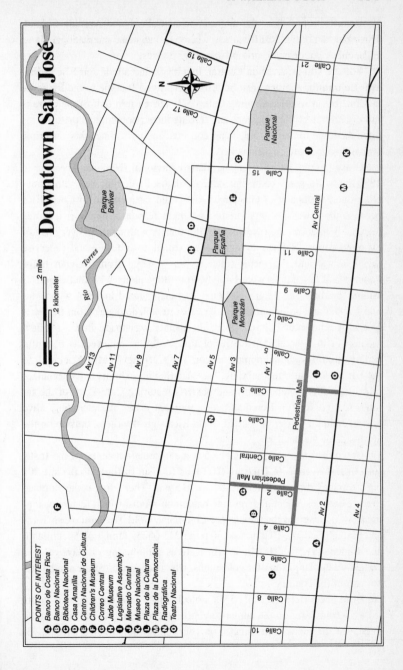

Downtown San José

POINTS OF INTEREST
- Ⓐ Banco de Costa Rica
- Ⓑ Banco Nacional
- Ⓒ Biblioteca Nacional
- Ⓓ Casa Amarilla
- Ⓔ Centro Nacional de Cultura
- Ⓕ Children's Museum
- Ⓖ Correo Central
- Ⓗ Jade Museum
- Ⓘ Legislative Assembly
- Ⓙ Mercado Central
- Ⓚ Museo Nacional
- Ⓛ Plaza de la Cultura
- Ⓜ Plaza de la Democrácia
- Ⓝ Radiográfica
- Ⓞ Teatro Nacional

Río Torres

Parque Bolívar

Parque España

Parque Nacional

Parque Morazán

Pedestrian Mall

0   .2 kilometer
0   .2 mile

Look to your left at the intersection of Calle 1 and Avenida Central. Three blocks north is **Radiográfica**, where you can make international phone calls, check your e-mail, or send and receive faxes.

You are still on Avenida Central. In a block and a half you'll see **Librería Lehmann**, another great bookstore. Next you'll come to the **Plaza de la Cultura** on Avenida Central, Calles 5/3. The eastern half of the plaza is full of children chasing pigeons and feeding them popcorn, and the center is often the stage for street comedians, concerts, and fairs. Since this is a prime tourist area, beware of pickpockets.

Cross the plaza to the famous **Teatro Nacional** (National Theater). In 1890 the world-renowned prima donna, Adelina Patti, appeared with a traveling opera company in Guatemala, but could not perform in Costa Rica because there was no appropriate theater. In response, newly rich coffee merchants financed the construction of a theater with a tax on every bag of exported coffee. Belgian architects were called in to design and supervise the building, and the metal structure was ordered from Belgian mills. Painters and decorators were brought from Italy, along with that country's famous marble. The Teatro Nacional was inaugurated in 1894 with Gounod's *Faust* and an opening-night cast that included singers from the Paris Opera. A source of cultural pride, the theater was made into a national monument in 1965. Extensive restoration work has renewed its beautiful ceiling paintings and sumptuous decor. The **Café del Teatro Nacional**, to the left as you enter the building, has changing art exhibits and specializes in exotic coffee combinations and desserts featuring Café Britt, of the famous Coffee Tour in Heredia. Take a moment to see the incredibly alive bust of Joaquin Gutierrez, one of Costa Rica's great writers, outside on the north side of the theater.

Down the grassy steps on Calle 5 is the information center of the **Instituto Costarricense de Turismo (ICT)**, or Tourism Institute, to the left. It's open Monday through Saturday, 9 a.m. to 5 p.m. There, too, is the entrance to the plaza's excellent underground exhibition rooms, which feature changing shows, as well as the famous pre-Columbian **Gold Museum** (open Tuesday through Sunday, 10 a.m. to 4:30 p.m.; 223-0528; admission $4, children and students $1.50). This little gem features shimmering displays of gold crafted by the Diquis master goldsmiths, who once inhabited the southwestern part of the country

Head north (left) on Calle 5. In a block you'll pass three upscale crafts stores: **Atmósfera**, on the corner to your right, **Magia**, on your right in the middle of the block, and **Suraja**, on your left at the corner of Avenida 3.

They feature excellent wood carvings, ceramics, and art, as well as furniture, bowls, and boxes made of tropical hardwoods. All merit a browse.

Parque Morazán is on your right. At its center is the domed **Music Temple**, purportedly patterned after Le Trianon in Paris. On the northwest corner of the park is the **Aurola Holiday Inn**, with mirrored panels reflecting San José's changing skies.

Three blocks north of the Music Temple is the entrance to **Parque Bolívar**, the location of San José's **zoo** (open Tuesday through Friday, 8 a.m. to 4 p.m.; weekends, 9 a.m. to 5 p.m.; admission $1). Monkeys, crocodiles, and birds live there, as well as some felines. At the beginning of the zoo is an interactive exhibit for kids.

East of the Music Temple is the green **Escuela Metálica**, a turn-of-the-20th-century school building built entirely of metal that was shipped from France. The story goes that the prefabricated school was destined for Puntarenas, Chile, but was mistakenly delivered to Puntarenas, Costa Rica. Next comes **Parque España**, which is filled with venerable and beautiful trees.

Continue to Avenida 7 and the tall National Insurance Institute (INS), which houses a fine exhibit of jade, ceramics, and art in the **Jade Museum** on the 11th floor (open Monday through Friday, 8 a.m. to 4:30 p.m.; 287-6034; admission $2, under 12 free). This museum rivals the National Museum in its extensive exhibits of pre-Columbian jade, gold, and ceramics. Modern art is also displayed in the outer gallery, and the eleventh-floor location provides a good view of San José and the mountains beyond. The Jade Museum should be high on your list of places to visit.

Continuing east on Avenida 7, you will pass the **Casa Amarilla** with its wide stairways. It houses the country's Department of Foreign Relations. This building and the park in front of it were donated by Andrew Carnegie. On the east side of the park is the former National Liquor Factory, founded by President Juan Rafael Mora in 1856. It has recently been converted into the **Centro Nacional de la Cultura**, an impressive museum and theater complex with delightful places for sitting, walking, or taking pictures (open Tuesday through Saturday, 10 a.m. to 5 p.m.). The **Museum of Contemporary Art and Design** (257-9370), inside, has exciting exhibits from all over the world.

Up a gentle hill on Avenida 7, you'll pass the Mexican Embassy on the left and arrive at the intersection of Avenida 7 and Calle 15. Turn right toward the **Biblioteca Nacional** (National Library). On its western side is the **Galería Nacional de Arte Contemporáneo** (open Monday through Saturday, 10 a.m. to 1 p.m., 2 p.m. to 5 p.m.), which often has good exhibits. Across the street is the other entrance to the Centro Nacional de la Cultura.

The library faces the largest of San José's city parks, **Parque Nacional**. In the center of the park is the massive **Monumento Nacional**, which depicts the spirits of the Central American nations driving out the despicable *filibustero* William Walker. The statue was made in the Rodin studios in France and shipped to Costa Rica.

Across the street from the park you will see a statue of **Juan Santamaría**, the national hero, holding aloft his torch. The elegant, white Moorish **Legislative Assembly** building he fronts houses the Costa Rican Congress. Inside is a small library and an exhibit recounting momentous decisions in Costa Rica's legal history.

Two blocks south of the Parque Nacional, on Calle 17, is the **Museo Nacional** (open Tuesday through Sunday, 8:30 a.m. to 4 p.m.; 257-1433; admission $4, students and children under ten free), housed in the former Bellavista Fortress. There are bullet holes in the turrets from the 1948 civil war. Inside are a lovely courtyard and large exhibits of indigenous gold and ceramics, religious objects, colonial furniture, and art. Definitely worth a visit.

The museum overlooks the **Plaza de la Democracia**, built by the Arias administration to receive visiting presidents during the historic Hemispheric Summit in 1989. Here you will see a statue of former president Don Pepe Figueres, hero of the 1948 civil war, and the abolisher of the army. His human stance and expression show that the citizens of this very small country know their leaders well. One block west on Avenida Central is a branch of Pop's, Costa Rica's excellent chain of ice cream stores. Nothing like a refreshing ice cream cone when you've been on your feet.

CREATIVE ARTS

Costa Ricans are well known for their interest in culture and the arts. The Ministry of Culture stimulates activity by sponsoring theater, choral music, opera, dance, literature, poetry, art, sculpture, and film.

The **International** or **National Festival of the Arts**, held each year in March and April, showcases national actors and musicians one year, and international artists the next. The 2000 festival featured theater groups from Bolivia, Chile, Guatemala, Colombia, Uruguay, Russia, Spain, and Brazil; folkloric dance and ballet from Russia, Italy, and Nicaragua; musicians from the United States and France; film from Canada; poetry, narrative, and drama workshops; and performers in all categories from Costa Rica. Tickets sell out early. Get more information at www.festivalcostarica.org, e-mail: festart @racsa.co.cr, or by calling 223-6361 or 223-6961.

MUSIC

Costa Rica's National Youth Symphony was inaugurated in 1972 by ex-President Figueres's famous quote: "We need to concern ourselves not only with the standard of living but the quality of life as well. Why have tractors without violins?"

Many of the young musicians trained in the Youth Symphony have graduated to participate in the National Symphony, which performs in the **Teatro Nacional** (Avenida 2, Calle 3; 221-1329) on the Plaza de la Cultura. Internationally famous guest directors and soloists are often featured. Entrance fees are kept low so that people at all economic levels may enjoy the concerts. The least expensive seats are in the *galería* section, which is up three flights of stairs through an entrance on the east side of the theater. The *butacas* are in the first tier of boxes above the *luneta* (orchestra) section. The *palcos* (box seats) are on the second tier. The symphony season starts in March and ends in December. Call or check the newspapers or the sign out front for current show times.

Teatro Melico Salazar (Avenida 2, Calle Central; 222-2653), across from the Parque Central, is slightly less grandiose than the Teatro Nacional, but often hosts performances by famous international musicians.

The world-renowned **International Music Festival**, presented each July since 1990, has been compared to the Aspen and Salzberg Music festivals. Concerts starring artists from all over the world are given at the National Theater and the elegant Club Unión in San José, and at beautiful hotels throughout the country, such as the Chalet Tirol in Heredia, the Fonda Vela in Monteverde, and Villa Caletas near Jacó. Tickets are sold through Credomatic (224-6266, fax: 234-6208).

Radio for Peace International is a worldwide shortwave radio station that provides provocative informational programming on topics important to world peace and justice. It provides daily news from the United Nations in English, Spanish, German, and French (and in other languages soon). Its studios are on the campus of the University for Peace in Villa Colón (249-1821, fax: 249-1095; in the U.S.: 503-252-3639, fax: 503-255-5216).

Costa Rica has a number of gifted folk singers and musicians, who regularly perform at some of the bars and theaters listed below. Look for posters around town or announcements in *The Tico Times* for concerts by some of the country's most creative contemporary performers: **Cantares** researches the history of Costa Rican music from all over the country, and writes songs with an ironic political twist; **Luis Angel Castro** sings *nueva trova* and calypso; **Canto América** adds to Afro-Caribbean rhythms with trumpets and flutes; **Adrián Goizueta and his Grupo Experimental** combine heartfelt lyrics with political statements and a great Latin beat; the contemporary string and percussion group, **Probus**, explores the edges of violin and cello repertoire; **Manuel Obregón** brings magic to the piano; and the very popular violin, guitar, and percussion group, **Editus**, which recently won a Grammy award for back-up work with Rubén Blades, has a New Age yet distinctly Latin tilt to its sensitive compositions. All of these musicians have produced CDs that make great souvenirs, and most of them can be heard at the music festivals in Monteverde (see the Northern Zone chapter) and Playa Chiquita (see the Atlantic Coast chapter). Highly recommended.

THEATER

Ticos are great actors. Even if you don't understand Spanish, it might be worth it to go to the theater to see the creativity that they bring to the stage. The English-speaking community also puts a lot of energy into its **Little Theater Group**, which presents musicals and comedies several times a year. Check *The Tico Times* for performance and audition information.

The Tico Times and the "Viva" section of *La Nación* will tell you what is playing in local theaters. Admission is usually about $5. Theater addresses are listed below:

Teatro de la Aduana: Calle 25, Avenidas 3/5; 251-8305

Teatro del Angel: Avenida Central, Calles 13/15; 222-8258

Teatro Bellas Artes: East side of University of Costa Rica campus; 207-4327, 207-5487

Teatro FANAL and Teatro 1887 in the CENAC: Calle 11, Avenidas 3/7; 257-5524

Teatro Giratablas: across from Pollos Kentucky in Barrio La California; 253-6001

Teatro Laurence Olivier: Avenida 2, Calle 28; 222-1034

Teatro La Mascara: Calle 13, Avenidas 2/4; 255-4250

Teatro Lucho Barahona: Calle 11, Avenidas 6/8; 223-5972

Teatro Nacional: Calle 3, Avenida 2; 221-5341

Teatro Melico Salazar: Avenida 2, Calles Central/2; 221-4952, 222-2653

Teatro Vargas Calvo: Calles 3/5, Avenida 2; 222-1875

FILMS

North American movies dominate the film scene here, and are usually shown three to six months after they appear in the United States, with Spanish subtitles. Check schedules in *The Tico Times* or *La Nación*. First-run movies are about $2-$3.

The **Sala Garbo** (Avenida 2, Calle 28; 222-1034) features excellent international films with Spanish subtitles. Next door, the **Teatro Laurence Olivier** offers films, plays, and concerts, as well as a gallery and coffee house. Local jazz groups play in its Shakespeare Bar. Take the Sabana–Cementerio bus (Calle 7, Avenidas Central/2) and get off at the Pizza Hut on Paseo Colón. The two theaters are one block south. You can walk to them from downtown in 25 minutes.

The **University of Costa Rica** in San Pedro runs an excellent, cheap international film series during the school year (March to December), Tuesday through Sunday nights. The movies are shown in the auditorium of the *Estudios Generales* building. Check current listings in *The Tico Times* or call **Cine Universitario** (207-4271).

ART

The Ticos converted their former air terminal into the **Museum of Costa Rican Art** (open Tuesday through Sunday, 10 a.m. to 4 p.m.; 222-7155; admission $2). This tastefully done museum displays the work of the country's finest painters and sculptors, as well as international exhibits. Located in La Sabana at the end of Paseo Colón. **Café Ruiseñor**, on the back porch, serves delicious coffee and European pastries.

Following local tradition, the National Liquor Factory downtown has also been converted to an impressive art center. FANAL (Fábrica Nacional de Licores) has become **CENAC** (Centro Nacional de la Cultura), a major gallery and theater complex (open daily, 10 a.m. to 5 p.m.; Avenida 3, Calles 15/17; 257-5524.

Galería Namu (open Monday through Saturday, 10 a.m. to 6 p.m., Sunday by appointment; Avenida 7, Calles 5/7; 256-3412) specializes in indigenous and women's art from around the country. The gallery hopes to give a forum to these artists so they may earn the recognition they deserve, and has already presented their beautiful artwork at galleries in New York.

See "Walking Tour" above for some of San José's many public galleries. Check *La Nación* and *The Tico Times* for exhibits at the galleries downtown. The Centro Cultural Costarricense-Norteamericano and the Alianza Francesa (see below) have monthly art exhibits. Their openings are a wonderful place to meet people and enjoy free wine and *bocas*.

NIGHTLIFE

While long-term residents and native Ticos often gripe about a lack of night-life, there's plenty to do after dark in San José. Besides dozens of theaters and cinemas, night owls can sample a wide variety of bars, discos, and all-night cafés.

The area bordered by Calle 4 on the west, Avenida 9 on the north, Calle 23 on the east, and Avenida 2 on the south is the heart of downtown night-life in San José and is usually quite safe. Of course, you should use common sense when walking around: keep your purse close to you; don't act drunk and out of control; and be extra-alert on deserted streets. Some of the night-spots listed here are in San Pedro, a ten-minute bus ride from downtown (Avenida 2, Calles 5/7).

BARS

Most bars offer a traditional *boca*, or small plate of food, along with your drink. *Ceviche* (raw fish "cooked" in lime juice), fried fish, chicken wings, little steaks, and rice and beans are common *bocas*; they are usually free. You'll find a variety of local beers, and most are pretty good. We recommend Imperial, Pilsen, or the more expensive, locally brewed Heineken.

The **All-Star Bar and Grill** (open daily, noon to 2 a.m.; 225-0838), across the street from the San Pedro Mall, brings in all the NBA, NFL, and soccer games on its giant TV screen. There's live music and dancing some weekends, and delicious chili and other American grub at reasonable prices.

Caccio's (100 meters east and 200 north of the San Pedro Church, near the railroad tracks; 283-2809) is a popular college bar, with two-for-one beers on Tuesday and Saturday, and free pizza *bocas* from 8 to 10 on Thursday night.

Chelles (open daily, 24 hours; 221-1369): As far as atmosphere goes, there's not much, but if you're a people watcher, you'll enjoy hanging out at Chelles. Probably because it remains open all the time, Chelles has be-come a landmark. You'll see actors, musicians, and dancers from the Na-tional Theater there having a midnight snack. You'll see middle-aged Costa Rican men amusing each other with toothpick tricks. You'll be asked to buy wilted roses from intriguing old ladies and persistent young boys. There are free *bocas* with every drink. For those who tire of the glare of Chelles' bare light bulbs, there is **Chelles Taberna** (open daily, 4 p.m. to 2 a.m.; 222-8060) around the corner, where you can hide in booths. The Taberna has better *bocas*, too. Chelles Lite is at Avenida Central, Calle 9; Chelles Dark is at Calle 9, Avenidas Central/2. *Overpriced*.

By day, **El Cuartel de la Boca del Monte** (open daily, 6 p.m. to 3 a.m.; Saturday and Sunday, 6 p.m. to 3 a.m.; Avenida 1, Calles 21/23; 221-0327) is one of the most popular singles bars in San José. The *bocas* aren't free, but they're good. *Pricey*.

La Esmeralda (open Monday through Saturday, 11:30 a.m. to 3:30 a.m.; Avenida 2, Calles 5/7; 221-0530) is lots of fun. It's the home of the Mariachi Union. Groups of musicians stroll between the tables while their vans wait outside to transport them to emergency serenade sites. We'll never forget the best party we ever went to in Costa Rica—our landlady's 80th birthday. After eating, drinking, and dancing until one in the morning, we were ready to retire, but that's not the way Ticos celebrate birthdays. At 2 a.m. the mariachis arrived to serenade her with guitars, harps, trumpets, and violins. But we digress. La Esmeralda offers good, reasonably priced food as well as an enjoyable time, but don't expect much from their "Mexican" dishes.

La Maga (open daily, 6 p.m. to 2 a.m.; San Pedro, 50 meters west of ICE; 280-9361) is a unique café/bar/theater, with a collection of literary and art magazines in wall racks. La Maga attracts the University literati, the hipoisie, and their teenybopper groupies.

Bar La Terraza in Hotel Colonial del Sol (100 meters south and 100 meters west of the Plaza del Sol in Curridabat; 225-9474) is one of the only places where you can go to dance and still be able to hear what your date is saying. Featuring live acoustic music a couple nights a week in a subdued atmosphere, this bar has a small outdoor dance floor surrounded by tropical foliage.

El Pueblo, in Barrio Tournón near the entrance to the Guápiles Highway, is a huge maze of Spanish Colonial–style alleyways and tiled roofs. You can spend hours wandering around there, getting lost and spending money. **Los Balcones** (open daily, 5 p.m. to 2 a.m.) features live music, from Latin fusion to Andean to *nueva trova* to jazz. The music starts at 9:30 p.m., Monday through Thursday, and 8:30 p.m., Friday and Saturday. There is a small bar where you can hear authentic Argentinian tango. A skating rink and three discotheques also await you at El Pueblo. **Lukas** (open daily, 24 hours; 233-8145) is a popular place to go for a moderately priced late dinner or snack. **Rías Bajas** (open Monday through Saturday, noon to 3 p.m., 6:30 p.m. to midnight; 221-7123), one of San José's most elegant seafood restaurants, is also there. At the **Cocina de Leña** (open daily, 11:30 a.m. to 3 p.m.,

6 p.m. to 11:30 p.m.; 223-3704), you can eat native Costa Rican dishes in an authentic campesino atmosphere, for twice the price of the Mercado Central. There are many more restaurants and nightclubs at El Pueblo to try out, as well as boutiques, galleries, and offices. Most nightspots have a cover charge, especially on weekends and holidays. El Pueblo is located north of downtown, across from the Villa Tournón. Walk, or take a Calle Blancos bus from Calle 1, Avenida 5.

Shakespeare Bar (open daily, 5 p.m. to midnight; Avenida 2, Calle 28; 257-1288) is under the Laurence Olivier Theater at the Sala Garbo complex. It's a nice spot to visit before or after a play or movie. There's a baby grand that often hosts a jazz pianist or combo.

DISCOTHÈQUES

Costa Rica's discos are not haunted by the specter of John Travolta, but are lively places to work on losing those rhythmic inhibitions. While some specialize in salsa and merengue, many mix in a fair selection of reggae and U.S. pop for those whose hips and footwork are not up to snuff.

While partner dancing is a novelty in the United States, it has a long tradition and a set of rules down here. The more serious salsa discos and salons try to encourage a sense of style and frown upon T-shirts and sneakers. Women who go alone or in groups should expect and be prepared for relentless pickup attempts. Women do not usually invite men onto the floor.

If you're not familiar with Latin music, here are some brief descriptions. *Salsa* is fast, lively Latin dance music. *Merengue* is similar, but basically Dominican with slightly less fancy footwork. *Cumbia* is Colombian, basic 4/4 dance music, and is also lively. *Boleros* are slow romantic ballads. *Rancheros* are a North Mexico version of country music. *Reggae* is mellow Jamaican music, with the words often in English. *Soca* is fast Caribbean dance music, a cross between merengue and reggae. Some places play Spanish-language rap, sometimes called *Punta*.

Cocoloco (in El Pueblo; 222-8782) attracts an older crowd. The emphasis here is on dancing, despite the small floor.

El Gran Parqueo (in Desamparados) is one of San José's classic dance salons, catering to working- and middle-class Ticos. Instead of comfy lounge furniture, they set out rickety chairs on their cement floor. Live bands mix up *salsa, merengue, boleros,* and *cumbia.*

Infinitos (in El Pueblo; 223-2195) offers three discos for the price of one. Separate rooms cater to different musical tastes. **Tobogán** is an outdoor covered area with a huge dance floor, also in El Pueblo.

La Plaza (just across from El Pueblo) has a large dance floor and attracts a young, lively crowd.

Risas (on Avenida Central, Calle Central; 223-2803) is a reasonably priced disco with a slide. It caters to a younger crowd. Patrons receive credit toward a drink with the cover charge.

At **Salsa 54** (Calle 3, Avenidas 1/3; 221-3220) it's worth the cover just to watch some of Costa Rica's best dancers strut their stuff on the raised stage. There are two adjoining discos, one featuring romantic music and *boleros*, the other dedicated to pop and techno tunes for the younger crowd. It's one of the most affordable discos.

GAY/LESBIAN NIGHTLIFE

For women, good *salsa/merengue* and a management that has supported many causes over the years make **La Avispa** (closed Monday; Calle 1, Avenidas 8/10; 223-5343) the first stop on a nightlife tour of San José. Men are welcome there, too, especially on Tuesday. It features three dance floors, a snack bar, pool tables, big-screen TV, and lots of local flavor. La Avispa attracts mostly locals and is popular as the country's first lesbian-owned bar.

For men, **Deja Vu** (Calle 2, Avenidas 14/16; 223-3758) is probably the hottest dance bar in Latin America, with pop, alternative, and techno music. It features a café, quiet bar, souvenir shop, and two large dance floors. On Saturday you'll usually find high-quality dancers and drag shows. Deja Vu attracts a younger, more upscale crowd than La Avispa. The management has invested thousands of dollars and many hours of work in support of gay and lesbian causes.

San José's many small, safe, and comfortable neighborhood gay and lesbian bars include **La Tertulia** in San Pedro (100 meters east and 150 meters north of the Church), the **Blue Moon Bar** in Los Yoses (75 meters west of Spoon), **Buenas Vibraciones** and **Puchitos** (Paseo de los Estudiantes, Calle 9), **Los Cucharones** (around the corner from La Avispa downtown), and the **Kasbah Bar and Restaurant** (150 meters north of the Hotel Europa), which also has an internet café.

RESTAURANTS

COFFEE SHOPS

Below are some of the best places we've found to eat a quick meal or have a cup of coffee. They are all rather pricey by Tico standards, but at any of them you can eat lunch for less than $5 and have coffee and a pastry for under $2.50. The traditional Tico way to serve coffee is in two separate pitchers, one filled with strong black coffee and the other with steaming hot milk. You can mix them to suit your taste. Many establishments have stopped this practice for economic reasons, but Giacomín has retained the tradition. Decaffeinated coffee is available only in those restaurants that serve Café Britt, Costa Rica's export-quality coffee. Most places only offer black or camomile tea, although many excellent herbal teas are manufactured here. You can always bring your own and ask for a pot of hot water at restaurants. Incidentally, the concept of smoking and nonsmoking areas in restaurants is just being introduced. If it matters to you, stick to vegetarian restaurants.

Azafrán (open daily, 9 a.m. to 7 p.m.; 232-7409) makes delicious sandwiches, lasagna, cannelloni, and desserts. The food can be ordered to go, and they offer an excellent catering service. Their *torta Azafrán* has to be one of the best cakes of all time. Located in Rohrmoser.

Boston Bagel Café (open Monday through Saturday, 7:30 a.m. to 6 p.m.; Sunday, 7:30 a.m. to 2 p.m.; 232-2991) has the best bagels we've tasted here or in the U.S. They come in 12 flavors, and the café serves them with pastrami, four flavors of cream cheese, and other delicacies. Located on the road to Pavas across from La Artística, and in San Pedro in the Plaza Calle Real next to Rosti-Pollo (283-8633). Recommended.

Delimundo (open daily, 8 a.m. to 8 p.m.; 289-9160) is a great deli located in Plaza Colonial on the road to Santa Ana in Escazú. They have bagels, hummus, salads, pastries, a variety of fresh fruit drinks, and well-brewed coffee, all in a clean, efficient environment.

In Barrio Amón, **La Esquina del Café** (open daily, 8 a.m. to 9 p.m.; Avenida 9, Calle 3 bis; 258-2983) is a small, quiet café with an in-house coffee roaster and grinder. Connoisseurs will be delighted by the gift-size packets of coffee from the country's different microregions. They offer an inexpensive lunch special that includes coffee and dessert.

Giacomín (open Monday through Saturday, 8 a.m. to noon, 2 p.m. to 7 p.m.; 225-0356) has an upstairs tea room; it's a nice place to enjoy coffee and pastries or homemade bonbons. It is next to the Automercado in Los Yoses.

Café Ruiseñor (open Monday through Saturday, 8 a.m. to 7 p.m.; Sunday, 11 a.m. to 7 p.m.; 225-2562) is a lovely place that serves delicious pastries and light meals made with pure, healthful ingredients. It has some outdoor tables. Located in Los Yoses, 150 meters east of Automercado—a 20-minute walk from downtown toward San Pedro. They also operate the café/restaurant at the Museo de Arte Costarrianse in La Sabana (251-3168).

Ritmos Culinarios (228-7978) is the place to go in Escazú for a light lunch featuring healthful gourmet ingredients. They have a cooking school and a gourmet food shop. It's pricey, but worth it. They are located on the right on the road to San Rafael de Escazú.

Vía Veneto (open daily, 8 a.m. to 11 p.m.; 234-2898), across from the Indoor Club in Curridabat, has espresso and cappuccino coffees, delicious pastries, and ice cream desserts. We recommend these over the Italian entrées they serve.

INTERNET CAFÉS

There are at least 16 internet cafés in San José. We will mention some of the more interesting ones:

Browsers (open Monday through Saturday, 9 a.m. to 8 p.m.; 228-7109; www.browsers.co.cr), in the Plaza Colonial shopping center in Escazú has a pleasant art-deco atmosphere and serves as a gallery for local art.

CyberCafe Las Arcadas (open Monday through Friday, 7 a.m. to 11 p.m.; weekends, 7 a.m. to 7 p.m.; 233-3310; www.searchcostarica.com/cy bercafe) is a popular spot for tourists, who can people-watch at their indoor or outdoor tables in the Las Arcadas building in front of the National Theater. A cheaper, no-frills, no-food version is on the second floor of Las Arcadas (233-3558).

Another downtown café with 20 computers is the **Internet Club** (open daily, 24 hours; 221-7927), 25 meters north of the Caja on Calle 7, Avenidas Central/2.

San Pedro's **Internet Café** (open daily, 24 hours; 224-7295; www.inter netcafecr.com) is a smoky, late-night hang-out with computer games. It's not much on atmosphere, but has quick and dependable service.

The smaller **Y2K Netcafe** (open Monday through Saturday, 8 a.m. to 7 p.m.; 283-4829; www.y2knetcafe.com), 200 meters east of U Latina, is a little cheaper, and you can share the computer with a friend for the price of one.

INEXPENSIVE EATERIES

The **Mercado Central** (Avenidas Central/1 and Calles 6/8) is filled with inexpensive places to eat—many of them, like the Marisquería Ribera, recommended for good food. The only problem with the market is that the restaurants are usually so crowded, you don't feel you can sit down and relax. Go in the late afternoon when things are winding down so you aren't competing with hundreds of hungry workers on their lunch hour.

Our favorite hole-in-the-wall place is the **Soda Amón** (Calle 7, Avenidas 7/9) where you can get a delicious *gallo pinto con huevo* for about $2, and a great *casado* for about $3. It has been there forever, always with the same humble, friendly Tico hosts. Recommended.

Café Rosé (open weekdays, 7:30 a.m. to 9 p.m.; Saturday, 9 a.m. to 2:30 p.m.; 258-2703) serves generous plates of honest Tico food. The service on their daily *casado* specials ($3) is lightning quick. They even have a non-smoking area. Located downtown on Calle 7, Avenidas 2/Central. Recommended.

Kontiki (open daily, 11:30 a.m. to 10 p.m.; 224-6848), in the southeastern *barrio* Zapote, has tasty Caribbean cuisine. It's on the north side of the Zapote bull ring, 250 meters west of the PriceSmart.

Don Wang (open daily, 11 a.m. to 3 p.m., 5 p.m. to 11 p.m.; 233-6484) has become famous for its Sunday *dim sum* brunches. Three or four of their plump Chinese dumplings cost under $2. Don Wang is on Calle 11, Avenidas 6/8.

Besides the Mercado Central, you'll find the highest concentration of inexpensive *sodas* in **San Pedro**, the neighborhood bordering the Universidad de Costa Rica. After lunch, you can browse in the area's many bookstores or stroll the shady campus. To get there from San José, catch one of the buses that leave from Avenida 2, Calles 5/7/9. The bus should say "La U" or "San Pedro" in its front window (15 cents).

Il Pomodoro (open daily, noon to 11 p.m.; San Pedro, 50 meters north of the church; 224-0966; and in Escazú; 289-7470) has thin-crust pizzas and inexpensive pasta dishes. Popular with students and professors.

By the way, if you must, Pizza Hut, Burger King, McDonald's, Kentucky Fried Chicken, and Taco Bell all have branches here. They are fast, but not as cheap as local places. The best thing about them is that they usually have clean, easy-to-find bathrooms—a boon in downtown San José.

VEGETARIAN RESTAURANTS

All of the restaurants listed here are inexpensive, offering prix-fixe lunches for under $3.

Bio Salud (234-2475), in the Plaza del Sol shopping center in Curridabat, a health food store with a vegetarian café and a resident herbalist.

El Encuentro (open Tuesday through Thursday, 8 a.m. to 6 p.m.; Friday and Saturday, 8 a.m. to 10 p.m.; 228-7742), serving great breakfasts, sandwiches, juices, desserts, coffee, and burritos, hopes to be a place where people of like beliefs can meet and share ideas. Located in the Centro Comercial Paco in Escazú.

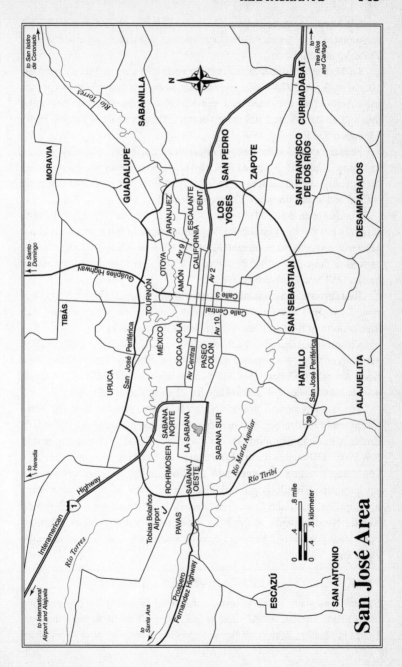

San José Area

Isla Verde (open weekdays, 11 a.m. to 11 p.m.; 296-5068) is a Chinese restaurant with vegetarian selections, located 300 meters west of the U.S. Embassy in Rohrmoser.

La Mazorca (open Monday through Friday, 11 a.m. to 7 p.m.; Saturday, 10 a.m. to 3 p.m.; 224-8069) serves macrobiotic fare and whole-wheat pastries. Across the street there is a minimarket with natural foods (including tofu and miso). Located 100 meters north, 200 meters east of the San Pedro Church in San Pedro.

Shakti (open Monday through Friday, 9 a.m. to 7 p.m.; Saturday, 10 a.m. to 4 p.m.; Calle 13, Avenida 8; 222-4475) serves generous, inexpensive, high-quality vegetarian meals. Their *plato del día* has soup, salad, a main course, and a fruit drink for $2. Recommended.

Tin-Jo (open daily, 11:30 a.m. to 3 p.m., 5 p.m. to 10 p.m.; 221-7605) certainly has the most interesting vegetarian menu in town, though it is not known as a vegetarian restaurant. Meat-free Chinese, Thai, and Indian dishes, as well as delicious sushi, are served in a quiet environment with classical music. On Calle 11, Avenidas 6/8.

Restaurante el Vegetariano (open Monday through Friday, 8 a.m. to 6 p.m.; 224-1163) is a small, macrobiotic joint popular with students, 125 meters north of the San Pedro church near the train tracks.

Vishnu (open daily, 7:30 a.m. to 9:30 p.m.; 222-2549) gives inexpensive, generous servings. It's crowded at lunch—get there early. There are five locations: Avenida 1, Calles 1/3; Calle 14, Avenidas Central/2; Calle 1, Avenida 4; Avenida 6, Calles 7/9; and in Heredia, 75 meters south of Fresas.

You can buy organic fruits, vegetables, grains, and coffee at the **Féria Orgánica** in Rohrmoser, 100 meters west and 500 meters north of the U.S. Embassy on Saturday morning and Tuesday and Friday afternoons, and in San Pedro 150 meters north of the church on Saturday morning. Call 232-2643. Supermarkets **Automercado** and **Yaohan** sell tofu, brown rice, and soy products; **Simbiosis** proffers macrobiotic items, vitamins, aromatherapy supplies, and Bach flower remedies in the Plaza Mayor in Rohrmoser; **Tienda Naturalmente** at the Plaza Colonial in Escazú carries vitamins, herbs, and goat milk, cheese, and pastries from the Dúrika reserve in the Zona Sur.

MODERATE TO EXPENSIVE RESTAURANTS

San José has many excellent restaurants. In the following list you will find many French, Italian, and Chinese places, but don't overlook those that specialize in Spanish, Korean, or Japanese cuisines. See the Central Valley chapter for excellent restaurants in a mountain setting less than an hour's drive from the city.

Moderate means that most entrées are under $8. *Expensive* indicates that entrées are $8 to $15. Wine can really increase the total price of a dinner, since wines in Costa Rica are imported and expensive. All restaurant bills include a 10 percent tip and a 15 percent tax. Tipping is not customary but is certainly appreciated, especially when the service is good.

Since getting around in San José is such a hassle, especially at dinnertime, we have arranged the following restaurants according to neighborhood:

DOWNTOWN/BARRIO AMÓN **Café Mundo** (open Monday through Thursday, 11 a.m. to 11 p.m.; Friday and Saturday, noon to midnight; Avenida 9, Calle 15; 222-6190), owned by a young Chicago chef, offers a reasonably priced, healthy menu featuring "Costa Ricanized" international dishes. There's also espresso and a nice selection of desserts. *Moderate*.

Fleur de Lys (open daily, 11:30 a.m. to 9:30 p.m.; Calle 13, Avenidas 2/6; 223-1206) specializes in Costa Rican cuisine. The restaurant is in the courtyard of the hotel of the same name, half a block from the Plaza de la Democrácia. *Expensive*.

Goya (open Monday through Saturday, 11 a.m. to 10 p.m.; Avenida 1, Calles 5/7; 221-3887) has good food and pleasant service. *Moderate*.

Tin-Jo (open daily, 11:30 a.m. to 3 p.m., 5 p.m. to 10 p.m.; Calle 11, Avenidas 6/8; 221-7605) is a friendly, creative Asian restaurant that serves spicy Szechuan, Thai, Indian, and Indonesian dishes. The kitchen accommodates vegetarians. Recommended. *Moderate*.

LOS YOSES/BARRIO ESCALANTE **Le Chandelier** (open Monday through Friday, 11:30 a.m. to 2 p.m., 6:30 p.m. to 11 p.m.; Saturday, 6:30 p.m. to 11 p.m.; 225-3980) offers fancy French cuisine. From Spoon in Los Yoses, 100 meters south, 100 meters east, and 100 meters south. *Expensive*.

L'Île de France (open daily, 6 p.m. to 10 p.m.; 234-7850) offers excellent traditional French cuisine and superb service. Even if you think you can't afford a full meal, stop in for a glass of wine and a delicious *crema de mariscos* and finish it off with a light, airy *parfait glace de maracuya*. But get there early—the place fills up with loyal patrons. Located in the relaxing garden court of the Hotel Le Bergerac, 50 meters south of the *"primera entrada Los Yoses."* *Expensive*.

Miro's Bistro (open Monday through Friday, noon to 10 p.m.; 253-4242) features good Italian food and brick-walled bohemian decor. It is a pleasant walk from downtown in Barrio Escalante, 300 meters north and 20 meters east of the *pulpería* La Luz, along the train tracks. *Moderate*.

Adventurous cuisine at **Paprika** (open daily, 6 p.m. to 10 p.m.; 400 meters west from the rear of the San Pedro Mall; 225-8971) includes wildly presented salads and entrées made with fresh ingredients. *Moderate*.

SAN PEDRO/CURRIDABAT   **Ambrosia** (open Monday through Friday, 11:30 a.m. to 3 p.m., 6 p.m. to 10:30 p.m.; Saturday, 11 a.m. to 10:30 p.m.; Sunday, 11 a.m. to 3:30 p.m.; 253-8012) is a quiet place for lunch, tea, or dinner, serving both vegetarian and nonvegetarian fare. All specialties are named after Greek deities. Located in the Centro Comercial de la Calle Real in San Pedro. *Moderate*.

Lai Yuin (open Monday through Saturday, 11 a.m. to 3 p.m., 6 p.m. to 11 p.m.; Sunday, 10 a.m. to 9 p.m.; 253-5055) specializes in Chinese seafood. Located in Curridabat, across from the Indoor Club. *Moderate*.

Marbella (open Tuesday through Saturday, 11 a.m. to 3 p.m., 6:30 p.m. to 10:30 p.m.; Sunday, noon to 5 p.m.; 75 meters east of the Banco Popular in the back of the Centro Comercial Calle Real in San Pedro; 224-9452) is an elegant Spanish restaurant that serves a diverse assortment of meat dishes unusual in Costa Rica—rabbit, lamb, and veal, for example. *Expensive*.

Ponte Vecchio (open Monday through Saturday, noon to 2:30 p.m., 6 p.m. to 10:30 p.m.; 200 meters west of San Pedro church, 25 meters north; 283-1810) offers intimate, attentive service and is a good place to propose marriage. Chef/owner is a New York City transplant and prepares the best Italian food we've tried in San José. Recommended. *Expensive*.

PASEO COLÓN/SABANA/PAVAS   **Casa Luisa** (open for lunch and dinner, Monday through Saturday; 296-1917) is a family-run restaurant with lovingly prepared Catalán cuisine. Make reservations for this popular restaurant, especially if you want the house specialty, *paella*. It's in Sabana Sur, 400 meters south of the Contraloría, and 40 meters east. *Moderate*.

Flor del Loto (open Monday through Saturday, 11 a.m. to 3 p.m., 6 p.m. to 11 p.m.; Sunday, 11:30 a.m. to 9:30 p.m.; 232-4652) serves delicious Hunan and Szechuan Chinese specialties. On the east side of the ICE (pronounced "ee-say") building, Sabana Norte. *Moderate*.

Fuji (open daily, noon to 2:30 p.m., 6 p.m. to 11 p.m.; 232-8122) is the Meliá Comfort Corobicí's Japanese restaurant, with tatami-covered, private dining rooms for six. Near the northeast corner of La Sabana. *Expensive*.

Grano de Oro (open daily, 6 a.m. to 10 p.m.; Calle 30, Avenidas 2/4, No. 251; 255-3322) is an excellent restaurant with a varied menu, in the delightful courtyard of the Hotel Grano de Oro. Recommended. *Moderate*.

Machu Picchu (open Monday through Saturday, 11 a.m. to 3 p.m., 6 p.m. to 10 p.m.; 222-7384) features authentic Peruvian *ceviche*, pisco sours, and *anticuchos.* A good introduction to Peruvian seafood. Located on Calle 32, Avenida 1, 125 meters north of Paseo Colón. *Moderate.*

La Masía de Triquell (open Monday through Saturday, 11:30 a.m. to 2 p.m., 6:30 p.m. to 10:30 p.m.; 296-3528) serves Spanish cuisine in an elegant colonial atmosphere. Located in Sabana Norte, 175 meters west and 175 meters north of the Nissan dealership. *Expensive.*

Shil La (open Sunday through Friday, 11:30 a.m. to 3 p.m., 6 p.m. to 10 p.m.; Saturday, noon to 9:30 p.m.; 290-8663) serves authentic Korean cuisine as well as sushi and sashimi. Located 25 meters north of Cemaco in Pavas. *Moderate.*

ESCAZÚ   **La Leyenda** (228-6486, 289-5604) is fast becoming legendary in Escazú for Mexican *alta cocina.* Located on the right, 600 meters toward San Rafael from the *cruce de Escazú.* Recommended.

María Alexandra (open Monday through Saturday, 11:30 a.m. to 2:30 p.m., 7:30 p.m. to 10 p.m.; Sunday, noon to 4 p.m.; 228-4876), located in the apartotel of the same name in Escazú, is a small restaurant that's quiet and intimate, with dependably good food and service. *Moderate.*

Monastere (289-4404) is a converted 19th-century monastery. The waiters, dressed as monks, reverently take your orders while you gaze out over the shimmering lights of the Central Valley. The food is as good as the view. Take the old road to Santa Ana past Escazú and turn left just past the U.S. Embassy residence. Signs lead you up the mountain from there. *Expensive.*

Q'tal (289-9335), next to McDonald's in Escazú, serves Costa Rican specialties and international cuisine with live music. *Moderate.*

LODGING

You will find lodgings scattered throughout metropolitan San José. Below is a list of each neighborhood's hotels. More detailed descriptions follow, organized by type and price.

DOWNTOWN

Many hotels are downtown—i.e., convenient for sightseeing and mobilizing for day trips. However, they can be noisy and the central city is badly polluted. We define "downtown" as the area between Avenida 7 and Avenida 12, Calle 20 and Calle 15. The cheaper hotels are located west of Calle 2, in an unsavory section of downtown. The hostels are on the east side, in a much nicer neighborhood.

Deluxe: Aurola Holiday Inn

Moderate: Europa; Fleur de Lys; Santo Tomás

B&B: Pensión de la Cuesta

Mid-range: Best Western San José; Diplomat; Doral; Gran Hotel Centroamericano

Inexpensive: Bienvenido; Boruca; Cocorí; Musoc

Hostels: Casa Leo; Casa Ridgway

BARRIOS AMÓN, OTOYA, AND ARANJUEZ

Quite a few hotels have sprung up in San José's historic northern neighborhoods. Most are restored turn-of-the-20th-century homes whose architecture includes high ceilings and enclosed courtyards, which allow the buildings to stay cool and fresh when it's hot outside. Barrios Amón, Otoya, and Aranjuez are safe, quiet (except for the city's ubiquitous traffic noise), and close to downtown restaurants, shopping areas, and museums.

Deluxe: Brittania; Casa Verde

Moderate: Don Carlos

B&B: Raya Vida

Mid-range: Aranjuez; Edelweiss; Hemingway Inn; Kekoldi; Rey Amon

BARRIO TOURNÓN

Across the Río Torres from Barrio Amón, Barrio Tournón offers one large hotel located on a busy thoroughfare.

Deluxe: Radisson Europa

BARRIOS BELLAVISTA AND CALIFORNIA

Just east of downtown in the hills, Barrios Bellavista and California are a bit quieter than downtown.

Moderate: Aparthotel Don Carlos

B&B: Ara Macao

Mid-range: Bellavista

PASEO COLÓN

This area, on the Paseo (Avenida Central between Calle 14 and Calle 42) and the two or three blocks north and south of it, is convenient for travelers who are coming from or heading west on the Interamerican Highway—stay here and you can avoid crossing town. Many car rental agencies have their offices here. Several fine restaurants are also in this area.

Moderate: Grano de Oro; Napoleon; Torremolinos

Mid-range: Cacts

EASTERN BARRIOS

Barrios Escalante, Dent, and Los Yoses are elegant embassy neighborhoods east of downtown toward San Pedro.

Moderate: Le Bergerac; Don Paco; Jade

Mid-range: Apartotel los Yoses

Hostels: Toruma

SAN PEDRO AND CURRIDABAT

This University area bustles with students during the March–December academic year, and is packed with good, inexpensive restaurants and nightspots. The campus is a pleasant area for exercising. Buses leave San Pedro frequently for the ten-minute ride downtown.

B&B: Maripaz; Residencia Saint-Pierre

Mid-range: Apartotel D'Galah; Ave del Paraiso

Inexpensive: Casa Agua Buena, La Granja

MORAVIA AND SANTO DOMINGO DE HEREDIA

The hotels in this windy, cool area are located in quiet residential neighborhoods.

Moderate: Bougainvillea

B&B: Casa Rosa Inn

LA URUCA

Although it's San José's industrial strip, this area has some pleasant facilities. La Uruca is about a third of the way to the airport from downtown, close to shopping.

Moderate: Best Western Irazu

Mid-range: Kalexma; Apartotel La Perla

PAVAS, ROHRMOSER, AND LA SABANA

The hotels in sunny, upscale Pavas and Rohrmoser, or ringing the green La Sabana, are convenient to the park.

Deluxe: Meliá Confort Corobici

Moderate: Apartotel El Sesteo; Tennis Club

B&B: Colours; La Sabana

Mid-range: Apartotel La Sabana

ESCAZÚ

This small village nestles in a valley to the southwest of San José. The road leading into town is lined with strip malls, but once you get into the village center and its nearby hills, Escazú regains its traditional campesino feel. Many bed and breakfasts are here; walkers will enjoy their proximity to beautiful country roads.

In addition to the accommodations below, you may want to check the listings in the following chapter, which covers the Central Valley area. The towns of Alajuela, Heredia, and Santa Ana are closer to the airport than San José and may be good places to stay on your way in and out of Costa Rica.

Deluxe: Camino Real; San Gildar; Tara Resort; Villas del Rio

Moderate: Amstel Country Inn; Apartotel Maria Alexandra

B&B: Casa Baker del Rio; Casa de las Tias; Las Golondrinas; La Posada del Bosque; Posada El Quijote; Tapezco Inn; Villa Escazú

Mid-range: Pico Blanco

LARGE DELUXE HOTELS

All of these luxury hotels have 100-plus rooms, and are fully equipped for conventions. In addition to tourists, their guests are often businesspeople and foreign dignitaries. All the hotels in this category boast elegant restaurants, bars, and casinos; most have pools and spas. All are wheelchair-accessible, unless indicated. Amenities in the rooms include private baths, hot water, air conditioning, bathtubs, hairdryers, phones, cable TV, security boxes, and small refrigerators. All have at least one nonsmoking section. Rates for double rooms range from $140-$350 and include taxes.

Aurola Holiday Inn ($140-$250; Avenida 5, Calle 5; 233-7233, fax: 222-2621; www.basshotels.com/holiday-inn, e-mail: aurola@racsa.co.cr) has a sauna, indoor pool, and gym, and is firesafe and earthquake-proof. Located downtown, across from Parque Morazán.

On the highway between Escazú and Santa Ana, **Camino Real** ($250-$800, including breakfast; located at the west side of the Multiplaza Shopping Center; 289-7000, fax: 289-8998; www.ticonet.co.cr, e-mail: camino real@ticonet.co.cr) is a very large complex that sports a pool, tennis courts, sauna and gym, and a beauty salon, as well as a complete business center for guests. A free shuttle runs to Escazú and downtown San José.

Rates in the large, well-appointed **Meliá Confort Corobicí** ($140-$150; 232-8122, fax: 231-5834; www.centralamerica.com, e-mail: corobici@ racsa.co.cr) include breakfast and use of the spa. On the northeast corner of La Sabana.

Radisson Europa ($160-$260; 50 meters west of Periódico La República; 257-3257, fax: 221-3976; www.crica.com/hotels, e-mail: eurohot@racsa. co.cr) is a modern hotel with an original design, a gym, a spa, and an outdoor pool. Rooms are spacious. Located at the beginning of the Guápiles highway in Barrio Tournón.

Villas del Río (bathtubs, air conditioning, pool, playground, gym, sauna; $140-$350; on the old road to Santa Ana on the eastern side of the country club; 289-8833, fax: 289-8835; www.villasdelrio.com), a gated townhouse complex in Escazú, maintains tight security for its guests—mainly executives and diplomatic personnel. Specifications are up to U.S. standards, including smoke detectors, 24-hour guard, and closed-circuit video monitoring. The ultramodern rooms have such amenities as hairdryers, VCRs, and phones with voicemail. Considering the quality of these apartments, the rates are quite reasonable. Weekly and monthly rates available.

SMALL DELUXE HOTELS

These are intimate luxury hotels, proud of the attentive service their smaller size makes possible. Far from the ambiance of the larger hotels, each of these small deluxe hotels has unique offerings and a more personalized feel. Amenities in the rooms include private baths, hot water, and phones, plus those mentioned below in each description. Rates for double rooms range from $100 to $290, including taxes. Note that there are similar accommodations in the moderate price range (see below).

Brittania (ceiling fans, bathtubs, air conditioning, cable TV, bar; $100-$130; Calle 3, Avenidas 9/11; 223-6667, fax: 223-6411; www.centralamerica. com, e-mail: brittania@racsa.co.cr) is a remodeled mansion in Barrio Amón, with high ceilings, spacious rooms, and a reasonably priced restaurant in the cool former wine cellar.

The **San Gildar** (wheelchair-accessible, air conditioning, bathtubs, cable TV, pool, bar; $110-$130, including breakfast; across from the country club, 250 meters to the northeast, on the road above Santa Ana; 289-8843, fax: 228-6454; www.hotelsangildar.com, e-mail: info@hotelsangildar.com) is a luxury/business hotel between Escazú and Santa Ana. The peach-colored complex has a pleasant, tree-filled courtyard with a pool and a restaurant. The best rooms are located on the third floor; their balconies look out into the treetops. The rooms in the reception area are not as private or quiet.

The **Tara Resort** (ceiling fans, some bathtubs, pool, restaurant, bar; $150-$290, including breakfast; one and a half kilometers above the Guardia Rural de San Antonio de Escazú; 228-6992, fax: 228-9651; www.tararesort.com, e-mail: taraspa@racsa.co.cr) is in an elegant antebellum-style mansion high in the hills above Escazú, a suburb of San José. It has a restaurant with grand views. For rejuvenation and refreshment, treat yourself to the services offered by the spa: low-impact aerobics, herbal healing, massage, facials, mud baths, aromatherapy, and herbal wraps.

MODERATE HOTELS

For what you'd spend in a lackluster roadside motel in the States, you can get elegant accommodations in San José, with excellent service, attentive tour-planning information, and great restaurants. Double-occupancy room rates for these hotels range from $60 to $100; some offer luxurious, pricier suites as well. In our opinion, you can get all the luxury you need in this price range, and the service will often be much more personalized. All these hotels accept children. Amenities include private baths, hot water, and, unless indicated, cable TV and phone. If you come in the Green Season, most of them give discounts.

Amstel Country Inn (ceiling fans or air conditioning, shared kitchen, pool, playground; $70-$90, including breakfast; 300 meters south of El Cruce Commercial Center; 228-1764, fax: 228-0620, in the U.S.: 800-575-1253; www.tourism.com/amstel, e-mail: escazu@racsa.co.cr) was once a private home. The gated entrance and quiet backyard preserve privacy in this busy section of Escazú.

Le Bergerac (ceiling fans, internet access; Calle 35, Avenidas Central/8; $80-$100, including breakfast; children under 12, $5; 234-7850, fax: 225-9103; www.bergerac.com, e-mail: bergerac@racsa.co.cr) is quiet and distinguished, with sunny, landscaped grounds run by dedicated hosts transplanted from Montreal. Several rooms have private gardens. The elegant French restaurant L'Ile de France is in the garden courtyard. Recommended.

The **Bougainvillea** (ceiling fans, some bathtubs, pool, restaurant, bar; $70-$80; 244-1414, fax: 244-1313; www.bougainvillea.co.cr, e-mail: info@bougainvillea.co.cr) is filled with Costa Rican and pre-Columbian art. Its quiet grounds have a pool, a conference room, a sauna, and tennis courts. Each room's private balcony overlooks the beautiful gardens or San José. The Bougainvillea name is associated with superb service and an excellent restaurant. Located 15 minutes from downtown in Santo Tomás de Santo Domingo de Heredia; microbuses provide a shuttle service between the hotel and San José. Recommended.

Located in Barrio Amón, **Casa Verde** (no smoking, ceiling fans, some bathtubs, cable TV; $70-$110; Calle 7, Avenida 9; phone/fax: 223-0969; www.zurqui.co.cr/crinfocus/verde, e-mail: casaverde@racsa.co.cr) is a lovingly restored Victorian home. Furnished with antiques and decorated with old timepieces, it is not ideal for families with small children, but it does offer one- and two-bedroom suites.

Don Carlos (wheelchair-accessible, ceiling fans, restaurant, bar; $60-$80, including breakfast; children under 12 free; Calle 9, Avenida 9, No. 779; 221-6707, fax: 255-0828; www.doncarlos.co.cr, e-mail: hotel@doncarlos.co.cr) is a well-run hotel in a pleasant historical neighborhood within walking distance of museums. It is filled with Costa Rican art, has a sun deck, gym, and shows tour videos, and its souvenir shop, Annemarie's, is one of the most complete and reasonably priced in San José. Guests are greeted with a special Don Carlos cocktail, and they have free access to e-mail services. Don Carlos also offers apartments with views in the exclusive Los Yoses section of San José ($400/week). Highly recommended.

Located on a quiet downtown street, **Fleur de Lys** (fans, most with bathtubs; $80-$110, including breakfast; children under 12 free; Calle 13, Avenidas 2/6; 222-4391, 223-1206, fax: 257-3637; www.hotelfleurdelys.com, e-mail: florlys@sol.racsa.co.cr) is a faithfully renovated mansion that has comfortable sitting areas on each floor as well as atriums. Rooms are graced by original works of art by Costa Rican painters and sculptors. There is also an excellent restaurant and pleasant porch-side bar. Near the National Museum. Recommended.

Grano de Oro (ceiling fans, bathtubs, hot tubs, bar, all rooms nonsmoking; $90-$270; Calle 30, Avenidas 2/4, No. 251; 255-3322, fax: 221-2782; www.distinctivehotels.com, e-mail: granoro@racsa.co.cr) is an elegant restored mansion located in a quiet neighborhood, yet close to restaurants, theaters, and shops. It has comfortable furnishings, deluxe baths, one of the best restaurants in the city, jacuzzis, and a sunny garden patio. If you have to stay in San José, this is the way to go. Highly recommended.

Hotel Jade (ceiling fans, cable TV, pool, bar; $80-$100, including breakfast; 250 meters north of the Subaru dealership; 224-2455, 225-3022, fax: 224-2166; www.ilisa.com/ho-jade) has spacious rooms in peaceful Barrio Dent, near San Pedro. A comfortable place for travelers on business and official missions.

Best Western Irazú (air conditioning, bathtubs, pool, some nonsmoking rooms; $80-$100, including continental breakfast, free local phone calls and internet access, free happy hour, free return transportation to airport; 232-4811, fax: 232-4549; e-mail: travel@costarica.net) is a large hotel with a convention center, casino, tennis courts, sauna, and bus service. Located 15 minutes west from downtown at kilometer 3 of General Cañas Highway, on the way to the airport. With the swimming pool and views of the Central Valley, this is a good value.

María Alexandra (no children under 13; kitchen, air conditioning, cable TV, pool, bar; $80-$100; 228-1507, fax: 289-5192; www.accommodations. co.cr) is quiet and very clean, featuring washing machines, a sauna, and an excellent restaurant. It is located in Escazú, west of San José, 100 meters north of Tega.

Secure and centrally located downtown, **Hotel Santo Tomás** (private bath, hot water, ceiling fans, some bathtubs, cable TV, phone, bar, nonsmoking; $70-$100; Avenida 7, Calles 3/5; 255-0448, fax: 222-3950; www.hotelst. co.cr, e-mail: hotelst@racsa.co.cr) is in a beautifully remodeled old home with many nice touches. The rooms are back off the street, a real boon in noisy downtown San José. Breakfast, half an hour of internet access, and tour planning are included in the rates. Airport pick-up on request.

Near the Sabana is the tropical oasis **El Sesteo** (ceiling fans, cable TV, pool, laundromat, conference room; without kitchen, $50-$60; with kitchen, $60-$90; rates include breakfast; 200 meters south of La Sabana McDonald's; 296-1805, fax: 296-1865; www.sesteo.com, e-mail: sesteo@racsa.co.cr). The rooms and apartments (comfortable but plain) surround the unheated pool and the lush garden. It's a great place to stay with kids, and there is a nice view of the hills from the buffet-breakfast area. Recommended.

Tennis Club (air conditioning, pool, restaurants, bar; $50-$70; 232-1266, fax: 232-3867) comes complete with tennis courts, a gym, a sauna, three pools, a bowling alley, playgrounds, and two restaurants. Located on the south side of La Sabana. A good value.

Torremolinos (pool, restaurant, ceiling fans, air conditioning; $80-$100; Calle 40, Avenida 5 bis; 222-5266, 222-9129, fax: 255-3167; www.central america.com/cr/hotel/torrem.htm, e-mail: torremolinos@centralamerica.com) is a large, quiet hotel near Paseo Colón and La Sabana.

BED AND BREAKFASTS

Bed and breakfasts are a growing trend in Costa Rica and can be found both in the city and the country. Even though there are many other hotels that include breakfast in their rates, the distinguishing characteristic of bed and breakfasts is that they are small and have a homelike atmosphere, usually with the owner in residence. All of the establishments listed below pride themselves on the personalized service they give to their guests in tour planning, car rentals, etc. Most will provide lunch and dinner on request and offer kitchen privileges. They range from basic to luxurious, with a wide variety of amenities, listed in each description. The **Established Bed-and-Breakfast Group** has a helpful "one call does it all" vacation-planning and reservation service to connect guests with the bed and breakfasts that are right for them throughout Costa Rica (contact Pat Bliss, 228-8726; www. catch22.com/~vudu/bandb, e-mail: crnow@amnet.co.cr). To call Costa Rica, dial 011-506, then the number.

Ara Macao (private bath, heated water, table fans, cable TV; $40-$50; 233-2742, fax: 257-6228; www.hotels.co.cr, e-mail: aramacao@hotels.co.cr) is very clean, with pleasant, sunny upstairs rooms, and a nice eating area. Near the National Museum in Barrio California, 50 meters south of the Pizza Hut.

Casa Baker Del Río (shared bath, hot water; $50-$60; with kitchen, $70-$80; phone/fax: 289-6819; e-mail: baker.del@racsa.co.cr) has spacious, comfortable rooms high in the hills of San Antonio de Escazú, with a magnificent view of the Central Valley, including the Poás, Barva, and Irazú volcanoes. The North American owners are knowledgeable about Costa Rica, and the food is delicious. A private suite with kitchen is also available. It's best to have a car if you're staying here, but rates include a taxi ride up the hill.

Casa de las Tías (no children under 12; private bath, hot water, ceiling fans, all rooms nonsmoking; $50-$80; 289-5517, fax: 289-7353; www.hotels. co.cr/casatias, e-mail: casatias@costarica.net), an ample wood-paneled house, sits at the end of a quiet street in Escazú. Each room is decorated with mementos of the owners' sojourns in Latin America as part of the foreign service. Airport pickup ($15) is available.

The comfortable, homey **Casa Rosa Inn** (no children under 13; private bath, hot water; $60-$80; in front of the main entrance of the Club La Guaria en Moravia, 150 meters south; phone/fax: 235-9743; www.costaricabureau. com/rosainn, e-mail: rainforest@costaricabureau.com) is located in an upscale section of Moravia. Some rooms have small private balconies. The hosts are an attentive English-speaking couple, the husband Cuban American and the wife Tica.

Colours (shared or private bath, hot water, ceiling fans, CD players, some cable TV, jacuzzi, pool, restaurant, bar; $100-$130, including breakfast and welcome cocktail; 150 meters west of Farmacia Rohrmoser; 296-1880, 232-3504, fax: 296-1597, in the U.S.: 800-277-4825, 305-532-9341, fax: 305-534-0362; colours.net, e-mail: colours@travelbase.com) is a gay guest house in Rohrmoser. They welcome lesbian travelers as well as men. Special trips and social events are planned throughout the year that cater to visitors and the Tico community. Owned by a Florida travel agency, they can plan your whole vacation, booking gay-friendly hotels and travel agents for side trips. Discounts for longer stays and cash payment.

Built on the lower slopes of an orchard, **Las Golondrinas** (private bath, heated water, kitchen; $40-$50; phone/fax: 228-6448) is a small private cabin located about two kilometers above the church in San Antonio de Escazú (call for directions). The friendly owners take advantage of their farm's fruits in season, and serve all sorts of jams and juices. It's best to have a car when staying here.

Maripaz (shared or private bath, hot water, table fans on request, all rooms nonsmoking; $30-$40; 300 meters south and 100 to the east of the *antiguo higuerón*; phone/fax: 253-8456; e-mail: giovolio@racsa.co.cr) is located in a friendly Costa Rican home in San Pedro. Convenient for those visiting the University of Costa Rica or the area's many nongovernmental organizations.

Located west of Parque Nacional, near museums and galleries, **Pensión de la Cuesta** (shared bath, heated water, some table fans, shared kitchen, e-mail service, cable TV in living room; $30-$40; Avenida 1, Calles 11/15; phone/fax: 255-2896, 256-7946; www.sunandfuntours.com, e-mail: lacuesta @sunandfuntours.com) has eight rooms (some rather dark) in an interesting old building—the rooms are filled with paintings and creative touches. The fun will be in hanging around with other guests in the light-filled living/ dining room.

Posada del Bosque (private bath, hot water, shared kitchen, nonsmoking; $60-$70; call for directions; 228-1164, fax: 228-2006; www.amerisol.com/ costarica, e-mail: posada@amerisol.com) is a quiet home-away-from-home on ample grounds in Escazú. This posada is run by Costa Rican owners who are world travelers and give true Tico hospitality. Breakfast is served in a gazebo; there is a do-it-yourself barbecue in the garden. Guests have access to the pool and tennis courts at nearby Bello Horizonte Country Club. Airport pickup ($15) and transportation to San José ($4) are available.

Posada El Quijote (private bath, hot water, ceiling fans, phone, cable TV; $60-$100; call for directions; 289-8401, fax: 289-8729; www.quijote. co.cr, e-mail: quijote@quijote.co.cr) is a family home with great views of the Central Valley and a comfortable sitting room with a fireplace. The fruit tree–filled yard has sitting areas with tables and benches. In Bello Horizonte de Escazú.

Raya Vida (shared or private bath, hot water, all rooms nonsmoking; $90-$100; Calle 15, Avenidas 11/13; 223-4168, fax: 223-4157; e-mail: raya vida@costarica.net) is in a very elegant and delightfully quirky house located at the end of a quiet street in Barrio Otoya. There are many unusual and artistic touches such as a small patio with fountain, a mirrored reading room, and free airport shuttle. Every seventh night is free. The owner runs a free bed-and-breakfast travel planning service throughout Costa Rica.

Residencia Saint-Pierre (private bath, heated water; $30-$40; 100 meters north and 50 meters east of the Banco Popular in San Pedro; 283-1526, fax: 283-0104; www.acepesa/jadetour/spierre, e-mail: lmartin@racsa.co.cr) is a modern home on a quiet dead-end street in San Pedro, managed by a cosmopolitan Francophone Tico host. It's close to the university and a major bus line.

Sabana (private bath, heated water, fans, cable TV; $50-$60; 100 meters north, 25 west and 175 north of the Chicote Restaurant; 296-3751, phone/fax: 232-2876; www.online.co.cr/sabana, e-mail: sabanabb@racsa.co.cr) accepts kids and provides a babysitting service. Rooms are small and crowded; all linens are anti-allergenic. The Tico family that runs this place will shower you with attention. Free airport pick-up.

The attractive, wood-paneled, chalet-style **Villa Escazú** (no children under 12, shared or private bath, hot water; $40-$60; with kitchenette, $200/week; phone/fax: 289-7971; www.hotels.co.cr/vescazu, e-mail: villaescazu@yellowweb.co.cr) offers lots of peace and quiet on its beautiful grounds. The North American hostess prepares gourmet breakfasts. In Escazú, west of San José (call for directions). Recommended.

MID-RANGE HOTELS

Hotel rates have gone down quite a bit in San José. You can get very pleasant lodgings for about half of what you would pay at home. A double room in these hotels ranges from $20 to $60, and they offer a wide variety of amenities. Some rooms are downtown; ask for a room off the street if you like quiet. When we say "TV" in this category, we mean just local-channel TV; cable TV is indicated when available. Many places in the B&B section have similar rates, as do homestays (see below). Be sure to look there too. All rates include taxes. Don't forget to ask for off-season discounts.

A good website to look at is www.hotels.co.cr. It takes you directly to the websites of many of the best hotels in this category. If you want to call directly, dial 011 and Costa Rica's area code, 506.

Aranjuez (solar hot water, shared refrigerator; shared bath, $20-$30; private bath, cable TV; $30-$40; children under 8 free; Calle 19, Avenidas 11/13; 256-1825, fax: 223-3528, in the U.S: 877-898-8663; www.hotelaranjuez.com, e-mail: aranjuez@racsa.co.cr) comprises several old-fashioned houses linked together in the safe neighborhood of Barrio Aranjuez. There are many sitting areas scattered throughout the hotel where people can gather and talk, and quiet gardens in the back. The Aranjuez is popular because of its low rates and the many services it offers—like free local phone calls, free e-mail, and discounts on tours—so make reservations well in advance. A generous buffet breakfast is included in the rate. This bargain is highly recommended.

Ave del Paraíso (heated water, cable TV; $50-$60, including breakfast; 350 meters north of the Fuente de la Hispanidad, San Pedro; phone/fax: 224-8515, 253-5138, fax: 283-6017; www.accommodations.co.cr, e-mail: apar aiso@racsa.co.cr), owned by a Polish-Tico family, is homey and quiet. A five-minute walk from San Pedro's many inexpensive restaurants and bars, this hotel borders the western side of the Universidad de Costa Rica's campus.

Bellavista (private bath, hot water, ceiling fans, restaurant, bar; $20-$30, including breakfast; Avenida Central, Calles 19/21; 223-0095, fax: 222-5731; e-mail: bellavista@hotels.co.cr) has chintzy charm but not a lot of fresh air. Most windows open onto a corridor. Fanciful *afro-caribeño* murals decorate the walls, and the baths are very clean. Near the National Museum.

The 70-room **Best Western San José** (private bath, hot water, air conditioning, most with bathtubs, phone, TV, pool, cafeteria, bar; $50-$60; Avenida 7, Calles 6/8; 255-4766, fax: 255-4613; e-mail: garden@racsa.co.cr) includes a full breakfast, free happy hour, free local calls, and free return to the airport. The north-facing rooms have a view of Irazú and Poás volcanoes. The hotel is centrally located but in a questionable neighborhood; hourly shuttle buses will whisk you away. A good value.

Cacts (shared or private baths, hot or heated water, ceiling fans, hairdryer on request, phone, some cable TV, cafeteria, all rooms nonsmoking; $40-$60, including breakfast; Avenida 3 bis, No. 2845, Calles 28/30; 221-2928, 221-6546, fax: 221-8616; www.tourism.co.cr, e-mail: hcacts@racsa.co.cr) is quiet, very friendly, and helpful with travel arrangements. Their recent addition has a sun terrace, and they are constructing a pool. Located in a neighborhood west of the Coca Cola.

Located across from the University of Costa Rica campus in San Pedro, **D'Galah** ($40-$50; $50-$60 with kitchen; rates include breakfast; in front of the Facultad de Farmacia; phone/fax: 280-8092, 253-7539, fax: 225-4852; www.ilisa.com/hotels, e-mail: dgalah@racsa.co.cr) is a quiet place offering a pool and sauna, a jacuzzi, a mudbath, and massage.

The **Diplomat** (private bath, hot water, phone, restaurant, bar; $30-$40; Calle 6, Avenidas Central/2; 221-8744, 221-8133, fax: 233-7474; www.accom

modations.co.cr) is a clean, well-run, centrally located hotel with a good restaurant. It's a favorite with foreigners. A good value.

Doral (private bath, hot water, ceiling fans, phone, TV, cafeteria; $30-$40, including breakfast; Avenida 4, Calle 8; 233-9410, fax: 233-4827; www.ho tels.co.cr/doral, e-mail: hdoral@racsa.co.cr) offers clean, bright, sunny rooms with original art. It's on a busy street, but the rooms are quiet. A good value.

Edelweiss (ceiling fans, some bathtubs, cable TV; $50-$60; Avenida 9, Calle 15; 221-9702, fax: 222-1241; www.edelweisshotel.com, e-mail: edel weiss@racsa.co.cr), a Swiss-owned hotel, is comfortable and elegant. Wallpaper and handmade furniture enhance the interior.

Europa Centro (air conditioning, some bathtubs, indoor pool, restaurant, bar; $50-$60; Calle Central, Avenidas 3/5; 222-1222, fax: 221-3976; www.zurqui.co.cr/crinfocus/europa, e-mail: europa@racsa.co.cr) is a distinctive European-style hotel featuring a light and airy atmosphere. Ask for an inside room.

Gran Hotel Centroamericano (private bath, hot water; $20-$30; Avenida 2, Calles 6/8; 221-3362, fax: 221-3714) has good wheelchair access and an inexpensive cafeteria open 6:30 a.m. to 2:30 p.m.

The **Hemingway Inn** (private bath, hot water, ceiling fans, cable TV, jacuzzi; $50-$60, including breakfast; kids over 3 $10; Avenida 9, Calle 9; phone/fax: 221-1804, 227-8630; www.hotels.co.cr/hemingway.html, e-mail: ernest@racsa.co.cr) comprises two connected old homes located on a busy street in Barrio Amón. Each room here is named for a North American writer; if you are a poet, request Allen Ginsberg's airy third-floor garret.

Kalexma (shared bath, heated water, table or ceiling fans, shared kitchen; $20-$30; with private bath, $30-$40; including breakfast; 50 meters west, 25 meters south of the Juan Pablo II overpass in La Uruca; phone/fax: 232-0115; www.kalexma.com, e-mail: info@kalexma.com) is a modest converted house in a residential section, a block off the highway to the airport. It is convenient for shopping and a 15-minute bus ride to downtown. The helpful owners will also teach you Spanish. Recommended.

Kekoldi (private bath, hot water, phones; $50-$60, including continental breakfast; Avenida 9, Calle 3 bis; 223-3244, fax: 257-5476; www.kekoldi. com, e-mail: kekoldi@racsa.co.cr), a gay-friendly restored corner house in Barrio Amón, is painted with refreshing pastels, and has beautiful murals throughout. A bit overpriced, except in off-season.

Casa Morazán (private bath, hot water, air conditioning; $50-$60, including breakfast; Calle 7, Avenidas 7/9; 257-4187, fax: 257-4175; e-mail: anakeith@racsa.co.cr) is the converted home of Minor Keith, of Atlantic

Railroad fame. Rooms are spacious and stylish. The double-paned windows keep out most of the street noise.

Apartotel La Perla (one or two-bedroom apartments, heated water, kitchen; $40-$50; $250-$290 weekly; 232-6153, fax: 220-4195; www.asuaire/ perla, e-mail: mcalvo@racsa.co.cr) has a friendly staff and is close to shopping. Located in La Uruca, 15 minutes by bus from downtown. A good value. Free airport pickup.

Pico Blanco (private bath, hot water, some refrigerators, pool, bar; $50-$60; suites, $60-$70; 228-1908, 289-6197, fax: 289-5189, in the U.S.: 916-862-1170, fax: 916-862-1187; www.helios.net/picoblanco, e-mail: pblanco@ costarica.net) is a mountain hotel with a great view, friendly atmosphere, clean, charming rooms, and a restaurant. In San Antonio de Escazú, eight kilometers west of San José. Recommended.

The **Pine Tree Inn** (private bath, hot water, ceiling fans, cable TV, phones, pool; $40-$50, including breakfast; 289-7405, fax: 228-2180, in the U.S.: 305-865-0614) has a very helpful staff and is within walking distance of many of Escazú's best restaurants. It is located in the exclusive Barrio Trejos Montealegre in Escazú, 150 meters northwest of Tega.

The small, colonial, very clean **Rey Amón** (private bath, heated water, cable TV, phones, half an hour free internet access; $30-$40, including breakfast; Avenida 7, Calle 9; 233-3819, phone/fax: 233-1769; www.yeess. com, e-mail: reyamon@yeess.com) is conveniently located. Streetside rooms have traffic noise, but others are quiet. It would be hard to find a better value in downtown San José.

Apartotel La Sabana (air conditioning, cable TV, phone, pool, kitchen; $50-$80, including breakfast; 220-2422, 296-0876, fax: 231-7386; crica.com/ hotels, e-mail: lasabana@racsa.co.cr) is a sunny complex on a quiet street near La Sabana, with clean, carpeted rooms, a laundromat, and a sauna.

The small, two-story **Tapezco Inn** (private bath, hot water, table fans, cable TV, phone; $50-$60, including breakfast; just south of the Escazú church; 228-1084, fax: 289-7026; www.tapezco-inn.co.cr, e-mail: camtapez@ racsa.co.cr) is in downtown Escazú. A tiny pool and sauna are situated in the upstairs dining room.

Apartotel Los Yoses (ceiling fans or air conditioning, cable TV, pool; $50-$100, children under 12 free; 225-0033, fax: 225-5595; www.apartotel. com, e-mail: losyoses@apartotel.com) is very clean. Their larger apartments can accommodate big families or groups, and they have a babysitting service. In Los Yoses, on the main thoroughfare 100 meters of the Fuente de la Hispanidad. A good value.

INEXPENSIVE HOTELS

These run $7-$20, double occupancy. All are downtown in the midst of traffic noise and gas fumes. We wouldn't want to be in most of these neighborhoods at night. Most of these rooms are basic but clean. If you want to enjoy San José's museums and nightlife, it might be more fun to splurge on something in the mid-range section or stay at one of the hostels or homestays (see below). Most of these hotels are close to the Coca Cola and the bus stops for Guanacaste, Manuel Antonio, Monteverde, and the Zona Sur, but a taxi within San José only costs $1-$2, so you don't have stay in this area in order to get to the buses on time. Don't forget that there are cheap places to stay in Alajuela and Heredia in case the idea of San José doesn't appeal to you, and most buses stop in Alajuela. To call the places below directly, dial 011-506 and the number.

Astoria (hot water; shared or private bath; $7-$12; weekly discounts; Avenida 7, Calles 7/9; 221-2174) is located in a semi-safe area of downtown, with small dark rooms.

Located one block from the Mercado Central, **Bienvenido** (private bath, heated water, shared refrigerator, restaurant; $12-$20; children under 12 free; Calle 10, Avenidas 1/3; phone/fax: 233-2161, 221-1872) is large, clean, friendly, and well-run. Most rooms are off the street, yet are light and fairly well ventilated. They change traveler's checks. Recommended.

The family-run **Boruca** (shared bath, heated water; under $7; Calle 14, Avenidas 1/3; 223-0016) is located near buses. The small, cubicle-like rooms don't have windows. It is secure, even though the neighborhood is not good. Very cheap—recommended for budget travelers.

If you plan to stay in San José for a week or more, **Casa Agua Buena** (no children under 14; shared bath, kitchen, washing machine, cable TV, phone; $90/week, $150-$280; apartment, $450/month; phone/fax: 280-9905, 390-5213; www.homestead.com/casaaguabuena, e-mail: rastern@sol.racsa.co.cr) is an inexpensive option. Guests share three houses in the pleasant Lourdes section of San Pedro and do their own cooking and cleaning. Although we were not able to visit before press time, this sounds like a very good deal.

Close to bus stops, **Cocorí** (private bath, hot water; $12-$20; Calle 16, Avenida 3; 233-0081, fax: 255-1058) has clean, light rooms but is not in a good neighborhood. Make sure you get an inside room. A good value.

Clean and well run, with a friendly staff, **Musoc** (shared or private bath, heated water, shared refrigerator; $12-$30; Calle 16, Avenidas 1/3; 222-9437, fax: 232-4373; www.westnet.com/costarica) is located next to the Coca Cola bus station.

HOSTELS

Although neither very private nor luxurious, hostels offer visitors a congenial atmosphere, with ample opportunities for meeting student and budget travelers. The managements of these hostels go out of their way to make guests feel welcome and comfortable. Both dormitory-style rooms and private rooms are available.

Casa Leo (heated water, shared kitchen; in dormitory-style rooms with shared bath, $8/person; in private rooms, $10-$12/person, some with private bath; Avenida 6, Calle 13; 222-9725) is in a clean converted home with good mattresses, run by a friendly German woman who speaks French, Spanish, German, and English. There is no checkout time. Casa Leo's sign is tiny; look for it across from Clinica Echandi, next to Acupuntura Kaminsky.

Casa Ridgway (heated water; no smoking; shared bath; $10/person; Avenida 6 bis, Calle 15; phone/fax: 233-6168; e-mail: camigos@racsa.co.cr) is a small *pensión* that helps to support the Quaker Peace Center next door. It has a convivial atmosphere, kitchen and laundry privileges, and dormitory-style bunks in some rooms. Make reservations in advance—it is often full.

La Granja (heated water, shared or private bath, $12-$20/person; phone/fax: 225-1073, 253-7113), run by a friendly family, will rent their washing machine and kitchen to guests. In San Pedro, 50 meters south of the *antiguo higuerón*.

Headquarters of the Costa Rica Youth Hostel Network, **Toruma** (hot water, all rooms nonsmoking; $12/person, including continental breakfast; discount with IYHF card; Avenida Central, Calles 29/31/33; phone/fax: 224-4085; www.hostelling.co.cr) is in an attractive remodeled mansion close to downtown. Men stay on one side, women on the other. All dorm-style rooms share baths. There are only two private rooms ($20-$30).

HOMESTAYS

This is a good way to get to know the local people and to practice your Spanish. To find a compatible family, call the language schools, look for signs at the University of Costa Rica, or use one of the contacts below. Be prepared for a lot of hospitality. If noise bothers you, check first to see if your family leaves the TV or radio on all the time. Amenities run the gamut and depend on the household you choose.

Bell's Home Hospitality (shared bath, $30 single, $45 double; private bath, $35 single, $50 double; 225-4752, fax: 224-5884; www.HomeStay.TheBells.org, e-mail: homestay@racsa.co.cr) matches you with a compatible Costa Rican family. Breakfast is included in the rates; dinner is $7 extra. Airport pickup is available ($15 for one person, $5 per extra person). Owners Vernon and Marcela Bell are excellent hosts and very generous with helpful information. Highly recommended.

Sra. Soledad Zamora (phone/fax in English: 280-7630; in Spanish: 224-7937) and her sister **Virginia** (225-7344) specialize in connecting longer-term renters with inexpensive rooms (Spanish speaking only).

MISCELLANEOUS INFORMATION

SOUVENIRS

Moderately priced souvenirs can be found at the government crafts cooperative, **Mercado Nacional de Artesanía** (Calle 11, Avenida 2 bis, behind the Soledad Church), as well as in the **Mercado Central** (Avenidas Central/1, Calles 6/8), **La Casona** (Calle Central, Avenidas Central/1), and **Souvenir** (Avenida 1, Calle 11). One of the most charming, complete, and inexpensive souvenir shops is in the converted home of one of Costa Rica's ex-presidents, now the **Hotel Don Carlos** (Calle 9, Avenida 9). You can see indigenous crafts at **Galería Namu** (Avenida 7, Calles 5/7).

If you have a little more money to spend, visit **Atmósfera** (Calle 5, Avenida 1), **Magia** (Calle 5, Avenidas 1/3), **Suraska** (Calle 5, Avenida 3), or **La Galería** (Calle 1, Avenidas Central/1), where more artistic items are sold, including the innovative woodwork of two North Americans, **Barry Biesanz** and **Jay Morrison**. Biesanz specializes in exquisitely crafted bowls and boxes, as well as furniture, which can be seen at his Escazú workshop (228-1811). Morrison's creative hardwood furniture is displayed at Magia and also at his showroom, **Tierra Extraña** (282-6697), in Piedades de Santa Ana. Faced with the dilemma of using precious hardwoods in danger of extinction for their work, both Biesanz and Morrison have reforested farms with the varieties they use, and Barry sells hardwood saplings at his showroom.

The beautiful handicrafts of Guatemala and El Salvador can be found on the second floor of **La Casona** (Calle Central, Avenidas Central/1) and at **Sol Maya** (on Paseo Colón across from Hospital San Juan de Dios).

If you don't want to spend money, don't even think of visiting **Angie Theologos' gallery** (225-6565) of irresistible, one-of-a-kind jackets and vests. The individually designed, lined jackets are crafted from Guatemalan textiles. Each one is a work of art. By appointment only. The gallery is in La Granja de San Pedro, east of San José.

BOOKS, NEWSPAPERS, AND MAGAZINES

English-language newspapers and magazines, including *The New York Times,* *Wall Street Journal,* *Miami Herald, Time,* and *Newsweek,* are sold throughout the metropolitan area. **Downtown,** there's the Candy Shop (Plaza de la Cultura), Hotel Aurola Holiday Inn (Parque Morazán), Automercado (Calle 3, Avenidas 3/5), Librería Francesa (Calle 3, Avenidas 1/Central), Seventh Street Books (Calle 7, Avenidas 1/Central), and Librería Lehmann (Avenida Central, Calles 1/3). **East of town** check out Revistas y Más (west of Muñoz & Nanne in San Pedro) and Staufer's (Plaza del Sol in Curridabat). On the **west side** there's Periódicos Americanos (across from the Hotel Corobicí in Yaohan's shopping center). **Agencia de Publicaciones de Costa Rica** (283-5551, 283-5269) offers home or office delivery of the above newspapers, as well as others from around the world.

The **Mark Twain Library** (open Monday through Friday, 9 a.m. to 7 p.m.; Saturday, 9 a.m. to noon; 225-9433) of the Centro Cultural Costarricense-Norteamericano in Barrio Dent has the latest newspapers and a special room for watching CNN. They also have computers for internet access. Francophiles can visit the **Alianza Francesa** (open weekdays, 8:45 a.m. to 11:45 a.m., 3 p.m. to 7 p.m.; 222-2283) on the corner of Calle 5 and Avenida 7, behind the Hotel Aurola Holiday Inn in San José.

The best source of local news in English, *The Tico Times* (258-1558, fax: 233-6378; www.ticotimes.co.cr, e-mail: times@racsa.co.cr; $1) is published Friday and available at the above places and at many hotels. Winner of the Interamerican Press Association award for distinguished service to the community, as well as other prestigious awards, *The Tico Times* offers a well-researched synthesis of weekly events in Costa Rica and Central America. It is without comparison in its coverage of local environmental and political issues and gives an excellent rundown of cultural activities.

With a convenient central location, **Seventh Street Books** (Calle 7, Avenidas 1/Central; 256-8251), run by two U.S. expatriates, boasts many shelves of contemporary English-language fiction and an excellent selection of books on tropical ecology and travel. They also buy and sell used books.

Mora Books (open 11 a.m. to 6:30 p.m., in the Omni Building, Avenida 1, Calle 3/5; 255-4136) offers a wide selection of used books, CDs, DVDs, comics, and magazines. They will buy or trade English and German books.

The **Librería Internacional** (300 meters west of Taco Bell in Barrio Dent; 253-9553) is a large trilingual (Spanish, German, English) bookstore with special selections of travel books, esoterica, art, and children's books, as well as a good fiction collection. It has branches in Rohrmoser (100 meters west and 25 south of El Fogoncito Restaurant), and in the Multiplaza in Escazú (288-1138).

For books in Spanish, **Macondo** (on the outside perimeter of the UCR campus, across from the main *Biblioteca*), in San Pedro, has an exhaustive collection of fiction and academic works. Many other small bookstores in that neighborhood sell interesting books as well. The grand *librerías* **Lehmann** (Avenida Central, Calles 1/3) and **Universal** (Avenida Central, Calles Central/1) carry translations from the English of U.S. bestsellers.

MEETING PLACES

The **Friends' Peace Center** (open Monday through Friday, 10 a.m. to noon, 1:30 p.m. to 6 p.m.; Calle 15, Avenida 6 bis; phone/fax: 233-6168; e-mail: camigos@racsa.co.cr) in San José is a training center for conflict resolution, and addresses issues involving human rights, community development, and ecology. It provides meeting space, activity coordination, a library, and educational programs, and hosts a weekly Quaker meeting (see "Religious Services" below). The staff of the center is made up of both Central and North Americans, most of them volunteers.

A variety of clubs meet regularly in San José and the Central Valley, including the Women's Club, Gringo Investment Club, Holistic Health Club, Bridge Club, Newcomer's Club, Republicans Abroad, Democrats Abroad, American Legion, Disabled American Veterans, Amnesty International, International Gay and Lesbian Association, La Leche League, Lions, Rotary, Women's Aglow Fellowship, Christian Women's Club, Canada Club, Coffee Pickin' Square Dancers, the Canoeing/Kayaking Club, AA, Al-Anon, OA, CODA, Alzheimer's Association, Birding Club, Cancer Support Group, the English-Spanish Conversation Club, PC and Mac Clubs, Singles Club, Songwriters Club, and the Women's International League for Peace and Freedom. Current hours and numbers are often listed in *The Tico Times*.

RELIGIOUS SERVICES

BAHA'I   The information center is in La Uruca (south side of the Catholic church; open Monday through Friday, 8 a.m. to 4 p.m.; 231-0647.

BHAKTI YOGA   The Sri Radha Raman Gaudiya Math Center for Meditation and Bhakti Yoga is at 1539 Calle 13, 100 meters north of Hospital Calderón Guardia (222-6386).

BAPTIST   English Sunday School services are Sunday at 9 a.m., worship at 10 a.m. at radio station El Farol del Caribe, 500 meters from the Parque de la Paz rotunda in San Francisco de Dos Ríos (237-7569; e-mail: tomwhill@racsa.co.cr). The Central Valley Baptist church is in Residencial Los Arcos, 500 meters east of the entrance to the Hotel Cariari, then straight 200 meters to the central kiosk (293-1060; e-mail: maxloya@racsa.co.cr). The San Pedro Christian fellowship meets at the Centro Bautista, two blocks east and one and a half blocks north of the San Pedro Church (267-6038).

CATHOLIC Saint Mary's Chapel (254-5807), adjacent to the Herradura Hotel, has an English mass Sunday at 4 p.m. The San Rafael de Escazú Church (232-6847) holds an English mass Saturday at 5 p.m.

EPISCOPAL English services are Sunday at 8:30 a.m. at the Church of the Good Shepherd (Avenida 4, Calles 3/5; 222-1560). Center hours are Monday through Friday, 8 a.m. to noon and 2 p.m. to 4 p.m.

ESCAZÚ CHRISTIAN FELLOWSHIP Church and Sunday school are Sunday, 5:30 p.m., in the annex to the Country Day School (282-0041).

HARE KRISHNA Headquarters are at the Finca Nueva Goloka Vrindavana on the Cartago–Paraíso Road. Sunday there is a banquet, and from 4 p.m. to 7 p.m. there are presentations (551-6752). They also have a center below the Theosophical Society (Avenida 1, Calles 11/15 (256-7392).

JEWISH Bilingual services are held Friday at 8 p.m. at Congregation B'Nei Israel (257-1785, 231-5243), 700 meters west of the Balcón Verde on the old road to Escazú. The congregation also has Hebrew school, preschool, teen studies, and social programs. Congregation Beit Menachem (296-6565) meets in Rohrmoser

MORMON Sacrament meetings are on Sunday at 9 a.m. with translators available. The temple is in Barrio Los Yoses (Avenida 8, Calles 33/35; 225-0208, 234-1940). The temple in Escazú, 400 meters west of the Banco Nacional, is also attended by many English speakers (Sunday at 9 a.m.).

QUAKER Bilingual worship services are Sunday at 11 a.m. at the Friends Peace Center (Avenida 6 bis, Calle 15; 233-6168).

THEOSOPHICAL SOCIETY There are nightly lodges (Avenida 1, Calles 11/15; 221-7246).

UNION CHURCH The church offers free bus service, nursery and children's church, and neighborhood Bible-study groups. English-language Sunday school is at 9 a.m., fellowship is at 10 a.m., and services are held at 10:30 a.m. It is located in Moravia, 100 meters east, 400 meters north, and 100 meters west of Lincon High School (235-6709).

UNITY   English-language services are at 10:30 a.m., 600 meters north of McDonald's (228-6051, 228-5476; wwprayer@racsa.co.cr) in Escazú. They also hold courses and lectures on a wide range of topics from yoga and meditation to education to bodywork and healing.

THE VINEYARD CHRISTIAN FELLOWSHIP   Sunday celebration at 5:30 p.m., 400 meters north of Los Antojitos Restaurant (289-6782) in Rohrmoser. Study groups convene in Rohrmoser, Cariari and La Sabana throughout the week.

SUPERMARKETS

Name-brand products from the U.S. are flooding Costa Rican markets. Because they are imported, they are very expensive. Right next to them on the shelf will be a comparable locally made product for half the price.

The **Más x Menos** supermarkets are open daily 8 a.m. to 8 p.m. Ask at your hotel for the nearest one. The **Automercado**, less crowded, cleaner, and more expensive than the Más x Menos, is also open all day. **Yaohan's** is a large Japanese-owned supermarket across from the Hotel Corobicí, Sabana East. It has a good produce section. On the east side, **Muñoz y Nanne** in San Pedro is also famous for its produce.

MUSEUMS

Most of the downtown museums are mentioned in our walking tour at the beginning of this chapter or in the Creative Arts section. A living museum is the **Pueblo Antiguo** (231-2001, phone/fax: 296-2212), a theme park of Costa Rican history and cultural traditions at the Parque Nacional de Diversiones in La Uruca, two kilometers west of the Hospital México. The park re-creates the city at the turn of the 20th century, as well as a rural town and a coastal village. Professional actors take you into the past in the **Vivencias Costarricenses** tour weekends from 10 a.m. in which they trace the roots of Costa Rican traditions and democracy in an entertaining one-hour presentation. Friday and Saturday nights from 6:30 to 9 p.m. you can enjoy a typical dinner and folkloric show, **Noches Costarricenses**, with a historical view of Costa Rican dance and music. Wheelchairs and baby strollers are available at the entrance. Kids will enjoy the amusement park on the same property. Proceeds from Pueblo Antiguo fund the local children's hospital.

ORCHIDS, BUTTERFLIES, BUGS, AND SNAKES

Orchid lovers should plan to visit during March when the **National Orchid Show** is held at Republic Tobacco in Zapote (223-6517, 224-4278). Butterfly enthusiasts will enjoy the **Insect Museum** run by the University of Costa Rica's Facultad de Agronomía (open Monday through Friday, 1 p.m. to 4:45 p.m.; 207-5318, 207-5647; $1.50). It is located on the University of Costa Rica campus in San Pedro, in the basement of the Artes Musicales building.

Spyrogyra (open daily, 8 a.m. to 4 p.m.; $6, $3 for children; 222-2937) is a butterfly garden just a ten-minute walk from downtown. Spyrogyra shares a wooded valley with the Bolivar Zoo, and our tour was punctuated with the roars of the African lion. You can easily forget you're in smoggy San José while visiting this verdant little corner. Visitors can spend as much time as they like browsing after the tour. Spyrogyra is located 100 meters south of El Pueblo. To walk there from downtown, follow Calle 3 north to Periódico La República, then turn right and walk about three blocks until you see Centro Comercial El Pueblo on your left. Turn right again and you'll see Spyrogyra at the end of the block. Take the Calle Blancos bus from Avenida 5, Calle 3, or the Periférica bus going east from Centro Colón on Paseo Colón.

If you want to be able to recognize a poisonous snake should you run across one in the wild, visit the **Serpentarium** (open Monday through Friday, 9 a.m. to 6 p.m.; weekends, 10 a.m. to 5 p.m.; Avenida 1, Calles 9/11; 225-4210; $3 for adults, $1 for children 6 to 13) in San José. Live native poisonous and nonpoisonous frogs, snakes, and reptiles are on exhibit here, along with some foreign snakes, such as the black cobra and a 19-foot python. At first we thought that the reptiles were very realistic plastic replicas because they move so little, but after a while we saw that their positions had changed slightly, so they must be alive. They also have some piranhas, which are fed Monday, Wednesday, and Friday at 5 p.m.

LA SABANA

San José has converted its outgrown international airport into a metropolitan park with sports facilities. The National Gymnasium was built on the southeast corner of the former airfield, the National Stadium on the northwest corner. A small lake, which had been filled in, is now restored, and the Air Terminal Building has become the National Art Museum. Residential districts have been built on three sides of La Sabana (which means "the savannah").

With jogging and walking paths; an Olympic swimming pool (open weekdays, 6 a.m. to 1:30 p.m.; 223-8730); tennis, volleyball, and basketball courts; and soccer and baseball fields, La Sabana is a favorite recreation area on weekends and a training ground for runners and joggers during lunch hours (showers are provided). There's a hill for kite flying and lots of trees for shady relaxation. People fly-cast in the lake. To get there, take the Sabana–Cementerio bus.

SEVEN

Central Valley and Surroundings

Costa Rica's Central Valley, or Meseta Central, is a large, fertile plateau surrounded by high mountains. Seventy percent of the country's population lives in this region, which centers around the towns of Alajuela, Heredia, and Cartago, as well as the city of San José. As you leave the more densely populated areas and drive toward the valley's western edge at San Ramón, or wind down through spectacular scenery to its eastern edge at Turrialba, you'll see large fields of sugarcane and corn.

Exploring the highlands leading to the volcanoes Poás, Barva, and Irazú, you will see hills full of coffee bushes, flower plantations, and dairy farms. People enjoy the varying climates of the Central Valley, ranging from year-round summer in the lower western towns of Alajuela, Santa Ana, and Villa Colón, to year-round spring at higher elevations.

A few years back, it was impossible to find lodging anywhere but in San José, but pleasant accommodations have sprung up all over the Central Valley. Since the Juan Santamaría International Airport is much closer to Alajuela and Heredia than to San José, it's possible to stay in or near these towns, avoiding the noise and pollution of the capital city.

You no longer need to go into San José to catch a bus to the provinces. Most of the direct buses to major tourist destinations like Guanacaste, Volcán Arenal, Manuel Antonio, and Monteverde pass through Alajuela on their way west, about 25 minutes after they leave San José. They do not go to the bus stations at the west side of Alajuela, but to a bus stop called *parada la Toyota*, 100 meters north of the big new Mas x Menos grocery store near the airport. The Soda Nandayure, which sells snacks at the bus stop, has a list of the buses that pass each day. There are usually plenty of seats on the morning buses from Sunday through Thursday, but it's safer to go to the San José terminals if you're leaving on a Friday or Saturday, or during holidays.

ALAJUELA AREA

Although only 20 kilometers from San José, **Alajuela** is 200 meters lower and considerably warmer. It is full of shady parks. Weekdays, old-timers sit in the Parque Central and entertain each other by thinking up nicknames for passersby. Sundays, the park fills with families, ice cream vendors, street entertainers, and kiosks selling balloons. The **Juan Santamaría Museum** (open Tuesday through Sunday, 10 a.m. to 6 p.m.), housed in the former jail one block north of Parque Central, features relics of the 1856 rout of William Walker, including his incursion order and defense plea in English.

RESTAURANTS   It's worth going downtown to eat at the following three restaurants: The **Pavo Real** (441-3274), on the road into town, is a good place for Chinese food; they have an international menu as well. Meat and seafood lovers will enjoy **El Cencerro** (441-2414), above McDonald's on the south side of Parque Central.

The **Herradura** (239-0033, fax: 239-2292), a resort lodging located on the highway to the airport, has three dining options. One of its restaurants, the **Sakura**, serves authentic Japanese cuisine, and includes a sushi bar. **Restaurant Sancho Panza** specializes in Spanish cuisine, and the Herradura also has a 24-hour **coffee shop**.

The **Marriott** (298-0000) in San Antonio de Belén, south of the airport, is the place to go for a sumptuous champagne brunch, served Sunday, 11:30 a.m. to 4 p.m., at the hotel's Villa Hermosa restaurant. There is everything from Mongolian stir-fry to pizza for the kids, plus a whole room just for desserts.

LODGING   There are a variety of accommodations in or near Alajuela. This is a convenient place to stay your first or last night in Costa Rica, much closer to the airport (about a $3-$6 cab ride to any of the hotels shown on the map) than San José, with less to worry about in terms of street safety. Downtown Alajuela can be noisy and not too clean, but the surrounding hills are nice.

The **Hotel Alajuela** (private bath, heated water, some ceiling fans; $40-$50; 441-1241, fax: 441-7912; e-mail: alajuela@racsa.co.cr) is on the south-west corner of Alajuela's Parque Central. Some newer rooms overlook the street and can be noisy. Most of the older rooms are windowless. There is a spacious lobby and a small garden.

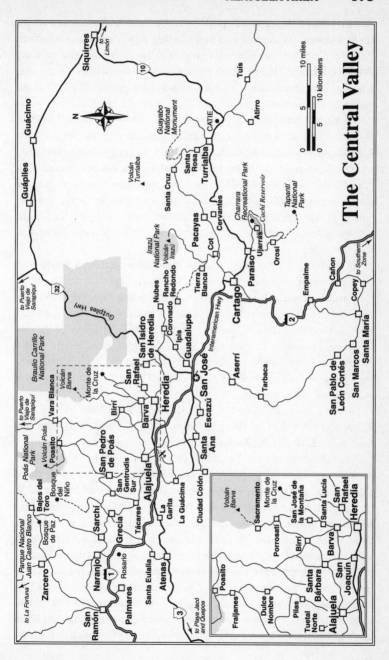

The Central Valley

A couple of blocks north, on what's called Calle Ancha, across from the Corte, **Pensión Alajuela** (heated water, ceiling fans; shared or private bath, $20-$30; phone/fax: 441-6251) is a good deal. The cramped lobby has a satellite TV, bar, and kitchen where ham-and-cheese sandwiches are the only offering, but behind that is an open-air patio for guests. The staff offers good advice on getting around.

La Guaria Inn (private bath, heated water; $30-$40, including breakfast; phone/fax: 441-9573, e-mail: laguaria@netscape.net) is clean and pleasant. It's 100 meters south of the Cathedral and 125 meters east. Recommended.

The German-owned **Hotel La Trinidad Puesta del Sol** (shared bath, heated water; $20-$30; 441-3259), located in a quiet neighborhood, is where a lot of foreign residents of Costa Rica stay when they are in the San José area. It's clean, friendly, has a cooking area for guests, and the price is right. It's in Alajuela's Barrio La Trinidad, across from Helechos Internacionales. Recommended.

In the villages surrounding Alajuela there are several more hotels, with more pastoral settings than those in downtown Alajuela.

Paraíso Tropical Inn (private bath, heated water, fans, cable TV; $50-$60, including breakfast and airport pickup; phone/fax: 441-4882) is an easy walk to Alajuela, located 200 meters from the Punto Rojo factory on the road to Tuetal. Four acres of gardens surround the clean, quiet rooms. Carlos Herrera, the helpful owner, worked in ritzy hotels in the States before opening this modest and secure B&B on his family's property. Camping available at $8/person. Recommended.

About a kilometer down the road to Tuetal is **Pura Vida** (private bath, heated water; $50-$70, including breakfast; 441-1157; www.costaricareserva tions.com), a friendly B&B with sunny rooms in the main house and bungalows with kitchens in a hillside garden. One bungalow has two bedrooms. To get there, tell the driver to go *"Mil quinientos metros de la fábrica de Punto Rojo, casa esquinera sobre el cruce de la carretera de Tuetal Norte y Sur."*

Located about a kilometer beyond Pura Vida is the Canadian-owned **Tuetal Lodge** (private bath, hot water, pool, restaurant; $30-$40; with kitchen, $40-$50; phone/fax: 442-1804; www.islandnet.com/~tuetal, e-mail: tuetal@ racsa.co.cr), whose cabins are spread through an eight-acre fruit orchard.

The American-owned **Las Orquideas Inn** (private bath, hot water, ceiling fans, some with air conditioning, pool; no children under 10; $60-$80; larger suites, $150-$160; breakfast included; 433-9346, fax: 433-9740; www. hotels.co.cr/orquideas, e-mail: orchid@racsa.co.cr) is on the road to San Pedro de Poás, about three kilometers northwest of Alajuela (ten minutes from the

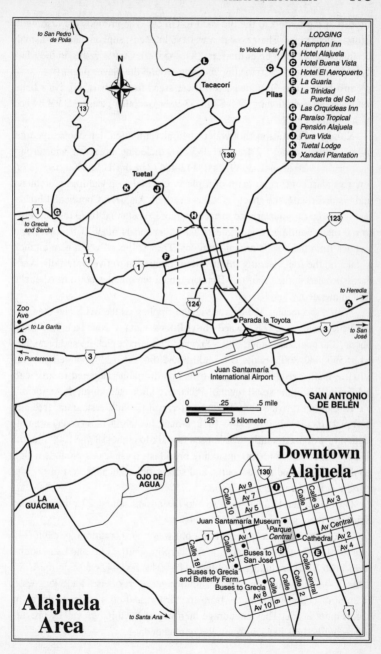

to San Pedro
de Poás

N

13

Tacacorí

L

to Volcán Poás

Pilas

C

130

LODGING
A Hampton Inn
B Hotel Alajuela
C Hotel Buena Vista
D Hotel El Aeropuerto
E La Guaria
F La Trinidad
     Puerta del Sol
G Las Orquideas Inn
H Paraíso Tropical
I Pensión Alajuela
J Pura Vida
K Tuetal Lodge
L Xandari Plantation

Tuetal

K **J**

1 **G**

to Grecia
and Sarchí

H

123

1

1 **F**

124

to Heredia

A

Zoo
Ave

to La Garita

D

3

to San
José

Parada la Toyota

to Puntarenas

3

Juan Santamaría
International Airport

**SAN ANTONIO
DE BELÉN**

0   .25   .5 mile
0   .25   .5 kilometer

**OJO DE
AGUA**

**LA
GUÁCIMA**

**Alajuela
Area**

to Santa Ana

**Downtown
Alajuela**

130

O

Av 9

Calle 3

Av 3

Calle 10

Av 7

Calle 1

Av 5

Juan Santamaría Museum

1

Av Central

Parque
Central

Cathedral

Av 2

Calle 18

Av 1

Calle 12

Buses to
San José

B

E

Av 4

Calle Central

Buses to Grecia
and Butterfly Farm

Buses to Grecia

Calle 4

Calle 2

Av 8

Calle 6

Av 10

1

airport) at the turnoff to the old road to Grecia. The grounds are lush, with tall trees and vines. Their new domes have kitchens, sunken baths and small skylights for looking up at the stars ($150-$160). Guests gather in the Marilyn Monroe bar to eat roast pig and sing around the player piano.

Just before Las Orquideas, you'll see signs for **Michele's** (private bath, hot water, air conditioning; $60-$70; 433-9864), another pleasant B&B owned by a German couple.

Xandari Plantation (hot water, natural ventilation, lap pools, open-air gym; children under 12 free; $170-$250, including breakfast and airport pick-up; 443-2020, 442-3939, fax: 442-4847, in the U.S.: 800-686-7879; www.xandari.com) is a dream of a place. Created by a California architect and his artist wife, the spacious villas overlook Alajuela. Continental breakfast is served on your private terrace. A more substantial breakfast buffet is in the main building, where guests can order meals made with spices and veggies from the hotel's organic gardens. They will pack you a picnic lunch to take on the trails leading through their plantation to five waterfalls. Xandari is located in the suburb of Tacacori, about ten minutes north of Alajuela. Recommended.

With a spectacular 360-degree view of rippling coffee fields and the Central Valley below, the U.S.-owned **Hotel Buena Vista** (private bath, hot water, phone, TV, pool, restaurant; $80-$90, including airport pick-up and breakfast; 442-8595, 442-8605, in the U.S.: 800-506-2304, ext. 1234, phone/fax: 442-8701; e-mail: bvista@racsa.co.cr) offers comfortable, carpeted rooms with balconies. It's in the small town of Pilas, five kilometers north of Alajuela.

El Colibri (private bath, heated water, ceiling fans, restaurant, free airport pickup; 441-4228, fax: 440-4628; e-mail: hcolobri@racsa.co.cr) is a collection of extended family-size houses (for six to eight; $800-$1000/month) and double rooms ($40-$50, including breakfast) on spacious grounds with a pool, basketball and tennis courts, and soccer field. Located west of the airport, near the Zeta Freetrade Zone.

On the General Cañas highway to the airport, about 20 minutes from San José, there are several major hotels.

The **Hampton Inn** (private bath, hot water, air conditioning, cable TV, free local calls, wheelchair access, free airport shuttle; kids and extra adults free; $100-$110, including breakfast; 443-0043, fax: 442-9532, in the U.S.: 800-426-7866; e-mail: hampton@hamptonhotel.co.cr) offers a lot to its guests. In spite of being two minutes from the airport and on a major highway, it seems quiet inside. They encourage their guests to "think green" by providing recycling bins in each room. Recommended.

The **Meliá Cariari Conference Center and Gold Resort** (air conditioning, cable TV; children under 12 free; $190-$570; 239-0022, fax: 239-2803, 800-336-3542; www.solmelia.es, e-mail: cariari@racsa.co.cr) offers an 18-hole, par-71 golf course, tennis courts, an Olympic-size swimming pool, exercise classes, a sauna, riding horses, a casino, bars, restaurants, a 1000-person convention center, and bus service to the airport. The **Villas de Cariari** ($500-$700/week; $1600-$2400/month; 239-1003, fax: 239-1341) are apartments with daily maid service near the Cariari Hotel complex.

Another large-scale resort and convention center, the **Herradura** (cable TV, pool, restaurants; children under 12 free; $150-$160; 239-0033, fax: 239-2292, in the U.S.: 800-832-0474; www.costasol.co.cr, e-mail: hherradu@sol.racsa.co.cr) has access to the Cariari's recreational facilities, but is slightly more elegant. In back of its new wing, with views of the mountains, is a wonderland of swimming pools: one is fed by a waterfall, another has four jacuzzis in it, another laps serenely on a sand-like beach, inviting you to swim up to the bar. The Herradura is also on the highway to the airport roughly 20 minutes from San José and has frequent bus service into town for guests.

Four and a half kilometers from the airport towards Puntarenas is the quiet **Hotel Aeropuerto** (private bath, hot water, air conditioning, TV, phone, pool; $70-$80, including breakfast; 442-0354, 441-2555, fax: 441-5922; www.novanet.co.cr/aeropuerto, e-mail: hotelaer@racsa.co.cr), with playground equipment and carpeted rooms. Airport pick-up is included in the rate.

The **Marriott Hotel and Resort** ($220-$240, including breakfast; 298-0000, fax: 298-0033; www.marriott.com) in San Antonio de Belén, just south of the airport, is built in the style of a colonial coffee hacienda. The stone arches, wrought-iron balconies, tiled roofs and mosaic staircases, the spacious courtyard, carved furniture and tapestries, and the small chapel are a welcome relief from the boring or pretentious architecture of most large hotels. The Marriott has four restaurants, 15 conference rooms, and a convention center. Add to this the pools, gymnasium, sauna, jacuzzi, tennis courts, golf-practicing course, an amphitheater, and a heliport, and you've got one of the most luxurious hotels in Costa Rica. Recommended.

GETTING THERE: In San José, buses leave continuously for Alajuela (Avenida 2, Calles 12/14). By car, take Paseo Colón out of town to the General Cañas Highway and watch for the Alajuela signs before the airport. The trip takes about 20 minutes.

SANTA ANA   Near the airport, in the sunny, warm outlying area of Santa Ana, are three fairly new hotels:

Posada Canal Grande (private bath, hot water, TV, phone, refrigerator; $70-$80, including breakfast; 282-4089, 282-4101, fax: 282-5733; www.nova net.co.cr/canal, e-mail: posadacg@hotmail.com), in Piedades de Santa Ana, is a new elegant Italian-owned inn with terraces and balconies framing the pool for maximum sun exposure, and a cool lobby furnished with leather armchairs and coffee tables. A restaurant serves dinner every night but Monday.

Albergue El Marañón (shared bath, solar hot water; $20-$30; private bath, $30-$40; phone/fax: 249-1761, 249-1271; www.cultourica.com, e-mail: cultourica@expreso.co.cr) is a pleasant B&B owned by a German-Tica couple who also run a language school for individuals or groups. Their tour company, Cultourica, focused on sustainable tourism, takes guests to community-run ecotouristic projects. There is a shady garden with hammocks strung beneath the fruit trees and a great view. El Marañón is located next to the church in Barrio La Trinidad, on a back road between Piedades and Ciudad Colón. It's about 15 minutes from the airport. Recommended.

Paraíso Canadiense (no children under 7; private bath, hot water, phone, ceiling fans, cable TV, kitchens, pool; $50-$60; weekly, $225-$250; monthly, $550-$600; 282-5870, fax 282-4981; e-mail: parcdn@hotels.co.cr) is quiet and secure, right off the highway in a rather sterile industrial sector in Pozos de Santa Ana. Apartments rent by the week or by the month. The hotel hosts a steady flow of Canadian snowbirds in winter months.

Salsa-starved gringos are finally able to satisfy their cravings at Santa Ana's **Tex-Mex Restaurant** (open Tuesday through Sunday, 11:30 a.m. to 11 p.m.). Mariachis drop by in the evening, but the main attraction is the excellent, plentiful food. This reasonably priced eatery with a bar and a big backyard for kids to run around in is located behind the church. As you enter Santa Ana from the Red Cross, turn left at the gas station. The church is straight ahead.

THE UNIVERSITY FOR PEACE   Founded by United Nations mandate in 1980 to "promote the spirit of understanding, tolerance, and peaceful coexistence among humans; stimulate cooperation among peoples and help overcome obstacles to peace and world progress," the **University for Peace** (249-1929; www.upeace.org) is the world's only truly international university. It offers degrees in Communications, Human Rights and Education, and Environmental Resources, all with an emphasis on how these subjects relate to humanity's search for peace. According to Interim Rector and acting UN Undersecreatry General Maurice Strong, it soon will be the headquarters of a global ombudsman institution that would "deal with conflicts which arise from environmental or resource-related issues . . . for example, transboundary pollution or conflicts over transboundary shared water systems."

The campus and surrounding park are also one of the best areas for **bird-watching** in the Central Valley. Trogons and toucans frequent the area. A trail that starts at the Disarmament Memorial, a half-kilometer beyond the campus, leads to a *mirador.* Park hours are weekdays from 8 a.m. to 4 p.m., and until 5 p.m. on weekends (admission $1). Ask the guard for a gate key to the *"sendero al mirador."*

GETTING THERE: By Bus: Take the Ciudad Colón bus from the Coca Cola (Calle 16, Avenidas 1/3). The six-and-a-half-kilometer road to the campus has fruit-bearing trees that attract a variety of birds.

By Car: Take the Escazú highway past Santa Ana to Ciudad Colón. Follow "Universidad para la Paz" signs to the turnoff for El Rodeo at the west end of Ciudad Colón and continue six and a half kilometers to the campus.

BUTTERFLY FARM   The Butterfly Farm (open daily, 9 a.m. to 3 p.m.; 438-0400, fax: 438-0300; www.butterflyfarm.co.cr, e-mail: cres@butterfly-farm.co.cr) is devoted to raising live butterflies for exhibit in Europe. Several tours are offered to suit visitors' varying interests. On the entertaining Butterfly Tour (two hours; $15, $7 for children; $25 including transport to and from San José, $14 for children), you learn about the relationships between the beautiful winged insects, their host plants, and their predators. The farm's owners have made it possible for all visitors to observe a butterfly emerging from its chrysalis by presenting an informative video during each tour. You can stay as long as you want to photograph the butterflies. Now you can combine the Butterfly Farm Tour with Café Britt's famous Coffee Tour in Heredia ($60 for both including transportation and lunch).

GETTING THERE: The Butterfly Farm is located southwest of the airport in La Guácima, de Alajuela, across from Los Reyes Country Club.

By Bus: To get there by bus, take the La Guácima Abajo bus at 11 a.m. from the stop marked San Antonio/Ojo de Agua (Avenida 1, Calles 20/22). The bus doesn't run on Sunday. Get off at the last stop, by a school. It's a one-hour trip. From the school, follow signs for 300 meters to the farm. There is a return bus at 3:15 p.m. For information about routes from Alajuela or Santa Ana, call The Butterfly Farm at 438-0115.

By Car: Coming from San José on the highway to the airport, turn left at the large intersection after the Hotel Cariari to San Antonio de Belén. Once past the church in San Antonio, turn right for one block and then left. From there you'll see unobtrusive little butterfly signs directing you to the farm, ten kilometers to the west through San Rafael and La Guácima.

LA GARITA–ATENAS–NARANJO AREA

A hundred years ago, La Garita was the checkpoint where ox carts hauling merchandise and coffee stopped on their Pacific Coast–San José journey. La Garita is now more a strip of attractions than an actual town. If you go to La Garita, you may want to stop at **La Fiesta del Maíz** (open Friday through Sunday), a restaurant where you can sample the wide variety of foods that Costa Ricans make from corn. Everything is delicious and homemade. The waitress will bring you little samples of the dishes if you ask.

The **Zoo Ave** (open daily, 9 a.m. to 5 p.m.; 433-8989; www.zooave.org, e-mail: zooave@racsa.co.cr; admission $9, children $1), 15 minutes west of Alajuela, houses the world's most comprehensive exhibit of Costa Rican wildlife, while also breeding and releasing more native species than any other zoo in Latin America. All the animals at Zoo Ave were former pets, or injured or confiscated wildlife. They are now healthy and living in a beautiful jungle environment, and are released to the wild whenever possible. If you missed seeing monkeys or crocodiles on your trip, you can catch plenty of them here. Birders visit Zoo Ave to familiarize themselves with the calls of the birds they want to see. There are even two male quetzales! Highly recommended. You also might want to stop at some of the *viveros* (greenhouses) near the Zoo Ave.

COUNTRY LODGINGS WITHIN HALF AN HOUR OF THE AIRPORT (Don't try to find these places by yourself after 5:30 p.m. when you are fresh off the plane.)

Chatelle (private bath, hot water, ceiling fans, phone, pool; $60-$70; with TV and kitchenette, $80-$90; breakfast included; 487-7781, fax: 487-7095; www.hotelchatelle.com, e-mail: chatelle@racsa.co.cr) is a country inn located about one kilometer to the left of La Fiesta del Maíz. It has a large open-air restaurant and conference room on landscaped grounds—and offers free airport pickup.

Fifteen minutes west of La Garita on a winding road is the sunny coffee-growing town of **Atenas**. Experts from *National Geographic* declared recently that Atenas has the best climate in the world. So far there hasn't been much tourist-oriented development in the area; the town has definitely retained its humble campesino ambiance.

Colinas del Sol (private bath, hot water, ceiling fans, kitchenette, pool, bar/restaurant; $50-$60; 446-6847, fax: 446-7582; www.hotels.co.cr/colinas, e-mail: colinas@hotels.co.cr) is a lovely project about half an hour from the airport in a quiet, rural location just east of Atenas. The spacious, airy rooms have terraces overlooking the pool or the green, rolling hills. They are a good value. It would be best to have a car to stay here.

Villas de la Colina (private bath, heated water, ceiling fans, pool; $30-$40; with kitchen, $40-$50; breakfast included; 446-5015, fax: 446-6635) with its comfortable villas top a hill planted with orchards and blooming gardens, is in Barrio Mercedes de Atenas, ten minutes by car off the main road. The owner, a friendly Costa Rican woman, rents horses, can coordinate delivery or take out from nearby restaurants, and will pick you up at the airport for about $20. If you drive, follow signs from Atenas or ask, since there are a few different ways to get there. A Barrio Mercedes bus leaves Atenas every couple of hours. Recommended.

Also off the main road, in Santa Eulalia de Atenas, is the comfortable ✪ **El Cafetal Inn** (private bath, hot water, ceiling fans; no smoking inside; $70-$100, including breakfast; 446-5785, fax: 446-7028; www.cafetal.com, e-mail: cafetal@racsa.co.cr); its owners, a Colombian-Salvadoran, English-speaking couple, are helpful and warm hosts. All rooms have expansive views of the Central Valley. There is a poolside coffee bar, and the owners cook elegant full-course dinners. Access is from Atenas or three kilometers south of the Interamerican Highway just after the Grecia turnoff, where a sign points to Santa Eulalia. Be prepared for lots of curvy roads either way.

In Rosario de Naranjo, just after the Rafael Iglesias bridge, is the turnoff to ✪ **Vista del Valle Plantation Inn** (private bath, hot water, ceiling fans, pool, jacuzzi; phone/faxes: 451-1165, 450-0800, 450-0900; www.vistadelvalle.com, e-mail: mibreho@racsa.co.cr), one of the most beautiful B&Bs we've seen. It sits on a coffee and citrus farm, on the edge of a forested 500-foot-deep gorge that is a protected nature reserve. A little road leads to the river below; there is also a trail that in the steepest part becomes a precipitous steel ladder. Private cottages (kitchen; $120-$150, including breakfast) are furnished in a simple, elegant Japanese style and surrounded by lovingly tended gardens. Some overlook the reserve, as does the poolside dining area. Rooms in the main house cost $110-$120. One cottage is "wheelchair friendly." Don't try to find this place at night. It's five kilometers from the main highway on a gravel road. Signs mark the way. Highly recommended.

GETTING THERE: Zoo Ave: To get to Zoo Ave by bus, go to Alajuela first from Avenida 2, Calles 12/14, then take a La Garita bus from there. By car, the zoo is three and a half kilometers to the right at the Atenas exit of the Interamerican Highway on a back road to Alajuela.

La Garita and Atenas: The Atenas bus leaves hourly from the Coca Cola in San José and passes La Fiesta del Maíz. By car, take the Atenas turnoff about half an hour from San José on the Interamerican Highway to Puntarenas. The Fiesta del Maíz is two and a half kilometers to the left. It's fastest to approach El Cafetal and Vista del Valle by continuing on the Interamerican Highway past the Atenas exits, unless you are already in Atenas.

SAN RAMÓN

San Ramón de Alajuela is a large agricultural center off the road to Puntarenas. Their *feria del agricultor* (farmer's market) on Saturdays is huge and worth going to for inexpensive fresh fruits and vegetables. Farmers markets are held on Saturday all over Costa Rica, even in San José.

The **San Ramón Museum** (open weekday afternoons), next to the plaza in the old Municipal Palace, features a replica of a campesino home from the turn of the century and recounts local history, from pre-Columbian times through local efforts to fight William Walker to the rise of famous native sons like former President José Figueres.

GETTING THERE: San Ramón is about one hour west of San José on the main road between San José and Puntarenas. Buses leave eight times a day from the Puntarenas terminal.

LOS ANGELES CLOUD FOREST   North of San Ramón is the Los Angeles Cloud Forest, a private reserve owned by ex-President Rodrigo Carazo. The 2000-acre sanctuary rivals Monteverde in its beauty and is easily accessible for a day trip from San José—a good alternative for those who don't want to make the long, arduous trip to Monteverde. The almost two-kilometer trail is paved with wood covered with chicken wire, a simple and practical way to prevent slipping. The entrance fee goes, among other things, to pay the salaries of a professional biologist to manage the reserve and guards to make sure that hunters do not bother the wildlife. Three-hour tours by an excellent naturalist ($24/person) begin at 9 a.m. and 1 p.m. daily. The cloud forest is worth a special trip.

✪ **Hotel Villablanca** (private bath, hot water, bathtub and showers with handholds; $110-$120; 228-4603, fax: 228-4004; www.villablanca-costarica. com, e-mail: info@villablanca-costarica.com), next to the reserve, consists of 20 *casitas*, charmingly decorated in the style of traditional campesino houses, each with its own fireplace, and a large central lodge where meals are served. Bunk bed lodging for students ($30) includes meals and entrance to the reserve. The highlight of Villablanca is the chapel, whose vaulted ceiling is covered with beautiful hand-painted tiles. Horses and mountain bikes can be rented. This is a suitable destination for seniors, and is a stop on Elderhostel tours, but it also attracts a more adventurous crowd with its Canopy Adventure ($38.50), a seven-platform glide through the treetops.

GETTING THERE: From the main highway's entrance to San Ramón, follow the main street through town, where good signs for Villablanca will direct you to the La Tigra road (200 meters west of the hospital). It's about 45 minutes away, all on a paved road. As you leave San Ramón, a winding road branches off to the right from the La Tigra road and takes you to Zarcero.

ZARCERO

Zarcero is one of the most charming Costa Rican towns, perched on the hills that divide the Central Valley from the San Carlos plain. At 1700 meters above sea level, its climate is fresh and invigorating. Its ruddy-cheeked inhabitants are famous for their peach preserves and homemade white cheese. In the past few years Zarcero has become the organic farming capital of Costa Rica, thanks to guidance from a Japanese volunteer from that country's version of the Peace Corps.

Cultural Interactions for Development (253-9935) offers a fascinating tour of organic farms, including a *trapiche* in San Ramon, combined with a trip to Volcán Poás.

But Zarcero's real claim to fame is the fancifully sculpted topiary in front of its picturesque little church: bushes shaped into gigantic green rabbits, a bullfight, a couple dancing, a monkey riding a bicycle, ox carts, and elephants. The topiary garden has been lovingly pruned by Don Evangelista Blanco, who says that God has been telling him what to sculpt for the last 35 years. He has posted little signs throughout the park with sayings like "You have doubted God, and yet he lives inside you." You can buy postcards at the park that help fund this unique treat. When we were there, a huge rainbow guided us down the country roads above Zarcero to the town plaza, then remained in a perfect arc directly over the church.

Just before you reach Zarcero, there is a group of restaurants and stands selling cheese, candied fruit, and flowers. If you want to stop for something to eat, the restaurants here are better than those in Zarcero itself. On the north side of the Zarcero church is the homey **Hotel Don Beto** (shared or private bath, heated water; $20-$30; phone/fax: 463-3137). Recommended.

Two kilometers north of Zarcero, just above the town of Laguna, with a lovely view of the whole area, are **Cabinas Pradera** (private bath, heated water, kitchens; $20-$30; 463-3959, 463-3346). The owner doesn't live at the cabinas, so ask at her husband's store, Abastecedor J y M, on the south side of the football field.

GETTING THERE: Buses leave hourly from San José for San Carlos from the Atlantico Norte station (255-4318) on Calle 12, Avenida 9, passing through Zarcero an hour and a half later. It's easy to catch a bus back to San José, or on to Volcán Arenal and the hot springs at Tabacón. By car, Zarcero is an hour and a half from San José. Take the Naranjo–Ciudad Quesada exit off the Interamerican Highway to Puntarenas.

SARCHÍ

The small town of Sarchí is the home of Costa Rica's traditional brightly painted ox carts. You can watch artisans creating beautiful wooden bowls, plates, furniture, and walking sticks decorated with animals and birds. With the influx of tour buses full of souvenir-hungry tourists, the main road through Sarchí has become pretty tacky. Although you can buy the same items in San José and Moravia, if you have a lot of wooden crafts on your gift list it is nice to go right to the source. The most inexpensive place to buy crafts is at the cooperative, on the right at the west end of town. In the center of town, the **Plaza de la Artesanía** is a pleasant place to shop for souvenirs. There are many different shops, and a restaurant that serves *comida típica*.

Vista del Valle (closed Wednesday; 454-3376), 15 minutes north of Sarchí toward Bajos del Toro, is a good place to stop for *comida típica* and great views.

GETTING THERE: Take the hourly Grecia bus from the Coca Cola. In Grecia, connect with the Alajuela–Sarchí bus. You can catch the latter bus in Alajuela, but it takes a long, roundabout route to Grecia. To get to Sarchí by car, take the Grecia exit off the Puntarenas Highway, 30 minutes west of San José. When you get to Grecia, turn left behind the church, left again (circling the church), then right for three blocks. The road going diagonally to your left is the road to Sarchí.

BOSQUE DE PAZ   Serving as a biological corridor between Poás and Juan Castro Blanco National Parks, **Bosque de Paz** is a pristine forest sanctuary owned by a Costa Rican family, about an hour due north of Sarchí near the town of Bajos del Toro. Well-maintained and -marked trails through the 1200-acre reserve range from a mild one-kilometer loop to a six-kilometer half-day trek to waterfalls. Quetzals nest here between December and February, orchids bloom most exuberantly in April, and troops of monkeys can be spotted all year. It is a favorite stop for Audubon Society birding tours. Your hike will most likely be accompanied by the flutelike song of the jilguero (black-faced solitaire). Iridescent purple hummingbirds flit around their feeders.

✪ **Bosque de Paz Lodge** (private bath, hot water; $105/person, including meals and tours; by reservation only; 234-6676, fax: 225-0203; www.

bosquedepaz.com, e-mail: bosque@racsa.co.cr) has comfortable, spacious rooms whose simple design blends with their beautiful natural surroundings. Genuine Costa Rican country food is served in the restaurant. Round-trip transportation from San José costs $70/person.

Seven kilometers north of Bajos del Toro is the **Catarata del Toro**, a large roadside restaurant that maintains half a mile of well-tended trails lined with crushed lava rock ($1), from which you can see the magnificent 300-foot El Toro waterfall. This is a great stop for a short hike to break up your trip to Arenal or Sarapiquí. They also rent rooms (private bath, heated water; $40-$50; 284-2258, phone/fax: 761-1355).

GETTING THERE: From Sarchí, follow signs directly north on a paved, winding road to Bajos del Toro. The entrance to Bosque de Paz is located to the left on the road that connects Bajos del Toro with Zarcero. You can also get there from Zarcero: the drive on the rough gravel backroad between Zarcero and Bajos del Toro has stunning views of the ancient oak forests of Juan Castro Blanco National Park. We drove it at the height of the rainy season with no problem (four-wheel drive recommended). Juan Castro Blanco is not set up for visitors, but Bosque de Paz encompasses the same kind of glorious high-altitude forest.

If you are continuing from here into the Northern Zone (west to Volcán Arenal or east to Sarapiquí), drive through Bajos del Toro and down to Río Cuarto in the San Carlos plains. The road was built by ICE, the Costa Rican electric company, to transport workers and materials to build a large hydroelectric plant, so it is well-paved the whole way down.

GRECIA AREA

The Grecia area offers many possibilities for day trips, by itself or including La Garita and Volcán Poás. Grecia was voted the cleanest town in Latin America, and its citizens take pride in maintaining that reputation. From its airy red metal church with delicate wooden filigree altars to the well-kept homes of its farmers, it still exudes the goodness and simplicity that many other parts of the country have lost. We enjoyed the chicken roasted over a wood fire at **Pollo a la Leña**, on the south side of Parque Central. **Soda El Oasis**, on the southwest corner of Parque Central, is a clean and pleasant family-style restaurant with attentive service, reasonable prices, and an ample menu.

The **Municipal Museum of Grecia** (open daily, 9 a.m. to 5 p.m.) now houses the Joyas del Trópico Húmedo (Jewels of the Rainforest) exhibit, part of a vast collection of moths, butterflies, beetles, and other insects. The iridescent creatures are displayed in geometric patterns, or arranged on velvet to highlight their jewel-like colors. The museum is located behind the municipal building, half a block north of Grecia's Parque Central (494-5620; $4, students and children half-price).

In the village of Poró, five minutes east of Grecia, is the **Mundo de las Serpientes** (World of Snakes) (open daily, 8 a.m. to 4 p.m.; 494-3700; adults $11, children $6), in which snakes from all over the planet are exhibited in outdoor concrete habitats. The young Austrian owners give a fascinating hour-long guided tour. They also breed endangered species for release into the wild.

In the sunny village of Rincón de Salas, 20 minutes from the airport, is ✪ **Posada Mimosa** (private bath, solar-heated water with back-up, ceiling fans, pool; $60-$70, including breakfast; $90-$100 with kitchen and two bedrooms; cabin for eight, $100-$110; house, $700/month; phone/fax: 494-5868, 494-2295, in Canada: 905-842-4598, fax: 905-842-6458; www.mimosa.co.cr, e-mail: mimosa@sol.racsa.co.cr), owned by a congenial retired British-Canadian couple, has beautiful tropical gardens and fruit trees. Almost half of the farm, descending to a stream below, is protected primary forest. Comfortably furnished rooms in the main house open onto a shady corridor. There are beautiful views of the Central Valley from here.

GETTING THERE: An hourly bus goes to Grecia from the Coca Cola. By car, head west on the Interamerican Highway past the airport and turn right at the well-marked Grecia intersection. To get to Posada Mimosa, go two kilometers toward Grecia, then turn right and go three kilometers to the first crossroads at the village of Rincón de Salas. Turn right again, and go two blocks to Posada Mimosa. Their yellow signs will guide you.

Sugarcane and coffee are the main crops in the Grecia area. A winding road through the hills to the northwest takes you to **Los Trapiches** (open Tuesday through Sunday, 8 a.m. to 5 p.m.; 444-6656; campground; admission $2), where on Sunday you can see how *tapa dulce*, the flavorful hard brown sugar of Central America, is made. A waterwheel activates the huge gears of a venerable Victorian cane press, imported more than a century ago from Aberdeen, Scotland. The cane juice is collected in enormous *pailas* (cauldrons) set into a brick vault in which a fire is built. As the liquid boils, it reaches different stages of consistency until it is ready to be poured into the flower pot–shaped molds. At one point the sugar can be whipped into different forms, called *sobado*. It is quite an interesting process to see, and you can spend the day there, picnicking or eating *comida típica* in the restaurant. There are swimming pools and a small lake for boating. Ticos love to go there on weekends, and there is live music on Sunday afternoon. Call before you go to make sure the *trapiche* is operating. To get there, drive three blocks past the church in Grecia and turn left onto Route 13, winding through the hills on paved roads to Santa Gertrudis Sur, following the Los Trapiches signs. A bus from the main terminal in Grecia—the Grecia–Poás bus—leaves hourly.

A few kilometers south of Los Trapiches, **Los Chorros** ("the jets"; 494-8312; admission $4) are two beautiful waterfalls, about 75 feet high. Numerous smaller jets of water pour from the rock cliffs between them. Rickety bridges hang over the river and there are several covered picnic areas. On weekends locals flock there to picnic and swim in the pools, but you'll have the place to yourself during the week. You pay the admission at a little building downhill from a small sign that indicates the entrance. There is also another entrance through a coffee field farther up the road to Santa Gertrudis.

Getting to the waterfalls requires a ten-minute hike along a well-maintained trail through a wooded gorge. At the entrance, take the lower trail straight to the river, or opt for the high trail and then veer left to the *mirador* for the overlook above the falls. The two trails meet at the main picnic area near the falls, so you can go in one way and come out the other. Only 20 minutes from Alajuela, this is an easy and delightful way to find relief on a hot day. The waterfalls come down with such force that a refreshing mist permeates the air at their base.

GETTING THERE: If you're coming from Los Trapiches, continue south along the gravel Santa Gertrudis–Tácares road for about 15 minutes until the road descends from the hills and makes a sharp right. Here you will see the gated entrance to a quarry on your left. During the week you can drive through the gate, veer left at the bottom of the hill, and park at the entrance to Los Chorros. The gate is closed on Sunday, so you have to leave your car in the makeshift lot outside and walk five minutes to the entrance.

If you're coming from Alajuela, drive west about 15 kilometers to Tácares. Turn right just past the Tácares church and bear left for three kilometers until the road makes a sharp left into the hills. You'll see the large gate on your right.

If you don't have a car, you can take buses as far as Santa Gertrudis or Tácares and then walk. A taxi from the Tácares church only costs $1.50. An interesting day trip for those who like to hike (or hitch) might be to take the bus to Santa Gertrudis from Grecia, hike to Los Chorros, continue walking to Tácares, then bus it back to Alajuela from there.

Above Grecia on the slopes of Volcán Poás is the 7600-hectare **Bosque del Niño** (Children's Forest), named so because it was purchased in 1979, the United Nations Year of the Child. A small area at the entrance has been planted with cypress and eucalyptus trees, and has camping and covered picnicking spots. If it rains, the ranger will probably let you camp under a pic-

nic *rancho*. Well-marked trails through the primary cloud forest above lead
to overlooks, waterfalls, and Poás National Park (eight kilometers and two
and a half hours). The ranger has seen all types of big cats in the park;
quetzals and *jilgueros* also abound. This park is still off the beaten track for
foreign visitors.

GETTING THERE: By Bus: From the Grecia bus terminal take a bus to San
Isidro at 9:30 a.m., noon, 1 p.m., or 4:30 p.m. These buses will drop you at the
turnoff for the Bosque; it's a four-kilometer (one-hour) hike through coffee plantations from there. Buses back to Grecia leave the turnoff approximately half an
hour later than the times given above.

By Car: Drive toward Santa Gertrudis del Sur (see Los Trapiches, above), and
turn left off the main road just past the Balneario Victoria towards San Isidro.
From there, signs clearly mark the way to Bosque del Niño.

VOLCÁN POÁS NATIONAL PARK

Poás is one of the few active volcanoes on the continent that is accessible
by a good road. The 37-kilometer trip from San José is marked by beautiful
scenery, with lookouts over the Central Valley. It is the most developed of
the national parks, with a visitors' center (including a museum, cafeteria,
and gift shop) and well-maintained nature trails.

The main crater of Poás is one and a half kilometers wide and 300 meters deep. There was a hot, sulfurous lake at the bottom, but it recently
evaporated due to increased volcanic activity. Active fumaroles are visible
from the lookout point above the crater. A 20-minute uphill hike takes you
to another lookout over jewel-like Botos Lake, which fills an ancient crater.

Volcán Poás is just coming out of an active phase, apparently part of a
40- to 45-year cycle. The volcano spewed a 4000-meter column of water
and mud in 1910, sending ash as far as Puntarenas. Lava flow increased
also in 1953. In May 1989, Poás shot ash a mile into the air, but still it is
quiet compared to other volcanoes, such as Arenal and Irazú.

Scientists believe that Poás has a relatively open passage from its magma
chamber to its huge crater, so it lets off steam more easily than other volcanoes and doesn't build up the pressure that causes large eruptions. Nevertheless, it is under close observation these days, and the park is sometimes
closed to visitors because of sulfur gas emissions from the crater, which combine with steam to make sulfuric acid. It's difficult to predict when Poás
will be emitting gases, just as it's difficult to predict when it will be clear
enough to see the craters. Basically, you just have to take your chances.

Volcán Poás National Park (open daily, 8 a.m. to 3 p.m.; call 192 or 283-8004 for information) protects the headwaters of several rivers, which feed the Río Tárcoles to the southwest and the Río Sarapiquí to the north. While the active crater is full of subtle, moonscape colors, the rest of Poás is intensely green, with a great variety of wildflowers, bromeliads, ferns, mosses, and lichen. One of the most interesting plants there is the *sombrilla del pobre* (poor man's umbrella), which has thick, fuzzy leaves up to two meters in width, designed to trap airborne algae. Hummingbirds are among the 26 species of birds most easily seen along the road or on the trails. Quetzals, the famed sacred birds of the Maya, also frequent Poás. Don't miss the 20-minute hike along Sendero de la Escalonia that connects the upper parking lot to the picnic area farther along the main road. It's a green mossy tunnel through a shaggy cloud forest. If you read Spanish you'll appreciate the poetic signs along the trail that anthropomorphize your surroundings.

The average temperature on misty Poás is 50 degrees, dropping as low as 22 and climbing as high as 70, so it is important to dress in layers. Bring rain gear. If you arrive too late in the day, clouds will be covering the crater, so the earlier you go the better. When it's clear, you can see Poás on the horizon to the northwest of San José. If you can't see it, it's probably too late to go.

Two and a half kilometers below the park entrance is the turnoff for ✪ **Lagunillas Lodge** (private bath, hot water; $20-$30, including breakfast; cell phone: 389-5842). The nine brothers and sisters who inherited this former dairy farm were aware of its ecological riches—bordering Volcán Poás National Park, with quetzals, toucans, and *jilgueros* inhabiting the 90 percent of it that is still forested—so they decided to attend to ecotourism, which they hope can maintain their inheritance. The sisters cook *comida típica* ($5) over a wood stove, and the brothers take visitors out for hikes and horseback rides ($8/hour) along the extensive trails. You can hike alone, but they feel it's safer to go with a guide. Rooms off the charming dining area are clean, nicely decorated, and inexpensive for the area. Water is heated by being piped through the back of the kitchen's woodstove, so you have to let them know in advance when you want to take a shower. Private cabinas away from the main building are under construction, as are ponds where you can fish for trout, pay for it based on weight and take it home or have it cooked there. The one-kilometer dirt road down to the lodge is very steep, but regular cars can make it. Recommended.

Souvenir y Cabinas Quetzal (private bath, heated water; $20-$30; 482-2090), located between Poasito and Lagunillas, is a small gift shop and restaurant with four plainly furnished rooms below it. The view from the guest rooms' large windows is a patchwork of cultivated fields, towns, and forest—an almost dizzying perspective of the Central Valley.

The road to Poás is lined with strawberry plantations and restaurants. Be sure to stop at **Chubascos**, one of the nicest places we know for native Costa Rican food. It is set in a hillside garden with covered outdoor tables. Their large *casado* can't be beat, especially accompanied by *refrescos* made from local strawberries and blackberries and followed by homemade cheesecake. It's about 16 kilometers above Alajuela.

Another highly recommended eatery is **Las Fresas** (open daily, 9 a.m. to 11 p.m.; 448-5567, fax: 448-6044), owned by an Italian family, where the pizzas are baked in a wood-heated brick oven. The steak at this elegantly cozy restaurant has received rave reviews. Las Fresas now rents rooms (private bath, hot water; $30-$40) in a hexagonal building covered on the outside with lava rock. Coming down from the volcano, you'll see many signs for Las Fresas on the road to San Pedro de Poás. It's about five kilometers below Fraijanes.

Churrascos Steak House is in Poasito, about ten kilometers from the park entrance. There's a gas station and a little supermarket there, too.

At Poasito, there's a six-kilometer road going east to **Vara Blanca**, along the Continental Divide on the pass between Poás and Barva volcanoes. Ticos who have cars drive up on weekends for family picnics in the grassy meadows along this road. Half a kilometer west of the junction with the Heredia–Sarapiquí road, at Vara Blanca (16 kilometers from Poás), is the turnoff for **Poás Volcano Lodge** (hot water; shared bath, $60-$70; private bath, $70-$90; breakfast included; phone/fax: 482-2194; www.arweb.com/poas, e-mail: poasvl@racsa.co.cr), an imposing English manor house 6175 feet above sea level, with cozy rooms and a sunken fireplace in the living room to take the chill off the air. About one kilometer off the road on a lush dairy farm, this bed and breakfast is especially suited for hikers and birders who like to roam the countryside. There are trails through the forested sector of the farm. The manager can connect you with neighbors who run horse tours through the mountains. To get there, take the Río Frio–Sarapiquí bus from the Terminal Atlántico Norte and get off in Vara Blanca (see below).

Just a few hundred meters toward Heredia from the junction, **La Suiza** (225-3243) offers inexpensive horseback rides to the spring that forms the head of the Sarapiquí river (three to four hours for about $15/person). You can call a day or two in advance and leave a message when you'll be coming; if you just stop in, they will need about an hour to get the horses ready. You can fill this time with a meal at the nearby **Restaurant Vara Blanca**, recommended for generous servings and friendly service.

Six kilometers north of Vara Blanca are **La Paz Waterfall Gardens** (221-1378; e-mail: wgardens@racsa.co.cr; admission $15), a private wildlife refuge with a restaurant and hummingbird, orchid, and butterfly gardens.

GETTING THERE: A bus to Volcán Poás leaves daily at 8:30 a.m. from Parque de la Merced in San José (Avenida 2, Calle 12; 222-5325). Buses leave from Alajuela's Parque Central on Sunday, continuously between 8 and 9 a.m. Get there early to reserve yourself a seat. The bus from San José arrives at the volcano around 11 a.m. Check with the driver for departure time. Many tour companies offer day trips to Poás for between $30 and $60 per person, but a taxi from Alajuela to Poás costs about $40 per taxiload (including waiting and return trip) and a taxi from San José costs about $50. Ask at your hotel for reliable *taxistas,* or call the Alajuela taxi company at 443-3030. If you're going to Vara Blanca, some Río Frío buses take this route (6 a.m., noon, 3 p.m.; Calle 12, Avenida 9).

By Car: Take the Alajuela turnoff from the General Cañas (Interamerican) Highway, about 15 minutes from San José. It goes past Alajuela's Central Park and the Juan Santamaría Museum. Stay on the same road until you get to Fraijanes Lake and Chubascos. About one and a half kilometers beyond the restaurant, you will connect with the road from San Pedro de Poás, which leads to the volcano. If you are near Heredia, take the Barva–Birrí road to Vara Blanca and turn left for six kilometers, then right at Poasito. If you are in Grecia, take the back road to Alajuela through Tácares, turn left at Hotel Las Orquideas to get to San Pedro de Poás, and continue on to the volcano. You can make a nice circular route, entering through Alajuela, and returning through Vara Blanca and Heredia. We highly recommend the Vara Blanca–Heredia route, especially for coming down; it is still beautiful and undeveloped, whereas the faster road from Alajuela has become too crowded and a lot of the beautiful farmland on that route is covered with gray screening that protects berry and flower agroindustries.

HEREDIA AND SURROUNDING TOWNS

Founded in 1706, **Heredia** has retained a friendly, small-town atmosphere. Its colonial 1796 **church** has a pretty facade and a peaceful garden. Here, too, is the Universidad Nacional which has a substantial student population. There are concerts Thursday nights in the music temple in **Parque Central**.

In the **Mercado Florense** (300 meters south and 50 meters west of the church) there's an inexpensive place to have a good seafood lunch. You'll also find some nice, clean restaurants behind the Mercado Central, across from the buses. **Mango Verde** (open weekdays, 9 a.m. to 6: 30 p.m.; 237-2526) is a vegetarian restaurant downtown on Avenida 7, Calle 5. **Fresas** (237-3915), a restaurant one block from the university, is clean and spacious with some outdoor tables. Servings are generous and inexpensive. **Le Petit Paris** (238-1721) serves crêpes and French cuisine in its garden near the university.

Located about 750 meters north of Colegio Santa Cecilia in Heredia, **Apartotel Vargas** (private bath, hot water, fans, TV, parking; $50-$60; 237-8526, fax: 260-4698) offers clean, fully equipped apartments on a quiet street. The upper rooms are lighter. Laundry facilities and airport pickup are available.

The stucco highrise **Hotel Valladolid** (private bath, hot water, air conditioning, hairdryers, phone, cable TV, kitchen; $70-$80; Calle 7/Avenida 7; 260-2905, fax: 260-2912; e-mail: valladol@racsa.co.cr) hosts dignitaries visiting the Universidad Nacional as well as tourists who seek urban luxury in a small-town atmosphere. From the top-floor jacuzzi, sauna, and solarium there are 360-degree views of the Central Valley, and at sunset, the Pacific Ocean is a bright sliver on the horizon. There is a bar on an upper floor and a so-so restaurant downstairs across the street. In the lobby, stop by the table of **Interviajes**, a locally owned tour agency that runs some of the more unique tours around.

Hotel Verano (shared bath, cold water; $12-$20; 237-1616), up three flights of stairs on the west side of the market in Heredia, is clean, friendly, and inexpensive. The same owners run **Hotel Las Flores** (private bath, heated water, secure parking; $20-$30; 237-1616) nearby. Recommended for budget travelers. **El Parqueo** (shared bath, cold water; $7-$12; 238-2882) is in the same block as the Verano. It is a little grungier, but has good mattresses and friendly owners.

GETTING THERE: By Bus: Buses to Heredia leave every five to ten minutes from Calle 1, Avenidas 7/9 in San José, 5:20 a.m. to 10:30 p.m. (through Tibás), and from Avenida 2, Calle 12 every 20 minutes (through La Uruca).

By Car: From downtown San José, you should have a good map and ask for detailed instructions. From the General Cañas Highway there are good signs from the turnoff near the airport.

SAN ISIDRO DE HEREDIA   A town to the east of Heredia, San Isidro de Heredia is visible throughout the area because of its white Gothic **church**. San Isidro and San Joaquín de las Flores are both known for their colorful Easter-week processions.

Across the river behind the church is a little road that goes uphill to the **Cerámica Chavarría** (268-8455), where Doña Frances turns out ovenproof stoneware and blends her own nonleaded glazes. Unique ripped openings in some of her bowls and vases give the pieces a tactile fluidity. Don't be concerned about transporting her work back home. Her pieces, well packed, have arrived intact to several continents. Call first.

GETTING THERE: Buses leave San José (Calle 4, Avenidas 7/9) for San Isidro de Heredia every half-hour. By car from San José, take Guápiles Highway toward Braulio Carrillo, and take the exit to the left about 14 kilometers from downtown, right after the Restaurant Las Orquideas. San Isidro is about four kilometers from the highway. You can snake your way to San Isidro along backroads from the Universidad Nacional in Heredia, but bring a good map and ask questions, as there are few signs.

MONTE DE LA CRUZ   The mountains above Heredia are full of evergreen forests and pastureland. It's exhilaratingly chilly year-round, and a bright, sunny day can turn into a rainy one in minutes, especially after noon. From these mountains you can see the sun glinting off the Gulf of Nicoya in the west. A hike to **Monte de la Cruz Recreation Area** (open daily, 8 a.m. to 4 p.m.; admission 75 cents) gives you an incredible panorama of the entire Central Valley and beyond. Take a picnic lunch, an umbrella, and a sweater. This large, well-maintained park has a slick basketball court, plenty of playground equipment, a soccer field, covered picnic tables, and trails permeated with the smell of evergreens. Many Ticos go there on Sunday. A restaurant is open 11 a.m. to midnight.

Take a left at the aforementioned fork and in about one kilometer you will arrive at the **Hotel Chalet Tirol** (hot water, bathtub, electric heating; $100-$110; children under 12 free; 267-6222, fax: 267-6229; www.chalet-tirol.com, e-mail: info@www.chalet-tirol.com). At 1800 meters (5900 feet), the hotel is surrounded by a private cloud forest reserve that borders Braulio Carrillo National Park. The older rooms are charming two-story, vine-covered cabins with handpainted Tyrolean designs, and the newer, larger rooms are in a cement building. Also offered are room service, the **Bugatti Pizza Parlor**, and an elegant French restaurant that opens at noon.

Three hiking trails are accessible from the hotel's private reserve, one of which leads to a moss-covered cliff where a dozen small waterfalls cascade into as many small pools before joining the river below. It's a beautiful place and amazing in that it's so close to San José. The other trails follow the Río Segundo into Braulio Carrillo amidst a carpet of ferns and ancient trees covered with orchids and bromeliads. Horseback tours ($48) to Cerro Chompipe in Braulio Carrillo are also available for guests and nonguests alike, with a day's notice. It's a great place for a day hike or for a weekend trip, and you can warm up with hot chocolate and pastry on the second floor of the Chalet's restaurant.

Añoranzas (open Wednesday through Saturday, noon to 11 p.m.; Sunday, noon to 6 p.m.; 267-7406), down a road on your left from the main road four kilometers above San Rafael, specializes in *comida típica* and has play equipment for kids.

GETTING THERE: Buses for this area leave from one block south of the Mercado in Heredia. For Monte de la Cruz and Chalet Tirol, take the San Rafael "Monte de la Cruz" bus, which leaves at 9 a.m., noon, and 4 p.m, during the week and every half-hour after 8 a.m. on Sunday (60 cents). The terminus is at a fork in the road, one kilometer from Chalet Tirol (left) or from Monte de la Cruz (right). The bus goes all the way to Monte de la Cruz on Sunday.

Monte de la Cruz and Chalet Tirol are about 35 minutes from San José by car. Take the San Isidro exit to the left about 14 kilometers down the Guápiles Highway right after the Restaurant Las Orquídeas. When you reach San Isidro, turn right uphill in front of the church and go two kilometers to Concepción (ignore any previous Concepción signs). Continue a few minutes more to San Rafael, and again turn right uphill at the church, to reach the road that goes through Los Angeles to Monte de la Cruz.

BARVA DE HEREDIA   The town of Barva, two kilometers north of Heredia, is one of the oldest settlements in the country. Its historic church and the houses near it have been restored.

The Museo de Cultura Popular (open weekdays, 8 a.m. to 4 p.m.; weekends, 10 a.m. to 5 p.m.; 260-1619; admission $1.50) in Santa Lucía de Barva, just outside of Barva, is a colonial-era Central Valley dwelling that has been carefully restored to showcase the best of traditional design. The seven stages of *bahareque*, or reinforced adobe construction, are demonstrated, and the cool house is proof that this is a practical technique in hot climates. Adobe construction without reinforcement has been illegal in Costa Rica since 1910, when an earthquake toppled many adobe houses, killing the people inside. The fruit tree–shaded *solar* (yard) is decked with traditional children's playground equipment: a plank seesaw, rope-and-stick swings, and homemade stilts. A *soda* serves economical and delicious *comida típica* on weekends, and a little crafts shop sells inexpensive children's toys. By car, follow the signs that start on the road to Barva from Heredia. Otherwise, take the Jardines de Santa Lucía bus which leaves every half hour from the Patronato, 100 meters north of Heredia's central plaza. Ask the driver to drop you off at the museum stop, a 500-meter walk from the museum itself. Signs mark the way.

Maker of Costa Rica's excellent export-quality coffee, **Café Britt** (open daily, 9 a.m. and 11 a.m; 260-2748, fax: 238-1848; www.coffeetour.com, e-mail: coffeetour@cafebritt.com; $20, by reservation only; discounts for children under 10 and students) has an educational tour of its operations, including a lively skit about the history and cultivation of coffee and a demonstration of the art of professional coffee tasting. Company representatives will pick you up at your hotel or in downtown San José ($5); call for information. You can also combine the coffee tour with a trip to the Butterfly Farm in La Guacima de Alajuela ($60 including transportation and lunch). To get there, continue uphill from McDonald's in Heredia, then follow the Coffeetour signs on the road to Barva. Recommended.

On the Barva–Santa Barbara road, Spanish *paella* master Vincent Aguilar prepares personalized *paellas* and other Mediterranean dishes at **La Lluna de Valencia** (phone/fax: 238-3965). His restaurant has become a gathering place for the international NGO crowd. He has revived the tradition of *la tertulia*, where people get together to discuss literature and ideas. The restaurant is located 50 meters from Pulpería La Máquina in San Pedro de Barva; open Friday and Saturday noon to 10 p.m., Sunday noon to 5 p.m.

La Rosa Blanca (private bath, hot water, pool, concierge service, non-smoking; $180-$280, including breakfast; children 3 to 12 half price; 269-9392, fax: 269-9555; www.finca-rblanca.co.cr, e-mail: info@finca-rblanca.co.cr) is near Santa Barbara de Heredia. Each room has a theme, and the architecture and handcrafted furnishings are full of fantasy and delightful, creative touches. The honeymoon suite features a tower room with a 360-degree view and a bathroom painted like a rainforest, with the water for the bathtub bubbling out of a rocky waterfall. Gourmet dinners are available for guests only ($25). Airport pickup can be arranged ($15). Recommended.

VOLCÁN BARVA

On the western edge of Braulio Carrillo National Park (see below) is Volcán Barva (closed Monday; admission $6). This ancient volcano, on whose slopes Heredia and its neighboring villages roost, offers a good heavy-duty hike through pastureland and, near the top, through cloud forest. You usually must walk about four kilometers from where the road gets too bad for most vehicles, and then it's an hour's hike from the park entrance to the 2900-meter-high Laguna Barva, a forest-rimmed green lake in the old crater. The vegetation is vibrant and full of birds. The other, smaller, Laguna Copey, is a 40-minute hike from the turnoff for Laguna Barva. The Copey trail crosses the divide from the Pacific side to the very moist, muddy Atlantic side. This trail is lined with flowering bushes and huge, primordial *sombrilla del pobre* plants, making it a pretty walk. Since there are two-thousand-year-old trees in the cloud forest surrounding the old crater, scientists surmise that the volcano has been dormant for at least that long. However, vulcanologists have been noticing some volcanic activity in the pass between Barva and Volcán Irazú, and speculate that Barva will act up again soon.

Quetzals are sometimes visible here. They migrate to forests more than 3600 feet above sea level, where they nest in the hollows of the tallest and oldest trees. Males and females share the incubation of eggs and the feeding of hatchlings. The females sit on the eggs at night and at midday, and the male sits with his beautiful green tail hanging out of the nest during the rest of the day. Also heard on Volcán Barva is the black-faced solitaire, which has been compared to the nightingale for the sweetness and delicacy of its song. If you want to see birds, you might do well to take a tour. **Jungle Trails** (255-3486, fax: 255-2782) specializes in hiking and birding trips to Barva. Bring rain gear, compass, and waterproof footwear, even in the dry season.

Camping is permitted in the pasture behind the administration building at the entrance to the park. There are two covered picnic areas with grills along the trail to the lake.

Note: Not a year goes by without some overconfident hiker getting lost in this area. The lucky ones are discovered by search parties or follow a stream down to the Atlantic plains. The others are never found. Do not stray from the trail. The forest is too dense and the terrain too hilly for you to navigate on your own. Know that the best strategy if you get lost is to stay put, rig a brightly colored shelter, drink water from the cups formed in bromeliads, and try to hunt small fowl or eat *palmito*, the heart of palm trees. In the event that no one knows you're missing (thus a search party will not be sent out), follow a stream downhill until you reach civilization.

Restaurante La Campesina, three and a half kilometers above Paso Llano, serves tasty, wholesome country food at outdoor tables overlooking the valley. **Restaurante Sacramento** (237-9596), four kilometers above Paso Llano, looks like a rather dingy bar when you enter, but has a lovely covered porch for dining on the left side. Its owner, Manuel, is a good person to talk to about the area. You might want to stop and admire the view from Sacramento's little church, just down the hill from the restaurant. Cabina rental signs are all along the road; most cabinas are in the $20-$30 range and are family size.

In the rainy season, the road beyond Restaurante Sacramento is impossible for regular cars. Even when we visited in the height of the dry season, the road beyond Sacramento was in such poor condition that we had to leave our vehicle and walk the remaining three kilometers to the park entrance. Some four-wheel-drive trucks were navigating the rutty, rock-filled road, however. Every once in a while, the Park Service smooths out the road, so check on road conditions before going (261-2619 or 283-8004). Even if you can't make it to the park, the scenery around Sacramento is worth the trip.

GETTING THERE: By Bus: To climb Volcán Barva you should catch the 6:30 a.m. San José de la Montaña–Paso Llano bus from behind the Mercado Central in Heredia. (Later buses leave at 11 a.m. and 4.p.m. On Sunday there is no 6:30 a.m. bus. Check schedules at 237-5007.) At Paso Llano (Porrosatí), you'll see signs for the park entrance eight kilometers uphill to the left. The crater lake is 2.6 kilometers beyond the entrance. Be sure to make it back for the 5 p.m. Paso Llano bus to Heredia. (There is also a 7:30 a.m. and 1 p.m. bus.)

By Car: Follow the road north of Heredia through Barva. Take the right fork north of Barva to lovely San José de la Montaña, with its peaceful church and charming country houses. Continue five kilometers beyond it and turn right at the signs for Braulio Carrillo. In a few hundred meters you'll arrive at Paso Llano. Turn left. The road after San José de la Montaña has quite a few potholes.

BRAULIO CARRILLO NATIONAL PARK

The founding of Braulio Carrillo National Park in 1978 represented a compromise between ecology and development. Environmentalists were concerned that the opening of a highway between San José and Guápiles would result in the ecological disasters that accompanied the opening of other roads in Costa Rica: indiscriminate colonization and deforestation. The government agreed to make 80,000 acres of virgin forest surrounding the highway into a national park.

The Guápiles Highway, opened in May 1987, makes Braulio Carrillo the national park most accessible by car. The scenery is inspiring. Hopefully, it is an education in itself for all the motorists who pass through it on their way to the Atlantic coast—mountains of untouched rainforest as far as the eye can see. And just 30 years ago, most of Costa Rica looked like that!

In order to hike the trails accessible from the highway, you must stop and pay the entrance fee ($6) at the visitors center (1.8 kilometers after the tollbooth if you're coming from San José, or 500 meters after the tunnel if you're coming from Limón). While you're there, ask which trails are accessible and patrolled at the moment. The forest is constantly evolving—trees frequently fall and block paths. It can be risky to try a trail that the rangers don't have resources to take care of. We took a lovely, solitary two-and-a-half-hour hike on the trail right near the visitors center. Views were as beautiful as the more crowded cloud forests in the country, but, unfortunately, loud semi-trailer truck noises competed with the flutelike song of the *jilguero* and probably chased other animals much deeper into the forest. The trails in Braulio Carrillo are usually muddy and steep, so wear appropriate shoes and bring rain ponchos.

GETTING THERE: Take the hourly Guápiles bus from the Atlántico Norte terminal (Calle 12, Avenidas 7/9; 258-2734; $1.50), and ask to be let off at the Oficina de Parques Nacionales, 1.8 kilometers after the *peaje* (tollbooth). By car, the trip from San José takes about 20 minutes on the Guápiles Highway.

Note: Avoid the *miradores*, the scenic lookout points along the highway—especially the ones that are out of view of the main road. Tourists have been robbed at these places, and the park does not have enough personnel to guard them.

Hotel Villa Zurquí (private bath, hot water, TV, some with kitchens or fireplaces, restaurant; $50-$80; 268-5084, phone/fax: 268-8856) is just two kilometers toward San José from the *peaje* (tollbooth). The grassy, cypress-dotted complex has separate chalet-style houses. Recreation opportunities include basketball courts and a gym. Their conference rooms can accommodate 30 to 40 people. Wheelchair-accessible.

CORONADO AREA   San José's northern suburb of Coronado, a traditional dairy area, has an imposing Gothic church towering over its central square. About one kilometer east of the Coronado church is the **Lone Star Grill** (open Tuesday through Saturday, 11 a.m. to 11 p.m.; Sunday, 11 a.m. to 6 p.m.; closed Monday; 229-7597, 292-1207). Homesick Texans and upscale Ticos flock to this secluded and cozy barbecue joint for fajitas, gorditas, and margaritas.

Above Coronado, **Rancho Redondo** is a beautiful place to go for a drive and a view of the Central Valley. Just follow the main road through San José's northeastern suburb of Guadalupe. Soon the houses start to thin out, and the crowded thoroughfare becomes one of Costa Rica's charming country roads, lined with the famous "living fenceposts." (The volcanic soil is so fertile that fenceposts sprout and turn into trees.) About 15 kilometers from San José, just before you reach Rancho Redondo, is a good spot to stop and look at the view.

Another nice drive involves heading out the same Guadalupe road, but taking the left fork at Ipís, about six kilometers from San José, arriving in about two kilometers at San Isidro de Coronado. From there, follow signs seven kilometers east to Las Nubes, misty mountains full of dairy cattle and strawberry plantations, where you'll find **Cronopios** (open Wednesday through Friday evenings; Saturday, noon to 11 p.m.; Sunday, noon to 6 p.m.; 229-6283, 229-0517), a cozy gathering place that serves moderately priced soups, salads, mini-pizzas, apple pie, and cocktails. It has a fireplace and a good collection of Latin American and North American music.

CARTAGO AND VOLCÁN IRAZÚ

Though **Cartago** was the birthplace of Costa Rican culture and the capital for 300 years, many of its historic buildings were destroyed in the earthquakes of 1823 and 1910. The 1910 quake prevented the completion of a cathedral in the center of town. The **ruins** of that church have been made into a pleasant garden. On August 2 every year, thousands of Costa Ricans walk from San José to Cartago in honor of *La Negrita*, the Virgin of Los Angeles, who appeared to a peasant girl in 1635. She has become Costa Rica's patron saint, and her shrine is surrounded by offerings from grateful pilgrims whom she has miraculously cured. Tiny metal arms, legs, hearts, and other charms decorate the walls inside **La Basílica de Nuestra Señora de Los Angeles**, an imposing structure on the east side of town.

GETTING THERE: Buses to Cartago leave often from Calle 5, Avenidas 18/20 (233-5350) in San José. It's a half-hour trip and the bus lets you off in the middle of bustling downtown. Walk east to the ruins and the Basílica. By car, just follow Avenida Central east of San José through the suburbs of San Pedro and Curridabat. That will put you onto the Autopista Florencio del Castillo (50 cents toll), part of the Interamerican Highway, which leads to Cartago.

PARQUE NACIONAL VOLCÁN IRAZÚ   Volcán Irazú (open daily, 8 a.m. to 3:30 p.m.; admission $6) is 32 kilometers north of Cartago. On a clear morning, the trip up its slope is full of breathtaking views of farmland, native oak forests, and the Central Valley below. The craters are bleak and majestic. On March 19, 1963, the day John F. Kennedy arrived in Costa Rica on a presidential visit, Irazú erupted, showering black ash over the Central Valley for the next two years. People carried umbrellas to keep the ash out of their hair, roofs caved in from the weight of piled-up ash, and everything was black. Since then the volcano has been dormant, but there were a few tremors in 1991. Gases and steam are emitted from fumaroles near the sulfurous lake that recently formed in the crater. It is said that you can see both the Atlantic and the Pacific from Irazú's chilly 3432-meter (11,260-foot) summit. This is true on occasion, but often the Atlantic side is obscured by clouds. You can get plenty of exercise there, hiking along the rim of the crater from the *mirador*. Irazú is at high altitude, so you might experience fatigue and lightheadedness.

As you get toward the top of Irazú, you'll see some magical old oak trees covered with lichen and bromeliads. The mossy pastureland there is a good place for a picnic. If you want to try to catch the view of both oceans, you must go early. Bring warm clothes and rain gear. There are clean restrooms at the top and a restaurant and souvenir shop offering soup, *tamales*, and gourmet coffees. Rain ponchos are available for rent.

On the way to or from the volcano in the town of Cot, be sure and stop at **Restaurant 1910** (open daily, noon to 10 p.m.; phone/fax: 536-6063). Their plentiful and varied buffet includes delicious salads and excellent Costa Rican and international entrées (about $10 including dessert). You can eat indoors or out. Be sure to see the historical photographs on the walls—1910 was the year of the earthquake that destroyed Cartago. Highly recommended.

The **Soda Típica Irazú** (open 8 a.m. to 6 p.m.; closed Monday; 224-6854, 530-0996) is a campesino-owned restaurant in San Juan de Chicua, farther up toward the volcano. They serve country specialties like *olla de carne* and *tamal asado* made in a clay oven, and have a souvenir shop and a great view.

Another good place to go for a day hike is **Area Recreativa Jiménez Oreamuno** (also known as Parque Prusia), a reforestation project started after the 1963 eruption. It's about halfway up the west side of the volcano, eight kilometers west of Tierra Blanca, near Prusia. The hike to the forest is very beautiful, through steep hills covered with oak and pine. Once there, you'll find trails and picnic tables. To get there, take Route 8 to Tierra Blanca and ask for directions from there.

GETTING THERE: By Bus: Buses to Irazú (551-9795, 272-0651; $4 round-trip) leave Saturday, Sunday, and holidays at 8 a.m. from Avenida 2 across from the Gran Hotel Costa Rica. You can also catch this bus at the Cartago ruins at 8:30. The bus leaves Irazú at 12:15 p.m., arriving in San José at 2 p.m. Other days you have to drive or take a tour.

By Car: Take the Interamerican Highway east to the Taras Intersection, two kilometers before the entrance to Cartago. There's a nondescript three-pronged monument there. Go left instead of turning right toward Cartago, then take the first left (there's no sign). The road signs after that are pretty good. Stay on the main road, veering left at the large statue of Christ. A taxi from San José should cost about $40 for one to four people. A taxi from Cartago costs about $20.

OROSI VALLEY

By car, you can take a day trip from San José through one of Costa Rica's most precious jewels, the Orosi Valley, south of Cartago. In just a few

Above: The once prosperous port of Puntarenas has the closest beaches to San José, 80 miles away, and its funky charm can still be found at the local market.

Below: The church of San Blas in Nicoya reflects the colonial influence of the Spanish conquistadores.

Left: Rincón de la Vieja National Park in northern Guanacaste has several hiking trails that lead to mud pools, hot springs, and other thermal activity.

Below: Playa Hermosa is one of Guanacaste's liveliest beaches, with small beachfront hotels. Various watersports are available and it's a great place to watch the sunset.

hours you can visit an amazing variety of sites, all surrounded by peaceful pastoral landscape. There are innumerable stops you can make, according to your interests, and the trip can be as quick as an hour or as long as a couple of days. Following is a description of a circular route from Cartago.

Two blocks after the Basílica in Cartago, make a right, then a left onto the main road that leads to Paraíso.

Six kilometers after Cartago, you will pass the turnoff on the right for **Lankester Gardens** (open daily, 9 a.m. to 3:30 p.m.; 552-3247; admission $4), which display the hundreds of varieties of orchids and bromeliads for which Costa Rica is famous. The labyrinthine gardens are run by the biology department of the University of Costa Rica. Orchids are abloom all year, but the best show is between February and May. They also have a butterfly garden. Recommended.

Next you'll come to the town of **Paraíso**, which is about seven kilometers from Cartago. Drive through town until you see the park, where you turn right. Continue straight down this street, which becomes a narrow country road. Before descending into the valley, you will pass two small lodges. The German-owned **Linda Vista** (shared bath, hot water; $30-$40, including breakfast; 574-5497, fax: 574-5534) is down a road to the right. It has an enclosed porch with a good view, and is a nice place for a family to stay. There is also a separate house with its own kitchen ($70-$80; children under 10 free). A bit farther down the hill is **Sanchiri Lodge** (private bath, hot water; $30-$40, including breakfast; phone/fax: 533-3210; www.cicr. or.cr/afiliados/sanchiri, e-mail: sanchiri@racsa.co.cr), a row of rustic wooden cabins on a hillside, each with a balcony and great view. A wooded glen has hiking trails. The family that runs the lodge has been on the land for five generations. There is a restaurant (open daily, 7 a.m. to 8 p.m.) with reasonably priced *comida típica*. Recommended.

Continue on to the **Mirador de Orosi**, a well-tended public park and picnic ground with another great view. It's easy to miss the entrance on the right after Paraíso, but the place is definitely worth a stop. An intimidating flight of steps goes uphill at the entrance, but you can take a path to the left, circle around by the *mirador*, and end up at the top without losing your breath.

Once you get to the floor of the valley, you will soon arrive at the town of **Orosi**. It has a colonial **church** whose beautiful wooden altar and shrines were carved with a special grace. This is one of the few churches in Costa Rica that has survived enough earthquakes to preserve its original atmosphere. A small museum of colonial religious history, **Museo Franciscano** (open daily, 9 a.m. to 5 p.m.; admission 75 cents, 25 cents for children) is next door.

There are two thermal swimming pools/recreation areas in town: **Balneario Termal Orosi** (open daily, 7:30 a.m. to 4 p.m.; admission $1.25), southwest of town, and **Los Patios** (open Tuesday through Sunday, 8 a.m. to 4 p.m.; 533-3009; admission $1.50), two and a half kilometers beyond Orosi. The pools are lukewarm, reputed to be medicinal, and full of kids and their families. Both have picnic areas and restaurants, and Balneario Termal Orosi has a basketball court and soccer fields. This is a worthwhile stop if you have young children. Weekdays are more tranquil here.

Near the Balneario Termal Orosi is **Montaña Linda** (shared bath, heated water, shared kitchen; $6/person; camping, $2.50/person; kitchen for guests, $1; meals, $2-$4; 533-3640, fax: 533-2153). This friendly backpackers' hostel offers a variety of services: laundry, bike and horse rentals, weddings, and an inexpensive language school with an emphasis on conversation. A five-day intensive course costs $99, including a dormitory room and two meals a day. A homestay is $5 extra per night. They will take you up to Irazú and other points of interest for $10, starting at 4 a.m. Staying here gives you a chance to be part of the life of this lovely little town. To get there, ask to be let off the Orosi bus at Super Anita Numero Dos, the local supermarket, then walk back half a block to Bar La Primavera. Turn left at the bar and go two and a half blocks.

The locally owned **Cabinas Media Libra** (private bath, hot water, TV; $30-$40; 533-3838, fax: 533-3737) are clean and loaded with amenities. The second-floor rooms look up to hills covered with a patchwork of coffee and bananas. The cabinas are 200 meters past the plaza and 25 meters to the right.

The **Orosi Lodge** (private bath, hot water, ceiling fan, refrigerator, TV; $30-$40; phone/fax: 533-3578; http://sites.netscape.net/timeveit), next to the Balneario Martinez on the east side of town, has verandas with stunning views of the Irazú and Turrialba volcanoes.

Five hundred meters north of the church, at the entrance to town, is **Las Torrejas** (private bath, heated water, fans; $30-$40, including breakfast; 533-3534), also a friendly place to stay.

As you no doubt will notice, Orosi is a fertile coffee-growing region. When we drove this circuit in January, we passed groups of young coffee pickers strolling home after a day in the fields. Costa Rican coffee farmers use the labor of kids on vacation from school and housewives getting some fresh air. Coffee fields are hot and full of stinging bugs, but coffee picking is also an opportunity to stray from daily routine, spend time with friends and neighbors, and bring in some supplemental cash. The pickers we saw after their day's work looked refreshed and jubilant.

TAPANTÍ NATIONAL PARK After you pass the coffee plant, you can take a right and drive ten kilometers over gravel roads (about 30 minutes) to Tapantí National Park (771-3155, 551-2970; admission $6). Make sure you bear left at the church after the electric plant; there's no sign. Tapantí protects the rivers that supply San José with water and electricity. It's a great place for birdwatching (black-faced solitaires, hawks, guans, to name a few) and river swimming. There are three trails, one a short trek to the Río Grande, another to a swimming hole, and another a two-kilometer circuit.

Tapanti has just been incorporated into Costa Rica's 26th National Park, which bears the unwieldy name of Tapantí–Macizo de la Muerte. By connecting tiny Tapantí to the 52,000-hectare Río Macho forest reserve, the new park extends to Chirripó National Park, which then connects to Parque International La Amistad, making a total of 75,696 protected hectares. This is an important step toward the goal of forming a Mesoamerican biological corridor so that species can migrate between Mexico and South America without interruption. Environmentalists are worried about proposed legislation that would open Costa Rica's national parks to hydroelectric dams, including three proposed projects in the new park. Keep abreast of the situation at www.preserveplanet.org.

The nearby **Kiri Lodge** (private bath, heated water; $30-$40, including breakfast; 551-3746, fax: 591-2839) has trout ponds, picnic huts, and a restaurant that specializes in trout. The family-run lodge has its own reserve. Since hiking and birdwatching are best early in the morning, it's a convenient place to spend the night. If you are traveling without a car, it's a pleasant (albeit long) hike, or you can hire a jeep-taxi in Orosi ($6 one way).

One kilometer from the Río Macho, the road to Tapantí passes the entrance to **Monte Sky** (by reservation only; 232-0884, 228-9892; admission $8, including tour), a private reserve whose Costa Rican owner considers it a spiritual retreat. Visitors are greeted by guides who present them with walking sticks and accompany them on hikes. The reserve stretches over 562 mountainous hectares; 80 percent is primary forest. Groups may stay in a renovated farmhouse (shared bath, cold water; $30-$40/person, including meals) that is rustic but peaceful, about half a kilometer uphill from the parking lot. There are also camping platforms in the forest. Taxis from Orosi will charge $5-$6 each way to Monte Sky. The road is passable with any type of vehicle, but those with low ground clearance should drive slowly to avoid rocks.

Also on the way to Tapantí is the two-kilometer entrance road to **Purisil Trout Farm** (open daily, 6 a.m.to 6 p.m.), pools teeming with huge rainbow trout surrounded by lush rainforest. You can fish for trout ($7/kilo), grill it right there and eat it at a picnic table with a gorgeous view. A 20-minute walk along a trail beyond the ponds leads to a waterfall.

Back on the main circuit, as soon as you cross the Río Grande de Orosi on a narrow suspension bridge, you will see a driveway to the left for the **Motel Río Palomo** (private bath, heated water, some with kitchen, pools; $20–$30; 533-3128, phone/fax: 533-3057), which has a huge, tour group–size restaurant (open daily, 8:30 a.m. to 5 p.m.), and has traditionally been the place for a fresh-fish lunch.

As you circle **Cachí Lake**, you'll see the entrance to **La Casona del Cafetal** (open daily, 11 a.m. to 6 p.m.; 533-3280) on the left. This open-air restaurant has a creative menu featuring trout, crêpes, and a wide range of coffee specialties made with coffee grown on the farm. They have a break-fast buffet on Sunday morning, after which you can take a refreshing stroll on lakeside trails. Near the restaurant you can see the work of self-taught woodcarver José Luís Sojo, whose massive creations are made from wood he has salvaged from the rivers or otherwise found. Each one of his pieces has a story and a message. Definitely worth seeing.

Several kilometers later, continuing around the Cachí Reservoir, you'll see the **Casa del Soñador** on your right. This whimsical, sculpture-filled house built by the late sculptor Macedonio Quesada is also worth a stop. His sons, Hermes and Miguel, fashion melancholy campesino and religious figures out of gnarled coffee roots. Some are for sale at moderate prices. Hermes can take you to see local petroglyphs.

Soon after is the **Cachí Dam** and the left-hand turnoff for **Ujarrás**, a small agricultural town in a peaceful setting, home to the ruins of Costa Rica's oldest church, **Nuestra Señora de la Limpía**. **Valle Viejo** (open 11 a.m. to 11 p.m.; closed Tuesday; 574-7576) is a friendly bar/restaurant on the main road, where we had a small, delicious, freshly caught fish for about $1.50. The *bocas* that are served with beer in the Cartago area are more like small meals than snacks. You pay for them, but they are very inexpensive and quite filling. Valle Viejo has live music on weekends.

GETTING THERE: By Bus: If you cannot rent a car, you can take either an Orosi bus (leaves every hour; 551-6810) from two blocks south of the southwest side of the church ruins in Cartago (Calle 6, Avenida 1), or a Cachí bus (leaves at 5:30 a.m., 6:15 a.m., 8:40 a.m., 11:15 a.m., and 1:30 p.m., returning from the town of Cachí at 3 p.m., 5 p.m., and 6 p.m.; 551-0644) one block east of the south-west corner of the ruins and half a block south. The Orosi bus passes Linda Vista and Mirador Sanchiri, and goes through Orosi (but get off at the park in Orosi if you want to hire a taxi for Tapantí). The Cachí bus will drop you off at the entrance to Ujarrás. Reliable *taxistas* in Orosi are Luis Arce (533-3343) and Carlos Mora (533-3862).

TURRIALBA AREA

Turrialba is becoming known worldwide as the perfect winter training ground for kayakers and whitewater rafters. The town, which used to be the main stopping place on the old San José–Limón road, suffered an economic depression with the opening of the Guápiles Highway, which bypasses the area completely. Now, however, it is a haven for international whitewater fans who rent houses there or stay with local families. Young Turrialbans are becoming interested in kayaking, and although many of them come from humble homes, some can buy used equipment from the foreign athletes who train there. Many local rafting companies have sprouted up, offering an even greater variety of trips than the companies in San José. **Loco's Tropical Tours** (556-6035; www.whiteh2o.com, e-mail: riolocos@racsa.co.cr) has been recommended by readers, as has **Rios Aventuras** (556-9617, in the U.S: 888-434-0776; www.costaricarios.com, e-mail: rmclain@racsa.co.cr), which offers canoe and kayak instruction as well as certification. **Aventuras Naturales** (225-3939, fax: 253-6934; www. toenjoynature.com) guides you on a Class III/IV trip to their **Pacuare Jungle Lodge**, which features individual bungalows nestled in the rainforest with a gourmet restaurant on the Pacuare river. You can only reach it by raft—there are no roads.

Don't be disappointed if your river rafting company calls off your trip because it has been raining. Sometimes *cabezas de agua* can develop when water becomes dammed behind fallen trees upriver and then releases with life-threatening power. Prudent companies will call off their trips when they see a potential for these conditions.

Halfway between Orosi and Turrialba, in El Duan de Tucurrique, Mike and Sally Swanson's **Kayak Costa Rica** (cell phone: 380-8934; members. aol.com/swanldmkc/kayak-costa-rica, e-mail: swanldmkc@aol.com) has three private cabins in its 300-acre reserve. They have an air-conditioned van, and like to plan trips for families, active adults, and seniors that include kayak instruction, hiking, biking, camping, and horseback-riding ($800-$1100/week, including meals).

Definitely off the beaten track, Turrialba has a life of its own beyond tourism, and its residents are open and friendly to visitors. The area offers many possibilities for an interesting day or weekend trip.

If it's hot, you might want to take a dip at **Balneario Las Américas** (admission 75 cents), two large pools for kids and adults that have a bar-restaurant. You'll see signs for it on the main road, a few blocks toward town from Restaurant Kingston.

Turrialba is the home of **CATIE** (Centro Agronómico Tropical de Investigación y Enseñanza; 556-6431, 556-0755, fax: 556-7948; e-mail: post master@catie.ac.cr). Established in the 1940s, it is one of the five major tropical research centers in the world. Its extensive library houses Latin America's largest collection of English-language literature on agriculture and natural resources.

CATIE's facilities include greenhouses, orchards, forest plantings, experimental agricultural projects, a dairy, an herbarium, seed conservation chambers, and housing for students and teachers. Seeds of fruit and nut trees, tropical forest species suitable for lumber, ornament, erosion control, shade, and pulpwood are available by writing CATIE, Turrialba, Costa Rica. CATIE publishes several bulletins in Spanish and a monthly newsletter in English.

Birders will find the purple-crested gallinet and other rare waterfowl around the lagoon at CATIE. There is a trail from behind the administration building to the Río Reventazón for more birdwatching. Call in advance (556-0568; e-mail: ssalazar@racsa.co.cr) to arrange an inexpensive two- to three-hour tour, which includes visits to their coffee and cacao plantations, and a chance to chew on a *coca* leaf. By car, drive toward La Suiza and Siquirres, four kilometers from Turrialba. A taxi charges about $2, and La Suiza buses leave hourly from the main terminal in Turrialba.

Parque Viborana (open daily; atención Apdo. 28-7150; cell phone: 381-4781, fax: 556-0427; admission $4), a 20-minute drive from downtown Turrialba in the village of Pavones, is one of the country's model wildlife rehabilitation and educational centers. Owner Minor Camacho worked in the venom extraction laboratories of the University of Costa Rica for over two decades before moving back to this area; he knows as much as anyone in the country about snakes. He is a man with a mission: to teach people about snake behavior so that they can avoid being bitten and thus avoid killing snakes. For instance, we learned that snakes are likely to be out the day after several days of heavy rains, because they want to dry out in the sun (see snake section in chapter 2). Exhibits here include well-designed terrariums for Costa Rica's most dangerous serpents and a large walk-in cage for nonvenomous boa constrictors. Don Minor has planted his small farm with flowers and trees that attract birds, and many species that had disappeared from the sugarcane- and macadamia-monopolized landscape are beginning to come back to his land. Recommended.

LODGING   The **Hotel Wagelia** (private bath, hot water, phone, some with table fans, others with air conditioning, TV, refrigerator; $50-$60; 556-1566, fax: 556-1596; e-mail: wcotom@racsa.co.cr), at the entrance to Turrialba, 150 meters west of the central park downtown, has clean, small rooms and a restaurant that offers an elegant menu with reasonable prices. Just outside of town in a more suburban setting is **Hotel Geliwa** (private bath, heated water, ceiling fans, pool, conference center; $40-$50 including breakfast; 556-1142, fax: 556-1029; e-mail: wcotom@racsa.co.cr).

Wittingham Hotel (shared and private bath, heated water, wall fans, TV; $7-$12; long-term discounts; 556-8822, 556-0013), on the main street through town, is friendly and accommodating to backpackers and has two stories of respectable though dark rooms. **Hotel Turrialba** (private bath, heated water, ceiling fans; $12-$20; phone/fax: 556-6654), 25 meters west of the Turrialba service station offers small neat rooms above the Digrasa supermarket.

Located on a curve in the Reventazón river, **Casa Turire** (private bath, balcony, cable TV, phone, pool; no children under 12; $140-$260; 531-1111, fax: 531-1075; www.hotelcasaturire.com, e-mail: turire@racsa.co.cr) is a unique plantation-style hotel. The elegant lodge is surrounded by thousands of acres of working fields in which coffee, macadamia nuts, and sugarcane are the main products. Here you'll find a pool, conference center, tennis court, and riding horses. The hotel also offers local tours. It is 15 minutes southeast of Turrialba.

Catering to birders, naturalists, and photographers, **Rancho Naturalista** (private and shared bath, hot water, good mattresses; $125/person, including meals, transportation, and tours; four-night minimum; 267-7138, 531-1516, in the U.S.: 800-593-3305; www.ranchonaturalista.com, e-mail: info@ranchonaturalista.com) sits high in the hills above Tuís, east of Turrialba. There are nature trails through their private virgin rainforest reserve, the habitat of four species of toucans, the snow-capped hummingbird, and many other bird and butterfly species. The comfortable lodge overlooks the wide valley. The restaurant's creative cookery is a special attraction. A week's stay is $750. Families can be accommodated. The same people own Tárcol Lodge at the mouth of the Tárcoles River (see Chapter Eleven), and packages can be designed to include some days there, as well.

RESTAURANTS   **Pasteleria Merayo**, near the bus station, is a good place to pick up a picnic lunch. **Soda Burbujas**, next to the Church, is famous for plentiful, low-cost meals. It's where the river runners go to stoke up for an active day. After your adventure, **Betico Mata's** has great *bocas* and beer, and **La Garza** is known for huge *casados* and good service. Just outside Turrialba is **Restaurant Kingston**, whose Limonese chef/owner has made it famous.

The charming and folkloric **Turrialtico** (open daily, 7 a.m. to 10 p.m.; 556-1111) is high on a hill about eight kilometers east of town. The spacious open-air dining room has a magnificent view of the valley. Native food is the specialty. Above the restaurant are comfortable rooms (private bath, heated water, playground equipment; $30-$40) with the same great view.

GETTING THERE: By Bus: Buses leave San José for Turrialba from Calle 13, Avenidas 6/8 (223-4464, 556-0073, 556-0148; $1.25). The trip takes an hour and a half.

By Car: The traditional route is through Cartago and Paraíso, then winding through sugarcane fields into Turrialba, about one and a half hours total from San José. There is also a delightful, paved back road that starts slightly south of the town of Cot on the slopes of Volcán Irazú, skirts Volcán Turrialba, and passes through the towns of Pacayas and Santa Cruz before arriving in Turrialba itself. This route takes less than two hours from San José.

GUAYABO NATIONAL MONUMENT

Guayabo National Monument (open daily, 8 a.m. to 3:30 p.m.; admission $6), on the slopes of Volcán Turrialba, is considered the most significant archaeological site in Costa Rica. It offers a glimpse into the harmony between people and nature that existed in pre-Columbian times. Birds abound in the ruins, which are set in premontane rainforest and dotted with the guava trees that give the town its name. *Oropéndolas* (related to North American orioles) hang their sacklike nests from tree branches. Water sings its song in ancient aqueducts.

Archaeologists have excavated only the central part of a 10,000-inhabitant city that existed from 1000 B.C. to about 1400 A.D. The exposed area is composed of circular mounds, which were the floors of large buildings raised to keep them dry; paved sidewalks, some of whose stones are decorated with petroglyphs; a large stone carved with stylistic representations of two Indian gods: the jaguar, god of the forest, and the crocodile, god of the river; a system of covered and uncovered aqueducts which still functions well; and the oldest bridge in Costa Rica, a flat rock, now broken in several places, which crosses one of the aqueducts. Several roads radiate from the center of the town. Spot excavations verify that some of them extend at least eight kilometers. It's theorized that the most important people—the chief, his family, and priests—lived in the center of town, and that common people lived outside.

There are many mysteries about the civilization that inhabited Guayabo. No one knows why the people left (just before the *conquistadores* discovered Costa Rica), nor why Spanish explorers never found or never kept records of finding the site. Yet the peace and beauty that reign in Guayabo echo a wise and gentle people.

From the *mirador*, you can see green grassy mounds and stone sidewalks nestled within the rainforest. Hawks and vultures swoop and sail in front of the striking four-layered backdrop of mountains. Across the road from the site, behind the campground, a steep trail leads down to the fast-flowing Guayabo River, where you can sit bathing

Oropéndolas

your feet and looking for birds. You can also walk up the road past coffee and sugarcane fields for views of the green Guayabo valley.

Park personnel orient visitors when they arrive, then give them a pamphlet to do a self-guided tour. Camping is allowed. Bring rain gear.

GETTING THERE: By Bus: From Turrialba, two buses a day (11 a.m. and 5 p.m., Monday through Saturday) leave the main bus terminal for Guayabo. They return at 5:30 a.m. and 12:50 p.m. On Sunday, the bus leaves Turrialba at 9 a.m. and returns at 4 p.m., so locals can spend the day up at the Monument.

By Car: From Turrialba follow the signs off the main highway through downtown, crossing the river on the old steel bridge. Stay on the main road till you see the sign indicating a left to the Park. It's a 19-kilometer trip and takes about 40 minutes. The road is paved except for the last four kilometers.

From San José you can choose to take the above-described back road from San José to Turrialba, via Pacayas and Santa Cruz. There's a short cut to Guayabo National Monument. Watch for a steep left down a gravel road a few kilometers after Santa Cruz at the Pulpería Arca de Noe. Drive approximately six kilometers on this road, then take a right. From here it's only four kilometers to Guayabo. If you want to drive back to San José this way, drive through the park till you reach a T intersection, make a left, then drive till you reach the paved road, where you make a right.

La Posada de la Luna, west of the church in Cervantes, halfway between Turrialba and Cartago, serves *comida típica* and delicious homemade desserts. Diners are surrounded by cases full of antique memorabilia: Spanish swords, pre-Columbian artifacts, Japanese *netsuke*—you name it, they've got it.

Volcán Turrialba Lodge ($90-$100, including all meals and tours; phone/fax: 273-4335; www.volcanturrialbalodge.com, e-mail: volturri@racsa.co.cr) is near the top of the Turrialba volcano; their special feature is horseback rides to the top. Access is only via four-wheel drive; they provide transportation from San José.

EL CAMINO DE LOS SANTOS

El Camino de los Santos is a mountainous region southwest of San José covered with well-groomed coffee farms. You can take a pleasant circular route by car, stopping for snacks and lunch, and, especially if you have children, at one of the two *balnearios* (pools) along the way.

You probably will want to start by heading toward Cartago on the *autopista*, then up the Interamerican Highway toward San Isidro. The turnoff for Santa Maria de Dota is at El Empalme, 29 kilometers from Cartago. Stop to buy the tart apples and hard balls of sharp, white *palmito* cheese produced here. Or warm up with a cup of *agua dulce* and a hot *tortilla de queso*.

Continue down the road on the right to **Santa María de Dota** (11 kilometers). In the plaza, there is a small monument to those who lost their lives in the 1948 Civil War. There's not too much more to do right in the town, but if you do stay, eat at **Las Tejas** (open Friday and Saturday, 6 p.m. to 10 p.m.; Sunday, noon to 11 p.m.), 200 meters east of the church. We stayed at the **Hotel Dota** (private bath, heated water, restaurant and bar downstairs; $7-$12; 541-1026), which we found to be just above acceptable—but it's the only full-time hotel in town.

COPEY   For hikes through narrow mountain valleys and native oak forests, following rushing rivers and mesmerizing waterfalls, spend at least a day in **Copey**, seven kilometers uphill from Santa María. Its brisk climate at 7000 feet above sea level is refreshing, especially if you're feeling worn out from the lowland heat. Treat yourself to a trout lunch at William Rodríguez's *soda* and buy crisp, local apples for dessert. The old wooden **church** in Copey is a national monument.

You can visit Don Fernando Elizondo's well-developed **trout farm** and buy his tinned trout. He doesn't allow fishing in his sluices, but there are several private lakes in the area where you can rent a pole and pull out a few.

Most places charge $5-$7 per kilo for what you catch. One of the most developed is **El Sosiego**, two and a half kilometers above Copey in Río Blanco.

◐ **El Toucanet** (private bath, hot water; children under 10 free; $50-$60, including breakfast; 541-1435; orbitcostarica.com/toucanet, e-mail: toucanet@orbitcostarica.com) is the only lodge in Copey, with cabins and a restaurant overlooking a peaceful forest and a rushing mountain stream. Owners Edna and Gary Roberts also rent out a more private two-bedroom cabin (private bath, hot water, kitchen; $40-$50, including breakfast) nearby. They can connect you with horse rentals.

A bit beyond El Toucanet, Urs and Isabel, a Swiss-French couple, offer horseback and hiking tours at **Finca Pelota de Roble** (541-1299). They will take you around the region, or even as far as Londres, near Quepos and Manuel Antonio—a two- or three-day camping trip. They also rent a rustic cabin that sleeps four (gas hot water, no electricity, woodstove; $12-$20, including breakfast; long-term rental possible) on the edge of the cloud forest. Great for birders. You must have four-wheel drive to get there. If you don't they will pick you up in Copey or Santa María.

Back to the drive along Camino de los Santos: From Santa María head west to San Marcos. At San Marcos, turn right toward San Pablo León Cortés. From here you should follow your map and ask directions when you get to intersections. The winding road dips into valleys and follows mountain crests through fertile farmland that hasn't suffered the same erosion (and as a consequence poverty and depopulation) other similar areas have, so you are really seeing Costa Rican rural life at its best.

When you come to Tarbaca, make a right to drop back into San José. You'll pass what seems like dozens of *miradores*, where *Joséfinos* come weekends and evenings to gobble down *chicharrones* and enjoy the view of the Central Valley. The first one you come to, after Tabarca, is one of the most popular. **Ram Luna**, on the left, is the most elegant and expensive. They have a special buffet on Wednesday night for about $20.

GETTING THERE: By Bus: You can catch the bus to Santa María from San José (Calle 21, Avenida 16 bis; 223-1002; $1.80) at 6 a.m., 9 a.m., 12:30 p.m., 3 p.m., and 5 p.m. Buses return to San José from the main square in Santa María six times a day. The trip takes about two hours.

Copey has its own bus service now, leaving from Santa María de Dota at 7:15, 9, and 11:30 a.m., and 12:30, 3, 5, and 7:30 p.m., returning at 4:30, 5:30, 7:15, and 9:15 a.m., 12:30 and 5 p.m. weekdays; on weekends buses leave at 8:30 a.m. and 5:15 p.m., returning at 8 a.m. and 3:30 p.m. You might want to confirm this unusual schedule at 541-1449.

To get to Copey without going through Santa María, take a San Isidro bus (Calle 16, Avenidas 1/3) to Cañón del Guarco, kilometer 58 on the Interamerican Highway. (You'll see the little yellow markers on the side of the road that tell you how many kilometers you are from San José.) From Cañón it's seven kilometers downhill on a dirt road to Copey. Santa María is another seven kilometers downhill. You can either walk or hitchhike. It's customary in that region for drivers to offer rides to people on the road. If you drive up from Santa María, make sure you have a four-wheel drive, or at least a powerful engine and a high clearance.

Buses to San Ignacio de Acosta from San José leave hourly (Calle 8, Avenida 12) and pass by all the *miradores*.

By Car: Head east of San José on the Interamerican Highway and drive toward San Isidro (not Cartago). At Empalme turn right toward Santa María, or continue to kilometer 58 and turn right to go directly to Copey. It takes about one hour to one and a half hours.

EIGHT

The Atlantic Coast

A trip to the Atlantic coast in Limón Province offers a chance to enjoy this area's wild beauty and the distinct culture that characterizes it. Much of the region is a jungle-covered lowland, which is skirted by a coastline dotted with beautiful white- and black-sand beaches. Limón is the least-populated province in Costa Rica, and its slow-moving way of life makes it a good place to visit for people who want to avoid touristy atmospheres. The Talamanca area, south of Limón, is best if you want to relax and sunbathe or snorkel, although, sometimes it is inundated by surfers. Naturalists will enjoy Tortuguero to the north, and anglers will gravitate to the lodges at Barra del Colorado, near the Nicaraguan border.

Limón Province is unique in its mix of ethnic groups. Afro-Caribbean peoples migrated to the Atlantic coast in the 19th century to fish, work on the railroad, and farm cacao and coconut, and they now comprise roughly a third of the province's population. A variety of English dialects are spoken here, including an elegant Jamaican English and the patois spoken by blacks. "What happen" (pronounced "whoppen") is the common greeting. Instead of saying *"adiós"* when they pass each other, people say "all right" or "okay." For a fascinating history of the region, read Paula Palmer's *What Happen*, in which elders of the black community tell their life stories (see "Recommended Reading" in Chapter Thirteen).

A relatively large population of indigenous Bribris and Cabécars inhabits the rainforests of Talamanca. They try to maintain their traditional lifestyle in harmony with nature. Limón also has many Chinese residents whose relatives immigrated in the 19th and early 20th centuries.

Note: Because the water system is not reliable, we recommend that while you're visiting the Atlantic coast area, you *avoid drinking tap water* (or any

213

water not bottled or boiled), fresh juice made with water or ice, and raw fruits and vegetables that cannot be peeled. We always bring a large plastic bottle of San José water on our trips. You might want to bring your own fruits and vegetables, too (previously washed, of course), because it gets a bit expensive to eat three meals a day on the coast.

PUERTO LIMÓN

Limón is Costa Rica's Atlantic port, in transition from funky seaport to gateway to some of the country's most beautiful beaches. The streets are full of people, bicycles, dogs, and the occasional vulture. Stevedores load containers of bananas and pineapples onto huge freighters at Moín, a few kilometers to the north. Moín is where independent boatmen dock for trips up the canals to Tortuguero.

The main attraction in Limón proper is the annual carnival that coincides with *El Día de la Raza*, renamed by the Ticos "El Día de las Culturas" to honor all of Costa Rica's heritages, on October 12. Brightly costumed *Limonenses* parade to the rhythm of drums, tambourines, pots and pans, maracas, and whistles. You're part of the parade too, drawn in by the irresistible Afro-Caribbean beat. The drinking, dancing, and carousing last several days. Make sure you reserve a hotel room in advance.

Another annual event, the February surfing championship takes place on **Playa Bonita** (known for its reef-beach break) just north of Limón. Surfers also like **Playa Portete**, just north of Bonita—it has the Caribbean's best right point. Both of these beaches are very dangerous for swimmers.

La Antillita has been recommended to us for its excellent lunches and dinners. Sometimes they have live Caribbean music.

You can stay just as cheaply in the more beautiful areas down the coast, so try not to get stuck in Limón for the night. If you do, **Parque Vargas** is pleasant, with its huge palms, and you can take a refreshing walk along the sea wall. Be careful in Limón after dark. Mugging is a danger. We were even stopped once by a uniformed person who seemed to be trying to trump up something about our identification in order to get a bribe. We played dumb and walked away. If you do stay in Limón, here is a rundown of several downtown hotels. All directions are from the central market, half a block north and one block west of the San José–Limón bus terminal.

LODGING   Three relatively nice hotels are located within a few blocks of the *mercado*. Across from the northwest corner of the *mercado* is the plain but very clean second-story **Hotel Teté** (private bath, hot water, ceiling fans or air conditioning; $20-$30; 758-1122, fax: 758-0707). Across from the

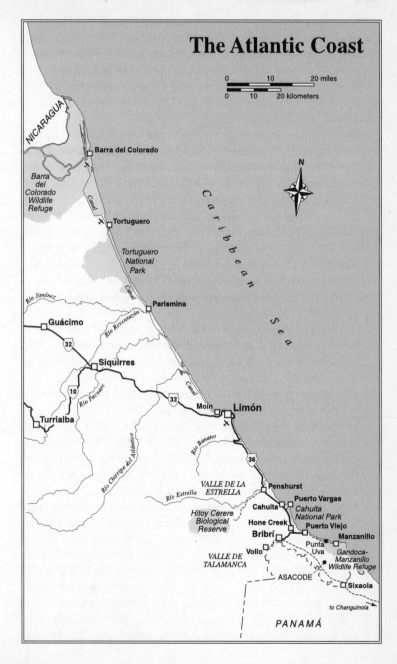

The Atlantic Coast

0   10   20 miles
0   10   20 kilometers

NICARAGUA

Barra del Colorado

Barra del Colorado Wildlife Refuge

Canal

Tortuguero

Tortuguero National Park

Caribbean Sea

N

Río Jiménez

Canal

Parismina

Guácimo

Río Reventazón

32

Siquirres

10

Río Pacuare

32

Moín

Limón

Turrialba

Río Banano

Río Chirripó del Atlántico

36

VALLE DE LA ESTRELLA

Penshurst

Río Estrella

Puerto Vargas

Cahuita

Cahuita National Park

Hitoy Cerere Biological Reserve

Hone Creek

Puerto Viejo

Bribrí

Manzanillo

Vollo

Punta Uva

Gandoca-Manzanillo Wildlife Refuge

VALLE DE TALAMANCA

ASACODE

Sixaola

to Changuinola

PANAMÁ

northeast corner of the *mercado* is the **Hotel Acón** (private bath, hot water, air conditioning, TV, phone; $30-$40; 758-1010, fax: 758-2924), a bit unfriendly, but with a restaurant and a big disco on the second floor. If you can get a room facing the sea, you will find the aging **Park Hotel** (private bath, wall fans, air conditioning, hot water, cable TV, phone; $40-$50; 758-3476, fax: 758-4364) very pleasant. It's located 250 meters east of the *mercado* and a block north of Parque Vargas.

Two mid-range hotels, both in generic buildings with partitioned-off, clean rooms, are the **Continental** (798-0532) and the **Internacional** (798-0545), with identical amenities (private bath, hot water; ceiling fans, $7-$12; air conditioning, $12-$20). They are two blocks north of the northeast corner of the market. Secure overnight parking is available.

Side by side are two inexpensive hotels in charming two-story 19th-century buildings: The **Cariari** (shared bath, cold water, wall fans; $7-$12; 758-1395) is filled with plants and some of the rooms have their own balconies. The **Palace** (cold water, fans; private bath, $12-$20; shared bath, $7-$12; 758-0419) has some very small, windowless rooms along endless labyrinthine hallways, but some others open onto the common verandah. Both are one block east of the *mercado*.

You might prefer to stay at one of the comfortable hotels north of Limón on the road to Moín, a short ride from downtown. From the *mercado*, drive straight north till you reach a T intersection, then turn right and follow the road that winds along the coast several kilometers to Moín, finally intersecting with the main highway back to San José. Buses leave frequently from the Radio Casino bus stop, a block north of the *mercado*.

The first hotel along this road is the **Hotel Maribú Caribe** (private bath, hot water, air conditioning, phone; $40-$50; 758-4010, 758-4543, fax: 758-3541). Its white, circular, thatch-roofed cabinas are perched on the only cliff in the area, and the complex resembles a tribal fort. The cabinas and pool are spotless, the restaurant overpriced. The hotel offers tours.

About a kilometer away, without the ocean view but in a luxuriant jungle setting crossed by several trails, is the **Hotel Matama** (private bath, hot water, air conditioning, phone; $60-$70, including breakfast; 758-1123, fax: 758-4499; e-mail: protected_forest@hotmail.com). The rooms are clean and tastefully decorated, but there is no cross-ventilation so you have to use the air conditioning. Tours are available, and the restaurant here offers Caribbean specialties on weekends. Across the street is the smaller-scale **Cocorí** (758-2930, fax: 798-1670) with rooms (private bath, hot water, ceiling fans; $30-$40) and apartments (private bath, heated water, table fans, kitchens;

$50-$60), as well as a breezy open-air restaurant. Both of these establishments are close to Playa Bonita—quite dangerous for swimmers but popular with surfers. **Quimbambu**, a restaurant on Playa Bonita, serves up good Afro-Caribbean specialties. The setting is nice and breezy enough that you might not mind the inflated prices.

Close to Moín is **Hotel Moín Caribe** (private bath, hot or heated water, ceiling fans, TV; $12-$20; phone/fax: 758-1112), with a restaurant downstairs and rooms above, a good choice for budget travelers coming from or going to Tortuguero via Moín, which is a short walk downhill.

GETTING THERE: By Bus: In San José, the buses for Limón (221-2596; $3) leave hourly from the Terminal Caribe at the north end of Calle Central. Buy tickets in advance for a weekend or holiday trip. To get to the area north of Limón, on the road to Moín, take the Moín or Villa del Mar bus near Radio Casino in Limón.

By Car: Driving to the Atlantic coast is fairly easy and enjoyable, unless you get behind a long line of trucks heading for the port. It takes about two and a half hours from San José. The first part of the drive is through the mountains of Braulio Carrillo National Park. It's hard to believe that when it's raining cats and dogs in San José, it can be clear and hot on the other side of those mountains. It's true, though, especially in September and October, usually the heaviest months of the rainy season. Try to go early in the day to avoid fog and rain. And if it has been raining a lot, ask around about landslides in Braulio Carrillo before you set out. If you want to break up your drive with a hike, stop at the park headquarters, 1.8 kilometers after the tollbooth. They will give you directions and current information. However, do not stop or leave your car anywhere else (thieves are common along the highway in the park). The second half of the drive is through the Atlantic lowlands, past towns with names like Cairo, Boston, and Liverpool. If you are driving to the area north of Limón, you can avoid Limón altogether. Before you get to Limón, take the Moín exit that goes diagonally to the left from the main highway. The road signs marking the exit are confusingly placed, but you'll see signs advertising the hotels. Turn right just before the entrance to the port facility.

TALAMANCA REGION

We recommend going south to the Talamanca region rather than staying in Limón. When we first went to Talamanca in 1975, there was no road. We took a two-hour train ride from Limón to Penhurst on the Río Estrella, where we were met by a man in a dugout canoe who ferried us across the river to a rickety bus. Then it was another hour on a dirt road to Cahuita, a small village where horses grazed on the grassy paths between houses. That has all changed, now that there are roads. Cahuita's grassy paths have become dusty streets, and the people of Talamanca find themselves thrust uneasily into the 21st century. Independent farming and fishing are giving way to a tourism-based economy, with some related drug culture and theft. Cahuita used to be where the action was, but now the action seems to have moved south to Puerto Viejo, and Cahuita has reverted to its relaxed pace. The beaches are uncrowded, and the weather, in June, September, and October especially, can be beautiful in contrast to the afternoon rains in the rest of Costa Rica.

At the Pacific beaches, the local culture takes second place to a tourist milieu created by highland Ticos and foreigners of all nationalities. Talamanca, however, is still terra incognita for most Ticos, so local culture remains intact. In 1975 a law was passed prohibiting construction within 50 meters of the shore. Then the point below Cahuita was declared a national park. The area south of Puerto Viejo has been made into a wildlife refuge. For these reasons, the beaches and coral reefs retain their pristine beauty.

In 1999 the Costa Rican government granted a U.S. oil company exploration and exploitation rights for 20 years in the ocean and mountains of this gorgeous area. Currently they are conducting seismic probes using some of the loudest manmade sounds in the ocean. These blasts can be detected 100 kilometers from the detonation site. Studies have shown that even slight deafness can hurt dolphins and whales, who depend on echo-location faculties for survival. Residents are also worried about future oil leaks and contamination during hurricane season to one of the country's most beautiful coral reefs. You can sign a petition against this oil exploration at www.puertoviejo.net.

Life on the Atlantic coast is definitely laid back. Because of this, it is a great place to relax. There are a few places that offer air conditioning and hot water, but service everywhere is generally very slow. When going to a restaurant, bring along some snacks to eat while you're waiting, or dance with your waiter or waitress.

Both Cahuita and Puerto Viejo now attract artisans and nouveau hippies, who occupy their own quarter of the beach and offer Guatemalan fashions and Bo Derek–style braiding services. To find them, follow your nose to the patchouli. Single women should know that they could become targets for hopeful *gringa*-chasers, who see them as possible trust funds or at least a good time for a weekend. Most of these guys are gentlemanly enough to accept a flat "no." Also, if you look slightly bohemian you might be offered coke or crack, which are taking their toll on the local youth. Be aware that there are lots of narco-police on duty. Many tourists have gotten into trouble for their naivete. One last warning: It is generally not a good idea to walk alone at night in solitary areas.

Despite these problems, we still love the Talamanca region and are hopeful that the people of this area can preserve their unique character in the face of change.

CAHUITA AND CAHUITA NATIONAL PARK

The town of **Cahuita** is a 45-minute drive or a one-hour bus ride down the coast from Limón. "Downtown" is a dusty intersection with a bus stop, noisy bars, and a small park with statues of the founding fathers, with Rasta-run restaurants sprinkled nearby. Two blocks south takes you to the entrance of Cahuita National Park. The first 400 meters of this beach can be dangerous to swim in. The currents can be very strong and unpredictable. When we were there in November 1999, the sea was as placid as a bathtub and many bathers were enjoying the water. Three blocks north of the bus stop is the Guardia Rural office and the beginning of the road to Black Beach.

CAHUITA NATIONAL PARK   Cahuita National Park is the primary reason that Cahuita has become the tourist destination it is. The park was established to protect the coral reef that extends 500 meters out from Cahuita Point. This spectacular underwater garden is home to 123 species of tropical fish, as well as crabs, lobsters, shrimp, sea anemones, sponges, black and red sea urchins, and sea cucumbers. Try not to touch the coral while you explore its nooks and crannies. Dissatisfied with the way the park was being administered in the early nineties, the citizens of Cahuita decided to administer the park themselves. Only a donation is asked at the park entrance in Cahuita, but the usual $6 park entrance fee is required at the Puerto Vargas entrance to the south.

To reach the reef, simply take a shady, scenic hike down the nature trail that starts from the entrance to the national park. It runs between the beach and the jungle, and is a good place to see wildlife. Tanagers, iguanas, sloths, and white-faced and howler monkeys are common along the trails. The freshwater rivers and estuaries are good places to spot caimans and herons. It's four kilometers by trail from the park entrance to the point and another three kilometers to the Puerto Vargas area of the park, where the campgrounds are. We don't recommend camping in the park.

Roberto Tour (755-0092), at the corner of the entrance road and the main street, has been recommended for snorkeling and dolphin-watching tours. **Cahuita Tours** (755-0232, phone/fax: 755-0082) can take you to the reef in a boat that has a glass window in the bottom. The trip takes an entire morning. (If it has been raining and the water is cloudy, it's not worth going out.) They can take you to Tortuguero or the local indigenous reserves. They also rent snorkeling equipment and binoculars; lead scuba and sport-fishing expeditions; run a taxi service; change travelers checks; and provide a public telephone. They're on Cahuita's main street, half a block from the Guardia Rural. There are chip telephones near the park entrance.

LODGING AND RESTAURANTS   There are cabinas all over town. Those near the entrance to the national park are noisier than those east of the main street or in the Black Beach area. For honeymooners or neo-honeymooners away on a tropical escape, we recommend the more remote cabinas. They require a walk to get to them, but the tranquility of a deserted beach is worth it. Many of the cabinas here are mom-and-pop establishments, with families erecting a few rooms in their back yards. While not the most deluxe accommodations, they are usually clean, with friendly owners. Staying at one of these places is a good way to give direct support to a community trying to raise its standard of living while maintaining its cultural values. You are also likely to learn more about local culture than if you stayed in foreign-owned cabins. The first few places are right at the entrance to the national park:

National Park Hotel (private bath, hot water, ceiling fans; $20-$30; 755-0244, fax: 755-0024) seems to be perpetually under construction. It's a multistory cement building next to one of the most popular eateries in town, the **National Park Restaurant** (open daily, 11 a.m. to 9:30 p.m.). Across the street is the spacious, Spanish-owned **Kelly Creek Hotel** (private bath, heated water, ceiling fans, mosquito nets; $30-$40; 755-0007; e-mail: kellycr@racsa. co.cr), built on filled-in wetlands. Their restaurant features Spanish cuisine.

The **Sol y Mar Restaurant** across the road offers hearty breakfasts and local specialties, and also has spacious, clean cabinas (private bath, heated water, table fans; $12-$20; 755-0237). The upstairs rooms have balconies with views. Recommended. They are owned by the family of Walter "Mr. Gavitt" Ferguson, Cahuita's famous calypso composer, whose songs often contain humorous commentary on the issues of the day. If you run into Mr. Gavitt at the restaurant, you might be able to buy one of his tapes.

Down the small road that cuts inland from Sol y Mar, **Cabinas Rhode Island** (private bath, cold water, table fans; $7-$12; 755-0264) has basic but clean cabinas, a good bargain for budget travelers. Behind them, at **Cabinas**

Atlantic Surf (private bath, cold water, ceiling fans; $12-$20; 755-0086), you'll find a two-story building with wood-paneled rooms and private balconies. Follow a trail to the left, bearing left, to the Austrian-owned **Alby Lodge** (private bath, cold water, mosquito nets, table fans; $30-$40; phone/fax: 755-0031), a collection of thatch-roofed A-frames with porches dotting a grassy meadow. There are lots of nice details here that will make your stay more comfortable, like mosquito coils and broom and dustpan provided in each room. It's a very peaceful place. Bring a flashlight. Recommended.

El Típico has fresh coral crabs. Make sure you ask them how much the seafood costs. The price on the menu is for the smallest size. Our large crab, though delicious, was almost twice as expensive ($7.50) as the menu price. **Roberto's**, on the main street at the entrance to town, is a good place for fresh fish. **100% Natural**, just down the street, has been recommended by locals. A few blocks down the main street, across from the Salón Comunal, the welcoming, candle-lit **ChaChaCha Restaurant** features huge servings of sea-

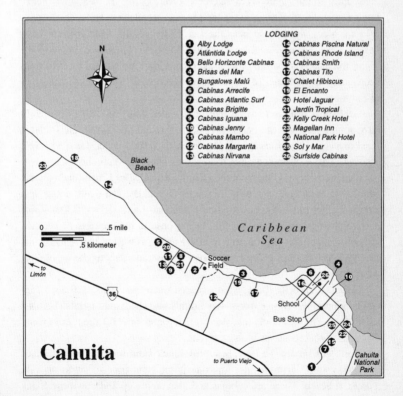

LODGING	
❶ Alby Lodge	⓮ Cabinas Piscina Natural
❷ Atlántida Lodge	⓯ Cabinas Rhode Island
❸ Bello Horizonte Cabinas	⓰ Cabinas Smith
❹ Brisas del Mar	⓱ Cabinas Tito
❺ Bungalows Malú	⓲ Chalet Hibiscus
❻ Cabinas Arrecife	⓳ El Encanto
❼ Cabinas Atlantic Surf	⓴ Hotel Jaguar
❽ Cabinas Brigitte	㉑ Jardín Tropical
❾ Cabinas Iguana	㉒ Kelly Creek Hotel
❿ Cabinas Jenny	㉓ Magellan Inn
⓫ Cabinas Mambo	㉔ National Park Hotel
⓬ Cabinas Margarita	㉕ Sol y Mar
⓭ Cabinas Nirvana	㉖ Surfside Cabinas

Black Beach

Caribbean Sea

0 .5 mile
0 .5 kilometer

Soccer Field

to Limón

36

School

Bus Stop

Cahuita

to Puerto Viejo

Cahuita National Park

food and pasta cooked with French-Canadian *savoir faire*. Try their Black Magic Woman dessert, made with chocolate chip ice cream, coffee liqueur, and cinnamon. Open for dinner only, closed Tuesday. Recommended.

Speaking of good food, don't miss the French cuisine at **Restaurant Piedmont** (open 6 a.m. to 8 p.m., 381-1076; www.greencoast.com) in Penhurst, a few kilometers north of Cahuita. Situated on the orchid farm of French botanist Pierre Dubois, the restaurant features fresh salads, soup, and seafood *cordon bleu* prepared by Pierre and his wife Judith. They will be glad to show you around their **Orchid Garden** ($5), where they are trying to save native orchid species by rescuing them from deforested areas and planting them in the wild. To get there, drive a few kilometers north of Cahuita and turn inland at Rancho Bonito (if you pass the Penhurst school and church, you've gone too far). Continue inland 500 meters, following the signs.

Back in Cahuita, another fun-loving French-Canadian place is **Cabinas Jenny** (private bath, heated water, ceiling fans, mosquito nets; $20-$30; 755-0256; e-mail: jennys@racsa.co.cr). Overlooking the sea, this breezy two-story building with good mattresses is a nice place to stay.

One block north, also near the sea, is **Brisas del Mar** (private bath, heated or cold water, wall fans; $20-$30; 755-0011). The clean, simple rooms are in the back yard of an older local couple, and are shaded by fruit trees found only in this area of Costa Rica, which have hammocks strung between them.

Surfside Cabinas (private bath, hot water, fans; $12-$20; 755-0246) have some rooms on the beach ($20-$30). Around the corner, the friendly, local owners of **Cabinas Smith** (private bath, heated water, fans; $12-$20; 755-0068) offer clean and quiet rooms, with small front porches.

One block to the right from the Guardia Rural, **Miss Edith** (open all day Monday to Saturday; open only for supper on Sunday, 755-0248) cooks up a storm, ladling out tasty, down-home Caribbean food—jerk chicken, spicy curry, fish soup with coconut milk. In response to the requests of her customers, she includes vegetarian fare in her menu, as well as native medicinal teas such as bay rum, *guanabana* leaves, *sorosi*, and lemongrass—good for what ails you.

Cabinas Arrecife (private bath, heated water, wall fans; $20-$30; 755-0081), around the corner from Miss Edith's, are shady and quiet. There's a small *soda*. The owner claims you can fish for snapper off the reef in front. Bikes and snorkels are available for rent.

North of Cahuita is a long, beautiful, **black-sand beach**. The water laps the grassy shore at high tide; low tide is the right time to swim or walk along the beach. There are cabinas and restaurants up and down the Black

Beach road. If you stay at the lodgings that are farther along the road, you should either enjoy walking, rent a bike, or have a car. What they lack in proximity to town, they gain in tranquility. Remember that it's not advised to walk along this road at night.

As you leave Cahuita and walk north on the Black Beach road, the first sign is for **Cabinas Tito** (private bath, cold water, table fans; $20-$30; 755-0286). These are very clean little houses with porches run by friendly owners. The road can be muddy; check before driving in.

El Encanto (private bath, hot water, ceiling fans; $40-$50; phone/fax: 755-0113) is a comfortable bed and breakfast run by a friendly couple from North America. Rooms have large windows and natural wood ceilings. The management can connect you with reef tours and fishing trips.

Located across the street, **Bello Horizonte** sells homemade cakes and natural fruit drinks. Behind the store are the **Bello Horizonte Cabinas**, where Leti Grant rents Caribbean-style wooden houses (private bath, heated water, ceiling fans, some kitchens; $20-$30; 755-0206) as well as rooms (shared bath, cold water; $7-$12). Ask for her in the Tienda. Her brother's family runs **The Pastry Shop**, on the left after the Tienda. They bake cinnamon rolls, cakes, and breads, and sell coffee, takeout only. Try the lemon bake.

The road that intersects 100 meters later will take you to the main highway. At the intersection is the Swiss-owned **El Cactus** (open from 4 p.m.; closed Monday), which specializes in pizza and pastas, and has been recommended by many visitors. Fifty meters to the right are the **Cabinas Margarita** (private bath, cold water, ceiling fans; $20-$30; 755-0205). These are quiet and basic, and are very clean.

On the north side of the soccer field is the **Atlántida Lodge** (private bath, heated water, ceiling fans, screens, pool; $60-$70; 755-0115, fax: 755-0213; e-mail: atlantis@racsa.co.cr). The lodge has well-kept grounds, though the rooms are nothing special. (This overpriced hotel is all over the internet, making it seem like it the only lodging in Cahuita. The internet can be misleading sometimes.)

At the next corner, one and a half kilometers from the bus stop, are **Restaurante Chao**, famous for soup and Caribbean cuisine, and the **Reggae Bar**. Here a road will take you inland to several European-owned places: **Restaurant and Cabinas Brigitte** (private bath, cold water, fans; $20-$30; 755-0053), cute little rooms and a popular restaurant (open 7 a.m. to noon, breakfast only.) Horse and bike rentals are also available.

Across the street are the **Cabinas Mambo** (private bath, heated water, fans, mosquito nets; $20-$30, a bit more for use of kitchen). Italian-owned

Cabinas Nirvana (with shared bath, cold water, $7-$12; with private bath, heated water, table fan, $20-$30; house for four, $40-$50; phone/fax: 755-0110) has attractive wood rooms with hammocks on their wide porches.

On this same road is **Cabinas Iguana**, our favorite place in Cahuita. There are natural wood rooms with porches (shared bath, heated water, mosquito nets, pool; $12-$20; private bath, refrigerator, $30-$40; 755-0005, fax: 755-0054; e-mail: iguanas@racsa.co.cr), and two houses (private bath, heated water, ceiling fans, mosquito nets, kitchens; one bedroom, $40-$50; three bedrooms, $50-$60). A clean swimming pool is in a secluded setting at the back of the property. The helpful Swiss owner runs a multilingual book exchange in the office; he will pick you up at the bus stop. They also offer kayak tours down the Sixaola river. Recommended. Next door is **Jardín Tropical** (heated water, no fans, kitchen; $20-$30; phone/fax: 755-0033), a couple of clean, quiet thatch-roofed cabinas with lots of windows. The owner also rents a house for $250-$600 per month.

Back down the main road is **Hotel Jaguar** (private bath, hot water, ceiling fans; $50-$70, including breakfast; phone/fax: 755-0238), the largest hotel in Cahuita. The rooms are spacious, but not much attention has been put into decor or landscaping. There are trails through the natural areas, and an international restaurant. Overpriced.

Bungalows Malú (heated water, ceiling fans, refrigerators; $30-$40; phone/fax: 755-0006) are artistically designed cabinas that incorporate driftwood and stone into the furniture and have porches with overhangs and benches. The owner is an Italian artist whose paintings also decorate the rooms. Her mama serves up Italian home-cooking in their open-air restaurant during the high season.

The locally owned **Cabinas Piscina Natural** (private bath, cold water, table fans; $12-$20; no phone) are named for a sandy-bottomed saltwater pool set in the coral outcrops on the grounds. It looks like a safe place for kids to cavort, and is a lovely, calm place to swim. The owner sells cold drinks, and there are picnic tables by the sea.

From here on, the establishments are farther apart.

The Swiss-owned **Chalet Hibiscus** (private bath, hot water, wall fans, pool, some with kitchens; $50-$100; 755-0021, fax: 755-0015; e-mail: hibis cus@racsa.co.cr) offers one- and two-bedroom bungalows with ocean views.

The most elegant option in Cahuita is the **Magellan Inn** (private bath, hot water, ceiling fans, pool; $70-$80; phone/fax: 755-0035). The carpeted rooms are quiet, the Canadian hosts are attentive, and the garden setting is serene. A path leads from the inn to the well-known **La Casa Creole**. Delicious French Creole and seafood dishes are served for dinner at this candlelit restaurant.

Ten kilometers north of Cahuita is the bird-filled **Estrella River delta**, with narrow waterways similar to those near Tortuguero. This area is a flyway for migratory birds—314 species have been counted. Luis and Judy Arroyo, proprietors of a comfortable bed and breakfast here, have worked hard to protect what is now a private wildlife sanctuary encompassing the delta. ❂ **Aviarios del Caribe Lodge** (private bath, hot water, table fans, laundry service; $70-$110; shared bunkbed rooms, $17/person, including breakfast; phone/fax: 382-1335; e-mail: aviarios@costarica.net) has large rooms downstairs and a screened-in library/dining room upstairs for relaxing between your canoe expeditions along the waterways. Even if you don't stay here, take the canal tour (6 a.m. or 2 p.m.) for $30. The morning tour includes breakfast. They are also an official rehabilitation center for injured or orphaned sloths. It costs $5 to visit the rescue center, where you can meet some of the inmates and see a film about these slow, sweet creatures. Recommended.

GETTING THERE: By Bus: Two of the MEPE buses to Sixaola (Sixaola Terminal, north end of Calle Central; 236-1220, 257-8129) will drop you off right in Cahuita (10 a.m., 4:30 p.m.; $5). The 6 a.m. (special price $7) and 1:30 p.m. buses will drop you off on the highway, a ten-minute walk from "downtown" Cahuita. Either way, the ride takes three to four hours. Buses return to San José at 7 a.m., 9 a.m., 11:15 a.m., and 4 p.m.

From the bus terminal 100 meters north of the *mercado* in Limón (754-1572), buses leave for Cahuita (90 cents) at 5 a.m., 8 a.m., 10 a.m., 1 p.m., and 4 p.m.

If you are staying at one of the hotels on Black Beach, you can get off at the first or second entrance to Cahuita and walk from there (not recommended at night). The first two entrances take you several hundred meters to the Black Beach road, and the last leads half a kilometer to the center of town.

There are several buses each day from Cahuita to Puerto Viejo and the beaches south of there. Schedules are posted in hotels and at Cahuita Tours.

Fantasy Tours (220-2126; www.fantasy.co.cr/fantasy_bus) has air-conditioned buses that leave San José daily at 8 a.m. for Puerto Viejo ($19). They will drop you off at the entrance to Cahuita.

By Car: From Limón it's pretty much a straight shot down the coast. Turn south at the first intersection as you arrive in Limón; there's a Texaco plant at the intersection. It's 45 minutes from there to Cahuita. Close to Cahuita the road is riddled with potholes, so drive carefully. Cahuita is about half a kilometer off the main highway; the first two marked entrances take you to the Black Beach area and the last takes you to the center of town.

HITOY CERERE BIOLOGICAL RESERVE **Hitoy Cerere Biological Reserve** (reservations: 283-8004) is definitely off the beaten track and has hardly been developed for visitors. Trails are overgrown and unmarked. But for hardy explorers, there are beautiful views, clear streams, waterfalls, and lots of birds to see. Day visits only. Researchers wishing to stay can make arrangements by calling. You have to take a Valle de la Estrella bus from Limón to get to Hitoy Cerere, which winds its way into the banana plantations. Get off at Finca Seis, the end of the line. Jeep-taxis there will take you ten kilometers farther for around $4 and leave you at the entrance. They will return to pick you up at an agreed-upon time and can take you back to Cahuita if you want (one and a half hours, $30). Samasati Nature Retreat (below) arranges tours to Hitoy Cerere.

SAMASATI NATURE RETREAT **Samasati** (private bath; $60-$70/person, including meals; 224-1870, 800-563-9643, fax: 224-5032; www.samasati. com, e-mail: samasati@samasati.com) is a private 250-acre rainforest reserve in the hills between Cahuita and Puerto Viejo. The intelligent, lively owners have created calming Japanese-style bungalows with a sleek Italian flair, where you can swing in a hammock on the porch and gaze out over acres of forest to the blue Caribbean. Rooms in the guest house (shared bath; $40-$50/person, including meals) do not have the views, but are cozy. There are also four fully furnished houses. Everyone shares the view and the congenial atmosphere at the open-air restaurant where delicious vegetarian meals are served buffet-style. An energetic movement meditation to music gets your juices flowing in the morning, and yoga classes and bodywork will soothe you after a day on the nature trails. They offer a ten-day eco-adventure that includes snorkeling, hiking to waterfall pools, river kayaking, and watching dolphins. This magical place is located ten kilometers south of Cahuita, then 800 meters inland on a gravel road, then uphill about ten minutes (four-wheel drive needed—they will meet you below if you don't have a car). Highly recommended.

PUERTO VIEJO

Puerto Viejo is 19 kilometers south of Cahuita, on paved road. A boom in tourism has taken place in the last few years and a plethora of restaurants and discos have opened in town; new hotels have sprung up along the road south to Manzanillo. Fortunately the development is low density, leaving most of the forest standing. The pristine beaches are some of the most beautiful in the country.

Costa Rican public attention turned to this area when Ana Cristina Rossi's compelling novel *La Loca de Gandoca*, about her struggles to brake tourism development in the Gandoca–Manzanillo Wildlife Refuge, came out in 1993. Look for it in San José bookstores.

Puerto Viejo on the web: Almost all our favorite places in this area have websites on **www.greencoast.com**, which promotes "responsible and organic tourism." You can also get quite a bit of information at **www.puerto viejo.net**.

Culture: The Puerto Viejo area is home to at least three different cultures: the English-speaking black farmers who grew cacao and coconut until a blight in the early 1980s ruined the cacao harvest, the indigenous people of the Bribri and Cabécar tribes who live in the foothills, and the Spanish-speaking immigrants who came to the area in search of land. Because the Talamanca region was so isolated from the rest of Costa Rica until recently, many of its cultural traditions are still alive.

Miss Sam takes piping hot journey cakes out of the oven around 6 every night but Sunday; get there on time because a line forms and locals and keyed-in tourists snap them up quick. Also check out the small bakery run by Mr. Patt.

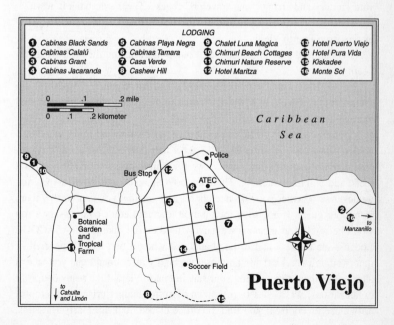

LODGING

❶ Cabinas Black Sands	❺ Cabinas Playa Negra	❾ Chalet Luna Magica	⓭ Hotel Puerto Viejo
❷ Cabinas Calalú	❻ Cabinas Tamara	❿ Chimuri Beach Cottages	⓮ Hotel Pura Vida
❸ Cabinas Grant	❼ Casa Verde	⓫ Chimuri Nature Reserve	⓯ Kiskadee
❹ Cabinas Jacaranda	❽ Cashew Hill	⓬ Hotel Maritza	⓰ Monte Sol

Caribbean Sea

Police
Bus Stop
ATEC
Botanical Garden and Tropical Farm
Soccer Field
N
to Manzanillo
to Cahuita and Limón

Puerto Viejo

Miss Dolly makes bread with coconut milk, which is good with her home-made guava jam. You can buy ginger biscuits, pineapple rolls, plantain tarts, *patí* and *pan bon* from local women such as Ivette, Doña Cora, and Miss Daisy. To locate these bakers, ask any resident. Doña Guillermina cooks family-style in her home.

Services: To learn more about the area, plan to stop by the office of the **Talamancan Ecotourism and Conservation Association** (ATEC) (phone/fax: 750-0188, 750-0191; e-mail: atecmail@racsa.co.cr), across from Soda Tamara in "downtown" Puerto Viejo. They put out two excellent publications: *Costal Talamanca: A Cultural and Ecological Guide* ($2.50), which describes the cultural heritage of the zone and provides visitor information and maps; and *Taking Care of Sibö's Gifts* ($7), in which the people of the Kekoldi reserve explain their way of life and their commitment to conserving nature. It also has a bird list of the area. ATEC is the local communications center, with a public phone and fax machine, e-mail service, and post office. They also have a spring water dispenser where you can fill your water bottles! It's usually open 7 a.m. to noon and 2 p.m. to 9 p.m., with some variations on weekends. There is also a public phone at Manuel León's *pulpería*.

ATEC and Manuel León's will change dollars for you. The Girasol will do your laundry and change your travelers' checks. There's no bank in town.

There is a **medical clinic and doctor** at the Hone Creek *cruce,* five kilometers from Puerto Viejo.

You can find announcements of 12-step meetings on the ATEC bulletin board.

Bull (750-0112), Delroy (750-0132), and Mr. Spence (750-0008) are the main taxi drivers in town. Bull usually meets the bus in his gray and maroon Trooper.

Organic tourism: ATEC will put together customized tours with local guides based on your interests ($15 for a half day, $25 for a full day) including early-morning bird walks, two-hour night hikes, snorkeling at coral reefs, and dolphin-watching. There are both Spanish- and English-speaking guides. Ask whether you will need boots and whether you can borrow them from your guide. If not, look for a pair at Manuel León's commissary. (You won't be sorry. The sneakers we naively used on our hike to the ASACODE Lodge—see below—had to be abandoned when a two-inch-thick shell of mud wouldn't crack off.) In any case, we highly recommend that you take at least one of these tours during your stay in Puerto Viejo. Like many nonprofit organizations, ATEC has been known to suffer budget crises and temporarily close its doors. If you find the office closed, look for Harry Hawkins, who specializes in medicinal herbs and Afro-Caribbean culture, or Martín Hernandez, who leads wildlife walks and ocean diving tours in Punta Uva. Tino Grenald of Manzanillo is the expert on the Gandoca-Manzanillo refuge, and Alex Paez takes people to the Kekoldi Indigenous Reserve and the iguana farm.

ATEC will also lead you on a 7- to 10-day transcontinental hike through unmarked traditional trails in the Talamanca mountains of Amistad International Park, or to the indigenous village of Yorkín. See www.greencoast.com for details. Don't attempt to do these hikes without a guide. Two independent hikers died in these mountains in 1999.

Talamanca Learning Adventures (www.greencoast.com) offers the natural and human community of Talamanca for hands-on learning about forest management, ecotourism, turtle protection, iguana farming and problems such as logging, banana plantations, coral reef degradation, and marine resources depletion. Contact Mauricio Salazar (750-0119) or Mel Baker (750-0052) for more information.

Along the stretch of beach before you get to town is the entrance to the **Botanical Garden and Tropical Farm** (open Friday through Monday, 10 a.m. to 4 p.m.; 750-0046; $2.50, $8 with guided tour; www.greencoast.com), where black pepper, tropical fruits, and spectacular flowering plants are grown. Colorful frogs live among the bromeliads. You can learn about chocolate production, sample fruits from all over the world, take a walk on a rainforest loop trail to a small waterfall with a pool, or climb 60 feet up in a strong *chilamate* tree to an observation platform. Wear sturdy shoes for the two-and-a-half-hour tour. To get there, walk 500 meters inland from the sign on the beach road, then bear to your right, following the signs.

Water sports: The area outside the reef in Puerto Viejo has become famous in surfing lore as **La Salsa Brava**. The waves are world-class from December to April. Another season opens up in June and July. During the high season, surfers on their way out often sell their boards to new arrivals. This avoids the tremendous hassle of taking surfboards on the bus. Some surfers hire a taxi or truck to haul their gear from Limón ($25-$30). This is cheaper than renting a car in San José, and most of the good waves are an easy walk from Puerto Viejo. La Salsa Brava is definitely not for neophytes. We have heard that at least one surfboard per day breaks on the reef.

In June, September, and October the sea is calmer and better for snorkeling and swimming. Nonsurfers will be able to enjoy Puerto Viejo a lot more in those months. Everything is less crowded, and the weather is generally beautiful.

Sea kayaking and snorkeling rentals are available from **Aquamor**, in Manzanillo. They also run inexpensive scuba diving tours and give a PADI certification course (391-3417; www.greencoast.com, e-mail: aquamor@ racsa.co.cr).

Horses and bikes: Other activities you can do on your own in the area include walking the beach trail between Puerto Viejo and Manzanillo, or renting a bike to pedal the flat, coastal road between these two towns. Being on a bicycle, even if you have rented a car, seems like the best method of locomotion in the area. Driving is no fun on the pothole-scarred road, and a bike can provide just enough breeze to keep you cool. El Parquecito and Tabú near the bus stop rent bikes, but you have to get there early. To rent horses, ask around for Don Antonio or Jesus.

Note for drivers and bicyclists: Do as the locals do and get off your bike to cross the small bridges along the beach road. It's very easy to lose your balance on the sandy concrete surface, and there are no railings to keep you from falling into the rocky river below. If you are driving, do so slowly: the bridges are unmarked and you can be on them before you know it.

Insects: Just to be on the safe side, we recommend that you invest in some mosquito coils (about $1 at the local *pulpería*) or bring mosquito nets (available in San José from La Gloria, a department store located at Avenida Central, Calles 4/6). Whether you will be bothered or not depends on the climatic conditions and the location and design of your hotel. Many hotels now offer mosquito nets. Check when you make reservations. If there are mosquitos, they will only bother you at night. Worse than mosquitos are no-see-ums in the sand, which bite your ankles around dusk. And watch out for mean biting ants in the grass.

LET ATEC DO IT

If you have trouble contacting the place where you want to stay in Puerto Viejo, call ATEC (750-0188, 750-0191, e-mail: atecmail@ racsa.co.cr) and ask them for the number or to transmit a message. Remember, do not go to this area without reservations during Christmas or Easter, and try not to go on weekends in the high season. In fact, Puerto Viejo is becoming too much of a scene—it's best to avoid it during the holidays.

Water: Make sure you have bottled water in your hotel to brush your teeth with and drink at night. Many hotels supply drinking water for guests. Make sure the bottle is filled before you settle in.

RESTAURANTS If you want a taste of the culture, try rice and beans cooked with coconut or jerk chicken at the popular, inexpensive **Soda Tamara** in the center of town. Tamara sometimes sells little rounds of unsweetened cacao—just the thing to take back to town for hot chocolate, which you can sip while you recall the misty beaches and reggae rhythms of the Talamanca coast. Stop by **Miss Sam's** front porch restaurant, two blocks inland, for her fluffy rice-and-beans served with a delicious cabbage *curtido* at rock-bottom prices. Recommended.

Several breakfast spots are across from the bus stop, next to the Sunset Reggae bar. **Café Red Stripe** was recommended by locals. Or try the homemade bread and jam at German-owned **The Place**. Or look for the Dutch-owned **El Café Rico** (open 8 a.m. to 8 p.m.), across the street from Casa Verde, where generous servings of delicious food are served all day. According to her flyer, **Veronica's Breakfast** (open daily during high season, 6 a.m. to noon, 750-0132) is "prepared out of her kitchen with love, only the way a mother can do it." You'll find her humble dining room a block inland from Stanford's. She also rents a small, funky cabin with a cooking area ($7-$12).

The Garden (5:30 p.m. to 9:30 p.m.; open during high season only; 750-0069) is another outstanding restaurant. It specializes in Asian, Caribbean, and Creole cuisines featuring vegetarian dishes and seafood. All breads and desserts are homemade. It is near the soccer field.

Hotel Puerto Viejo's **Piraña Restaurant** (open 6 p.m. to 9 p.m. Wednesday through Sunday, and for breakfast on weekends, 9 a.m. to noon) has a terrific reputation for California-style burritos. The mural at the entrance is worth seeing, too.

Stanford's Restaurant El Caribe is famous for fresh seafood, although it is often overcooked. Their disco is jumping Thursday through Sunday. **La Salsa Brava**, just beyond Stanford's, serves seafood with a Spanish touch.

Travelers craving Italian cuisine will have no problem satisfying their taste buds in Puerto Viejo. **Amimodo**, just south of town, offers authentic pastas and Italian-style seafood, gracefully served in their lovely open-air restaurant. **Caramba**, right in town, serves calzones, sandwiches, and pizza. **Marco's Ristorante**, down the street, is a popular music bar featuring rock, blues, and jazz and tasty Italian food.

Probably the most elegant and unique place in Puerto Viejo is **Celeste** (open 6 to 10 p.m.; closed Monday) run by French-Belgian chefs. Their menu includes cassoulet, *boeuf bourguignon*, Tunisian couscous, Bombay curry, and mousse or crêpes with ice cream and hot homemade chocolate sauce for dessert. They are located on the right at the entrance to the village. Unlike most restaurants in Costa Rica, they do not include the tip in their bill, but the excellent service certainly merits recognition. Recommended.

Ask when fresh fruits and vegetables are delivered to Puerto Viejo. You can buy them from the delivery truck as it makes its rounds or at the vegetable stands near the bus stop and at the Parquecito.

LODGING The ✪ **Chimuri Nature Reserve and Organic Farm** (shared bath, cold water, mosquito nets; $20-$30; 750-0428, phone/fax: 750-0119; www.greencoast.com, e-mail: atecmail@racsa.co.cr) borders the Kekoldi reserve and has typical Bribri thatch-roofed constructions set on a hill in a cool, shady forest. Vegetarian breakfasts and dinners with produce from the gardens are served at a large, central *palenque.* Chimuri is a great place to stay for those who like simplicity: living with nature, and getting to know the Bribri way of life. This is the home of **Talamanca Learning Adventures** (see "organic tourism," above). Look for the sign about 500 meters before arriving at the beach, about a half-hour's walk north from "downtown" Puerto Viejo. To reach the cabins you must walk 200 meters uphill from the road. Recommended.

If you make a left at Pulpería Violeta instead of veering right to Puerto Viejo, you'll drive along an intensely black beach and after about 300 meters you'll come to the following three beach establishments, all of which we recommend for their simplicity, tranquility, reasonable rates, and closeness to the sea. **Chimuri Beach Cottages** (private bath, heated water, kitchens, mosquito nets; $30; $195/week; 750-0119; www.greencoast.com, e-mail: atec mail@racsa.co.cr) are simple, lovely houses with porches and hammocks. Next door is **Cabinas Black Sands** (shared bath, cold water, mosquito nets; $10/person; 750-0124; www.greencoast.com, e-mail: bsands@racsa.co.cr)—private, tranquil, and right on the beach. The Indian-style, thatch-roofed structure has three rooms and a shared kitchen. Next to that is **Chalet Luna Mágica** (750-0115; e-mail: commander@racsa.co.cr), a house for four with an ocean view and a lovely private garden in front. It rents by the week ($200-$250) or month ($500-$600).

The next cabinas are in Puerto Viejo proper. We describe them in the order you would find them as you walk or drive into town.

The road into town becomes Puerto Viejo's main street. Located on the second corner, with a locked parking lot, is the friendly **Cabinas Grant** (wheelchair-accessible, private bath, heated water, table or ceiling fans; $20-$30; 750-0292).

A block toward the coast from Cabinas Grant is the **Hotel Maritza** (private or shared bath, heated or cold water, ceiling fans, some with refrigerators; $12-$30; phone/fax: 750-0003, fax: 750-0313; www.puertoviejo.net), which used to be the only place you could stay in Puerto Viejo. Its small second-story rooms have been supplemented by newer, modern cabinas set around a parking lot.

Catering to surfers and budget travelers, the **Hotel Puerto Viejo** (shared bath, cold water, ceiling fans; $7-$12; with private bath,; $12-$20; 750-0128) is a multistory wooden building offering rooms of various sizes. The rooms on the second story are better ventilated. They also have an air-conditioned apartment with hot water for $25. This is the home of Piraña, a great Mexican restaurant.

Farther down the same street are **Cabinas Tamara** (private bath, cold water, table fans, air conditioning; $50-$60, including breakfast; 750-0148), offering clean rooms with shady, furnished porches and a secure parking lot.

Nicely furnished and decorated, the **Cabinas Jacaranda** (shared or private bath, heated or cold water, table fans, mosquito nets; $12-$30; 750-0069; www.greencoast.com) share a building with the Garden Restaurant. Recommended for budget travelers.

Hotel Pura Vida (shared or private bath, hot water, ceiling fans; $20-$30; 750-0002, 750-0296; www.puertoviejo.net), across from the soccer field, is a good value. Built by the Swiss owner himself, it is tastefully designed, with large screened windows. Each room has a sink with hot and cold water, although some baths are shared. There is a communal kitchen as well. Recommended.

The **Kiskadee** (shared bath, cold water, no fans; $4-$5/person; 750-0075) is a real jungle experience. We're lousy birders, but even we couldn't help spotting scarlet tanagers and the yellow and black kiskadee for which the lodge is named, flitting through the heliconias by the side of the trail. There are two second-story rooms—one with double beds, one with bunks—and ample communal kitchen space below. Guests are asked to conserve water by using an outhouse during the day. Be sure to bring a flashlight. To get there, go to the right at the end of the block the Garden Restaurant is on, where you'll find the soccer field. Go to the northern corner and you'll see the Kiskadee sign. It is five minutes up a path through the jungle beyond the soccer field.

Climbing five minutes up another trail at the north corner of the soccer field, you'll soon arrive at **Cashew Hill** (shared bath, heated water, ceiling fans, mosquito nets; $12-$20; 750-0256), three hilltop rooms fanned by breezes and rented out by a young North American couple. The rooms share a kitchen. The outstanding view from the top of the hill includes the famous Salsa Brava surf break. This place is quiet, friendly, and surrounded by nature. Recommended.

One of our favorite places in town is the Swiss-Tica-owned **Casa Verde** (heated water, ceiling fans, mosquito nets; with shared bath, $20-$30; with private bath, $30-$40; 750-0015, fax: 750-0047; www.greencoast.com, e-mail: cabinascasaverde@hotmail.com), recommended for its very clean and nicely decorated rooms. One small house has its own kitchen, but shares a bath ($20-$30). There is a *rancho* to relax in, or you can venture behind the cabins to see the poisonous-frog collection. Laundry service, secure parking, money exchange and a coffee shop are among the many services offered at the Casa Verde.

As you leave town, set back from the road on the right is the clean and simple **Monte Sol** (shared or private bath, cold water, ceiling fans, mosquito nets; $20-$30; phone/fax: 750-0098; www.montesol.com, e-mail: montesol@racsa.co.cr), which displays a lovely painted mural of the area. The young German owner is a hairdresser. Next door is **Cabinas Calalú** (private bath, hot water, ceiling fans, mosquito nets, some with kitchens; $20-$30; 750-0042; www.puertoviejo.net). The thatch-roofed cabins are surrounded by trees.

GETTING THERE: By Bus: MEPE (Sixaola terminal, at the north end of Calle Central; 236-1220, 257-8129) runs buses daily between San José and Puerto Viejo (10 a.m., 1:30 p.m.; $5. There is also a 4 p.m. bus that goes all the way to Manzanillo, but we don't recommend getting there late the first time you go). The ride is about four hours. Their 6 a.m. Sixaola bus ($7) will drop you at the *cruce*, six kilometers from Puerto Viejo; you will have to walk, hitch, or wait for a local bus for the rest of the trip.

A bus leaves Puerto Viejo for Manzanillo at 7 a.m. and 4 p.m.

From the Talamanca bus stop in Limón (100 meters north of the *mercado*, 754-1572), catch the Sixaola bus at 5 a.m., 8 a.m., 10 a.m., 1 p.m., or 4 p.m. ($2.35), which stops in Puerto Viejo. You can also take the Manzanillo bus (6 a.m., 2:30 p.m.; $2.85), which passes through Puerto Viejo and follows the coastal road south of Puerto Viejo through Cocles and Punta Uva. Get there early to buy a ticket. Buses return from Puerto Viejo to Limón at 6 a.m., 8:15 a.m., 1 p.m., and 4 p.m. The Manzanillo bus returns at 7:45 a.m. and 4:45 p.m., passing through Puerto Viejo about half an hour later. You can check these schedules at ATEC or www.greencoast.com.

Fantasy Tours (220-2126; www.fantasy.co.cr/fantasy_bus) has air-conditioned buses that leave San José daily at 8 a.m. for Puerto Viejo ($19). They will drop you off at your hotel.

By Car: From Limón, it is about an hour to an hour and a half (depending on road conditions) to Puerto Viejo. When you reach Hone Creek there is a *cruce*, where the road curves to the right toward Bribri and the Panama border, and the road straight ahead continues six kilometers to Puerto Viejo. *Note:* Cars and buses are often stopped by the Guardia Rural and checked for Panamanian contraband as they leave Talamanca.

BEACHES SOUTH OF PUERTO VIEJO

Lovely hotels and cabinas are scattered all along the 15-kilometer road between Puerto Viejo and Manzanillo. We list them in appearance north to south. Most of them are clustered around **Punta Cocles** (four kilometers from Puerto Viejo), **Playa Chiquita** (five kilometers from Puerto Viejo), and **Punta Uva** (seven kilometers from Puerto Viejo). Punta Uva has the best swimming and is a gorgeous beach. All of these shady beaches have strong currents, but are safe if you don't go out too far. These are the kind of places to stay if you're looking for tranquility and less contact with village (and disco) life than you would get in Puerto Viejo. Since there are *pulperías* and restaurants dotting the coast, you won't have to return to Puerto Viejo for meals. Two buses a day travel this road, and some hotels offer shuttle bus or boat service into town.

Hotel Playa Chiquita hosts the **Caribbean Music Festival**, seven weekends of concerts by Costa Rica's most lively and innovative musicians. Transportation is provided at 7 p.m. from the Parquecito in Puerto Viejo so you can make it to the lodge on time for the 7:30 concerts. You'll be able to hear Cantoamerica, Luis Angel Castro, Duo Afrocosmos with Manuel Obregon, Maria Pretiz, and other wonderful groups. Definitely worth catching if you're in the area in February and March. For more information, call Wanda Paterson (750-0408, fax: 750-0062; e-mail: wolfbiss@racsa.co.cr).

RESTAURANTS   **El Principito** (open 8 a.m. to 10 p.m., 750-0495; e-mail: antic2m@aol.com) features the artful cooking of a French professional woman who opted for the simple life at the beach. In addition to her inexpensive *platos del día,* featuring creative soups and homemade bread, she offers internet access and laundry service. You'll see the familiar figure of the Little Prince on her signs just before the Cocles school and soccer field. **El Rinconcito Peruano**, on the right after the soccer field, doesn't look like much, but locals tell us their seafood preparation is truly sophisticated. **Elena's Bar**

and Restaurant on Playa Chiquita is recommended for fish and tasty sandwiches. The atmosphere is dominated by whatever is on their satellite TV. **Selvin's**, at Punta Uva, is the place to go for authentic Caribbean cooking (including fresh lobster) in a relaxed, friendly atmosphere.

LODGING   The Italian-owned **Escape Caribeño** (private bath, heated water, ceiling fans, refrigerators; $40-$50; phone/fax: 750-0103; www.green coast.com, e-mail: escapec@racsa.co.cr), tidy cabinas with porches and hammocks set in a garden across the road from the beach, and beach cabins designed to catch the sea breezes ($50-$60).

  Casa Blanca (private bath, hot water, ceiling fans, mosquito nets; $20-$30; phone/fax: 750-0001; www.puertoviejo.net) has clean white cement-block rooms, set about 100 meters inland. There is a kitchen for guests to use. The friendly owner rents water-sports equipment, including kayaks, boogie-boards, and snorkeling gear.

  Back on the main road, still heading south, **Cariblue** (private bath, heated water, ceiling fans; $60-$90, including breakfast; with kitchen and room for seven, $150; 750-0057; www.greencoast.com, e-mail: cariblue@racsa.co.cr), owned and managed by a friendly Italian couple, is back from the road in a tranquil, park-like setting. The individual wooden bungalows are private and polished, with nice touches like hammocks on the porches and creative mosaics in the bathrooms. They have a restaurant and souvenir shop. Recommended.

  Cabinas Garibaldi (private bath, cold water, wall fans; $7-$12; 750-0101), one of the original places to stay in this area, are basic and a bit shabby, but are right across the road from the beach.

  Set in a lush five-acre garden with a pond and resident sloths, **La Costa de Papito** (private bath, heated water, ceiling fans; $40-$60; kids free; 750-0080; www.greencoast.com, e-mail: costapapito@hotmail.com) offers individual wood bungalows with good mattresses, whose porches have hammocks and chairs to relax in. Horseback, hiking, and bike and snorkel equipment rental are available. A trail behind the cabins takes you up to a scenic *mirador*. A good value. Recommended.

  With balconies overlooking the beach, the **Villas del Caribe** (private bath, hot water, ceiling fans, kitchens; $80-$90; 750-0202, fax: 750-0203; www.villascaribe.net, e-mail: info@villascaribe.net) are two-story apartments with room for two to five people. The rooms are not well-ventilated. The person we talked to said that the windows do not have screens because the management fumigates every week.

Cabinas Dasa (shared bath, cold water, boiled drinking water, table fans; $7-$12; private bath, heated water, one with a kitchen, $20-$30; two-bedroom house, $300/month, 750-0358) rent three cabinas at Playa Chiquita, just past Villas del Caribe, right on the beach, with excellent snorkeling possibilities nearby.

Aguas Claras (private bath, heated water, ceiling fans, kitchens; $40-$90; 750-0180, 750-0131) has cute gingerbread cottages of different sizes in a grassy clearing. These are some of the most charming accommodations at the beach, with open-air kitchens and living rooms built in a colorful Caribbean style. Good for families or groups. Recommended.

Next on the right is the entrance to **Hotel Punta Cocles** (private bath, hot water, ceiling fans, air conditioning, pool; restaurant; $80-$90; with kitchens, $100-$110; 750-0017, fax: 750-0336; e-mail: puntacocles@express mail.net) which, with 60 guest rooms, is the largest project in the area. The poorly ventilated bungalows have private porches facing the jungle. A nature trail identifies local flora and offers a chance to birdwatch. This is the end of the line for the Fantasy Tours bus to Puerto Viejo (see the Getting There section).

Kashá (private bath, heated water, ceiling fans, some with kitchens; $60-$70, including full breakfast; phone/fax: 750-0205) offers three spacious duplexes set back in the forest, with a pool and jacuzzi. There is a restaurant/

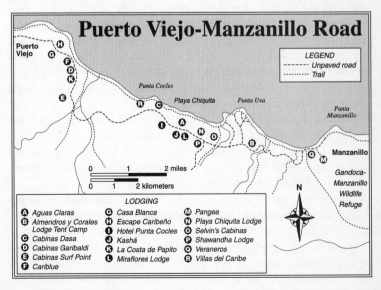

Puerto Viejo-Manzanillo Road

Puerto Viejo

Punta Cocles

Playa Chiquita

Punta Uva

Punta Manzanillo

LEGEND
- - - - - Unpaved road
.... Trail

0   1   2 miles
0   1   2 kilometers

Manzanillo

Gandoca-
Manzanillo
Wildlife
Refuge

N

LODGING

Ⓐ Aguas Claras	Ⓖ Casa Blanca	Ⓜ Pangea
Ⓑ Almendros y Corales Lodge Tent Camp	Ⓗ Escape Caribeño	Ⓝ Playa Chiquita Lodge
	Ⓘ Hotel Punta Cocles	Ⓞ Selvin's Cabinas
Ⓒ Cabinas Dasa	Ⓙ Kashá	Ⓟ Shawandha Lodge
Ⓓ Cabinas Garibaldi	Ⓚ La Costa de Papito	Ⓠ Veraneros
Ⓔ Cabinas Surf Point	Ⓛ Miraflores Lodge	Ⓡ Villas del Caribe
Ⓕ Cariblue		

bar. Daily tours to Monkey Point, Gandoca, and Manzanillo are offered in their Zodiac ($25-$45/person).

Next door is **Miraflores Lodge** (heated water, table fans; with shared or private bath, $40-$50, including breakfast; group rooms for four to ten, $8/person; phone/fax: 750-0038; www.puertoviejo.net), a tastefully decorated bed and breakfast with good mattresses and mosquito nets.

Six kilometers south of Puerto Viejo is the German/Tica-owned **Playa Chiquita Lodge** (private bath, cold or heated water, ceiling fans; $40-$50; 750-0408, fax: 750-0062; www.puertoviejo.net, e-mail: wolfbiss@sol.racsa.co.cr). The connected cabins are nicely designed and are shaded by exuberant vegetation. The lodge rents houses, snorkels, and offers boat tours to Manzanillo, and Punta Mona. Their international restaurant features herbs grown in their own garden. The secluded-seeming beach, down a path from the cabinas, has three tide pools where kids can enjoy themselves at low tide.

Across the road, the elegant, tranquil **Shawandha Lodge** (private bath, heated water, natural ventilation; $100-$110, including breakfast; 750-0018, fax: 750-0037) comprises several thatch-roofed A-frames set in the forest. Each large, half-moon bathroom is adorned with a different fanciful tile mosaic. A 200-meter path leads directly to Playa Chiquita. Their spacious, open-air restaurant features French-tropical cuisine.

About one kilometer farther down the road on the left are **Selvin's Cabinas** (shared bath, cold water, mosquito nets; $7-$12). Selvin also rents inexpensive apartments. **Selvin's restaurant** (closed Monday and Tuesday during peak season; open weekends only during the low-season) is one of the best in the area and specializes in fish and lobster dinners. They serve the local dish of rice and beans on weekends. The basic cabins are a boon for budget travelers since they are a short walk from the most beautiful part of the beach at Punta Uva. There is no phone. Recommended.

Various houses in this area are available for nightly and longer-term rental. See what is currently available on www.greencoast.com.

Two kilometers south of Selvin's, a road on the left takes you to the small community at **Punta Uva** and to some good picnic/parking spots at the beach. This is not as scenic or as swimmable as the beach near Selvin's.

GeoExpediciones has opened a unique facility, ✪ **Almendros y Corales Lodge Tent Camp** (private bath, cold water, table fans; $70-$80; 272-2024, 272-4175, fax: 272-2220), right in the middle of the Gandoca–Manzanillo Wildlife Refuge (see below). Elevated, screened-in huts, with vinyl Boy Scout tents permanently erected inside, complete with beds, cabinets, bathrooms, and a table and chairs, are scattered throughout the mostly intact jungle, connected by a boardwalk. The walkway leads to the beach. The entrance is beyond Las Palmas by a few hundred yards.

MANZANILLO

Seven kilometers beyond Punta Uva is the small fishing village of Manzanillo. The **Gandoca–Manzanillo Wildlife Refuge** protects a nine-kilometer beach where four species of turtles lay their eggs, including the giant *baula* (leatherback). The turtles' main nesting season is March through July. The refuge also includes two swamps important as wildlife habitats, a 740-acre forest, and 4000 hectares of coral reefs. The Gandoca River estuary is a nursery for tarpon, and manatees, crocodiles, and caimans are also seen there. Dolphins are often present offshore.

Get information, locate reliable guides, and donate what you can to the maintenance of this refuge at the turquoise and white gingerbread-style MINAE headquarters. Always go with a guide when you explore the jungle here.

A great new eco-tourism opportunity is now available in this area. For $13 a day (plus one-time $20 inscription fee; room and board included, minimum five-day commitment) you can be part of ANAI's effort to study and protect turtle nesting grounds in the Refuge. You live and eat with a local family, so you can practice Spanish during the day and get close to the turtles at night. For groups of ten or more, several other interesting community-based educational, sustainable development and scientific tourism options exist. Call ANAI at 224-6090, fax: 253-7524, e-mail: anaicr@racsa.co.cr. ANAI also accepts volunteers to work at its experimental farm and nature reserve south of the refuge, where plants from all over the world are tested for the possibility of crop diversification in Talamanca. This is part of an exciting community program that has gone on for more than 20 years. Serious volunteers with a background in botany or agriculture may live on the farm for free, but must provide their own food (minimum one-month commitment).

ATEC offers tours from Manzanillo to Punta Mona and Gandoca through the reserve, with **Florentino Grenald**, a local community leader with a great sense of humor. He can arrange dolphin watching, medicinal-herb walks, and bird- or insect-watching trips on foot or horseback, depending on your interests ($15 for four hours, $25 for a full day; 750-0398, 750-0191; www.green coast.com).

Aquamor (cellular: 391-3417, beeper: 225-4049; www.greencoast.com, e-mail: aquamor@racsa.co.cr) rents kayaks and snorkeling equipment, and offers inexpensive kayak tours, scuba diving and PADI certification. The owners, brothers Greg and Shawn Larkin, are the founders of the **Talamanca**

Dolphin Foundation, which works with MINAE to protect these wonderful creatures. They are trying to get the refuge extended to include the newly mapped reef and dolphin area offshore. Their love and respect for dolphins is reflected in their dolphin tour: dolphins are not chased, but allowed to approach boats out of their own curiosity. If conditions are right, you can swim with them. Aquamor has also set up buoys in shallow water that you can tie your kayak to, so that you can explore the reefs as long as you want. They welcome committed volunteers, especially those experienced with boats.

Locals gather in **Maxi's Bar** to play dominos, and tourists flock there for the Caribbean cuisine in the breezy second floor restaurant. **La Selva**, at the entrance to town, is also good and has faster service. **Miss Marva** also cooks for visitors in her home.

Pangea (private bath, heated water, ceiling fan; $30-$40, including breakfast; beeper: 224-2400 Pangea; www.radiomensajes.co.cr/pangea), 200 meters inland from Aquamor, is a friendly place to stay. **Cabinas Las Veraneras** (private bath, cold water, ceiling fans; $12-$20; 754-2298) are basic and *tranquilos*.

GETTING THERE: Two buses a day pass through Puerto Viejo and continue on to Manzanillo, one around 7:30 a.m. and the other around 4 p.m. (check exact times at ATEC or the Hotel Maritza). They can drop you off at your hotel of choice. Buses leave Manzanillo for Puerto Viejo and continue to Limón at 7:45 a.m. and 4:45 p.m., and will pick you up if you wait on the road outside your hotel. If driving, pay special attention to the bridges along the road. Some are on curves, some are in great need of repair, all are narrow. Careless drivers have drowned.

Deep in the forest behind the Gandoca–Manzanillo Wildlife Refuge is a remote, primary forest reserve owned by ASACODE (Asociación Sanmigueleña de Conservación y Desarrollo), a small farmers' association. They are dedicated conservationists who experiment with reforestation of native trees and harvest hardwoods selectively from their forest, dragging out the tree trunks with water buffalo to make the lowest impact possible. Besides being ecologically conscious, they are economically wise as well, processing the wood themselves to offer the more expensive finished product directly, bypassing middlemen. Easiest access is from Celia, a town off the Bribri-Sixaola road, but hikes in from Manzanillo can be arranged as well.

The ✪ **ASACODE Lodge** (shared bath, cold water, mosquito nets) in the middle of the reserve offers simple accommodations for groups. Tours of the reserve, including the experimental plots, canopy exploration areas, water buffalo pastures, and the sawmill, are available for groups ($37/person including meals). Call ANAI in San José (224-6090, fax: 253-7524, e-mail: anaicr@racsa.co.cr) or ATEC (750-0191; www.greencoast.com, e-mail: atecmail@racsa.co.cr) to arrange your visit. Only the hardy should attempt this trek; accommodations at the lodge are very simple, and there are plenty of mosquitos.

Bribri is a town between Puerto Viejo and the Sixaola, on the Panama border. There are a couple of good *sodas*, but otherwise it's a dull administrative center. A few kilometers away is an indigenous handicrafts co-op, **Rancho Grande**, that's worth visiting. The building itself is interesting, with floors and walls made from *rawa*, a traditional, sturdy construction material pulled from an endangered palm. They sell inexpensive baskets, gourds, and lances.

GETTING THERE: By Bus: from Puerto Viejo, take one of the several Sixaola daily buses that come from San José or Limón, and get off in Bribri. You'll have to take a taxi or walk the rest of the way.

By Car: Bear right and stay on the main road at the *cruce*, instead of going straight on the road to Puerto Viejo. Drive through Bribri until you come to a T intersection, near the *colegio* (high school). Turn right, and continue two kilometers to the town of Volio. Leave your car on the side of the road at the "Artesanía" sign, and walk about 300 meters to Rancho Grande. The path can be quite muddy and slippery, and you must cross a river on a hanging bridge.

PANAMA COAST

If your visa has run out and you want to leave Costa Rica for 72 hours in order to become a legal tourist again, **Bocas del Toro** on the Caribbean coast of Panama is a nice place to go. Christopher Columbus reached Bocas del Toro on October 5, 1502, on his fourth and last trip to the New World. The town is on Isla Colón at the northernmost part of the archipelago of the same name. The road that circles the island is great for biking or peaceful walks. There are two bike rental shops, one near the park and one at the Laguna Hotel. On Front Street behind the Park is the **tourist information office** of the Instituto Panameño de Turismo, housed in a stunning reproduction of a classic Bocas building. They have a great exhibit on the history and natural beauty of the area that is worth seeing. There is also useful information at **www.worldheadquarters.com** and **www.explorepanama.com**.

Bastimientos National Marine Park protects coral reefs and turtle nesting beaches on and around several other islands in the Bay, principally Islas Bastimientos and Zapatilla, with long fine-white-sand beaches. The snorkeling in the park is very good. You can hire a dugout canoe with a guide, or paddle around in a rented kayak. Several dive shops operate in Bocas; all can coordinate trips. There's a light turquoise speck in the bay—an island that sank during the April 1991 earthquake. You can go out and stand on it.

Make sure you bring U.S. dollars with you, for they are the currency used in Panama, and banks there won't change Costa Rican *colones*. There is now an ATM machine on the island.

LODGING   Among the most upscale lodgings in town is the **Hotel Laguna** (private bath, heated water, air conditioning; $50-$60; 507-757-9091, fax: 507-757-9092; e-mail: hlaguna@cwp.net.pa), across the main street from the water taxi drop off. The elegant wooden rooms are above the waterfront bar and restaurant. They also rent one suite with a kitchen. **Swan's Cay** (private bath, hot water, fans, air conditioning, TV; $60-$70; 757-9090; www.bocas.com), has an expensive restaurant and bar. **Cocomo On-The-Sea** ($40-$50, including breakfast; 757-9259; www.caribpro.com/cocomo, e-mail: cocomoonsea@cwp.net.pa) is a popular B&B with famous breakfasts, built over the water on Avenida Norte.

The **Hotel La Veranda** (shared or private bath, heated water, fans, mosquito nets; $20-$40; 757-9211; www.explorepanama.com, e-mail: heath guidi@hotmail.com) is a charming Caribbean-style home with a large gingerbread veranda running all around the second floor. It's a cozy, clean, relaxed place to stay, with a fully equipped, open-air kitchen available to guests. It's on calle 7 and avenida G, one block from the sea. Ask Heather, the owner, about a secret beach she knows of. On the same street, **Casa Max** (heated water; $20-$40; 757-9120) owned by a Dutch family, is also a good place to stay.

On the park, **Hotel del Park** ($20-$30) is new and promising, but had not opened yet when we were there.

For budget accommodations, try **Cynthia's Place** (shared bath; $7/person), next door to La Veranda. Its clean, has kitchen facilities, a nice veranda, and is popular with young people. The basic **Mondo Taitu** (shared bath; kitchen facilities; $7/person; 757-9425) on Avenida Norte is a backpackers' haven. **Pensión Angela** (shared bath) is on the sea down the street from Mondo Taitu. But the prize-winning budget place is **Tío Tom's** ($5/person) on Isla Bastimientos. It is quaint but clean, and built over the sea. The East German owners are great hosts and a lot of fun.

RESTAURANTS   **Heike's Tropical Garden** on the Park is the best deal in town for good food and atmosphere. Its clean bar attracts a fun crowd. They also rent rooms ($20-$30). At **Don Chicho's,** down the street, you can get a huge meal for $3.50. **Alberto's** has great homemade pizza and yummy seafood appetizers served on its veranda. **Orlando's**, next to Hotel La Veranda, serves a whole fish dinner for $4.50. The U.S.-owned **Buena Vista** serves deli-style sandwiches on it's over-the-water deck and is a favorite watering-hole at night.

GETTING THERE: If you have overstayed your tourist visa in Costa Rica, take care of that before you leave San José by visiting Migración or having a travel agency deal with it for you. Migra will charge a small fine for the time you were in the country illegally and will sell you an exit visa (about $44). You can obtain a tourist card ($10) after you cross the border, in Changuinola or in Bocas. It costs about 75 cents to leave Costa Rica if your visa is in order.

By Bus: Take the Sixaola bus from the Sixaola terminal at the north end of Calle Central in San José (6 a.m., 10 a.m., 1:30 p.m., 3:30 p.m.; $7; 236-1220, 257-8129). The 6 a.m. bus is direct. So is the 3:30 p.m., but then you'll arrive at night and won't be able to get all the way to Bocas. You can also catch it on the road outside Cahuita around 10 a.m., or at the Puerto Viejo *cruce* around 10:20. It's best to take the 6 a.m. bus so you can make this trip in just one day.

The 6 a.m. bus arrives at Sixaola around noon, which is 1 p.m. in Panama. Cross the border to Guabito on foot over a funky metal bridge, and from there take a taxi (20 minutes, $1) to Changuinola. From Changuinola take a bus (20 minutes, $1) to the port of Almirante. Take a water taxi (20 minutes, $3) from Almirante to Bocas del Toro—the last water taxi leaves Almirante at 5 p.m. (4 p.m. Costa Rican time). It takes about an hour and a half to get from the border to Bocas. It can cost as little as $11 per person to make the entire trip from Puerto Viejo. Make sure you start your trip as early as you can so you won't get stuck in Changuinola or Almirante for the night.

By Air: Aeroperlas, the Panamanian airline, has weekday flights from San José to Bocas for about $150 roundtrip (440-0093 in San José, 507 315-7500 in Panama).

TORTUGUERO NATIONAL PARK

Tortuguero National Park protects a unique series of natural inland waterways that are home to freshwater turtles; river otters; crocodiles; sloths; howler, spider, and white-throated capuchin monkeys; toucans; *oropéndolas*; parrots; morpho butterflies; and many other species. In addition, it is known as one of the world's richest fishing grounds for tarpon and snook.

Tortuguero is the largest nesting area in the Western Hemisphere for the green sea turtle. These turtles return to Tortuguero every two to four years to mate offshore and dig their nests. Although their feeding grounds can be as far away as Florida and Venezuela, none of the 26,000 turtles tagged in Tortuguero has ever been found to mate at any other beach. Green turtle nesting season is from July through mid-October. The leatherbacks come in fewer numbers and are less regular about their arrivals, but they usually nest in March, April, and May. But you might see nesting turtles at any time of year. Their flipper marks look like tractor treads, showing up as wide black lines on the beach at night.

Tortuguero has been famous for its turtles—and as a source of their meat, shells, and eggs—since the 1600s, when the Spanish set up cacao plantations on the Atlantic coast. Turtles were valued as a meat source on early ships, because they would stay alive if they were kept out of the sun and sprinkled with water. Turtle soup became a delicacy in England around the end of the 1800s. Large-scale turtle export from Tortuguero started in 1912, and by the 1950s, the green turtle faced extinction.

Long-term biological research on the green turtle, started by the Caribbean Conservation Corp. (CCC) in 1954, has helped greatly in understanding and preserving this species. Dr. Archie Carr, the founder of CCC, wrote an entertaining and informative book, *The Windward Road* (see "Recommended Reading" in Chapter Thirteen), about his wanderings in search of the green turtles' nesting ground, which finally led him to Tortuguero. Thanks to international interest in Carr's work, Tortuguero was declared a national park in 1970 by the Costa Rican government.

Today Tortuguero is the premier center for turtle research in the world. Leatherbacks are beginning to be researched as well as green turtles. Despite this, it is estimated that poachers still get 80 percent of the turtle eggs in the area. The CCC needs volunteer turtle taggers, but their program is more expensive than ANAI's in Manzanillo (see Puerto Viejo-Manzanillo section in this chapter).

When we were in Tortuguero in March, we saw two huge *baulas* (leatherback females) laboriously digging holes in the soft brown sand by the light of the full moon. Witnessing this age-old ritual left us with a deep respect for the primordial instincts of all creatures, including humans. The turtles lay about 100 eggs at each of several nestings per season. The eggs incubate for approximately 60 days, then the baby turtles bite through the rubbery shells and clamber out of the nest, heading straight for the ocean, which they try to reach before dawn. Once they hit the water, their instinctive navigational powers direct them to the open sea. Research has shown that turtle hatchlings are attracted to the light reflected off the sea. When researchers block their view of the sea and set up a light source in another direction, the turtles head toward it.

The CCC has built a biological field station and a new **Natural History Visitors Center** at the north end of Tortuguero village. In addition to beautiful photographs and interpretive material on the area's wildlife, the center

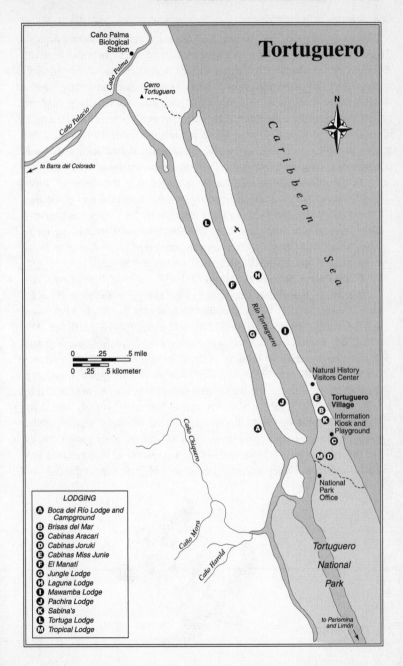

Tortuguero

Caño Palma
Biological
Station

Cerro
Tortuguero

Caño Palma

Caño Palacio

to Barra del Colorado

Caribbean Sea

N

Río Tortuguero

0   .25   .5 mile
0   .25   .5 kilometer

Caño Chiquero

Caño Mora

Caño Harold

Natural History
Visitors Center

**Tortuguero
Village**

Information
Kiosk and
Playground

National
Park
Office

Tortuguero

National

Park

to Parismina
and Limón

LODGING
ⓐ Boca del Río Lodge and
   Campground
ⓑ Brisas del Mar
ⓒ Cabinas Aracari
ⓓ Cabinas Joruki
ⓔ Cabinas Miss Junie
ⓕ El Manatí
ⓖ Jungle Lodge
ⓗ Laguna Lodge
ⓘ Mawamba Lodge
ⓙ Pachira Lodge
ⓚ Sabina's
ⓛ Tortuga Lodge
ⓜ Tropical Lodge

features a lifesize model of a mother turtle laying her eggs, and shows an excellent video about sea turtles. Another video describes threats to turtle nesting grounds on Costa Rica's west coast. Student research assistants and naturalists are available to answer questions and tell you about volunteer programs. The center also sells T-shirts, books, laminated field guides to the birds of Tortuguero, and other wildlife gifts. Proceeds help fund the CCC's conservation programs. The visitors center is open from 10 a.m. to noon and 2 p.m. to 5:30 p.m. Monday through Saturday, and 2 p.m. to 5 p.m. Sunday. Given advance notice, the center will stay open after hours for groups. Admission to this excellent small museum is about $1.

In the information kiosk near the playground at the center of Tortuguero village, there is a fascinating exhibit on the cultural history of the area, illustrated by Deirdre Hyde. To learn more about the human inhabitants of Tortuguero, where they came from and how they made their living for so many years before tourism discovered the area, read *Turtle Bogue* by Harry LeFever (see "Recommended Reading" in Chapter Thirteen).

Caño Palma Biological Station (381-4116, admission $2) near Cerro Tortuguero, eight kilometers northwest of the village, is another research facility founded in 1991 by the Canadian Organization for Tropical Education and Rainforest Conservation (COTERC: in Canada: 905-831-8809, fax: 905-831-4203; http://home.interhop.net/~coterc, e-mail: coterc@interhop.net). The station preserves 40 hectares of tropical lowland forest and is conducting several studies, including the identification of every plant in the area. Tourists are welcome at the station, and many of the boat tours provided by lodges visit it. COTERC has a campaign to buy more property beside the station to expand their wildlife reserve, home to monkeys, jaguars, sloths, margays, anteaters, tapirs, river otters, caimans, toucans, green parrots, hawks, and poison-dart frogs. One acre costs $125, a quarter of an acre costs $35. Their Partners in Preservation Project protects wildlife habitat through ani-

Green sea turtle

mal sponsorship for as little as $15. Their volunteer program is open to any-one who is fit, over 18, and able to adapt to remote field station conditions. Volunteers assist biologists, help run the station, and lead tours. Minimum stay is two weeks. Volunteers have some free time each day to enjoy the sta-tion's kayaks and hammocks ($100/per week for room and board).

Locally guided turtle walks: Recognizing that no conservation effort can succeed without full support from the human community, the CCC, in part-nership with the National Parks Service, has trained local people as turtle guides. Young men who in earlier times might have become turtle hunters are learning a new way to make their living from the town's unique natural re-source. They have formed a cooperative and take small groups (ten people) onto the beach to see the turtles in their peak nesting season from July to October. The guides are familiar with the stages of the nesting process; they only let people approach once the mother turtle is so fully absorbed in laying her eggs that the observers' presence will not disturb her. Turtle tag-gers are also at work on the beach, and visitors must retreat to about 30 feet away from the turtles while the tagging is going on.

The turtle walks are undertaken in two shifts, at 8 p.m. and at 10 p.m. Only 100 people are allowed on the beach at one time, so the guides queue early to buy permits for night tours. You can hook up with a guide during the day at the main dock, at the information kiosk, or through your hotel, and arrange to meet at 8 p.m. or at 10 p.m. Guided turtle walks cost $10. Most package-deal hotels do not include the turtle tours in their rates, be-cause the tours only take place July 1 through October 15.

We recommend seeing the green turtle nesting in Tortuguero rather than visiting the leatherbacks at Playa Grande in Guanacaste, because the green turtle population is greater and more stable than that of their larger cousins. Several thousand greens visit Tortuguero each year, compared to several hundred leatherbacks at Playa Grande. In addition, there are many beautiful beaches (like Playa Grande) in Costa Rica, but the jungles and rivers of Tor-tuguero are unique in their richness and should not be missed.

The area north of Limón, like most of the Atlantic coast of Nicaragua, is a water-based society. All travel is by boat. In 1974, a series of canals was built to connect the natural inland waterways between Limón and Barra del Colorado, thus allowing coastal residents to get to Limón without the hazards of sea travel. In 1979, the government established a twice-weekly launch service up the inland waterway, but due to mechanical difficulties, the flat-bottom boat has stopped running. The difficulty of getting in and out of Tortuguero has begun to wear on local residents, who see boatloads of tourists zooming up and down the canals while they can't afford to travel (some community-minded hotels and tour operators take local people to Limón when there is space on their boats). It also means that they must pay higher prices for food, because local *pulpería* owners have to pay high prices for transport. In January 1996, the Municipality of Pococi, a small town inland from Tortuguero, paid for the clearing of a road bed through at least one and a half kilometers of national park land, ending seven kilometers from the village. The road project was stopped by the government, and a suit filed against the municipality is still being fought in the courts. Locals began using the road again, especially in the dry season, and in March 1999 Environment Minister Elizabeth Odio ordered a 10-foot deep ditch dug across the road bed. Protesters began filling in the ditch by hand until the government sent park officials to guard it. Local people who have benefitted from tourism realize that building a road will threaten the pristine conditions in which wildlife thrives, but they also see that their families cannot afford transportation as it now stands.

Touring by boat: The best way to enjoy the exuberant vegetation and abundant wildlife of Tortuguero's canals is to rent a *cayuca*, or dugout canoe (about $2/hour, three hours for $10/person with a guide). Pamfilo, Tina, Castor, Reynaldo Hooker, Chico Torres, Bill Sambola, and Alberto Taylor are some of the villagers who rent out *cayucas*. (They also serve as guides.) *Cayucas* are quite stable and easy to paddle. Paddle around for awhile to see if your dugout is the right size for you and make sure it is of solid, one-piece construction and not caulked together. Check also that it has a plastic bailer.

You have to pay $6 admission to the park at the administration office (300 meters south of the information kiosk) before you set off in a *cayuca*. The main waterway of the park is inland from the canal that comes from Moín. Paddle south. You will see smaller waterways branching off that you can explore. If you go out without a guide, ask where the currents are most gentle. The current in the Río Tortuguero can be quite strong.

To make your boat trip more comfortable, bring the following:

Thick-soled athletic shoes	Lightweight long-sleeved
Socks	and short-sleeved shirts
Insect repellent	Towels
Sunblock	Lunch in waterproof bags
Broad-rimmed hat	Drinking water
or visored cap	Swiss army knife
Umbrella for sun or rain	Flashlight
Lightweight plastic poncho	
or picnic cloth for rain	

Motorboats to tour the canals are also available in town and from the lodges. These are okay for going fast, but the noise disturbs the quiet beauty of the jungle streams, and you might scare away any wildlife before you can see it. Daryl Loth, an enthusiastic Canadian expat, is an exception. He has a quiet electric motor in his boat, and enjoys giving educational tours of the area, emphasizing not only wildlife observation but insight into the community. He lives across from the Jungle Shop; you can e-mail him at safari@racsa.co.cr.

Elvin Gutierrez has a small Boston whaler for fishing trips ($50 for two people, including refreshments and guide; fax: 233-2243, or ask at the Jungle Shop). Modesto Watson takes up to four people fishing for $50 (phone/fax: 226-0986; www.tortuguerocanals.com, e-mail: fvwatson@racsa.co.cr).

Camping is allowed in the park, but remember that Tortuguero has one of the highest annual rainfalls in the world: more than 200 inches a year. *Terciopelo* (fer-de-lance) snakes are not uncommon on land, especially at night. There is a nature trail on the narrow piece of land between the large canal and the sea. It is a bit less swampy in the dry season.

Note: If you want to go swimming, Tortuguero is not the ideal place. The beach offers very little shade, has rough, dangerous surf, and is frequented by sharks.

LODGING AND RESTAURANTS   Many people splurge on a tour to Tortuguero because the logistics seem difficult. But it is quick, easy, and cheaper to fly there on SANSA or Travelair and stay in one of the hotels in the village. Compare $50 and 20 minutes by air with $40-$45 by bus, taxi, and boat through Limón and Moín (six hours travel time). If you want to return via the canals, it is easier to arrange boat transportation *from* Tortuguero than *to* it. The boat trip up the canals from Moín takes about three to five hours, depending on the condition of the canals, and is noisy and boring for some. It is worthwhile if you have a good guide. If you go on a tour you'll stay at one of the hotels in the "Tour Package Hotels" listed on the next page.

Note: There is no bank in Tortuguero, and many local hotels and guides do not take credit cards or travelers' checks, so be sure and change money before you get there. Some shops and restaurants will take credit cards if you make a purchase, but they don't have the cash flow to handle money changing.

There are several inexpensive hotels in the village. **Brisas del Mar** (shared bath, cold water, no fans; under $7), known as *El Bochinche* (The Commotion) in honor of a memorable fight that took place there once, has cheap, dark cabinas right on the beach. It doesn't serve food, but it has a bar and holds dances there Wednesday and Saturday nights. Next door is **Sabina's** (cold water; with shared bath, no fans, under $7 to $20; with private bath, table fans, $20-$30), the largest place in town. She is often grumpy with tourists, but her cabinas are clean and some have good ocean views.

On the south side of the soccer field, beyond the information kiosk and the playground, is **Cabinas Aracari** (private bath, cold water, wall fans; $12-$20; 798-3059) nice, clean cabinas surrounded by a garden with native fruit trees: mango, avocado, water apple, and cashew. There are bars on the windows, a thoughtful touch for travelers' peace of mind. The owner, Doña Bachi, who lives behind the cabinas in a blue house, is the essence of down-home motherliness. Recommended.

Tropical Lodge (private bath, cold water, fans; $20-$30; 221-6839, fax: 257-7735, cell phone: 389-7258; e-mail: tourarena@racsa.co.cr), 200 meters south of the main dock, has rather dark, rough wood cabins near the river. The use of a canoe comes with each room. The Chilean owner runs many tours of the area.

Cabinas Joruki (private bath, cold water, fans; $10/person, $23/person including meals), on the river on the south side of town, serves excellent Caribbean food in its restaurant.

At the northern end of the village are **Cabinas Miss Junie** (private bath, hot water, ceiling fans; $30-$40; 710-0523), the nicest in town. Each room has its own pastel color theme, with walls and bed linens that blend harmoniously. The tiled bathrooms are impressive. Miss Junie gained fame over the years as the cook at the CCC, and now has her own restaurant. If you want to sample her cuisine, you must let her know in advance, so that she can give your meal the preparation it deserves. Recommended.

The **Vine Coffee House**, in the middle of the village, serves sandwiches, pizzas, and desserts to be savored with Café Britt, Costa Rica's gourmet coffee. Some tables in the back overlook the river, and the Tico/gringa owners make sure good music is always playing—from Vivaldi to Stan Getz to Bob Marley.

Aside from Miss Junie's, Joruki, and the Vine, we found the few restaurants in the village to be lackluster. And at some places we visited, the waitresses added up the bill in their heads and ended up overcharging us. The situation was resolved peacefully by simply asking for a *factura* (a written bill). When they wrote it down and added it up, the numbers came out right. One distinct advantage of taking a tour package to Tortuguero is that the food at most of the lodges is great, and is geared to foreign preferences (more fresh fruit and vegetables, less fat).

There are several souvenir shops in the village. **El Paraíso Tropical**, an unmistakable purple building that you can see from the water, has many things that you'd find in souvenir shops in San José, and not many locally made articles. The **Jungle Shop**, a few houses to the south, across from The Vine, has better-quality, more interesting, and more tasteful things for sale, as well as cold drinks, and donates a percentage of its profits to the local school.

✪ **El Manatí** (private bath, heated water, reading lamps, fans; $30-$40, including breakfast; 383-0330, fax: 239-0911), one and a half kilometers north of the village, across the canal, also accommodates budget travelers. The owners have started a community project to save the sea cow (manatee). At 1600 pounds, it is the largest mammal in Costa Rica. They are enlisting the help of tourists and guides to help them locate these aquatic mammals that inhabit the coasts and rivers of both sides of the tropical Atlantic. Some scientists claim that manatees are distant relatives of the elephant. These shy creatures and a related species, the dugong, are said to have given rise to the legend of the mermaid. When frightened, they can stay under water for as much as half an hour, but usually they stop grazing on aquatic plants and seaweed long enough to surface every ten to fifteen minutes. That is when they become vulnerable to the propellers of the dozens of motor boats that ply the canals. The lodge is the center for manatee and crocodile research in the area. Earthwatch is coordinating volunteer programs to help with this; call 226-0986 for information. The lodge is simple, peaceful, and unpretentious—a good place for families since the owners have young children. In addition to their regular rooms, they have a couple of two-bedroom cabins, and rent canoes and kayaks for tooling into the village and around the park. They often coordinate transportation and guided tours with Modesto Watson, an excellent guide (226-0986; www.tortuguerocanals.com, e-mail: fvwatson@racsa.co.cr).

Boca del Río Lodge and Campground (385-4676) has tent-cabins with hammocks and mosquito nets (no beds), supplied with cooking utensils, ice chests, barbecue grills and firewood for $5 per person. The shared bathrooms have cold water. They also rent a nicely tiled room with heated water for $30-$40, including breakfast and lunch.

TOUR PACKAGE HOTELS   All of these lodges offer two- and three-day packages that include food, lodging, tours of the canals via motorboat, and ascent of Cerro (Mount) Tortuguero. Most tours include bus and boat transportation between San José and Tortuguero, and all offer an air transport upgrade. Tour prices are given per person.

Mawamba Lodge (private bath, hot water, ceiling fans, pool; 223-2421, fax: 255-4039; www.costaricabureau.com, e-mail: mawamba@costaricabureau.com) has pleasant cabinas and a large, airy dining room that serves very good food. Just one kilometer north of Tortuguero village on the ocean side of the canal, it's one of the two lodges from which you can walk to the village or the ocean. There is a large, fanciful pool with a waterfall, near a bar where tropical drinks are served. With its air-conditioned conference room and resident multilingual biologist, it's a good setting for seminars or small conventions. The rustic cabinas blend in with the environment in a way that some large hotels do not. Packages: two days/one night: $201; three days/two nights: $252.

Next door, **Laguna Lodge** (private bath, hot water, ceiling fans, swimming pool with jacuzzi; cellular phone: 225-3740, fax: 283-8031; www.laguna lodgetortuguero.com, e-mail: laguna@racsa.co.cr) is owned by the brother of the owner of Mawamba, a noted Costa Rican poet and author. It has the same congenial atmosphere as Mawamba but is smaller and more peaceful. The food is terrific. A two-day, one-night package costs $187 ($110 for students), a pretty good deal. They offer three-day packages for $234 ($130 for students). Recommended.

Tortuga Lodge (private bath, heated water, ceiling fans; 257-0766, 222-0333, fax: 257-1665; www.expeditions.co.cr, e-mail: costaric@expeditions. co.cr) is on 125 acres of the forested spit, two kilometers from the village across the canal from the airstrip. Tortuga Lodge was the first nature lodge in this area. Architecturally, it has expanded in a tasteful, harmonious way, and maintains its tradition of excellent service. A new riverside dining room adds a special tone to the atmosphere. The pool has an environmentally friendly purification system that doesn't irritate the eyes. Their tour boats use electric motors unless high water or strong currents preclude their use. Packages: two days, one night with air transportation, $379-$499. Recommended.

Cotur takes you by bus and launch to the largest hotel in the area, **Jungle Lodge** (private bath, hot water, ceiling fans; 233-0155, 233-0133, fax: 233-0778; www.tortuguero.com, e-mail: cotour@racsa.co.cr), with comfortable rooms, a swimming pool, and covered walkways between buildings. Package: three days, two nights, $150. Room rates include free use of canoes.

Pachira Lodge (private bath, hot water, ceiling fans, $80/person, including meals; 256-7080, fax: 223-1119; www.pachiralodge.com, e-mail: paccira@racsa.co.cr) is Tortuguero's newest hotel. Located on the canal to Barra, across from the village, its spacious, airy dining room wins our award for architectural excellence. The individual rooms are decorated in a traditional Caribbean style, with many attractive touches. Their three-day/two-night tour costs $239; two days and one night with boat transportation: $176. Early morning tours are $10.

GETTING THERE: If you are traveling on your own, it's often easier to fly into Tortuguero and arrange boat transportation for the return trip once you are there. If it is turtle season, reserve a hotel room in advance. There are also some interesting ways of getting to Tortuguero from Moín.

By boat from Moín: Modesto and Fran Watson offer flexible tours in their canopied **Riverboat Francesca** (two days/one night from Moín, including lodging and meals at El Manatí or Laguna, and an early-morning tour of the National Park: $130-$145; three days/two nights can be arranged; roundtrip transportation between San José and Moín optional and $40 extra, including a hearty breakfast; phone/fax: 226-0986; www.tortuguerocanals.com, e-mail: fvwatson@racsa.co.cr). Modesto has an eagle eye for animals and pointed out caimans, toucans, an osprey, jacanas, basilisk lizards, monkeys, sloths, a pair of scarlet macaws (a rare sight on the Atlantic coast), a roseate spoonbill, freshwater turtles, and lots of waterbirds on our trip up the canals. Modesto and Fran recently purchased a pontoon boat which has very little draw, and thus can navigate the canals when the water level is low. They also use a quiet, fuel-saving four-stroke motor. Recommended.

Alexis Soto of the **Tropical Wind II** (758-4297, fax: 790-3059, cell phone: 387-8951, beeper: 297-1010) provides roundtrip transportation from Moín to Tortuguero for $45, but you may have to sit and wait for his boat to fill up to get that price. **Arena Tours** (221-6839, cell phone: 389-7258; e-mail: tourarena@racsa. co.cr) arranges low-cost tours to Tortuguero.

By boat via the Río Suerte: The cheapest way to get to Tortuguero is with Rubén Aragón, **Bananero** (cell phone: 382-6941, beeper: 296-2626 #127-714), who has a boat service from Tortuguero to El Geest de Casa Verde on the canal to Barra and on to Cariari, a small town north of Guápiles. Take the 6 a.m. or 9 a.m. San José–Cariari bus ($2.50) from the Sixaola station at the north end of Calle Central. Once in Cariari, catch the bus to El Geest ($2) at noon. Bananero meets the bus and leaves for Tortuguero at 1:30 p.m. ($8). On the return trip, he leaves Tortuguero at 7 a.m. and gets you to El Geest between 8:30 and 9:30, depending on the level of water in the canals, to catch a bus that arrives in Cariari to meet the 11 a.m. San José bus. Bring snacks in case you don't have time to stop for a meal in Cariari or El Geest. You can see lots of birds and animals on this trip, too. ASOMEP (The Association of Eco-tourism Micro-Businesses of Pococí, 767-7991) runs a two-day tour to Tortuguero via Cariari and the Río La Suerte for about $60, not including food.

By boat from Sarapiquí via the Río San Juan: **Oasis Tours** (766-6108, 766-6260, cell phone: 380-9493; www.tourism.com, e-mail: oasis@tourism.com) runs a two-day, one-night tour ($175) to Tortuguero from Puerto Viejo de Sarapiquí via the Río San Juan on the Nicaragua border. The boat trip takes about five hours. Oasis offers secure parking in Puerto Viejo while you're away. They also do a five-day trip by car to Poas and Arenal volcanoes, then by boat to Tortuguero ($1000 for two).

By Air: Travelair ($51 one way; $93 roundtrip; 220-3054, fax: 220-0413; www. centralamerica.com, e-mail: travelair@centralamerica.com) flies to Tortuguero every morning at 6:45 a.m. SANSA ($50 one way; 221-9414; http://relee.webwize.com/travel/sansa) leaves for Tortuguero daily at 6 a.m. If you are visiting Tortuguero on your own, this might be a quick and easy way to travel at least one way.

PARISMINA

Parismina is a small fishing village about halfway between Limón and Tortuguero. Turtles nest in this area as in Tortuguero, but are much more vulnerable to poaching because they are outside the national park. Just south of Parismina, the private **Pacuare Reserve** (233-0451, fax: 221-2820, cellular: 391-9975; e-mail: desmag@racsa.co.cr) operates a volunteer program to patrol the beaches and help with scientific research during the March-to-July nesting season. Volunteers pay about $100 per week for the experience, including room and board. You can rent a comfortable house that sleeps up to six ($50/person including meals and boat transportation; no electricity, minimum three nights) and relax at the private beach in front of the house.

Parismina is known in fishing circles for the **Río Parismina Lodge** (private bath, hot water, ceiling fans and air conditioning; package deals only; phone/fax: 236-7480, in the U.S.: 800-338-5688; e-mail: rioparismina@costaricabureau.com), a luxury fishing resort set in five acres of tropical gardens, with nature trails in the forest behind the lodge. Rates run from $1650 for Saturday through Tuesday, to $2550 for a week of fishing. The three-day non-fishing price is $1450. All packages include two nights at a first-class hotel in San José, luxury accommodations and gourmet meals at the lodge, fishing guide and licenses, and transport to and from the lodge.

BARRA DEL COLORADO

Barra del Colorado, at the northeast end of Costa Rica, is a sleepy, rainy, car-free town occupying opposite banks near the mouth of the Río Colorado. The west bank of the river has the poverty-stricken village, the east bank has the expensive lodges. There is excellent fishing in the river, nearby canals, and the Caribbean Sea. All of the hotels here specialize in fishing.

Tarpon season is from January to June and September to December. Snook run from October to January and also in May. The rainy season on the Atlantic coast is unpredictable, so bring a good windbreaker and sweatshirt. The lodges usually provide raingear. The beach in Barra is too rough for swimming, snorkeling, or scuba diving, but it is a nesting ground for sea turtles from July through September.

The **Barra del Colorado Wildlife Refuge**, at 92,000 hectares, is the second largest in Costa Rica. If you fly to Barra, you'll see its importance. Everywhere between the Central Mountains and the Atlantic Coast, the land looks like an animal whose pelt has been shaved in large patches. Bright green spots littered with fallen trees finally give way to the beauty of the rich coat of billowing dark-green treetops extending north into Nicaragua. It is a great relief to see that this one expanse of virgin forest has been saved. SINAC (National Conservation Areas System) operates on a shoestring budget, with ten poorly equipped guards to patrol this huge area and to keep its monkeys, sloths, jaguars and birds safe from hunters and loggers.

Because Barra is traditionally known as a fishing area, it is less crowded with naturalists than nearby Tortuguero, but its lagoons and streams offer just as many opportunities to commune with nature, often in a less regimented way, at least at this point. Researchers estimate that the reserve has 700 different kinds of orchids.

LODGING   **Tarponland Lodge** (private bath, heated water, ceiling fans; $40-$50, including meals; 292-2963, cell phones: 383-6097, 382-3350), right on the airstrip, is the only Tico-owned place in Barra. The basic rooms are not bad, and they have a funky swimming pool. Fishing trips cost $275 per person.

The **Río Colorado Fishing Lodge** (private bath, hot water, ceiling fans, some air conditioning; $380/person/fishing day; $100/person/non-fishing day; prices do not include transportation and licenses; $1420 for six days and five nights, including three days of fishing, transportation and licenses; in the U.S. and Canada: 800-243-9777, in CR: 232-8610, fax: 231-5987; www.rio coloradolodge.com, e-mail: tarpon4u@mindspring.com) was one of the original lodges that gave Barra del Colorado its name as a world-class fishing destination. The lodge is a survivor from the days before Costa Rica got fancy, when fishing places at the beach were simple and shabby but had a certain charm. Its maze of covered walkways and rooms winds around courtyards full of caged animals (monkeys, a deer, a tapir, pheasants, parrots, scarlet macaws, a *tepiscuintle*). Our kids loved it. As do most other lodges in Barra, it has a bar with a free happy hour, cable TV, and VCR. The fishing fleet is outfitted with sonar fish finders, radios, and skilled guides. The lodge offers a two-day non-fishing tour that leaves San José for an early morning trip to Poás volcano, then heads to Puerto Viejo de Sarapiquí to board a riverboat for a four-hour cruise northeast to the Río San Juan, which borders Nicaragua and flows into the Caribbean at Barra del Colorado. After a night at the lodge, the tour continues down the canals and back to San José. From July to September, the tour stops in Tortuguero on the return, to try to catch a glimpse of a leatherback or green turtle nesting.

The best Barra accommodations are at the **Silver King Lodge** (private bath, hot water, ceiling fans; $435/person/fishing day; $130/person/non-fishing day; prices do not include transportation; packages from $1810; in CR: phone/fax: 381-1403; in the U.S.: 800-847-3474; e-mail: slvrkng@racsa.co.cr). Each spacious room has two huge orthopedic mattresses, real closets and a large bathroom with plenty of hot water. Rates include free beer, soft drinks and local liquors, and complimentary laundry service—a real boon in Barra's wet weather. The gourmet food is excellent and plentiful, with attention to good service, and the staff is friendly. The most memorable part of our stay there was the green-lighted hot tub with jacuzzi—the perfect end to a cool, misty day of buzzing around Barra in speedboats. They also have a swimming pool with a waterfall. Their fishing fleet is as well equipped as the rest of their operation. Lures can be purchased at the lodge or you can ask in advance for a list of recommended ones. Rods and reels are free of charge (not for fly-fishing). For the non-angler, they offer canoe and kayak rentals, guided or not.

A few minutes more down the waterway is the homey **Casamar** (private bath, hot water, ceiling fans, free bar, free laundry, VCR room; $320/day, $2195 for a seven-day trip, including transportation; 433-8834, 381-1830; in the U.S.: 800-543-0282; www.casamarlodge.com, e-mail: info@casamar lodge.com), with well-designed, comfortable duplex cabinas. Mango trees shade the grounds; howler monkeys provide the sound effects.

Anglers will enjoy a sojourn aboard the **Rain Goddess** (shared bath, hot water, fans; three-day package $1750, five-day package $2250, three-day nature tour $475; 231-4299, fax: 231-3816; www.bluwing.com), a 65-foot houseboat that anchors where the fish are. The air-conditioned, carpeted staterooms have comfortable beds. Guests can enjoy a barbecue on the roofed upper deck or dine in the main salon with its VCR and open bar. Twin 135-hp gas engines provide silent running, and there is a cellular phone with international and local service. On any given trip they may fish the Barra Colorado area, Tortuguero, and Parismina, or up the Colorado and San Juan rivers. They also go to Lake Silico, Lake San Juanillo, and the Río Indio, amid the forests of southeastern Nicaragua. Experienced guides include Peter Gorinsky, fly-fisherman and naturalist extraordinaire. They also offer a three-day/two-night nature tour that starts with land and boat transport from San José to Bird Island, their private six-acre wildlife preserve, then a cruise down the

Río Colorado, anchoring for the night in Samay Lagoon, near Barra. The *Rain Goddess* visits Tortuguero the next day and night, and the tour ends with a jungle walk and a visit to a banana plantation on the third day. There's a library of natural-history books on board.

GETTING THERE: Most of the lodges in this area have tour packages that include transportation from San José.

By Air: SANSA has daily flights to Barra (6 a.m.; $61 each way; 221-9414, fax: 255-2176; http://relee.webwize.com/travel). See Chapter Four, "Local Transportation—Planes" for reservation procedures and policies.

By Bus and Boat: **Oasis Tours** (766-6108, 766-6260, cell phone: 380-9493; e-mail: oasis@arweb.com) runs a two-day, one-night tour to Barra or Tortuguero ($175) from Puerto Viejo de Sarapiquí via the Río San Juan on the border of Nicaragua. The boat trip to Barra takes three to four hours. Oasis offers secure parking in Puerto Viejo while you're away. We saw several huge crocodiles on this trip.

The people of Barra del Colorado go in and out by way of Puerto Lindo and Cariari. Direct buses for Cariari leave the Sixaola bus terminal in San José six times a day (north end of Calle Central; $1.75), or you can take one of the frequent local buses from Guápiles. A bus leaves Cariari at 2 p.m. for Puerto Lindo (three hours). A boat takes you from Puerto Lindo to Barra by 6 p.m. To return to Cariari, take a 4:45 a.m. boat to Puerto Lindo and you'll arrive in Cariari by 9 a.m. ($7.50, one way).

NINE

The Northern Zone

Costa Rica's agriculturally rich Northern Zone extends from the Atlantic plains in the east to the Nicaraguan border in the north, and to Lake Arenal and the Tilarán mountain range in the west. More and more visitors include a visit to the Northern Zone's towering rainforests and the spectacular Arenal Volcano in their itinerary. We find this verdant area one of the most friendly and inviting in the country.

With the creation of the new Liberia airport, you could visit Guanacaste's beaches and National Parks, then head east around Lake Arenal to La Fortuna and Sarapiquí, making your connections by boat or bus to Tortuguero or the beaches of Talamanca and avoiding the crowds and pollution of San José.

THE GUÁPILES AREA

After the opening of the highway through Braulio Carrillo National Park in 1989, the Guápiles area became the gateway to the Atlantic coast. It is the commercial and social center for local vegetable farmers and the banana companies that work thousands of acres of surrounding land.

Part of what we like about this area is that there is still a large rainforest covering the mountains south and west of Guápiles. The climate is considerably more pleasant than the lowland forests. With a higher elevation (1500 to 2000 feet), it's cooler and there aren't as many mosquitos. The proximity to the capital allows tourists to make day trips from San José. There are an ever-increasing number of mini-ecotourism projects in the Guápiles area that we recommend visiting.

Note: The area is crossed by dozens of crystalline rivers that deepen into tempting swimming holes. Several of the lodges in the area offer river-swimming, and the riverside restaurants on the highway advertise *balnearios* as well. The rivers' steep descent from the mountains makes many of them subject to flash floods, and unwary swimmers have been killed by *cabezas de agua*. If it's cloudy in the mountains above, it's safer not to swim. If it's sunny, dive in!

Descriptions of the area's attractions follow, in the order that you will find them traveling from San José to Guápiles.

Descending from Braulio Carrillo National Park, you'll see a sign on your right for the **Rain Forest Aerial Tram** (open daily from 6 a.m. to 3:30 p.m., by reservation only); make reservations two days in advance, by phone or online. Rates are $49.50 for walk-ins; $24.75 for children over five and card-carrying students (children under five are not allowed on tram); $78.50, including breakfast or lunch and transportation from your hotel, from San José; 257-5961, fax: 257-6053; www.rainforesttram.com, e-mail: info@rain foresttram.com). Six-person gondolas, hanging from a 1.3-kilometer cable, glide silently through the forest at heights ranging from three feet off the ground to mid-canopy to 120 feet, above the tallest trees, affording a view formerly available only to birds, monkeys, and scientists brave enough to climb into the treetops. The ride lasts 80 minutes. Birds are most visible before 8 in the morning or late in the afternoon (conditions permitting, you can usually stay until dark, but you must arrive at the site by 2 p.m.). Animals can sometimes be spotted on the hour-long hike that follows the tram ride, but the main attraction here is the rainforest flora. There are more spectacular rainforest sites in Costa Rica, but this is an informative and easy introduction for those short on time or endurance. The Aerial Tram now has attractive cabins (private bath, hot water, $80/person including meals and tramride) to stay in. They also make special arrangements for handicapped access.

Several open-air, always-open restaurants lie along the highway near Guápiles. Our favorite, **Casa de Juancho**, serves dishes prepared with a light Caribbean touch. The popular **Ponderosa** specializes in steak, but will accommodate vegetarians. **Restaurante Río Danta** (open 6:30 a.m. to 4:30 p.m.; 710-7282) two kilometers after the Ponderosa on the right, is owned by Mawamba Lodge in Tortuguero, and is where their tour buses stop for breakfast or lunch on the way. It has an international menu and a pleasant garden setting with a charming bridge across the Río Danta leading to nature trails.

A gravel road on the right, 100 meters toward Limón from the Ponderosa, leads to two lodgings right in the forest. ✪ **Casa Río Blanco** (private bath, hot water; $60-$70, including breakfast; other meals available by request; bar; 382-0957, fax: 710-2264) one and a half kilometers from the highway, is a small bed and breakfast with comfortable rooms right on the river. There are several rainforest trails to explore. At least ten species of hummingbirds regularly sip from the feeders on the shady reading porch. A covered outdoor platform gives a romantic view of a small waterfall. Tree canopy researcher Don Perry has designed an ascending system that even novices can use to climb 125 feet up a *pulsinia armada* ($20). Casa Río Blanco's North American owner can get you discounts on trips to Tortuguero, for kayaking, whitewater rafting, and the Aerial Tram. Right before the lodge there is a hill that's a bit of a struggle to get up, but the road is pretty good after that. A taxi costs about $7 from Guápiles, or you can stop at the Ponderosa and ask them to radio the lodge to pick you up. Recommended.

Ten minutes more along the same road, **Happy Rana Lodge** (private bath, hot water; $40-$60, including breakfast; cell phone: 385-1167, fax: 710-6309, in the U.S.: 520-743-8254; e-mail: happyranalodge@netscape.net) offers accommodation in screened wooden cabins elevated ten feet above the jungle floor to maximize cool forest breezes and minimize humidity. The owners, a Tico-gringa couple, will accompany visitors on hikes on their own property and to a waterfall several hours up the river ($10); they also lend inner tubes for river floats. The lodge has a pristine spot on the river with a little beach and a calm swimming hole (great for kids); there you can be alone with the soothing sound of the river and the birds and morpho butterflies that idle by. The Río Blanco is the most beautiful clear emerald green; a hanging bridge leads to trails on the opposite side. With fewer creature comforts than the Casa Río Blanco, the Happy Rana offers an undiluted experience of nature. Recommended.

In the frontier village of Buenos Aires de Guápiles, ✪ **Las Cusingas** (admission $5; cellular: 382-5805) is a small botanical garden packed with medicinal plants, ornamentals, bromeliads, and fruit trees. Owners Jane Segleau Earle and Ulíses Blanco give an informative tour emphasizing the traditional medicinal uses of plants. Behind the garden stretch several acres of majestic rainforest. White-faced monkeys followed us along the 30-minute trail to the chilly Río Santa Clara. Campesino-style meals are available at Las Cusingas, and a rustic but comfortable **cabin** (private bath, cold water, kitchen; $20-$30) sleeps four. Reiki treatments are offered. To get there, drive past the main entrance of Guápiles to the Santa Clara gas station. Turn right and follow the passable gravel road four kilometers. Just past the school you will see the gate for Las Cusingas on your right. Your vehicle should have high-ground clearance. A taxi will take you there from Guápiles for $7. Recommended.

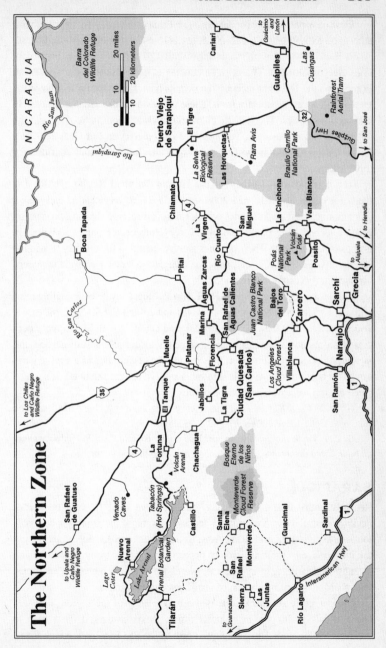

The Northern Zone

Costa Flores (open Monday through Friday; Saturday by appointment; admission $15; 716-6457, 716-6065, fax: 716-6439; e-mail: costaflo@racsa. co.cr) is a 120-hectare heliconia farm with 120 varieties of this breathtaking family of flowers. The farm's mainstay is exportation of cut flowers to Europe and the U.S., but recently the owners have landscaped a section of the garden and added a butterfly farm. There are ponds with fountains and finely masoned pathways. The tour includes information about heliconias and the cut-flower export business. The farm is 15 kilometers east of Guápiles. Turn left at Guácimo, and at the first stop sign, turn left again and continue for three kilometers.

The **Agricultural College of the Humid Tropical Region** (EARTH is the acronym in Spanish; 255-2000, fax: 255-2726; www.earth.ac.cr) has a giant campus east of Guácimo, with a rainforest reserve, banana processing plant, paper-making plant, and plastic recycling center open to visitors in groups of ten or more. Their bananas are the second in the country to win the prestigious "ECO-O.K." seal, which is awarded to banana growers using environmentally responsive methods.

Across the highway from EARTH, **Río Palmas** (private bath, ceiling fans; with cold water, $40-$50; with hot water and color TV, $50-$60; 760-0305, 760-0330, fax: 760-0296) is a well-designed complex with handsomely decorated rooms and a thatch-roofed lounge enclosing a beautiful garden and swimming pool. A clear stream runs next to the restaurant and a simple playground. There are nature trails through a reserve behind the hotel. It's a nice place to stop for a meal or for the night.

GETTING THERE: By Bus: Buses leave every hour from the Atlántico Norte station on Calle 12, Avenidas 7/9, ($2, 256-8963).

By Car: Drive northeast from San José on the Braulio Carrillo Highway about an hour. From downtown, take Calle 3 north to the highway entrance.

SARAPIQUÍ

Recently, tourism and the banana industry have been fighting neck-and-neck for first place in Sarapiquís's economy. Some of the country's best ecotourism experiences, like Rara Avis, Selva Verde, and La Selva, are seeing the importance of their decision to preserve rainforests through tourism and scientific research as they become islands in a sea of banana plantations, with their attendant heavy use of fertilizers and pesticides.

Puerto Viejo de Sarapiquí is the major town in the region, and was Costa Rica's main port in colonial times. Boats embarked from here to cruise down the wide Río Sarapiquí, north to the Río San Juan, which forms

Costa Rica's border with Nicaragua, and from there to the Atlantic. During the years of Contra activity in northern Costa Rica, the area was closed to tourists, but now the rivers are open again. You can find out a lot about this region at www.sarapiquirainforest.com.

The **Banco Serfín** across from the plaza gives quick service to tourists. The public boat to the Nicaraguan border leaves every day at 11 a.m., returning at 5 a.m. from the village of La Trinidad ($4). **Trinity Lodge** (private bath, cold water; $7-$12; 259-1679), at the confluence of the Sarapiquí and the San Juan, is a decent place to stay, but there's not much to do. They rent horses for $1 per hour.

Oasis Tours (766-6108, 766-6260, beeper: 296-2626, cell phone: 380-9493; e-mail: oasis@tourism.co.cr) specializes in trips up the Sarapiquí. Their boats leave daily at 8:30 a.m. and 1:30 p.m. for the two-and-a-half-hour *paseo* ($15). You can connect with them through your hotel for $25. They also offer a two-day trip to Tortuguero by way of the Sarapiquí and the San Juan for $175 per person including lodging, meals, and tours, and they will watch your car while you are away. The trip to Tortuguero from Puerto Viejo de Sarapiquí takes about five hours. They also offer a four-day Arenal-Tortuguero tour ($1000 for two including all meals). We saw a huge crocodile on this trip.

Note: If you go by this route, you'll need to show your passport and pay $5 at the Nicaraguan border guard station on the Río San Juan.

Aguas Bravas (296-2626, 292-2072, fax: 229-4837; www.aguasbravas. co.cr) runs rafting expeditions on the Río Sarapiquí, the Río Toro and the Río Peñas Blancas, and a gentle river float with natural history information for people of all ages. They also run a nature camp for 10- to 17-year-olds that features hiking, horseback riding, rope courses, rapelling, mountain biking and rafting. In La Virgen, 12 kilometers south of Puerto Viejo, Rancho Leona's **Kayak Jungle Tours** offers a one-day kayak trip for beginners ($75) on the Sarapiquí or one-day trips on local rivers for more advanced kayakers ($75). They have double kayaks, so children can come along. All trips include two nights' lodging at Rancho Leona.

A must-see in the Sarapiquí region is the stained glass at **Rancho Leona** (phone/fax: 761-1019; www.rancholeona.com, e-mail: kayak@rancho leona.com). Leona draws jungle birds, butterflies, and frogs, and her husband Ken crafts them into world-class stained-glass lamps and windows. Stop in for a BLT or a vegetarian lunch and let them show you around. They also make jewelry from native seeds, and T-shirts of Leona's designs. These amazing artists share their skills with visitors in a series of art retreats, a wonderful way to experience Costa Rica. Participants visit local families, hike to waterfalls, draw tropical flowers and animals, soak in hot springs, paint landscapes and riverscapes, draw old timers, and visit the Atlantic coast. Find current schedules on their website.

A few kilometers to the east of Puerto Viejo (on the road to the Guápiles Highway) is **MUSA**, a collective of local women who grow, sell, and promote the use of native medicinal herbs. They will give you a tour of their farm ($1/person) and explain the uses of the different plants. They also offer excellent *romero* (rosemary) and *manzanilla* (chamomile) shampoos, facial soaps, packets of dried herbs, and other preparations. The farm is in El Tigre, on the road to Las Horquetas. It is open every day until 5 p.m., but closes for lunch from noon to 1 p.m. If you don't have a car, take a San José or Río Frío bus from Puerto Viejo at 9 a.m., 10:30 a.m., 12:30 p.m., or 2:30 p.m.

PUERTO VIEJO LODGING AND RESTAURANTS   The town of Puerto Viejo has several hotels. **Mi Lindo Sarapiquí** (private bath, heated water, ceiling fans; $20-$30; 766-6074; www.sarapiquirainforest.com) is next to the soccer field. It is a newer building with bright, sunny rooms upstairs and good food and service in the restaurant below.

El Bambú (private bath, heated water, ceiling fans, TV, phones, security boxes, guarded parking; $50-$60, including breakfast; 766-6005, fax: 766-6132) is comfortable and airy, with good mattresses. Downstairs you'll find a bar and restaurant built around a stand of giant bamboo.

Andrea Cristina Bed & Breakfast (private bath, heated water, table fans, small kiddy pool; $30-$40, including breakfast; phone/fax: 766-6265), owned by one of Sarapiquí's foremost environmental activists, is shady and quiet; its quaint A-frame and cottage rooms have a European flavor. Special rates for families.

The best budget hotel is four kilometers west of Puerto Viejo on the road to Chilamate at **Cabinas Yacaré** (shared or private baths, cold water, table fans, restaurant; $7-$12; 766-6691)—very clean, and simply decorated. Take a Cristo Rey bus from Puerto Viejo to get there. They leave every 45 minutes.

LA SELVA   This 1560-hectare research station and biological reserve of the Organization for Tropical Studies (OTS) has brought fame to Sarapiquí because of its enormous variety of tropical plants and animals. In an effort to secure the large hunting territories needed by jaguars and pumas, Braulio Carrillo National Park was extended to meet it, forming a corridor from Volcán Barva (2500 meters above sea level) to the lowlands (30 meters) at La Selva. More than 400 species of birds either live in or migrate to La Selva from the highlands, including toucans, *oropéndolas* (golden orioles), tinamous, and umbrella birds. More than 300 different species have been observed there in a single day by the Audubon Society Birdathon. Research and education are the reserve's top priorities.

One of the many courses offered at La Selva is not for biologists, but for the world's decisionmakers: government and business leaders who need to understand tropical ecology in order to guide their countries along the soundest environmental paths.

Groups or individuals can roam La Selva's 57 kilometers of well-kept trails through primary and secondary forest, and its arboretum. The best way to visit is to stay overnight (shared bath; $50-$60/person, including meals and one half-day tour; call the San José office at 240-6696, fax: 240-6783; e-mail: reservas@ots.ac.cr).

You can also go for half-day tours ($20/adult, $10/ages 3 to 12) that leave every day at 8 a.m. and 1:30 p.m. A cafeteria-style lunch is $5 extra. Call the station at least a day ahead for reservations (766-6565, fax: 766-6535; e-mail: laselva@sloth.ots.ac.cr).

OTS runs a bus ($10 one way) to La Selva from its San José office on Mondays at 7 a.m. La Selva is about five kilometers east of Puerto Viejo; look for the sign opposite the Lapa Verde restaurant. From that turnoff it is about two kilometers to the main administration building. A taxi will charge about $3.25 to La Selva from Puerto Viejo, or you can take any bus from Puerto Viejo to Río Frío or San José via the Guápiles highway and walk from the main road.

RARA AVIS   Back when people were first learning of the destruction of rainforests worldwide, but didn't know what to do about it, Amos Bien, an ecologist and former manager of La Selva, had a brilliant idea. He decided that the best way to convince people not to cut down rainforests was to demonstrate that it was economically sound to conserve them through tourism and sound land management. The result of Amos Bien's efforts is the now-famous Rara Avis, a 1500-acre forest reserve near the small village of Las Horquetas, southeast of La Selva. Through its excellent tours, visitors get a short course in how the rainforest works, why it is being cut down, and how it can be restored—without feeling that they have been in school. Now that Rara Avis has mastered ecotourism, it is able to focus on other types of rainforest conservation projects. Currently underway are a butterfly research and production project and a greenhouse for seedlings of endangered tree species and orchids.

Various accommodations are available at ✪ **Rara Avis** (764-3131, fax: 764-4187; www.rara-avis.com, e-mail: raraavis@sol.racsa.co.cr), Costa Rica's original rainforest lodge. The comfortable, eight-room **Waterfall Lodge** and

River Edge Cabin (private bath, hot water, no electricity; $70-$80/person, double occupancy) are both close to a gorgeous three-tiered waterfall. The River Edge Cabin is especially designed for birdwatchers. **El Plástico Lodge** (shared bath, hot water; $40-$50/person, double occupancy) is more rustic but still comfortable. For the intrepid, the **Treehouse** ($140-$170/person, double occupancy) allows guests to spend a night 100 feet above the ground on a tree-top platform. The base is a 15-minute walk from the Waterfall Lodge, and the ascent, undertaken with help from an expert, is with ropes and a harness. Prices for each include three hearty meals, guided tours, and transportation from Las Horquetas. Discounts for children, residents, students, hostel card–holders, and researchers are available.

Because transportation to Rara Avis is difficult, you need to make reservations. They will help you arrange transportation from San José. If you want to handle it on your own, you must arrive by 8:30 a.m. in Las Horquetas, which is 15 kilometers north of the Guápiles Highway on the Río Frío–Puerto Viejo turnoff. At 9 a.m. a tractor-pulled *chapulín* leaves Las Horquetas for Waterfall Lodge, 15 kilometers away. (Don't attempt this adventure if you have a bad back.) The trip takes three hours. It is impossible to get to Rara Avis any other way, except by horse (available through Rara Avis), which takes longer and involves walking the last three kilometers, because the road is covered with logs. Rara Avis is in the process of improving the road so that part of the trip can be made by jeep, reducing travel time to two hours and allowing for two trips a day. Check with them on current conditions.

OTHER RAINFOREST LODGES   To the east of Puerto Viejo is ✪ **El Gavilán Lodge** (private bath, hot or heated water; $50-$60/person, including breakfast; 234-9507, cell phone: 383-5627, fax: 253-6556; www.gavilan lodge.com, e-mail: gavilan@racsa.co.cr) on the Sarapiquí river. Here you'll find a private dock, a swimming hole, an outdoor cool-water jacuzzi, fruit trees, and an orchid collection on the landscaped grounds. Two kilometers away is a 100-hectare private forest reserve where visitors can hike or go on horseback tours. The lodge serves delicious meals emphasizing fresh fruits, salads, and tropical fruit drinks. No alcohol is served.

✪ **Selva Verde Lodge** (private bath, hot water, ceiling fans; $60-$70/person, double occupancy, including meals, children under 12 free, 12- to 15-year olds half price; 766-6800, fax: 766-6011, in the U.S.: 800-451-7111; www.holbrooktravel.com) in Chilamate, five minutes by car west of Puerto Viejo, is a complex of covered walkways leading to a riverside dining room, an open, airy lounging area with hammocks and a conference room. Its comfortable cabins are raised on pillars to jungle (and bird's-nest) level. Guests may roam trails in the secondary forest reserve. You must go with a guide to visit the butterfly garden ($5) and the primary forest reserve. Early-morning birdwalks are offered for guests, and three- to four-hour walks with naturalist guides leave at 8:30 a.m. and 1:30 p.m. Both guests and nonguests can join the hikes for $15 per person, including boots.

Selva Verde's owners, long concerned with the well-being of the local community, have established the **Sarapiquí Conservation Learning Center** (766-6482; e-mail: lrngcntr@racsa.co.cr), with the only library in the area, a day-care center, and English and environmental education classes. Volunteers are welcome to further the center's projects, and hotel guests can contribute by donating money to the center's scholarship fund.

✪ **La Quinta de Sarapiquí Lodge** (private bath, hot water, ceiling fans, pool; $50-$60, children under 12 free; phone/fax: 761-1052; laquintasara piqui.com), on the Río Sardinal one kilometer off the main Puerto Viejo–La Virgen road, has lush gardens that attract a variety of birds. Guests can visit their butterfly garden, ride horseback or fish in their tilapia pond for free.

✪ **Centro Neotrópico Sarapiquís** (private bath, ceiling fans, phones, internet connection, $90-$100, children half price, meals $25/day; 239-1627, 761-1004, fax: 239-2738, 761-1415; www.sarapiquis.org, e-mail: magistra@ racsa.co.cr) is a beautiful ecolodge on the banks of the Río Sarapiquí, patterned on a 15th century pre-Columbian village. It is a project of the Landscape Foundation, a group of European architects who wish to evoke the interrelationship of humans and nature through their circular structures with soaring thatch roofs, each of which houses eight spacious rooms with French doors that open to covered terraces outside. Furnishings are antiques or artisan-made. The restaurant terrace overlooks the river and the Tirimbina rainforest reserve. Cuisine includes fresh fruit raised in the gardens and edible flowers, once part of the indigenous diet. The use of solar energy and natural wastewater treatment make this a truly ecologically sound project.

The 300-hectare **Tirimbina Reserve** is connected to the lodge by a bridge across the Sarapiquí. Visitors can explore an island in the river or learn about the rainforest from a naturalist guide who accompanies them on a suspended walkway spanning a gorge in the reserve. Groups leave daily at 8 a.m. for the two-and-a-half-hour hike ($12, children $6). An interactive cultural and ecological museum is under construction, as is a research and education center. This project, with its integral, educational vision, promises to be a great draw for ecotourism in this region.

In the village of La Virgen, ✪ **Rancho Leona** (phone/fax: 761-1019; rancholeona.com, e-mail: rleona@sol.racsa.co.cr), 12 kilometers southwest of Puerto Viejo, has a restaurant that offers eggplant parmesan, BLTs, and vegetarian dishes. The rancho has a family environment, with good music, games, and a library. They offer internet access and a computer network for Starcraft fans. Leona and Ken, the owners, have an art studio where they design and make T-shirts, stained glass, and jewelry out of native seeds. They can point you toward a beautiful waterfall nearby, or toward good hiking for serious adventurers. Lodging (shared bath, solar-heated water, hot tub, sauna; $12-$20) is simple and unique.

GETTING THERE: By Bus: Buses to Puerto Viejo de Sarapiquí leave several times a day from the Caribe terminal in San José at the end of Calle Central. The 6:30 a.m., noon, and 3 p.m. buses travel the scenic route above Heredia. The trip takes a little over three hours. The 8 a.m., 10 a.m., 11:30 a.m., 1:30 p.m., 3:30 p.m., and 4:30 p.m. buses take the Guápiles Highway through Braulio Carrillo and turn north to Las Horquetas, La Selva, and Puerto Viejo, where they end. This trip takes only an hour and a half. You will have to change buses or get a taxi to go to Chilamate or La Virgen if you take the latter route. Be sure to take the bus to Puerto Viejo de Sarapiqui, not Puerto Viejo de Talamanca.

If you are coming from Monteverde or Guanacaste and want to explore Sarapiquí without going back to San José, you can take buses to Tilarán and then from Tilarán to San Carlos. To do this, you will have to spend the night in San Carlos or La Fortuna (see below). The San Carlos–Río Frío bus leaves at 5 a.m. and 5:30 p.m. and takes about three hours to reach Puerto Viejo. Aguas Bravas (766-6574) offers transfers from Sarapiquí to La Fortuna for $20. Also, check out www.costarica pass.com for private bus routes all over Costa Rica.

By Car: A scenic route above Heredia winds around the northeast side of Poás Volcano to the northern plain and passes through La Virgen, Chilamate, and Puerto Viejo before reaching La Selva. (Don't go this way if you tend to get carsick.) It is one of the most beautiful rides you can take, passing by the powerful La Paz waterfall on a hairpin turn, with vistas of the forests of Braulio Carrillo to the east. This route takes two and a half hours from Heredia, all on paved road. To combine this trip with a visit to Poás, go straight instead of turning right at Vara Blanca, travel about six kilometers to Poasito, and turn right. You should be at Poás in about 20 minutes. Recommended.

A quicker, less winding route is along the Braulio Carrillo Highway from San José. Turn left on the road to Puerto Viejo after you descend out of Braulio Carrillo National Park. The new road to Puerto Viejo from the turnoff is smooth, wide, and virtually straight, taking you through cow pastures and oil palm plantations and passing Las Horquetas, the entrance to Rara Avis, on its way to La Selva and Puerto Viejo.

You can get from Volcán Arenal to Puerto Viejo in under two hours, avoiding San Carlos, if you turn left at El Tanque, eight kilometers out of Fortuna, then take the turnoff to Muelle (Route 4), following signs to Aguas Zarcas and turning right at each turn. At Aguas Zarcas, 23 kilometers west of San Carlos, turn left to San Miguel, and left again to La Virgen, Chilamate, and Puerto Viejo, all on paved roads.

SAN CARLOS

Ciudad Quesada is a bustling commercial center located in the San Carlos plain of central Alajuela Province, one of Costa Rica's most agriculturally productive zones. The countryside is a vibrant green with pastoral, rolling hills. Within half an hour of Ciudad Quesada there are several resort hotels and interesting ecotourism destinations.

Termales del Bosque ($5, phone/fax: 460-1356; e-mail: termales@racsa. co.cr) is a great place for the travel-weary to stop on their way to La Fortuna. After a short hike through this 100-hectare forest reserve, you arrive at a series of thermal pools of different temperatures next to a rushing stream. There is a stone sauna cantilevered over the river, a place to change with showers and lockers, a little building for massage and mud treatments, and a rustic snack bar. Everything has been left as natural as possible, so you bathe under the canopy of the trees. Don't spend more than 20 minutes in the warm baths before immersing yourself in the river to cool off. Up near the road is a restaurant, a canopy tour (five platforms, three traverses, and a rappel) and rather sterile but comfortable rooms (private bath, ceiling fans, $50-$60, including breakfast). It's seven kilometers east of San Carlos in San Rafael de Aguas Calientes on the road to Aguas Zarcas. Recommended.

On the other side of the Río San Rafael, set back from the road in forest shade, sits Costa Rica's foremost health spa, **El Tucano** (private bath, hot water, some bathtubs, air conditioning, cable TV, phones; $90-$100; 460-3152, fax: 460-1692; e-mail: tucano@racsa.co.cr). El Tucano offers mini-golf, tennis courts, horseback rides, and tours. Its elegant European-style spa, graced with marble fountains, is staffed by a team of Romanian physiotherapists, schooled in massage, hydrotherapy and mud treatments. They have supervised detoxification programs that can last several weeks or more. Health spa clients get special package rates in the off-season. The natural warm mineralized waters of the area are channeled into a swimming pool. Jacuzzis, a sauna, a gym, a beauty salon, and a gift shop full of Italian bath and beauty products complete the luxurious scene. This 100-room hotel also has a conference center. The food was not great when we were there, but the impending arrival of a Spanish consortium might change that.

Just beyond El Tucano is the **Zoológico La Marina** (open daily, 8 a.m. to 4 p.m.; admission $1.50), a private zoo with a wide selection of Costa

Rican fauna living in conditions a bit better than the Bolívar zoo in San José. Officially recognized by the Wildlife Department, La Marina now accepts injured or illegally held animals for rehabilitation and special care.

GETTING THERE: By Bus: San José–San Carlos buses ($1.50) leave almost every hour, 5 a.m. through 6 p.m., from the Atlántico Norte station on Calle 12, Avenida 9. It's a three-hour trip. Try to get a Directo bus—it makes fewer stops. Take any of the following buses from the Ciudad Quesada terminal: Río Frío, Puerto Viejo, San Miguel, Pital, Venecia, or Aguas Zarcas.

By Car: Take the Naranjo exit, about an hour down the General Cañas Highway from San José, and continue north through Zarcero to San Carlos. For information about Zarcero, see the Central Valley chapter. Signs in Ciudad Quesada will direct you to the Aguas Zarcas road just north of the cathedral. San Rafael de Aguas Calientes is about ten minutes away, La Marina is about 20 minutes away, and Aguas Zarcas just a few minutes more.

Sixteen kilometers south of the Nicaraguan border, ✪ **La Laguna del Lagarto Lodge** (shared bath, heated water, ceiling fans, $50-$60; private bath, $60-$70; 289-8163, phone/fax: 289-5295; www.worldheadquarters.com/cr/hotels/lagarto, e-mail: lagarto@racsa.co.cr) is a prime birdwatching spot, with 350 species sighted, including the endangered green macaw. The comfortable rooms sit on a hill overlooking a rainwater lake filled with orchid-draped dead trees. You can paddle in a canoe through this rather eerie waterway into the rainforest. Ten miles of trails lead through 500 hectares of primary rainforest and nontraditional agricultural plantations (pepper, heart of palm). Also offered are horseback rides through the pasture area of the farm, and a three-hour boat ride up the Río San Carlos to the Nicaraguan border. The lodge is remote, and you should probably have four-wheel drive to get there by car. The roads are well-paved to Pital, then it's 23 kilometers on a well-maintained gravel road to Boca Tapada, then 6.4 kilometers to the lodge. From Ciudad Quesada, buses leave almost hourly for Pital, where you can connect with the Pital–Boca Tapada bus at 9:30 a.m. or 4 p.m. From San José, a bus leaves the Atlántico Norte terminal (Calle 12, Avenida 9) for Pital every day at 5:30 a.m. and 12:30 p.m., connecting with the 9:30 a.m. and 4 p.m. buses to Boca Tapada. If you arrange it in advance, the staff will pick you up in Boca Tapada; otherwise, a taxi from Boca Tapada is $24 for the remaining 6.4 kilometers to the lodge. The lodge can arrange transportation from San José for $75/person.

Located in Platanar, between Florencia and Muelle, ✪ **Hotel La Garza** (private bath, heated water, ceiling fans, air conditioning, refrigerators, phones, jacuzzi, pool; $80-$90; 475-5222, fax: 475-5015) has a lovely site on the hilly banks of the Río Platanar, and is named for the flocks of herons that use the river as their daily migration path. The quiet bungalows are located across a hanging bridge from the restaurant. Each has a porch and hammocks overlooking the river. Half-day guided horseback rides ($30-$40) take you through the pastures of the dairy farm across the river; the farm includes a 350-hectare forest reserve, one of the few remaining in San Carlos.

In Muelle de San Carlos, the **Tilajari Resort Hotel** (private bath, hot water, air conditioning, ceiling fans, pools; $90-$100; 469-9091, fax: 469-9095; e-mail: tilajari@tilajari.com) also serves as a country club. It offers tennis, racquetball, volleyball, and basketball courts, a sauna, a conference room, a game room, a bar, and a restaurant. The well-groomed lawns are interspersed with stands of bamboo and other tropical plants; rooms overlook the Río San Carlos. The Tilajari offers horseback riding and guided walking tours through a private forest reserve as well as tours of the Juan Castro Blanco cloudforest reserve. Located 22 kilometers north of Ciudad Quesada.

GETTING THERE: By Bus: Catch a bus in Ciudad Quesada to Platanar, Los Chiles, or Boca Arenal; one of these leaves approximately every half hour.

By Car: Follow the road towards Florencia, where you turn right (north) to reach Platanar and Muelle.

CAÑO NEGRO WILDLIFE REFUGE

Caño Negro Wildlife Refuge comprises the Río Frío and Caño Negro Lake, which grows and shrinks seasonally. The wetland refuge was created to protect the diverse aquatic birds that live and breed there including the northern jacana, which builds its nest on lily pads; the endangered *jabiru*; black, long-necked, and sharp-billed anhingas; and roseate spoonbills, the only pink birds in Costa Rica. Caño Negro is home to the country's largest colony of olivaceous or neotropical cormorants, glossy black birds that fish in groups then dry out their wings in the sun. Birding is best between January and April. Sloths, iguanas, and three types of monkey inhabit the trees on the shores of the Río Frío; you will probably see caimans and turtles, and maybe even the gar fish, a prehistoric relic with a caiman-like snout, and a hard exoskeleton. Fishermen are enthusiastic about the lake because of the tarpon, snook, rainbow bass, machaca and drum that abound there. Park rules prohibit fishing from April through July.

The village of **Caño Negro** is within the Refuge, right on the western side of the lake. It still has not been impacted by tourism, because most of the tours that say they are going to "Caño Negro" actually go to the bustling border town of Los Chiles, 19 kilometers northeast of the village, where a fleet of canopied tourist boats takes people to the eastern edge of the refuge, but not inside it, so they won't have to pay the park entrance fee. Here we have the dilemma of ecotourism. Because it has been "left out" of the tourist boom, the village and the shimmering lake have the pure, untouched feel of the Costa Rica of twenty years ago, without the plethora of billboards and "tourist info centers" that plague places like La Fortuna. The mayor and the park director are trying to open the area to tourism in a principled way. Even though new Swiss and Italian fishing lodges were being built when we were there, we hope this tiny village can avoid the pitfalls that have transformed other sleepy little towns into tourist traps. Refuge staff have been working to involve residents in conservation and protection activities; they participate in maintaining turtle and caiman nurseries, and a butterfly garden, which you can visit near town. The park office can set you up with a guide.

There are a couple of *sodas*, and rustic lodging at ✪ **Albergue Caño Negro** (shared bath, cold water, mosquito nets; $7-$12; beeper: 224-2400 for Alvaro Arguedas Molina, 461-8464, message in Spanish, fax: 471-1198; e-mail: alvaroarguedas@biesanz.com), whose informative owner, Don Alvaro Arguedas, offers wildlife observation boat rides ($25/person including park entrance) through the reserve, and fishing trips for $10/hour, or a full day of fishing, including meals and lodging, for $100. Take repellent. The **Kingfisher Lodge** (private bath, fans, $12-$20; beeper: 233-3333 for Carlos Sequeira Sibaja), located just beyond park headquarters, has very nice, clean cabins with screens and good air circulation. Recommended.

GETTING THERE: By Bus/Boat: From Upala, the bus leaves at 11:15 a.m. and 3:45 p.m., and takes about two hours to reach Caño Negro ($2). The San José–Los Chiles bus leaves at 5:30 a.m. and 3 p.m. There is a Los Chiles–Caño Negro bus at 2 p.m. It's a good idea to call the Soda La Amistad (461-8464) in Caño Negro to confirm these schedules. Spanish only.

By Car: There are two ways to get to Caño Negro. Take Route 4 northwest from El Tanque to San Rafael de Guatuso (**Rancho Ucurín**, on the left just beyond Guatuso is a good place to stop for lunch). Drive 25 kilometers (1/2 hour) north of Guatuso to the small town of Colonias de Puntarenas and take the marked gravel road to the right for another 26 kilometers (an hour and a quarter drive). Because there are a lot of potholes and many speed bumps between Guatuso and Colonias, it's probably better to take the Los Chiles road—Route 35 north from Muelle. Seven kilometers before you get to Los Chiles, a National Park sign indicates the road to Caño Negro on the left. It's 19 kilometers (1 hour) on a pretty good gravel road from there.

CAVERNAS DEL VENADO   The Cavernas del Venado (cell phone: 284-9616) are alive with thousands of bats, cave fish, crickets, and spiders. Located an hour's drive north of La Fortuna, they are more accessible than the caves of Barra Honda (see the Guanacaste chapter), but are not for the faint-hearted. To explore them, you must wade through a rushing underground river, which is only knee- to ankle-high in dry season, but rising as high as a meter in the rainy season. At some points, you must crawl on your hands and knees. Guides accompany visitors on the hour-and-a-half tour ($6/person). Kids are welcome as long as they don't get too scared of the river or the dark. Boots, flashlights, face masks, and helmets are included in the admission, as well as soap and showers for after the hike. It's important to bring a change of clothes. The caves were closed for two months in 1998, after several visitors came down with histoplasmosis, a fungus infection that affects the lungs, causing flu-like symptoms, which can be transmitted by exposure to bat droppings. Studies have shown that the incidence of histoplasmosis within the caves is low, but now the Ministry of Health requires wearing protective gear and showering afterwards. Hotels and tour agencies in La Fortuna, an hour away, offer excursions to the caves, or you can drive there yourself. Call ahead in order to have a guide waiting for you when you get there—otherwise you might have to wait for him.

On the way to the caves, **Cabinas Las Brisas** (shared bath, cold water; $7-$12) is a clean and inexpensive place to stay in the nice little town of Venado.

GETTING THERE: It's better to approach from the east, as all but the last two kilometers before the caves are paved. From Lake Arenal the road is entirely unpaved, and sometimes disappears in the middle of a cattle pasture. Drive north from El Tanque towards San Rafael de Guatuso about 30 minutes. Turn left at a turnoff marked Jicarito. From there it's 15 minutes to the picturesque village of Venado. The driveway to the caves is marked by a sign on the right, on a gravel road 2 kilometers beyond Venado. A bus leaves Ciudad Quesada at 2 p.m. for Venado, arriving at 4:30 p.m.

Due west of Ciudad Quesada, on the San Ramon–La Fortuna road, are three beautifully situated rainforest lodges:

Chachagua Rain Forest Hotel (private bath, hot water, ceiling fans, restaurant; $90-$100; 231-0356, fax: 290-6506; www.novanet.co.cr/chachagua, e-mail: chachagua@novanet.co.cr) is a comfortable mountain ranch about half an hour south of La Fortuna, two kilometers off the main San Ramón–La Fortuna road. Trails lead through a private forest reserve, and horseback tours around the farm are possible. A stream passes between the spacious, wood cabins and the open-air restaurant; it is channeled into a shallow, cement-bottomed pool that is especially good for kids. It's a nice getaway for families.

About an hour south of La Fortuna is **Valle Escondido Lodge** (private bath, hot water, bidets, ceiling fans, pool, jacuzzi; $70-$80; 231-0906, fax: 232-9591; www.valleescondido.com, e-mail: valle@ns.goldnet.co.cr), a hotel/

restaurant on the La Tigra road. It sits on an ornamental plant farm nestled on the side of a steep valley, with views of the northern plains and neighboring forest reserves. There are tours with agronomists through the cultivated fields and the packing plant, as well as hikes on trails through the forest-covered sections of the farm. Mountain bikes and horses are available for rent. The rooms are comfortable; some are carpeted. The restaurant specializes in excellent Italian dishes. If nothing else, it's a great place to have lunch on your way to or from the volcano.

Hotel Villablanca, a renowned cloud forest lodge, is also along this road. See our description in the Central Valley chapter under "San Ramón."

GETTING THERE: From the Central Valley, turn north at San Ramón, 55 minutes west of San José. Follow the signs for "Villablanca" through town. Valle Escondido is roughly halfway between San Ramón and La Fortuna, and Bosques de Chachagua is only about half an hour south of La Fortuna.

From Ciudad Quesada, continue west past Florencia to Jabillos, where you turn left to get to the San Ramón–La Fortuna road. Once there, turn right to Chachagua and left to Valle Escondido.

VOLCÁN ARENAL

Volcán Arenal is the quintessential volcano. Its perfectly conical shape emerges from Alajuela's gentle green hills. From time to time, loud explosions are heard, a gray, brown, orange, or blue mushroom cloud of gases and steam billows out of the top, and you can watch the ejected boulders as they bounce down the slopes. Although the volcano is capable of inspiring intense fright and awe in visitors, inhabitants of nearby **La Fortuna de San Carlos** and the dairy farms at the volcano's base seem to live with relative peace of mind.

Arenal was dormant until the late 1960s, and the only people who suspected that it was a volcano were those who had scaled it and found a crater and steam vents at the top. But few listened to them, until a series of earthquakes began shaking the area late in the evening of July 28, 1968. The following morning, Arenal blew, sending out shock waves that were recorded as far away as Boulder, Colorado. All damage occurred roughly five kilometers west of the volcano, where people were knocked down by shock waves, poisoned by volcanic gases, and struck by falling rocks. Lava flows eradicated the town of Pueblo Nuevo, and by the end, 78 people had died. Three new craters formed during the explosion.

Arenal is most impressive at night—in the dark, bursts of fire and red-hot rocks shoot hundreds of feet into the sky. Incandescent material cascades down the slopes, especially on the north side. In the daytime, you only see steam and hear the volcano's terrible roar. There are explosions every few hours during Arenal's active phases, but it can go for months without activity. Very often the volcano is shrouded in clouds and it's hard to see anything— even if it's active. When we were there in October 1999, the volcano would rumble every few minutes, and lava would ooze down its northwestern side. The day after we left there was a major explosion with huge clouds of ash.

Note: Although the volcano is not dangerous at a distance, it is very perilous to climb. One tourist was killed and another burned in July 1988, when they hiked too near the crater, foolishly trusting Arenal's placid appearance between explosions. If they had seen it explode before climbing, they probably would never have begun. They also unwittingly risked the lives of 15 Costa Rican Rural Guards and Red Cross workers who heroically searched the volcano to retrieve the body of its victim. The volcano is not safe to scale even part-way. There are steam vents and abysses, and lava sometimes descends quite far down the side. *Do not climb this volcano.* Even observation areas can be deadly. On August 23, 2000, a tour guide was fatally burned and a tourist and her daughter seriously injured when a sudden pyroclastic avalanche of hot gases, rocks, and mud opened up on Arenal's northeast slope above Los Lagos. This was the strongest eruption since 1968. The guide and his tourists were in an area previously regarded as safe when the avalanche traveled toward them at 80 kilometers per hour.

Between La Fortuna and Lake Arenal there are a few spots worth checking out:

The **Catarata La Fortuna** is a beautiful waterfall five and a half kilometers from the town of La Fortuna. If you have the time, it's a nice walk. There are two ways to get there. At the back of the church you'll see a sign pointing south to the La Fortuna–San Ramón road. Go one kilometer toward San Ramón and turn right up a country lane. There is one hill about halfway there; it's roughly paved with rocks, and you can negotiate if your engine is powerful enough and you don't mind a few dents in your chassis. An easier way to get there is to stay at Cerro Chato Lodge or La Catarata (see below) and walk, drive, or ride horseback two or three kilometers. There is a parking lot and information office at the entrance (open daily, 8 a.m. to 4 p.m.; $1.50). If you want to walk down to the bottom of the falls, keep to the right on the ravine trail. The trail has steps built into it at the steepest parts, and there are guardrails. The force of the waterfall is such that swimming is not possible, but the hike is an exhilarating workout—it took us about 45 minutes to descend and huff and puff back up again.

Los Lagos (phone/fax: 479-9126, fax: 479-8009; admission $3) is a park on the lower slopes of Arenal, six kilometers northwest of La Fortuna. The lower of Los Lagos' two sections has pools (with hair-raising slides, volcano fountain, jacuzzi, etc.), a restaurant, and **cabins** (private bath, heated water, air conditioning, direct TV, phones, refrigerator; $60-$70, including breakfast). To the right at the entrance is a reptile zoo, a crocodile farm, and ponds for fishing.

Two kilometers farther into the park, up steep cement tracks through pastureland, you will reach the first of two beautiful lakes. The first emerald-green lake has paddleboats and you can swim in it as well. There are covered picnic tables with grills and water taps, good bathrooms, and a *soda* open weekends. Just above here is the site of the August 2000 avalanche, so visit at your own risk.

There are three choices for enjoying the thermal waters that spring out of the volcano. However, you should be aware that the area was the site of a 1975 hot avalanche deposit (the ongoing source of heat for the thermal waters) and vulcanologists consider the location hazardous and at risk for future hot avalanches. In fact, during stronger-than-usual explosions on May 5, 1998, and October 25, 1999, lava flowed to within 500 meters of Tabacón. Four hundred tourists and employees were evacuated, but business was back to normal within 48 hours. With that in mind, you can die happy at **Tabacón Resort** on the left (open daily, 10 a.m. to 10 p.m.; $16/person, children $9). Here a stream is channeled into a veritable thermal wonderland: 12 pools of varying temperatures and depths; one waterslide; benches tucked under waterfalls; jacuzzis and individual tubs. There is a great restaurant (open daily, noon to 10 p.m.), with a creative and varied menu including vegetarian dishes. The place seems a bit hectic out front, especially when you see all the tour buses parked there, but there is plenty of room once you get onto the lushly landscaped grounds to find your own little stream and a warm waterfall to massage your shoulders. There are several cold pools and showers to cool off in. The management recommends that you alternate hot with cold water every 15 minutes to avoid high or low blood pressure. Two paramedics are employed by the resort. It is definitely worth the entrance fee, especially if you stay into the evening to watch the volcanic fireworks. While at Tabacón, you can visit their **Iskandria Spa** and get a massage or mud wrap ($40-$50), a facial ($25-$40), or a combination of all three ($110; www.tabacon.com).

Across the street you'll find the budget thermal springs, with the same water but in a creek that's terraced into sandy-bottomed pools. Entrance fees here are $5; there are changing rooms, showers, and toilets. Farther on toward the lake, there is a widening in the road where you can pull off and clamber down to the free hot springs (slippery trails, no bathrooms). The latter two hot springs lack a view of the volcano.

To get to the hot springs from La Fortuna (if you don't have a car), take the 8 a.m. bus to Tilarán. The driver will let you off at any of the hot springs or parks. A taxi to Tabacón costs about $5.

Three kilometers beyond the springs, as the road curves around the volcano, you'll come to a turnoff on the left to **Arenal National Park** (479-9654). If you pay the entrance fee ($6/person), you can drive farther up and view the volcano from there. Their four-kilometer "Los Tucanes" trail leads through the area devastated by the 1968 eruption. Because the volcano is often obscured by clouds, the park has a beautiful visitors center where you can watch videos of the more spectacular displays and find out about the history of the volcano, the hydroelectric production of Arenal Dam, and the flora and fauna of the area. The center is down a road to the right a bit beyond the guardhouse, which takes you to nature trails and several lookout points with terrific views of both the volcano and Lake Arenal. Birding is especially good in this area. A taxi from La Fortuna to the park costs about $12.

Advertised as the "rapid transit system," the horseback ride to Monteverde has become very big business in La Fortuna, and many tour groups are springing up to get some of the action. The only way to get to Monteverde by road is to drive or take a bus around the north side of Lake Arenal to Tilarán, and then take the very bad Tilarán–Santa Elena road or go down to

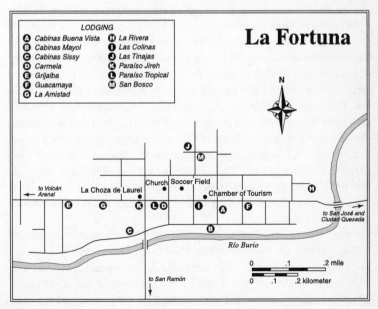

La Fortuna

LODGING

Ⓐ Cabinas Buena Vista
Ⓑ Cabinas Mayol
Ⓒ Cabinas Sissy
Ⓓ Carmela
Ⓔ Grijalba
Ⓕ Guacamaya
Ⓖ La Amistad
Ⓗ La Rivera
Ⓘ Las Colinas
Ⓙ Las Tinajas
Ⓚ Paraíso Jireh
Ⓛ Paraíso Tropical
Ⓜ San Bosco

N

to Volcán Arenal ←

La Choza de Laurel

Church

Soccer Field

Chamber of Tourism

Ⓗ

to San José and Ciudad Quesada

Ⓔ Ⓖ Ⓚ ⒻⒹ Ⓘ Ⓐ Ⓕ

Ⓒ Ⓑ

Río Burio

0 .1 .2 mile
0 .1 .2 kilometer

to San Ramón

the Interamerican Highway south to the Lagarto entrance and an hour and a half uphill from there. However, there are horse trails between El Castillo, on the south side of the lake, and San Gerardo, a lookout point 13 kilometers from Monteverde from which you can see the volcano. The horseback ride can be done in four hours. A taxi then drives you to your Monteverde hotel. People have told us that this trip, although beautiful and enjoyable, is hard on the horses—in fact, we have heard about horses dying on the trail. One problem is that the short *criollo* horses that are used by most companies have to walk in knee-deep mud, especially during the rainy season, and get overworked. We talked with **Desafío**, one of the major adventure tour companies in the area, and they assured us that they use bigger horses, and the horses get four to seven days off between trips.

The Monteverde horseback trip is a steep, muddy ride in which several rivers must be forded. Do not do it in the rainy season. The mud is too deep and slippery and the river crossings can be dangerous because of flash floods. The tours cost $65 one way and include a fruit snack, but be sure to get some breakfast before you go. The companies will take your bags and cars up to Monteverde if you don't mind someone you don't know driving your rental car. We would be interested in hearing feedback about this trip from our readers. E-mail us at info@keytocostarica.com.

The main tour operators in town are **Aventuras Arenal** (half a block east of El Jardín restaurant; 479-9133, fax: 479-9295), **Sunset Tours** (open daily, 7 a.m. to 8 p.m, offices next to the Rancho La Cascada restaurant; 479-9415, fax: 479-9099; www.sunset-tours.com, e-mail: info@sunset-tours.com), where you can make international phone calls, and **Desafío**, which specializes in rafting and adventure travel and offers internet access (open daily, 7 a.m. to 8 p.m.; phone/fax: 479-9464; desafiocostarica.com, e-mail: desafio@racsa.co.cr). The tours offered by these operators and the many "tourist information offices" in town include a volcano and hot springs night tour, horseback riding to the Catarata La Fortuna, mountain biking in the National Park, a boat tour of the Caño Negro Wildlife Refuge, boating and fishing on Lago Arenal, a visit to the Cavernas de Venado, rafting on the Sarapiquí river (a three-hour drive east), and a float down a smooth river with lunch at a *campesino* home and rainforest hiking.

Note: Because there are so many hotels in La Fortuna, the competition is fierce. Hotels often send people to meet the buses and convince tourists to go one way or the other. Don't be swayed by these people. They also will try to sell you tours, but never accept a tour from someone who doesn't have an office and a business permit, in case something goes wrong and you need somewhere to go to complain.

Renting a bike is a good way to get mobile if you don't have a car in this area. It's a hilly but lovely ride from La Fortuna west to the springs and the lake. Bikes are for rent at **Ciclo Cali**, on the left as you head west leaving Fortuna. If you lack stamina, taxis are relatively cheap and plentiful ($5) from Fortuna to the hot springs.

LA FORTUNA RESTAURANTS   These are some of our favorite places to eat in La Fortuna: **Cafetería El Río**, a block south of the soccer field, is simple, family-run, and has great *gallo pinto* with homemade tortillas in the morning; **El Jardín**, right on the main street near the bus stop, has historically been the place for good, inexpensive Tico-style food. Their *plato del día* is cheap and comes lightning fast. **La Choza de Laurel**, on the main road after the church, offers *casado* plates with traditional *picadillos*; it has nice decorative touches and the waitresses are dressed in colorful *campesina* attire. It also has the local administered public phone. **Rancho La Cascada**, a large thatch-roofed restaurant across from the football field, is the most elegant restaurant in town, but seems to cater mostly to tour groups. **Monpik** has a good ice cream parlor a few doors down, across from the plaza. **Hotel Pizzería and Spaghettería Vagabondo**, one and a half kilometers beyond La Fortuna on the left, just after Cabinas Rossi, serves genuine Italian food, and their rooms are very nice too (private bath, hot water; $30-$40; 479-9565; e-mail: vagabond@racsa.co.cr). For a flavorful, well-prepared meal on your way to or from the hot springs or the volcano, visit the large, thatch-roofed **La Pradera** (open daily, 11 a.m. to 11 p.m.; 479-9167) three kilometers west of La Fortuna. **El Novillo**, on the left just before Tabacón Lodge, is the place to go for grilled meats.

LA FORTUNA LODGING   These are the nicest accommodations ($30-$90) in La Fortuna, listed from east to west (the cheaper ones follow on the next page). All have good mattresses, new furnishings, and views of the east (nonactive) side of the volcano:

Las Cabañitas (private bath, hot water, ceiling fans, pool, restaurant; $80-$90; 479-9400, 479-9343, fax: 479-9408), a few hundred meters east of town, across the road from the gas station, are comfortable, tile-roofed *casitas,* finely crafted in the traditional manner.

Villa Fortuna (private bath, hot water, fans, pool, $30-$40; with air conditioning, refrigerator, $40-$50; with kitchen and room for four or five, $50-$60; phone/fax: 479-9139), has spacious cabins with porches and rocking chairs in a large, bird-filled yard. It is on the right as you approach town, just beyond Las Cabañitas. Recommended.

Our favorite place to stay in La Fortuna itself is **Cabinas La Rivera** ($30-$40, including breakfast; 479-9048), owned by a German-Tica couple, with beautiful gardens full of fruit trees, flowers and herbs, a small pool and barbecue area with a great view of the volcano, a kitchen area for guests, and clean, simple rooms. It's quieter than most places in town because it's off the main road. To get there, take the first right coming into La Fortuna from the east, turn right again and go 300 meters along the dirt road. Recommended.

Guacamaya (private bath, hot water, air conditioning, small refrigerator; $30-$40; 479-9393, fax: 479-9087; www.cabinasguacamaya.com, e-mail: info@cabinasguacamaya.com) has grown from a couple of cabins in the owners' backyard to a row of comfortable, modern rooms.

The best thing about **San Bosco** (private bath, heated water, ceiling fans; $30-$40; with air conditioning, $40-$50; 479-9050, fax: 479-9109; www. arenal-volcano.com, e-mail: fortuna@racsa.co.cr) is the observation deck above the hotel. Apartments for groups are available ($80-$100). This is a cool, shaded place to sit and contemplate the great green pulsing giant. They have recently added a pool, jacuzzi, and gym.

Across the main drag from the church, **Paraíso Tropical** (private bath, hot water, ceiling fans, air conditioning, refrigerators; $20-$50; 479-9222, fax: 479-9722; e-mail: partro@racsa.co.cr) has wood-paneled rooms behind the owners' house, as well as more modern rooms. The second-story rooms have volcano views.

Paraíso Jireh (air conditioning, bathtubs, hot water; $40-$50, including breakfast; 479-9004, fax: 479-9549; www.arenaljireh.com, e-mail: jireh@ expressmail.net) offers helpful area maps and has an open Bible on a stand in each room.

Two more of our favorite places are located down a dirt road to the south, one and a half kilometers west of La Fortuna. Located at the base of the volcano, both have the advantage of being at a slightly higher altitude than La Fortuna, thus cooler. They are also off the main road enough to avoid sounds of grinding gears that are audible from almost all of the previously mentioned hotels. Both provide easy access to the Catarata La Fortuna. **Cerro Chato Lodge** (private bath, hot water; $40-$50, including breakfast; 479-9494, cell phone: 384-9280, fax: 479-9575) has tidy grounds and offers a special rate of $30 per person for the first night, including a horseback tour to the falls. They also offer a two-day tour for $120 that includes transportation to and from San José, visits to Sarchí, Zarcero, Tabacón, the La Fortuna falls, a night tour of the volcano and lake, meals, and lodging.

✪ **La Catarata** (private bath, hot water; $40-$50, including breakfast; phone/fax: 479-9522, 479-9612; www.agroecoturismo.net, e-mail: araocr@ mail.com) is an endeavor run by a cooperative of campesinos who have created a medicinal herb plantation with a solar herb dryer, a butterfly farm, and a project to raise endangered *tepiscuintles* and release them into the wild. They also raise orchids, tilapia, and organic vegetables. Even if you don't stay in their quiet, comfortable cabinas, you can tour their project for $1, have lunch or dinner at their restaurant, and have them point you toward the Catarata La Fortuna, only two and a half kilometers away. The downhome breakfast included in their rates will last you all day. This hotel also has a great place to camp ($2/tent). Recommended. To get there, go one and a half kilometers west of La Fortuna. Take a dirt road on the left just before Cabinas Rossi and go another one and a half kilometers, bearing left.

Budget hotels ($10-$30): The following lodgings are clean, inexpensive, decent places for budget travelers in the town of La Fortuna. Unless noted, all have private baths, heated water, and fans. Most offer secure parking lots. They appear in order, east to west:

Right at the bus stop, **Cabinas Buena Vista** (hot water; $12-$20; 479-9027, 479-9326) are new and clean. Second-story rooms have volcano views. A good value.

One block south of the gas station, **Cabinas Mayol** (private bath, hot water, pool; $20-$30; 479-9110) has a pool for adults and one for kids, good water pressure in the showers, good mattresses, and nice gardens, with the sound of the Río Burió in the background. Recommended.

One block west, **Las Colinas** ($20-$30; phone/fax: 479-9107; www.ac commodations.co.cr, e-mail: hcolinas@racsa.co.cr) is a three-story hotel whose front rooms have volcano views.

Las Tinajas ($20-$30; 479-9308; e-mail: mcastro@racsa.co.cr) is very clean and has nice furnishings.

Across from the church and owned by a large family, **Carmela** ($20-$30; with refrigerator and room for four, $40-$50, two room apartment with kitchen, $70-$80; 479-9010; www.hostelling-costarica.com) has rooms of all shapes and sizes. Those in the back are quieter.

Across from La Choza de Laurel are two cabinas side by side: **La Amistad** ($20-$30; 479-9364, fax: 479-9342), and **Grijalba** ($20-$30; 479-9129). Some of the cheaper rooms in front have no windows. The new, more expensive rooms in back are very nice.

Cabinas Sissy (with shared bath, $5/person; private bath, $7/person; 479-9256, 479-9356) is an excellent deal. It's squeaky-clean, well-run, and even has little plants in the hallway. It's on a quiet back street off the main drag. Recommended for budget travelers.

Because volcano watching is best at night, we recommend getting a hotel with a view of the active side of Arenal. These hotels are listed below.

Three sets of cabinas, all with excellent views of the current lava flows on the north side of the volcano, are another two kilometers to the west of those listed above. Since they are six to nine kilometers from La Fortuna, you will probably want a car if you plan to stay here. **Volcano Lodge** (private bath, hot water, ceiling fans, air conditioning, pool, $80-$90, including breakfast; 460-6080, fax: 460-6020; e-mail: mcastro@racsa.co.cr) features comfortable rooms with volcano views and an outdoor, warm-water jacuzzi where you can soak your travel-weary muscles while watching lava ooze down the side of Arenal. **Arenal Paraíso** (private bath, hot water, ceiling fans, refrigerator, pools, jacuzzi; $50-$60; with balcony, TV, air conditioning, $80-$90; 460-5333, fax 460-5343; www.arenalparaiso.decostarica.co.cr, e-mail: arenalpa@racsa.co.cr) has trim wooden cottages with open porches— breakfast is served across the street. ✪ **Montaña de Fuego** (private bath, hot water, wall fans, $80-$90; junior suites with refrigerators, $100-$110, kids under ten free; 460-1220, fax: 460-1255; www.costaricabureau.com/montana defuego.htm, e-mail: mntnadefuego@costaricabureau.com) is a bit fancier, with glass-enclosed porches and its own restaurant, Acuarelas. Both Arenal Paraíso and Montaña de Fuego have forest reserves and offer tours on horseback.

Another two kilometers toward Lake Arenal is **Tabacón Lodge** (air conditioning, cable TV; $130-$140, including breakfast and access to Tabacón resort; 256-1500, fax: 221-3075; www.tabacon.com, e-mail: sales@tabacon. com), a luxury hotel across from the famous hot springs. Hot water is piped into the tubs and showers from the springs. Each room has a terrace with a close-up view of the volcano. Considering that the price includes unlimited access to Tabacón, the rates are quite reasonable for luxury accommodations. Recommended.

Continuing around the volcano, you come to the entrance of the National Park on the left. Going two kilometers beyond the park headquarters and climbing a steep hill on the south side of the volcano, you'll arrive at the ✪ **Arenal Volcano Observatory** (hot water; with volcano views, $110-$120; without views, $70-$80; budget rooms with shared bath and common sitting room with fireplace, volcano view from porch, $40-$50; children under ten free; meals $45/day; 257-9489, 695-5033, fax: 257-4220; www.arenal-ob servatory.co.cr, e-mail: info@arenal-observatory.co.cr). This site was chosen by Smithsonian vulcanologists who wanted a safe vantage point from which to study the volcano's activity. There is a small museum with a seismograph monitoring current action. When there is an eruption during the day, you are close enough to see boulders bouncing down the sides of the volcano, but if there are no eruptions, you are better off viewing the incandescent lava flows on the northwest side at night. The climate is cool and fresh, and there are tours and self-guided hikes up the old lava flows, to a nearby waterfall, and to the Cerro Chato, a dormant volcano. A bouncy hanging bridge leads to the newer luxury rooms with volcano views. If you cannot afford to stay, $2 will get you a day's access to the trails and a seat on the restaurant's well-appointed viewing deck. Birding is great there. Though the road to the entrance is bumpy, the steep road up to the lodge from the entrance is paved.

Before you get to the observatory entrance, there is a turnoff to the right for the hilltop ✪ **Linda Vista del Norte** (private bath, hot water; $60-$70, including breakfast; 479-9623, fax: 479-9443; www.costaricabureau.com/lindav, e-mail: lindav@costaricabureau.com), a family-owned restaurant and hotel with a fantastic view of the volcano *and* the lake. Half of the rooms don't face the volcano, so request one that does; the restaurant terrace provides great views for all. *Casados* at the restaurant are well prepared and feature tilapia raised in Lake Arenal. Linda Vista offers a five-hour horseback and hiking trip to the volcano ($20/person), as well as a large natural reserve on the family farm. You have to ford two small rivers on the way to the lodge, but regular cars can make it. We have heard that the walls are thin here, but hopefully you'll be on the same schedule as your neighbors. Recommended.

GETTING THERE: By Bus: From San José, buses (255-4318; $4) leave the Atlántico Norte terminal for La Fortuna every day at 6:15 a.m., 8:40 a.m., and 11:30 a.m., returning at 12:45 p.m. and 2:45 p.m. From Ciudad Quesada you can catch a La Fortuna bus at 6 a.m. and 10:30 a.m. From Monteverde or Santa Elena, catch the 7 a.m. bus to Tilarán. In Tilarán, catch the San Carlos bus at 12:30 p.m. It will drop you in La Fortuna. To get to Monteverde from La Fortuna, take the 8 a.m. bus to Tilarán (3 hours), have lunch in Tilarán, then board the 12:30 bus for Santa Elena (2 hours, $2).

Fantasy Tours (220-2126, in U.S.: 1-800-272-8854, in Canada: 1-800-453-6654, current schedule at www.fantasy.co.cr/fantasy_bus) has daily air-conditioned buses to Arenal from San José, Tamarindo, Liberia, Playa Flamingo, and Playa Jacó. Any trip costs $19. Buses leave at 8 a.m. and return at 2 p.m. If you are coming from somewhere other than the above-mentioned towns, see www.costaricapass.com. These private buses are less complicated than taking public transportation. Your hotel can make reservations for you.

Don Taco of Cabinas Don Taco in Monteverde (645-5263) takes people by taxi, boat, and jeep to Monteverde ($75 for two, $115 for three or four). The trip takes three hours—that's even faster than the horseback ride. Ask about it at the Hotel Las Colinas in La Fortuna. **Mirador San Gerardo**, near Monteverde, provides a similar service (phone/fax: 645-5087, cell phone 381-7277). **Sunset Tours** (479-9415, fax: 479-9099; www.sunset-tours.com, e-mail: info@sunset-tours.com) can also set this up for you.

Another option (four-wheel drive transport that goes around the lake) is offered by **Cabinas Paraíso Tropical** in La Fortuna (479-9222) for $25/person (minimum two people). We have heard that their driver, Alexander, is excellent.

By Car: A direct road connects La Fortuna with San Ramón de Alajuela. From San José, follow the Interamerican Highway west and turn north at San Ramón, 55 minutes west of San José. Follow the signs for Villablanca through town, then north along a lovely road. This road borders a reserve that protects a beautiful rainforest southeast of Monteverde and conserves the water supply for the town of San Ramón. It ends right in La Fortuna. Alternate routes are: through Naranjo, Zarcero, and Ciudad Quesada; through Heredia, Varablanca, San Miguel, and Aguas Zarcas; or from Monteverde or Guanacaste by way of Tilarán and Lake Arenal.

By Air: SANSA (221-9414, fax: 255-2176; $50 one way) has a daily San José–La Fortuna flight as well as one from Tamarindo ($56). Check current schedules at relee.webwize.com/travel. Travelair (232-7883, 220-3054, fax: 220-0413) also has a daily San José–La Fortuna flight. Check schedules at www.centralamer ica.com/cr. The La Fortuna airstrip is new. It's out in the middle of a cane field and lacks facilities. See Chapter Four for reservation information.

LAKE ARENAL

Lake Arenal is a large reservoir at the foot of the volcano. The original Laguna Arenal was the source of a river whose waters flowed east to the Atlantic. Dams built for a hydroelectric energy plant enlarged the lake and diverted the waters. Now they flow from the northwest side of the reservoir to irrigate Costa Rica's dry Pacific coast.

Many people enjoy boating and fishing on the lake. The lake also offers the best windsurfing conditions in the country, if not in all of Central America. The lodges on the west side of the lake specialize in windsurfing and rent equipment.

LODGING   Lake Arenal's eastern and northern banks are flanked by a road that passes by all the lodgings listed below. It's easiest to have a car if you want to stay at one of these places. You can do it on a bus, however, although you won't have the same mobility for eating out and getting around. Just get off the San Carlos–Tilarán bus where you want to stay, and expect to remain there till the next bus comes along. It's pretty easy to hitchhike with tourists along the lake. Just watch for Suzuki Sidekicks, the ubiquitous four-wheel-drive rent-a-cars.

After La Unión, the road around the lake has some unpaved patches until you hit Nuevo Arenal. The road is a great way to connect Volcán Arenal, Sarapiquí, and Tortuguero with Monteverde and the beaches and parks of Guanacaste. Be sure to call ahead and check on its condition before setting out.

The lake is dammed at its southeastern tip, 20 kilometers from La Fortuna. Just north of the dam, **Arenal Lodge** (private bath, hot water; with view, $70-$80; with view, some with kitchens, $130-$160, including breakfast; 228-3189, fax: 289-6798; www.arenallodge.com, e-mail: arenal@racsa.co.cr) is a comfortable place, high on a hill two and a half kilometers from the main road. There is a lovely view of Volcán Arenal from the dining room and most guest rooms. A library with leather chairs and a fireplace, an outdoor jacuzzi, and a pool table contribute to the clubby atmosphere. Fishing trips on the lake are $250 per day.

After about 14 kilometers you will come to an imposing Swiss chalet–style hotel, painted on the outside with romantic scenes from the heroic lives of Costa Rica's Juan Santamaría and a mysterious Swiss-German hero. **Los Héroes** (private bath, hot water, pool, phones; $60-$120, including breakfast; phone/fax: 284-6315, fax: 228-1472; e-mail: heroes@racsa.co.cr), adorned with Swiss memorabilia and a Swiss restaurant, is owned by a Swiss-Tica couple. The small rooms are plainly decorated. The owners are putting together a small railroad (made in Switzerland) that will go through tunnels and across bridges to take guests into the rainforest at the back of the property. They also have a small chapel for weddings.

Two kilometers to the west, in La Unión de Arenal, **Toad Hall** (open daily, 8 a.m. to 4 p.m., cell phone: 381-3662, fax: 471-9178) is a nontraditional general store with a fabulous selection of local and national handicrafts (Cecilia Figueres' fanciful ceramics, hand-sewn dolls made by a local *campesina*, indigenous masks, and spears, to name a few). There is a used-book nook and a delightful restaurant that has outside tables overlooking the lake and a healthy menu featuring organic vegetables, fruit drinks and smoothies, and espresso. Recommended.

Next door to Toad Hall, the Belgian-owned **Marina Club Hotel** (private bath, hot water, ceiling fans, one with kitchenette, restaurant, pool; $80-$130, including breakfast; phone/fax: 284-6573; e-mail: marina@skynet.be) includes in its price the use of horses and canoes. Its originally decorated units are private, and guests can enjoy a view of the lake from the beds.

After two more kilometers you get to **Sabor Italiano Restaurante y Refugio Artesanal** (cell phone: 385-1474), about eight kilometers from Nuevo Arenal. The pizzeria supports the work of a family of artistic Italians, and the small open-air restaurant is decorated with their weavings, paintings, and fanciful wood sculptures. They rent two small houses with kitchens and hot water for $50.

Arenal Botanical Gardens (open daily, 9 a.m. to 5 p.m.; closed Sunday afternoons; fax: 694-4273; exoticseeds.com; admission $8) is one of the most lovingly designed that we've visited. It showcases a complete collection of plants from around the world. On a sheltered hillside four kilometers after Nuevo Arenal, there is a self-guided tour that takes you through the lush garden, and the owner is usually on hand to answer questions or share plant anecdotes. There's also a butterfly garden. It's an easy lakeside stroll from Villa Decary. Recommended.

Two kilometers down the road (and only two kilometers from Nuevo Arenal) is **Villa Decary** (private bath, hot water, ceiling fans; $60-70; with kitchen, $80-$90; one-bedroom bungalows with kitchen and a great view of the lake, $130-$140; fax: 694-4330, cell phone: 383-3012; www.villade cary.com, e-mail: info@villadecary.com), with large, clean, comfortably furnished rooms whose balconies overlook the lake below. The North American hosts are warm, gracious, interested in their guests, and eager to help with recommendations for further travel. Within moments of our arrival we saw seven species of small, jewel-like birds. About a hundred meters from the hotel a troop of howler monkeys sojourned by the lake, oblivious to our presence. Rates include breakfasts with homemade preserves. No credit cards. Recommended.

The prosperous town of **Nuevo Arenal** was founded by ex-inhabitants of the old Arenal when that town was submerged by the lake in the 1970s. It is cool and breezy there. Most locals are afraid to swim in the lake; there have been several drownings, usually due to the victim not knowing how to swim or being inebriated. Bikes are for rent for $1.25 an hour near the church. Ask at Omar's grocery store.

We spent an unforgettable morning with Gordo from **Establo Arenal** (694-4092). He takes you up to a ridge where you can see heart-shaped Lago Coter on one side and Lake Arenal on the other. He sings *rancheros* as he rides along, and embodies the joyful sprit of the *vaquero guanacasteco*. His bright, friendly daughter Alexandra often comes along, an excellent horsewoman at 12 years old. All hotels in the area arrange horseback trips with Gordo. His operation is a genuine Tico experience. Another great horseman is Lucas, 694-4357.

You should treat yourself to a meal at **Tramonti** (open Tuesday through Sunday, 11:30 a.m. to 3 p.m., 5 p.m. to 9:30 p.m.; 694-4282; located in a subdivision accessible from the southern entrance to town), whose Italian owners bake their pizza in traditional wood-burning ovens. There is a German bakery on the right as you enter Nuevo Arenal. Our favorite place is **El Caballo Negro** (open daily, noon to 8 p.m.; 694-4515) on the right, three kilometers west of Nuevo Arenal. This open-air restaurant in a garden setting

Arenal Area

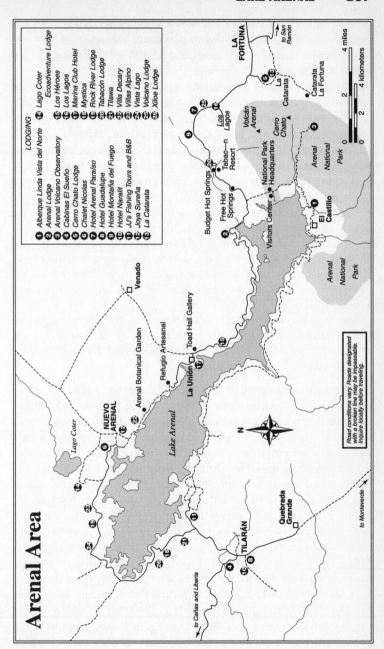

LODGING
1. Alberque Linda Vista del Norte
2. Arenal Lodge
3. Arenal Volcano Observatory
4. Cabinas El Sueño
5. Cerro Chato Lodge
6. Chalet Nicolas
7. Hotel Guadalupe
8. Hotel Arenal Paraíso
9. Hotel Montaña del Fuego
10. Hotel Naralit
11. J's Fishing Tours and B&B
12. Joya Sureña
13. La Catarata
14. Lago Coter
15. Ecoadventure Lodge
16. Los Héroes
17. Los Lagos
18. Marina Club Hotel
19. Mystica
20. Rock River Lodge
21. Tabacón Lodge
22. Tilawa
23. Villa Decary
24. Villas Alpino
25. Vista Lago
26. Volcano Lodge
27. Xiloe Lodge

Road conditions vary. Roads designated with a broken line may be impassable. Inquire locally before traveling.

LA FORTUNA
to San Ramón

Catarata La Fortuna

La Catarata

Volcán Arenal

Cerro Chato

Los Lagos

Tabacón Resort

National Park Headquarters

Budget Hot Springs

Free Hot Springs

Visitors Center

El Castillo

Arenal National Park

Arenal National Park

Lake Arenal

La Unión

Toad Hall Gallery

Refugio Artesanal

Arenal Botanical Garden

Venado

NUEVO ARENAL

Lago Coter

TILARÁN

Quebrada Grande

to Cañas and Liberia

to Monteverde

N

4 miles
4 kilometers

(with a hammock for post-prandial siestas!) features hearty European and vegetarian home cooking using organic ingredients. The owner and her triplet daughters have rescued many animals, and the girls sell their artwork to pay for the animals' upkeep. Recommended.

The Canadian-owned **Joya Sureña** (private bath, hot water, ceiling fans or air conditioning, restaurant/bar; $60-$70, including breakfast; 694-4057, fax: 694-4059) has attractive, light-filled rooms and colorful murals illustrating the history of the site. In addition to the pool, gym, jacuzzi, sauna, and tennis court, the grounds include fruit and nut orchards, a conference room, and sitting areas for watching wildlife. To get there, turn left onto a rocky road at the gymnasium at the northern entrance to Nuevo Arenal. The hotel is one and a half kilometers east of town.

GETTING THERE: By Bus: All of the lake lodgings and Nuevo Arenal are served by the Tilarán–Ciudad Quesada bus, which leaves Ciudad Quesada at 6:30 a.m. and 3 p.m. and passes through La Fortuna around 8 a.m. It returns from Tilarán at 7 a.m. and 12:30 p.m. You can ask to be let off anywhere along this route. More frequent buses from Tilarán to Nuevo Arenal stop at all the hotels in the northwestern section of the lake. From Nuevo Arenal you can get a taxi to places east of town.

By Car: From La Fortuna, drive around the volcano, then bear right to skirt the lake's northern shore. The full distance from La Fortuna to the town of Arenal is 47 kilometers, but it could take as long as an hour and a half to drive, given the curves and possible bad road conditions.

The northwestern shore of Lake Arenal has become a mecca for windsurfers, providing the most stellar conditions for this sport that you will find in Central America. You can get a lot of information about wind conditions at www.windsurfer.com. Even if you do not windsurf, consider spending a night on the lake if you plan on encircling it on your way to or from Volcán Arenal.

✪ **Chalet Nicholas** (private bath, hot water, table fans; $60-$70, including breakfast; non-smokers only; phone/fax: 694-4041; e-mail: nicholas@ sol.racsa.co.cr) is a small bed and breakfast run by a friendly North American couple in their home. They will accompany guests on hikes through a large public reserve bordering their own reforested farm, or down to the lake for swimming and birdwatching. They can also arrange horseback trips. On a clear day, you can see a distant view of Volcán Arenal from every room. Visitors should like dogs, because the owners have several Great Danes.

Lago Coter Eco Lodge (private bath, hot water, ceiling fans; meals, $37/day; 257-5075, fax: 257-7065, in the U.S.: 888-326-5634; www.eco-lodge. com, e-mail: information@eco-lodge.com) has individual cabins with lake and volcano views from their private balconies ($70-$80) and comfortable hotel rooms ($50-$60). They offer two-day, one-night packages including meals, horseback riding, and kayaking on Lago Coter for $120-$130 per person. In addition to a canopy tour, hiking, horseback riding, water sports, and volcano trips are offered. The lodge's rainforest nature trail is completely lined with wooden planks, so you won't slip and slide. Access to the lodge's site on a small mountain lake is via a three-kilometer gravel road in good condition.

Villas Alpino (private bath, heated water, kitchen; $30-$40; 284-3841, allow five days for response) are attractive, efficiently designed bungalows for four with a great view of the lake. Good value.

Rock River Lodge (private bath, heated water; $50-$100; phone/fax: 695-5644; e-mail: rockriver@racsa.co.cr) has nice rooms with wide porches for enjoying the view. A comfortable restaurant/bar with a fireplace adds to the ambiance. The lodge offers mountain-biking trips and can arrange windsurf equipment rental.

Vista Lago (private bath, heated water; $30-$40; 661-1363, 661-1840) has cabinas creatively designed with stone-masoned baths and porches. The **Soda Macha**, across a little bridge in the village of Rio Piedras has good *comida típica*.

Nearby **Tico Wind/Bic Windsurfing Center** (open December through April; 695-5768, in the U.S.: 800-678-2252, fax: 503-343-7507) rents equipment ($45/day or weekly rates) and gives lessons to those proficient in "waterstarting."

Xiloe Lodge (private bath, heated water; $12-$20; with kitchen, $30-40; 259-9806, 259-9192, fax: 259-9882) rents small cabins. Its **Restaurante Equus** (open Tuesday through Friday at 4 p.m.; Saturday and Sunday, 10 a.m. to 11 p.m.) features barbecued chicken. They have dances every weekend.

The rooms at **Mystica** (private bath, hot water; $40-$60; cell phone: 382-1499, fax: 695-5387; members.aol.com/mysticacr) are comfortable and have delightful artistic touches. The flowering vine–covered porches have distant views of the volcano across the lake. Their restaurant serves breakfast from 7:30 a.m. to 9:30 a.m. From 12 p.m. to 9 p.m. they offer homemade pasta, fresh salads, and excellent pizza, enlivened by fresh tomatoes and herbs grown in their garden.

The last hotel is the North American–owned **Hotel Tilawa** (private bath, hot water, ceiling fans, pool, tennis court; $80-$120; with kitchens, $130-$140; seven-day package rates; 695-5050, fax: 695-5766, in the U.S.: 800-851-8929; www.hotel-tilawa.com, e-mail: webmaster@costaricanet.net). Their **Windsurf Center** on the banks of the lake, a kilometer away, offers both guests and walk-ins windsurf equipment rental for $45-$55 per day.

Soon you will see signs for Tilarán to the right and Tronadora to the left. If you are on your way to Monteverde or Guanacaste, turn right to go into Tilarán. There are more lakeside lodges on the road to Tronadora:

Just before the turnoff for the campground, you will see the sign for **JJ's Fishing Tours and B&B** (phone/fax: 695-5825). JJ (Juan José Chaverría) speaks perfect English and can take you by boat or jeep to the volcano and hot springs or fishing ($150 for a four-hour trip, including lunch and refreshments). He offers special packages for guests in his bed and breakfast (private bath, heated water, ceiling fans; $50-$60). He also arranges fishing trips including airport transfers and other details.

Down the road is a big, new, Dutch-owned project called **Las Palmas** (695-5764) with covered soft and hard tennis courts, a heated swimming pool with a removable roof, and a sauna, gym, and restaurant overlooking the lake. Cabinas were under construction when we were there.

GETTING THERE: Buses for Tronadora leave Tilarán six times a day. By car, the trip takes about 15 minutes.

TILARÁN

Fifteen minutes beyond the lake is the clean, pleasant mountain town of Tilarán, with its streets full of cowboys and churchyard trees full of songbirds.

Leaving Tilarán through Quebrada Grande on the road to Monteverde, you can see three sources of non-fossil-fuel energy: the large white windmills that catch the wind off Lake Arenal to the northeast, the three fumaroles at the Miravalles geothermal plant to the north, and the candy-striped surge tank of the Arenal hydroelectric plant. The Costa Rican government is committed to finding alternative sources of energy by the year 2020. On a clear day you can also see four volcanoes from this site: Tenorio, Miravalles, Rincón de la Vieja, and Orosi.

La Carreta Restaurant (695-6654), behind the Cathedral, is a real treat. Its North American owners use garlic and spices to liven up their pizzas and pastas and make unforgettable sandwiches with homemade bread. Try the "Dennis" sandwich made of eggs, onions, and jalapeños, or the garlicky dorado salad. Their guestbook is full of comments from travelers who have had one gallo pinto too many and really appreciate their creative cookery. Open for breakfast, lunch, and dinner every day except Sunday morning. While you are waiting for your meal, browse in their unique gift shop. They can give you directions to a nearby *finca* with a ceiba tree whose trunk is 30 feet wide, 100 feet in circumference.

Cabinas El Sueño (private bath, heated water; $20-$30; 695-5347), half a block from the northwest corner of the park, has a nice interior garden and sitting area. **Hotel Naralit** (private bath, heated water, ceiling fans, some TVs, some carpeted; $20-$40; 695-5393), across the street from the cathedral, is the most comfortable place to stay in Tilarán. Recommended. **Hotel Guadalupe** (private bath, heated water, wall fans, TV; $20-$30; 695-5943), one block south of the Cathedral, is very new and clean with a nice atmosphere. Good value; recommended. All of the above hotels have guarded parking.

GETTING THERE: By Bus: It's a four-hour trip to Tilarán from San José (Calle 14, Avenidas 9/11; 7:30 a.m., 9:30 a.m., 12:45 p.m., 3:45 p.m., and 6:30 p.m.; 222-3854; $3). If you are traveling to Tilarán from Monteverde, catch the 7 a.m. bus from the cheese factory (a two-and-a-half-hour trip on bumpy but passable roads). You can continue on to La Fortuna by connecting in Tilarán to the 12:30 p.m. San Carlos bus. The bus from San Carlos to Tilarán passes through La Fortuna around 8 a.m., arriving in Tilarán around 11 a.m. You can continue to Monteverde on the 12:30 p.m. Santa Elena bus.

By Car: From the Interamerican Highway, turn into Cañas and continue 22 kilometers up into the mountains on a good paved road.

From Monteverde: Passable gravel roads connect Tilarán with Monteverde. In the rainy season, ask first about the best route and current road conditions.

From La Fortuna: It's a pleasant two-hour drive, longer with stops at the attractions along the shores of Lake Arenal. The road conditions are not great between the volcano and the town of Arenal. Between Arenal and Tilarán the road is in good shape.

MONTEVERDE

During most of the two-hour ascent east from the Interamerican Highway to Monteverde, you climb through deforested, eroded pastures. This would be Costa Rica's future without conservation: unbridled tree-cutting and cattle-grazing until nothing is left but dust in the dry season and mudslides in "winter." When you arrive at the misty heights of Monteverde, you see the other possibility, which, thanks to the work of a growing number of conservationists, has become reality. Here the land is still productive for farmers and, with large patches of forest untouched and thick windbreaks between pastures, there's plenty of moisture and less erosion. The contrast between the two areas is staggering.

The road from the Interamerican Highway to Monteverde is graded but unpaved. The worst stretch is at the very beginning. Monteverde residents, in an attempt to protect the simple, friendly lifestyle that has made their community such a special place, have fought against paving the road, believing that easier access would ruin the peaceful ambiance of the area. Many communities in Costa Rica have developed tourism quickly over the last few years because they desperately need the business, but often much is lost in the process.

Monteverde, because it has always concerned itself with social issues, is perhaps more articulate about these problems than most other rural villages being overwhelmed by tourism. A group of Alabama Quakers who felt that Costa Rica's disarmament policy was in line with their pacifist tradition started dairy farming in Monteverde in the early 1950s. Visiting biologists found the cloud forest above their community rich in flora and fauna, and the Quakers, along with the Tropical Science Center, had the foresight to make it a reserve.

Monteverde is not a place you can visit in one day. You need a day for travel and recovery each way, plus at least two days to visit the Monteverde Reserve and other nearby attractions.

Bring rain gear, warm clothes, and good socks. Most hotels rent rubber boots. Be sure to dress in layers for the trip up and down. You forget when you are in cool, windy Monteverde how swelteringly hot you'll be by the time you get to the Interamerican Highway.

VOLCANO VIEWING FROM MONTEVERDE Although many people make a circuit from Volcán Arenal to Monteverde by way of Tilarán, it is not widely known that you can see the volcano from the hills north of Monteverde. Part of the reason for this is that clouds on the rainy Atlantic slope often obscure the view. But when it is clear, the view of the volcano behind the forested slopes of the Children's Eternal Rainforest is awe-inspiring. We know of four places from which you can see this lovely sight: by hiking to the observation tower of the Santa Elena Reserve or the San Gerardo station in the Bosque Eterno, or by walking or driving (four-wheel drive is necessary) to Mirador San Gerardo or the Vista Verde Lodge. The latter two are about a 45-minute drive from Monteverde. More information below.

MONTEVERDE CLOUD FOREST PRESERVE At Monteverde Cloud Forest Preserve (field station open daily, 7 a.m. to 4 p.m.; reservations: 645-5112; e-mail: montever@racsa.co.cr; admission $8.75, discount for students with ID, no charge for children under 12; $1 boot rentals), you can walk along the well-maintained trails with a self-guiding pamphlet available at the field station for $2. But we recommend taking at least one guided tour, as you will be shown wonders that your eyes alone would probably never catch. Call 645-5112, or 645-5122, or e-mail montever@racsa.co.cr to arrange a three- to four-hour guided tour ($15.25 plus entrance fee) the night before you

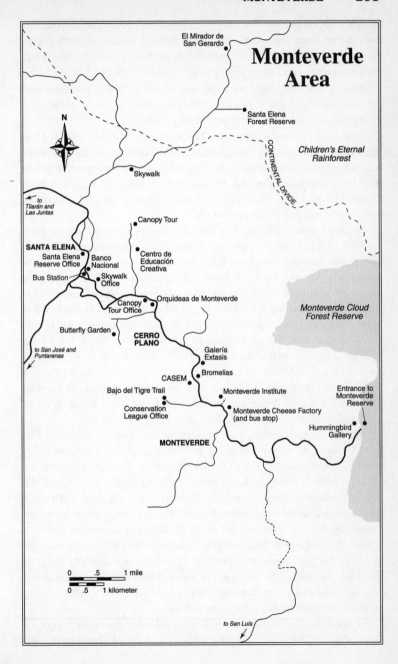

Monteverde Area

El Mirador de
San Gerardo

Santa Elena
Forest Reserve

CONTINENTAL DIVIDE

*Children's Eternal
Rainforest*

N

Skywalk

to
Tilarán and
Las Juntas

Canopy Tour

SANTA ELENA

Centro de
Educación
Creativa

Santa Elena
Reserve Office

Banco
Nacional

Bus Station

Skywalk
Office

Orquideas de Monteverde

*Monteverde Cloud
Forest Reserve*

Canopy
Tour Office

Butterfly Garden

**CERRO
PLANO**

to San José and
Puntarenas

Galería
Extasis

Bromelias

CASEM

Bajo del Tigre Trail

Monteverde Institute

Conservation
League Office

Monteverde Cheese Factory
(and bus stop)

Entrance to
Monteverde
Reserve

Hummingbird
Gallery

MONTEVERDE

0   .5   1 mile

0   .5   1 kilometer

to San Luís

want to visit the reserve. The tour, given by naturalists with years of experience in the cloud forest, includes a slide show of amazing wildlife photographs by Michael and Patricia Fogden, and helps support the preserve. The preserve's tours are done in groups of nine people. Your hotel can help you arrange a private tour, but it won't include the slide show. If you don't take the preserve's tour, but want to see the slides, there is a daily showing at 4:30 p.m. (admission $3, minimum of four people).

In order to protect the forest, only 150 people can be in the preserve at one time. If you'd like to miss the crowds, avoid the peak hours of 8 a.m. to 10 a.m. The least crowded months are between May and December, although it is rainier during that time, and the quetzals are less active. Or arrive at dawn (5 a.m. to 5:30 a.m.), which is the best time to observe the bird population, and pay the entrance fee on the way out.

Quetzals feed on the tiny, avocado-like fruits of *aguacatillo* trees. They are most visible in the early morning from January through June, especially during the mating season from February to May, but we talked to happy tourists who had seen them in November and December, too. The Monteverde Preserve's popularity has given impetus to the preservation of several other similar areas nearby, but this reserve is still the best place to see quetzals, due to its altitude and the maturity of its forest (quetzals like to live in old trees).

Beautiful, strange frogs also used to live in the cloud forest. The golden toad, once endemic to the Monteverde area, was remarkable for its color and the poison glands behind its ears, but it has not been observed for the last few years and is feared to be extinct. Biologists believe that global warming has caused a general drying trend in the cloud forest, depriving the frogs of the gentle mists that were vital to their existence.

When you arrive and pay your entrance fee, you'll see the preserve's **Visitors Center**. There you will find a relief map that shows you the entire area, including Lake and Volcán Arenal. The center also features several interactive wildlife paintings, illustrating the quetzal migratory cycle and the lives of nocturnal and diurnal animals. There is a souvenir shop, and a small restaurant that serves sandwiches, fruit drinks, and a very good vegetarian *casado*. Bathrooms are across the road. The Fogdens' slideshow is shown next door to the famous Hummingbird Gallery, on the right as you leave the preserve. The guided nature walks depart from there. In addition to the beautiful fauna and flora, other highlights of a hike in the preserve are a cascading waterfall, a mirador with stunning views of the area, and a 300-foot-long suspension bridge spanning the forest canopy.

If you like to live in nature, you'll enjoy hiking to the **rustic lodges**, El Valle, Eladio's, and Los Alemanes, within the preserve. The lodges have

THE CANOPY TOUR, SKYWALK, & SKYTREK

For those who tire of being earth-bound there are three other ways of exploring the cloud forest: the Canopy Tour, the Skywalk, and the Skytrek. For the **Canopy Tour** you are strapped into a harness, then you take a short hike through the forest until you come to a hollow strangler fig; you climb up inside it to reach a platform at its top. Your harness is then attached to a pulley system on a steel cable, and you zoom among the treetops to another platform 75 feet above the ground. There you climb a tower to another platform and zoom off again. After one more zoom you rappel down the last tree. Our seven-year-old was afraid to cross the first time, so a guide went across with her; the next crossings she did by herself. The kids loved this trip. The Canopy Tour office is in Cerro Plano, just after Johnny's Pizzeria on the way to Monteverde. They provide transportation to the Cloud Forest Lodge, where the tour takes place (645-5243, phone/fax: 257-5149; www.canopytour.co.cr; $50, student and child discounts).

The **Skywalk** (open 7 a.m. to 4 p.m.; fax: 645-5238; www.monteverde.co.cr; admission $8) is for those who aren't quite up to the Canopy Tour. It is a two-kilometer walk through a series of easy, well-maintained trails that lead to five narrow bridges with cyclone fencing on the sides, suspended as much as 120 feet above the ground. As with any wildlife tour, you should go early in the morning if you want to see animals. During the high season, visitors can hire bilingual guides (not as experienced as those in the Monteverde Reserve) who leave at 8 a.m. and 1 p.m. ($20/person, including entrance fee; reservations required). The hike takes about an hour and a half at a leisurely pace.

At the same forest is **Skytrek**, a much longer cable ride than the canopy tour ($35). Young kids cannot go on it because you need to weigh a certain amount to have the momentum to slide. The Skywalk office is just outside Santa Elena near the Serpentarium on the road to Monteverde, but the reserve itself, which protects 563 acres of forest, is on the road to San Gerardo, a 20-minute ride from Santa Elena. You can get there in a regular car, but you'll probably end up with a couple of dents on your undercarriage. The 7 a.m. jeep to the Santa Elena reserve passes by the Skywalk.

bunk beds with foam padding and gas stoves. Hikers must bring food and bedding. You can stay at the lodges for $3.50-$5 per night, plus the daily entrance fee. Volunteers who want to help with trail maintenance can stay at the Preserve Field Station ($14/person, including meals; 645-5122, fax: 645-5034; www.cct.or.cr, e-mail: montever@racsa.co.cr).

GETTING THERE: The preserve is a lovely 45-minute uphill walk from "downtown" Monteverde; farther from most hotels. Only La Colina, Fonda Vela, Mariposa, and Villa Verde are within 20-30 minutes' walk from the entrance. A bus ($1) leaves Santa Elena at 6:15 a.m. and picks up passengers all the way through Monteverde to the Preserve, where it arrives at around 7 a.m. It returns to Santa Elena at noon and makes the run again at 1 p.m., returning to Santa Elena at 4 p.m.

RESERVA SENDERO TRANQUILO   Reserva Sendero Tranquilo (open December through May; 645-5010) is the 200-acre private reserve of the Lowther family. Visitors must go with one of their excellent bilingual guides (reservations required; $20/person, including entrance fee). Visitors are usually pleased with the amount of wildlife they see. The tour often ends with a visit to the cheese factory and the crafts cooperative, CASEM. Recommended.

SANTA ELENA FOREST RESERVE   The 765-acre Santa Elena Forest Reserve (open daily, 7 a.m. to 4 p.m.; 645-5390; e-mail: reserve@monteverde info.com; admission $7, $4 for students), located six kilometers northeast of the nearby town of Santa Elena, has 12 kilometers of trails, with one leading to an 11-meter observation tower overlooking forest canopy; on clear days, you have a view of Arenal Lake and Volcano. There is a 45-minute self-guided trail; detailed ethnobotanical information is available for the tagged plants on the wayside. Arrange for guides ($15) beforehand through your hotel, or by calling 645-5014. You can rent boots there. Owned and maintained by the Santa Elena high school, this reserve helps to fund courses in environmental education, biology, language, and tourism. The Santa Elena Forest Reserve is an inspiring, community-run effort that should be a model for conservationists trying to integrate sustainable development with wilderness preservation. The reserve's information office has a *soda* (open daily, 7 a.m. to 4 p.m.) and small local crafts shop. A jeep leaves the Banco Nacional in Santa Elena each morning at 6:45 a.m., 10:30 a.m., and 1:45 p.m. for the Santa Elena Reserve (make reservations by calling 645-5014, 645-5236, 645-5390; $2 each way). It also passes by the Skywalk and can leave you three kilometers from Mirador San Gerardo (see below). A taxi from Santa Elena should cost about $7.

MIRADOR SAN GERARDO   On the way to the Santa Elena Forest Reserve, a fork to the left leads three kilometers to the private 100-hectare reserve at ⊙ **Mirador San Gerardo** (phone/fax: 645-5087, cell phone: 381-7277; www.electricmall.com/mirador, e-mail: miradoro@racsa.co.cr), famous for its spectacular views of Arenal Lake and Volcano during the dry season. One-day visits on horseback can be arranged; these include a hike to the reserve's waterfalls and lunch in the rustic dining room ($40). Lodging is also offered (heated water; dorm-style with shared bath, or individual cabin with private bath, $60-70, including breakfast). Meals in the restaurant are moderately priced. The owners also offer a horseback ride to Volcán Arenal ($65/person). It's a scenic and unique way to travel between these two popular destinations. Don't expect to enjoy this trip during the rainy season.

THE CHILDREN'S ETERNAL RAINFOREST   Children from all over the world have been inspired by the efforts of a group of Swedish fourth-graders who organized the first Children's Rainforest campaign in 1987, in response to a presentation at their school by a biologist who talked about growing deforestation in the Monteverde area. Since then, schoolchildren and adults from 44 countries have raised money to buy more than 50,000 acres of rainforest on the Atlantic slope to the east of the Monteverde Cloud Forest Reserve. This land, now the largest private reserve in Costa Rica, is called the Children's Eternal Rainforest (Bosque Eterno de los Niños, or BEN), in honor of the children of the world who have helped protect this special place.

Two rustic stations in the forest offer lodging for groups of students or tourists. The **Poco Sol Station** (dorm-type setting, shared bath), accessible from La Tigra, south of La Fortuna, is near a waterfall, hot mineral springs, and a mountain lake, with excellent hiking and wildlife observation opportunities. The **San Gerardo Station** (private bath, hot water when the generator is working; $30/person, including meals) offers a breathtaking view of Arenal Volcano and Lake Arenal. It can be reached in a two-hour downhill hike from the Santa Elena Reserve, but you cannot go without reservations. The station has comfortable bunkbeds and sleeps four to a room. The trails, and the chances of seeing the volcano, are best in the dry season. Highly recommended for those who enjoy hiking. Call (645-5003) for reservations to either station.

The only section of the Children's Rainforest currently open to walk-in visitors is the **Bajo del Tigre Trail** (open daily, 8 a.m. to 5 p.m.; admission $5, $2 for students with ID, including trail map). The entrance is down a side road on the right about 100 meters past Stella's Bakery and CASEM as you enter Monteverde—watch for the sign. Our favorite is the Murciélago trail, which goes along the canyon's edge. Bajo del Tigre has a **Visitors Center**, with a spectacular view of the Gulf of Nicoya, and a **Children's Nature**

Center, designed to help kids discover the wonders of a tropical mountain rain forest.

The **Monteverde Conservation League** (645-5003, fax: 645-5104; e-mail: acmmcl@racsa.co.cr; Apdo. 10581, 1000 San José), with an office at the entrance to the Bajo del Tigre trails, administers BEN. Besides ongoing projects in environmental education, reforestation, protection, and biological research, the League also has an ambitious plan to link up remnant patches of forest to create green corridors that will ensure the continued existence of habitats for migratory birds and butterflies. Donations for the League's important work are welcome.

BUTTERFLIES AND ORCHIDS   The **Butterfly Garden** (open daily, 9:30 a.m. to 4 p.m.; admission $7, students $5, children $3; 645-5512; www.best.com/~mariposa) is a section of forest at a lower altitude than the Monteverde Reserve that has been covered with a fine screen. There you can see all the different butterfly species that inhabit the zone, including the beautiful blue morpho. You're likely to see more butterflies on a sunny day than on a cloudy one. Guides give a fascinating explanation of the habits of each species, with ample botanical information as well. At the entrance is a free exhibit about the butterfly's life cycle. To get there, follow the small butterfly-shaped signs that start across from the Hotel Heliconia in Cerro Plano. Take the dirt road to the right 600 meters, turn left, then go another 300 meters.

Orquideas de Monteverde (645-5510; admission $5, children under 12 free) exhibits more than 400 species of orchids near the home of Monteverde's leading orchid expert, Gabriel Barbosa. Visitors are presented with magnifying glasses so they can observe *platystele gunnermanoides,* the world's smallest flower. At least 40 orchid species will be in bloom at any given time in the garden, located in Cerro Plano, next to Johnny's Pizza.

EDUCATION, ART, AND MUSIC IN MONTEVERDE   The **Monteverde Institute** (645-5053, fax: 645-5219) offers courses on a variety of topics for college students and adults. They also place volunteers in reforestation programs, reserve maintenance, and local ESL programs. See Chapters Two and Three for more information.

The **Monteverde Music Festival** (admission $12, children free), held from 5 p.m. to 7 p.m. every evening between mid-January and mid-March, is a wonderful chance to hear some of Costa Rica's best musicians. Concerts range from classical string quartets and brass ensembles to New Age, jazz, Afro-Caribbean, and folk groups. Don't miss it.

The Centro Panamericano de Idiomas' **language school** (645-5026; www.cpi-edu.com, e-mail: info@cpi-edu.com) is located on the road into

Monteverde, just before the gas station. They will arrange homestays with local families for you.

Monteverde Studios of the Arts (645-5434, in the U.S.: 800-370-3331; www.mvstudios.com, e-mail: mstudios@racsa.co.cr) is a summer program that combines the talents of local and international artists, dancers, potters, jewelers, photographers, cooks, storytellers, stringed instrument makers, stained-glass crafters, yoginis, masseuses, and personal-growth experts who give one-week workshops in Monteverde.

For arts and crafts, be sure to stop by **CASEM**, a cooperative of local women who make beautiful embroidered and handpainted clothing and souvenirs portraying quetzals, golden toads, and other cloud-forest flora and fauna. It's located on the right next to the food co-op as you enter Monteverde. Across the street, above **Meg's Stables** (645-5052), is the studio/gallery of Monteverde artists Stella Wallace and Meg Laval.

Marco Tulio Brenes' **Galeria Extasis** (645-5548) is nestled in the forest down a road to your right as you leave Monteverde. Using only wood from fallen trees, this local sculptor elaborates on the work already done by insects and fungi; his pieces follow the natural form and beauty of the wood. You can also see his work at the Hummingbird Gallery.

Patricia Maynard's **Hummingbird Gallery** (645-5030), near the entrance to Monteverde Reserve, exhibits Michael and Patricia Fogden's photographs from around the world. The Fogdens spend months at a time with sloths, frogs, snakes, insects, and birds, trying to get just the right shot. You'll never see better wildlife photographs. The framed photographs are not for sale, but slides and postcards are. The gallery sells beautiful Guatemalan textiles, locally made batiks, woodcrafts, ceramics, jewelry, tapes, posters, books, and T-shirts.

Bromelias, also owned by Patricia, is a similar store and gallery in the heart of Monteverde. It features the work of former Monteverde resident Sarah Dowell, celebrating the flora and fauna of Costa Rica. To get there, bear left immediately after Stella's, and you'll see it on the left after about 100 meters.

The famous **Monteverde Cheese Factory** (open Monday through Saturday, 7:30 a.m. to 4 p.m.; Sunday, 7 a.m. to noon) sells cheddar, jack, gouda, and other cheeses. You can also buy ice cream, fresh milk, and *cajeta* (delicious milk fudge) there. An observation room off the store allows you to watch the workers as they go about making cheese in the factory's huge vats.

Chunches (phone/fax: 645-5147), in the village of Santa Elena, could be the best-stocked bookstore in rural Costa Rica, with a great selection of literature in Spanish and English for children and adults, naturalist books, art and office supplies, and very useful topographical maps. It's also a laundromat ($5/load, washed and dried) and serves espresso, popcorn, and fresh-squeezed orange juice.

The **Centro de Educación Creativa** (phone/fax: 645-5161; e-mail: cecclc@sol.racsa.co.cr), is a bilingual school whose main focus is environmental education. Children maintain organic gardens, a recycling center, compost bins, a native tree nursery and a trail system, and study in the rainforest itself for a half-day every week. With more than half the students on scholarship, the school needs volunteers and stateside collaborators.

You can learn a lot about Monteverde online at www.monteverdeinfo.com, www.costaricabureau.com, and www.costaricanet.net.

HOTELS AND RESTAURANTS   The Monteverde area is made up of several small communities. **Santa Elena**, the bustling commercial and transportation center of the area, is the first town you come to on the road from the Interamerican Highway. Most of the budget accommodations are here, but some nice, quiet hotels are as well, like the upscale Monteverde Lodge and the helpful, affordable Arco Iris. North of Santa Elena, in the communities of **Cañitas** and **San Gerardo**, there are inexpensive rural lodgings, like Miramontes, Mirador San Gerardo, and Eco-Verde Lodge. South of Santa Elena on the four-kilometer road to Monteverde is the community of **Cerro Plano**, where most of the hotels are located. There are only six hotels in the community of Monteverde itself. There are accommodations in each area for all budgets. At the lowest end, campers can pitch their tents at several hotels and use their facilities for a modest fee. If you're tempted to do this, be aware that temperatures are low and wind and precipitation are high most of the year. *Note:* Christmas and Easter are booked months in advance.

SANTA ELENA HOTELS AND RESTAURANTS   Many of the *pensiones* here will cook for you and make you box lunches, or you can eat at the central, popular **El Daiquirí** (open daily, 6 a.m. to 10 p.m.; 645-5133), or the clean, inexpensive **Café Morpho** (645-5818) across from the bus stop. If you just want a snack, stop at **Chunches** around the corner to the right of the bus stop. The main landmark in Santa Elena is the Banco Nacional (National Bank), where you can change money or cash travelers checks (bring your passport). Directions are given from there.

The locally owned **Camino Verde** (shared bath, $5/person; private bath, $7/person; phone/fax: 645-5916), across from the bus stop, gives lots of information, sells tickets and provides transportation to the Santa Elena Reserve, and changes dollars daily until 9 p.m.

Three hundred meters east (uphill) from the Banco Nacional are two sets of cabins owned by brothers. The bright blue, spiffy **Cabinas Don Taco** (private bath, heated water; $20-$30, including breakfast; phone/fax: 645-5263) are carpeted and fuzzily furnished. Both the breakfast room and the enclosed porch have views of the Gulf of Nicoya. Don Taco runs the rapid-transit system from Monteverde to La Fortuna (see Getting There, below). **Cabinas Marín** (heated water; shared bath, $7-$12; private bath, $12-$20; 645-5279) are clean rooms behind the family's house. Rooms are bright green downstairs, varnished wood upstairs.

Back in town, **Pensión Santa Elena** (shared bath, shared rooms, $5/person; private bath, heated water, $7-$12/person; suite for six, $40; community kitchen; 645-5051, fax: 645-6060; www.monteverdeinfo.com/pension.htm, e-mail: mundonet@racsa.co.cr) has been recommended by several readers for helpful service and friendly atmosphere. They offer inexpensive internet access, international phone and fax service, and laundry service ($2). Some rooms are near the street, others are in the former Pensión Marbella, back from the road.

Pensión El Tucán (heated water; shared or private bath; $20/person; 645-5017, fax: 645-5462), 100 meters south of the Banco Nacional, has pleasant rooms above a *soda*. They also rent a few more secluded rooms (private bath; $20/person) down the street.

With very small upper-story rooms, **Pensión Colibrí** (shared bath, heated water; under $7/person), 75 meters south of the Banco Nacional, then 50 meters down a side street to the east, is run by a friendly couple who cook and offer horseback tours of the area.

At the end of that street on a grassy hillside is ✪ **Arco Iris Eco-Lodge** (private bath, hot water; $30-$50; 645-5067, fax: 645-5022; www.bbb.or.cr/lodges/arcoiris, e-mail: arcoiris@racsa.co.cr), a circle of private cabins, set in beautifully landscaped grounds. They will lend you binoculars so you can birdwatch right on the property, from nature trails near a small creek. Internet access and international phone and fax service are also offered, as well as same-day laundry service. Their restaurant has home-baked goods and lots of fresh vegetables. You must make reservations for meals at least two hours beforehand. The German owners provide lots of information for their guests and are committed to running their lodge in the most environmentally friendly manner possible. Recommended. A three-minute walk from downtown Santa Elena toward Monteverde, ✪ **Finca Valverde** (private bath with tubs, hot water; $70-$90, including breakfast; students: $40/person, including meals; 645-5157, fax: 645-5216; www.monteverde.co.cr, e-mail: info@monteverde.co.cr) is owned by a large local family, and has duplex wood cabins with lofts and porches, set back from the road in the forest. There's good bird-watching from the cabins themselves.

Monteverde Lodge (hot water, bathtubs; $110-$120; 257-0766, 645-5057, fax: 257-1665, 645-5126; www.costaricaexpeditions.com) is located on a road to the right at the entrance to Santa Elena. The lodge, built especially to accommodate tour groups from Costa Rica Expeditions, is spacious, beautifully designed, and comfortable. It features an indoor atrium with a large jacuzzi. The grounds include a botanical garden. A multimedia slide show incorporating sounds of the rainforest is shown several times a week ($5).

SAN GERARDO AND CAÑITAS HOTELS AND RESTAURANTS   One and a half kilometers above Santa Elena, on the way to the Skywalk and Santa Elena Forest Reserve, **Sunset Hotel** (private bath, hot water; $30-$40, including breakfast; 645-5048, 645-5228) is nicely landscaped and has fantastic views of the Gulf of Nicoya. There are birdwatching trails on their 35-acre reserve. The beautiful, glassed-in restaurant serves moderately priced dinners to non-guests (who must make reservations).

About six kilometers farther down this beautiful but bumpy road, and one kilometer before the Mirador San Gerardo, is the turnoff to **Hotel Vista Verde** (private bath, heated water, restaurant; $70-$80, including breakfast; cell phone: 380-1517; www.vistaverdelodge.com, e-mail: info@vistaverde lodge.com), with an incredible view of Arenal Lake and Volcano from each room and a nearby waterfall with swimming hole on their private reserve. You should have four-wheel drive to get to these two places. The manager of Vista Verde will pick you up in Santa Elena for about $10. Taxis cost $14. They do an Arenal horseback ride too.

In Cañitas, on the road to Tilarán, **Miramontes** (private bath, hot water; $40-$50, 645-5152, fax: 645-5297; www.multicr.com/miramontes, e-mail: miramont@racsa.co.cr) has a fine restaurant serving Swiss, French, and Italian specialties and homemade strudel. Their wood-paneled rooms are comfortable and reasonably priced, and the lodge runs a free shuttle to Santa Elena. Recommended.

Nestled in a private cloud forest reserve six kilometers from Santa Elena, **Albergue Eco-verde** (shared or private bath, hot water; $20-$30; 385-0092, 661-8126, 286-4203; www.agroecoturismo.net, e-mail: cooprena@racsa.co.cr) is a project initiated by a local *campesino* cooperative. Quetzals frequent the old-growth forest around the lodge, and trails lead to *miradores* where you can see Volcán Arenal. Accommodations are rustic and country cooking is served in their restaurant. You need four-wheel drive to get here, or take a taxi from Santa Elena. Call for directions—getting there is not a simple process.

CERRO PLANO HOTELS AND RESTAURANTS   Along the winding road between Santa Elena and Monteverde Reserve are most of the area's hotels. There is usually enough friendly traffic to try hitching, at least part of the way. Taxi service from this area to the Monteverde Preserve costs about $6 and can be worth it if you want to conserve your energy for hiking, or you can take the bus (see Monteverde Preserve, above).

About a kilometer off the road, nestled in a hilly forest, is the **Cloud Forest Lodge** (private bath, hot water; $60-$70; 645-5058, fax: 645-5168; www.costaricabureau.com/cloudforest.htm, e-mail: cloudforest@costaricabu reau.com). Its reserve is where the Canopy Tour takes place; lodge guests receive a discount. There is plenty of good hiking right around the lodge. Look for the turnoff on the left almost one kilometer outside Santa Elena. The lodge has a stunning view of the Gulf of Nicoya.

With large, comfortable rooms featuring either sunset-view terraces or fireplaces, ✪ **El Sapo Dorado** (private bath, hot water; with fireplace, $80-$90; with refrigerator and terrace, $90-$100; 645-5010, fax: 645-5180; www. costaricabureau.com/sapo, e-mail: elsapo@racsa.co.cr) is one of the area's finest hotels. A five-kilometer self-guided nature trail behind the hotel circles through a private cloud forest reserve. Their gourmet restaurant, open to the public, serves generous helpings of fantastic food and sinful desserts in an elegant setting, with excellent service. The carefully prepared cuisine is low in fat, sugar, and salt, and covers all tastes, from steak to vegetarian dishes to pizza for the kids. Highly recommended.

Along the main road as you approach the community of Cerro Plano is **Johnny's Pizzería** (open daily, 11:30 a.m. to 9 p.m.). Johnny's offers a salad bar and crispy, wood stove–baked pizzas, with some ingredients coming from the backyard vegetable garden. Around the corner, a hundred meters towards the Butterfly Garden, the **Restaurant De Lucía** (open daily 11 a.m. to 9 p.m.; 645-5337) serves light lunches; dinner specialties are steak and fish filets with a Chilean flair, with a few vegetarian dishes.

Nicely landscaped and with a comfortable, homey atmosphere, **Helico-nia** (private bath, hot water, bathtubs, jacuzzi; $80-$120; 645-5109, 645-5005, 645-5145, fax: 645-5007; www.centralamerica.com/cr/hotel/heliconia.htm, e-mail: heliconia@racsa.co.cr) has carpeted second-story rooms in the main lodge, and more private cabins out back. Guests get free admission to their bird sanctuary near the Santa Elena Reserve. **El Establo** (private bath, hot water; $40-$60; 645-5110, 645-5033, fax: 645-5041; e-mail: establo@ticoweb. com) is owned by a woman who came to Monteverde as the youngest Quaker of the original group. Enlarged black-and-white photos give a sense of the area's history. Beds have warm comforters, and the lobby has a fireplace-heated sitting area. Their sunny, quiet garden reading room with desk space is a good place to write letters.

About 100 meters farther along the main road, you'll find a road to the right, which leads to two of the most basic and inexpensive hotels near Monteverde. **Pensión Manakín** (shared or private bath, heated water; $10-$30/person; phone/fax: 645-5080; e-mail: manakin@racsa.co.cr) offers clean rooms in a family's modest but chaotic home. Next door is **Pensión El Pino** (shared or private bath, heated water, laundry sink; $10-$20/person; phone/fax: 645-5130), a small rooming house next to the owners' home. Meals are served on request. For $1 extra they will take you to the Monteverde Preserve.

The beautifully landscaped **Hotel de Montaña Monteverde** (private bath, hot water; $80-$90; 645-5046, fax: 645-5320; e-mail: monteverde@tico net.co.cr) has a sauna and jacuzzi overlooking the Gulf of Nicoya, a restaurant, some homey wooden cabins with forest views, other rooms with Gulf views, and a private reserve with nature trails.

On the left is the entrance to **Cabañas Los Pinos** (private bath, hot water, kitchen; one bedroom, $40-$50; two bedrooms, $60-$70; three bedrooms, $80-$90; 645-5252, fax: 645-5005) offering cabins in a peaceful setting—a good value, and the only cabins in Monteverde that have kitchens.

The chalet-style **Belmar** (private bath, hot water; $80-$90; 645-5201, fax: 645-5135; www.centralamerica.com/cr/hotel/belmar.htm, e-mail: belmar @racsa.co.cr) has beautiful views, comfortable rooms, and a good restaurant. Its entrance is uphill from the gas station on the left.

As the main road drops into a valley, you'll find the **Bar La Cascada** (open daily, 6 p.m. to 1 a.m.) with a nice view, lots of wood and windows, and moderate prices. It is the area's only disco; they often have live bands.

At this point, you still have not arrived in the community of Monteverde, and when you do you might not realize it, because Monteverde is not what we usually think of as a town. Most houses are back in the woods where you don't see them, and are connected by footpaths. Monteverde residents are more likely to be receptive to tourism if their privacy is respected, so please pay attention to gates, fences, and posted signs.

MONTEVERDE HOTELS AND RESTAURANTS   On the right as you enter Monteverde, ✪ **El Bosque Lodge** (private bath, hot water; $40-$50; 645-5221, phone/fax: 645-5129; www.bosquelodge.com) is a bargain in its price range. Rooms are clean and comfortable; there are beautiful gardens and a nice, grassy camping area ($2.50/person). Their restaurant serves well-prepared, healthy meals. A few meters down the road is a well-stocked food store and CASEM, the crafts cooperative. Also here is **Stella's** (open daily, 6 a.m. to 6 p.m), a bakery/coffee shop full of delicacies we are not used to finding in Costa Rica: apple pie, brownies, strudel. Fresh, organic produce from the greenhouses out back appears in their salads, and you can construct your own sandwich.

Out on the road again, you'll see the cheese plant up ahead, marked by a sign with a big silver cow's head between two mountains. **La Colina Lodge** (shared bath, heated water, $30-$40; private bath, $40-$60, including full breakfast; 645-5009, phone/fax: 645-5580; www.costaricanet.net/lacolina lodge, e-mail: lacolina@racsa.co.cr) is about 200 meters beyond the bridge to the right, where the road turns left to go to the preserve. This is the remodeled Flor-Mar, one of the oldest *pensiones* in Monteverde. We weren't able to see the changes before press time, but it sounds like the additions of a downstairs fireplace and upstairs verandas have given the venerable pension a welcome facelift. The new owners also own Hotel La Colina in Manuel Antonio.

A few hundred meters up the hill toward the preserve is the ❂ **Hotel Fonda Vela** (private bath, hot water; $90-$110; 257-1413, 645-5125, fax: 645-5119; www.centralamerica.com/cr/hotel/fondavel.htm, e-mail: fondavel@ racsa.co.cr), which has lovely large rooms, some with views and balconies, and an excellent **restaurant** with a large, dramatic design and huge windows that make it a bit chilly at night. The lodge also has a comfy TV room and ping-pong tables. The owners rent horses and offer rides to neighboring San Luis; there is a short trail through patches of primary forest.

Across the road is the simple **Hospedaje Mariposa** (private bath, heated water; $20-$30, including breakfast; 645-5013), a good value for its close proximity to the Monteverde Preserve. **Hotel Villa Verde** (private bath, hot water, some kitchens; $50-$60; suites with kitchens, $90-$100; 645-5025, fax: 645-5115, e-mail: estefany@sol.racsa.co.cr), farther up the hill, is only a 15-minute walk from the preserve. We have heard that a new place, the **Trapp Family Lodge** (private bath, heated water; $60-$70; 645-5858, fax: 645-5990; www.ticoweb.com/trappfam, e-mail: trappfam@racsa.co.cr) is closer, but we haven't seen it yet.

All of the above hotels will bag breakfasts and lunches for birders and hikers, and prepare vegetarian meals on request. Laundry services, horse rentals, transportation to the preserve, and tours to nearby points of interest are also available through the hotels.

Monteverde Cloud Forest Preserve is a 30-minute uphill walk from the Fonda Vela. The **Preserve Field Station** sometimes has room in its dormitories (shared bath, heated water; $14/person, including three meals; 645-5122, fax: 645-5034; www.cct.or.cr, e-mail: montever@racsa.co.cr) for students or researchers. You must make reservations with a 30 percent deposit 45 days in advance.

Only 45 minutes by horseback or car from all the attractions in the Monteverde area, the ✪ **San Luis Ecolodge** (phone/fax: 645-5277; www.costarica bureau.com/ecolodgesanluis, e-mail: ecolodgesanluis@costaricabureau.com) is a working farm and biological reserve in the scenic San Luis Valley. Owners Drs. Diana and Milton Lieberman are both well-known tropical biologists who specialize in patterns of ecological regeneration. The atmosphere here is different from similar research stations, where working scientists have little to do with lay visitors: the researchers are eager to share their findings with guests, and articulate in discussion of on-site projects. Guests are encouraged to become familiar with the area's campesino culture; tours to neighboring reserves and through the valley's farms often include stops at family homes, where guests are invited in for coffee and can share thoughts with people they would probably never meet otherwise. Three types of lodging are offered: a dorm-style converted milking barn (shared bath, hot water; $50-$60/person); bungalows (private bath, hot water; $60-$70/person); lovely secluded rooms ($80-$90/person) about a kilometer from the main lodge, with balconies overlooking the forest and valley and the sound of a rushing stream in the background. All rates include meals and activities. Children 7 to 12 pay $35, under 7 free. Recommended.

GETTING THERE: By Bus: Direct buses leave the Atlántico Norte terminal in San José (Calle 14, Avenidas 9; 222-3854; $5) every day at 6:30 a.m. and 2:30 p.m., leaving Monteverde for the return trip at these same hours. Buy tickets in advance. You will get to Santa Elena before you get to Monteverde, so if you aren't staying in Santa Elena, just stay on the bus and ask the driver to let you off at your hotel. The bus does not go beyond the Cheese Factory, so if you are staying at La Colina, Fonda Vela, Mariposa, Villa Verde, or the Preserve, make arrangements to be picked up. Beware of theft on this bus, especially on the way up. Make sure your large luggage gets safely into the luggage compartment underneath the bus and keep valuables with you at all times. We have heard many stories of someone who poses as a bus employee, and tells vulnerable-looking tourists that they may not keep their backpacks with them, but must store them in another place. Later their backpacks are gone. This said, we have ridden this bus many, many times, and have never had any problems. The warning is to keep you alert, not to discourage you from taking this most economical way of reaching Monteverde. This bus is full of interesting people, and often the four-hour trip passes very quickly if you get into a good conversation.

Note: Seats on the Monteverde–San José bus are reserved. You can get on a nearly empty San José–bound bus at the Cheese Factory without a ticket, but you will have to get off and purchase one when the bus arrives at the Santa Elena bus station. If there are a lot of people that have already bought tickets ahead of you, you may end up without a seat—not a pleasant experience.

A daily bus from Puntarenas to Santa Elena leaves Puntarenas (bus stop on the oceanfront, one block from the San José–Puntarenas terminal) at 2:15 p.m., turns off the Interamerican Highway at Río Lagarto around 3:30 p.m., and arrives in Santa Elena around 5:30 p.m. If you are coming from the north, any San José–bound bus will let you off at Lagarto, where Monteverde-bound buses pass around 3:30 p.m. and 5:30 p.m. It's also pretty easy to hitchhike from Lagarto. If you are coming from Manuel Antonio, take the 10:30 a.m. Quepos–Puntarenas bus to connect with the Puntarenas–Santa Elena bus. The bus returns from Santa Elena at 6 a.m.

If you are coming from the Arenal area, you can catch an 8 a.m. bus in La Fortuna to Tilarán (3 hours). Eat lunch in Tilarán (at La Carreta, behind the church) and then catch the bus for Santa Elena at 12:30 p.m. (2 hours, $2). To do this in the opposite direction, catch a bus at the Cheese Factory for Tilarán at 7 a.m., then get on the Tilarán–San Carlos bus at 12:30 (it passes through La Fortuna).

From Tamarindo, Flamingo, or Liberia, you can take the **Fantasy Tours** buses ($19, make reservations through your hotel), get off in Tilarán and catch the 12:30 p.m. Tilarán–Santa Elena bus. **Interbus** goes to Monteverde (283-5573; www. costaricapass.com).

If you are coming from Guanacaste, take a bus to Cañas and then to Tilarán, and proceed as above. Or get off at the Las Juntas turnoff, take a taxi into Las Juntas ($2.50), spend some time exploring the old gold mines (see Guanacaste chapter), then take the bus that passes through Las Juntas on the way to Monteverde around 3 p.m. ($2), It takes you all the way to the Cheese Factory by 5 p.m.

To get to Guanacaste from Monteverde, take the 5 a.m. bus to Puntarenas via Las Juntas or the 5:30 a.m. Santa Elena–Las Juntas bus. Both let you off at La Irma on the Interamerican highway, where you can flag down a Guanacaste bus.

By Jeep: Hotel Paraíso Tropical in La Fortuna takes you by jeep around the lake to Monteverde (479-9222, $25/person, minimum 2 people).

By Jeep, Boat, and Taxi: **Don Taco** (645-5263) will pick you up at your La Fortuna hotel, take you on a 25-minute boat ride across Lake Arenal, then take you in his jeep for a bumpy two-hour drive uphill to Monteverde (and vice versa). He leaves Monteverde daily. This is the fastest way to get to or from Volcán Arenal ($75 for two, $115 for three or four). Mirador San Gerardo also performs this service (645-5087, 381-7277), as do several tour agencies in La Fortuna.

By Car: Most people turn off the Interamerican Highway at Río Lagarto, about a half-hour north of the Puntarenas turnoff. Go uphill from there for one and a half to two hours. This gravel road is the best tended of all the access routes. **Base Tres** is a friendly bar at Lagarto where you can stop for a drink or a snack on the way up.

An alternate route that is a bit shorter if you're coming from San José is to look for the right-hand turnoff to Sardinal, 20 kilometers after the Puntarenas turnoff. Drive to the central plaza of the small town of Sardinal, then make a left and continue on to Guacimal, where the road joins the Lagarto route.

If you have four-wheel drive, you can travel by car from Tilarán to Monteverde by way of Quebrada Grande, San Rafael, Cabeceras, and Santa Elena. During the rainy season, the bus can make it through when cars can't. The trip takes two hours. But, the route of choice is through Las Juntas de Abangares. The road is paved for half of the distance to Monteverde. After the paved road ends, you'll come to a fork with a big sign for El Dos and a small sign that points to San Rafael on the right. Be sure to take this right fork, because if you go to El Dos, you'll be heading down the mountain again to Tilarán. We have heard that the unpaved part of this route is in bad condition, but that could change. Check with your hotel on the best route to take before setting out.

TEN

Guanacaste Province

Guanacaste has always been important to the cultural and economic life of Costa Rica, but the creation of the new Daniel Oduber Quiros International Airport just outside Liberia marks a new stage in the province's development. Because of Guanacaste's dry climate and flat terrain, the Liberia airport is easier for planes to approach than Juan Santamaria, and it's less likely to be closed because of unfavorable weather conditions. In fact, visitors can avoid the crowds and pollution of San José altogether by arriving at Liberia, visiting Guanacaste's beaches and national parks, heading east to Volcán Arenal and the rivers of Sarapiquí, and continuing on to Tortuguero or Talamanca on the Caribbean coast by boat, car, or bus. They can also go south to Monteverde or Manuel Antonio in three or four hours from Liberia. (See the Central Pacific, Northern Zone, and Atlantic Coast chapters for more details.)

Guanacaste was a separate province of Spain's Central American empire until 1787, when it was given to Nicaragua. In 1812, Spain made Guanacaste part of Costa Rica so Costa Rica would be large enough to be represented in the colonial government, which ruled from Guatemala. After independence, both Costa Rica and Nicaragua claimed Guanacaste. *Guanacastecos* were divided, too. Liberians, whose founders were Nicaraguan cattle farmers, wanted to join Nicaragua. Nicoyans were in favor of joining Costa Rica. Nicoya won in a vote, and an 1858 treaty declared Guanacaste part of Costa Rica. Costa Ricans celebrate annexation of Guanacaste on July 25.

Guanacaste's long period of autonomy, sizeable indigenous population, and geographic isolation from the Meseta Central have contributed to make it a unique province in Costa Rica. Many "Costa Rican" traditions originated here. The people, dark-skinned descendants of the Chorotega Indians, are possibly closer to their cultural and historical roots than are other Costa Ricans, and there is a special campesino richness in their friendly manner.

Most of Guanacaste has been converted into pastureland for beef production. The deforestation of the region has altered its climate and ecosystems, causing occasional droughts. But Guanacaste is beautiful, nonetheless. Brahma bulls lounge under the graceful, spreading shade trees that gave the province its name. The brilliant yellow blossoms of the *corteza amarilla* dot the plains in February, and in March the light red blossoms of the *carao* (carob tree) brighten the landscape. The waters of Guanacaste's beaches are clear and gentle, and the dry climate helps keep mosquitos to a minimum.

When you stop for *refrescos*, be sure to try some typical Guanacastecan grain-based beverages: *horchata* (rice), *resbaladera* (barley), and *pinolillo* (roasted corn) are all sweet, milky drinks. *Tamarindo* is made from the sticky fruit found in the pod of the tamarind tree. If you're prone to iron deficiency, buy a bottle of *miel de carao*, the iron-rich syrup made from the carao tree's pods. It doesn't taste too good, but it's very effective.

LAS JUNTAS DE ABANGARES

Las Juntas de Abangares, the old gold-mining capital, is a historic part of Costa Rica that is just beginning to open up to tourism. From 1884 to 1931, its mines attracted workers and gold seekers from all over the world, including North and South Americans, Europeans, Chinese, Russians, Lebanese, and Jamaicans. The multiracial background of the residents of Las Juntas distinguishes it from the rest of Guanacaste. Also, unlike the rest of Guanacaste, it is mountainous, with a cool climate.

The **Eco Museo** has trails through tropical dry forest to the top of an old gold mine built into the beautiful Río Abangares. The old mine structure bears a striking resemblance to a Mayan ruin rising out of the forest. To get there, turn right at the **Monumento a los Mineros** in front of the historic **Caballo Blanco Cantina** in Las Juntas, which has a good collection of turn-of-the-20th-century artifacts, and marks the road to Monteverde. Go four kilometers to a fork in the road, where there is a sign. It is a nice, shady walk from town, and you can stop at **La Sierra**, the original base camp of the gold-boom years, for a *refresco*. Taxis and horses can also be hired in Las Juntas.

A longer trip can be taken to **Boston**, where independent gold miners are working cooperatively. They will show you the whole mining process and take you into their candlelit tunnels. You'll need four-wheel drive or a horse in rainy season; at other times the road is passable.

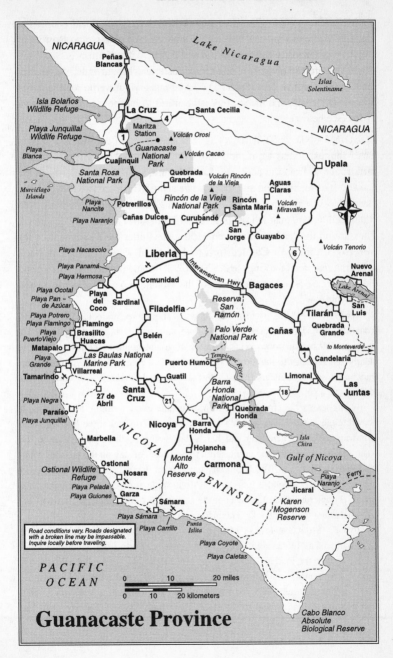

Guanacaste Province

Mina Tours (662-0753, fax: 662-0010), owned by a local couple descended from gold miners, will take you to the Eco Museo and Boston, as well as to see a salt-drying operation and nearby coffee farms.

If you are traveling between Guanacaste and Monteverde, we recommend going through Las Juntas. The Las Juntas–Monteverde road is paved for half of the trip, and the scenery is beautiful. A bus now connects the two towns (see below).

LODGING AND RESTAURANTS   The best place to eat in Las Juntas is **Los Mangos**, across from the church—though it lacks *ambiente*. **La Familiar**, across from the park, and **La Golosina**, around the corner from the Caballo Blanco, are good and inexpensive *sodas*. There are two inexpensive, clean places to stay in Las Juntas: **Cabinas El Encanto** (private bath, cold water, ceiling fan, guarded parking; $7-$12; 662-0677) are nicely decorated. They are on the road to Monteverde, 50 meters after the Monumento a los Mineros. **Cabinas El Cayuco** (private bath, cold water, ceiling fan, pool, restaurant, guarded parking; $12-$20; 662-0868) are plainer but still a good value. They are 50 meters to the left of the Monumento a los Mineros, as you are leaving town.

GETTING THERE: By Bus: Las Juntas is about three hours (145 kilometers) from San José. Direct buses leave at 10:45 a.m. and 5:10 p.m. from Calle 12, Avenidas 7/9 in San José ($2; 256-8598). If you're going by car, the turnoff is clearly marked on the Interamerican Highway. Las Juntas is only an hour from Puntarenas and 30 minutes from Cañas, so you could make it your base for exploring this area.

A bus leaves the cheese plant in Monteverde every morning at 5:30 a.m. It goes through Santa Elena, arriving in Las Juntas at 7:15 and at the Interamerican Highway at 7:30. There you can hail a bus going north to Liberia or to the Nicaraguan border, hail one going south to San José, or stay on the bus and get to Puntarenas at 8:30 a.m. The return bus leaves from Puntarenas at 1:15 p.m., arriving in Las Juntas around 3 p.m. and in Monteverde at 5 p.m. From Guanacaste, get off the Interamerican Highway at the Las Juntas turnoff (named "la Irma" after a restaurant there) and take a taxi ($3) into town.

By Car: From San José or Liberia, get off the Interamerican Highway at the well-marked Las Juntas sign. From Monteverde, go north from Santa Elena and follow signs to the road to Tilarán. At the Finca Bello, the road splits; take the left fork to Las Juntas, and follow signs from there. When driving to Monteverde from Las Juntas, after the paved road ends you will come to a fork with a small sign pointing to San Rafael to the right. Take the right fork. The trip from Las Juntas to Monteverde takes an hour and a half by car.

Above: The quickest way to open a fresh young coconut is with a swift blow from a machete.

Right: Colorful pottery from the kilns of near-by Guaitil is displayed at a roadside stand near Nicoya.

Top: Rainforest canopy

Top right: Ginger flower

Middle left: Philodendron

Bottom right: Crotons

CAÑAS AND RÍO COROBICÍ

Cañas is a busy, hot town where you might stay en route to somewhere else. Fifty meters from the Interamerican Highway (turn in at the Hotel El Corral), the **Nuevo Hotel Cañas** (private bath, hot water, ceiling fans, air conditioning, cable TV, phone; $35; 669-1294, fax: 669-1319) has light-filled rooms around a swimming pool.

It's worth traveling two and a half kilometers north to the peaceful **Capazurí** (private bath, cold water, ceiling fans; $20-$30, including breakfast; phone/fax: 669-0580), whose name means "deer" in the indigenous Chibcha language. Rooms are simple; despite some highway noise, it has a nice family atmosphere. Be sure to ask Don Jorge, the friendly owner, about his fascinating role in the Civil War of 1948. He and his wife can also explain to you how Costa Rican democracy works, since they are the heads of the election tribunal in their area. Camping is permitted in the groves near the main house ($3/person).

Four kilometers north of Cañas on the Interamerican Highway is **Safaris Corobicí** (phone/fax: 669-1091), which offers raft trips down the smooth Corobicí river. Two-hour trips are $37 per person, three-hour trips are $45, and a half-day tour costs $60 (children under 14 half-price). These are scenic floats on which the guide does all the work, and are good for breaking up the monotony of a long trip to the coast. As with any wildlife observation tour, you will see more if you go early or late in the day. You will also avoid being out in the hot sun.

Down a gravel road from Safaris Corobicí is **Las Pumas** (donation requested), a large collection of felines and birds. Most of the cats were confiscated from private owners who had them illegally; many were brought to the shelter with serious injuries and illnesses. Some of the veterans have been in captivity for 20 years. An overly friendly caretaker offered to take us into the cages of some of the tamer cats so we could take pictures, but it's dark in the cages and the owners are adamant about not using a flash because it hurts the animals' eyes. We saw margays, ocelots, pumas, jaguars, macaws, parrots, parakeets, and a cockatoo.

Centro Ecológico La Pacífica (heated water, ceiling fans, pool; $70-$80; 669-0050, fax: 669-0555) is a shady, green oasis in the midst of Guanacaste's heat. More than 200 different bird species have been observed in its woods and near the Río Corobicí, which flows through the ranch. The center has tastefully designed cabinas, a lovely pool, and a restaurant with an international menu. It is located north of the road that goes to Safaris Corobicí.

Right on the river just after the entrance to La Pacífica, **Rincón Corobicí** (669-1234, fax: 669-0303) is also a cool, pleasant place to stop—for a few hours or the whole day. Its Swiss-owned restaurant specializes in beef and seafood, and there is a souvenir shop, a playground, clean baths, a small campground, and a trail along the riverside.

GETTING THERE: Five buses run daily to Cañas ($3; Calle 16, Avenidas 3/5; 222-3006). By car, Cañas is about three hours from San José, right off the Interamerican Highway.

Three kilometers north of the Río Corobicí crossing, a road on the right heads to Upala between **Tenorio** and **Miravalles** volcanoes. We spent a memorable afternoon driving through this beautiful area. It is undeveloped, but the views of the volcanoes as you approach and then cut between them are spectacular. Just past the volcanoes, Lake Nicaragua and the Solentiname Islands are visible to the north.

The view is even better from **Albergue Heliconias** (private bath, heated water; $10/person; 466-8483; www.agroecoturismo.net, e-mail: cooprena@racsa.co.cr), a community-based eco-tourism project on the slopes of Volcán Tenorio, just outside the village of Bijagua. They have simple rooms with two bunkbeds in each one, and a **restaurant** specializing in *comida típica.* They also have a laboratory for the use of researchers or study groups; it houses a collection of the area's amazing insects. You can take a fairly easy one-kilometer hike through their private reserve, or a more difficult one up to the dormant volcano's crater, which becomes a lake in the rainy season. If you have your own four-wheel-drive vehicle, they will lead you on a very inexpensive tour to the **Río Celeste** ($12/group plus $2 entrance fee/person) on the other side of Volcán Tenorio. This involves an hour's ride on rough roads, then a couple of hours' hiking through primary forest to the waterfall. The Río Celeste is named after its unique blue color, which probably comes from volcanic minerals. A bit further upstream are hot springs and boiling pots of mud. This trip is offered for a much higher price in La Fortuna. The lodge, run by friendly *campesina* co-owners, is about 40 minutes north of Cañas. When you get to the village of Bijagua on the nicely paved road to Upala, turn right at the signs for the lodge and go two kilometers on a bumpy dirt road. A taxi from Bijagua costs about $4. To make reservations, leave a message for Albergue Heliconia at 224-2400, and they will call you back.

BAGACES AREA

Bagaces is a sunbaked colonial town halfway between Cañas and Liberia. It is the gateway to Palo Verde National Park and the area around Volcán Miravalles. At the town's entrance, **Albergue Bagaces** (private bath, cold water, table fans; $20-$30; 671-1267, fax: 666-2021) is a breezy hotel/restaurant right on the Interamerican Highway. Rooms are large, some suitelike with sofa and chairs. In Bagaces, the best place to eat is **Soda Fuentes**, two blocks to the left of the plaza.

GETTING THERE: Bagaces is about 20 minutes north of Cañas, on the Interamerican Highway. A Liberia bus (Calle 14, Avenidas 1/3; 222-1650; $3) will drop you off in Bagaces.

PALO VERDE NATIONAL PARK

In addition to being a resting spot for 60 migratory and 200 native bird species, **Palo Verde** (admission $6) has 15 different types of habitat for mammals, amphibians, and reptiles, many of which can be observed relatively easily. During the dry season, animals stay near the few permanent springs in the area, one of which is only 100 meters from the park's administration building and campsite. The best observation spot for birds is in the swamp across from the OTS headquarters. The best months to go are January, February, and March.

Palo Verde is on the east side of the mouth of the **Tempisque**, Guanacaste's major river. Stretching along the banks of the river is a plain that floods during the rainy season and dries to a brown crisp in the dry season. Away from the river rise bluffs dotted with limestone cliff outcrops. The park administration is set in an old hacienda at the base of the bluffs; a couple of trails begin there and go up to lookout points.

Palo Verde became known as an important bird refuge when it was still a large cattle ranch. When it was granted park status, the cattle were removed. Over the years, vegetation formerly grazed by the cattle started to grow up and overrun the wetlands. The cattle were recognized to have become a natural part of the ecosystem and were reinstated selectively. Cattle are also an important element in reducing fire hazards, since they eat vegetation that makes the park prone to fires. Being able to graze their cattle in the park helps local campesinos, who in turn do fire prevention work.

If you call the park administration (671-1062, 671-1290) beforehand, they will help arrange a boat trip with neighboring boatmen to **Isla de Pájaros** ($55 for up to four passengers), an important nesting ground for many showy waterbirds, including the roseate spoonbill, glossy ibis, anhinga, and several species of egrets and storks.

Be aware that tour boats should remain 50 yards from the island and no one should try to startle the birds into flight, because that endangers their nestlings. If your tour does not obey these rules, notify the park director or the Audubon Society.

The **Organization for Tropical Studies** has a research station one kilometer before the park administration. Each room has a bunk bed and a reading lamp (though lamps attract insects at night). Food is plentiful and good. Arrangements must be made as far in advance as possible through OTS in San José ($40/person, including food and orientation; 240-6696, fax: 240-6783; e-mail: reservas@cro.ots.ac.cr). OTS can arrange transportation by taxi from Bagaces to their station.

Camping is allowed in the park, or you can stay in the park's new **visitors center** (shared bath, cold water; $25, including meals). Even though there is potable water, bring water, a flashlight and insect repellent for either facility. Make reservations in advance through the **Tempisque Conservation Area** office in Bagaces (open weekdays, 8 a.m. to 4 p.m.; 671-1062, 671-1290; e-mail: yolandar@ns.minae.go.cr), which directs all the parks and reserves in the region. It's right on the Interamerican Highway, next to the Bagaces gas station.

GETTING THERE: Turn left at the gas station in Bagaces, north of Cañas. The park administration is 30 kilometers (one hour) from there. Signs mark the way. A taxi from Bagaces costs about $25. There is a small building at the entrance to the park, and some housing for personnel beyond it, but don't get off there, because it's about eight more hot, dry kilometers to the administration building.

During the dry season, the adventurous can enter the area from the Nicoya Peninsula. Take a bus from Nicoya to Puerto Humo (11 a.m. and 2 p.m., returning at 5:45 a.m. and 12:45 p.m.; 70 cents). Local boatmen there will take you across for a minimal fee and indicate which way to hike to get to the park station. Don't try this route in the rainy season—the whole plain is swamped.

Palo Verde is now an easier overnight destination for "soft ecotourists" (people who love nature but appreciate comfort), thanks to ❂ **Rancho Humo** (private bath, hot water, bathtubs; $90-$100, meals $22.50/day; 255-2463, fax: 255-3573, 385-0387; e-mail: ecologic@.racsa.co.cr), which sits high above the Río Tempisque on a grassy bluff. Room balconies overlook the river and its fertile plain. Views are also expansive from the conical-roofed hilltop restaurant, which serves delicious meals. They rent horses and mountain bikes for $5 per hour and run tours to Palo Verde, Guaitil, and Barra Honda. Reservations required. To get there, follow road signs from the ferry or Nicoya—they will lead you down gravel roads for about 45 minutes from either place. There is a private airstrip as well. The bus from Nicoya to Puerto Humo passes the entrance to Rancho Humo; it leaves Nicoya at 11 a.m. and 2 p.m., returning from Puerto Humo at 5:45 a.m. and 12:45 p.m.

RESERVA AGROECOLOGICA DE SAN RAMON   **Reserva Agroecolog-ica de San Ramon** (formerly Lomas Barbudal) is a community-run reserve where there are birds, monkeys, waterfalls you can hike to, and rivers with pools you can swim in shaded by graceful trees. Stop by the Tempisque Conservation Area (admission $6; 671-1062; e-mail: yolandar@ns.minae.go.cr) office next to the gas station in Bagaces before heading out. Camping is allowed in the reserve, which is open only during the dry season. Bring your own food and water. Soon after passing Bagaces on the Interamerican Highway, heading north, there is a dirt road on the left for the reserve. After six kilometers on the dirt road, you'll come to the entrance. A taxi to the reserve from the bus station in Bagaces costs $20-$25, roundtrip. They will wait for you for a couple of hours.

VOLCÁN MIRAVALLES   Dormant, tree-covered Volcán Miravalles looms behind Bagaces. The Costa Rican Electric Company has a geothermal project on its slopes, with deep bores into the earth to tap the extreme heat from magma veins and convert it into electricity. With prior arrangement, groups can visit the plant and get an informative guided tour from ICE, the Electric Company. Ask for Mainor Pérez (673-0100).

In Fortuna de Bagaces, two kilometers beyond the geothermal installations, is **Centro Turístico Yoko** (673-0410, fax: 673-0770), which has a nice restaurant and a large swimming pool filled with thermal water of varying temperatures.

GETTING THERE: By Car: Drive north from Bagaces about 20 minutes (9.4 kilometers) then turn right at the sign for the "Proyecto Geotérmico." Fortuna and the plant are a few kilometers beyond that. Roads are nicely paved in this area.

LIBERIA

Liberia, the historic capital of Guanacaste's beef industry, is taking its place as the site of Costa Rica's second international airport (see "Getting There" below). The city is unique in Costa Rica for its distinct colonial feel. Many of the old houses are made of adobe, the traditional building material of this hot, dry area, and have orange tile roofs, which help keep the temperature cool inside. You'll notice that some of the corner houses have a door on each side of the corner. This is known as the *puerta del sol*. The door on the east side lets in the morning sun, while the door on the south side lets in the afternoon sun. Liberia is bright and hot, so bring a hat or use your umbrella.

A small museum dedicated to the *sabaneros*, Guanacaste's cowboys, the **Casa de Cultura** (open Tuesday through Saturday, 8 a.m. to noon, 2 p.m. to

5 p.m.; 666-4527), three blocks south and one block east of the church, is also a very helpful tourist information center.

The **Regional Museum of Guanacaste**, rather poorly housed on the south side of the old Comandancia (open weekdays, 8 a.m. to 5 p.m.; 666-5193), showcases the archeological collection of former president Daniel Oduber. Most interesting are the stone *metates* and sacrificial burial stones carved into figures of pelicans, iguanas and bats, and the carved stone figure holding a head as a trophy.

Souvenir Frogs (open daily, 8:30 a.m. to 6:30 p.m.; 666-3541) on the west side of Parque Central, features Chorotega pottery, local wood crafts, and regional music cassettes.

Tourists can make international phone calls at **ICE** (open weekdays, 7:30 a.m. to 5 p.m.; Saturdays, 8 a.m. to noon), 50 meters south of the Banco Nacional on the right.

RESTAURANTS   **Las Tinajas**, in the same block as Frogs, has pleasant outdoor tables where you can drink beer and munch *bocas* on hot Liberian afternoons. **Rancho Dulce**, a small, very clean *soda* 25 meters south of the church, serves good ice-cold fruit *batidos*. **Da Beppe**, two blocks toward town on the boulevard from the highway, serves delicious Italian food; the service is very professional. **Pizza Pronto**, one block toward town from the Casa de Cultura, has a wood-fired clay oven and a pleasant garden atmosphere. **Pókopí**, across from Hotel El Sitio, has a varied menu that will be familiar to North Americans. The discotheque **Kurú** next door has a gigantic TV screen with a satellite dish and will show U.S. sports events on request. Not to be missed is **Café Europa**, a German bakery and café on the left just past the airport.

LODGING   There are gas stations on each corner where the main road to Liberia intersects the Interamerican Highway. (They are the surest places to get fuel on holidays.) At this intersection are **Hotel Boyeros** (private bath, hot water, air conditioning, phone, pools, restaurant open 24 hours; $30-$40; 666-0722, fax: 666-2529), and **Hotel El Bramadero** (pool; with fans, $20-$30; with air conditioning, $30-$40; 666-0371, fax: 666-0203; www.accommodations.co.cr), which has quieter rooms in the back away from the pool. **Hotel El Sitio** (private bath, hot water, air conditioning, pool, restaurant; $70-$80, including breakfast and airport pickup; 666-1211, fax: 666-2059; www.bestwestern.co.cr, e-mail: htlsitio@racsa.co.cr) has huge concrete walls around its spacious, shady grounds, making for a peaceful environment despite its proximity to the highway. It is now part of the Best Western chain.

The **Hotel La Siesta** (private bath, cold water, air conditioning, TV, security boxes, pool, restaurant; $20-$30; 666-0678, fax: 666-2532) is clean and quiet. Recommended. **Hotel Daysita** (private bath, heated water, ceiling fans, pools; $20-$30; $30-$40, including breakfast; 666-0197, fax: 666-0927) has a lot of nice touches and a family atmosphere. A discotheque is located beneath their reasonably priced international restaurant.

The quiet neighborhood near the Casa de Cultura has several good options for budget travelers in converted historical homes. All offer guarded parking. **Hotel Liberia** (private bath, cold water, fans; $12-$20, including breakfast; phone/fax: 666-0161), has quiet rooms in the back, a souvenir shop, and a bar/restaurant. It is half a block south of the church. The **Posada del Tope** (shared bath, cold water, ceiling fan, kitchen privileges; $7-$12; phone/fax: 666-3876; www.accommodations.co.cr), one block south, is in an impressive historic building, but the rooms are not that great. Still, the owners are friendly and the price is right. **La Casona** (shared bath, cold water, ceiling fans; $7-$12; 666-2971) another block and a half to the south, has nice tiled bathrooms, cable TV in the lobby, and e-mail service for guests. This friendly little place seemed like a good value for budget travelers.

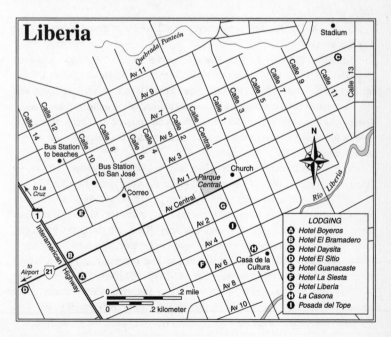

Liberia

Stadium

Quebrada Panteón

Av 11

Av 9

Av 7

Av 5

Av 3

Av 1

Parque Central

Church

Av Central

Av 2

Av 4

Av 6

Av 8

Av 10

Calle 14

Calle 12

Calle 10

Calle 8

Calle 6

Calle 4

Calle 2

Calle Central

Calle 1

Calle 3

Calle 5

Calle 7

Calle 9

Calle 11

Calle 13

Bus Station to beaches

Bus Station to San José

to La Cruz

Correo

Interamerican Highway

1

21

to Airport

Casa de la Cultura

N

Río Liberia

0   .2 mile

0   .2 kilometer

LODGING
- **A** *Hotel Boyeros*
- **B** *Hotel El Bramadero*
- **C** *Hotel Daysita*
- **D** *Hotel El Sitio*
- **E** *Hotel Guanacaste*
- **F** *Hotel La Siesta*
- **G** *Hotel Liberia*
- **H** *La Casona*
- **I** *Posada del Tope*

LIBERIA RENT-A-CAR AGENCIES

Budget Rent A Car (667-0126), Dollar Rent A Car (668-1061), National Car Rental (666-5594), Sol (666-2222), and Toyota (666-0016) have car rental agencies in Liberia and provide transportation to and from their offices for customers. Make advance reservations in the dry season.

Hotel Guanacaste (private bath, cold water, window fans, some with air conditioning, parking; $20-$30; discount for youth hostel card-holders; camping $4/person; 666-0085, fax: 666-2287), has rooms reminiscent of a very basic youth hostel; the small fans in the high windows didn't look too effective. On the plus side, they have some courtyards with gardens, a good restaurant, and a convenient location—two blocks south of the municipal bus terminal, yet in a quiet part of town. An enthusiastic staff can help with travel arrangements. They run a handy bus service to Rincón de la Vieja and Santa Rosa National Parks ($20 roundtrip), and are the local Tica Bus headquarters for trips to Nicaragua.

Note: During the dry season, you need to make reservations for all Liberia hotels.

GETTING THERE: By Bus: Buses leave the San José Pulmitán station at Avenidas 1/3, Calle 14 ten times a day (222-1650; $2.75). Buses connect Liberia with Playa del Coco, Playa Hermosa, Puntarenas, Bagaces, Canas, La Cruz, and the Nicaraguan border. Schedules are clearly marked at the municipal bus station, five blocks north and two blocks east of the main entrance to Liberia. Pirate taxi drivers have been known to tell tourists that the posted bus schedules are wrong: always check with the bus companies.

Note: Buses from Liberia to San José may be stopped for passport checks, so bring at least a copy of your passport and make sure your visa is in order.

By Car: Take the *autopista* north from San José. You can take a circular route through Liberia, Santa Cruz, and Nicoya, the gateways to the Guanacaste beaches, and come back on the Tempisque ferry. Roads are paved along that circular route, making it a two-hour trip by car from Liberia to the ferry.

By Air: SANSA flies to Liberia from San José every day at 11:45 a.m., returning at 12:50 p.m. ($61 one way; 221-9414, 666-0017, fax: 255-2176). Travelair flies daily to Liberia at 8:20 a.m. by way of Tamarindo ($92 one way; $152 roundtrip; 220-3054, fax: 220-0413; e-mail: travelair@centralamerica.com). See Chapter Four for additional information about reservations and flight itineraries.

BEACHES NEAR LIBERIA

PLAYA DEL COCO   The most centrally located of the beaches near Liberia, Playa del Coco's waters are filled with small craft. This is where the nightlife is, so it's not the place to go if you want solitude and relaxation. However, it does have some of the least expensive restaurants and cabinas in the area. (Virtually all the hotels in this area offer substantial off-season discounts.) It also has a large and involved community of international residents.

The 36-foot catamaran **Spanish Dancer** ($50; 670-1107, 390-9451; e-mail: dancer@racsa.co.cr) leaves the pier each day at 9:30 a.m. ($50 including lunch) and 2:30 p.m. ($45) for a four- to five-hour cruise, including a stop at a deserted beach for lunch and a swim, and frequent turtle and dolphin sightings. The afternoon cruise returns at sunset. Snorkeling gear is included.

A couple of scuba diving operations offer day and overnight trips, PADI certification, airfills, equipment sales, and boat charters for surfing or fishing trips. **Mario Vargas** (670-0351) has recently been taken over by a European couple, whose office is located on the right as you enter town. The Canadian-run company **Deep Blue** (670-1004) has its office in the Hotel CocoVerde.

Hotel y Spaghetería Pato Loco (private bath, hot water, ceiling fans; $30-$40; 670-0145; e-mail: patoloco@racsa.co.cr), on the left as you enter town, is run by an Italian-Dutch couple. The food is great and very reasonably priced. Their candlelit restaurant, **L'Angoletto di Roma**, is open 6 p.m. to 9 p.m., closed Thursday. They also rent a two-bedroom apartment with air conditioning for $250 per week and $600 per month.

Café internet 2000 (on the left 150 meters before the Ocotal turnoff) has several computers and printers, and great coffee and snacks.

One of the best *sodas* in town is **Los Almendros**, a block from the beach on the left. Their cook formerly worked for the plush Hotel Ocotal. Other good bets for seafood are **Los Cocos**, on the left as you arrive at the beach, and **Papagayo**, beside the bank (if it is full, go somewhere else—service is slow). The Mexican-style restaurant, **Tequila**, a block and a half before the beach, is good and inexpensive.

In the heart of the action and right on the beach are the relatively clean **Cabinas El Coco** (cold water, fans; $20-$30; with air conditioning, $30-$40; 670-0276, 670-0110, fax: 670-0167). The sound of the waves muffles the noises from the neighboring disco, but not completely. Less expensive and noisier rooms are in back. Ask for a breezier and quieter front room on the second floor. This place has been spruced up and gets our vote for the Quintessential Funky Beach Hotel and Restaurant in Playa del Coco.

Turn right (north) off the main road, about 150 meters before the beach, to reach some of Coco's quieter lodgings. Soon you will come to the Italian-owned **Hotel Villa Flores** (private bath, heated water, ceiling fans, pool, gym; $40-$50; with air conditioning, $50-$60; breakfast included; phone/fax: 670-0269), built of dark stained wood. This is a comfortable facility with a wraparound balcony upstairs and cool sitting rooms downstairs. They offer boat tours as well. Another half-kilometer down the road is **Villa del Sol** (private bath, hot water, ceiling fan, some with air conditioning, pool; $40-$50, including breakfast; phone/fax: 670-0085; www.villadelsol.com, e-mail: villa sol@racsa.co.cr), a beach home with a large grassy yard, tropical greenery, and well-ventilated rooms upstairs. The personable owners are knowledgeable about the area. They also rent beach houses by the week or month. Recommended.

Back in town, on the south side of the soccer field, **Hospedaje Celi** (shared bath, cold water, table fan, kitchen privileges; $7-$12; 670-0365) has the cheapest rooms we found. The basic facilities are part of the owner's home. **Cabinas Coco Palms** (private bath, hot water, ceiling fans, pool; $40-$50; with kitchen, $50-$60; with kitchen and air conditioning and room for five, $110-$120; 670-0367, fax: 670-0117) has clean, quiet rooms in the back and a small restaurant for guests near the pool. We don't know what the decibel level is from the gringo bar and restaurant next door, but in the daytime it was very peaceful.

Overlooking Playa del Coco, about a ten-minute drive from the beach, is ✪ **Rancho Armadillo Estate** (private bath, hot water, ceiling fans, air conditioning, some bathtubs; $69; with all meals and alcohol included, $89; with kitchen, $99; 670-0108, fax: 670-0441; www.ranchoarmadillo.com, e-mail: info@ranchoarmadillo.com), whose crusty Texan owner barbecues burgers on demand, pulls in live football and basketball with his huge satellite dish, and, the day we visited, sent someone down to Coco for a dozen blocks of ice that were thrown into the swimming pool to the delight of all the gringo guests. Guest rooms are in comfortable replicas of Guanacaste-style *casonas*. And best yet, the setting in the hills above the beach features a beautiful view and cooling breezes.

GETTING THERE: Buses leave San José (Calle 14, Avenidas 1/3; 222-1650, five-hour trip) every day at 8 a.m. and 2 p.m., returning from Playas del Coco at 8 a.m. and 2 p.m. Buses leave Liberia for Playa del Coco (one-hour trip) six times a day, returning one hour later. By car, Playa del Coco is about half an hour southwest of Liberia.

Fantasy Tours (220-2126, 800-272-8854; www.fantasy.co.cr) runs a shuttle to Coco, Ocotal and Hermosa from San José for $19 one way. Arrangements must be made in advance through your hotel.

PLAYA OCOTAL   Playa Ocotal is a shady cove four kilometers (a 40-minute walk or ten-minute drive) south of Playa del Coco, with a cup-shaped valley that is quickly filling up with luxury homes. Perched high on a hill above the beach, **El Ocotal** (hot water, ceiling fans, air conditioning, phone, cable TV, refrigerator; $100-$180, airport pickup in Liberia $25, children under 12 free; 670-0321, fax: 670-0083; www.centralamerica.com/cr/hotel/ocodive.htm, e-mail: elocotal@racsa.co.cr) is the most elegant hotel in the area. Even if you can't afford its sportfishing, tennis, and swimming facilities, you can visit the restaurant for a meal or sunset drinks and enjoy the beautiful view. They offer scuba-diving packages. Not recommended for people who have difficulty walking (the steep walkways have no railings).

On the way to Playa Ocotal, you'll see signs for **Villa Casa Blanca** (private bath, hot water, ceiling fans, air conditioning, pool; $70-$80, including breakfast; honeymoon suites with jacuzzis, $100-$110; condo, $110-$120; 670-0518, phone/fax: 670-0448; e-mail: vcblanca@racsa.co.cr), a charmingly decorated and well-run bed and breakfast. They rent kayaks and horses, organize diving and snorkeling trips, and are very helpful. Recommended.

We've heard good things about **Fusion Massage Natural Spa** (670-0250).

GETTING THERE: You'll need to walk or take a cab to Ocotal from Playas del Coco ($4), or take the Fantasy Tours bus (see above).

PLAYA HERMOSA   With gentle waves and clear water, Playa Hermosa, nine kilometers north of Playa del Coco, has gotten quite built up lately. **Bill Beard's Diving Safaris** (phone/fax: 672-0012; www.diving-safaris.com, e-mail: diving@racsa.co.cr), mentioned as the #2 diving operation in the Indo-Pacific Region in *Scuba Diving Magazine,* has its headquarters here, and sets up diving packages through all the good hotels in the area, with special green-season rates. They offer morning excursions to two local dive sites every day ($60 if you bring equipment, $75 if you rent theirs). They are inside the Codovac complex, near the beach.

Down the first road on your left as you enter Playa Hermosa is **Villa del Sueño** (private bath, hot water, ceiling fans, pool; $40-$60; phone/fax: 672-0026; www.villadelsueno.com, e-mail: delsueno@racsa.co.cr), with spacious rooms designed for good cross-ventilation. The gracious, friendly French-Canadian owners get together in the evenings and play music for guests. Their restaurant serves delicious meals at fair prices. They arrange personalized tour itineraries and airport pickups, and also run **El Oasis**, an air-conditioned condo project nearby (one-bedroom apartments, $100-$110; efficiency units, $90-$100). Recommended.

A steep drive uphill to the left will take you to **La Finisterra** (hot water, ceiling fans, pool; $60-$70, including breakfast; 672-0237, fax: 670-0293; www.finisterra.net, e-mail: finisterra@hotmail.com), a windy restaurant with a great view that features reasonably priced grilled meats and seafood. Open 7 a.m. to 10 p.m. Rooms are upstairs. Call ahead to get a lift up the hill.

Right on the beach is the well-known **Hotel Playa Hermosa** (private bath, hot water, ceiling fans; $30-$40; phone/fax: 672-0046). The screened rooms have been spruced up by the new Italian owners, and the gardens surrounding the Italian restaurant are pretty.

Once you get to the beach, there are several restaurants and hotels.

Aquasport (672-0050) rents snorkeling gear, kayaks, windsurfers, pedal boats, beach paraphernalia, waterskiing boats, and canoes. In addition to its sports facilities, Aquasport has a restaurant serving excellent seafood dinners, and a well-organized grocery store. Nearby, **Ecotours** (672-0175, fax: 672-0146) runs tours throughout Guanacaste and rents beds in the owners' house (shared bath, cold water, fans, mosquito nets; $20-$30). **Gaviota Tours** (672-0143) specializes in tours to Palo Verde, Guaitil, Arenal, and Nicaragua.

A few doors south of Aquasport is **Playa Hermosa Inn** (private bath, hot water, ceiling fans; $50-$60; with air conditioning, $70-$80, including breakfast; 672-0063), a large, remodeled beach house with spacious rooms, closet space, kitchen privileges, and a pool. They rent one kitchen-equipped apartment ($110-$120, seven-person capacity). About 100 meters north of Aquasport is the French Canadian–owned **Hotel El Velero** (private bath, hot water, ceiling fans, restaurant and bar, pool; $80-$90; 672-0036, phone/fax: 672-0016), a two-story villa with balconies, red-tiled corridors, and breezy, spacious rooms. They rent a sailboat for diving and snorkeling, and have a gift shop.

The posh **Condovac La Costa** (heated water, air conditioning, cable TV, kitchen, pool; $110-$120; 221-2264) overlooks Playa Hermosa and is crowded with vacationing Ticos. If your beach requirements include a disco, you'll get it here—plus a restaurant; sportfishing facilities; water-sports rentals; tennis courts; and golf-cart-like vehicles to transport you up and down the hill. **Hotel Sol Playa Hermosa** (hot water, air conditioning, pools; $140-$160; two-bedroom villas, $260-$300; 257-0607, fax: 223-3036) dominates the hillside above Condovac.

PLAYA PANAMÁ   Playa Panamá, with usually gentle waters and tidepools full of sea urchins, used to be the end of the road, the best place for camping and being alone. However, for more than 20 years the Costa Rican Tourism

Institute, which owns the property, has been plotting to create a fun-in-the-sun resort area, the Golfo Papagayo Project.

Unfortunately, this region, covered in tropical dry forest, presents a grey, leafless landscape in the dry season, making the Guanacaste sun seem even hotter than it is. A little farther south and a little farther north, the landscape is greener and less forbidding. A whole lot of watering will have to be done to make this area as attractive as its southern neighbors, and water has always been scarce in Guanacaste.

If you go sailing, windsurfing or use Hobie cats in this area, or anywhere in Guanacaste, be aware that it can suddenly become extremely windy, especially after noon. We've heard comments from readers who have gotten into dangerous situations because they were not warned about this.

The two existing megaprojects in Papagayo are "all-inclusive"—meals, transportation, and services are put together into one package. Tourists are flown in to Líberia, bused to their resort, fed there, and bused out to various tours until it is time to get on the plane again. It's the perfect hygienic vacation, without the messiness of being in a "foreign country."

The Italian-owned **Costa Smeralda** (private bath, hot water, bathtubs, hairdryers, air conditioning, cable TV, phone, pool, tennis court, restaurant; $90/person, including meals, drinks, and taxes; children under five free; 670-0044, fax: 670-0379; e-mail: smeralda@racsa.co.cr) has luxurious, glass-fronted rooms that sprinkle a well-irrigated green hillside and overlook the Gulf.

Blue Bay Village Papagayo (private bath, hot water, ceiling fans, air conditioning, satellite TV, refrigerator, phone, pool, spa; $110/person, children 4 to12, $45, including meals, drinks, tips, shows, water sports, children's program; guaranteed ocean view is $10 more; 233-8566, 670-0033, fax: 221-0739) is owned by a Mexican conglomerate that has similar resorts in Cancún and Puerto Vallarta. Tourists are bused from the 160 garish yellow-and-orange cabinas to the pools, spa, and gym. When we visited this site while it was under construction, we watched cattle meandering across the hotel's small beach—a taste of pure Guanacaste that has now become an anachronism in the Gulf of Papagayo. The cafeteria-style food was not very good, and there was an institutional feeling about the whole project.

GETTING THERE: By Bus: A Tralapa bus leaves San José (just south of the Atlantico Norte bus station on Calle 14 Avenidas 7/9; 223-5859, 666-1249, five-hour trip; $3.50) for Playas Hermosa and Panamá at 3:20 p.m., returning at 5 a.m. From Liberia ($1), there are five buses daily: 7 a.m., 11:30 a.m., 3:30 p.m., 5:30 p.m., and 7 p.m., returning at 6 a.m., 10.a.m., 4 p.m., and 5 p.m.

By Car: Playas Hermosa and Panamá are a few minutes north of Playa del Coco. Signs indicate the turnoff to the right. Roads are well paved until Playa

Panamá, unpaved beyond that to Smeralda and Blue Bay. There is a gas station along the way, after you pass the turnoff for Sardinal. Taxi service to or from Playa del Coco to Playa Hermosa should cost around $5.

BEACHES NEAR BELÉN

Some of Costa Rica's most famous beaches are accessible from the small highway town of Belén. This area attracts sun worshipers, sportfishing enthusiasts, and surfers, and is home to increasing numbers of U.S. expatriates, who have formed colony-like communities with English-language newsletters, bilingual schools, softball teams, and stores stocked with U.S. foods.

Flamingo is the most ritzy, definitely the place to go if you or your yacht need luxury accommodations. The sand there is whiter (less volcanic) than at many other beaches. Surfers like Playas Junquillal, Negra, Avellana, and Grande.

The beaches at Brasilito, Potrero, and La Penca are calm and the best for children. Many sportfishing operators anchor in Flamingo and Tamarindo. Because the land near the beaches is largely deforested, naturalists do not usually enjoy this part of Guanacaste, except for turtle observation at Las Baulas National Marine Park on Playa Grande (which we don't recommend, because the turtles are disappearing) and mangrove exploration in the estuary between Tamarindo and Playa Grande.

BRASILITO AND CONCHAL   Brasilito is a small town on a gray-sand beach that is no great shakes. It is home to **Costa Rica Riding** (654-4106; e-mail: crriding@racsa.co.cr), which leads a five-day horseback tour for experienced riders that covers 42 beaches in Guanacaste, staying in four beachside resorts ($1200 including meals). Half an hour south on foot is **Conchal**, a beach remarkable for its hill of shells. Brasilito has several small cabinas, but Conchal until recently had none—you could only camp there—and it was the Ticos' best-kept secret. Now it is the site of the **Meliá Playa Conchal Beach and Golf Resort** (private bath, hot water, ceiling fans, air conditioning, satellite TV; $215-$700, kids under 12 free; 654-4123; www.accom modations.co.cr): 368 deluxe bungalow suites, lavish baths, a par-72 golf course, expansive free-form pool, water sports, tennis courts, health club, five restaurants, four bars, casino, and discotheque. We have not heard good reports about the food here, but otherwise it seems to be one of the better-run megaresorts in the area. Prices include roundtrip transport from Tamarindo airport.

Just before you reach Brasilito, on the main road, are **Cabinas Caracol y Nany** (private bath, cold water, ceiling fans; $30-$40; 654-4320), simple rooms near the road and pleasant new rooms around a garden 50 meters inland. Camping ($2/person) is allowed on the grounds and there is a shaded cooking/washing area for guests with a little grill. Recommended for budget travelers.

We often heard local residents singing the praises of **Spaghettería Il Forno,** a reasonably priced Italian restaurant set back from the road on the right as you enter Brasilito.

Right in town and on the beach is the German-owned **Hotel Brasilito** (private bath, cold water, ceiling fans; $30-$40; 654-4237, fax: 654-4247; www.brasilito.co.cr, e-mail: compes@racsa.co.cr), a nice old wooden building with an attractive open-air restaurant right on the beach and a couple of rooms overlooking the ocean. They can arrange boat, diving, and horseback riding trips, and offer internet access.

Leaving Brasilito, you'll pass the **Camarón Dorado** on the left, a somewhat pricey restaurant that's known for its seafood. Be clear on how much the catch of the day costs before you order.

FLAMINGO   Five minutes north of Brasilito is the entrance to **Playa Flamingo**. One of Costa Rica's most exclusive beaches, Flamingo sports its own marina and landing strip. Several businesses offer water-sports rentals, and many sportfishing operations headquarter there as well. Book fishing tours through your hotel. Relaxing sailing excursions to nearby islands for snorkeling ($55) or sunset cruises ($45) are offered by **Papagayo Pete** (654-4911, fax: 654-4064; e-mail: papagayopete@hotmail.com). Big hotels rise up on a point beyond the beach, but Flamingo itself is a beautiful, untouched curve of white sand, lined with shady trees, one of the nicest beaches in the area. Since the coastline belongs to everyone in Costa Rica, you can enjoy the beach without staying in Flamingo. **Marie's** (654-4136) is the best restaurant in town, with California-Mexican and seafood specialties.

Hotel Aurola Playa Flamingo (private bath, hot water, air conditioning, ceiling fans, TV, phone, hairdryers; 233-7233, 654-4010, fax: 233-9583, 654-4060; www.accommodations.co.cr) has smallish rooms in the hotel complex itself ($110-$120), poolside rooms for $140-$150, suites for $260-$270, and apartments for $290-$300. They have two restaurants, three pools, and four bars.

In addition to its standard rooms, the nearby **Flamingo Marina Hotel** (private bath, hot water, air conditioning, fans, satellite TV; $100-$110; 290-1858, 654-4141, fax: 231-1858, 654-4035; www.flamingomarina.com, e-mail: tickledpink@flamingomarina.com) offers suites that have their own terraces with jacuzzis and bars ($150-$160) and pristine oceanfront apartments for four ($280-$300). This hotel overlooks the marina and bay, is 300 meters from the main beach, and has a restaurant, the **Sunrise Café**, and pool. They provide roundtrip shuttle service from San José ($64) or from the Tamarindo or Liberia airports ($20).

The **Presidential Suites** (private bath, hot water, air conditioning, ceiling fans, kitchens; $140-$150, $900/week; 654-4126, 654-4483, fax: 654-4486) are hillside apartments that sleep four; their terraces overlook the bay.

PLAYA POTRERO   Across the bay from Flamingo, and six kilometers north of Brasilito, is Playa Potrero. This rather barren beach seems to have become the culinary capitol of the area. Some restaurants even send shuttle buses over to Flamingo to gather up tourists looking for something special to eat. A French restaurant, **El Grillo** (open 5 p.m. to 9 p.m.; 654-5417) is supposed to be one of the best places there, as is the **Bahía Potrero Restaurant and Bar** (654-4555), known for its seafood specialties. **Cafe by the Bay** is a small coffee shop in front of a well-stocked **grocery store** at the entrance to town. They serve breakfast, lunch, and Italian specialties for dinner. **Richard's American Restaurant and Bar** (654-4445) serves steak, pasta, and seafood. **Stella's** has Japanese and Thai dishes. **Pleamar**, on the beach between Potrero and Flamingo, serves good *ceviche*.

Mayra's Camping y Cabinas (cold water, table fans, private bath; $20-$30; 654-4213), right on the beach, is quiet and has a nice family atmosphere. Camping among the dwarf palms in the yard costs $3.50 per person.

Behind the grocery store is **Windsong Cabinas** (private bath, hot water, fans, air conditioning; $40-$50; 654-4291), clean, white rooms with kitchenettes. Weekly rates are available—a good value.

The quiet **Cabinas Cristina** (private bath, heated water, ceiling fans, kitchens, small pool; $30-$40; with air conditioning, $50; phone/fax: 654-4006) are 250 meters inland. Dishes, silverware, and cooking utensils are available if you leave a deposit.

The Italian-owned **Cabinas Isolina** (private bath, heated water, ceiling fans; $30-$40; with kitchen, $40-$50; 654-4333, fax: 654-4313) are right on the road. A path leads 150 meters to the beach.

PLAYA LA PENCA   This small beach has whiter sand than Potrero and is framed by rocky outcrops on both sides. The waters are calm at the north end of the beach, but we were warned about strong currents at the south end (in front of Cielomar).

The oceanfront **Cielomar** (private bath, some with heated water, ceiling fans, air conditioning; $60-$70, including breakfast; 233-9451, 654-4194), formerly the private beach home of a family from San José, is lovely and tranquil and serves familiar American food in its restaurant.

Casa Sunset (private bath, heated water, ceiling fans, one with kitchen; $40-$50, including breakfast; phone/fax: 654-4265) offers simple, nicely designed white cabins, a small pool, and a beautiful view of the bay and its Isla de Plata. They have an open-air cooking area for guests to use. The owners, dedicated parents of many dogs, rent horses and arrange cruises and snorkeling trips.

PLAYA PAN DE AZÚCAR   This pretty beach offers some shade, a rocky area for snorkeling, and a sandy area for swimming. It's 15 minutes (five kilometers) north by car from Playa Potrero.

One of the oldest lodgings in the area, the recently remodeled **Hotel Sugar Beach** (private bath, heated water, air conditioning, ceiling fans, pool; children under 12 free; $120-$160; with kitchen, $220-$230; 654-4242, fax: 654-4239, 800-458-4735; www.sugar-beach.com, e-mail: info@sugar-beach.com) has spacious rooms and pleasant grounds on a rise overlooking the sea. We prefer the standard rooms; they are quite reasonable in the green season. There is a great view from the restaurant/bar, where many pet birds entertain the guests; a 25-foot boat for charter trips; and sports equipment. They also rent beach houses for 8 to 10 people.

GETTING THERE: By Bus: Direct buses from San José leave the Tralapa station (Calle 20, Avenidas 1/3; 221-7202; $5.20, six-hour trip) at 8 a.m. and 10 a.m. The earlier one goes as far as Flamingo, the later to Potrero.

Fantasy Tours (220-2126, 800-272-8854; www.fantasy.co.cr) runs a shuttle to Flamingo from both Jacó and Arenal for $19 one way, $25 from San José.

Buses leave the Folclórico station in Santa Cruz for Flamingo at 6:30 a.m. and 3 p.m., passing through Brasilito and going all the way to Potrero.

From Playas del Coco, Hermosa, or Panamá, take a returning bus from your beach and get off at Communidad (also called Tamarindo Bar) where the road from Coco meets the road from Liberia. There you can intercept a Santa Cruz or Nicoya bus. In 15 minutes you'll be in Belén, where at least seven buses a day stop on their way to Playas Brasilito, Flamingo, and Potrero.

A $5 taxi van runs between Flamingo and Potrero. Your hotel can call it for you. Shuttles to Tamarindo and Las Colinas Golf course cost $10.

There is no bus service north of Potrero.

By Car: If you're traveling by car, you'll see the turnoff for the beaches about a block after you pass the plaza of Belén. A winding road leads to the village of Huacas, where you turn off to the right. Turn right again after about 200 meters to go to Playas Flamingo, Brasilito, Potrero, and Pan de Azúcar. The trip from Belén to Brasilito, the closest beach, takes about 45 minutes by car or an hour by bus, and is on paved road. The road is unpaved after Playa Flamingo, as is the road to

Playa Grande. There are a couple of gas stations in Filadelfia, about halfway between Comunidad and Belén.

Note: If you are snorkeling anywhere in northern Guanacaste, beware of the *Pelamis platurus*, a small, thin sea snake with yellow and black stripes whose venom is lethal in 15 to 30 minutes and has no antidote. Fortunately, they have a very small mouth in which their teeth are set far back and, like most animals, won't bother you if you don't bother them. There have been no reports of fatal run-ins with this snake in Costa Rica, but it does live here, and we would think twice about snorkeling with children in this area.

LAS BAULAS NATIONAL MARINE PARK AND PLAYA GRANDE

The *baula* (leatherback) sea turtle is the largest reptile in the world, around five feet in length, some weighing over a ton. Until recently their migration pattern has been a mystery to turtle researchers. Scientists have attached radio transmitters to leatherbacks and discovered that they follow the crests of underwater mountains. Around 450 leatherbacks (down from 700 in 1992) came in 1997–98 to nest on the beach at **Playa Grande** from October through March, making it one of the most important leatherback nesting sites in the world. Because turtles return to the same beach over and over again to nest, it is necessary to keep those beaches as clear as possible. Recent studies have shown that the presence of humans does indeed affect turtle reproduction. The thin line of light on the ocean horizon guides turtle hatchlings as they scramble towards the sea, and the illumination of human development, either on the beach or in the hills behind it, can confuse them, preventing them from reaching the water before their limited energy stores are depleted. Peaceful Playa Grande is the scene of a battle to protect the venerable and voiceless turtles' right to nest where their instincts demand.

Playas Langosta and Ventanas, the Tamarindo Estuary and Playa Grande form **Parque Nacional Marino Las Baulas**. National marine parks protect the first 50 meters of land beyond the high-tide line. The exact status and coverage of these areas is in dispute, partly because the government has not paid for the expropriated lands that were made into the park. Given the amount of development on all the beaches within the protected area, the park could cost millions of dollars—money that the already impoverished national park system does not have.

That point aside, since the area is officially protected, turtle watching is more regulated than it used to be. In the old days, excursion buses from the Central Valley would bring fun-loving Ticos who would ride on the mother turtles' backs. Instead of 150-plus people gathering around a nesting turtle, observers of this primordial ritual must now go with guides from the local community.

We recommend a visit to **El Mundo de la Tortuga**, ($5, children under 10 free) the leatherback turtle museum in Playa Grande, near the park entrance. This lovely new project gives you earphones with recordings in English, Spanish, French, or German to guide you through an award-winning presentation on the leatherbacks, their life cycle, and the challenges they face. In fact, we recommend going to the museum rather than observing the turtles themselves, because the numbers of leatherbacks at Playa Grande are diminishing. Turtle observation is less harmful at Tortuguero on the Atlantic coast, where there are no lights on the beach and the green turtles come in far greater numbers.

If you feel you can't live without seeing the turtles at Playa Grande, we recommend the Mundo de la Tortuga tour ($25; with bus transportation to Playa Grande from Tamarindo, $30; 653-0471). The time of the turtle tours is determined by the phase of the moon and the hour of high tide. Signs are posted each day with the new time. Radio-carrying guides roam the beach until they spot a turtle. They alert the group guides, who then round up their flock of 15 or fewer, and the group walks down the beach to observe the nesting turtle. Sometimes you have to walk for a kilometer or more at high tide, so expect to get your feet wet. It is preferable to wear dark colors to make you invisible and long pants to protect you from bugs. When we were there last, the presence of our group striding along the beach trying to reach "our" turtle caused two mother turtles who were emerging from the surf to turn around and go back. A movement is underway to convince the park to make a trail up in the brush off the beach so that this will not happen. Once you reach your turtle, you might have to wait awhile until she is ready to be observed. During the egg-laying process, because of the scarcity of turtles, your group might have to move away from the turtle you are watching and share it with another group. The observation ends when the mother turtle starts camouflaging her nest by throwing sand over it with her flippers; the leatherbacks can be distracted during this part, and observers can get a face full of sand. At Tortuguero, you can watch the camouflage process, too.

Before becoming a national park, Playa Grande had already established a reputation as a favorite spot for surfers because of its long waves (avoid September, October, and late May). As is true with most beaches that are good for surfing, Playa Grande is not good for swimming. Playa Grande should not be considered a recreational beach. Camping is not allowed.

Note: If you are staying in Playa Grande, it is possible to walk along the beach during the day and catch a river-taxi over the estuary to Tamarindo. Be aware, however, that the park is closed during the night because of the turtles, so you will not be able to walk back to Playa Grande at night.

Hotel Las Tortugas (private bath, hot or heated water, fans and air conditioning, pools, jacuzzi; $40-$80; phone/fax: 653-0458, 653-0423; www.tamarindo.com, e-mail nela@cool.co.cr) has been designed to have the least possible negative effect on nesting turtles, with no ocean views toward the south and no lights shining on the beach. Staff and owners are dedicated conservationists, and keep a lookout for danger to turtles. A network of trails runs along the estuary and beaches. The hotel has a good restaurant, and arranges fishing, scuba diving, estuary tours by canoe or motorboat, and night turtle tours. A taxi to the hotel from Santa Cruz costs about $20, and the hotel offers a boat taxi to Tamarindo on request. Recently the turtle-viewing season has been shortened because of the diminishing number of turtles. Even if tourists are staying at this hotel on Playa Grande, they cannot watch the turtles if the parks department has ruled against it.

If you take a left just before reaching Las Tortugas, you can drive 15 minutes through dense overgrowth to a vacation cottage development. If you turn left, you will come to **Cantarana** (private bath, hot water, ceiling fans, pool; $60-$70, including breakfast; 653-0486, phone/fax: 653-0491), very attractive rooms around a lush garden with a lovely pool. The German owners pride themselves on homemade bread and the other tasty offerings from their open-air restaurant. They are on the estuary near one of the park entrances. **Hotel Villa Baulá** (private bath, hot water, ceiling fans; $60-$70; with refrigerator and two bedrooms, $90-$100; 257-7676, fax: 257-1098, phone/fax: 680-0769), farther along this road, is a wooden complex comprising several thatched bungalows, a couple of two-story units with guest rooms, a pool, and a restaurant. All rooms are well ventilated by sea breezes, though sea dew on the screened windows make the rooms a bit humid. The hotel offers horse and bike rentals and an estuary tour in kayaks.

GETTING THERE: By Bus: The 10 a.m. San José–Flamingo bus (Calle 20, Avenida 1/3; 221-7202; $5.20) stops in Matapalo first. Buses leave Santa Cruz for Matapalo at 10:30 a.m. and 2:30 p.m., returning at 5:30 a.m. and noon. From Matapalo you'll have to either walk or take a taxi to Playa Grande.

By Car: Go straight on the gravel road going west from Huacas instead of turning right (north) for Brasilito and Flamingo. At the end of the soccer field in Matapalo, turn left for Playa Grande. It's about 15 minutes along a gravel road. If you're coming from Tamarindo, go to Villareal, turn left and then left again at the

Rancho Las Colinas Golf Course signs. When the road Ts in Matapalo, turn left, then take the next left fork to the golf course. Follow the road next to the golf course to Playa Grande.

TAMARINDO

Tamarindo is a wide, white-sand beach with a large estuary—a favorite with surfers and windsurfers. Leatherback turtles nest at Tamarindo from October to March (as well as Playa Grande to the north). As they scramble to the ocean from late December to May, many baby turtles have been inadvertently crushed by beachgoers because it is hard to see the hatchlings in the dry, loose sand high up on the beach. Be sure to walk near the waterline, where it is easier to spot them.

Papagayo Excursions (phone/fax: 653-0254), at the entrance to town, offers sportfishing, scuba diving, turtle tours during the nesting season, and nature safaris by boat or horseback. They also will take you on day trips to some of Guanacaste's national parks. **Coopetamarindo** (653-0201), at the entrance to Tamarindo, offers shuttles across the estuary to Playa Grande, and will take you on mangrove/estuary tours ($18/person) and, in season, to observe nesting turtles ($25/person). Check the life-jacket situation before you embark. We recommend going to **El Mundo de las Tortugas** museum in Playa Grande instead of taking the turtle tour (see Playa Grande section, above).

Agua Rica Diving Center (phone/fax: 653-0094) will take you out to see the turtles while they are still in the water. They offer full SSI certification as well as a "resort course." They do night dives, snorkeling, and sail and dive cruises. Their office is on the left at the entrance to Cabinas Marielos.

Housed in a large thatch-roofed rancho on the road to Playa Langosta, **Iguana Surf** (653-0148; www.tamarindo.com/iguana, e-mail: iguanasurf@aol.com) rents surfboards, boogieboards, Hobie cats, and sea kayaks. They offer snorkeling tours by kayak or boat to a nearby island. They can also take you to the Langosta estuary, south of Tamarindo, and have a surf taxi to nearby Playas Negra and Avellanes, favorites with surfers. We have heard rave reviews about their restaurant, which specializes in seafood.

You can study Spanish in Tamarindo at **Wayra Language School** (653-0359, fax: 653-0059; www.spanish-wayra.co.cr, e-mail: spanishw@racsa.co.cr), on the road to Playa Langosta. They offer three- and four-day survival courses as well as one- to four-week courses and teach Latin dancing in the evenings. The owners will arrange housing for students.

Tamarindo has an **24-hour medical emergency center**: get details through your hotel.

RESTAURANTS   On the left as you enter Tamarindo is the **Panaderia de Paris** (open 6 a.m. to 7 p.m.), a bakery owned by a French family. They also own the **Restaurant Français Crocodilo** (open 5 p.m. to 10:30 p.m.; 653-0255) next door, named for a nine-foot crocodile that lives at the river mouth. Their disco, **Club 24**, is open from 11 p.m. to 4 a.m.

Frutas Tropicales, on the left just after the entrance to town, is reasonably priced, simple, clean, and very popular. Open all day.

Soda el Arrecife, on the circle in "downtown" Tamarindo, offers huge servings of fish, rice, beans, french fries, and salad for about $2.50. They are also open for breakfast. The pizzeria next door isn't great, but the **Fiesta del Mar** (open 24 hours a day; 653-0139), just beyond, specializes in tasty native food cooked over a wood fire; **Nogui's**, just on the beach around the bend, offers moderately priced salads, sandwiches, grilled meats, and seafood, with sundaes for dessert. **Bar y Restaurante Zully Mar** (653-0023) is one of the original restaurants on the beach, and still is good for seafood. **Blue Maxx Café** (653-0647) serves filling surfer-style breakfasts.

At the turnoff for Playa Langosta, **Las Meridianas** has an excellent reputation for reproducing the cuisine of Tuscany. It's on the pricey side ($16 for lunch, open 11 a.m. to 11 p.m.). Vegetarians will enjoy the **Arcoiris**.

Supermercado El Pelícano (open Monday through Saturday, 7 a.m. to 7 p.m.; Sunday, 9 a.m. to 5 p.m.) has gourmet coffee, fresh-baked breads, deli sandwiches, cookies and pastries, health-food products, herbs, organically grown vegetables, books and newspapers, cigars, wine, and beer. They are at the crossroads to Playa Langosta.

The **Iguana Grill**, on the road to Playa Langosta, is popular for breakfast and lunch. **Cantina Las Olas**, down the street, serves Mexican food.

Hotel Capitán Suizo serves excellent international cuisine and **Hotel Jardín del Edén** serves French and Italian specialties.

LODGING   Formerly an active fishing village, Tamarindo is now the site of many hotel development projects. All hotels offer substantial off-season discounts; off-season usually means May through mid-November. You can find out a lot more about most of the places listed below on the Tamarindo website, www.tamarindo.com.

Halfway between Villareal and Tamarindo are two lodging facilities. **Monte Fresco** (private bath, hot water, ceiling fan, kitchen, satellite TV; $60-$80, including breakfast; 653-0241, fax: 653-0243; e-mail: samoniqe@racsa. co.cr) is a small Austrian-owned hilltop farm that has neat apartments and a pool. Their raison d'être is *Samonique*, their sailboat, which they charter out for sunset cruises ($45), half-day cruises ($60, including snorkeling and all you can eat or drink), and longer excursions, including trips to Isla del Coco.

The owner of Hotel Santo Tomás in San José rents out his family's three-bedroom **beach house** (heated water, kitchen; $150-$240; 255-0448, fax: 222-3950). Guests have use of a canoe for estuary explorations, as well as boogieboards.

As you enter Tamarindo, you'll find the **Best Western Vista Villas** (private bath, hot water, air conditioning, ceiling fans, kitchens, pool; $100-$230, including breakfast; 653-0118, fax: 653-0115, 800-292-3786; www.central america.com.cr/hotel/vista.htm, e-mail: tamvv@racsa.co.cr), large apartments with views, which sleep four to eight. The apartments have special closets for your surfboard. They rent water-sports equipment. The **Pueblo Dorado** (heated water, air conditioning, pool; $50-$60; phone/fax: 222-5741, 653-0008, fax: 653-0013) has small, clean, comfortably furnished rooms intimately arranged around a courtyard. The Dutch-owned **Hotel El Milagro** (private bath, hot water; with ceiling fans, $50-$60; with air conditioning, $60-$70, including breakfast; 653-0042, fax: 653-0050; www.elmilagro.com, e-mail: elmilagro@elmilagro.com) offers several rows of cabinas. Restaurant customers can use the pool.

A five-minute walk up the hill from El Milagro is the French/Italian–owned luxury hotel, **El Jardín del Edén** (private bath, hot water, ceiling fans, air conditioning; $120-$130; with kitchens, $140-$150; kids 5 to 12, $15; phone/fax: 653-0111, 653-0137; www.bestofcostarica.com/jardineden). These stuccoed, tile-roofed rooms and apartments have a distinct Mediterranean feel. There are pools (one with a swim-up bar) and a jacuzzi. The restaurant has a tempting prix-fixe menu. A 100-meter footpath leads to the beach.

Back on the main beach road is **Cabinas Marielos** (private bath, cold water, ceiling fans; $30-$40; phone/fax: 653-0141). Clean, they have nice gardens. Doña Marielos takes pride in her place, from the fine woodwork on her newest cabins to the aura-cleansing ylang-ylang trees in the gardens and her orchid collection. She offers many guest services: safety deposit boxes, laundry service, a pleasant communal kitchen, guarded parking, and surfboard rentals. Recommended.

The **Tamarindo Diriá** (private bath, hot water, air conditioning, ceiling fans, satellite TV, phone, refrigerator; $130-$140, including breakfast; 653-0032, phone/fax: 653-0031) is a comfortable place to stay, especially with kids, although the rooms are on the small side. The hotel has shady grounds, tennis courts, a game room, a casino (open in high season), and a restaurant. It gets crowded in tourist season. Local people sell jewelry and animals made out of shells at the hotel's beach entrance.

Cabinas Zully Mar (private bath; with cold water and ceiling fans, $30-$40; with ceiling fans and refrigerator, $40-$50 with heated water, air conditioning, and refrigerator, or new rooms, $50-$60; 226-4732, fax: 286-0191, phone/fax: 653-0140; www.accommodations.co.cr) are in "downtown" Tamarindo, where the road ends in a clutch of bar-restaurants on the beach. Zullymar has been transformed from a row of dark cabinas to a grandiose structure resembling an Italian villa. The dank old rooms still exist, but the new rooms are lighter and airier, and have balconies.

Before you arrive at the downtown cul-de-sac, you can veer left, uphill. Beyond this turnoff, if you go right at the next Y in the road beyond Tamarindo Resort, you'll be on the Calle Real, the road to Playa Langosta, where German, Swedish, and North American beach-lovers have built some of the nicest places in Tamarindo. The bright, white **Casa Blanca** (private bath, hot water, ceiling fans, kitchens, pool; studio, $70-$80; apartment for six, $130-$140; house for eight, $200-$220; phone/fax: 653-0073, in the U.S.: 360-371-3560, in Canada: 604-253-1252; e-mail: csimmons@sol.racsa.co.cr) has comfortable, airy apartments and a pool set in a lovely garden. The friendly **Casa Cook** (private bath, hot water, ceiling fans or air conditioning, kitchens, pool; one-bedroom cabinas, $120-$130; two-bedroom villa, $230; 653-0125, in the U.S.: 510-846-0784, fax: 510-426-1141; www.tamarindo.com/cook, e-mail: casacook@racsa.co.cr) farther down the road on the right has one-bedroom apartments on the beach and an upstairs villa overlooking the pool. They welcome families.

Farther along on the right is the comfortable **Capitán Suizo** (680-0853, fax: 653-0292; www.tamarindo.com/capitan, e-mail: capitansuizo@ticonet.co.cr), with rooms (private bath, hot water, ceiling fans or air conditioning; $100-$120, children 4 to 12, $5) and larger bungalows (private bath, hot water, ceiling fans, refrigerator; $140-$150). There is a pool, and an open-air restaurant near the beach has a good salad bar. The multilevel hotel is built around lush gardens and has a relaxed but sophisticated atmosphere. **La Casa Sueca** (private bath, hot water, ceiling fans, kitchens; $80-$90; phone/fax: 653-0021; www.tamarindo.com/sueca, e-mail: vikings@sol.racsa.co.cr), just around the corner from the Capitán Suizo, has charming, spacious rooms with kitchens and offers monthly rates.

Our two favorite places in Tamarindo are near the end of the road: **Sueño del Mar** (private bath, hot water, ceiling fans, $130-$140; matrimonial suite, $170-$180; phone/fax: 653-0284; www.tamarindo.com/sdmar, e-mail: suenodem@racsa.co.cr) is owned by a North American gourmet cook specializing in healthy cuisine. The hotel embodies what the owner most liked of the many architectural styles she encountered in her travels. You'll find double-thick adobe-style walls and uniquely sculpted Bali-style open-roof showers, to name just a couple of the wonderful features. They specialize in beach weddings and special occasions. The hotel is on rocky Punta Langosta, at the extreme south end of Tamarindo's beach. (From Capitán Suizo it is five more minutes south; take a right after the Cala Mar Hotel project.)

Villa Alegre (private and shared baths, hot water, ceiling fans or air conditioning; $120-$140; one-bedroom villas with kitchens, $180, including breakfast; 653-0270, fax: 653-0287; www.tamarindo.com/alegre, e-mail: vialegre@racsa.co.cr) is an oasis of peace and tranquility. Behind its high white walls, the friendly, helpful owners have created a spacious yet welcoming retreat with a lovely pool and rooms furnished with fabric and art from their worldwide adventures. Their gourmet breakfasts, served on the terrace, are memorable, as is the untouched stretch of Playa Langosta that fronts the villa. Group rates are available for small workshops or seminars. Some rooms are wheelchair accessible.

Back to the Y at Tamarindo Resort: veering left will get you to the following places:

Arcoiris Restaurant and Cabinas (private bath, heated water, ceiling fans, hammocks on porches; $30-$40; with kitchens, $40-$50; 653-0330) are rainbow-colored cabins, each with its own funky interior decor. The owners are creative young Italians, who own a tattoo studio, teach karate and yoga, and give shiatsu massages.

Bella Vista Village Resort (private bath, heated water, ceiling fans, kitchens, pool; $90-$110; phone/fax: 653-0036; e-mail: belvista@racsa.co.cr) is owned by a down-to-earth California couple. The resort comprises cylindrical, two-story efficiency *ranchos*. Each *rancho* accommodates four to five people.

Nearby is **Stella's** (closed Sunday), a popular Italian restaurant, as is **La Pachanga**, down the street.

GETTING THERE: By Bus: Empresa Alfaro buses to Tamarindo leave San José (Calle 14, Avenida 5; 222-2160, 222-2666, 223-7685; $4.75) daily at 3:30 p.m., returning at 5:45 a.m.; on Sunday, there is another return bus at 1 p.m. Buy tickets early, especially on weekends and holidays.

Buses leave Santa Cruz for Tamarindo daily at 10:30 a.m., 1:30 p.m., and 3 p.m., returning at 6 a.m. and noon. Check schedules at 680-0401 or 653-0167.

From Playas del Coco, Hermosa, or Panamá, take a returning bus from your beach and get off at Comunidad (also called Tamarindo Bar), where the road from Coco meets the highway from Liberia. There you can intercept a Santa Cruz or Nicoya bus. In 15 minutes you'll be in Belén, where the Santa Cruz–Tamarindo bus passes shortly after leaving Santa Cruz according to the schedule listed above. See Guanacaste map at the beginning of this chapter.

Fantasy Tours (220-2126, in the U.S.: 800-272-8854, in Canada: 800-453-6654; www.fantasy.co.cr/index8.html) has daily air-conditioned buses to Tamarindo from San José, Liberia, La Fortuna (near Volcán Arenal), and Playa Jacó ($19). Make reservations through your hotel.

By Car: If you are coming from Santa Cruz, drive north on the highway until you cross the bridge on the north end of town, then make a sharp left. It's about 16 kilometers to 27 de Abril on a paved road with plenty of potholes (the first two kilometers are gravel). At the fork in the road, just before 27 de Abril, turn right for another 14 kilometers on a gravel road to Villareal. Here you turn left for the last four kilometers to Tamarindo.

If you are coming from points north, turn right off the main highway at Belén. A winding road leads to the village of Huacas, about 25 kilometers away; there you turn left for Villareal (14 kilometers), just five minutes from Tamarindo. This route is paved as far as Villareal. If you are coming from Flamingo or Potrero, it is hard to catch this turnoff, because all the signs that point to Tamarindo are facing oncoming cars from Liberia. But follow signs to the Rancho Las Colinas Golf Course and Villareal and you'll be on the right track.

By Air: SANSA (221-9414, fax: 255-2176; $61 one way) has four flights daily to Tamarindo from San José, and one flight from La Fortuna near Volcán Arenal ($56). Travelair (232-7883, 220-3054, fax: 220-0413; $92 one way, $152 roundtrip) flies to Tamarindo from the Pavas airport near San José three times a day. Check schedules at www.centralamerica.com/cr/tran/travlair.htm. Ask your hotel to arrange transportation from the airstrip. See Chapter Four for reservation information.

SANTA CRUZ

Santa Cruz is the home of much of Costa Rica's folklore. The music department of the University of Costa Rica has a special branch there, devoted to researching and celebrating traditional songs, dances, and instruments.

Just a 15-minute drive from Santa Cruz, through the beautiful hill country that is the heartland of the Nicoya Peninsula, are the villages of **Guaitil** and **San Vicente**, where local artisans have revived the art of Chorotega-style pottery making. With little use of a wheel, they recreate every known original design from native clay and natural paints and colors. Pieces range in price from $2 to $30. The pottery is displayed at the local shop and in front of homes. Stop for a chat with the artisans, and you'll feel the warmth and goodness of the Costa Rican campesino. On the road to Guaitil, stop for lunch at **Sol de Vida** (680-0713), where all the food is cooked with sun-power. The women who run this restaurant go all over the country teaching other women how to build solar ovens. Food that is slow-cooked in a solar oven doesn't stick or burn, retains more flavor and nutrients, and leaves the cook free to do other things, as well as saving energy. Buses leave Santa Cruz for Guaitil every two hours; to drive there, head towards Nicoya and take the left after you cross a bridge leaving Santa Cruz. Recommended.

Coopetortillas (open 5 a.m. to 7 p.m.; 680-0688), 250 meters south of the church, is our favorite place to eat in Santa Cruz. It has grown from a tortilla factory to a popular restaurant featuring typical Guanacaste food. We don't know if you get emotional about huge hand-patted tortillas made from freshly ground corn, but this is a rare treat in Costa Rica, and well worth the $2 they charge for a hearty breakfast of *gallo pinto* with eggs and *café con leche*. Highly recommended. **Jardín de Luna** (open daily, 11 a.m. to 3 p.m., 5:30 p.m. to 11 p.m.; 680-0819, on the north side of the Parque Central) is the best we found of the plethora of local Chinese restaurants.

There is an open-air **farmers' market** at Plaza los Mangos on Saturday mornings and under the trees on the block behind the church on Monday mornings. Another block south is the **hospital**, which offers 24-hour emergency care.

LODGING   **Hotel Diriá** (private bath, hot water, air conditioning, table fans, TV, phone; $40-$50; 680-0080), at the entrance to Santa Cruz near the highway, is the fanciest option in town, a large hotel whose rooms enclose gardens and pools.

Close competition comes from **Hotel la Calle de Alcalá** (private bath, hot water, air conditioning, phones, local TV, pool, restaurant; $40-$50; with jacuzzi, $60-$80; 680-0000, fax: 680-1633) a fancy hotel one block east of the Tralapa bus stop in Santa Cruz. They don't have reading lamps and the air conditioners are noisy, but there is room service.

Hotel La Pampa (private bath, cold water, TV; with fans, $20-$30; with air conditioning, $30-$40; 680-0586) is clean and attractive, 50 meters west of the southwest corner of Plaza Lopez. A good value.

Cabinas Permont (private bath, cold water, ceiling fan or air conditioning; $12-$20; 680-0425) is a very clean establishment by the highway on the southeast side of town. Look carefully for the sign; it's on the left as you leave Santa Cruz for Nicoya. Recommended.

GETTING THERE: By Bus: Ten daily Tralapa buses go to Santa Cruz (half a block west of the Coca Cola; 221-7202, 680-0392; $5; buses leave hourly from Liberia and Nicoya for Santa Cruz).

By Car: Santa Cruz is about five hours from San José. The Tempisque Ferry route is more scenic and about 50 kilometers shorter than going via Liberia. Ferries leave every hour on the hour from the landing 25 kilometers west of the Limonal turnoff on the Interamerican Highway (just north of the turnoff to La Juntas de Abangares). Each vehicle crossing on the ferry pays $3 for the ride, and each passenger 35 cents. A bridge is being built that will eliminate the ferry. It is scheduled for completion in 2001.

Guaitil is 12 kilometers southeast of Santa Cruz and 19 kilometers northeast of Nicoya. The road is paved between Santa Cruz and Guaitil, unpaved between Guaitil and Nicoya.

BEACHES NEAR SANTA CRUZ

This area gives more of a sense of Costa Rican rural life than the more populous beaches farther north. The hotels are just as nice—quieter and often more reasonably priced than in nearby Tamarindo, and not that much harder to get to. With off-season discounts, prices can be half of those listed here.

PLAYA JUNQUILLAL

This wide, almost deserted beach has high surf and strong rip currents. Once when we were there, locals were sighting sharks. At the southern and northern ends are tidepools big enough to snorkel in.

The Canadian-owned **Iguanazul** (private bath, hot water, ceiling fans, pool; $80-$90; with air conditioning, $110-$110, including breakfast; phone/fax: 653-0123, 653-0124; www.iguanazul.com, e-mail: reservations@igua nazul.com) is one kilometer north of Playa Junquillal on a cliff overlooking the ocean. It has good food, good music, and friendly people. You can rent snorkeling and surfing equipment and horses here. Sportfishing, river rafting, and waterfall trips are also available, and this isolated 24-room hotel could be rented as a whole for a retreat. To get there, get off the Junquillal bus at the arched Iguanazul entrance and walk one kilometer toward the beach. Their website has excellent directions for cars.

Next door is a real boon for campers, **Camping Los Malinches** ($5/person; phone/fax: 653-0429). Owned by a cultured Costa Rican gentleman who taught for many years in California, it has a lovely view from its shady campsites, and the cleanest bathrooms and showers we've seen at any Costa Rican campground. The Green Tortoise bus tours stay here. Although you have to hike for a kilometer to get to the campsite from the road, once you are there it's a short walk to the great restaurant at Iguanazul. In front of Los Mal-inches and Iguanazul the beach is mostly rocky tidepools, but sandy Playa Blanca is just 200 meters north.

Just before arriving in Junquillal, you'll pass the lovely **Guacamaya Lodge** (private bath, hot water, ceiling fans, pool; $40-$50; 653-0431; www.guacamayalodge.com, e-mail: info@guacamayalodge.com), which has at-tractive screened rooms and a Swiss restaurant on its hilltop perch. They also rent a two-bedroom house for $120 a night. A good value.

El Lugarcito (shared bath, hot water, ceiling fan; $50-$60, including breakfast; phone/fax: 653-0436), up a rise to the left, is a Dutch-owned B&B, bar, and scuba diving center. They also arrange hiking trips to Arenal.

Arriving in Junquillal proper, you'll come first to **El Malinche** (shared bath, cold water, table fan, $7-$12; private bath, ceiling fan, $12-$20; $4/per-son to camp; 655-0433), the cheapest place to stay. Doña Aydee and Don Pedro, the owners, also have a nice little grocery store open daily from 6 a.m. to 9 p.m. and serve as the public phone and the Tralapa bus ticket office. We couldn't see the rooms, but the little grassy campsite looked nice and the bath-rooms were okay. Next door, the German-owned **Hotel Hibiscus** (private bath, heated water, ceiling fans; $40-$50, including breakfast; phone/fax: 653-0437) has well-designed and -decorated bungalows. Across the street, with gardens leading to the beach, is **La Puesta del Sol** (653-0442), an attractive Italian restaurant open in the evening.

Hotel Playa Junquillal (private bath, heated water, fans; $30-$40; 653-0432; www.playa-junquillal.com, e-mail: hotel@playa-junquillal.com), right on the beach, has simple but clean rooms with nice decorative touches, friendly management, and a classic Tico beach restaurant that's the local hangout, open 8 a.m. to 10 p.m. They provide inexpensive showers and toi-lets for campers, but the rooms are a bit overpriced.

The beach road ends at the **Hotel Antumalal** (private bath, hot water, ceil-ing fans, pool, tennis court; $70-$80, including breakfast; phone/fax: 653-0425), whose large thatched restaurant is at the top of a hill, cooled by breezes and with an ocean view. The grounds are pleasant and shady and the rooms have terraces with hammocks.

GETTING THERE: By Bus: A bus leaves the local terminal in Santa Cruz for Junquillal at 7 p.m., returning at 5 a.m. A direct Tralapa bus (Calle 20, Avenidas 3/5; 221-7202; $4.50) leaves San José at 2 p.m. and returns at 5 a.m. The trip takes five and a half hours. Check schedules at El Malinche (653-0433).

By Car: To reach Junquillal from Tamarindo by car, continue south 18 kilo-meters to the 27 de Abril crossing. Turn right onto an unpaved road and go another 12 kilometers. Turn left at Paraíso. The hotels are four kilometers from there. If you are coming from Liberia, it is faster to take a turnoff to the right just before you reach Santa Cruz (follow the signs). If you are coming from Nicoya, turn left after you cross a small metal bridge as you leave Santa Cruz. From there, it's 19 kilometers to 27 de Abril. Turn left and proceed as above. You'll feel a lot better if you have a sturdy car with high clearance on these bumpy roads.

By Air: See Tamarindo section for flight information. A taxi from Tamarindo to Junquillal costs about $35 and takes about 45 minutes. Some hotels will pick you up if you're staying for several days.

PLAYA NEGRA

Just north of Playa Junquillal, Playa Negra has been a secret destination for surfers for many years. This beach was featured in *Endless Summer II*, and is known for its hollow right barrel. The beach itself is quite pretty, with lovely shade trees all along the coast.

Within walking distance from the beach, **Pablo Picasso's** (cold water; with private bath and wall fans, $7-$12/person; air-conditioned rooms with kitchens, $40-$50; cell phone: 382-0411) is a lively surfer spot; the restaurant serves gringo food. Camping is allowed ($4/tent). On the beach, **Hotel Playa Negra** (private bath, hot water, ceiling fans, restaurant, pool; $60-$70; cell phone: 382-1301, cell fax: 382-1302, phone/fax: 293-0332) has well-designed circular bungalows, a circular swimming pool, and a breezy circular restaurant on the beach. **Las Hermanas Bakery, Deli and Restaurant** specializes in hearty breakfasts and lunches.

GETTING THERE: By Bus: No public transportation goes all the way to Playa Negra. See the Junquillal bus directions and get off in Paraíso, where you can hitch, hire a car, or walk the rest of the way (about five kilometers).

By Car: For Playa Negra, drive to Paraíso as described in the "Getting There" section for Junquillal. In Paraíso, turn right (instead of left for Junquillal) and drive along the gravel road. In 15 minutes you will be at Playa Negra. It's best to have four-wheel drive in the rainy season, and a high clearance at any time of year.

NICOYA

While Liberia is the transportation and commercial capital of Guanacaste, Nicoya is the cultural capital. Its church (open 8 a.m. to noon, 2 p.m. to 6 p.m.), dedicated to San Blas, was built in 1644 and is an adobe monument to the austere faith of the Spanish colonists. Next to it is a lovely, shady square abloom with flowers.

Café Daniela, an open, airy restaurant on the main thoroughfare one block from the park, has freshly baked goods, pizzas, and ice-cold *refrescos*, plus a full Tico menu, including a vegetarian *casado* and carrot juice. **El Presidente**, 25 meters east of the plaza, serves generous portions of tasty fried fish and Chinese food. We counted 11 Chinese restaurants in Nicoya. A **Monpik** ice cream store is on the plaza.

LODGING   There are several inexpensive places to stay in the center of town. All directions are given from the central park.

Las Tinajas (private bath, cold water, ceiling fans; $7-$12; 685-5081), next to the Plaza de la Anexión supermarket, has some rooms off the street that might be quieter than other places in town.

The **Pensión Venecia** (shared or private bath, cold water, table fans; $7-$12; 685-5325), across from the church, is clean and basic with a nice airy sitting area.

Hotel Curime (private bath, hot water, pool; ceiling or table fans, TV, $30-$40; with air conditioning and refrigerators, $40-$50; 685-5238, fax: 685-5530), south of town on the road to Playas Sámara and Nosara, has some rooms with folding screens that can be pulled out to give each bed privacy. You'll find a recreation complex, including a large pool, tennis, volleyball and basketball courts, a playground, and a restaurant.

GETTING THERE: By Bus: Buses to Nicoya leave San José from Empresa Alfaro (Calle 14, Avenida 5; 222-2160, 222-2666, 223-7685; $4.50) eight times a day. You must buy tickets in advance. If your bus takes the Tempisque ferry route, follow the flock to the ticket booth and then jump on the boat right away so you don't get left behind.

By Car: It's a much shorter drive from San José to Nicoya via the Tempisque ferry. Take the Interamerican Highway and look for the ferry signs right after the turnoff for Las Juntas, at Limonal. The ferry landing is 25 kilometers to the west. Buy tickets ($3/car and 35 cents/passenger) while in line. The ferry leaves every hour on the hour and returns on the half hour. A bridge over the Río Tempisque is scheduled to be completed in 2001.

It's about 20 minutes from Santa Cruz to Nicoya on the paved road and an hour on the scenic old road that passes through Santa Bárbara and Guaitil. Buses run hourly between Santa Cruz and Nicoya.

THE MONTE ALTO FOREST RESERVE ✪ Monte Alto is a community-based conservation effort near the town of **Hojancha**, a cool, coffee-growing region in the hills southeast of Nicoya. In response to increasing water shortages, the community banded together in 1992 to buy 290 hectares of land, which they have left untouched. Mother Nature has already begun the regenerative process that will insure the survival of the Río Nosara and thus the community itself. Hojancha won the WHO Healthy Community Prize in 1998. Visitors can hike within the reserve and stay at the lovely wooden **lodge** the community has built (shared bath, cold water; $8/person; 659-9089; www.agroecoturismo.net, e-mail: cooprena@racsa.co.cr). You can bring your own picnic, or call in advance and they will cook for you. A small visitor's center displays old farm implements and has pictures of the animal and bird species in the area. There is a meeting room, a barbecue, and an orchid garden (best between December and February). During their annual April celebration, they run the old *trapiche* to show how sugar is made. They have a couple of short loop trails, and a steep four-kilometer climb to a *mirador* where you can see both sides of the Nicoya Peninsula. Recommended.

GETTING THERE: The 14 kilometers from Nicoya to Hojancha are scenic and the road is nicely paved. The six kilometers from Hojancha to the reserve are best done with four- wheel drive, especially in the rainy season. There are four small streams to cross. Be sure to arrive before sundown so people can easily direct you to the reserve. Everyone in the community knows where it is.

A bus leaves San José (222-2160, Calle 14, Avenida 5) for Hojancha at 2:30 p.m. daily, returning at 7:30 a.m. There is also bus service from Nicoya.

NOSARA, SÁMARA, AND CARRILLO

NOSARA   **Playas de Nosara**, one of the only ecotouristic beaches in Guanacaste, is an international community with many North American and European residents who have set aside half their land as a wildlife reserve and park. The Nosara Civic Association governs the community and so far has been successful in keeping out large developers. You won't find many hotels right on the beach here, because the residents respect and obey Costa Rican laws concerning development within the Maritime Zone, unlike many other more touristy beaches in the country. The maritime zone fronting four kilometers of beach is protected by the forest service. Nosara is a short drive from the **Ostional Wildlife Refuge**, which protects an important olive ridley turtle nesting ground (see below). Because of these reserve areas, Nosara is generally much greener than the rest of Guanacaste. No hunting has been allowed there for decades, so birds and wildlife are plentiful. It is common to see coatimundis, armadillos, howler monkeys, and even the jaguarundi, a cat that looks black from a distance but actually has a gray diamond pattern on its fur. Parrots, toucans, cuckoos, trogons, and pelicans are also easily observed. Humpback and gray whales can be seen offshore during the winter months. The beaches have community-maintained shelters for picnicking and camping.

Note: Bring a flashlight for walking around at night.

Playa Pelada is a small, S-shaped beach. Its volcanic outcrops house tidal pools and a blowhole that sends up a surprising shower and spray during high tide. There are coral reefs and tidepools on **Playa Guiones** that are good for snorkeling and safe for children at low tide. Surfing is best at Guiones and at the mouth of the **Nosara River**.

Canoeing or kayaking on the Río Nosara and through the mangroves on Ostional, moonlit horseback rides on the beach or to a local waterfall, and fishing and snorkeling trips are available through Tony and Beata Kast's **Casa Río Tours** (682-0117, fax: 682-0182; e-mail: casarionosara@nosara.com). Canoes and kayaks are also available for rent. Recommended. Surfing lessons are offered at **Corkey Carol's Surf School**, based at the Harbor Reef Hotel (see below).

We used to recommend that you rent a car to visit Nosara, but if you stay at a hotel in the Bocas de Nosara beach area, you'll be in walking distance of Swiss, French, Italian, Costa Rican, and creative Californian restaurants, and might not need a car. Ask your hotel if they can pick you up at the airport or at the bus stop. Most hotels can arrange for you to pick up a rental car in Nosara for a $40-$50 service charge.

First we describe the lodgings and restaurants closest to Playa Guiones, then we move northward to those close to Playa Pelada and inland, to the village of Nosara. (This is the order in which you will find them if you drive in from Nicoya.) You'll find useful information as well as a good map of the area at www.nosara.com.

Near the southern end of Playa Guiones, **La Dolce Vita** (open daily, 11 a.m. to 11 p.m.; 682-0107) is worth the hike (or drive) from where you are staying. They serve gourmet Italian pizza, pasta, and seafood.

The **Gilded Iguana** (open daily, 10 a.m. to 6 p.m.; 682-0259, 680-0749) is famous for its Black Panther cocktail, named after the local jaguarundi. It offers a Tex-Mex menu Tuesday through Saturday and hosts a traditional bridge game on Friday. They also rent furnished efficiency apartments (private bath, hot water, fans, kitchenette; $40-$50) 125 meters from the beach. They have a fax service, and offer sportfishing, sea kayaking, and horse rental. To get there, as you come from the south, take the next left after the road to the Nosara Civic Association.

Housed in an airy, elegant mansion with a sea view, **Nosara Yoga Institute** (682-0071, fax 682-0072, in the U.S.: 888-803-0580; www.nosara yoga.com, e-mail: yogacr@racsa.co.cr) is dedicated to professional training for teachers and practitioners in the fields of yoga and bodywork. The turnoff from the main road is at the big round yellow "Nosara Civic Association" sign; from there, follow the small frog markers bearing left.

The Bocas de Nosara area has several friendly places near the beach. The first is **Café de Paris** (682-0087, fax: 682-0089; www.cafedeparis.net, e-mail: info@cafedeparis.net), which bakes French bread and croissants for its poolside restaurant (open daily, 7 a.m. to 11 p.m.). Their well-designed, light and airy rooms (private bath, cold water, ceiling fans, $40-$50; with kitchen and hammocks, $60-$70; with hot water and air conditioning, $70-$80 for four; bungalow for 6, $140; all rates include breakfast) offer a variety of configurations for families and groups. A few hundred meters toward the beach is **Villa Taype** (private bath, hot water, pool, restaurant, disco/bar; with ceiling fans or air conditioning, $70-$80; bungalows that sleep six, $80-$90; breakfast included; phone/fax: 682-0188, fax: 682-0187; www.villataype. com, e-mail: info@villataype.ocm), with lovely landscaped grounds, two pools, tennis courts, and many activities for the whole family. Smaller rooms with shared bath are available for long-term guests ($30). Across the street is **Casa Tucan** (private bath, hot water, fans or air conditioning, kitchenettes, pool, airport pick-up; $70-$80; phone/fax: 682-0115; www.casatucan.net, e-mail: info@casatucan.net), a friendly hotel and restaurant owned by California chef Richard Moffat. Besides the creative cookery he dreams up each day, he is a wealth of information about the area. Around the corner is **Alan's Surf House**, a friendly, inexpensive place to stay.

Just past Alan's is **Harbor Reef Lodge** (private bath, hot water, ceiling fans, air conditioning; $70-$100; with kitchens, $100-$110; 682-0059, fax: 682-0060; www.harborreef.com, e-mail: hbrreef@racsa.co.cr), which offers well-designed rooms with many amenities, some with private porches. Meals are served in the tastefully decorated restaurant. They are home base for the 31-foot sportfisher *Black Marlin II*. They also have a handy general store.

Back on the main road, turn left at the open-air pizzeria, **Giardina Tropical**, and follow signs to **Villa Romántica** (private bath, hot water, ceiling fans, refrigerator, pool; $60-$70, including breakfast; phone/fax: 682-0019; www.nosara.com/casaromantica, e-mail: casroma@racsa.co.cr). This small Swiss-owned hotel is where the international community goes when they want a special meal by candlelight. Delightful salads, filling Swiss, Italian, and seafood specialties, delicious desserts, and fine wines make up the menu.

The main road winds around a bit after the pizzeria, then you come to **Rancho Congo** (private bath, heated water, ceiling fans; $20-$30; phone/ fax: 682-0078) on the left, a pleasant B&B owned by Monika Theil. Even without the generous breakfast included in the rates, this would be a best deal in Nosara.

Heading toward Playa Pelada, the following lodgings are within a five-minute walk from the beach:

Perched on a hill, with breezy balconies, original artwork on the walls, and ocean views, **Almost Paradise** (private bath, hot water, wall fans; $40-$50, kids under 12 free; phone/fax: 682-0173; e-mail: almostparadise@iname. com) is a homespun hotel with a restaurant specializing in German dishes and vegetarian food. Stop in for afternoon tea and cake. The helpful German owner is a former television journalist who has planted her hillside garden with fruit trees that attract a variety of animals.

Views from the palatial **Hotel Playa Nosara** (private bath, heated water, ceiling fans; $60-$80; phone/fax: 682-0122, 680-0495; www.nosarabeach hotel.com, e-mail: uscontact@nosarabeachhotel.com), high on the point that divides Playas Guiones and Pelada, are magnificent, but the hotel has been partially under construction as long as we can remember. Now its restaurant has become like a Byzantine palace in an Escher drawing, with endless arches, terraces, and stairways under an observatory-like dome with a tall minaret that dominates the skyline of Nosara. Nearby, **Olga's Bar**, in a lovely setting right on the beach, serves meals and drinks and provides campers with water. (Check your bill there, though.)

Owned by a Swiss couple, **Rancho Suizo** (private bath, heated water, wall fans; $50-$70, including breakfast; 682-0057, fax: 682-0055; www.nosara. com/ranchosuizo, e-mail: rsuizo@infoweb.co.cr) has clean rooms, a jacuzzi, a Swiss restaurant, and a barbecue grill at their beachfront **Pirate Bar**. Rates include breakfast, a welcome cocktail, and use of boogieboards, bicycles, and snorkeling equipment. They are building an aviary for guests to take wild bird photos inside.

Coatimundi

Hotel Estancia Nosara (private bath, heated water, refrigerators; with ceiling fans, $40-$50; with air conditioning, $50-$60; phone/fax: 682-0178; www.nosara.com/estancia, e-mail: estancia@nosara.com) is one kilometer inland from the beach, and has a good restaurant, a pool, and a tennis court.

At the summit of a rocky hill, with a terrific view of the meandering Nosara River and the beaches north of Nosara, is ✪ **Lagarta Lodge** (private bath, hot water, ceiling fans, pool; $60-$70; 682-0035, fax: 682-0135; www.nosara.com/lagarta, e-mail: lagarta@racsa.co.cr). This secluded, peaceful private reserve descends to the river, and nature trails lead at low tide to the turtle beach at Playa Ostional. Look for signs at the foot of the hill, near the entrance to Estancia Nosara. You definitely need a car to get to this hotel.

Heading inland towards the village of Nosara, **Casa Río Nosara** (private bath, cold water, table fans, mosquito nets; $20-$30; phone/fax: 682-0117, fax: 682-0182; e-mail: casarionosara@nosara.com) offers simple accommodations in two-level thatched A-frames. Barbecues around the campfire and a kitchen for guests make this an ideal place for budget travelers, backpackers, or those who enjoy the simple life. The owners, a friendly German couple who obviously enjoy what they do, provide a variety of canoe and kayak tours on the Nosara River, as well as snorkeling and horseback riding.

NOSARA VILLAGE   The village of **Nosara** is about five kilometers inland from the beaches. There are a gas station and a couple of food markets in town, and disco dancing on Saturday nights. Several restaurants in the town serve inexpensive Tico meals. **Rancho Tico** has been recommended, and we like **Restaurant Nosara**, across the street from the soccer field. Also in town is **Rey de Nosara Spanish School** (682-0215; www.nosara.com/reydenosara, e-mail: reydenosara@hotmail.com), with a shady outdoor classroom overlooking the river. **Tuanis Tours** (682-0265) on the plaza takes people to see the *arribadas* at Ostional. The **Nosara Office Center**, 150 meters north of Super Nosara, has copiers, fax machines, and e-mail access.

As you approach town from the beaches, you will first come to **Cabinas Chorotega** (shared or private bath, cold water, ceiling fans; $12-$20; 682-0129), a friendly, very clean place with a patio perfect for evening conversations with other guests. There is a restaurant next door. A few hundred meters closer to town are the **Cabinas Agnnel** (private bath, cold water, ceiling fans; $12-$20), built on two sides of a gravel parking lot. These cabins are clean but there's not a lot of cross-ventilation in the rooms. The owner's brother sometimes rents bikes—ask at the service station.

GETTING THERE: By Bus: A direct bus from San José leaves the Alfaro terminal (Calle 14, Avenida 5; 222-2666, 223-7685; $6) at 6 a.m. daily, returning at 12:45

p.m. From Nicoya, a bus leaves daily at 1 p.m., returning at 6 a.m. Check schedules at 682-0236. The trip from Nicoya to Nosara takes about two hours by bus.

By Car: From Nicoya, follow the road southwest toward Sámara and Nosara. After about 30 kilometers, you will come to a Y intersection. Veer right and continue another 27 kilometers (about an hour) on a bumpy gravel road to Nosara. Most of the bridges on this route are in good repair, but there may be a couple of small streams to ford. You can also take the coastal road that runs between Sámara and Nosara. Rumors abound about how bad this road is, but we found it freshly-graded even in the rainy season. The only thing that slowed us down was a herd of cattle that surrounded us, but that is what gives Guanacaste its charm. Be sure to ask about road conditions before setting out. A high-clearance vehicle is necessary. The San José–Nosara trip takes six to eight hours via the Tempisque ferry.

By Air: SANSA flies to Nosara (221-9414, fax: 255-2176; $61, one way) Mondays, Thursdays, and Saturdays via Playa Sámara. Ask your hotel to arrange transportation from the airport. If you fly into Oduber International Airport in Liberia, you'll be two and a half hours from Nosara by car. Adobe Rentacar will deliver a car to you at the Nosara airport for no charge (www.adobecar.com).

OSTIONAL WILDLIFE REFUGE   Just north of Nosara, Ostional Wildlife Refuge protects the breeding grounds of *lora* (olive ridley) turtles, which arrive in great numbers between the third quarter and the new moon between the months of April and December. In November 1995, 500,000 arrived in one wave. The people of Ostional are allowed to harvest turtle eggs during the first 36 hours of the *arribada*, since the eggs laid during that period are usually dug up and crushed by subsequent waves of mother turtles. The eggs are sold to bars across the country to be gulped raw as *bocas*. After the first 36 hours, community members guard the beach to make sure that the rest of the eggs are laid without disturbance. You can find more information at www.gema.com/turtles.

Ostional is the only beach in the world where locals are permitted to market turtle eggs, so we've been disappointed to learn that anomalies in the way the eggs are distributed have caused struggles and social problems in the community. We have heard that it is best to visit Ostional in a tour rather than on your own if you plan to go at night. However, it is possible to see a lot of turtle activity between 5 and 8 a.m. In addition, 45 days after an *arribada*, the women and children of the town gather at dawn to help the baby turtles get from their nests to the sea. This is one moment when tourists are welcome to participate. Call the village *pulpería* (682-0267) to find out when the baby turtles are due to hatch.

GETTING THERE: By car, during the dry season, you can ford the river between Nosara and Ostional.

PLAYA SÁMARA   Playa Sámara is a large half-moon bay with shallow, gentle waters. It's popular with swimmers and windsurfers, and is a favorite weekend destination for Costa Ricans during the dry season. **Coast to Coast Adventures** (652-0552) will take you mountain biking, sea kayaking, hiking, horseback riding, and surfing in the area, or caving at Barra Honda National Park. The **Vaca Loca** offers scuba diving tours ($45-$65) and classes, rents bikes ($25/day, tandem $40), serves pizza in its restaurant, and rents rather nice rooms (private bath, fans; $20-$30; phone/fax: 656-0265; www.samarabeach.com). **The Flying Crocodile** (656-0483; e-mail: flycroco @racsa.co.cr), run by a German pilot with an excellent safety record, takes people flying in ultralights in the dry season. His family also has very nice cabins near Bahía Montereyna, a mostly deserted beach (shared bath, table fans, $20-$30; private bath, hot water, ceiling fans, $40-$50) with open-air cooking facilities for guests. They also rent cars, motorcycles, and bikes. To get there, turn left at the large gas station on the road to Nosara about 25 minutes north of Sámara.

Because it is now easily accessible (only 40 minutes from Nicoya on a good paved road), Sámara is quickly becoming crowded with new hotels and vacation homes. Make reservations if you want to visit on a weekend between December and April. Substantial discounts are available in the green season. You can find out a lot about this area at www.samarabeach.com.

The **Sol y Mar**, across from the soccer field on the main street, is a clean, reliable place to go for *gallo pinto* or a *casado* (open daily, 6:30 a.m. to 10 p.m.). Their Bob Marley record has a scratch on it that they seem to ignore for long periods of time. **Bar y Restaurante El Ancla**, right on the beach, 50 meters past the **Super Sámara**, is the place to go for seafood. See below for more interesting places to eat.

Close to the intersection of the road to Nosara with the road from Nicoya are **Cabinas Magaly** (cold water, table fans; shared bath, $7-$12; private bath, $12-$20; 656-0052, fax: 656-0368, attn. Cabinas Magaly), simple rooms with a shady front yard, rocking chairs, and hammocks. You may camp in the field next door for $2 per person.

Just off the road from Nicoya, at the first left-hand turn (down the Puerto Carrillo road), are two German-run places. **Belvedere** (private bath, hot water, table fans; $30-$40, including breakfast; 656-0213) has small neat rooms downstairs from the owners' lodgings, three A-frame chalets, and an outdoor jacuzzi. Rising three stories on the hill that backs the town, the imposing **El Mirador de Sámara** (private bath, hot water, fans, kitchens; $60-$70; 656-0044, fax: 656-0046; www.miradordesamara.com, e-mail: mdsamara@

racsa.co.cr) has views of the coast from the restaurant, and the large comfortable apartments are a bargain for Guanacaste.

One block closer to the beach on a side street is **Casa Naranja** (private bath, heated water, ceiling fans; $40-$50, including breakfast; 656-0220; www.samarabeach.com, e-mail: casanaranja@samarabeach.com), a bit of Paris in the midst of the tropics. Suzanne, the cultured Parisian owner, cooks one French main dish each night and serves crêpes, French ice cream and pastries, and fantastic homemade orange marmalade. She also plays the piano for guests, and hopes that her tropical garden will become a *salón* of sorts. This is certainly the most interesting place in Sámara. Recommended.

The Quebecois-owned **Casa del Mar** (hot water, ceiling fans; with shared bath, $30-$40; with private bath, some with air conditioning, $50-$60; breakfast included; 656-0264, fax: 656-0129), one block closer to the beach, is a tranquil and clean establishment featuring an Italian restaurant. Down the street is **Casa Valeria** (private bath, hot water, kitchen for guests; $30-$40, including breakfast; 656-0511, fax: 656-0317; www.samarabeach. com, e-mail: valeria@samarabeach.com), with rooms near the street and nice little bungalows right on the beach. The French-run **Restaurant Delfín**, next door, serves fresh fish and lobster in a delightful beachfront atmosphere. They also rent rooms above the restaurant (shared bath, heated water; $30-$40, including breakfast; 656-0418). The front room has a balcony overlooking the sea. At the end of the street, **El Acuario** is where tourists and locals gather on Fridays to hear live music and do the *salsa, merengue*, and *cumbia*. The rooms upstairs have good mattresses (cold water, fans; with shared bath, $7-12; with private bath, $12-$20). Next door, the clean, airy **Apartamentos Acuario** (private bath, heated water, ceiling fans; $70-$80; phone/fax: 656-0038) sleep up to six. Ask Angela or Flaco, the managers, about houses they have for rent.

Heading south, beachfront accommodations are accessible both from the beach (keep your eyes open for signs) and the parallel gravel road that passes by the Belvedere and Mirador de Sámara.

One of Sámara's original hotels, **Brisas del Pacífico** (private bath, hot water, ceiling fans, pools, jacuzzi; $60-$70; bungalows, $80-$90; with air conditioning, $110-$120; 656-0250, fax: 656-0076; www.brisas.net, e-mail: labrisa@racsa.co.cr) is well designed and comfortable. The upper units with the best views have a concrete corridor behind them that seems to amplify sound.

Villa Stephanie (private bath, heated water, ceiling fans, kitchen; $20-$30; 656-0411) has two inexpensive apartments 50 meters from the beach.

Fénix Hotel–On the Beach (private bath, hot water, pool, ceiling fans, kitchens; $50-$60, kids free; 656-0158, fax: 656-0162; www.samarabeach. com/ps08.html, e-mail: confenix@racsa.co.cr) is a small, friendly place where you can really relax to the sound of the waves. The owners, a couple from Seattle, seem just tickled pink with their life on the beach and are delighted to share their discoveries with their guests. Local fishermen stop by with fresh fish that you can cook in your own kitchen, and children bring baskets of warm *emapanadas* to sell. It's a mile from the center of town so it's quiet at night. Recommended.

Villas Playa Sámara (private bath, hot water, ceiling fans, pool, jacuzzi, restaurant, bar; $110-$120; with kitchen, $140-$240; meals $75/day; 656-0100, fax: 656-0109) is a large beach resort located three kilometers south of town. Dozens of tile-roof stucco villas that house up to six guests each are scattered over the grassy grounds. The resort offers diving and sportfishing packages, and a honeymoon special: three nights including meals, $422 per couple.

GETTING THERE: By Bus: A direct bus from the Alfaro terminal in San José serves Sámara daily at 12:30 p.m., returning at 4:30 a.m., except on Sundays when it returns at 1 p.m. (Calle 14, Avenida 5; 222-2666, 223-7685; $5-$6). It's a six-hour trip. Buy tickets several days in advance for three-day weekends. Empresa Rojas buses (685-5352) leave the Nicoya bus station for Sámara at 10 a.m., 12 noon, 3 p.m., 4 p.m., and 5 p.m., and all but the last one continue south to Carrillo, so you can get off at hotels along the beach. They return from Sámara at 5:30 a.m., 6:30 a.m., 7 a.m., 11:15 a.m., and 4:30 p.m. Check schedules at 685-5032.

By Car: The trip from Nicoya is approximately 40 kilometers and takes 45 minutes on paved roads. To drive to Sámara from Nosara you have to ford a couple of rivers that are ankle-deep in the dry season. We drove there in a four-wheel drive in the rainy season with no problem.

Olive ridley turtle

By Air: A SANSA flight goes to Playa Carrillo, a 15-minute drive from Sámara (221-9414, fax: 255-2176; $55). It leaves San José daily at 7:30 a.m., stopping in Punta Islita on the way three days a week. SANSA provides a $3.75 minibus service from the airstrip to your Sámara hotel. Travelair flies to Playa Carrillo (232-7883, 220-3054, fax: 220-0413; $82 one way, $134 roundtrip) daily at 1 p.m., returning at 1:50 p.m. Check schedules at www.centralamerica.com/cr/tran.

PLAYA CARRILLO Playa Carrillo, just a 15-minute drive south of Sámara, is a beautiful white-sand beach with waters kept calm by a reef outside a small semi-circular bay. Majestic palms at the beach's edge provide shade for campers and day-trippers. **Popo's Surf Camp and Seakayaking** (656-0086) offers four-to six-hour sea-kayak and rubber-duckie trips through the estuaries of the Río Ora ($45, including lunch). He'll tell you where the secret surfing spots are.

El Mirador (open daily, 10 a.m. to 10 p.m.) is a large open-air bar and restaurant at the entrance to the village of Carrillo. Up on a seacliff, it receives refreshing breezes and has a great view. Reasonably priced jumbo shrimp, lobster, and whole fried fish star on the menu, and there's no better place for watching the sunset. The owners also run **Cabinas Congo Real** (private bath, hot water, ceiling fans; $12-$30; with kitchens, $50-$60; phone/fax: 656-0307), cute cabinas that creatively use the possibilities of a narrow lot in town so that each has its own plant-filled patio. Cabins can easily be made into suites to accommodate families. Recommended. Next door, **Apartamentos Colibrí** (private bath, heated water, ceiling fans; $40; with kitchens and room for four, $50; 656-0656; www.samarabeach.com) was just being completed when we were there.

In rows descending the hilly southern rim of the bay are the comfortable units of the exclusive resort and sportfishing hotel **Guanamar** (private bath, hot water, ceiling fans, air conditioning, satellite TV, pool, bar, restaurant; $110-$120; suites that sleep four, $180-$190; children under 12 free; two-night honeymoon package, $190-$310, depending on the season; 239-2000, 656-0054, fax: 239-2405; www.costasol.co.cr/guanamar, e-mail: herradu @racsa.co.cr). Many rooms, and the restaurant/bar complex, have ocean views. Packages, including sportfishing trips and transportation, are available.

Two kilometers inland from Puerto Carrillo, and one and a half kilometers from Camaronal, the next beach south of Carrillo, is **El Sueño Tropical** (private bath, heated water, ceiling fans, pools; $60-$70; two-bedroom apartments with kitchens, $90-$100; with air conditioning, $10 more; rates include breakfast; children under 12 free; 656-0151, fax: 656-0152; www.samara beach.com/ps12.html, e-mail: tropical@samarabeach.com). This small Italian hotel, with a renowned Italian restaurant (open daily, 6:30 p.m. to 9:30 p.m.), is on a hilltop next to an appealing pool.

GETTING THERE: By Bus: Some of the Nicoya–Samara buses continue to Carrillo. Call 656-0047 or 685-5032 to check schedules. There is also a bus from Hojancha (see above) to Carrillo. Call 659-9167 or 656-0047 for current schedules.

By Car: From the Nicoya–Sámara road, turn left immediately before arriving in Sámara, at the Marbella, Belvedere, and Mirador hotels. It's 15 minutes and about five kilometers from there to Carrillo.

By Air: See "By Air" under the Sámara section, above.

PUNTA ISLITA   Eight kilometers south of Carrillo, **Punta Islita** (private bath, hot water, fans, air conditioning; $160-$350; three-bedroom villas with private pools, $400-$500; 656-0471; for package rates call 231-6122, fax: 232-2183; www.puntaislita.com) is a remote luxury resort (driving range, gym and spa, conference room, pool, mountain bikes, kayaks, horseback riding, and sportfishing). They also offer boat tours to Sámara, Carrillo, Cabo Blanco, and a large tropical dry-forest reserve combed by trails. Punta Islita is most easily accessible by air. SANSA flies there on Tuesday, Friday, and Sunday, leaving San José at 7:30 a.m. If you decide to drive to Punta Islita, take a four-wheel-drive vehicle and consult with the management about the best route.

GETTING THERE: By Car: The road south of Carrillo was a mess when we were there in October 1999, but as always, we were assured it was about to be graded. Don't expect to make it to Punta Islita from Carrillo in the rainy season unless a bridge has been built over the Río Ora. To get there from San José, Punta Islita recommends taking the ferry from Puntarenas to Playa Naranjo (see Central Pacific Chapter), driving west to Jicaral and taking the road from Jicaral south to Playa Coyote. They do not tell you how bad the road is. We turned back because it was such slow going. In the dry season you can drive all the way from Carillo to Playas Santa Teresita and Malpais, near Cabo Blanco, if you have four-wheel drive and go at low tide. (See Central Pacific chapter.)

BARRA HONDA NATIONAL PARK

El Cerro Barra Honda is part of a flat-topped ridge that juts up out of the dry cattle-grazing land of the Nicoya Peninsula. People used to call the ridge a volcano because it's covered with large white limestone rocks piled around deep holes that look like craters. In the 1960s and '70s speleologists discovered that the holes were entrances to an intricate series of interconnected caves, some as deep as 240 meters. The caves are so spectacular that the area was made into a national park in 1974.

When the region was under the sea millions of years ago, marine animals deposited calcium carbonate that hardened and became limestone. Later, when the land was pushed up out of the ocean, rainfall combined with carbon dioxide and dissolved the limestone to hollow out the caves. In a process similar to how icicles form, dripping water carrying calcium carbonate formed stalactites and stalagmites that resemble curtains, pipe organs, fried eggs, and pearls.

In the **Nicoa cave**, speleologists discovered human skeletons that were quite old—a stalagmite was growing on one skull. It is assumed that indigenous people used this cave as a *cenote* (chamber for religious rituals), since some artifacts were found near the skeletons. Fortunately, the deep vertical drops at the entrances have discouraged all but the best-equipped spelunkers from entering, so the caves have suffered almost no vandalism.

The 62-meter deep **Terciopelo** cavern is the only one open to the general public. Three local guides must accompany you—whether you visit alone or with a group. In addition to the $6 park entrance fee, they charge $12 per descent for groups of up to eight people, and $31 for groups of more than eight. All equipment is included. To get there, first walk one hour to the cave entrance; then, assisted by your guides and the equipment (harness, ropes, helmets, ladder), rappel down into it. The descent includes a 50-meter free fall. Visitors who suffer from vertigo, claustrophobia, or hypertension are not allowed to go down. You must wear pants and good shoes with closed toes, and bring your own drinking water and flashlight.

Arrange your descent in advance, by visiting the park headquarters the day before or by calling the Conservation Area Office in Nicoya (686-6760).

Even if you can't get down into the caves, a visit to Barra Honda is rewarding. You can explore the flat top of the ridge on trails where birds screech, iguanas stand motionless, and howler and white-faced monkeys fill the trees. The lookout point reached by following the seven-kilometer **Sendero/Los Laureles** trail affords wide views of the peninsula and the Gulf of Nicoya. You can take a six-kilometer hike (guide required) to a waterfall decorated with lacy calcium carbonate formations.

In the dry season it's very hot, so wear a wide-brimmed hat and bring a canteen. An unprepared European couple died several years ago from dehydration and heat exhaustion during their hike through the park.

LODGING   The park offers inexpensive and simple meals and lodging (private bath, cold water; $6/person) in dormitory-style rooms that accommodate up to eight. Meals cost about $10 per day, but you have to let them know in advance if you want them to cook for you.

About 15 minutes away by car, in the town of Santa Ana, **Palenque El Guácimo** (private bath, cold water; $7-$12) has a pool and an indigenous-style restaurant specializing in fried ribs. This is a countryside getaway for Nicoya residents.

More luxurious accommodations can be found at **Rancho Humo**, an hour's drive from Barra Honda. (See the listings earlier in this chapter, under "Palo Verde National Park.")

GETTING THERE: You can catch a bus at noon from Nicoya to the village of Santa Ana (an hour-and-a-half trip) and walk one kilometer to Barra Honda National Park. The bus returns the next morning at 7 a.m. A taxi from Nicoya to the park costs about $10.

Barra Honda is a half-hour from Nicoya by car. Take the main road east and make a left when you see signs for Barra Honda village. Follow signs to the park. You can also come from the east via the Tempisque ferry and turn right at the Barra Honda turnoff. The road to the village is full of potholes. Beyond that, the dirt road to the park gets narrower and bumpier, but national park signs clearly mark the way.

NORTH OF LIBERIA

RINCÓN DE LA VIEJA NATIONAL PARK

Rincón de la Vieja is one of Costa Rica's richest and most varied parks. The centerpiece is a broad massif formed by the Rincón de la Vieja and Santa María volcanoes, with nine craters that melded about a million years ago. Its flanks are pocked by mudpots and fumaroles, which help the volcano vent its heat. The crater that is currently active cups a steaming lake, and periodically erupts, sending hot mud and volcanic ash into the sky and down the rivers to the north of the volcano. Its most active episode in recent history was between 1966 and 1970, but in 1995 and 1998 eruptions caused its campesino neighbors to flee their volcano-side homes. The damage has always occurred on the northern slopes of the volcano because the southern rim of the crater is higher than the northern rim. All lodging and park attractions are on the south and west sides. For current information, call the Guanacaste Conservation Area in Santa Rosa National Park (666-5051, fax: 666-5052; www.acguanacaste.co.cr).

The park is a watershed for 32 rivers, many of which empty into the Tempisque. Three hundred species of birds have been identified there, as well as deer, collared peccaries, coatis, pacas, agoutis, raccoons, jaguars, two-toed sloths, and three species of monkeys. When we were there in April 1998, we easily observed toucans, manakins, and *urracas*.

There are two entrances to the National Park: Rincón–Las Pailas, above the village of Curubandé, and Rincón–Santa María, five kilometers beyond the village of San Jorge. The Las Pailas entrance offers the more spectacular thermal sites, while Santa María has trails through a forest that is unusually moist for Guanacaste, due to its Atlantic exposure, and offers easier access to the thermal springs.

RINCÓN–LAS PAILAS Las Pailas (The Cauldrons) is a 124-acre wonderland of pits of boiling hot water; vapor geysers that stain the rocks around them red, green, and yellow because of the iron, copper, and sulfur in the steam; minivolcanoes that emerge spontaneously, last a few days or weeks, then dry out, leaving a conical pile of mud; fumaroles, which are deep holes that emit billows of sulfurous vapor; and seven bubbling pots of gray mud called the *Sala de Belleza* (Beauty Salon). Face masks made from this smooth glop are supposed to have rejuvenating and refreshing powers, but the Parks Service no longer allows you to reach in and pull out a stick covered with the mud because too many beauty-seekers have been scalded. Albergue Rincón de La Vieja and Hacienda Guacipelín, on the way to Rincón, have access to mud baths you *can* go to (see below).

Note: In Las Pailas, the dry, crusty earth around the mudpots is brittle and thin in some places; unsafe areas are clearly marked. Be sure to stay away from any area that has warning signs and fences. People have been burned when the ground under them gave way and they fell into boiling water or mud. Don't believe anyone who tells you about "shortcuts" off the marked trails. Sulfur fumes can cause bad headaches for some.

The Río Blanco forms a lovely swimming hole that's reachable by following a path to the left, about 100 meters beyond the ranger station. It's 800 meters to the swimming hole. At the ranger station you can get a map that shows you how to get to **Catarata La Cangreja**, a 75-foot waterfall with a gorgeous blue-green pool at its base and **Cataratas Escondidas**. You can see two of the waterfalls from the rim of a canyon, and can reach a third by walking along a creek.

Note: Signs along streams and pools in the park state that the water is drinkable (*agua potable*), but that refers to the concentration of minerals in the water and not to the absence of bacteria. We have heard of people getting severe intestinal upsets from these streams.

The park is great for hiking because it is largely untouched, and the trails are not too steep and are dry most of the year. Unlike the slippery, muddy cloud forests and rainforests, Rincón is a transitional area between dry forest and cloud forest. The trails get a bit muddy only at higher altitudes, right before the forest gives way to rocky, windblown volcanic terrain.

If you want to hike to the volcano's craters, and Von Seebach peak, 7.7 kilometers from the ranger station, start out by 10 a.m. in order to be back by nightfall. If you'd like to go at a more relaxed pace, it's best to camp overnight. March and April are the best months for this, but it is always wise to bring rainsuits, warm clothes, several changes of clothing wrapped in plastic, good hiking boots, a waterproof tent, and a compass. We saw a well-prepared group of campers in July who had made the trip with no problem.

Note: It's a good idea to hire a guide from a local hotel or tour company if you are going to the volcano, because the paths are not clearly marked in the rocky terrain near the top, and thick mists come up frequently. If you go without a guide, the Park Service recommends that you turn back when you emerge from the forest to the barren crater area if you see that the crater is obscured by clouds. In the dry season the lava flows at the top can be extremely windy. You can contact guides through the park administration, 666-5051, fax: 666-5020.

LODGING   The **camping spots** ($1.50/person) are in a shady river glen, a five-minute walk from the park administration center.

Albergue de Montaña Rincón de la Vieja (students, $50-$60; with private bath, $70-$80; meals about $30/day; 666-0473, fax: 666-1887; www. guanacaste.co.cr, e-mail: rincon@racsa.co.cr) is a rustic and relaxed lodge located two kilometers from the Las Pailas entrance to the park. Rooms have porches with hammocks or rocking chairs. The main lodge has cozy areas for reading or meeting other travelers. Meals are served family-style. Los Azufrales, the sulfurous hot springs within the park, can be reached on a 45-minute hike. Be sure to pay the park entrance fee. They offer half-day to full-day hiking and horseback expeditions. **Top Tree Trails** is their canopy exploration venture, a series of 17 platforms and 11 cables that glide you through the tree tops in a four-hour tour ($50). Try to go with as small a group as possible so you won't have to wait too long between glides. You have to be in good shape physically and emotionally to do 11 cables. Daredevils can do the tour at night and sleep on the last and biggest platform. They offer a two-night package including meals for $99/person, and other packages including tours.

Several kilometers before you get to the park, **Hacienda Guachipelín** (private bath, cold water, no fans; $30-$40, including breakfast; $20-$30 in bunkhouse; 442-2818, fax: 442-1910, cell phone: 284-2049; www.guachi pelin.com, e-mail: tbatalla@racsa.co.cr) is a classic Guanacaste cattle ranch converted into a lodge. Rooms in the main building are clean and simple. There is a cool porch to sit on, a comfortable TV room, and a family-style dining area. The larger bunkhouse rooms are not as nice, but they're good for families or groups. Camping is allowed on the grounds for $1.50 per person. There is a hot mud pool about half an hour from the lodge. You can cover yourself with mud, let it dry in the sun, wash it off in a tank of water, then take a final dip in a cold river nearby. They offer a half-day horseback tour to Las Pailas, a waterfall, and the mud baths with a Spanish-speaking guide for $28 plus the park entrance fee. Their **Canopy Tour** lets you glide on cables to platforms attached to the walls of a lush nearby canyon ($50; www.canopytour.com).

Located about five minutes from the Interamerican Highway on the road to Rincón is the well-appointed **Posada El Encuentro** (private bath, heated water, fans, pool; small cottages, $70-$80; junior suites, $90-$100; rates include breakfast; cell phone: 382-0815, fax: 666-2472; www.arweb.com/encuentro, e-mail: encuentro@arweb.com), a bed and breakfast owned and managed by a German-Tico family. The land surrounding the lodge is rather desolate, but the lodge itself is clean and airy and full of very nice touches, including original paintings in each room. Chess boards, croquet and other games, a telescope, and equipment to make fondue and pizzas are available for guests to enjoy. They offer a two-night package that includes a tour to Rincón ($287 for two), or will provide you with all the equipment you need for camping in their private rainforest patch ($30 in a tent that sleeps four; food extra).

GETTING THERE: By Bus: Hotel Guanacaste (666-2287) in Liberia runs a bus to and from the Las Pailas entrance to Rincón for $16 roundtrip (not including the $6 entrance fee or $1.50 toll on the road to the park). They leave at 7 a.m. and return to pick you up at 5 p.m. Make reservations. No public buses run all the way to the Rincón–Las Pailas entrance, but a bus leaves Liberia for Curubandé daily at 2 p.m., returning the next morning at 6 a.m. You could walk or hitch the remaining eight kilometers from there, especially if you were planning to camp overnight. (If you're not planning to camp or stay in a nearby lodge, this alternative won't work.) Otherwise you must take a jeep taxi from Liberia ($25 one way).

By Car: Go four and a half kilometers north of Liberia on the Interamerican Highway to the turnoff for Curubandé. You'll see signs directing you to the Las Pailas entrance of the park. It's 12 kilometers to Curubandé over a fairly good gravel road, interesting because it was cut through deposits of white and pinkish pumice. From Curubandé, it's about three kilometers farther up to Hacienda Guachipelín, another three to the turnoff to Albergue Rincón de la Vieja and two more to the park entrance. Just beyond Curubandé you have to pay $1.50 to enter the part of the road maintained by Hacienda Guachipelín. It takes about 45 minutes to drive from the Interamerican Highway to the park entrance.

RINCÓN–SANTA MARÍA   This entrance to the park has a park administration center and a small historical exhibit, with campsites nearby. Fifteen kilometers of trails are explorable on your own, but you should not walk to Las Pailas without a guide, since it's easy to get lost.

Three kilometers from the Santa María entrance are **Los Azufrales**, hot sulfur springs at a perfect bathtub temperature, right next to a cold stream to splash in (don't let the sulfurous water get in your eyes, and don't stay in longer than five minutes before alternating with the cold water).

San Jorge, three kilometers toward Liberia from the park entrance, is home to **Rinconcito** (shared bath, cold water; $18/person; with private bath, $24/person, including meals; cell phone: 380-8193, beeper: 224-2400, leave message for "Rinconcito"), a modest cement-block house with several rooms on a working dairy farm. Guests can wake up early and milk the cows with the *peones*. Tours are available to the park and to the Miravalles volcano geothermic project and its mudpots and thermal springs.

GETTING THERE: No buses run to San Jorge or the Rincón–Santa María entrance (25 kilometers). The road is passable only with four-wheel drive. Rinconcito offers roundtrip transportation ($30/four) in their jeep.

Fifteen kilometers on the other side of the Rincón–Santa María entrance to the park from San Jorge, ✪ **Santa María Volcano Lodge** (private or shared bath, heated water; $30-$40; meals $20/day; 235-0642, fax: 272-6236, cell phone: 381-5290, 385-5450) is in the small town of Colonia Blanca. The main farmhouse has been remodeled, and there are chalet-style cabins as well. Horseback or four-wheel-drive excursions are available to Rincón–Santa María or Volcán Miravalles, or through nearby farms, where guests can hike through rainforest and swim or fish in rivers. Since it is located on the humid Atlantic slope, the lodge is surrounded by luxuriant greenery. (March, April, and May are the only months of the year when it doesn't rain every

Collared peccary

day.) The owner rents out neighboring farmhouses as well, large enough for families. It's easier to reach this lodge through Bagaces than through Liberia.

GETTING THERE: Buses leave Bagaces for Aguas Claras at 6:30 a.m. and 2 p.m. From Liberia, the bus to Aguas Claras leaves at 6 a.m. and 1:45 p.m. The owner can pick you up there if you request.

By Car: Drive north of Bagaces to Aguas Claras, about an hour on a paved road. You will pass the entrance to the Miravalles geothermal plant just after Guayabo (see above). At Aguas Claras, turn left at the sign for the lodge, and drive seven more flat kilometers on a good gravel road.

SANTA ROSA NATIONAL PARK

While most of Costa Rica's parks aim to preserve virgin forest, **Santa Rosa National Park** (666-5051, fax: 666-5020; www.acguanacaste.ac.cr) not only protects the little remaining tropical dry forest, but tries to promote its regeneration. This park encompasses almost every ecosystem that exists in Guanacaste. The latest addition to the park is a large tract of pastureland, overgrazed and biologically bankrupt, where biologists are applying research findings about how forests propagate themselves. Seeds for forest regeneration are primarily carried by the wind, and by mammals and birds who eat seeds and then defecate in treeless pastures. By encouraging this kind of seed dispersal and burning fire lanes to control the spread of wildfires, the scientists are allowing the dry forest to renew itself. Instead of making the park off-limits to local campesinos, who formerly eked out an existence as ranch hands, the park hires them as caretakers, research assistants, and guides. The addition, by the way, includes the location of the clandestine airstrip that figured in the Iran-Contra fiasco. The North American owner of this land just won a legal dispute with the Costa Rican government over the expropriation that made it part of the park, and will be paid $16 million for the property.

The three times that Costa Rica has been attacked by military, the invaders were defeated at the **Hacienda Santa Rosa's Casona** (big house). These days the *casona* is a museum with historical and environmental education exhibits. Near the museum is a trail you can follow for a short natural-history jaunt.

There is **camping** (minimal fee) in a central area of Santa Rosa, with water, toilets, showers, and nice big shade trees. The ranger will tell you which parts of the park are especially rich in wildlife at the moment. Lodging and meals at the **Centro de Investigación** (research station) can be arranged by calling the above numbers. You can eat lunch with the park personnel if you give them three hours' notice.

A 12-kilometer trail will take you to **Playa Naranjo**, a long stretch of white sand that you can usually have all to yourself. Near the ranger station, right off the beach, there is a camping area, an outhouse, and a windmill-pumped water well for washing, but not for drinking. You have to bring your own drinking water. Off Playa Naranjo is **Witch Rock**, famous with surfers the world over for creating the perfect wave.

The six-kilometer **Carbonal** trail takes you through dry forest, rock formations and mangroves. It starts 300 meters before the ranger station at Playa Naranjo.

If you don't want to go all the way down to the beach, the trail to **Mirador Valle Naranjo**, where you can get a panoramic view of the coast, starts from a point six kilometers down the road to Playa Naranjo. It takes about half an hour to hike the one and a half kilometers to the *mirador.*

The road to Playa Naranjo is probably a creek in the rainy season, and is only open to vehicles from December 15 to April 1. We have heard that this road has been greatly improved, but call the park before driving it, because when it is in bad condition the typical four-wheel-drive Suzuki Sidekick rent-a-cars routinely get stuck near the beach. The rangers have to call a tow-truck from Liberia to get them out, which costs the tourists $150. **Bahía Junquillal**, at the Cuajiniquil entrance, about five minutes north of the main entrance to Santa Rosa on the Interamerican Highway, is a lovely place to camp and much easier to drive to, though it's not as wild (see below). The walk to Playa Naranjo takes three hours, and you must start early because of the heat.

Santa Rosa is home to a wide variety of easily observed animals, including three types of monkeys: loud howler monkeys, agile spider monkeys, and white-throated capuchin monkeys. You'll also see vultures, falcons, and the *urraca*, a blue-and-white jay, which has a feather on top of its head that looks like a curled ribbon on a birthday present. This bird's beauty is contradicted by its obnoxious squawk. Twenty-two species of bats inhabit the park, including two vampire varieties (they rarely attack humans—their victims are almost always livestock). Pelicans, gulls, herons, and sandpipers are the most common birds on the beach. Cicadas buzz from tree branches, so loud you sometimes have to shout to be heard.

There are collared and white-lipped peccaries whose reputation for ferocity is misleading, according to a Santa Rosa biologist we talked to. Peccaries are actually afraid of humans and flee when they are near. White-tailed deer wander in the savannah, coatimundis prowl around the forests, and caimans live in the estuaries of Playa Naranjo. As in most areas of the Pacific coast, iguanas are everywhere.

Leatherback and green turtles nest in the park from October to March, but most common are Pacific ridleys. For the last several decades 200,000 turtles have nested yearly at **Playa Nancite**, the next beach north from Playa Naranjo. During the 1997 season, it is estimated that only 60,000 arrived. Their *arribadas* (arrivals by sea) take place on moonless nights, with the largest (thousands at a time) arrival in October. After an approximately 45-day incubation period, the baby turtles hatch and crawl into the sea. About two percent survive all the hazards of turtle "childhood" to become adults.

Playa Nancite is covered with turtle eggshell fragments and a few shells and skeletons of unfortunate mother turtles who didn't make it. You can't stay at Nancite overnight without a permit—it serves mainly as a biological research station. Only 15 people are allowed on the beach at one time.

GETTING THERE: By Bus: Buses that go to La Cruz and Peñas Blancas on the Nicaragua border pass the entrance to Santa Rosa. They leave San José (Calle 14, Avenidas 3/5; 257-6484) at 4:30 a.m. ($5, direct), 5 a.m., 7:45 a.m., 1:20 p.m., and 4:10 p.m. ($3.75, indirect). You have to buy tickets in advance. Because of the tremendous heat, it's better to take a San José–Liberia bus, stay overnight, then take a La Cruz (not Santa Cruz) bus from Liberia at 5:30 a.m. (check the bus schedule the night before). Ask to be let off at the "entrada a Santa Rosa." You must walk or hitchhike about seven kilometers to the *casona* and camping area before you start the 12-kilometer hike to Playa Naranjo. It's easy to hitchhike this distance in the dry season because there are many people going to and from the park.

By Car: Santa Rosa is only 20 minutes north of Liberia on the Interamerican Highway, to the left. The entrance to the Murciélago Sector, through Cuajiniquil, is about five minutes (ten kilometers) beyond Santa Rosa, also to the left.

The formerly inaccessible **Murciélago** sector of Santa Rosa has some lovely beaches that are easier to get to than those in the southern part of the park. **Bahía Junquillal Wildlife Refuge**, north of the picturesque inlet of **Cuajiniquil**, protects a calm bay that is good for swimming and snorkeling, a tropical dry forest, and a mangrove swamp. Three species of turtles lay eggs there. There is a lovely campground, with showers and toilets ($3.50/person). This is one of our favorite camping and swimming spots, but beware of the jellyfish. Bring your own water.

Cabinas Santa Elena (shared bath, cold water, natural ventilation; under $7), located above a *pulpería* near the fishing village of Cuajiniquil, is very basic but clean. Two rooms are available for tourists. The rest are rented to local fishermen, who can take you on boat tours ($20-$40/boatload) of the local estuary—which is rich in birds and wildlife—or nearby beaches and islands. The cabins are about four kilometers south of Bahía Junquillal; the *pulpería* below is a good place to get supplies.

Frigates

West of Cuajiniquil on the Santa Elena peninsula are peaceful **Bahía Santa Elena** and **Bahía Playa Blanca**, accessible by car only in the dry season. Fishermen will also take you around the peninsula to the **Murciélago Islands**, but the boat trip must be done during the rainy season to avoid the strong "summer" winds. There is a camping and picnic area with baths and potable water at the Murciélago ranger station, eight kilometers west of Cuajiniquil. Confirm that there is space at 666-5051, fax: 666-5020. From the campground you can hike 600 meters to a swimming hole, **Poza del General**. It's easy to spot monkeys, birds, and iguanas in this area. Bahía Santa Elena and Playa Blanca are 12 and 18 kilometers beyond the campground.

GETTING THERE: Buses to Cuajiniquil leave Liberia daily at 5:45 a.m. and 3:30 p.m., returning at 7 a.m. and 4:30 p.m. There is also a 12:30 p.m. bus from La Cruz (see below), which returns at 6 a.m. It takes about an hour to walk to the Bahía Junquillal campground from Cuajiniquil. If you're going by car, keep on the Interamerican Highway five to ten minutes beyond the Santa Rosa turnoff, then turn left on the nicely paved road to Cuajiniquil (seven kilometers). Playa Junquillal campground is four kilometers to the north of Cuajiniquil on a good gravel road. The Murciélago campground is eight kilometers southwest of Cuajiniquil, Bahía Santa Elena is 12 more kilometers southwest on a difficult road, and Playa Blanca is another six kilometers beyond that. These last three trips are best done in the dry season with a four-wheel-drive vehicle.

GUANACASTE NATIONAL PARK

Guanacaste National Park was created in 1989 to protect the migratory paths of animals that live in Santa Rosa, so it extends from the Interamerican Highway east to the Orosi and Cacao volcanoes. Many species of moths procreate in the high mountains during the dry season, then fly down to spend the rainy season at a lower, warmer altitude. The *zahino,* a wild pig, retreats from the volcanoes to the dry forest in January to search for seeds of the *encino* (evergreen oak) tree. Scientists studying the wildlife in Santa Rosa have found that in order to protect these and other animals, the environments so necessary to their existence must also be protected. The whole Guanacaste Conservation Area now protects 220,000 hectares of land.

Although Costa Rica has about .001 percent of the world's landmass, it has 5 percent of the world's biodiversity. For instance, an estimated 3800 species of moths live in Santa Rosa alone. Studying all of them would take years. However, under the auspices of **InBio** (see "The Outdoors") local park employees are being trained in biological inventory techniques by some of the best scientists in the world. By all reports, the program is a tremendous success, due to the sharp powers of observation of the campesinos, their familiarity with the region and its wildlife, and their motivation to learn a new career that was not open to them until a few years ago (45% of the conservation area's employees are women). People from parks all over the country are being trained in the same techniques. All specimens will be turned over to InBio in Santo Domingo de Heredia, which hopes to identify every plant and animal species in Costa Rica.

The main reason visitors come to Guanacaste National Park (admission $6) is to see the petroglyphs, over 800 of them, in the Pedregal sector on the west side of Volcán Orosi. The intricate line drawings etched in rocks date from about 500 A.D. The road to the Maritza biological station, near Pedregal, goes off to the east at the same intersection where you turn west to go to Cuajiniquil. The 18 kilometers from the Interamerican Highway to Maritza take about an hour to drive. There is lodging at Maritza for organized groups or courses, but no campground (www.acguanacaste.ac.cr).

LA CRUZ

The region around La Cruz, near the Nicaraguan border, is still off the beaten track for tourists. There are spectacular views from the well-designed **Restaurante Ehecatl** at the mirador in La Cruz, situated on high bluffs overlooking Bahía Salinas. Try their excellent and inexpensive shrimp salad. *Ehecatl* means "god of wind" in Chorotega—there is always a strong breeze there.

La Cafeteria, half a block east of the Central Park, is a good place to stop for breakfast. The owner, Ricardo Bolaños, is a naturalist guide; he will be glad to give you a personalized tour of Guanacaste's parks and beaches or of southern Nicaragua (679-9276).

Cabinas Santa Rita (shared bath, small rooms; $7-$12; private bath, cold water, fans, $12-$20; with air conditioning, $20-$30; 679-9062, phone/

fax: 679-9305) has well-kept, spacious rooms across from the Tribunales de Justicia. You can leave your car there if you want to take side trips by bus. Good value.

Right on the edge of the cliff, with a stunning view of Bahía Salinas, is **Villa Amalia** (private bath, hot or heated water, satellite TV, pool; no children under 14; $30-$40; phone/fax: 679-9181), originally built as a gallery for the paintings of American artist Lester Bounds. His widow, Doña Amalia, is a charming hostess. The rooms are eclectic; all have their own sitting areas. Recommended.

GETTING THERE: By Bus: Buses to La Cruz leave at 5 a.m., 7:45 a.m., 1:20 p.m., and 4:15 p.m. from San José (Calle 16, Avenida 3; 257-6484). The trip takes four and a half hours. Return buses are at 5:30 a.m., 5:45 a.m., 8 a.m., 11 a.m., 3:30 p.m., and 4 p.m. Buses leave Liberia for La Cruz and the Nicaraguan border at 5:30 a.m., 8:30 a.m., 9 a.m., and 11 a.m., noon, and 2 p.m., 6 a.m., and 8 p.m. It's a one-hour trip. By car, La Cruz is a straight shot up the Interamerican Highway from Liberia.

South of La Cruz is the turnoff for **Los Inocentes** (private bath, solar-heated water, pool; $70-$80/person, including meals; phone/fax: 679-9190, 265-5484, fax: 265-4385; www.arweb.com/orosi, e-mail: orosina@racsa.co.cr), the large estate of the Víquez family near Volcán Orosi. This was one of the first *haciendas* to open its doors to tourists, and served as inspiration to many of the area's lodges. The food and service at Los Inocentes are excellent, and one comes away with a sense of the graceful lifestyle of the Costa Rican gentry. Both overnight guests and day visitors may take a two-hour horseback or tractor ride through the ranch ($20/person, including lunch) on one day's notice. To get there, turn right at the security post about five minutes north of the turnoff to Cuajiniquil (the sign points to Upala and Santa Cecilia). After 15 kilometers, turn right at the "Los Inocentes" sign. Follow the gravel road 270 degrees around to the main lodge.

SIDE TRIPS TO SOUTHERN NICARAGUA

If your 30- or 90-day Costa Rican visa is about to expire, and you want to get legal again, take a quick trip to Nicaragua while you're in this part of the country. Tourists who leave the country for 72 hours can come back with a renewed tourist visa. (Officially you need to be out of the country for 72 hours, but in practice, you can leave on a Friday and come back on a Monday).

Don't let your visa expire. Because of the illegal immigration of thousands of Nicaraguans seeking work in Costa Rica, passport checks are frequent north and south of Liberia. If you are traveling by bus in this area, it's good to have your documents in order. If your visa has already expired, you must have an **exit visa** in order to leave Costa Rica ($44 if you leave by land, plus approximately $2 for each month you've overstayed). You must get the exit visa at *Migración* in Barrio La Uruca west of San José, or in Liberia (open weekdays, 8 a.m. to 4 p.m.; 400 meters east and 25 north of the Almacen Suma; 666-0713). Or a travel agent will get it for you. Going to Migración can take most of a day, so it's worthwhile to pay a travel agent. They charge $4-$8 plus the cost of the visa. If your tourist visa is still valid, you only have to pay about 30 cents to leave, and you don't need an exit visa.

Note: Be sure and get your passport stamped as you re-enter Costa Rica. If you do not get it stamped, your trip will have been in vain, you'll still be illegal, and you'll have to pay the higher exit visa charge when you return to your home country.

Most nationalities do not need visas to enter Nicaragua, but you must have six months validity left on your passport in order to cross the border. It costs $2 to leave Nicaragua by land, and $25 by air.

An item you may be asked to present on re-entry (we weren't) is your ticket out of Costa Rica (or $200) to prove that you're not going to lollygag in the country beyond your welcome. If you don't have a ticket out, you can always step next door to the office that sells bus tickets from the border to Managua—tickets are relatively cheap and it'll get you out of a pickle.

Since Costa Rican car-rental agencies won't allow you to drive their vehicles into Nicaragua, we give extensive public transport directions. You can park your rented car at Cabinas Santa Rita in La Cruz, provided you lock it up and don't hold the management responsible if it gets broken into. The police at the border will also watch your car for about $2/day. Don't overpay them.

San José–La Cruz buses continue 15 kilometers to the Nicaraguan border. They pass through La Cruz at 6:30 a.m., 9:30 a.m., 10 a.m., noon, 1 p.m., 3 p.m., 5:30 p.m., and 6:30 p.m. A taxi from La Cruz to the border costs about $4. Exchange rates are about the same on both sides of the border. You can also take the Tica Bus (221-8954; leaves San José at 6 or 7:30 a.m.) for about $9. The 6 a.m. bus stops in Granada. Both the 6 and 7:30 a.m. buses pass through Rivas. Buy tickets at least a day in advance and bring your passport. As of August 2000, you could get $12.44 *córdobas* for a dollar. Check current exchange rates at www.oanda.com. Food is slightly cheaper on the Tico side, but the view from Nicaragua's border cafeteria is far nicer.

Try to avoid getting to the border between 10 a.m. and noon because the Tica Buses arrive between those hours and you'll have longer to wait in line. Fill out a form and turn over your passport at Window 8, 9, or 10. It will be passed internally to a window to the left where it will be stamped by the Tico official (25 cents). You then walk about 800 meters and wait for a bus or *taxi colectivo* (50 cents for either one), which takes you four kilometers to the Nicaraguan Migración. Entrance fees are $7 for U.S. citizens, $2 for other nationalities that don't require visas, and $25 for those that do (like Canadians). Processing the paperwork costs another $1. Try to have exact change in dollars. If the immigration officials run out of change, they will send you to wait in the bank line, greatly slowing down your progress.

There are many young men and boys who act as guides through Nicaraguan immigration, and will help you carry your bags. Even if you tell them that you don't need help, they will help you anyway, because they need money. The young man who helped us seemed trustworthy. He asked for a donation of whatever we thought was right (we gave him 12 *córdobas,* the equivalent of a dollar). You should not turn your passport over to your guide, only to the people behind the windows.

Making calls in or from Nicaragua requires some training. The first thing to know is Nicaragua's national area code—505. Any calls made from countries outside of Nicaragua will start with 505. All of the local area codes begin with 0. When dialing from inside Nicaragua, you will always dial this zero unless you're calling a number in the same local area code. When dialing

Top left: Coati
Middle left: Howler monkey
Bottom left: Tiger heron
Top right: Dinosaur lizard
Bottom right: Jaguar

Above: A popular way to get a closer look at Volcán Arenal is by renting horses at local stables. After a while you dismount and clamber over the lava flow.

Below: The Río Corobicí flows slowly through southern Guanacaste; it is an easy, gentle river-rafting trip and a popular place to watch birdlife along the banks.

from outside Nicaragua, drop the zero. For example, to dial San Juan del Sur's Casa Internacional Joxi within San Juan del Sur, dial 45-82348; from Granada, you dial: 045-82348. From San José you would dial: 00 (Costa Rica's code for international calls) 505-45-82348.

SAN JUAN DEL SUR   A small fishing village on the Pacific coast, San Juan del Sur is 43 kilometers from the border at Peñas Blancas. Surfboards, bicycles, boogieboards, windsurfers, vans, and pickups are available for rent. Gorgeous sunsets, bodysurfing, and swimming in the small cove are free. Bring bug repellent and/or a mosquito net to town with you in case the wind (or your table fan) dies.

Skipper Chris Berry leads day-long sailing excursions on his boat, **Pelican Eyes** (458-2344; www.sanjuandelsur.org). For $50 ($25 for children under 12), you will spend the day swimming, fishing, and sailing to deserted beaches and, in November and December, checking out the olive ridley, hawksbill, leatherback, and Pacific green and black turtles. Tour fee includes an open bar on the boat and a chicken barbecue on the beach for lunch. Minimum ten people.

Surf Nicaragua (458-2492; www.nicasurf.com, e-mail: ddagger@bwi. com.ni) takes you to the best surfing spots in the area. Most of them are still deserted and only accessible by boat.

The **San Juan del Sur Spanish School** (505-244-4512, in the U.S.: 805-667-9941; www.sanjuandelsur.com, e-mail: nss.pmc@prodigy.net) faces the ocean. Classes are interspersed with bike, boat, and horseback trips to neighboring beaches, and classes in dancing, cooking, music, and art.

RESTAURANTS AND LODGING   **Ricardo's Bar** (www.sanjuandelsur. com), "where you surf by the surf," offers internet access, big breakfasts, seafood dinners with lots of interesting appetizers, and high-stakes Monopoly. **Marie's** (open nightly except Tuesday, 5:30 p.m. to midnight; weekends, 8:30 a.m. to noon) is a small European-owned restaurant one block north of the Hotel Estrella. It was too crowded for us to find a table, and the music, though tasteful, was too loud. But it definitely seemed to be the place to go. Around the corner is the **Cheesecake Cafe**, open for breakfast 7 a.m. to 11 a.m. every day but Monday.

In town, **Hotel La Estrella** (shared baths outside, cold water, table fans; $4/person; 045-82210) is in a classic old building with balconies overlooking the bay. It's reminiscent of Costa Rican beach hotels of 20 years ago. Unfortunately, La Estrella has gotten pretty rundown—and partition walls don't leave much room for privacy.

The Norwegian-owned **Casa Internacional Joxi** (cold water, screens on the windows; with shared bath and table fans, $7-$12; with private bath and air conditioning, $20-$30; children 4-14, half off; 045-82348), half a block east of Hotel La Estrella, is a comfortable and friendly place to stay. The breakfast pancakes are delicious, especially the *manuelitas:* crêpes stuffed and covered with fruit salad in a light sour cream sauce. Lunch and dinner are available if you order early in the day. The owner, a former sea captain, pulls the latest news off the Internet; guests can send and receive e-mail, and change traveler's checks. The rooms have good mattresses, closets, towels, shampoo, and even stoppers in the sinks! Recommended.

Near the bus stop, two blocks inland from the Hotel Estrella, are several budget hotels: **Guest House and Soda Elizabeth** (shared or private baths, cold water, fans; $7-$12; 045-82270) is a pleasant, simple place with a restaurant. New second-story rooms have cross-ventilation and views. A few doors down, **La Fogata** (shared or private bath, cold water, fans; $7-$12; 045-82271) has a large restaurant. Some of the walls don't seem to be too solid. Half a block toward the beach from the bus stop, **Hospedaje Los Almendros** (shared bath, cold water, fans; $3/person; 045-82388) offers rooms around a plant-filled courtyard.

There are two classy new places in San Juan del Sur and more are being built. The rather sterile but nicely decorated **Royal Chateau** (private baths, with fans, $30-$40; with air conditioning, $40-$50; 045-82551) is one block inland from the bus stop, and **Casablanca** (private bath, cold water, fans; $40-$50; phone/fax: 458-2135; e-mail: casablan@ibw.com.ni) has a pool and clean, spacious rooms in a remodeled private home right on the beach. It's one of the nicest places in San Juan.

GETTING THERE: From the border, take any bus going north (they will be heading to either Rivas or to Managua) and get off at La Virgen. Wait there for a bus from Rivas to take you to San Juan del Sur. Taxi cabs from the border cost $15; bargaining is appropriate. From Rivas, buses leave from the market every 45 minutes between 6 a.m. and 6 p.m. Cabs cost around $6. From Granada, take a Rivas bus one block south of the Mercado Central. If the Rivas bus has gone, take a bus to Nandaime and ask to be let off on the highway before you enter town so you can catch a Managua–Rivas bus. These buses sometimes continue to San Juan del Sur.

RIVAS   Continuing up the Pan American Highway from the San Juan del Sur turnoff, the first town north is Rivas, site of the 1856 battle in which Juan Santamaría set fire to the stronghold of William Walker's troops, losing his life and becoming Costa Rica's national hero. Today it is a sleepy, friendly town, without, perhaps, the allure of neighboring towns. Rivas is an important transportation hub.

If you need to stay the night to catch an early morning bus, **Hotel Nicarao** (private bath, cold water, air conditioning or table fans; $30-$40, including breakfast; 045-33234), one block west of the central park behind the Banco Nacional, is comfortable. Its long tile hallways echo ferociously, however, so weekends can be noisy. Still, the location is perfect for access to the buses, and it's not in the reputedly dangerous neighborhood near the highway where most of the *hospedajes* are found.

A reader has recommended the friendly **Hotel Turístico Mar Dulce** (private bath, ceiling fans, TV; $20, including breakfast; 045-33262) on the beach in San Jorge, Riva's port on Lake Nicaragua.

GETTING THERE: Buses leave the border every hour and a half or so for the 45-minute trip to Rivas; cabs cost $10 and get you there in 30 minutes.

ISLA DE OMETEPE   Legend says that the two volcanoes rising out of Lake Nicaragua on Isla Ometepe are the breasts of a beautiful princess who, like Juliet, fell in love with a prince from a rival tribe and then committed suicide with her lover (who became the Isla Zapatera on the way to Granada). Whether the legend is true or not, the sight of the two volcanoes in the lake is awe-inspiring. This tranquil, picturesque island has gained popularity in recent years. Because of Ometepe's isolation and Nicaragua's poverty in general, most of the island's 35,000 residents get around by bicycle, horse, or bus. Women still carry things on their heads, and buses have to stop to let herds of cattle go by.

Moyogalpa is on the island's western side, just one hour away from the mainland by boat. Stop at the shady, clean, and quiet **Cabaña 1908** for breakfast, lunch, dinner, or a snack. We loved the *empanadas de queso*—cheese melted between flour tortillas, served with fresh, homemade salsa. It's a block inland from the dock, on the left.

None of the hotels in Moyogalpa are as nice as the places at Playa Santo Domingo on the eastern side of the island (see below). **Hotel Cari** (cold water; private baths with fan, $12-$20; air conditioning, $20-$30; 045-94263) is behind the banana trees that you'll see to the right as you approach Moyogalpa. Though the rooms are small and plain, the restaurant is a great place to hang out. On the right as you enter Moyogalpa is the **Hotel Omotepetl** (private baths, cold water, fan or air conditioning; $12-$20; 045-94276, fax: 045-94132), which is also nice, though it's not on the water. Rooms are larger here than at the Cari. We didn't get to eat there, but the huge plates of food served from their kitchen looked and smelled delicious. They are also the

Toyota rent-a-car center. Recommended. The same gracious lady who owns the Ometepetl owns the **Hospedaje Moyogalpa** (shared bath, cold water, fans; $2.50/person) next door, for budget travelers, and the **Casa Hotel Ixtian** on Playa Santo Domingo.

Hospedaje Ali (cold water, fans; with shared bath, $3-$4/person; with private bath, $5-$6/person; 045-94196), 300 meters from the lake, has a patio/restaurant with hammocks. **Pensión Jade** (cold water, shared bath; $2-$3/person), one block east of the Ali, is the cheapest bed in town and has a nice patio, but is pretty run-down. Ask for a *tijera* (scissor) cot if you don't like a lumpy mattress.

Ecotur Ometepe (045-94118) offers various guided tours of the island, including the museum of pre-Columbian art and history it helped establish in the town of Altagracia. Ecotur is located at the Fundación entre Montañas headquarters, in a building covered with murals, 200 meters east and 175 meters south of the dock, across from the Enitel (telephone) office.

Both volcanoes on the island are hikeable. **Concepción** (1610 meters) is still active, so you can't go to the top. (Even so, hiking as far up as you can will take seven to eight hours roundtrip.) The easiest route is along the north face, starting in Altagracia. **Volcán Madera** (1395 meters) is considered an extinct volcano; there is a lake in its crater. Quite a bit of the pre-Columbian pottery found on the island comes from the Madera side, and petroglyphs are still visible there. If you are in good condition, it takes about four hours to scale Madera. Don't attempt to hike these hills and forests by yourself. Any hotel in the area can connect you with guides.

Altagracia is on the island's east side, and is served by boats from Granada and by bus from Moyogalpa. The **Museum of Altagracia** (admission 80 cents) has pottery and historical information about the island's earliest inhabitants. Pass by the front of the local cathedral to see a few more carved pre-Columbian statues.

The **Hospedaje Central** (shared or private bath, cold water, fans; $7-$12; 0552-6072) is spotless, with a spacious courtyard and some of the nicest cabins we've seen in the country. The attentive owner offers a tour of Altagracia for $6. There's a game room, conference room, store, and restaurant for guests. Recommended.

Santo Domingo beach is south of Altagracia on the road that connects the two halves of Ometepe. Here you can bathe in Lake Nicaragua with its calm, warm water and very gradually sloping bottom—it's about chest-deep 100 yards out. We took a memorable swim in the warm, windy lake at twilight, looking back at the sun setting behind Volcán Concepción, with the broad, forested Volcán Madera to the south.

Villa Paraiso (shared baths, cold water, fans; $7-$12; individual cabins with private bath, $20-$30; 045-34675) has beautiful gardens, a second-floor balcony looking over the lake, and a restaurant with scrumptious meals, including vegetarian items and fresh lake fish. The conscientious owners, a Nicaraguan doctor and his Austrian wife, furnish bottled drinking water for guests. For groups of three or more, they offer hikes to the lake atop Volcán Madera ($15), horseback rides to see the petroglyphs ($15), and tours of the island ($50/carload). This is definitely our favorite place on Ometepe. Call ahead to reserve a room. Recommended.

The **Santo Domingo** (shared baths, cold water, fans; $7-$12; 045-34675—same number as Villa Paraiso: they're owned by brothers) is a much older, typical beach hotel with a tightly winding spiral staircase and a thatched porch with hammocks. A little darker than Villa Paraiso, but nice. Both hotels rent horses and bikes.

GETTING TO THE ISLAND: To Moyogalpa: We recommend taking a taxi from the border so that you can get to Ometepe in time to get to the beach on the eastern side before dark. It is cheaper to get a taxi from the border to Rivas's port, San Jorge ($12) than to San Juan del Sur ($15). Another alternative is to take the 5:30 a.m. Managua-bound Transnica bus from San José (Calle 22, Avenidas 3/5; 256-9072, 221-0953; $10). This comfortable bus has a bathroom, gives you snacks and shows movies. Make reservations in advance. Ask to be let off at the Shell station in Rivas, and take a taxi to San Jorje ($2).

Boats leave from San Jorge six times daily, at 10 a.m., 11 a.m., noon, 2 p.m., 3:30 p.m., 5 p.m., and 6 p.m., returning at 6 a.m., 6:30 a.m., 7 a.m., 7:30 a.m., 8 a.m., 1:30 p.m., and 4 p.m. (045-34779, 045-94116; $1). The boatride from San Jorge to Moyogalpa in the *Reina del Sur* can be described as "colorful" or "har-rowing" depending on your orientation. The century-old boat was overloaded with sacks of cement as well as its full complement of passengers when we took it. It rolled from side to side, and we got soaked. It was a very windy day, but no-body else seemed to think the trip was out of the ordinary. The water calmed down after the wind was blocked by Volcán Madera's ample girth to the south. Sometimes a limited number of people are allowed on the boat, so buy your tick-ets as soon as you arrive at Ometepe Tours in San Jorge. Ometepe Tours has been known to give misleading information about the availability of hotel rooms in Moyogalpa, in an attempt to direct tourists to their own businesses, so don't ask them to book rooms for you.

To Altagracia: Boats leave Granada for Altagracia at 11 a.m. and 2:30 p.m. on Tuesday and 10 a.m. and 2:30 p.m. on Friday and Sunday. The trip takes four hours and costs $3. Call the boat company in Granada at 055-6457 or 055-6439.

To Santo Domingo: Try to get to San Jorge early, so you can catch the 2 p.m. boat to Moyogalpa. A bus to Altagracia meets the boat in front of the Hospedaje

Moyogalpa, around the corner to the right from the dock. In an hour or so, you'll be in Altagracia, where the bus backtracks to Santo Domingo on its way to Balgüe. You'll get to Santo Domingo around 5 p.m. A taxi will have you there in less than an hour and will cost $15-$20.

GRANADA

Founded in 1524, Granada is the largest city on Lake Nicaragua. It is full of history. If you have been disappointed by the sparseness of Spanish colonial buildings and churches in Costa Rica, you'll be pleased to find that Granada is full of them. The Central Park has kiosks that serve snacks, and signposts with shocking pink tourist-orientation maps. If you are lucky enough to be in Granada on the days cruise ship tourists arrive from San Juan del Oriente's port, you'll find Parque Central and the Plaza de la Independencia alive with artisans, mariachi bands and folkloric dancers. You can also catch these kinds of festivities every Friday night in Parque Central at the community *serenata*. Local restaurants sell the best they have to offer at food booths, and mariachis stroll among the tables.

Horse-and-buggy taxis ($6/half-hour) are used for transportation. Hiring one is a great way to get to know the city. When you are walking in Granada at night, beware of the bicyclists. They rip through the streets and sidewalks at top speed, without lights.

The **Casa de Cultura** (open 8 a.m. to noon, 2 p.m. to 8 p.m.; closed Sunday), in a beautiful old mansion facing the central park, offers classes to the general public: everything from children's karate to women's job training. Come here for poetry readings, art festivals, and dance, theater, and music performances; posters in front announce current cultural events.

Casa Xalteva (phone/fax: 0552-2436; www.ibw.com.ni~casaxal, e-mail: casaxal@ibw.com.ni) is a Spanish language school at 103 Calle Real Xalteva in the heart of Granada. According to their website, their values include "a respect for all individuals and cultures; a commitment to grassroots democracy and environmentally-sound development; support for peace and social justice; and a strong belief in the spiritual dimension of human existence and harmony with the natural world." There was a strong current of similar values that made Nicaragua in the 1980s an inspiring place to be. We are glad to see that in today's Nicaragua, which is opening so rapidly to tourism and development, there are still projects honoring the best of what the revolution was about.

A one-and-a-half-block walk north of the cathedral leads to another cultural center, **El Centro Cultural Internacional "Casa de los Tres Mundos."** Walk in and see their current painting exhibition, or buy a book. Their beautiful, quiet courtyard has a public phone, and is the hub of weekend cultural events—dance and orchestra concerts, poetry readings, film festivals, jazz groups, ethnic music.

Continuing in the same direction, the **Museo de San Francisco** (admission $1.25) is well worth a visit. From the cathedral, it is two blocks north and one block east. Built in 1524 as a convent, the museum houses a room full of Nicaraguan paintings done in the *primitavista* style: bright and beautiful representations of peasant life, mostly painted by residents of the islands of Solentiname. An interesting collection of pre-Columbian Chorotega Indian statues was found on Isla Zapatera, south of Granada, which was once used as a burial ground and ceremonial center. Walk all the way through to the back of the convent to see the statues.

The **municipal market**, which covers several blocks, is located three blocks south of the cathedral. It is a wonderland of spices, fresh vegetables, pretty dresses for little girls, handmade tortillas, and smoke rising from open fires as women cook huge cauldrons of soup. It makes the San José market look like a department store. Recommended.

Lake Nicaragua (originally "Cocibolca" in the Nahuatl language) covers 274 square kilometers, and is the only lake habitat in the world for freshwater sharks. To get there, walk east down Calle Calzada from the cathedral about a kilometer, or take a cab an extra kilometer to the dock if you want to go for a boat ride. (Bring insect repellent in case the wind dies down—the lakefront can be very buggy.)

The beautifully designed **Centro Turístico** stretches for a kilometer along the lakefront. Tile-covered restaurants specializing in fresh fish are interspersed with playgrounds and benches. On weekends there is a lot of live music and dancing—*muy alegre*. At the very end of the Centro, you can catch a small boat ($10/hour for one or two people, $17/hour for a group) that will take you on a tranquil tour of some of the more than 350 volcanic islands deposited there by Volcán Mombacho. These small, green islands are inhabited by both the very rich and the very poor. If you take the boat tour, you can ask your boatman to take you to an *isleta* for a downhome fish or chicken lunch with a local family, accompanied by an ice-cold beer or soft drink. It's customary to invite the boatman to join you for lunch.

RESTAURANTS   Restaurants are amazingly plentiful for a Nicaraguan city. For the best paella, the Spanish-owned **El Mediterraneo**, in a refurbished Spanish colonial mansion, is our choice. All tables are near the lush indoor patio and its bubbling fountain—expect to eat under the stars. Nice desserts here, too. It's pricey but tasty.

Dona Conchi's on Calle de Cisne is a charming, intimate restaurant, also Spanish-owned. If you ask nicely, Dona Conchi may play her castanets for you to her favorite CD. The decor is warmed by candlelight every evening, and small booths and cushioned benches share the edges of her lovely garden and fountain. Here are the best salads in town—ample enough alone for a dinner. Homemade soups are great, but look for other more hearty entrées as well—maybe *filete roquefort*, a bowl of pasta, or chicken in orange sauce. Try carrot or black forest cake for dessert. Nice *sangria*, too. After dinner, browse in the restaurant's "Coco Loco," a gift shop with a sampling of Nica artistry: ceramics, glass, handmade purses, decorative pillows, candles.

Two authentic Italian restaurants round out Granada's international flavor. At the **Alhambra**, Paolo and Lidia serve wonderful pasta meals that end with traditional Italian *digestivos*. On Calle Altravesada, just across the little bridge, look for Vera and Antonio's **Osteria** for excellent northern Italian cuisine—good bread and wine, too.

Sergio's Taqueria is a fun place to sample some Mexican specialties—chicken or beef tacos, burritos (huge ones), and beef pastor. Sergio's family as the wait staff for the tiny outdoor/indoor café is part of the charm. You'll see the taqueria on Calle de Calzada—look for small cantina tables and stools outside.

LODGING   Be sure to make reservations if you plan to visit Granada on a weekend.

The newest and best hotel in Granada is the **Casona de los Estrada** (private bath, hot water, ceiling fans, air conditioning; $100-$130; 552-7393, fax: 552-7295; www.casonalosestrada.com, e-mail: gensa@munditel) on Calle El Arsenal, just off Parque Central. Here you'll find Granada's finest restaurant, with unusually efficient service and menu selections not found in other dining establishments.

One of the two best-known hotels in town is the fancy **Hotel Alhambra** (private bath, cold water, air conditioning, cable TV; $30-$40; $40-$50 for rooms with balconies facing the park; 0552-4486, fax: 0552-2035; e-mail: hotalam@ns.tmx.com.ni), on the west side of the central park. This large hotel has just added a pool to its list of attractions. The other is **Hotel Granada** (private bath, heated water, air conditioning; $30-$40; 0552-2974, fax: 0552-4128), which has larger rooms. It is not as central, but is closer to the Centro Turístico (one block west of the lake on Calle Calzada).

A mid-range alternative is the **Hotel Casa Colonial** (shared bath, cold water, fans; $12-$20; 0552-4115), one block north and half a block west of the Hotel Alhambra. This elegant old building has a beautiful courtyard with quiet rooms in the back. The rooms are nothing special, but they appear to have good mattresses.

Another Night in Paradise (shared baths, heated water, fans; $12-$20, 552-7113; e-mail: ugogirl@tmx.com.ni) is a homey guest house owned by a former Peace Corps volunteer and run by a multilingual Dane. There's an upstairs veranda with hammocks, cable TV, rocking chairs, and a cool lake breeze. Guests can use the well-equipped kitchen and the book and video library. It's on Calle Calzada, across from the Cruz Roja.

The funky but serviceable **Hospedaje Central** (shared or private bath, cold water, fans; $2-$3/person; 0552-5900), two blocks east of the cathedral and owned by an accommodating gringo named Bill, draws travelers from all over the world. Their restaurant is popular with local expats for its different-than-Nica fare and two-for-one drink specials. It's the place to go for a chess game at an outdoor café table.

GETTING THERE: From Rivas: Frequent buses leave the Rivas market for Granada. The trip takes one and a half hours and the last bus leaves Rivas at 6 p.m.

From Ometepe: Boats leave Altagracia (the east side of the island) for Granada on Tuesday and Friday at 10 p.m. and Sunday at 10 a.m. ($3, four-hour trip). *Warning:* Boat schedules are subject to change without notice. You can call the boat company in Granada at 0552-6457 or 0552-6439.

GETTING BACK TO THE BORDER: All of the towns mentioned in the Nicaragua section of this chapter use Rivas as their local bus hub. Buses start leaving Rivas for the border at 8:30 a.m. If you're in the vicinity of Granada and want a direct ride back to San José, you can take a Tica Bus (0552-4301, fax: 0552-2899; $10). They pass through Granada on their way from Managua at 7 a.m. and 8 a.m. daily. Buy tickets one or two days in advance, and bring your passport. Their office is located half a block south of the Hospital San Juan de Diós on the road to Masaya and is open from 6 a.m. to 6 p.m. Or you can return on the 7 a.m. Transnica bus, which arrives at the Shell station outside Rivas around 8:30. There is an exit fee of $2, plus $1 for the municipality.

ELEVEN

The Central Pacific Zone

Puntarenas Province extends along the Pacific Coast from Guanacaste to the Panamanian border. The Central Pacific Zone roughly corresponds to the northern part of the province, from the town of Puntarenas to the Nicoya Peninsula, to Quepos and Manuel Antonio National Park, about halfway down Costa Rica's Pacific Coast. Like Guanacaste, the Central Pacific is famous for its beaches—from the rocky coves of Montezuma on the Nicoya Peninsula to the half-moon jewels of Manuel Antonio.

The climate of the Central Pacific is not as dry as that of Guanacaste, however. You'll feel the heat and the heaviness of the moist, tropical air, so be prepared to slow down and let your body adjust to the change. Bring sunblock, insect repellent, and an umbrella to use in the sun or in case of sudden showers.

Note: Sanitary conditions are generally good on the Pacific Coast, but if you don't want to take chances, bottled water is readily available. Don't swim in estuaries or rivers; most of them are polluted. However, the heavy surf and currents of the Pacific keep the beaches free of contamination. (Be sure to read the section on how to handle rip currents in Chapter Five.)

PUNTARENAS

The town of Puntarenas was Costa Rica's main port for most of the 1800s. The treacherous terrain between San José and the Atlantic Coast made an eastern port impossible until the railway was completed in 1890. So oxcarts laden with coffee rumbled down to Puntarenas, from which the precious beans were shipped to Chile, to be re-exported to Europe. In 1843, English Captain William Le Lacheur landed in Puntarenas on the way back from a business failure in Seattle, Washington. Worried about the danger of sailing with an empty ship, he traveled five days by mule to San José, hoping to find some cargo for ballast. It turned out that coffee had been over-produced that year, and growers were desperate for new markets. Even though he was a stranger and had no money to give them, the growers entrusted him with a weighty shipment. He came back two years later with the payment, and a thriving trade with England was established.

Traditionally the vacation spot for Ticos from the Central Valley, Puntarenas underwent a facelift in late 1999 when it inaugurated new facilities to receive thousands of cruise ship passengers during their September to May season. A tourist information and communications center, a crafts market, a restaurant, and an amphitheater are housed in airy well-designed buildings across from the huge new dock on the ocean side of downtown. The town has the closest beach to San José, but unless you're fond of funky seaports or are into sailing, you won't want to spend your vacation there. If you choose to visit en route to somewhere else, it is pleasant to stroll along the Paseo de Turistas, feel the sea breezes, and watch the sun set behind the mountains of the Nicoya Peninsula.

The main reason foreign tourists go to Puntarenas is to catch a ferry boat to Playa Naranjo or to Paquera en route to Tambor and Montezuma, or to make bus connections from Guanacaste and Monteverde to Manuel Antonio.

The town is only four blocks wide for most of its length, because it is built on a narrow spit. Fishing boats and ferries dock on the estuary side; a beach runs along the Gulf of Nicoya side. The Ministry of Health warns against bathing in the estuary. The beaches in town have been cleaned up in the last few years and recent tests show they are now safe for bathing.

Calypso Tours takes you around the gulf in a luxurious Manta Raya, a speedy yacht with on-deck pools and trampolines and a spacious air-conditioned cabin with a bar ($99, including transportation to and from San José; wheelchairs can be accommodated; 256-2727, 661-0585, fax: 233-0401; e-mail: calypso@centralamerica.com). The crew offers fresh tropical fruit snacks, and serves ceviche and a gourmet lunch on Tortuga Island, where you can swim and snorkel or zip through the forest canopy on a cable. Weekdays the beach is more tranquil than weekends. Returning to Puntarenas, the boat passes several of the Gulf's islands, including the Islas Negritos Wildlife Refuge, a main nesting ground for pelicans and frigate birds. Calypso can also take you to their private nature reserve at Punta Coral on the Nicoya Peninsula. They've been offering tours for 25 years and really know how to make their guests feel pampered.

Veleros del Sur (cell phone: 284-2203, 661-2186) has a large fleet of sailboats and motorboats docked in Puntarenas; they can be chartered to take you anywhere you wish, including Isla del Coco.

On the oceanfront, between Calles 21 and 23, **La Caravelle** serves expensive food in an elegant setting. Nearby, **El Jorón** (open 10 a.m. to midnight; closed Tuesday) is popular among locals and visitors alike for beer and *bocas*. The restaurant at the **Hotel Las Brisas** has a clean kitchen, is well lit and breezy, and serves some tasty Greek specialties. **La Yunta** (open noon to midnight), in a charming older building with a wide veranda overlooking the sea, serves good traditional *tico* food, specializing in seafood and steak.

LODGING   If you want to stay cool, yet need to be near Puntarenas, just 35 minutes northeast is **Vista Golfo de Nicoya Lodge** (hot water; shared bath, $30-$50; private bath, $50-$60; children three to twelve 50 percent off; phone/fax: 639-8303; www.vista-golf.com, e-mail daniel@vista-golf.com), above the mountain town of **Miramar**. The lodge, with a beautiful view of the Gulf, features a hot tub and pool fed by a natural spring, a reasonably priced restaurant, and horseback tours to a nearby gold mine ($20). Direct buses leave Puntarenas for Miramar at 7:15 a.m., 10 a.m., 2 p.m., and 4:30 p.m., returning at 6:30 a.m., 9 a.m., noon, and 3 p.m. The lodge is a ten-minute drive from Miramar up a narrow, winding road with many potholes.

The **Gran Hotel Chorotega** (cold water, ceiling fan; shared bath, $12-$20; private bath, $20-$30; 661-0998), a three-story building diagonally across from the Banco Nacional, is the best of the low-cost options in the crowded, funky downtown area. It's clean and well-run, with secure parking, a refrigerator for guests, and laundry service. Try to get an inside room. It's a couple of blocks from the municipal market and passenger ferry dock—convenient for the early-morning passenger boat to the Montezuma area.

The hotels along the beachfront have more pleasant surroundings. **Hotel Tioga** (private bath, air conditioning, pool; with cold water, $40-$50; with hot water, $50-$60; breakfast included; 661-0271, fax: 661-0127) is comfortable and well maintained, with a cafeteria.

The other places are at the western end of the Paseo de los Turistas, near the dock for the car ferries. Operated by a Canadian and his Tica wife, **Casa Dulia** (shared bath, cold water, table fans; $30-$40; 661-1292), in front of the small triangular Parque Lobo, is a homey B&B in a renovated wooden house. **Las Brisas** (private bath, heated water, air conditioning, pool; $50-$60; 661-4040, fax: 661-2120) is clean, with large, plain rooms and effective, no-nonsense management. **Hotel Yadran** (private bath, hot water, cable TV, air conditioning, phones, pool; $70-$80, including break-

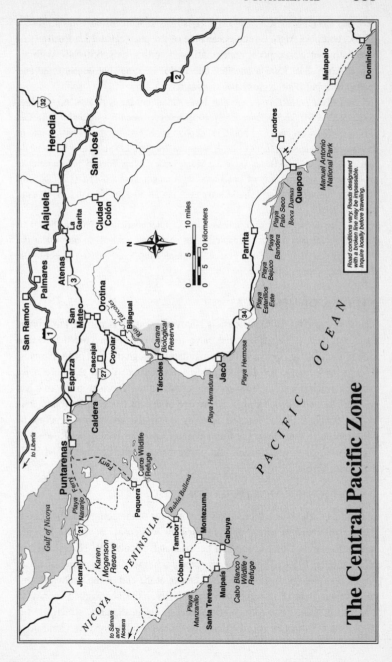

The Central Pacific Zone

Road conditions vary. Roads designated with a broken line may be impassable. Inquire locally before traveling.

PACIFIC OCEAN

Gulf of Nicoya

NICOYA PENINSULA

Matapalo
Dominical
Manuel Antonio National Park
Londres
Quepos
Boca Damas
Playa Palo Seco
Parrita
Playa Bandera
Playa Bejuco
Playa Esterillos Este
Playa Hermosa
Jacó
Playa Herradura
Tárcoles
Carara Biological Reserve
Río Tárcoles
Bijagual
Orotina
Coyolar
Cascajal
San Mateo
Atenas
La Garita
Ciudad Colón
San José
Heredia
Alajuela
Palmares
San Ramón
Esparza
Caldera
Puntarenas
Playa Naranjo
Ferry
Ferry
Paquera
Curú Wildlife Refuge
Bahía Ballena
Tambor
Montezuma
Cabuya
Cóbano
Cabo Blanco Wildlife Refuge
Malpaís
Santa Teresa
Playa Manzanillo
Karen Mogenson Reserve
Jícaral
to Sámara and Nosara
to Liberia

2
32
3
1
27
17
21
34

N

0   5   10 miles
0   5   10 kilometers

fast; 661-2662, fax: 661-1944) is a garish resort with restaurant, bar, disco, casino, and pool, right on the ocean side of the point. **Hotel La Punta** (private bath, hot water, pool, restaurant; with ceiling fans, $30-$40; with air conditioning, $40-$50; phone/fax: 661-0696) is somewhat deteriorated and overgrown, but it's the closest to the car ferry.

GETTING THERE: By Bus: San José–Puntarenas buses (Calle 16, Avenidas 10/12; 222-0064; $2.50) leave every 40 minutes between 6 a.m. and 7 p.m. Get there early on weekends and holidays. *Directo* buses take two and a half hours. In Puntarenas, the bus stop is at Calle 4, Avenidas 2/4 (661-2158). Return buses begin departing at 4:15 a.m. Buses leave the Monteverde Cheese Factory for Puntarenas daily at 5:30 a.m. (by way of Las Juntas de Abangares) and 6 a.m. (via Lagarto). Buses to Puntarenas from Liberia leave at 5 a.m., 8:30 a.m., 10 a.m., 11:15 a.m., and 3:15 p.m.

By Car: Drive west from San José on the Interamerican Highway about two hours. The entrance to Puntarenas may not be clearly marked, so turn off at the green highway sign for "Zona Franca." Coming from San José, if you get to the Recope fuel station, you've gone too far.

NICOYA PENINSULA

The southern edge of Guanacaste's Nicoya Peninsula is part of Puntarenas Province. This is because ferries have traditionally connected the eastern side of the Gulf of Nicoya with the mainland through the port of Puntarenas. Except for flying to the Tambor airstrip, the fastest way to get there is by boat, although it's still a time-consuming adventure. Tourism in the area has centered around Playa Naranjo, where one of the car ferries from Puntarenas docks; Bahía Ballena, located midway down the coast; the beaches of Montezuma to the south; the Cabo Blanco Absolute Biological Reserve at the very tip of the peninsula; and, most recently, the beaches of Malpaís and Santa Teresa.

THE KAREN MOGENSON RESERVE

In contrast to the beach tourism offered on most of the peninsula, the **Karen Mogenson Reserve** offers opportunities for wilderness adventure that are rare in this area. Doña Karen and her husband, Nicolas Wessberg, came to Nicoya in the 1950s. They were instrumental in the 1963 founding of Costa Rica's first biological reserve, Cabo Blanco, at the end of the Nicoya Peninsula. When Doña Karen passed away in 1993, she bequeathed money to ASEPALECO, a grass-roots conservation group in the area, which used it to buy the 600-hectare reserve that protects the local watershed. Conditions inside the reserve are still quite primitive, and it can only be reached by horse or on foot. There are two trails to a rustic cabin in the reserve—one trail has waterfalls along the way and the other has beautiful views of the Gulf of Nicoya. The cabin sleeps ten, or you can camp in the reserve. Meals can be arranged. In order to get there call the ASEPALECO office in Jicaral (650-0201, fax 650-0607; e-mail: asepalec@racsa.co.cr). They will meet you at the Playa Naranjo ferry and drive you to the reserve ($20/carload). Recommended for people who really want to get off the beaten path. Volunteering is a possibility.

PLAYA NARANJO

A weekend in Playa Naranjo can be one of the easiest possible beach getaways. Instead of driving four or five hours to Manuel Antonio or Guanacaste, you can drive or take the bus two hours to Puntarenas, take the hour-long ferry between the verdant islands of the Gulf, and really feel like you're on an adventure. Just a few hundred meters from the ferry landing toward Paquera is the **Hotel Oasis del Pacífico** (private bath, heated water, ceiling fans, pools; wheelchair accessible; $40-$50; phone/fax: 661-1555; e-mail: wilhow@racsa.co.cr), with spacious, peaceful grounds, a large pool, and a kids pool. Kayaks are available for rent. The hotel provides transportation to and from the ferry landing and is a good place for families or those who want to relax in a hammock next to the beach. Recommended.

A couple of hundred meters toward Jicaral from Playa Naranjo is the pleasant, clean **Hotel El Paso** (cold water, pool, private bath, ceiling fan or air conditioning, TV, restaurant; $20-$40, including breakfast; phone/fax: 661-2610). A good value. Use of their small pool costs $2, an option you might want to exercise to break up the trip. Also here is a compact complex including a gas station, convenience store, and bar/restaurant.

Travel notes: Since the advent of the car ferries from Puntarenas south to Paquera, there is really no reason to go to Playa Naranjo except for the tranquility of Oasis del Pacífico. This is reflected in the deteriorated state of the road between Playa Naranjo and Paquera. But if you want to get from Guanacaste to the Nicoya Peninsula in the rainy season, you have to go through Playa Naranjo. The roads coming into Playa Naranjo from Guanacaste are nicely paved, so even if it looks longer on the map, it's quicker to go from Samara or Nosara to Montezuma by way of Playa Naranjo rather than dealing with the even rougher roads along the Guanacaste coast and, especially, the Río Ora and the Río Bongo, which are impossible to cross in the rainy season. Staying in Playa Naranjo is convenient if you are coming from Guanacaste en route to Montezuma—in fact, you should not drive south from Playa Naranjo after dark, unless the road has been greatly improved.

GETTING THERE: A ferryboat (661-1069, 661-3834; $1.40/adult, 75 cents/child, $10/car) leaves Puntarenas five times daily, with exact schedules varying according to the season. To reach the dock, drive right through downtown Puntarenas on the same street you came in on, until you see a little sign directing you to turn right. The dock is near the northwestern tip of the spit. Make sure you take the Naranjo ferry, not the Paquera/Tambor one: both leave from the same dock. Hungry seagulls follow the boat and catch food thrown at them in midair. Pelicans are plentiful, especially on the Puntarenas side. Snacks are sold on board. We arrived too late to get on the returning 1 p.m. ferry one Sunday, so parked our car in the line for the next ferry, locked it, and went swimming in the lovely pools of the Hotel Oasis del Pacífico (see above). We were then treated to a beautiful trip back across the gulf in the moonlight, which transformed the steel hulk into a romantic ocean liner.

Note: If you have a car, be sure to get in line at least an hour before the ferry leaves from either end, as only a limited number of cars can fit. It is especially crowded on weekends and during the dry season. Drivers only are allowed to board the ferry in their cars. Passengers must walk on.

By Bus: There are no buses south to Paquera.

PAQUERA AND CURÚ WILDLIFE REFUGE

Paquera is one hour from Playa Naranjo by car (on a terrible gravel road), or an hour from Puntarenas on either of two car ferries: the Naviera Tambor or Ferry Peninsular. You can also get there on the *lancha,* a smaller boat that carries people only. The ferry landing is a 15-minute drive east from Paquera itself, a small town that has gas stations, food and clothing stores, and pharmacies. The commercial center for the beach towns and farming communities on the lower Nicoya Peninsula, Paquera is not where you'd want to spend your vacation, but it's convenient for visiting Curú or if you need to spend a night near the ferry docks.

Twenty minutes north of Paquera, in a lush horseshoe valley below the road, is **Hotel Bahía Luminosa** (private bath, hot water, pool, wall fans or air conditioning; $80-$90, including breakfast; 381-2296, 641-0386, 800-700-7768; www.bahialuminosa.com, e-mail: info@bahialuminosa.com), with both hilltop and poolside cabinas. Water-sports activities like sportfishing, diving, windsurfing, or canoeing through a local mangrove swamp can be coordinated through the hotel, as well as horseback rides to nearby waterfalls.

In Paquera, the **Cabinas Ginana** (private bath, cold water, ceiling fans, restaurant; $7-$12; 641-0119) are clean and inexpensive. Bring mosquito coils. **Cabinas El Paraíso** (private bath, cold water, table fans; $7-$12; 641-0240, fax: 641-0234), across from the Guardia Rural after you turn right toward Cóbano, are very clean and have a nice *soda*. The owner will pick you up at the ferry.

Located on a private farm seven kilometers south of Paquera is the **Curú Wildlife Refuge** (phone/fax: 200-5020; $5). Its beach is home to thousands of phantom crabs, one of which stole my watch while I was enjoying the warm, gentle waters of the picturesque, cup-shaped bay. Luckily, we spotted the watchband at the bottom of the nearest crab hole, and we fished it out with a stick. Snorkeling is supposed to be good there, but we didn't stay long enough to find out because no-see-ums and other nasty biting bugs were making mincemeat of us.

A recent study rated Curú as the ecologically richest reserve on the Nicoya Peninsula, due to its diversity of habitats, including mangroves, rainforest, and a lagoon, which is the only one left on the peninsula. The farm has banana plantations that are specifically for wildlife, so it's not difficult to see howler and white-faced monkeys, coatimundis, iguanas, and more than 150 species of birds from the 11 different hiking trails. Three kinds of turtles nest on the beach. Because the reserve is on private land, it is a good idea to call before arriving. (Leave plenty of time to do this because the phone connections are very poor.) There are primitive showers and toilets near the beach, and very rustic accommodations ($25/person including food) for groups of students and researchers. The bus from Paquera passes the entrance, which is easy to miss—if you're coming from the north it's on the left next to a green house on stilts.

BAHÍA BALLENA

The waters of this deep, round bay on the southeastern end of the Nicoya Peninsula are gentle and warm, but are not very clear near the shore. This bay is the site of one of the largest beach hotel and condo projects in Central America, owned by the Spanish chain Barceló. You'll see the guarded entrance to the hotel and the brightly painted condos lined up in rows as you enter Tambor. You'll also notice that the road is in perfect condition between Barceló's ferry landing in Paquera and their hotel. The government welcomed the giant project as a source of much-needed foreign currency, but there is still a heated national controversy over whether this is the type of tourism development that Costa Rica should be inviting.

LODGING   Hotel Barceló is near the village of **Tambor**, on the southern rim of the bay. The beach is nice for kids because the dark brown sand is spongy and the bay is shallow, with gentle waves. We've never noticed any biting insects there. A river to the north sometimes fills the water with leaves, but beyond the breakers it's cleaner.

Tambor Tropical (private bath, hot water, ceiling fans, kitchen, no children; $140-$180; 683-0011, fax: 683-0013; in the U.S.: 503-363-7084, fax: 503-371-2471; e-mail: tambort@aol.com) has spacious, hexagonal, Samoan-style houses made from beautiful but endangered hardwoods, which encircle a pool/jacuzzi. Each room accommodates two people. Horseback tours up the Río Panica to some scenic waterfalls are offered through the hotel.

Next door, **Hotel Dos Lagartos** (cold water, ceiling fans; with shared bath, $12-$20; with private bath, $20-$30; phone/fax 683-0236) is clean, friendly, low-key, and quiet (and has good mattresses). From the beach in front of the hotel you can see two points in the distance that resemble crocodiles or lizards, hence the name.

Inland from the beach, **Pulpería Super Lapa** is a well-stocked and friendly grocery store. Meals are plentiful, inexpensive, and good at **Cristina's**, next to Super Lapa. Cristina also rents rooms (cold water; with shared bath and wall fans, $12-$20; with private bath and ceiling fans, $20-$30; phone/fax: 683-0028) above the restaurant.

Tango Mar (289-9328, 289-8652, 683-0002, 683-0001; fax: 289-8218, 683-0003; www.tangomar.com, e-mail: reservations@tangomar.com) is a unique resort on a beautiful stretch of beach south of Bahía Ballena. It has a variety of accommodations (all with hot water, ceiling fans, and air conditioning; $190-$250; four- and five-bedroom villas, $1200): some on the beach, some with views, some with private jacuzzis. All rates include a lavish breakfast. Green season packages run $499-$999 for three nights, including breakfast and dinner. Tango Mar boasts a seaside golf course and offers sportfishing, sailing, surfing, scuba diving, tennis courts, and beach volleyball. They'll arrange to have you picked up in Paquera, or you can fly from San José to the airstrip at Bahía Tambor. By car, follow the signs south of Tambor. Reservations are required.

GETTING THERE: By Bus and Boat: The *lancha* ($1.50) to Paquera, a rustic passenger ferry, leaves the dock behind the market in Puntarenas at 6 a.m., 11 a.m., and 3 p.m. Buses for Tambor, Cóbano, and Montezuma meet the ferry. The boat returns to Puntarenas at 7:30 a.m., 12:30 p.m., and 5 p.m. Buses leave Montezuma to meet the ferry, so ask at your hotel what time they pass Tambor.

By Car and Boat: From the dock on the estuary side at the tip of Puntarenas, take the Naviera Tambor ($1.50 for passengers that ride on top of the boat, $3 for air-conditioned cabin with snack bar, $10 for cars; 220-2034, ext. 746) or the older Ferry Peninsular ($1.50 for passengers, $10 for cars, 661-3674) The car ferries leave about four times a day, six times a day when both are working (the Ferry Peninsular is currently undergoing repairs). Get there an hour early. Only drivers can drive onto the ferries—all other passengers must walk on. The trip takes an hour and a quarter. The landing is a 15-minute drive from Paquera on a poorly paved road. After that, the roads are perfectly paved. Drive through Paquera and follow signs to Bahía Ballena. It takes about 45 minutes to drive from the dock to Bahía Ballena.

If the Paquera car ferry is too crowded, you might want to take the Playa Naranjo car ferry (see above). After arriving at Playa Naranjo, you must drive an hour to Paquera, along a deteriorated but passable gravel road. The scenery is quite beautiful, typical Nicoya Peninsula countryside.

By Air: SANSA (221-9414, fax: 255-2176; $50 one way) flies to Tambor from San José at 10:05 a.m. and 2:40 p.m., returning at 10:50 a.m. and 3:25 p.m. Travelair (232-7883, 220-3054, fax: 220-0413, 800-948-3770; $69 one way, $109 roundtrip) flies to Tambor every day at 11:30 a.m. and 12:10 p.m. See Chapter Four for more information.

MONTEZUMA

Like other beautiful places in Costa Rica, Montezuma is having to adjust to its sudden fame as a tourist destination. Enchanted visitors have spread the word about its lovely rocky coves and waterfalls. Because of the rocky coastline, it is not ideal for swimming, but the many tidepools lend themselves to a refreshing dip. Of all the beach towns in Costa Rica, Montezuma is the one that has attracted the strongest "alternative" community, with a thriving population of hippie farmers, natural-foods producers and consumers, itinerant artisans, and the like.

Montezuma was for many years known as a campers' free haven, but now things are changing. Local residents are finally tired of cleaning up after inconsiderate campers, and worry about contamination of the ocean and beaches, since there are no public sanitary facilities available. So if you are planning to camp in the area, either do so at the one public campground (often full) at the northern end of the first beach ("Rincón de los Monos," $1.75/person; tents rent for $3-$6).

The first few rocky bays to the north of the village have very strong currents, especially during high tide. **Playa Grande**, about 30 minutes north by foot, is calm and shallow, the best and safest place for bathing. At the far end of Playa Grande is a picturesque waterfall where you can sit and watch pelicans dive. Several locals offer horseback trips here. Read our cautions about riding horses in hot climates (see Chapter Five); there is a tragic history of horses in this area being mistreated and overused. Ask your hotel owner which guides they recommend.

There are **boatmen** in Montezuma who provide transportation across the gulf to Puntarenas, Jacó, Manuel Antonio, and Dominical, or around Cabo Blanco to Carrillo, Sámara, and Nosara (see Guanacaste chapter). Contact them through the information kiosk across from Hotel Moctezuma. Fresh fruits and vegetables (some organic!) are delivered to Montezuma several times a week.

There is a series of gorgeous waterfalls about 30 minutes out of town with pools that are nice for swimming. People like to cliff-dive here, but it's dangerous, so be very careful. Several people have slipped and fallen to their deaths in recent years. To get there, walk along the road to Cabo Blanco until you get to Restaurant La Cascada (about ten minutes). At the bridge, scramble upstream over the rocks for half an hour to an hour. You should be sure-footed to attempt this hike. We used to recommend that people wear shoes that could get wet, but we've heard reports of many a twisted ankle on this slippery, rocky stream bed, so good hiking boots would be the best choice.

LODGING   In the dry season, Montezuma books up; call for reservations. As in most beach towns, hotels here offer significant discounts, sometimes up to 50 percent, in the "green season" (May through November). "Downtown" Montezuma can be very noisy at night due to the mighty sound systems at the two bars.

You'll see a couple of places as you drive toward Montezuma from Cóbano. The turnoff for ✪ **The Nature Lodge Finca Los Caballos** (private bath, hot water, fans, pool; $60-$90; phone/fax: 642-0124; www.accommodations. co.cr/nature, e-mail: naturelc@sol.racsa.co.cr) is about halfway between Cóbano and Montezuma. Rooms are tastefully designed and comfortable, and the breezy open-air restaurant has an international menu with a Latin flair and a lovely view of the ocean in the distance. Organic produce is used as much as possible. A private two-bedroom house on the property rents for $440 per week. Excellent horseback trips are offered, as well as a quieter and more relaxing atmosphere than in downtown Montezuma. Recommended.

The German-owned **Horizontes de Montezuma** (private bath, hot water, table fans, pool; $50-$70; 642-0534; www.horizontes-montezuma.com, e-mail: horizontes@mail.ticonet.co.cr) has spacious rooms with private balconies and hammocks. It also has a Spanish school.

Located on the bluff above Montezuma, high above the ocean but only 600 meters from downtown, **Linda Vista** (private bath, heated water, table fans, refrigerators; $30-$40; with kitchens, $140/week, $600/month; 642-0274, fax: 642-0104; e-mail: montemar@racsa.co.cr) has great views but not much atmosphere.

As you enter town, to the right is **El Jardín** (private bath, cold or heated water, ceiling fans, some with air conditioning, refrigerator; $50-$60; phone/fax: 642-0074). These spacious rooms have wide, tiled balconies and porches with hammocks. The houses up the hill sleep four and provide views ($400/week). Across the street is ✪ **Hotel La Aurora** (shared bath, cold water, ceiling fans, unscreened windows, mosquito nets, communal kitchen, $20; with private bath, $30; rates include morning coffee, tea, purified water; phone/fax: 642-0051), with a hammock-strewn balcony upstairs where it's easy to meet fellow travelers. The owners, a German-Tico couple, are passionate community activists. The hotel is in front of the shady, well-maintained town playground—a boon for families with kids.

Hotel El Tajalín (private bath, heated water, ceiling fans; $50-$60; with air conditioning, $60-$90; 642-0061, fax: 642-0527; www.tajalin.com, e-mail info@tajalin.com) overlooks the park and has ocean views from its third floor café. The owner is very helpful to his guests.

Next door is **Hotel Montezuma Pacific** (private bath, both cold and heated water; shared refrigerator; with fans, $20-$30; with air conditioning, $30-$40; 642-0204, 222-7746), which has a nice upstairs porch. The owner provides transportation between San José and Montezuma for a very reasonable price (see "Getting There," below).

The main street of Montezuma has become a brightly painted block of souvenir stands, trendy beach boutiques, travel agencies, an ice cream shop and a laundry. In the midst of all this is ✪ **El Sano Banano** (open 7 a.m. to 9:30 p.m.), a pleasant natural-foods restaurant that shows high-quality videos on a large screen at night. It also prepares sack lunches. This is the unofficial tourist meeting place in town. If you are a birder, inquire here about birdwatching tours in the area. The friendly owners rent out peaceful round bungalows (private bath, some hot water, fans, coffee maker; $75; and rooms, $55; with kitchen and room for eight, $120-$150; 642-0272, fax: 642-0068) set in their forested preserve behind the second beach to the north (a tenminute walk from downtown). You cannot drive there, but the owners will transport your luggage. Because of the walk, these cabins are not the best for little children, but older kids are welcome. Be sure and get there by 4 p.m. so you can check in and do your first beach walk before dark. The bungalows are very near the beach, and the surf is strong. Some people find the sound of the waves too loud, but we found it an incredible lullaby. Also here is a lovely new swimming pool with a waterfall that massages your shoulders. Recommended.

Hotel Moctezuma (cold water, ceiling fans; with shared bath, $7-$12; with private bath, $12-$20; phone/fax: 642-0058) tends to be noisy because it has a bar downstairs and another next door, but it has a good restaurant and a wide veranda upstairs overlooking the ocean. It is clean and professionally run. **Pizzería Del Sol** nearby has hearty breakfasts, homemade breads, and mouth-watering pizzas. Their outdoor tables are in the heart of town—a good people-watching spot. **Cabinas Mar y Cielo** (private bath, cold water, fans; $20-$30; phone/fax: 642-0261) are on a rocky point behind Chico's Bar and the **Mamatea Delicatessen** (open 7 a.m. to 9 p.m. daily), a well-stocked mini-market. A road to the left leads to **Cocolores** (open 11 a.m. to 11 p.m.). This European-owned restaurant specializes in delicious seafood curry, ceviche (the best we have ever tasted), and pasta, but also makes tasty sandwiches and salads and has a wonderful oceanside atmosphere. Recommended.

Up the road a bit and on the left is **Luz de Mono** (phone/fax: 642-0010; e-mail: luzdmono@racsa.co.cr) a large restaurant and bar with artistic bas-relief murals of monkeys doing all sorts of naughty things. In back are rooms (private bath, heated water, fans, screened windows; $50-$60) with a moat around them and little stair-bridges over the moat.

South of downtown, along the coastal road (the one that leads all the way to Cabo Blanco), are several more places to stay. The farthest are only a five- to ten-minute walk from downtown, and all are accessible by car:

Cabinas El Tucán (shared bath, cold water, wall fans; $12-$20; 642-0284), across from El Jardín, are owned by one of Montezuma's original residents, Doña Marta Rodríguez, who spent many years managing other people's hotels before finally building her own. El Tucán has a taxi service that will take you anywhere in Costa Rica. **El Caracol**, 100 meters south of the village, serves seafood and *casados*.

Pensión Las Arenas (shared bath, fan; $7-$12; 642-0308), on the beach to the south, has small rooms that are okay if you have quiet neighbors. Their restaurant is among the palm trees on the beach side of the cabinas. *Comida típica* is served in this beautiful setting. The friendly local owner of **Hotel Liz** (shared bath, cold water, ceiling fans; $12-$20; 642-0568) rents small but comfortable rooms near the ocean. The beach rooms in both of these places have more air.

Los Mangos (pool, restaurant; phone/fax: 642-0259, 642-0076) has comfortable precious-wood bungalows (private bath, hot water, ceiling fans; $80-$90 for up to three) dotting a hillside orchard, as well as a two-story house near the road (cold water, shared or private bath; $20-$30). Down the street, the highly recommended **Playa de los Artistas** specializes in Mediterranean-style seafood.

Across the street is **Hotel Lucy** (shared bath, cold water, natural ventilation or table fans; $7-$12; 642-0273). In 1993, just as we were about to leave town, some friends informed us that the municipality had a bulldozer on its way to destroy Lucy's. Like many other establishments at Montezuma, Lucy's is built within 50 meters of the high-tide line, a zone the Costa Rican government has wisely established as an inviolable public area. But destroying Lucy's would be a case of selective enforcement. Since the owner of Lucy's is a feisty guy without connections to politicians, his hotel was targeted. We went to Lucy's that morning and saw half of the town staked out in front of the hotel in defiance of the approaching bulldozer. Along with the dozer came several rural guards and the mayor of Cóbano. The crowd successfully intimidated the officials; Lucy's still stands.

The well-maintained, friendly **Hotel Amor de Mar** (cold or heated water, table fans; with shared bath, $30-$40; with private bath, $30-$80; phone/fax: 642-0262; e-mail: shoebox@racsa.co.cr) features quiet rooms, some with verandas and ocean views, has spacious grounds, its own private tidepool, and hammocks overlooking a stream that flows into the ocean. They also rent a house ($500/month) for up to six people. The restaurant (open for breakfast and lunch) serves homemade bread. It's located a few hundred meters south of Lucy's, across the street from the waterfall trailhead. Recommended.

Three kilometers from Montezuma is Playa Cedros, a good beach for beginning surfers. Just before you get to Playa Cedros you'll see signs for **Las Rocas** (642-0393; www.parquecaboblanco.com, e-mail: lasrocas@racsa.co.cr), owned by a young European family who offer rooms above their home (shared bath, cold water; $20-$30) and apartments in a two-story house (private bath, cold water, fans, kitchen; $40-$70; kids under 8 free). They have free snorkeling and fishing equipment for guests and provide bikes for riding into town. They can also tell you how to get to a nearby hidden waterfall. Las Rocas is a five-minute walk from the Río Cedros, a good place for kids to romp.

GETTING THERE: By Bus and Boat: From the dock behind the *mercado* in Puntarenas take the *lancha* (passenger ferry) to Paquera (see schedule below). Several public buses wait for the *lancha* at Paquera. Be sure to take the one marked Montezuma ($3.50), which makes the trip down bumpy roads, through beautiful country, in about two hours. If you want to take the 6 a.m. boat, you'll have to spend the night in Puntarenas. Buses leave Montezuma for Paquera at 5:30 a.m., 10 a.m., and 2 p.m. You can also take the more comfortable car ferry (see below). Buses don't always meet the car ferry, but you can get a taxi into Montezuma for about $25 per carload. It's much faster than the bus.

By Private Bus and Boat: During the dry season (December–April) there's a great new option for getting to Montezuma in a quick (five hours) and efficient way. On Monday, Wednesday and Friday, Hotel Montezuma Pacific (222-7746) will pick you up at your hotel in San José and drive you to the car ferry where you walk on. They leave their van in Puntarenas and meet you with another van on the other side. This avoids having to get to the ferry early and having to wait to disembark. They return to San José on Tuesday, Thursday, and Saturday. For $25 one way, this is a great service.

By Car and Boat: It is not really necessary to have a car to go to Montezuma, but if you do, take the Naviera Tambor or the Ferry Peninsular. The two car ferries leave from the same dock in Puntarenas, which is on the north side of town, near the far end of the spit. Drive through town on the same street you come in on, until a sign directs you to turn right. If in doubt, ask.

You have to leave your car and go inside the terminal to buy your tickets. Be sure you are in the line for cars if you want a car ticket, for passengers if you want a passenger ticket. On Barceló's Naviera Tambor you can opt for a first class seat in the air-conditioned (freezing) snack-bar and TV lounge. Otherwise, you ride on rather uncomfortable benches on top of the boat. The older, funkier Ferry Peninsular (in dry dock for repairs at press time) doesn't offer a first-class option. The car ferries leave four times a day. Call 661-2084 or ask your Montezuma hotel for current schedule information. Cars start boarding about 50 minutes before departure time, so drivers should get there an hour early at either end. Only drivers can drive onto the ferries—all other passengers must walk on. The trip takes an hour and a quarter, with another 15 minutes to disembark. The landing is a 15-minute drive from Paquera on a poorly paved road. After that, the roads are perfectly paved. Once you land on the peninsula, follow the road through the town of Paquera. Signs and pavement lead as far as the Hotel Playa Tambor; from there it's a straight shot 45 minutes on good gravel road to Cóbano, where you make a left for the final seven kilometers (15 minutes) downhill to Montezuma. The trip from Paquera takes about two hours. The nearest gas station to Montezuma is in Cóbano.

You can also take the more frequent and slightly cheaper car ferry from Puntarenas to Playa Naranjo, which makes five roundtrips a day, with schedules depending on the season (call 661-1069, 661-3834). From Playa Naranjo, drive one hour over a bad road south to Paquera, make a right at the T-intersection in downtown Paquera, and continue with directions above.

By Air: The nearest airstrip to Montezuma is in Tambor, about an hour from Montezuma by car ($20-25 in a taxi). Ask the airline or your hotel in Montezuma to help coordinate transportation in advance. SANSA flies to Tambor from San José (221-9414, fax: 255-2176; $50 one way) twice daily during the dry season, November to April, leaving San José at 10:05 a.m. and 2:40 p.m. and returning 45 minutes later. Travelair flies to Tambor every day at 11:30 a.m. (232-7883, 220-

3054, 800-948-3770, fax: 220-0413; $69 one way, $109 roundtrip), by way of Tamarindo, returning to San José at 12:10 p.m. See Chapter Four for information about making reservations on SANSA and Travelair.

CABUYA AND CABO BLANCO WILDLIFE RESERVE

A road continues south from Montezuma through Cabuya and on to Cabo Blanco Wildlife Reserve. Cabo Blanco was the first national reserve in Costa Rica—its founding in 1963 was the initial step in the development of the country's extensive national park system. Preserved with the encouragement of Swedish biologist Nicolás Wessberg and his wife, Karen, who were concerned about the encroaching deforestation that was threatening the area's rich and varied wildlife, it is an "absolute reserve," which means most of the area is accessible only to scientific researchers.

Stop at the "Area Turistica" building to get an entrance permit (open 8 a.m. to 4 p.m.; closed Monday and Tuesday; $6). You can take a fairly strenuous two-hour hike up the Sendero Sueco and down to Playa Cabo Blanco (bring food and plenty of water). You'll see lots of howler monkeys. (Don't stand directly underneath them—they like to pee on sightseers.) There are pelican colonies on the point, which has beautiful pinkish coral sand. If you don't want to go that far, you can hike three and a half kilometers on the Sendero Sueco to the *mirador*, where you can see the tip of the peninsula. Another trail is the semicircular Sendero Danés, which takes about an hour to complete.

If you are interested in marine biology, a fascinating opportunity to study the marine ecosystems of this area, which have been off-limits to humans for almost 40 years, is now available. Milton and Diana Lieberman, researchers from the University of Georgia who founded the San Luis Ecolodge near Monteverde, have established the **San Miguel Marine Research Center** (shared bath, cold water, bunk beds; $30-$40/person, including meals; 642-0093) within the reserve. You do not have to be a professional biologist—lay people with a sincere interest in this very special region are welcome, as long as they come in a group.

A minibus leaves Montezuma for Cabo Blanco daily at 8 a.m., 2 p.m., and 6 p.m., returning to Montezuma at 7 a.m., 1 p.m., and 5 p.m. A taxi costs about $6.50. Driving there takes about 45 minutes.

LODGING   There are a handful of hotels between Montezuma and Cabuya. The spacious triple-occupancy rooms of **Hotel Cabo Blanco** (private bath, heated water, ceiling fans, air conditioning, TV, pool, kayaks, bar/restaurant; $20-$30; 642-0332) have a beautiful oceanfront site and helpful management.

Just a bit farther, near the town of **Cabuya** two kilometers before the reserve entrance, is an island that holds an indigenous cemetery. You can walk to the island at low tide (wear water walkers because of the rocky sea floor). Snorkeling is good there during the dry season, and reef-protected areas and tide pools make for safe swimming. In the center of Cabuya, **El Ancla de Oro** (private bath, cold water, fans; $12-$30; house with kitchen, $150/week or $400/month; phone/fax: 642-0369; www.parquecaboblanco.com, e-mail: lamont@racsa.co.cr) offers thatch-roofed cabins with mosquito nets and hammocks. The friendly owners, a Tico-British couple, rent bikes and horses and have a shop with local handicrafts. Their restaurant specializes in lobster served in garlic butter, and they serve Mexican food once a week. The two-night package is a pretty good deal: $56 per person including breakfast and dinner, entrance fee to Cabo Blanco, and pick-up in Montezuma.

At the main intersection in the town of Cabuya, hang a left (toward the beach) then a right to the Tico-owned **El Yugo** (private bath, cold water, ceiling fans, kitchen; $12-$20; 642-0303). Its individual houses have kitchens and baths downstairs and sleeping areas upstairs. Boat tours and horseback rides are available.

MALPAÍS AND SANTA TERESA

The long white beaches at Malpaís and Santa Teresa are renowned among surfers, and have been a well-kept secret among the area's aficionados. Swells are especially high at Santa Teresa, but nonsurfers will enjoy the tidepools and shell-strewn beach. These are some of the more isolated beaches in Costa Rica, and the bad roads prove it. Their beauty can be worth the trip for those who want to get away from more heavily traveled areas.

Easier access has become possible with the improvement of the road from Cóbano, but the steep gravel road can be hairy in the rainy season. A few rivers must be forded, and the road is quite deteriorated in places, but you can make it in a four-wheel drive. First we'll talk about lodging to the south on Malpaís. Santa Teresa is to the north.

LODGING   The road from Cóbano intersects with the coastal road at **Frank's Place** (pool; phone/fax: 640-0096; e-mail frank5@racsa.co.cr), just 200 meters from a good surfing spot and the main area for beach camping. Over the years, Frank has studied what surfers need, and provides good, clean, cheap rooms (shared bath, cold water; $8/person) and a wide range of other possibilities (private bath, some with kitchens; $20-$50; private house, $60). His corner kiosk also has internet, phone and fax access and a Sansa reservation center. Recommended for budget travelers.

Howler monkey

Turning left (south) for Malpaís, in about a kilometer you'll see the North American–owned **Malpaís Surf Camp** (pool, restaurant; 640-0061; www.malpaissurfcamp.com), which also offers a variety of options. If you've brought a tent, camping is $5 per person. Their breezy ocean-view ranchos (shared bath, cold water; $35 for up to four) have gravel floors and are open on all sides, with bamboo curtains for privacy. There are swings in the rooms and a big wooden trunk to store things in. There are also small bunk bed rooms ($25) and spacious, elegant pool-side cabinas (private bath, hot water, ceiling fans, screened windows; $65). During the high season they do nightly pig roasts. They offer many services, from surfing instruction and board rental to laundry and baby-sitting. They welcome families, and their van will take you to or from Tamarindo or San José ($250 for up to eight people).

Next on the right is **El Atardecer**, a friendly gathering place for gringos and ticos who enjoy a laid-back lifestyle. They rent rooms, have a bar and restaurant, and encourage music-making in the evenings.

Further south is **Laura Mar** (private bath, cold water, ceiling fans; $20-$30; 640-0080), with a row of simple rooms across a grassy lot from the beach. Next is the clean **Bosque Mar** (private bath, heated water, ceiling fans, kitchen; $20-$30; phone/fax: 640-0074). Across the road from Bosque Mar is a culinary treat: **Albimat Dulce Magia** (closed Tuesday) serves fresh fruit juices and authentic Italian fare, including pastas and pizza, for very reasonable prices. They have bocce ball, Italian TV, and a roller-skating rink in the back yard that also doubles as a basketball court and an outdoor dance floor with live music.

Turn off the main road from Albimat to **Mar Azul** (private bath, cold water, table fans, screens, some with kitchens; $12-$40; phone/fax: 640-0098): simple, Tico-style cabins at a beachside location, with a restaurant, Foosball, and billiards. Camping costs $2/person. They have a public phone.

The coastal road ends at **Sunset Reef Marine Lodge** (private bath, hot water, ceiling fans, air conditioning, pool, jacuzzi; $110; phone/fax: 640-0012; www.altatravelplanners.com). This hotel, although in a beautiful location, seems overpriced for what you get at the end of a long and very deteriorated road. They rent bikes and kayaks and arrange sportfishing trips.

If you turn north at the intersection of the Cóbano road and the coastal road (at Frank's Place), you head toward Santa Teresa. About 800 meters away, the **Trópico Latino** (private bath, hot water, ceiling fans, pool; $50-$60; children under 12 free; phone/fax: 640-0062, 888-401-7337; e-mail: tropico@centralamerica.com) is a beautiful retreat, with spacious, well-ventilated rooms and an open-air restaurant. Only the front cabinas are right on the beach. They offer horseback riding, scuba, snorkel and fishing trips, and surfboard rentals.

A bit farther, the breezy **Cabinas El Bosque** (private bath, cold water, kitchens; $12-$20; 640-0104) are perched on a forested hill. Each has a kitchen downstairs and a bedroom above. The A-frame structures are nothing special, and it's about a ten-minute hike up to them, but their shady location makes the place worthwhile.

Two hundred meters farther, on the ocean side of the road, look for the friendly **Cabinas Zeneida's** (shared bath, cold water, table fans; $8/person; 640-0118). The comfortable rooms are kept very clean. There is one family-size cabina and a camping area. We have heard numerous recommendations for the inexpensive, delicious food at Zeneida's. She obviously cares about her guests, and has a basketball court for days when the waves aren't good. Recommended for budget travelers.

About three kilometers from Frank's Place, **Cabinas Playa Santa Teresa** (private bath, cold water, ceiling fans, some kitchens; $20-$30; phone/fax: 640-0137) are clean quarters with a shady plant-filled front yard 150 meters from another of the area's prime surfing spots. The German owner is friendly.

Our favorite place in this area is **Milarepa** (private bath, hot water, ceiling fans, pool; $90-$100; phone/fax 640-0023; www.ticonet.co.cr/milarepa), which *is* worth the bumpy drive. Four bungalows, decorated with a relaxed grace, feature antique Indonesian canopy beds that are draped with filmy mosquito nets, giving them a medieval air. Folding wooden doors lead to beach-front stone terraces. Bamboo curtains roll down to block the sun and wind if needed. The outside is invited in, yet you are sheltered in a lovely way. Even the bathrooms are open to the sky, with lush tropical gardens inside. Tide pools in front are safe for kids at low tide. Milarepa's restaurant features cuisine from the south of France, with meals served at a leisurely pace and topped off by excellent coffee and homemade desserts. Recommended.

GETTING THERE: Follow directions in the Montezuma section for arriving at Cóbano. Two buses leave Cóbano daily to Malpaís and Santa Teresa ($2; 10:30 a.m. and 2:30 p.m.) from the town's main intersection. Scheduling is unreliable in the rainy season. In the high season, one more bus follows the same route at 6:30 p.m. Before driving your own car, check with the hotels about road conditions. It takes half an hour to drive the eight kilometers from Cóbano to Malpaís. You can drive from the southern end of Malpaís to Cabuya and Cabo Blanco in the dry season, but the road was closed when we were there in November.

If you want to explore the road going west to Río Negro and Manzanillo from Cóbano on your way to Playa Sámara in Guanacaste, keep asking people if you're going the right way—there are no signs. We would have made it to Sámara in about four hours by jeep if we hadn't hit Río Ora at high tide. You can avoid this by heading inland at Pueblo Nuevo, crossing the river on a bridge at Santa Marta, and heading down the coast again after the bridge. In the rainy season this route is impassable. It's best to go back to Paquera and Playa Naranjo, then on paved roads to Nicoya and then to Sámara and Nosara.

OROTINA AND ENVIRONS

Orotina, southeast of Puntarenas, is known mainly for its bountiful orchards—the best mangos come from there, and local farms produce papayas and avocados too. Fruit stands are all along the road throughout the area.

Just two kilometers from Orotina toward Atenas, the pleasant town of San Mateo is the setting for the U.S.-owned **Rancho Oropéndola** (private bath, heated water, ceiling fans, kitchen; $50-$60, including breakfast; phone/fax: 428-8600), a country hotel whose spacious cabins are set around a pool. The more expensive rooms have screen-enclosed terraces overlooking a green gorge.

Near Orotina in the tiny town of Cascajal is **Dundee Ranch Hotel** (private bath, hot water, ceiling fans and air conditioning, TV, pool, restaurant/bar; $80-$90, including breakfast; 267-6222, 428-8776, fax: 267-6229; www.dundee-ranch.com), a former cattle ranch with large tracts of tropical dry forest. Guests stay in a luxurious reconditioned ranch house and take excursions through the *finca* and mangroves on horseback or by tractor-tram. A lowland area on the grounds turns into a lake during the rainy season, and there is a boardwalk with decks for comfortable observation of water birds.

CARARA BIOLOGICAL RESERVE

Located near Orotina, Carara Biological Reserve is one of the closest wildlife observation spots to San José. It is in a transitional area between the dry climate of Guanacaste and the humid climate of the southern coast. It has wildlife common to both regions, including macaws, toucans, trogons, waterfowl, monkeys, crocodiles, armadillos, sloths, and peccaries. Jaguars, pumas, ocelots, margays, and jaguarundis are also present, but rarely seen. Birders stand on the bridge over the Río Tárcoles about 5 p.m. to witness the scarlet macaws' nightly migration from the Carara forest to the mangroves at the mouth of the river. You can see crocodiles from this bridge as well. No camping is allowed in the reserve. Tourists are only allowed on certain trails, but can go with professional guides into restricted areas. Many tour companies in San José and Playa Jacó offer guided tours to Carara. Your hotel can set one up for you. If you have a car, make sure that you leave it in a well-guarded spot, as there have been break-ins near Carara.

TÁRCOLES

Most people visit Carara on their way to or from the beaches south of there. But if you want to stay nearby, there are several options. In the fishing village of Tárcoles, about four kilometers from the entrance to Carara, **Cabinas Carara** (private bath, cold water, table fans, pool; $20-$30; 224-0096) are located across the street from the church, right on the ocean (but no one swims there since the water's dirty). There's a restaurant, pool, and Foosball tables. The grounds often flood when it rains.

Down a gravel road five kilometers north of Tárcoles is an important destination for any birdwatchers worth their binoculars: **Tárcol Lodge** (shared bath, hot water, table fans; $100-$110/person, including transportation, meals, and tours; phone/fax: 267-7138), built on the edge of a sandflat at the mouth of the Río Tárcoles. From the porch of this humble two-story, screened-in wooden house, you can watch the scarlet macaws fly into the mangroves across the flat every evening, and admire the hundreds of water birds that feed in the sandflat at low tide. Most guests are part of the week-long Rancho Naturalista package (see the Turrialba section of the Central Valley chapter), but overnight guests can often be accommodated here as well. Guests are encouraged to stay for at least three days so the guides can take them to Carara, on the Río Tárcoles, and to a nearby giant waterfall. Serious birdwatchers only.

The riverside complex at **Villa Lapas** (private bath, hot water, ceiling fans and air conditioning; $89/person, including meals, snacks, and drinks; 637-0232, fax: 637-0227; e-mail: hvlapas@racsa.co.cr) is composed of beautifully cared-for gardens, an open-air restaurant, a pool, and adobe-style rooms. The rooms are a bit stuffy and this deep river valley can be dank in the rainy season. The hotel protects a natural reserve that follows the Río Tarcolitos (there are two kilometers of trails), bordering Carara Biological Reserve to the south. It's easy to find: the sign is on the left as you head toward Jacó, and it's 600 meters from the highway turnoff.

If you continue up the Villa Lapas road, after about four kilometers you will come to the small community of **Bijagual**, where there is a 200-meter waterfall. The Vindas family (661-1787) conducts tours to the waterfall at 9 a.m. and 1 p.m. daily for $35, including a typical lunch and roundtrip transportation from Jacó. Camping facilities are available and there are several "natural jacuzzis" to cool off in. If you just want to hike (admission $10 for the 45-minute hike), call 236-4140 or fax 236-1506, atención Daniel Bedard. By bus, get off the Jacó bus at the Villa Lapas sign and hitchhike in. The local bus gets there too late for good hiking.

The backcountry near Bijagual is beautiful and unspoiled. **Arbofilia**, a widely respected organization specializing in grassroots ecological regeneration, operates a field station in the town of El Sur de Turrubares, a tiny village bordering Carara National Park, and five kilometers northwest of Bijagual. For hearty, hard workers with at least two weeks to spare, there are volunteer opportunities here. Call or fax them if you are interested, at 240-7145, or visit their website: www.sustainablefutures.com.

GETTING THERE: To reach Carara or Tárcoles by bus, take a Jacó or Quepos bus from San José or Puntarenas. Get out at the entrance to Carara, or for Tárcoles, at "Invu de Tárcoles." Walk 15 minutes into town (another hour at least to Tárcol Lodge). By car, you will pass the entrance to Carara on your left. For Tárcoles, turn right opposite the entrance to Villa Lapas, then right again at the T-intersection.

CENTRAL PACIFIC BEACHES

PUNTA LEONA   This unique development is striving to combine environmental conservation with intense tourist development. Seventy hectares of primary rainforest have been registered with the Ministry of Natural Resources as a private reserve, and the hotel has allowed Universidad Nacional researchers to build artificial nests for scarlet macaws in the forest. Researcher Chris Vaughn estimates that about 300 macaws may live in the Carara–Punta Leona area, with 16 or 17 chicks hatching each year. The nests at Punta Leona are protected from poachers to help this endangered bird population expand. Free guided nature walks are offered daily, as well as lectures on Costa Rican history, culture, and ecology.

You must drive through two gates and several kilometers of rainforest to reach **Selva Mar** (private bath, hot water, ceiling fans and air conditioning, phone, cable TV; $90-$100; 231-3131, fax: 232-0791; www.hotelpunta leona.com, e-mail: info@hotelpuntaleona.com), Punta Leona's jungle hotel. The three-story condo complex **Leona Mar** (suites with kitchens; $160-$230) is on a cliff above Playa Blanca. There are also one- and two-bedroom apartments ($90-$150). Guests have access to the two white-sand beaches, by far the most beautiful and clean in this area. The resort offers several pools, playing fields, basketball and volleyball courts, trails through the rainforest, several restaurants, a discotheque, and vans and buses to ferry you around from one point to another. For families with children of various ages and interests, Punta Leona could make everyone happy. Watch for the turnoff to Punta Leona on the right, a few kilometers south of Tárcoles.

VILLA CALETAS   Built in a charming French Colonial style and perched on a hilltop 1000 feet above the Pacific with magnificent views, **Villa Caletas** (private bath, hot water, air conditioning, ceiling fans, cable TV, phone; in main building, $150-$160; in more private villas, $200-$350; 257-3653, phone/fax: 222-2059; www.hotelvillacaletas.com, e-mail: caletas@ticonet. co.cr) is real elegance. Its two restaurants specialize in excellent French and international cuisine. The pool is constructed to form an optical illusion: looking across it, the division between pool and ocean blends in a deep blue. The 150-person Greek amphitheater has been the scene of many sunset weddings. Each luxury suite has its own crystal-clear swimming pool in a lush private garden (three-night honeymoon packages run $708-$1095 including breakfast, a champagne dinner, and transfers to and from San José). Villa Caletas sponsors an international classical music festival every year from July 25 to August 15. The entrance is between Punta Leona and Playa Herradura, then it's about three kilometers up on a paved but precipitous road. Recommended.

PLAYA HERRADURA   Besides Puntarenas and Punta Leona, Playas Jacó and Herradura are the closest swimmable beaches to San José. Playa Herradura is right after the Río Caña Blanca, about seven kilometers north of Jacó, and three kilometers down a paved road from the main highway. It is smaller than Jacó, its waves are gentler, and it has more shade and good trees for hammocks. The north side of the bay is now dominated by **Los Sueños**, a giant golf and tourism complex with a 200-slip marina, built by the Marriott chain. We must say that Marriott in Costa Rica has proven to be a creative and dynamic force, and Los Sueños is no exception. Before they even began digging the foundations for the condos, they hired a biologist and planted trees that attract scarlet macaws. Half of their 1100-acre property will remain untouched. The golf course is being built following recommendations from the Audubon Society and will be free of chemical pesticides. They work in conjunction with the public school in Jacó to teach English and provide training in tourism. We hope that the other complexes springing up all over Costa Rica's Pacific coast will follow their example.

Los Sueños Marriott Beach and Golf Resort (private bath, hot water, air conditioning, ceiling fans, pool; $220-$240; 298-0000, fax: 298-0033; www.marriotthotels.com) is patterned after a Spanish colonial village and displays all the fine attention to detail that characterizes the San José Marriott.

Some low-cost cabinas are still hanging around the south side of the bay: **Cabinas Herradura** (private bath, cold water, air conditioning or ceiling fans, kitchen; $7-$12/person; 643-3181, fax: 643-3578), on the beach, are modest, family-style accommodations. Some cabinas have room for five people. **Cabañas del Río** (private bath, cold water, table fans, kitchen, restaurant; $12-$20; phone/fax: 643-3275), neat *casitas* with two bedrooms upstairs and a small porch, are about 200 meters from the beach. They rent a boat for fishing or snorkeling trips.

Soda y Baños Juanita is a friendly place to stop for a meal. Open all day, every day.

GETTING THERE: See below under Jacó for bus directions. Get off at the entrance to Herradura; taxis wait for the bus, or the owner of Cabinas Herradura will pick you up if you call. By car, watch for the turnoff about 13 kilometers south of the Tárcoles turnoff, after you descend from the high point where the Villa Caletas road branches off.

PLAYA JACÓ   Playa Jacó has not been known as an ecotourism destination. It had a "fun and sun" reputation, and, as the closest readily accessible beach to San José, that is still true. But people are starting to plant trees and flowers that attract birds and butterflies, and there are many tours in the area that will connect you to nature. For instance, **Escuela del Mundo** (643-1064; www.speakcostarica.com) lets you earn college credit for a four weeks of Spanish lessons interspersed with hiking, horseback riding, kayaking, and sessions on travel safety and planning, Costa Rican foods, history, culture, flora and fauna, salsa dancing, and more. It's a great way to get to know the country in a congenial setting. One- and two-week courses are also offered, but not for credit. Students live in attractive but very inexpensive quarters at the school (see below), which is within walking distance of the beach and downtown. Other packages for families, surfers, and artists are available. Recommended.

Kayak Jacó ($45 for a half-day tour; phone/fax: 643-1233; www.kayak jaco.com, e-mail: neilka@racsa.co.cr) takes you to a secluded, gentle beach for a paddle along the coastline combined with snorkeling, or to the Río Tulín, where you sit on top of the kayaks and drift down the shallow river where birds and crocodiles abound. No experience necessary. This tour is great for families, but bring sun-hats and sunscreen. For those who want more, advanced instruction in sea and whitewater kayaking is available. **Diana** (643-3808) is an energetic and knowledgeable guide on her horseback tour of forests, beaches, and waterfalls out of nearby Playa Hermosa ($35), where you can also glide through the forest canopy (see "Playa Hermosa" section, below).

Ocean Adventures (phone/fax: 643-1885, 643-1305; e-mail: fishjaco@ racsa.co.cr) boats you to Tortuga Island for snorkeling and a picnic lunch, with plenty of chances to fish along the way ($400 for up to six people). They customize trips for families and provide transport to Tambor and Montezuma. Fishing trips cost $325 for a half day. Billfishing is good near Jacó and costs $550/day. In the dry season scuba diving is rewarding and they have a state-of-the-art surface-supplied air system—a 150-foot hose that connects you to the boat so you can dive in 15- to 20-foot water where decompression is not a problem and PADI certification is not necessary ($250 for four people).

J.D.'s Watersports (257-3857, 800-477-8971; www.centralamerica.com/ cr/tours/jd.htm), based in Punta Leona, picks you up at your hotel and takes you on a Jungle River Cruise, exploring the Tarcoles River and mangrove estuary. They can also teach you to scuba dive or take you sportfishing or on a cruise at sunset.

Surfers use Jacó as a base for trips to nearby beaches like **Boca Barranca** (a very long left), **Playas Tivives** and **Valor** (rights and lefts), **Escondida** (accessible by boat from Herradura), **Playa Hermosa** (the site of an annual surfing contest—very strong beach break, three kilometers south of Jacó), and **Playas Esterillos Este**, **Esterillos Oeste**, **Bejuco**, and **Boca Damas**, which are all on the way to Quepos. Many hotels give surfers discounts from May to December, and there are several surfing teachers in town.

Note: It's not wise to swim in the estuary or near river mouths. The rip currents at Playa Jacó can be dangerous, as can sudden large waves. People drown there each year. The southern end of the beach is cleanest and safest.

RESTAURANTS   In northern Jacó, **Hotel Copacabana** shows NFL and college football, serves draft beer and seafood cuisine, and has jam sessions on Saturday nights. In central Jacó, **Rene's Euro Deli** (across from the Tropical Paradise; 643-1747) sells imported cured meats, cheeses, chocolates and baked goods. **Padang-Padang** (open 7 a.m. to 9 p.m.; closed Monday; next to the Fuji film center; 643-1848) is named after a famous surfing beach in Indonesia and is decorated with artwork and wood carvings from that area. The Colombian owners make fish in coconut sauce, oriental food, and vegetarian specialties. **Planet Jacó** (open daily in high season, 1 p.m. to 10 p.m.), on the corner of Calle Bohio, has tasty roast chicken. Down the street, past the Centro El Paso, **Wishbone** (open 11:30 a.m. to 3 p.m. and 5 p.m. to 10 p.m.; closed Wednesday; 643-3406), is a popular restaurant that shows surfing videos and serves hearty portions of pizza, burritos, chimichangas, and stuffed potatoes. **Maravillas Naturales** (643-1113) offers internet access, bicycle rentals and homemade ice cream and smoothies on weekends. **Marisquería El Recreo**, across from the Mas por Menos, is good for Tico-style seafood. **Chatty Cathy's**, next door, serves the kind of breakfast or lunch surfers need to keep them going all day. **Disco La Central** is down the next street, a block from **Terraza El Hicaco** (643-3226), a beachside seafood restaurant.

Heading into the southern section of town, the simple, typical **Estrella de David** near the bridge serves good, cheap meals. For casual fine dining on the oceanfront, visit **Las Sandalias Restaurant** (open daily, 7 a.m. to 2:30 p.m.; Friday through Sunday, 6 p.m. to 8 p.m.) at the Club del Mar, all the way at the end of the beach. Part of the charm of Las Sandalias is the possibility of engaging in conversation with the owners, knowledgeable world travelers Philip, Marilyn, and Simon Edwardes. Recommended.

CAR RENTALS   Now that the road between Jacó and Quepos is improved, the possibility of staying in lower-priced Jacó and making day trips to Manuel Antonio (90 minutes one way) is more feasible. There are plenty of car rental agencies in Jacó, and the driving is less nerve-racking because the roads are relatively straight and flat and in good condition. **Zuma Rent-acar** (phone/fax: 643-3207; e-mail: zumaway@racsa.co.cr) in central Jacó has good rates and is responsive to clients' needs. **Elegante Car Rental** (643-3224; e-mail: elegante@racsa.co.cr) is also a good bet. There is a gas station on the main highway near the southern entrance of town. We have heard complaints about Economy Rentacar.

SERVICES   South of Elegante Rentacar, **Souvenir Cocobolo** (643-3486) has a wide variety of souvenirs and rents surf boards, bikes, motorcycles, beach umbrellas, boogie boards, and snorkeling equipment.

The **International Phone Center** (open 7 a.m. to noon, 1 p.m. to 7 p.m.; 643-3094), behind Zuma Rentacar, lets you make international calls and send faxes with or without a calling card, as do **AR Internet Service**, across from Ferretería Macavi, and **ICE**. The **Serenity Spa** (open 9 a.m. to 6 p.m.; closed Sunday; 643-1624), behind Zuma Rentacar, offers massage, facials, salt-glows, and volcanic mud treatments.

For day trippers, **Camping Madrigal** rents showers and changing rooms at the southern end of the beach. **Puro Blanco Laundry** (643-1025) will pick up your clothes at your hotel and return them clean and nicely folded. In the center of town, the **Rayo Azul** supermarket is a good source for groceries; they also have an ice cream stand in front. Next door, **Ciclo Jacó** rents bikes ($1.50/hour).

LODGING   There are plenty of hotels, cabinas, and campsites in Jacó. Many have kitchenettes complete with utensils. Although Jacó does not have the dramatic views that you see from the hills near Manuel Antonio, it has many more lodgings that are right on the beach. So if you like the sound of the waves, you might prefer Jacó. Just make sure you're not within earshot of Disco La Central. Most hotels give substantial discounts during the off-season, and Jacó is often sunny when it's raining in San José. All of the following establishments are off Jacó's main boulevard, which runs parallel to the beach. We'll mention them in order of their appearance, north to south.

The German-owned **Hotel Pochote Grande** (private bath, hot water, ceiling fans, refrigerator, pool; $60-$70; 643-3236, fax: 220-4979; www.centralamerica.com, e-mail: pochote@racsa.co.cr) has a restaurant, shady grounds, and good-sized rooms with lots of windows.

Cabinas Antonio (private bath, heated water, ceiling fans; $20-$30; 643-3043) is clean, relatively quiet, and a good bargain for this area.

South along the boulevard is **Hotel Best Western Jacó Beach** (private bath, hot water, air conditioning, satellite TV; $100-$110; 643-1000; www.bestwestern.co.cr), which features a large, doughnut-shaped pool; a discotheque and a noisy bar on the beach; tennis and volleyball courts; and rentals of cars, bikes, mopeds, and surfboards. Between members of the hotel's club and the numerous Canadians who arrive on special charters, this hotel is one of the busiest all year. **Jacó Princess** (private bath, hot water, ceiling fans, air conditioning, kitchens, satellite TV, pool; $120-$130; 643-1000, in the U.S.: 800-948-3770; www.centralamerica.com/cr/hotel/jacobch.htm) is a dense condo development next door. Between the hotel and the condos is a shopping center with a modern branch of the Banco de Costa Rica, a tie-dye shop, fast-food and ice-cream joints, and the **Zarpe Bar**, recommended for its good *bocas*. This is also the San José bus stop and ticket office.

Across the Río Copey and inland a bit are the tranquil, nicely designed cottages that make up **Villas Estrellamar** (private bath, hot water, pool, TV, phone, ping-pong; with ceiling fans, $40-$50; with air conditioning or kitchens, $60-$70, rates include breakfast; 643-3102, fax: 643-3453; www.hotels.co.cr/estrellamar).

One of the least expensive and best places to stay is at the **Escuela del Mundo** (private bath, ceiling fan, kitchenette, pool, $20; $80/person/week double occupancy; 643-1064; www.speakcostarica.com) if they have room between study sessions. Better yet, take a session yourself (see description above). The attractive rooms are located in a residential neighborhood on the east side of town.

The Austrian-owned **Villas Miramar** (private bath, hot water, ceiling fans, kitchen, pools; $60-$70, including breakfast; 643-3003, fax: 643-3617; www.hotels.co.cr/miramar), in a garden setting, is one of the loveliest and most tranquil places in Jacó. It is located down the next road to your right. **Apartotel Flamboyant** (private bath, hot water, ceiling fans, kitchen; $40-$50; 643-3146; fax: 643-1068; www.accommodations.co.cr) is tastefully designed and right on the beach.

The road going inland will take you to **Las Gaviotas** (private bath, heated water, ceiling fans, cable TV, kitchens; $60-$70; 643-3092, fax: 643-3054), which has clean and pretty rooms for five people, with patios and a pool.

Camping El Hicaco ($2.50/person in your own tent; 643-3004) has campsites near the beach and an oceanside restaurant specializing in seafood. Just south, on the beach, is **Aparthotel Girasol** (private bath, hot water, ceiling fans, air conditioning, kitchens, pool; $90-$100, kids under 12 free; 643-1591, in the U.S. 800-923-2779; www.girasol.com), which offers modern one-bedroom apartments that sleep four.

Cabinas Alice (private bath, heated water, ceiling fans; $30-$40; with kitchens, $40-$50; 643-3061) are toward the beach from the Red Cross. Doña Alice's husband, Don Antonio, cooks good food that's served by their son at shady outdoor tables.

Apartotel Sole d'Oro (private bath, hot water, ceiling fans, pool, kitchen; with ceiling fans, $60-$70; with air conditioning, $70-$80; 643-3441, phone/fax: 643-3172) is a row of neat apartments parallel to the beach, but half a block away, with a pool and grassy area at the end. Half a block toward the beach, **Apartamentos El Mar** (private bath, hot water, ceiling fans, kitchen, pool; $20-$30; 643-3165, fax: 272-2280) are secure, clean, and spacious.

The main boulevard veers inland heading toward the Quepos highway. Turn right at the church to enter Jacó's more peaceful southern section. Across from the unsightly tower of the Jacofiesta are **Chalets Santa Ana** (private bath, hot water, ceiling fans, screens; $20-$30 for up to three people; with kitchen and room for five, $40-$50; phone/fax: 643-3233), basic rooms with a pool—a good deal for groups.

The peaceful **El Colibrí** (private bath, solar-heated water, ceiling fans, pool, jacuzzi; $40-$50; phone/fax: 643-3419, 643-3770, fax: 643-3730) stretches from the road to the beach, and offers clean, spacious rooms. Hammocks are strung outdoors under shady ranchos.

Kangaroo (private bath, hot water, ceiling fans, pool; $30-$50, including breakfast; phone/fax: 643-3351) is a hostel-type place owned by a dynamic young German who escorts his guests on mountain-biking adventures and rents bikes. His restaurant specializes in European favorites like crêpes.

La Paloma Blanca (private bath, hot water, ceiling fans, some kitchens, some air conditioning, pools; $40-$80; 643-1893, fax: 643-1892; e-mail: iwann@mailcity.com) has spacious, nicely designed rooms with verandas overlooking the beach.

Camping Madrigal ($2.50/person; 643-3521) has shaded campsites with toilets, showers, makeshift tables, and barbecue pits.

On a quiet cove at the southern end of the beach is the **Club del Mar** (phone/fax: 643-3194). The "economy" apartments (private bath, heated water, ceiling fans, kitchen; $60-$70) we stayed in are comfortable and spacious. "Standard" rooms ($70-$80; $5 extra for air conditioning) differ in that they have hot water from a tank and optional air conditioning. But if you can, splurge for a "superior" room (hot water, bathtubs, refrigerator, air conditioning, no children under 14; $80-$90)—these are tastefully decorated and have private balconies with lovely sea views. There is a good restaurant, a pool, a dartboard, and even a book and game library. Swimming is probably safer here than at any other part of the beach. Highly recommended.

GETTING THERE: By Bus: San José–Jacó buses (223-5567; $2) leave the Coca Cola at 7:30 a.m., 10:30 a.m., and 3:30 p.m., returning at 5 a.m., 11 a.m., and 3 p.m. They add extra buses on holidays and weekends. The trip takes three hours. When the bus arrives in Jacó, it makes a big loop along the boulevard from south to north, so you can get off at your hotel/campground of choice. Buy your ticket back to San José a day or two before you want to leave, because (especially on weekends) return tickets go fast. And get to the bus stop (across from the Best Western) early on weekends, because you'll be waiting with a big crowd of *Joséfinos*. Buses leave Jacó for Quepos at 6:30 a.m., 12:30 p.m., and 4 p.m., returning from Quepos at 4:30 a.m., 10:30 a.m., and 3 p.m. Catch Puntarenas–Quepos buses to Jacó at 5 a.m., 11 a.m., or 2:30 p.m. near the former Puntarenas train station. They return to Puntarenas at 6:30 a.m., 12:30 p.m., and 5 p.m. Catch these buses across from the Mas por Menos.

Fantasy Tours (in Costa Rica, 800-326-8279) runs a daily bus between San José and Jacó, with connections to Liberia and Tamarindo, for $19 per trip. Guests at the Best Western Jacó Beach pay $15. They also have connecting buses from Jacó to Arenal, Liberia, Playa Flamingo, and Tamarindo ($19).

By Car: Herradura and Jacó are a two-hour drive from San José on a winding road through beautiful countryside. Take the Atenas turnoff on the Interamerican Highway to Puntarenas. The road is in fairly good repair most of the way through the mountains and offers some magnificent views. Near Orotina, you can buy watermelon, mangos, and sugarcane juice. After Orotina, the road becomes a four-lane highway for a few miles. Be careful when a median forms at underpasses, as you can easily get in the wrong lane if you're not alert. After the turnoff for Jacó (again, pay attention—it's easy to miss it and find yourself en route to Caldera/ Puntarenas), the road becomes a two-lane highway again, with sea views on one side and green rice fields on the other. You'll pass the entrance to Carara Biological Reserve (see above) about 20 minutes before Jacó. If you feel more comfortable with less-winding roads, continue west along the Interamerican Highway from San José all the way to Puntarenas, then drive south to Jacó. You can continue on to Quepos (70 kilometers farther), Dominical, and points farther south on the same road.

PLAYA HERMOSA   Surfers like Playa Hermosa for its consistent, strong break. There are southern swells between April and December, with the biggest waves in June and July. All the lodgings here are right on the beach. This is not a good beach for children because of the wild waves.

La Terraza del Pacífico (private bath, hot water, air conditioning, adult and children's pools; $90-$100 for up to three people; 643-3222, fax: 643-3424; www.terraza-del-pacifico.com) is a nicely decorated hotel with strong lights for night surfing, an attractive restaurant and a pool with a bar in the middle. They are the base for **Chiclet's Tree Tour**, a cable-glide between 14 platforms suspended in the treetops 60 to 132 feet above the forest floor ($55).

Fuego del Sol (private bath, hot water, ceiling fans, air conditioning, pool; $80-$90 including breakfast; kids under 12 free; 643-3737, fax: 643-3736; www.fuegodelsol.com) is our favorite at Playa Hermosa. The well-designed rooms have balconies and fanciful decorations on the walls, the gardens are lovely, and there is a world-class gym. They have a week-long package ($650/person double occupancy including two meals/day and airport pickup) that takes surfers to different beaches in the area.

Las Olas (private bath, heated water, ceiling fans, kitchens, pool; $30-$50; 643-3687; www.cabinaslasolas.com) is a friendly, gringo-run surfers' hostel with some rooms in the main house and a row of thatched A-frames. There's also a small restaurant on the beach. Next door **Vista Hermosa** (private bath, heated water, ceiling fans, air conditioning, kitchens, pool; $30-$40; 643-3373; www.surf-hermosa.com) offers rooms for up to eight. **The Backyard** (open Thursday through Sunday, noon to midnight; 643-3936) is a breezy bar and restaurant overlooking the waves. **Natural Mystic** (closed Monday) is a soda and mini-market next door.

GETTING THERE: Playa Hermosa is ten minutes by car from the south end of Jacó. Without a car, walk, hitch, or wait for a Quepos bus on the main road.

ESTERILLOS ESTE   A rough beach 27 kilometers south of Jacó, Esterillos Este is home to some peaceful French Canadian–run retreats. Just 20 minutes south of Jacó and 45 minutes north of Manuel Antonio, this area would be a great base for trips to both with plenty of tranquility in between. **Auberge du Pélican** (hot water, ceiling fans, pool; shared bath, $30-$40; private bath, $40-$50; fax: 779-9236; www.aubergedupelican.homestead.com) is a well-designed place to go when you really need a break. They pay attention to detail in a way that many places don't: the main lodge is totally screened in; two cabins, the restaurant, and the grounds are wheelchair accessible; and rooms have built-in counters and benches. The restaurant serves lots of fresh fruit and salads, and there's a shuffleboard court and board games. The owners or local fishermen will take guests out for fishing trips. Recommended. **Flor de Esterillos** (private bath, hot water, ceiling fans, kitchenettes, pool, restaurant; $40-$50; fax: 779-9141) is a cluster of spacious cabins connected by sidewalks and surrounded by flowering bushes. Their **Restaurante Tulú** (open 8 a.m. to 8 p.m.) is a great place to have a relaxed lunch.

GETTING THERE: By Bus: The San José–Quepos or Puntarenas–Quepos buses will drop you off at the entrance to town. See Quepos "Getting There" for schedules.

By Car: The beach is one kilometer off the highway. The turnoff is clearly marked.

By Plane: See Quepos for SANSA and Travelair schedules.

PLAYA PALO SECO   Just south of the town of Parrita, five kilometers off the Costanera, **Palo Seco** is home to another French retreat, **El Beso del Viento** (private bath, heated water, fans, kitchens, pool, cable TV; $50-$60; 779-9674, fax: 779-9575; e-mail: bviento@racsa.co.cr). The attractive apartments have spacious, tiled kitchens and good cross-ventilation. They sleep up to six people ($100). The Parisian owners offer kayaks and bikes for rent, and there is a lovely pool. Children are welcome. The owners have two teen-age boys, and the whole family seems to be enjoying their little paradise.

GETTING THERE: Take the San José–Quepos or Puntarenas–Quepos bus (see below in the "Quepos" section), and get off at Parrita. Take a taxi from Parrita to Playa Palo Seco (about $4). By car, follow signs five kilometers down a pretty good gravel road from Parrita. Palo Seco is about a half hour's drive from Esterillos Este.

QUEPOS AND MANUEL ANTONIO

Before you get to the inspiring vistas of Manuel Antonio, you pass through the bustling former United Fruit banana port of **Quepos**, where lodging is general less expensive and cleaner than the low-cost alternatives near the beach. It's about another three miles to the reason why you're here: Manuel Antonio National Park.

When you first glimpse the sea from the hills above Manuel Antonio, the word "paradise" might cross your mind. These hills have become one of Costa Rica's most elegant destinations. **Manuel Antonio National Park**, one of the smallest in the country, is the area's crowning glory. The park is one of the few remaining habitats of the *mono tití* (squirrel monkey). According to *The Tico Times*, the 682-hectare park "cannot sustain a big enough *tití* population to avoid inbreeding. The only chance of survival this unique species has is to breed with neighboring troupes outside the park. However, rapid development that has taken place around the park . . . is leaving the monkeys increasingly isolated from each other." Added to this is the problem that lands within the national park are currently for sale, because the government has not yet paid for them. New tourism projects are under construction at the entrance to the park on filled-in wetlands. The area is still beautiful, but for the above reasons we will not mention large tourism projects in this area.

Howler and white-faced monkeys, two-toed sloths, coatimundis, and raccoons frequent the beaches, which are shaded by leafy trees. Manuel Antonio includes one of the best beaches on Costa Rica's Pacific coast for swimming and snorkeling, as well as trails where you can hike for at least a full day.

The wedge-shaped piece of land that is now Cathedral Point was once an island. A neck of land connects it to the beach. This rare phenomenon is known as a *tombolo*: a deposit of sand that builds up over thousands of years and finally connects an island to the mainland. North-flowing currents pushed water and sand through the opening between the island and the beach, and then flowed on to Punta Quepos, farther north, which forced the water back. The sand-bridge was formed after about 100,000 years of this action. Grass and shrubs gained a foothold on it, followed by the present-day trees that keep the formation from returning to the sea. The Manuel Antonio tombolo is one of the most perfect in the world.

The indigenous people who lived in Manuel Antonio 1000 years ago observed that while female green turtles were laying their eggs in the sand at high tide, the male turtles were waiting for them in the water. They fashioned balsawood models of female turtles to attract the males into an area surrounded by rocks. The males would stay with the decoy females and be trapped by the rocks when the tide went out. These pre-Columbian turtle traps are still visible on either end of Manuel Antonio Beach at low tide.

A trail takes you through the jungle to the top of Cathedral Point, where you can look down the vertical cliffs to the blue ocean 300 feet below. You start from Playa Espadilla Sur (the second beach) and take a circular route, about an hour from start to finish. At low tide, you can also begin or end on Playa Manuel Antonio, the third beach. The trail is very steep in some parts and muddy and slippery in the rainy season, so don't go alone. Sandals are probably the most appropriate footwear.

Snorkeling is a rewarding adventure at Manuel Antonio. In the dry season, when the water is clear, you'll see iridescent, peacock-colored fish, conservative pin-striped fish, and outrageous yellow fish with diaphanous capes, all going in and out between the coral rocks—especially at Playa Escondida, a half-hour walk beyond Playa Manuel Antonio. Fins and a mask are all you need. If you burn easily, watch out—you'll lose track of time staring at the fish while the sun is reddening your back. It's best to wear a T-shirt in addition to waterproof sunblock.

Manuel Antonio

The entrance to the park is a 200-meter walk south of the end of the Quepos–Manuel Antonio road, and is clearly indicated ($6). You have to cross a stream that changes width and depth with the tides. Try to go at low tide, because you have to wade across. Around high tide the water is waist-high. Locals will take you across in small rowboats (40 cents/person). Be sure to take food and water with you into the park, because it is a hassle to go in and out. If you do wish to leave the park for lunch, the ranger will stamp your hand so you can re-enter without paying again.

Camping is no longer allowed within the park.

Note: Do not leave your belongings unattended on the beach. If anyone offers to guide you through remote areas of the park, they should have an official ID card, or be in a park service uniform. Perhaps more of a risk than *ladrones* are the white-faced monkeys on the beach. They have become very bold about stealing food and will grab your backpack and carry it up into a tree if you don't keep an eye on them. When they are through investigating your bags, they will unceremoniously drop them—not good for cameras or binoculars.

If you long to visit this still-beautiful area, try to go in the off-season (May through November). As we've stated elsewhere, you'll still have most of the day to play, you can relax with a book in your hammock if it rains, there are substantial discounts on lodging in most hotels, and you'll be able to enjoy Manuel Antonio in its more pristine, uncrowded state.

For good updated information on Quepos and Manuel Antonio, look for www.maqbeach.co.cr; www.manuelantoniopark.com; or www.biesanz.com on the web.

ACTIVITIES **Quepolandia** (777-1984; e-mail: oasisme@racsa.co.cr) is the English-language newspaper for the Quepos-Matapalo-Dominical area. They run a helpful information center near the Banco Bar and publish a restaurant guide. Read their online version at www.quepolandia.com. **La Buena Nota** (open 8 a.m. to 5 p.m.; 777-0345, 777-1002) is a well-stocked beachwear and gift shop that sells *The Tico Times* and *The New York Times* and publishes a useful pamphlet with a map of the area, current bus schedules, and tips on water safety. It's on the Manuel Antonio road, close to the beach between Karahé Hotel and Cabinas Piscis.

Iguana Tours (777-1262, phone/fax: 777-0850, fax: 777-0574) offers sea-kayaking ($65) and whitewater-rafting ($60-$85) tours down the Río Savegre as well as sportfishing and horseback tours. The offices are across from the soccer field in Quepos. **Equus Stables** (777-0001) can take you on a two-hour guided mountain-and-beach horseback tour ($35). The full-day **Canopy Safari** ($80, including breakfast, fruit snacks, and lunch) swings you through the treetops over a waterfall and pool that you can swim in later.

The **Pura Vida** (777-0909, fax: 777-0779; $45) cruiser leaves the Quepos dock daily at 3 p.m. Kick back with drinks, grilled chicken, dancing and tropical fruit as the boat cruises to Biesanz beach, where they stop for a swim or snorkel. Then the captain heads out in search of dolphins. On the way back, the boat stops again for guests to savor the moment the sun drops into the sea.

Now, thanks to several new projects, you can combine learning about the rainforest with your trip to Manuel Antonio; you could spend your whole vacation there. **Rainmaker**, run by Si Como No, is a private 1500-acre reserve protecting part of the Quepoa biological corridor used by migrating birds and animals. It also protects the streams that supply some of Manuel Antonio's water. In a well-run tour, visitors learn about rainforest botany on a guided hike along one of these streams to several magnificent waterfalls, ending at a swimming hole. Suspension bridges strung between giant trees give a bird's-eye view of the rainforest ($65 including transportation, lunch, and tropical fruit snacks; 777-1250).

In **Londres**, 13 kilometers inland from Quepos, **Brisas del Nara** (779-1235, 779-1049) offers horseback tours to nearby waterfalls ($48, including transportation, breakfast, and lunch; $38 half day). They have special horses for kids. Nearby, **Quinta Tucan B&B** (private bath, heated water; $55, including three meals; phone/fax: 779-1379) has excellent birdwatching from the porches of its cabins on the banks of the rushing Río Naranjo. While there, you can visit a family-run organic spice farm or hike through nearby rainforest reserves.

Run by an agricultural cooperative that has been together since the early 1970s, **El Silencio** (private bath, some heated water; 771-1938, phone/fax: 779-9545, cellular: 380-5581; www.agroecoturismo.net, e-mail: cooprena@racsa.co.cr) is a fledgling eco-tourism project, about an hour inland from Manuel Antonio, that also protects the watershed. They work with Jardín Gaia (below) as a release point for green and scarlet macaws. They have a breezy restaurant, clean cabins, nature trails, orchid propagation projects, and a butterfly garden. Volunteers pay $70 a week. To get there, turn left at kilometer 22 of the Quepos-Dominical road, and continue another six very bumpy kilometers to the village of El Silencio.

Jardín Gaia (daily tours at 9 a.m. and 4 p.m.; 775-0535, 777-1004; www.csn.ul.ie~gwh/jg, e-mail: wildlife@racsa.co.cr), on the Manuel Antonio road, is a conservation project for many endangered species. The animals have been confiscated from poachers. Educational material provided at the cages describes Jardín Gaia's impressive program to rehabilitate their patients and (when possible) reintroduce them to their natural habitats. Recommended. The Jardín needs volunteers. See Chapter Two for more information.

SOUVENIRS   **L'Aventura**, across the street from the Hotel Kamuk, displays tasteful and creative clothes, pottery, wood, leather and jewelry, and **Romero**, a few doors down, also sells local crafts. **Regalame** (pronounced ray-ga-la-may: a very Costa Rican way of saying "give me") is another popular gift shop located next to La Marquesa Restaurant on the oceanfront. They have another branch in the small shopping center next to the Si Como No in Manuel Antonio. Two blocks north of the soccer field in Quepos is **La Botánica** (closed Sunday; phone/fax: 777-1223), an enticing shop that sells packets of organically grown herbs and spices such as vanilla, cinnamon, cardamon, and pepper. While you're looking around you can sip a cup of their tea *du jour*. If you're under the weather, they might be able to mix up an herbal remedy. If you're interested in the workings of a self-sustainable farm, you can drive or take a taxi to their place near Londres, several kilometers inland. The U.S. expatriate who owns it will show you around. His wife, a friendly, bilingual Tica, runs the shop; ask her for directions.

Development is occurring in Manuel Antonio at an alarming rate. Some students at the local private elementary school have created the **Amazing Arts Art Gallery** (at the Hotel Mono Azul; 777-2252), where they sell their artwork to raise money for buying land so the birds and monkeys they love can still have a home. So far they've bought two acres of this pricey real estate, and have launched an Adopt-a-Tree program: you buy a tree as a gift or in memory of someone, they plant it and send a picture to you or the giftee. They've got lots of other ideas for linking with school-age kids around the world. See their website: www.amazingarts.org.

LANGUAGE SCHOOLS   **Escuela de Idiomas D'Amore** (phone/fax: 777-1143; www.escueladamore.com, e-mail: damore@racsa.co.cr) offers a Spanish immersion course in a pleasant building overlooking the sea on the road to Manuel Antonio. Students are housed with local families in not-so-elegant Quepos. If you have the discipline to study in such a heady tropical environment, this school might be a great learning vacation. At least one correspondent was very pleased with it.

SPORTFISHING   *Marlin Magazine* named Quepos the second best location in the world for "all around action." **HighTec Sportfishing** (cell phone: 388-6617, 777-1682 nights) will take you out, and The Banco Bar, El Gran Escape, and the Dos Locos (see below) will cook your catch.

IMPORTANT NUMBERS   *Hospital*: 777-1397, 777-0020; *Red Cross*: 777-0118; *Police*: 117 or 777-0196; *OIJ* (investigative police): 777-0511; *Taxi*: ASOTAQUEPOS: 777-1693, 777-1068; 777-0425; 777-1191, 777-0734

CAR RENTALS   You really do not need a car once you are in Manuel Antonio, because buses are frequent and taxis are cheap ($4-$10 to go anywhere in the area). But if you want to fly here and rent a car to drive down the coast, Elegante (777-0115, in the U.S.: 800-283-1324) is the only agency with an office in town (next to Café Milagro in Quepos). They will meet you at the plane or at your hotel. It costs about $30 extra to drop the car off in San José. Adobe Rentacar also will deliver a car to you in Quepos (www.adobecar.com).

LAUNDROMATS   The **Casa Tica**, in the Mercado at the bus station, will do your laundry for you. There is a coin-op laundry near the beginning of the Manuel Antonio road, just as you start to go up.

LODGING, RESTAURANTS, AND NIGHTLIFE

QUEPOS LODGING   Low-cost lodging in the town of Quepos is cleaner and more comfortable than many of the cheapest rooms near the beach—with some exceptions. Unfortunately, theft is becoming more and more common. Many hotels are putting in security boxes for valuables; be sure and use one if you can. People boarding the Manuel Antonio bus in Quepos are common targets. A taxi to Manuel Antonio from Quepos costs about $4, or about half that if you hail it when it's coming back to Quepos. Lodging and dining facilities extend from the airport five kilometers east of Quepos through town and south along the seven-kilometer road to Manuel Antonio. Whether or not you have a car should not determine how you choose your hotel, as it does in other areas, because there is frequent bus service between Quepos and Manuel Antonio. We list hotels and restaurants according to location. Note: The beach at Quepos is polluted. Do not swim there.

The ✪ **Hotel Rancho Casa Grande** (private bath, hot water, fans, air conditioning, phones, cable TV, restaurant, pool, jacuzzi; $120-$130; 777-0330, 777-1646, 777-1020, fax: 777-1575; www.accommodations.co.cr) is owned by the family of one of Quepos' first pioneers. It is known for attentive service and the owners' hospitality. It features rows of tastefully decorated one- and two-bedroom *casitas* bordering a grassy area and pool. The grounds include a 180-acre gallery forest (secondary and primary growth) with level, self-guided nature trails, a pool and jacuzzi, and a pricey but excellent restaurant. Rancho Casa Grande is outside Quepos, across the road from the airport, but shuttle vans take guests to Manuel Antonio or Quepos upon request.

The following lodgings are located roughly between the bus station and the waterfront. This is the bustling section of Quepos. This area is also convenient to supermarkets. Rooms in Quepos tend to be noisy, so bring earplugs.

Hotel Ramus (private bath, cold water, table fans; $12-$20; phone/fax: 777-0245) has a nice plant-filled balcony, but the rooms are a bit dark. Across the street are two more hotels. **Hotel Melisa** (private bath, cold water, wall fans; $12-$20; phone/fax: 777-0025) is well maintained; there's an ice cream parlor out front. **Hotel Malinche** (private bath; with cold water, ceiling fans, $12-$20; with hot water, air conditioning, $20-$40; phone/fax: 777-0093) has two types of rooms—nice older wooden ones for less, and carpeted ones (some with balconies) for more.

The luxurious waterfront **Hotel Kamuk** (private bath, hot water, air conditioning, phones; $70-$180, including breakfast; 777-0379; fax: 777-0258; www.maqbeach.com), provides a break from the sleepy, banana-port-of-the-past feeling of Quepos. A casino, a pool, and an international restaurant top off the amenities.

Hotel Sirena (private bath, hot water, air conditioning, restaurant, pool; $50-$60; children under 12 free; 777-0528, fax: 777-0171) is a small, comfortable hotel run by two helpful brothers. It's half a block off the waterfront up the first street after the bridge into town. Besides the Hotel Kamuk, it has the only pool in downtown Quepos.

The following places are away from the waterfront. First we'll talk about those north of the soccer field.

On the northwest corner of the soccer field, near the post office, **Cabinas Doña Alicia** (private or shared bath, cold water, ceiling fans; $7-$20; 777-0419) are recommended for their cleanliness and the friendly owners. Some of the cabinas have three rooms, handy for families.

El Cisne (private bath, heated water, wall fans, refrigerator, TV; $20-$30; 777-0719, 777-1570), two blocks north of the church, has psychedelic cement floors. Kitty-corner from El Cisne is **Ramacé** (private bath, cold water, table fans, refrigerator; $12-$20; with air conditioning, $20-$30; 777-0590), with spacious, bright rooms next to the owners' house.

Across from the bus station, a local family runs the **Hotel Sánchez** (shared or private bath, heated water, wall fans; $7-$12; 777-0491). The rooms are simple but roomy.

Now we come to the hotels south of the soccer field, along the road in Quepos to Manuel Antonio. If you stay at one of these places, you can wave down the Manuel Antonio bus along the way, or ask at the hotel where to wait for it.

Closest to the waterfront are the **Cabinas Hellen** (private bath, cold water, ceiling fans, refrigerator; $20-$30; 777-0504), built off the back of a family's house, with a nice atmosphere.

On a street that branches off to the right is **Villas Cruz** (777-0271, fax: 777-1081). They rent one villa for up to six people on the hill right above their house (private bath, ceiling fans, kitchen, TV; $40-$50) with stairs that may not be suitable for small children, and several rooms next door to their home (private bath, cold water, ceiling fans, refrigerator; $20-$30).

Hotel Quepos (shared and private baths, cold water, ceiling fans; $12-$20; 777-0274) has small, second-story rooms with hardwood floors. It is across from the soccer field. They give discounts for extended stays.

The German-owned **Hotel Villa Romántica** (private bath, hot water, ceiling fans; $40-$70, including breakfast; phone/fax: 777-0037), tucked in on the right as you leave town, has a pool and shady sitting area.

QUEPOS RESTAURANTS AND NIGHTLIFE   A popular oceanfront place for both tourists and locals, **Restaurante Isabel** (open all day) offers a full menu. Owned by a transplanted gringa, **El Gran Escape** (closed Tuesday) next door has some of the best food in town. Mexican food is their specialty, but they also serve a hearty breakfast buffet and desserts. **La Marquesa Bar and Restaurant**, in the next block, has good, cheap *casados*. Around the corner, the Texan-owned **Banco Bar**, housed in a former bank, is known for authentic Tex-Mex cooking and great burgers and sandwiches. While on the oceanfront, check out **Café Milagro**, one block north of La Marquesa, which roasts and distributes pure Tarrazú coffee, the best that Costa Rica has to offer. For an extra buzz, accompany your cup or glass with a rich, chewy brownie. You can't always find decaf in Costa Rica, but they have it. Their delicious breakfasts feature bagels, croissants, and Belgian waffles. They have a branch in Manuel Antonio across from the Barba Roja. A traditional stop for a *refresco* or fresh-fish lunch in Quepos is **El Kiosko**, a small, open-air place on the oceanfront three blocks from the entrance to town. **Club Banana**, just beyond the wharf, is another favorite for good, inexpensive Tico food.

The market at the bus terminal is a good place to grab a quick bite to eat and to stock up on fruits and vegetables. The **Quepoa** on the south side of the market has tasty seafood. Half a block toward the ocean, **Dos Locos** has Mexican food and a lively open-air atmosphere with live music Wednesday and Friday. Try their Guaro Sour, a creative new use of the local firewater.

Escalofrio, next door, serves brick oven pizza and ice cream. **Gastronomía L'Angulo**, across the street, serves a variety of pizzas and sells imported cheese, olives, wine, and pesto. Toward the ocean from north side of the market is **Pizza Gabriel**, which has good food and is run by a friendly local owner. **El Bolognese**, one block north, next to the fire station, is another place to go when you're in the mood for Italian.

Internet and video cafes: The **Quepos Post Office**, on the north side of the soccer field, has **Punta.com**, then there's **Quepos Net Café**, upstairs from Iguana tours across from the soccer field. **Internet Tropical**, next to Quepolandia, near the Banco Bar, serves delicious sandwiches and great tropical fruit drinks. **Americano Video** rents videos and has a big-screen viewing room so you can watch them there if you need to. They also develop film and sell photo supplies. They are across from the bus station, above the Super Mas grocery store.

El Gran Escape, El Banco, and Dos Locos broadcast TV sports.

For dancing, head to the **Bahía Azul**, on the water across from El Gran Escape, the **Arco Iris**, just north of Quepos, or **Las Marracas**, near the wharf.

MANUEL ANTONIO LODGING AND RESTAURANTS   Near Manuel Antonio the most beautiful places to stay are in the hills between Quepos and the park. There you'll find small, elegant hotels owned by tropics-lovers of many nationalities.

Make reservations three months in advance for Christmas or Easter, and at least one month in advance during the rest of the tourist season (December through April). Most of these places offer a 20-50 percent discount during the green season (May to November). If you're trying to save money, keep in mind that this area as a whole is not for budget travelers. Those who can afford $70-$150 per day will find some of the most beautiful accommodations in the country, but if you're looking for budget beachfront places, go south to Dominical or the Golfito area or east to the Caribbean coast.

House rentals: If you have more time to spend, you might want to rent a house by the week or month. For example: Fully equipped houses and apartments with breathtaking ocean views rent for about $200-$600 per week or $700-$2000 per month during the high season, and half that in the low season. Contact **La Buena Nota** (777-1002, 777-0292), **Sheryl** (777-0481, fax: 777-0451), or **Condominios Biesanz** (228-1811; www.biesanz.com); **Sula Bya-ba** (phone/fax: 777-0547) rents Japanese-style apartments by the week ($250-$750), as do **Bungalows Las Palmas** (phone/fax: 777-1269). Most hotels give discounts for longer stays.

We will mention facilities in order of their appearance on the road between Quepos and Manuel Antonio.

The family-run **Cabinas Pedro Miguel** (private bath, cold water, ceiling fans; phone/fax: 777-0035) have two types of lodging: a two-story construction with carpeted upstairs rooms that overlook the ocean ($20-$30), and funky large rooms with kitchens and a wall-sized screened window overlooking jungle ($50-$60, sleeps four). There's a small pool.

Across the road, the European-owned ✪ **Hotel Plinio** (private bath, hot water, ceiling fans, pool; breakfast included; computer access for guests; 777-0055, fax: 777-0558; www.hotelplinio.com, e-mail: plinio@racsa.co.cr) has single-story jungle-view rooms ($50-$60; with air conditioning, $60-$70), and suites of either two ($70-$80) or three levels ($90-$100), featuring raised king-size beds from which you can enjoy a coastal view. The hotel is surrounded by lush foliage, and has recently acquired a 70-acre forest reserve with a nature trail that leads up the mountain to a 15-meter observation tower. It has one of the most popular dinner restaurants (open daily for breakfast and dinner) in Manuel Antonio, offering delicious pasta, lasagna, eggplant parmigiana, and Thai specialties. Its homemade bread is worth a trip in itself. Call for reservations.

Next on the right, the **Mono Azul** (private bath, heated water, ceiling fans, some with air conditioning, pool; $40-$50, including breakfast; phone/fax: 777-1954; www.maqbeach.com, e-mail: monoazul@racsa.co.cr) is owned by a vivacious North American. Her restaurant (open daily, 7 a.m. to 10 p.m.) delivers delicious pizza, burgers, fish, salad, and homemade cake anywhere in the area. The atmosphere is relaxed, the owner is very helpful. As one writer put it, the Mono Azul is "just like home, only you don't have to do the dishes." This is the home of the Amazing Arts Art Gallery, mentioned above. Recommended.

A small road leads to the left to **Villas Mymosa** (private bath, hot water, ceiling fans, air conditioning, kitchens, pool; $70-$120, phone/fax: 777-1254; www.villasmymosa.com, e-mail: mymosa@racsa.co.cr), one- and two-bedroom condos that sleep up to six, around a large pool.

Each room in the multi-story **Hotel California** (private bath, hot water, ceiling fans, satellite TV, kitchen; $50-$110; 777-1234, phone/fax: 777-1062; www.hotel-california.com, e-mail: hotelcal@racsa.co.cr) is illustrated with a mural of a different national park, and prices depend on the quality of the view. Up top is a sunset terrace, and below are a pool/jacuzzi and an open-air restaurant. Their budget bungalows are individual cabins without kitchens set in a garden ($40-$50).

Midway up the road's steepest hill is the entrance to **Hotel Las Tres Banderas** (private bath, hot water, air conditioning, TV with VCR, pool,

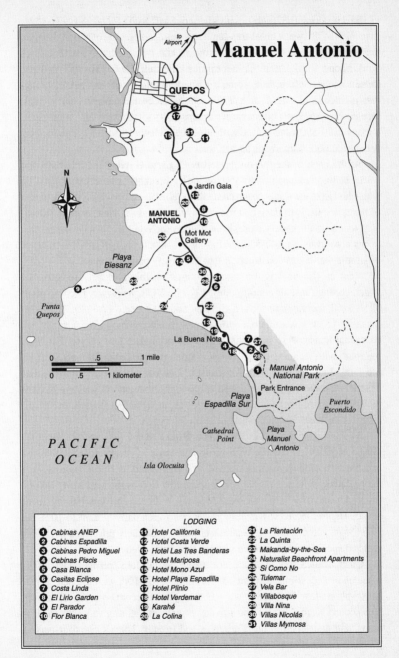

Manuel Antonio

to Airport

QUEPOS

N

Jardín Gaia

MANUEL ANTONIO

Mot Mot Gallery

Playa Biesanz

Punta Quepos

0   .5   1 mile
0   .5   1 kilometer

La Buena Nota

Manuel Antonio National Park

Park Entrance

PACIFIC OCEAN

Playa Espadilla Sur

Cathedral Point

Puerto Escondido

Playa Manuel Antonio

Isla Olocuita

LODGING

❶ Cabinas ANEP
❷ Cabinas Espadilla
❸ Cabinas Pedro Miguel
❹ Cabinas Piscis
❺ Casa Blanca
❻ Casitas Eclipse
❼ Costa Linda
❽ El Lirio Garden
❾ El Parador
❿ Flor Blanca

⓫ Hotel California
⓬ Hotel Costa Verde
⓭ Hotel Las Tres Banderas
⓮ Hotel Mariposa
⓯ Hotel Mono Azul
⓰ Hotel Playa Espadilla
⓱ Hotel Plinio
⓲ Hotel Verdemar
⓳ Karahé
⓴ La Colina

㉑ La Plantación
㉒ La Quinta
㉓ Makanda-by-the-Sea
㉔ Naturalist Beachfront Apartments
㉕ Si Como No
㉖ Tulemar
㉗ Vela Bar
㉘ Villabosque
㉙ Villa Nina
㉚ Villas Nicolás
㉛ Villas Mymosa

jacuzzi, restaurant; $70-$80; with kitchen, $110-$120; 777-1284, 777-1521, fax: 777-1478; www.hotel-tres-banderas.com, e-mail: info@hotel-tres-ban deras.com). The hotel owes its name to the owners from two countries working in a third nation. Farther up this killer hill, **La Colina** (private bath, heated water, ceiling fans, some air conditioning; pool, restaurant; break-fast included; 777-0231, fax: 777-1553; www.costaricapages.com, e-mail: lacolina@racsa.co.cr) offers garden rooms ($40-$50), apartments with kitch-enettes ($80-$90) and suites with an ocean view ($80-$100) around their two-tiered pool with swim-up bar.

At the crest of the hill on the left is **El Lirio Garden** (private bath, hot water, ceiling fans, pool; $40-$50, including breakfast; phone/fax: 777-0403, fax: 777-1182; www.maqbeach.com/ellirio, e-mail: ellirio@racsa.co.cr). Some of the spacious, well-designed rooms have a distant sea view. A good value.

Near a small grocery store, **Flor Blanca** (private bath, heated water, fans or air conditioning; $40-$50, including breakfast; phone/fax: 777-1633) is of simple wallboard construction, but has nicely painted rooms.

Next on the right is the gated entrance to **Tulemar** (private bath, hot water, ceiling fans, air conditioning, TV with VCR, hairdryer, kitchen, pool; $250-$260, including breakfast; children under 12 free; 777-0580, 777-1325, fax: 777-1579; www.tulemar.com, e-mail: tulemar@racsa.co.cr), luxurious octagonal houses with skylights, which accommodate four people. Far from the road, with stunning ocean views, a small private beach 800 meters from the bungalows, and kayaks for guests, Tulemar offers the quintessential Manuel Antonio experience. Their three-night honeymoon package ($1000 including airfare from San José) includes champagne and flowers on arrival, a sunset sailboat tour, and a barbecue on the beach.

At the top of the hill is the **Barba Roja** (open 7:30 a.m. to midnight; closed Monday), a favorite with visitors because of its gringo-style lunches and dinners, such as burgers, nachos, and BLTs, and its sinful desserts—try the macadamia pie à la mode! Above the Barba Roja is the **Mot Mot Gallery** (open 4 p.m. to 9 p.m.; closed Monday), with tasteful exhibits by local artists. Behind them, at **Karola's** restaurant (open daily, 7 a.m. to 10 p.m.; 777-1557), you can drink margaritas or enjoy reasonably priced Mexican and seafood specialties in a garden setting. Recommended.

Casa Blanca (private bath, hot water, ceiling fans, refrigerators, pool, wheelchair accessible; with air conditioning, $90-$100; with kitchen, $140-$150; phone/fax: 777-0253; www.hotelcasablanca.com, e-mail: cblanca@ racsa.co.cr) is an intimate and private gay resort catering to gay men, les-bians, and their open-minded relatives and friends. There's one four-person suite with a kitchen that goes for $200-$210. This is also the site of the Miranon center, devoted to spiritual growth.

At Casa Blanca there's a road to the right leading to three exclusive hotels. The area's original luxury hotel, **Hotel Mariposa** (private bath, hot water, ceiling fans, pool, some suites with jacuzzis; $140-$180; 777-0456, in the U.S: 800-416-2747; www.lamariposa.com, e-mail: htl.mariposa@msn.com) offers beautiful views from private balconies. Ask for the villas or the upstairs rooms; avoid the "garden view" rooms. The French owners pride themselves on their *haute cuisine* restaurant. The view and the setting could make any meal an unforgettable experience, and we have heard the restaurant is excellent.

Down a steep gravel road, one kilometer to the right from the Mariposa, is **Makanda-by-the-Sea** (private bath, hot water, ceiling fans, kitchen, pool; $140-$210; 777-0442, fax: 777-1032; www.makanda.com, e-mail: makanda@racsa.co.cr), secluded villas with wide balconies and a sunset ocean view set in a 12-acre nature reserve. Our first choice. No children. Honeymoon packages available. Makanda's **Sunspot Grill** is gaining a reputation as *the* place to go for lunch or dinner.

At the end of the road is **El Parador** (private bath, hot water, ceiling fan, air conditioning, phone, cable TV, some with kitchens and jacuzzis; $170-$320; children under 12 free; 777-1411, fax: 777-1437; www.hotelparador. com, e-mail: parador@racsa.co.cr), modeled after the traditional Spanish country inns but with some contemporary features, including a heliport, conference center, gym and spa, pool, tennis court, and mini-golf course. The main building is designed to show off a large collection of European antiques, some dating from the 17th century. The rooms are comfortable with the standard amenities of a luxury hotel.

If instead of continuing toward El Parador you make a left and head down a steep dirt road, you will arrive at **Nature's Beachfront Aparthotel** (private bath, hot water, ceiling fans, kitchen; $30-$70; $120-$130 for seven people; 777-1473, 777-1475; www.maqbeach.com, e-mail: beachfront@maq beach.com), small, simple apartments in a two-story house, right on the northern end of Playa Espadilla.

Returning to the main road, past a rather dense highrise hotel, are the comfortable and well-designed **Villas Nicolás** (private bath, hot water, ceiling fans, pool; $70-$90; with kitchen, $90-$200; 777-0481, phone/fax: 777-0451; www.maqbeach.com, e-mail: nicolas@racsa.co.cr), with private terraces. The floor plans of the various-sized villas give an open, airy feel. Some have beautiful ocean views. Recommended.

✪ **Sí Como No** (private bath, hot water, ceiling fans, air conditioning, kitchenette or wet bar, pool, jacuzzi, restaurant/bar; $170-$270, including breakfast; children under 6 free; 777-0777, fax: 777-1093, 800-282-0488; www.sicomono.com, e-mail: sicomono@racsa.co.cr) is a wonderland of gardens, waterfalls, and cascading pools. Our kids loved the waterslide and the **Rico Tico**, a swim-up bar and grill serving California-style food and icy fruit smoothies as well as the air-conditioned restaurant, **Claro Que Seafood**. They even have a 46-seat movie theater under the lobby, free for guests of the hotel or restaurants. They welcome gay and straight people alike. Their two-night honeymoon package costs $598. This luxury resort is a showcase of eco-friendly alternative technologies for saving energy and water (double-paned windows and insulated ceilings, low-voltage lighting, solar-heated jacuzzi, self-cleaning pool, graywater recycling system, etc.). Recommended.

Next to it is a small shopping center that houses **Pickles**, a good deli that rents coolers and will make you a delightful picnic basket for the beach. Be sure to try their marinated roast chicken and world-class sandwiches. You can check your e-mail here at **Net Café**.

Set in a lush garden, **La Plantación** (private bath, heated water, ceiling fans, kitchens, pool; $150-$320; 777-1332, fax: 777-0432, 800-477-7829; www.bigrubys.com, e-mail: quepos@bigrubys.com) is a gay-friendly hotel that offers small houses with shady porches and hammocks. **Casitas Eclipse** (private bath, hot water, ceiling fans, air conditioning, pools; $100-$110; with kitchen, $120-$140; houses, $250-$260; 777-0408, phone/fax: 777-1738; www.crica.com/hotels, e-mail: villatucan@sand.net) features whimsical Mediterranean-style houses, with three pools and a romantic Italian restaurant, **El Gato Negro**.

La Quinta (private bath, ceiling fans, pool; with cold water, $30-$40; with heated water, view, and kitchen, $50-$60; phone/fax: 777-0434) is quiet, with private terraces and beautiful views of the park from its spacious grounds. On the slope between this driveway and the main road is the Costa Rican–owned **Villa Nina** (private bath, hot water; with ceiling fan, $50-$60; with air conditioning, $60-$70, including breakfast; 777-1628, phone/fax: 777-1497; www.accommodations.co.cr, e-mail: vilanina@racsa.co.cr). Breakfast is served to guests on their own individual balconies. With a clean pool and breezy thatch-covered bar, Villa Nina is small and well cared for.

Hotel Costa Verde (private bath, hot water, ceiling fans, screens, kitchen, pool, restaurant; $70-$80; larger rooms near pool, $100-$110; 777-0584, 777-0187, fax: 777-0560; www.maqbeach.com, e-mail: costaver@racsa.co.cr) has balconies, lovely views, and two miles of nature trails. Guests can connect with the internet at the **Cantina Bar and Grill** here. The rooms on the road can be noisy at night.

BEACH AREA LODGING AND RESTAURANTS The following hotels have easy access to Playa Espadilla, a long beach known for its dangerous rip currents. Access to the national park is from the south end of Espadilla. Some of Manuel Antonio's least expensive rooms are in this area, although several comfortable, luxurious hotels are here too.

Karahé (777-0170, phone/fax: 777-1072; www.karahe.com, e-mail: infor mation@karahe.com) offers three types of rooms: the villas (private bath, solar-heated water, ceiling fans, refrigerators, air conditioning; $80-$90), which have magnificent views, but you must walk up more than a hundred steps to get to them; the newer "deluxe" rooms near the road (private bath, solar-heated water, air conditioning; $90-$100), which have terraces; and the junior suites (private bath, solar-heated water, air conditioning; $110-$120). The suites, which also have terraces, are across the road, near the pool and 200 meters from the beach. Breakfast is included in all rates. The solar showers are hottest in the afternoon.

Next on the right is **Buena Nota**, a well-stocked newsstand and beach shop. Above the shop are some two-bedroom apartments for rent ($100-$110). Call 777-1002 for information.

Cabinas Piscis (cold water, restaurant; phone/fax: 777-0046), shaded by tall trees, has simple cabinas with porches and rocking chairs (private bath, table fans; $30-$40) and dormitory-style rooms (shared bath, ceiling fans; $20-$30). A little trail leads 100 meters through a field to the beach.

Hotel Verdemar (private bath, hot water, ceiling fans, air conditioning; $70-$80; with kitchens, $80-$100; 777-1805, fax 777-1311; www.maqbeach. com, e-mail: verdemar@racsa.co.cr) has pleasantly decorated rooms with a pool and a raised wooden walkway to the beach.

With shady tables on the beach, the **Restaurant Mar y Sombra** is the traditional place to eat on Playa Espadilla. It's about 500 meters north of the entrance to the national park; you'll see the entrance from the main road as well.

Next comes a row of restaurants (not recommended) and souvenir shacks where you can rent surfboards, umbrella chairs and snorkeling equipment. Many vendors in this area sell bottled water, and we highly recommend that you bring some. A road to the left in the middle of these establishments leads to the following hotels, some of the best at the beach: **Cabinas Espa-dilla** (private bath, heated water, fans, kitchen, some with air conditioning; $50-$70; 777-0416) has clean cabins in a tranquil garden atmosphere. Owned by the same family, the newer **Hotel Playa Espadilla** (hot water, air conditioning, kitchens; $80-$90; phone/fax: 777-0903; www.maqbeach.com, e-mail: spadilla@racsa.co.cr), down the street on the left, has light, spacious rooms with tiled floors. Recommended. Across the street from Cabinas Espadilla, the Swiss-owned **Costa Linda** (cold water, table fans; shared bath, $12-$20; phone/fax: 777-0304) is basic, but rooms are clean and neat, and the bathrooms have been tiled and greatly improved. Recommended for budget travelers. Contact them for motorcycle tours throughout the country.

The **Vela Bar** offers seafood and vegetarian specialties with a Spanish touch. Their rooms (private bath, ceiling fans, security boxes; with cold water, $40-$50; with hot water and refrigerator, $50-$60; 777-0413, fax: 777-1071; www.maqbeach.com, e-mail: velabar@maqbeach.com) are set in the trees behind the restaurant.

The **Villabosque** (private bath, hot water, ceiling fans, air conditioning, hairdryers, restaurant; $80-$90; 777-0463, fax: 777-0401) overflows with plants in the courtyard, and has an elevated pool (not too safe for small kids).

At the end of the lane, **Cabinas ANEP** (private bath, cold water, ceiling fans; under $7/person; 777-0565) is a basic retreat for the public employees' union. During the week, when there aren't many public employees on vacation, they rent to the public.

GETTING THERE: By Bus: A direct San José–Manuel Antonio bus (223-5567; $5) leaves the Coca Cola at 6 a.m., noon, and 6 p.m., returning at 6 a.m., noon, and 5 p.m. Buy tickets in advance on weekends and holidays and purchase return tickets as soon as you arrive. The Quepos ticket office (777-0263) is open Monday through Saturday, 7 a.m. to 11 a.m., 1 p.m. to 5 p.m.; Sunday, 7 to noon. This bus will pick you up at your hotel on its way from Manuel Antonio to Quepos, but you must be out on the road to flag it down. (Do not let anyone but the bus driver load or unload your baggage. Try to keep it with you if possible. Things have been stolen from the luggage compartment.) One driver on this route makes the trip in three hours, a fact that defies conventional concepts of space and time. We have heard of several people who have become quite religious on this bus. The bus will let you off at the airport near San José if you ask.

San José–Quepos buses leave from the western end of the Coca Cola at 7 a.m. and 10 a.m., and 2 p.m., 4 p.m., and 5 p.m., returning at 5 a.m. and 8 a.m., and 2 p.m. and 4 p.m. (223-5567, 777-0263; $3). These buses are slow and make many stops. The trip takes four hours. (Watch out for pickpockets at the Coca Cola.)

Quepos–Manuel Antonio: From the southeast corner of the market, take a 20-minute bus ride (30 cents) seven scenic kilometers to the entrance of the park. They leave every hour or two (schedule posted in bus station ticket booth or call 777-0263). Service is continuous on weekends during the dry season. Watch out for robberies in the tumult to get on this bus.

Quepos–Puntarenas buses leave at 4:30 a.m., 10:30 a.m., and 3 p.m., returning at 5 a.m., 11 a.m., and 2 p.m. (All of the above buses pass by Playa Jacó, an hour and a half north from Quepos.)

Buses leave San Isidro de El General (771-2550) for Quepos at 7 a.m. and 1:30 p.m., passing through Dominical. They return from Quepos at 5 a.m. and 1:30 p.m.

Fantasy Tours (220-2126; www.fantasy.co.cr) has buses from San José (departs at 9 a.m. daily) or Jacó (departs at 1 p.m. daily) to Manuel Antonio for $19. From Jacó their connecting buses to Arenal, Liberia Flamingo, and Tamarindo, leave at 8 a.m., all for $19. Recommended if you feel too shaky in your Spanish to take the public bus.

By Boat: Manuel Antonio is included in the itinerary of the luxurious **Temptress Cruise** (220-1679, fax: 220-2103, in the U.S.: 305-871-2663, fax: 305-871-2657), which spends a week sailing from Curú on the Nicoya Peninsula to Drake Bay, Corcovado, Isla del Caño, and the Golfo Dulce and comes complete with naturalist guides. Half-week trips are also available.

By Car: The trip from San José is about three and a half hours if you take the Atenas turnoff and drive the narrow, winding road through the Aguacate mountains. This route is scenic and gives you a glimpse of rural life. You can buy sugarcane juice and fruit along the way. If you feel more comfortable with better highways, go all the way to Puntarenas, follow the signs to Jacó, and continue on to Quepos. It only takes a half hour longer, even though it looks much farther on the map.

By Air: SANSA has eight flights a day to Quepos during the high season (221-9414, fax: 255-2176; $35 one way). Buy tickets at least two weeks in advance during dry season. SANSA will transport you from its San José office to the airport, and a private bus ($2.50) will deliver you to your hotel in Quepos or Manuel Antonio, and pick you up to get you to your return flight. SANSA also has a Quepos–Tamarindo flight, leaving Monday, Wednesday, and Friday at 10:25 a.m. and returning at 11:30 a.m. ($37.50 one way). Travelair (220-3054, fax: 220-0413; $50 one way, $80 roundtrip) has flights to Quepos daily, at 7:45 a.m., 9 a.m., 1 p.m., and 4 p.m. in high season and 9:10 a.m. in low season, all returning half an hour later. (Some of their flights continue on to Palmar Sur, the point of departure for Drake Bay, and to Puerto Jiménez, gateway to the Osa Peninsula.)

MATAPALO

Twenty-five kilometers south of Manuel Antonio along the bumpy Costanera Sur road is Matapalo, a small, quiet beach town set in the middle of a seemingly unending stretch of beach. (One section of Matapalo is on the road, and its oceanside twin, with all the cabinas and restaurants, is a couple of kilometers away on the beach.) The surf here is not what you would call gentle, but it is much less rough than it is at Dominical, about 15 kilometers farther south (see Southern Zone chapter).

In the pueblo, enjoy good Tico food at **Soda Mango** (behind the soccer field) where there is also a public phone and fax. Down the road a bit is **Bar Deportivo**—pool tables, lots of local color, and Don Toto's famous *ceviche* on Saturday and Sunday.

Just at the beach road, across the little bridge south of the football plaza, is a wonderful restaurant and equally fantastic *pulpería*. **La Pulpería Espiral** has lots of items that gringos and Europeans want but can rarely find— especially in remote areas like this one. Next door, **Express del Pacífico** serves up very fine cuisine, hand-tossed pizzas, rotisserie chicken, and a few Tico dishes.

The first place you come to on the beach is **El Oasis**, clean economical cabins with an adjacent bar/restaurant serving Tex-Mex and Gringo food along with a few Tico dishes.

The Swiss-owned **El Coquito del Pacífico** (private bath, cold or hot water, ceiling fans, pool; $55-$65; phone/fax: 284-7220) has spacious, bright cabinas with good screens and reading lamps. Their restaurant has a Swiss chef.

A French restaurant, **La Terraza del Sol**, is a few hundred meters north. Reservations recommended (779-9255).

Almost a kilometer farther north, **La Piedra Buena** (private bath, cold water, ceiling fans, mosquito nets, some kitchens, restaurant; $30-$40; fax: 771-4441), owned by an industrious Swiss woman, is a wooden duplex set back from the beach in a groomed sand yard (with geese) and a house closer to the road. Beatrice, the owner, is an excellent chef—readers have written us with rave reviews of her cuisine.

Just next door is the **Jungle House** ($20-$50), with American-owned rooms and lovely new cabins, which can also include kitchenettes if you want. Direct TV, pool table, and direct beach access are included in the amenities.

El Castillo ($35-$60, including breakfast and transportation Quepos–Matapalo; phone/fax: 777-1984; cellular: 392-3460; e-mail: oasisame@ racsa.co.cr) is a bed and breakfast in the hills with awesome views of Playa Matapalo and an in-house trained chef to cook meals aside from breakfast if you like.

GETTING THERE: By Bus: Take a San Isidro bus from Quepos at 5 a.m. or 1:30 p.m., or a Quepos bus from San Isidro at 7 a.m. or 1:30 p.m.

By Car: Drive south along the gravel Costanera Highway from Manuel Antonio, or north from Dominical (see Southern Zone chapter). Travel time can be from one to two hours, depending on road conditions; ask before you set out.

TWELVE

Southern Zone

Costa Rica's *Zona Sur*, or Southern Zone, encompasses the southern half of coastal Puntarenas Province (from Playa Dominical to the Osa Peninsula, to Punta Burica on the Panamanian border), as well as the mountainous southern half of San José Province and inland Limón and Puntarenas provinces, including Chirripó National Park and La Amistad International Park, which extends across the border into Panama. For hikers, naturalists, anglers, and those who want to get off the beaten track, this area has a tremendous amount to offer.

Despite its reputation nationally as a center of agroindustry (bananas, pineapples, palm oil, coffee), it has a larger percentage of national parks and forest reserves than any other region of Costa Rica. It also has the largest concentration of indigenous people, especially the Guaymís and Borucas, centering around the towns of Buenos Aires and San Vito. Because the area is not really on the tourist trail, budget accommodations are plentiful. The Southern Zone is also becoming known for small, aesthetically designed nature lodges that fund private reserves where you can get up close and personal with monkeys, macaws, and dolphins.

CERRO DE LA MUERTE

The Interamerican Highway, which becomes San José's Central Avenue, crossing the city from west to east, turns right at Cartago to connect the Central Valley with the Southern Zone. It winds into the mountains that surround fog-shrouded Cerro de la Muerte, the highest pass on the Interamerican Highway. These mountains were the scene of the beginnings of the

1948 Civil War—the late Don Pepe Figueres' farm, La Lucha Sin Fin (The Endless Struggle), is located off this road (see Chapter One).

For information on side trips from the Interamerican Highway, to Santa María de Dota, and the charming mountain village of Copey above it, see the Central Valley chapter.

As you wind around **Cerro de la Muerte**, you will see the lush vegetation become stunted and then diminish. When taking this trip, dress in layers and try to go early in the day, before fog and rain reduce the visibility to zero. This can happen even in the dry season. Landslides are also a very real danger during heavy rains. If you are cold in your car and intimidated by the driving conditions, imagine how Costa Ricans hiking or driving ox carts must have felt before the road was built. That's why this area is called "Mountain of Death." Several high-altitude mountain lodges are on or near Cerro de la Muerte:

○ **Albergue Mirador de Quetzales** (shared bath, heated water; $20-$30/person; private bath, $30-$40; including dinner, breakfast, and morning tour; 381-8456; www.ecotourism.co.cr, e-mail: recajhi@racsa.co.cr) virtually guarantees that you will see quetzales in their reserve between November and May. The Serrano Obando family guides are intimate with the birds' hangouts and habits, but even if you're unlucky, the guided hike is lovely and punctuated with curiosities: huge *cipresillo* trees that naturally hollow out in their old age, and marine fossils in the rocks beside one of their creeks. Most visitors spend the night in the rustic-but-homey A-frame cabins because quetzal sightings are most likely in the early morning, but you can also stop in for a guided or a self-guided tour ($6) and a delicious *campesino* lunch. To get there, go one kilometer west after you turn off the Interamerican Highway at marker 70. Recommended.

Several roadside cafeterias on the Cerro specialize in quick *comida típica* for bus passengers. The classic **La Georgina**, in Villa Mills, bakes doughy apple pie and tender carrot muffins, and also rents basic rooms with electric blankets (shared bath, $3/person; private bath, heated water, $7-$12; 770-8043), above the restaurant. On a rare clear day you can see Volcán Irazú to the north and Chirripó to the south.

SAN GERARDO DE DOTA   San Gerardo de Dota, a narrow, pristine mountain valley at 6900 feet, has become a mecca for birders, hikers, and trout fishers. The first lodge you come to is the **Trogon Lodge** (private bath, hot water; $50-$60; meals $25/day; 223-2421, fax: 222-5463), with duplexes of dark-stained wood overlooking lovely flowering gardens next to a stream where you can catch your dinner. One and a half kilometers of trail lead

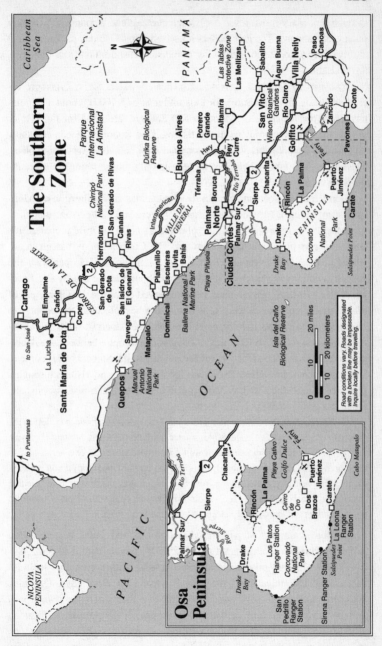

through a primary-forest reserve in which quetzals and woodpeckers, among other birds, abound. The lodge offers horseback trips. One-day packages ($72) and two-day tours ($166), including roundtrip transportation from San José, are available.

Cabinas El Quetzal (private bath, heated water; $20-$30/person, including meals, 50 percent off for kids under 8; 541-1007), about a kilometer before the Albergue de Montaña Río Savegre, are good for families or groups that come to enjoy nature or fishing. Don Rodolfo Chacón can show you around the area and put you in contact with neighbors who rent horses. The cabins lack atmosphere, but the guests-only dining room has a beautiful river view.

Don Efraín Chacón and his family rent cabinas at ✪ **Albergue de Montaña Río Savegre** (private bath, heated water; $60-$70/person, including three meals; cell phone: 390-5096, phone/fax: 771-1732). Be prepared: it's cool, and gets downright chilly at night. The Chacón family has taken advantage of the crisp weather to grow apples, plums, Chilean papayas, and peaches, which you sample in meals. Trout abound in the nearby Río Savegre. Over 170 bird species have been observed from the 16 kilometers of hiking trails here. This is known as one of the best places in the country to observe quetzals, who live there year-round. The Albergue hosts the Quetzal Education Research Complex, a cooperative venture between the Albergue and Southern Nazarene University in Oklahoma. Students who come to study quetzals share information with local residents and visitors through a series of public talks at the Albergue. Be sure to make reservations: the lodge has grown quite popular lately.

GETTING THERE: Take a San Isidro bus (see below) and ask to be left at the *"entrada a San Gerardo"* at the 80-kilometer mark on the Interamerican Highway. San Gerardo is nine kilometers downhill from there, a scenic two-and-a-half to three-hour walk. Don Efraín's family can pick you up ($20 roundtrip) if you are staying at their place. If you are driving from San José, follow the directions in "Getting There" for San Isidro de El General, and make sure your vehicle has a powerful engine as the road is extremely steep and narrow. It is paved in the steepest parts.

Avalon (camping $6/person; shared room and bath, heated water, $9/person; private room, shared bath, $20-$30; private bath, $30-$50; 380-2107) is a 375-acre private cloud forest reserve with a view that includes San Isidro, Dominical, and the Osa Peninsula on clear days. Quetzals, *jilgueros*, and the three-wattled bell-bird live there, and the owner will arrange professional birding hikes ($70/group), or nonprofessional guided hikes ($3-$7/person). The wooden cabins are well designed and comfortable, with many thoughtful touches. Guests can warm up in a wood-fired hot tub while gazing at the panoramic view or the stars. The day-use fee is $3. Access is via a bumpy 3.8-kilometer road from the village of División at kilometer 107 on the Interamerican Highway. Regular cars can make it, but you must drive carefully. Homecooked meals are available for $3-$9. Volunteers who work three hours a day can stay for $30-$40 a week including meals. Mountain biking, horseback riding, trout fishing, and massages are also available. División is about 40 minutes from San Isidro. If you are carless, you can get a taxi at the Soda Arco Iris on the right as you enter División ($4-$5), or call ahead and horses will be brought to meet your bus ($4).

SAN ISIDRO DE EL GENERAL

The **Valle de El General** is one of Costa Rica's natural jewels. When the fog clears after you pass Cerro de la Muerte, the surrounding small towns in the valley offer beautiful flowers and a lovely climate.

The bustling, fast-growing town of **San Isidro de El General** is the gateway to Chirripó National Park and Playa Dominical. The clean public market in San Isidro is a delight, offering an array of beautiful fruits and vegetables, and good, inexpensive places to eat. **Soda Popeye** (pronounced pop-ayay) is one of the best in the market. There is a farmers market behind the Escuela del Valle Thursday afternoons and Friday mornings.

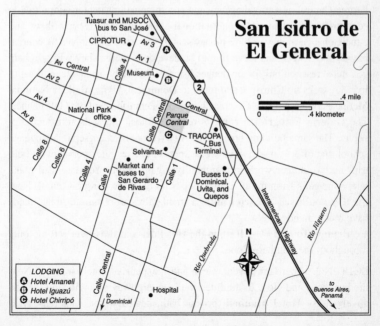

San Isidro de El General

Tuasur and MUSOC bus to San José
CIPROTUR
Av 3
Av 1
Av Central
Calle 4
Av 2
Museum
Av 4
Av Central
Av 6
National Park office
Calle Central
Parque Central
TRACOPA Bus Terminal
Selvamar
Calle 8
Calle 6
Calle 4
Calle 2
Market and buses to San Gerardo de Rivas
Calle 1
Buses to Dominical, Uvita, and Quepos
Río Quebrada
Interamerican Highway
Río Jilguero

0 — .4 mile
0 — .4 kilometer

N

LODGING
Ⓐ *Hotel Amaneli*
Ⓑ *Hotel Iguazú*
Ⓒ *Hotel Chirripó*

Calle Central
to Dominical
Hospital
to Buenos Aires, Panamá

Twenty minutes (by car) before arriving in San Isidro, you can stop at the friendly **Vista del Valle** for a panoramic view and well-prepared, inexpensive *comida típica*. They serve fresh-squeezed orange juice. You can eat inside the homey restaurant or out on the balcony. They sell original crafts, including painted wooden platters, sun hats, and woven baskets, and have a cute little cabin with a great view and a balcony (private bath, hot water; $60, including breakfast; 384-4685).

On the central plaza, the **Restaurant/Bar Chirripó**, at the hotel of the same name, is a favorite for local gringo residents. **El Tenedor** (closed Monday) is a good restaurant right off the central plaza, 50 meters toward the Hotel Iguazú, and so is **El Jardín**, also just off the plaza. The local branch of the Universidad Nacional runs an interesting **museum** (open Monday through Friday, 7 a.m. to noon and 1 p.m. to 5:30 p.m.; Saturday 7 a.m. to noon), 200 meters west and 75 meters north of the church. They also have a gift shop and theater complex. Readers have recommended the Canadian-owned **Restaurante Las Estrellas**, on the northeast corner of the central park in Palmares, south of San Isidro, for "generous servings of excellent food in a fun atmosphere."

Selvamar (771-4582, fax: 771-8841; www.chirripo.co.cr/selvamar, e-mail: selvamar@racsa.co.cr), on the east side of the Hotel Chirripó, facing the Parque Central, is a travel agency and communications center committed to ecotourism. You can make international calls, send and receive faxes and e-mail, change money or have money sent to you, send documents by courier, buy airline tickets, and leave film to be developed there. They will also help you make reservations for any lodges listed below. They specialize in three- to five-day treks up Chirripó, and tours to Dominical, Uvita, Ballena National Marine Park, Drake Bay, Corcovado, the Osa Peninsula, and the Golfo Dulce. The **Galería Fotográfica** exhibits nature photos, and sells film and souvenirs. The same building houses **SEPA** (www.online.co.cr/sepa), a language school that offers one- to three-week Spanish classes interspersed with field trips and volunteer work in community organizations. You can also make telephone calls from the ICE, two blocks north of the Parque Central. Near the ICE you'll see **Mexico Lindo**, a small Mexican restaurant that friends have recommended.

Brunca Tours (771-3100), in the Hotel del Sur, runs river rafting tours throughout the Southern Zone.

LODGING   There are several clean and inexpensive hotels in town. Near the bus stops and close to the Interamerican Highway you will find the relatively noisy **Hotel Amaneli** (private bath, heated water, wall fans; $12-

$20; 771-0352) and the quieter **Hotel Iguazú** (wall fans, cable TV; with shared bath and heated water, $7/person; with private bath and heated water, $12-$20; 771-2571). **Hotel Chirripó** (hot water, no fans; with shared bath, $7-$12; with private bath, $12-$20; 771-0529) is the least expensive, and is much quieter.

Six kilometers south of San Isidro, on the left, is the large, comfortable **Hotel del Sur** (private bath, solar-heated water, fans or air conditioning, phones, TV, pools; $30-$60; 771-3033, fax: 771-0527), with well-tended gardens, tennis courts, playground equipment, large conference rooms, and a good restaurant. Their *ceviche de camarón* is fresh and filling. Quiet cabins that sleep five are at the back of the property (refrigerators, heated water; $50-$60). A good value.

By far the most peaceful alternative is the friendly ❂ **Albergue de Montaña Talari** (private bath, heated water, refrigerator, pool; $40-$50, including breakfast; phone/fax: 771-0341; www.crica/chirripo, e-mail: talari pz@sol.racsa.co.cr; closed in September and October), a small, unpretentious farm on the banks of the Río El General, eight kilometers (15 minutes) from San Isidro toward Chirripó National Park. The attentive Tica-Dutch hosts can arrange four-day treks up Chirripó ($189). Another three-day package features a hike up Paraguas Peak in Chirripó's buffer zone, and two nights at Talari ($124). Their restaurant offers good food at reasonable prices, and even has a piano. Recommended.

Rancho La Botija (private bath, heated water; $50-$60, including breakfast; 771-4582, 382-3052) has a very clean restaurant, a swimming pool open to non-guests, and, so far, one cabin. Some mysterious rocks with petroglyphs are down a path at the base of the property; the inscriptions are thought to be maps of the Talamanca mountains, showing the trails to the Caribbean side. You can swim in the pool and tour the rocks for $5 (children $3).

GETTING THERE: By Bus: Comfortable buses leave San José for the three-hour trip to San Isidro once an hour on the half hour from two bus companies along the same block (Calle 16, Avenidas 1/3; MUSOC, 222-2422, Tuasur, 222-9763; $3.25). Buy tickets in advance, especially on weekends and holidays. Buses back to San José leave hourly. (San Isidro: Tuasur, 771-0419; MUSOC, 771-0414.)

By Car: Follow San José's Avenida Central toward Cartago, then follow signs to San Isidro. There is a tricky spot just before Cartago where you should continue straight ahead on a smaller road toward San Isidro instead of following the freeway left into Cartago. The trip is a precipitous 125 kilometers, and takes three hours. Do not try to rush this trip, because there is almost always some delay on this part of the Interamerican—road work, or an accident. Once, some non-uniformed *campesinos* moved dayglo cones into the road. We could see some heavy machinery in the distance. They told us we would have to wait for an hour. Then they tried to sell us bags of potato chips. After a while we figured out that the machines were not blocking the road up ahead, and that the two men had stopped us so they could sell us chips. We continued on our way.

CHIRRIPÓ NATIONAL PARK AND ENVIRONS

San Gerardo de Rivas and **Herradura** are small mountain villages at the entrance to Chirripó National Park. Most people stop on their way to the famous Cerro Chirripó, but even if you are not up to climbing the mountain, the scenery in this area is beautiful and birds of all kinds are abundant. Not to be missed is the wood sculpture of Rafael (Macho) Elizondo of El Pelícano (see below). This prolific artist sees birds, people, and animals in wood and stone, and does what is necessary to bring out what he sees. He does not sell his *artesania*, but sometimes trades with other crafters. Highly recommended.

Narrow gravel roads follow the Chirripó Pacífico river and the neighboring Río Blanco through scenic valleys lined with vegetable, coffee, and dairy farms, perfect for invigorating day hikes. You can see quetzals halfway up the mountain; it's best to go with a guide who can show you where they nest. There is a hot spring in a lovely natural setting nearby: walk half a kilometer up the road to Herradura, then 20 minutes uphill through the pastures ($1.50 for adults, 75 cents for kids; pay at a small *soda* near the springs). It's clean, thanks to entrance fee revenue, and the bathtub-like temperature is maintained with a trickle of cold water from another stream above. Any of the hotels listed in this section can provide you with specific directions and guides for exploring this verdant area.

LODGING   The above-mentioned **El Pelícano** (shared baths, heated water; $20-$30; cellular: 382-3000, 771-4582; e-mail: selvamar@racsa.co.cr) has wood-paneled rooms with comfortable beds and valley views above a restaurant high on a hill. The entrance to the lodge is up a steep hill paved with rocks; it would help to have a car with fairly high clearance.

Cabinas Marín (shared bath, heated water; $7-$12), next to the ranger station, have nine rooms behind their *soda/casa/pulpería*, and plan more. Leave a message at the *pulpería*, 771-1866.

Francisco Elizondo offers simple, clean lodging at his ✪ **Posada del Descanso** (shared bath, heated water, laundry service; $7-$12; private bath, $20-$30), 400 meters toward San Gerardo from the ranger station. He is a font of information and can take you on tours of the area, including his own *finca*. Don Francisco has won the *Carrera a Chirripó* several times, running up and down the mountain in three and a half hours! He provides taxi service ($16) back to San Isidro if you miss the bus. Reserve through CIPROTUR in San Isidro (771-6096) or leave a message at the *pulpería* (771-1866) and he will call you back.

Roca Dura (shared or private bath, heated water; $7-$12) is a multi-story cabina/*soda* built on top of a giant boulder overlooking the river. It's right in town, across from the soccer field.

La Villa (shared bath, cold water; $7-$12; 771-1199, leave message in Spanish for Olger or Mirna) has simple rooms on the banks of the rushing Río Blanco in "downtown" Herradura. The owners cook for guests; they also rent horses.

CLIMBING CHIRRIPÓ   Chirripó means "Land of Eternal Waters." It is regarded as sacred land by the local indigenous people, who do not venture up the mountain. The area is magnetically charged. Watches and compasses can be affected. Then there are the *nímbolos*, or dwarves, that play tricks on you up there. The old rangers have lots of stories. The trek up Chirripó can be painful, tiring, frustrating, and freezing, but it's so satisfying to reach the summit, which is really the top of this part of the world, being the highest peak in southern Central America at 12,503 feet. A climb up Chirripó, with only one day at the summit, will take a minimum of five days, including transportation to and from San José.

Making reservations for lodging within the park: The weeks before Easter and before New Year's are the Ticos' favorite time to climb Chirripó, because they are on vacation and the weather is usually dry, so it is usually crowded at those times. The *Carrera a Chirripó* is in mid-February, so it might be hard to get reservations then, too. No matter when you want to go, you must make reservations, because they allow only a limited number of trekkers into the park at one time. Call or visit La Amistad Conservation Area office in San Isidro (150 meters west and 50 meters south of the Parque Central, in front of the Cámara de Cañeros; phone/fax: 771-3155, 771-5116) to make your reservations. Once they confirm that there's space, you must deposit the fee for your stay in their bank account and fax them the receipt. Charges per person include $6 per day admission and $6 per day for lodging in the new *albergue* near the top of the mountain. The *albergue* has two bunkbeds with vinyl-covered mattresses and four security boxes in each room. There are shared baths. You can rent blankets ($1), sleeping bags ($2), and camping stoves ($2) at the top. There is potable water, but you do have to bring your own food.

Kingfisher

Porters: There is an association of local men who will lug your back-pack and equipment up the mountain by horse ($20-$25 for up to 15 kilos or 33 pounds) in the dry season or on their backs (a few dollars more) in the rainy season. This will probably make your hike a lot more enjoyable. To arrange for *porteros*, you must get to San Gerardo the day before you plan to hike and ask around to find who's available, or call 771-1866. This service is not for hikers with inferiority complexes—just as you're struggling up another hill halfway up the mountain, you will meet the man who hauled up your stuff whistling gaily down the trail. Payment is made when you arrive in San Gerardo de Rivas.

Guides: Trails are well-marked, so there's no problem in going alone, but there are many advantages of going with a bilingual guide. You learn more about the history, legends, wildlife, and plants of the area. You don't have to make any arrangements yourself, and don't have to carry anything. While other tired hikers are struggling to boil water with their campstoves at the top, you'll be treated to gourmet meals, prepared by someone experienced in high-altitude cooking. Selvamar (771-4582; www.chirripo.com) and Talari (771-0341; www.crica/chirripo) offer guided tours up the mountain.

Check-in: To climb Chirripó, check in at the ranger station, near the final bus stop in San Gerardo de Rivas. It's open 5 a.m. to 5 p.m. If you want to leave before 5 a.m., as we did, check in the day before. Don't start any later than 8 a.m.—start earlier if it's raining or windy. You cannot enter the park after 10 a.m.

What to bring: The summit area is above timberline, so once you get there you can always see where you are as long as inclement weather and fog do not envelop you. Watch out for lightning and falling trees. Be sure to bring:

• A water bottle, at least one liter per person, to replenish all the liquid you'll lose sweating.

• Warm clothes and a warm sleeping bag. It gets very cold at night— between minus 5°C (23°F) in the windy dry season, and 3°C (37°F) in the rainy season. Bring or rent extra blankets. I slept in a Polarguard sleeping bag with one blanket inside it, another on top, another underneath, all my clothes on, and a friend beside me. I was almost warm. You can rent blankets and sleeping bags at the top.

- Snacks for the hikes. Dried bananas and peanuts are good for energy when you're climbing. Carrots proved to be our lifesaver on the Cuesta de Agua. They quench your thirst and give you something to do slowly and steadily as you climb that never-ending hill.

- A kerosene or alcohol burner to cook your meals. Because of recent forest fires, building fires in the park is no longer allowed. You can rent camping stoves at the top.

- A poncho to keep you dry during the daily multiple rainshowers. Veteran Chirripó climbers warn against getting wet during the hike. It might seem okay while you are heated up on the trail, but it can be dangerous when you get to the top.

- Binoculars and a camera (200 ISO film).

The hike: The first day is long and grueling. Hikers make the 14 straight uphill kilometers to the lodge in anywhere from seven hours to two days. It took us 11 hours; we left at 4:30 a.m. The average time is seven to nine hours. Follow the road through San Gerardo, across two bridges. Half a kilometer past the second bridge, follow the sign that directs you up through a coffee field. This is the *termómetro* shortcut, and connects with the main trail, which is well marked. Signs every half kilometer give the altitude and distance to the summit.You will be slapping flies, sweating, and slipping on your long haul, but if you can take your mind off these annoyances, you'll enjoy your surroundings.

The trail climbs through a dense cloud forest, where *jilgueros* (black-faced solitaires) sing their amazing song—which sounds like it's blown through a flute made of glass. The song is simple, but very fine. The birds like to stay up in the highest treetops, so they're difficult to spot. The *jilguero*'s natural habitat is the cloud forest. Sadly, as people destroy the cloud forests in Costa Rica, they are destroying the *jilguero* as well.

The first opportunity to get potable water is at "Llano Bonito" (Lovely Plain). This is four or five hours into the hike. There is a rustic hut here where you should stay only if you are sick or injured. The park service doesn't like to have hikers stay here because there is no ranger to supervise. After Llano Bonito comes **La Cuesta del Agua** (Water Hill), which is the longest haul of them all—it takes two to three hours to climb. It ends at **Monte Sin Fé**

(Faithless Mountain), where you walk into a new kind of landscape. Almost 20,000 acres of Chirripó, including Monte Sin Fé, were ravaged in April 1992 by a fire started by careless hikers.

Next you have to climb **La Cuesta de los Arrepentidos** (Repentant's Hill), then the trail traces around the side of a mountain. Soon you'll see **Los Crestones** (The Outcrop) on the top of a ridge straight ahead. These are huge, sharp rocks that look like they were folded accordion-style. The lodge is in the valley just below them.

Herradura Route: You can travel a different route altogether that takes off from Herradura. It passes over Cerro Urán and then Chirripó. You have to camp two nights before arriving at the Chirripó lodge. This is a new trail and you must hire a guide. Tell Parques Nacionales that you plan to take this route. Rodolfo Elizondo is a local guide who makes this trip. It is also offered by Selvamar in San Isidro.

No matter which route you take, arriving at the lodge is a relief. If you're lucky, someone will have a pot of water boiling and will offer you a cup of hot tea.

Mornings are clear in the summer, then the valley fills with fog. Wisps of fog drift in until they crowd together and form dense clouds. Visibility decreases, and at 2 or 3 p.m. it rains for about 45 minutes, so be sure you're on the trail by dawn. Besides having a better chance to see both the Atlantic and Pacific oceans, you'll get to enjoy this time of day—the sun touches the frost-covered leaves and grasses, the ice melts, the plants stretch, and whole meadows squeak softly.

Day hikes from Los Crestones: There are many places to explore on day hikes. Of course you should go to the summit of Chirripó, two hours up the same trail. You pass through the **Valle de los Conejos** (Rabbit Valley). *Lagartijas* (spiny lizards, endemic to this area) now occupy the valley. Each lizard has a different sheen that perfectly matches the rock it suns itself on. On the top of Chirripó you can see both the Pacific Ocean and the Caribbean Sea if the clouds haven't rolled in by the time you get there. There's a register to sign in a metal container at the summit cairn. Below the summit is **Lago Chirripó**. You can swing by it on your way down.

The lake-filled **Valle de las Morrenas** (Valley of the Moraines, or glacier lakes) is on the other side of the peak. If you want to continue hiking in that direction, you can pass over Cerro Urán and continue along the **Camino de los Indios** (Indians' Path), a trail known and used almost solely by the locals. Talk to Parques Nacionales in San José for a special permit and hire a guide for this hike.

Other day-hike possibilities are **Cerro Ventisqueros**, the second-highest mountain in southern Central America, whose trail leads from the main trail a bit below the Valle de los Conejos. This is a very steep hike. You can also hike from the lodge to **Los Crestones**. The top of the ridge above the valley is reached by going up to the left of Los Crestones. Follow the ridge left to **Cerro Terbi**, a mild 15 minutes. There's a register there, too. To make this hike a roundtrip, continue on the ridge a few hundred meters and descend on a trail that goes through a steep chimney and ends up in Valle de los Conejos. You can also continue walking along Terbi's curving ridge, ascending and descending the peaks, and go down into Valle de los Conejos when you get tired.

Note: When you go on your day hikes, take a map, a compass, a flashlight, a sweater, a rain jacket, snacks, and water.

GETTING THERE: By Bus: From the terminal near the market in San Isidro, buses leave for San Gerardo de Rivas at 5 a.m. and 2 p.m.; $1. The trip takes an hour and a half. When asking which of the many buses to take, specify San Gerardo de *Rivas*, because there's another San Gerardo. To be able to start your hike before dawn, arrive a day early and spend the night in San Gerardo de Rivas. The 10:30 a.m. bus from San José will get you to San Isidro in time to catch the 2 p.m. bus to San Gerardo. If you miss the bus, a taxi will take you to San Gerardo for about $16. Buses leave San Gerardo for San Isidro at 7 a.m. and 4 p.m. As mentioned above, Francisco Elizondo of Posada del Descanso can take you to San Isidro for $16.

By Car: It's about 45 minutes from San Isidro to San Gerardo de Rivas. Take the paved road, which you'll see going uphill on your left just south of San Isidro, after the second bridge (there's a small sign for Parque Nacional Chirripó). It's nine kilometers to the town of Rivas. San Gerardo de Rivas is 11 kilometers on good gravel roads from there.

DOMINICAL AND THE COSTANERA SUR

The scenery along the Costanera Sur Highway south of Playa Dominical is reminiscent of California's Big Sur coast—with lush tropical vegetation, of course. Soon the Costanera will become the major north-south route through Costa Rica, connecting Puntarenas with Ciudad Cortés in an easy couple of hours. The gravel road between Manuel Antonio (Quepos) and Dominical, although it can be driven throughout the year, is still bumpy, but the road between Dominical and Cortés is almost fully paved.

Dominical is an important surfing destination (see www.crsurf.com, a Dominical-based webpage), and most of the cabinas on the beach in the town itself are designed to attract surfers, complete with blaring rap music.

Even without a car, you can get to several places on the bus that offer more peace and quiet than the town.

Parents of teenagers might be interested to know about the **Wild Waters Surf Camp** (www.wildwaters.com, e-mail: wwsurfcamp@aol.com). They run ten-day sessions in June, July and August for kids ages 11 to 17. Sessions include surfing instruction, skateboarding, rafting and horseback trips. Counselors are snowboarding and skiing instructors in Colorado in the U.S. winter months. Parents can drop their kids off and continue traveling on their own.

The area has numerous beaches, many with rough waves and strong currents. Swimming at the long beach at the village of Dominical can be dangerous, though surfers love it. On the other hand, the warm, reef-protected waters of Ballena National Marine Park, half an hour's drive to the south, are perfect for swimming and snorkeling. The small beaches near Costa Paraíso and Cabañas Escondidas (below) are also safe for swimming, as is Playa Hermosa, just before Ballena Park.

Kayak Joe (787-0121) runs sea kayaking tours. He charges $35-$50 (depending on the number of people) for a half-day tour exploring the coast and sea caves. He suits his instruction to the level of his students: adrenaline rushes for the more advanced, patience and encouragement for beginners.

The area's numerous and spectacular waterfalls provide a refreshing break from the sea level's sweltering climate. **Don Lulo's Cataratas Nauyaca** (771-3187, fax: 787-0006; $40) takes you on horseback from Platanillo, a small town between San Isidro and Dominical, to two beautiful waterfalls with a large swimming hole. Breakfast, lunch, and a snooze in a hammock are offered at Don Lulo's ranch. Hotel Bella Vista (below) also offers horseback rides to the falls as well as boat excursions for fishing and whale and dolphin watching (see below). The two private biological reserves in the area offer even more to do. (See descriptions below of Hacienda Barú and Rancho La Merced.)

On your way into Dominical, you'll pass **Tropical Waters** (787-0031; e-mail: crinfo@racsa.co.cr), a tourism and rental office where you can make reservations for local hotels, particularly those in out-of-the-way mountain and river locations, and find out about car and house rentals (one-week minimum), or sign up for sea-kayaking, fishing, horseback riding, or hotels in Drake Bay and the Osa Peninsula.

Halfway along the 17-kilometer road between San Isidro and Dominical are the well-designed **Cabinas Tinamaste** (private bath, hot water, ceiling fans, kitchen; $20-$30; cell phone: 382-8660), whose wide porches overlook the mountains and ocean far below. This would be a nice place to relax after too many days on the road. With the view and the fully equipped kitchens, it's quite a bargain. Recommended. Make reservations.

On the way to Dominical in Platanillo, the **Restaurant El Barú** offers good roast chicken and grilled meats. **Paraíso Tropical** (private bath, heated water, refrigerators; $60-$70; phone/fax: 770-5080), also in Platanillo, is a nice place to stop for a meal. Restaurant customers can also take a swim in their pools; one has a waterslide. Their two-room cabinas are nicely decorated and quite peaceful.

DOMINICAL   Dominical itself is not a particularly charming beachside village, but it is where most of the lodging and restaurants are concentrated. There are a couple of supermarkets in Dominical, but no banks. Water quality in the town is poor except in places that have their own wells; bottled water is available.

As you approach Dominical from San Isidro, you follow the peaceful **Río Barú**. If you go right instead of left to cross the bridge into the village, you'll come, in about a kilometer, to the area's only gas station, where you can buy tide tables, fishing supplies, film, maps, and *The Tico Times*. They cash traveler's checks if they have enough money on hand. They also repair flat tires.

A bit farther north, ✪ **Hacienda Barú National Wildlife Refuge** offers self-guided tours ($2-$4) on several trails (one of which has a birding tower), rainforest and lowlands tours on their 830-acre private reserve ($20-$35), tranquil kayak trips ($60) through the mangroves at Playa Hatillo to the north, and horseback trips in the jungle and on the beach ($25 for three hours). One trip ($60) involves camping in a tent on a platform in a jungle clearing. This gives you a good opportunity to look for nocturnal mammals. A trip up the 100-foot-high treetop observation platform costs $35 per person.

Hacienda Barú also operates **Cabinas Hacienda Barú** (private bath, heated water, ceiling and table fans, mosquito nets, kitchen, restaurant; $60-$70, including breakfast; 787-0003, fax: 787-0004; www.cool.co.cr/usr/baru/baru.html, e-mail: baru@cool.co.cr), three-room cottages on a grassy field close to the reserve and about 400 meters from Playa Barú (rough surf and dangerous currents).

A few minutes upriver from the village of Dominical is the **Villa Río Mar Resort** (private bath, hot water, ceiling fans, refrigerator; $90-$100; 257-1138, 787-0052, fax: 787-0054) with pool, jacuzzi, mini-gym, tennis court, etc. The thatched bungalows have spacious porches with mosquito-net curtains and a terrace sitting area with hammocks.

Leticia Porras rents a house ($40/day; weekly and monthly rates; Apdo. 126-8000 Pérez Zeledón) along the cool Río Barú, a kilometer or so inland from town. Find her at the Posada del Sol (fax: 787-0024) in Dominical.

Another half-kilometer up the river road, you will come to a narrow hanging bridge over the Barú. We wouldn't recommend driving over it, as it swings and groans under the weight of a car, but it is quite beautiful and makes a nice stroll from Dominical.

The **Plaza Pacífica** shopping center, just south of the entrance to town along the Costanera, includes **Banana Bay**, a souvenir shop with a selection of clothing and gifts from the world around, and **Dos Hermanos**, a well-stocked supermarket open 8 a.m. to 6 p.m. daily. **Kayak Joe** bases his kayak tours from **Zona Libre**, a funky little outdoor bar here that serves chili dogs, nachos, and beer. The **Funky Orchid Boutique** (787-0061), next to the Dominical police station, sells clothes, jewelry, artwork, and crafts.

There are three public phones in town: at Cabinas Nayarit, by the soccer field in front of Restaurante San Clemente, and in front of the Roca Verde (see below). To use them, you must purchase a phone card at San Clemente for 200, 400, or 3000 *colones*.

Heading toward the beach, you'll see the **Deli Del Río**, a bakery and pizzeria, open from 5 p.m. to 9 p.m. The next major establishment you come to here is **Restaurant San Clemente**, with inexpensive Tex-Mex specialties. Pool tables, surfing videos, and a satellite TV define the ambience. There is also a public phone. Across the street is **Restaurante su Raza** where a television and inexpensive food attract crowds of Ticos and gringo tourists every night.

Nearby is **Posada del Sol** (private bath, heated water, wall fans, screens; $20-$30; two-bedroom apartment with kitchen, $40-$50; fax: 787-0024), clean and pleasant, and with its own well-water supply. **La Residencia** (shared bath, heated water, ceiling fans, screens; $20-$30), across the street, has clean, small rooms in a family home.

Veering right at the Y in the road will take you to a couple of cabinas in front of the best surf break on the beach. **Cabinas DiuWak** (private bath, heated water, ceiling fans, jacuzzi; $20-$30; with kitchen, $30-$40; phone/fax: 223-8195) is a surfers' information center. **Tortilla Flats** (private bath, heated water, ceiling fans or air conditioning; $60-$90 for up to three people; phone/fax: 787-0033) has good Tex-Mex specials. **Cabinas San Clemente** (private bath, heated water, ceiling fans; in the basement, $12-$20; nicer and larger, $20-$60; $10 more with air conditioning; phone/fax: 787-

0026, 787-0055) are fairly nice rooms run by a transplanted California surfer, the owner of Restaurant San Clemente. They rent surfboards. The **Restaurant Atardecer** at the beach offers pitas, falafels, and smoothies.

About a kilometer south of Dominical, where a small estuary bisects the beach, **Roca Verde** (private bath, hot water, ceiling fans, air conditioning; $90-$100; 787-0036, fax: 787-0013; www.doshermanos.com, e-mail: roca ver@racsa.co.cr), has a popular restaurant that serves barbecue, holds popular disco dances on Saturday, and brings in *mariachis* on Sunday. You can book fishing, snorkeling, and wildlife observation boat tours here.

Two kilometers from Dominical, the **Costa Paraíso Lodge** (heated water, ceiling fans; $50-$60; private bath, kitchen, $60-$80; 787-0025; www.domin ical.net, e-mail: costapar@racsa.co.cr) is quiet and secluded. Picturesque rock formations on the beach in front of the hotel form a lagoon; nearby beaches, protected by a reef, are safe for swimming. The less expensive rooms are in the owner's home and include breakfast. The tastefully decorated cabinas are designed for natural ventilation and have hammocks on the porch. You can also rent rooms by the week or the month. Recommended.

GETTING THERE: By Bus: Dominical is served by two bus lines from San Isidro. The San Isidro–Uvita line leaves the Empresa Blanco terminal near the Interamerican Highway in San Isidro for Uvita every day at 9 a.m. and 4 p.m., passing through Dominical an hour later. It returns at 6:45 a.m. and 2:45 p.m. A slower Uvita bus leaves San José daily at 3 p.m., stopping in Dominical at 9 p.m., and returning through Dominical at 6 a.m. The San Isidro–Quepos bus leaves Empresa Blanco at 7 a.m. and 1:30 p.m., arriving in Dominical an hour later. From Quepos, take the 5 a.m. or 1:30 p.m. San Isidro bus, which passes through Dominical two hours later. Check schedules at your hotel.

By Car: Dominical is about 45 minutes from San Isidro on a nicely paved road. Follow the signs through San Isidro. If you are coming from Quepos ask about road and bridge conditions before leaving. The Quepos–Dominical trip takes about an hour and a half.

ESCALERAS AREA

About three kilometers south of Costa Paraíso, a road to the left climbs steeply up to the Escaleras area. Several lodges, cooled by mountain breezes and affording breathtaking views of the Pacific, can be found here. The road is an inverted U; the other end meets the Costanera just beyond Cabañas Escondidas (below). Access is often only possible in a four-wheel-drive vehicle; most of the lodges will pick you up in their own vehicles, or by horse if you prefer. You can also hike, but it's quite steep. Before driving up, radio your lodge (from Restaurant San Clemente or Punta Dominical) to ask which side of the U is in better condition. Lodges in this area still do not have telephones, so book them through **Selva Mar** (777-4582, 771-8841; e-mail: selvamar@sol.racsa.co.cr) or **Tropical Waters** (phone/fax: 787-0031; e-mail: crinfo@sol.racsa.co.cr), a Dominical-based communications center that also rents furnished houses.

Finca Brian y Emilia (private bath, solar hot water, screens; $52/person/day, including meals and farm tour; book through Selva Mar, or write Apdo. 2-8000 San Isidro de El General), two and a half kilometers up the road from the first entrance, is much more than a place to stay. Sample the smorgasbord of 65 species of exotic fruit and nut trees on Brian's guided tour of the farm. The fruits are being grown experimentally to offer tree-crop alternatives for the region. A heated, stream-fed pool awaits guests after their hikes. Cabins are rustic and surrounded by jungle vegetation. Give them a week's notice if you want to stay or participate in tours.

✪ **Bella Vista Lodge** (private bath, solar-heated water, natural ventilation, pool; $50-$60, including breakfast; with kitchen, $60-$70; cell phone: 388-0155 or book through Selva Mar or Tropical Waters) has a beautiful view of the ocean from high atop the Escaleras road. Accommodations are simple but comfortable, and the lodge has a wide, breezy veranda. The two-bedroom house down the hill is probably quieter than the rooms in the main lodge. Woody, the owner, delves into his Cajun roots and cooks up some mighty fine dishes in his homey, inexpensive restaurant. He runs tours with local guides to the Barú waterfall. He also runs boat excursions for whale, dolphin, and turtle watching, swimming, and snorkeling. You can book these tours through the Roca Verde in Dominical.

Nearby are the elegant **Villas Escaleras** (private bath, hot water, kitchens, screens, pool; no children; $150-$350, three-night minimum; $750-$1800/week; phone/fax: 771-5247), whose tasteful details include vaulted ceilings, polished purple-heart floors, and Spanish tiles in the baths. The beautiful villas sleep two to eight and have a 160-degree coastal view. Reservation policies are very strict.

Located above the Villas Escaleras on a small private farm, **Villa Cabeza de Mono** (kitchen, pool, maid service; $120-$130; $800/week; 787-0023) sleeps five to seven and comes with its own version of the beautiful Escaleras view. It's a nice place to retreat from the world for a while. Four-wheel drive is necessary.

Back on the Costanera, in the middle of the inverted U, there is a road heading up one kilometer to ✪ **Pacific Edge** (private bath, cold water; $50-$60, $5 extra for kitchenette; book through Tropical Waters), which has individual rustic but comfortable cabins with broad, covered porches and an open-air restaurant featuring Thai cookery and fresh shrimp. The cheery owners, a British-U.S. couple, can arrange catch-and-release fishing trips with local fishermen and show you the way to a beautiful waterfall at the bottom of their gorge. With advance notice they will pick you up from the bus stop (the Uvita bus from San Isidro) on the Costanera, or in Dominical. Four-wheel drive is necessary.

Heading down to the Costanera again, you'll find the turnoff to **Cabinas Punta Dominical** (private bath, heated water, ceiling fans, screens; $50-$60; 787-0016, fax: 787-0017), on a rocky point overlooking the ocean. The cabinas are well designed, private, comfortable, tranquil, and fanned by ocean breezes, and there's a good restaurant. Although there is a beach north of Punta Dominical, there are a lot of fishing boats, and the river is polluted, so swimming is not recommended.

Three and a half kilometers south of Punta Dominical is **Cabañas Escondidas** (private bath, heated water; $40-80; phone/fax 282-3848; www.crdirect. com/retreats; four-day special including meals, massage, and adventure hike, $215/person), a natural resort with three cabins near a small, secluded beach. Massage, yoga and tai chi classes, jungle walks, horseback, and snorkeling trips are offered. The restaurant features gourmet international cuisine with organic fish, fowl, and eggs, and plenty of vegetarian dishes. Recommended.

Beyond Escondidas, **Las Casitas de Puertocito** (private bath, hot water, ceiling fans, pool; $40-$50, including breakfast; with kitchens, $50-$60; 771-4582, fax: 787-0048; www.amerisol.com/costarica/lodging/lascasitas) are thatch-roofed fourplexes; the sleeping lofts have ocean views. A candle-lit restaurant serves pasta and seafood dishes with fine Italian wines. They are about ten minutes away from a beach and a waterfall.

GETTING THERE: By Bus: The lodges on the main road are right on the San Isidro–Uvita bus line. A bus leaves the Empresa Blanco terminal in San Isidro (just off the Interamerican Highway) daily at 9 a.m. and 4 p.m., arriving in Bahía by about 11 a.m. and 6 p.m. If you are staying at one of the lodges on the Escaleras horseshoe, ask the management to help coordinate transportation from the coastal road. Schedules change, so be sure you check.

By Car: The Costanera Sur road between Quepos and Dominical is still unpaved; it's in good condition, although the rough gravel is hard on tires. South of Dominical the road is paved.

BALLENA NATIONAL MARINE PARK

Ballena National Marine Park is one of Costa Rica's newest national parks, and one of only two marine parks. The first 50 meters inland from the high tide line are part of the park; the rest is ocean.

The park protects the largest coral reef on the Pacific side of Costa Rica and the Ballena Islands, where humpback whales are seen with their young between December and April. Local boatmen can take you out to the reef for snorkeling, skindiving, fishing, or birdwatching. Frigate birds, brown boobies, and ibises all nest on Isla Ballena. If it's sunny and hasn't been raining lately, snorkeling and skindiving on the reef (near the village of Bahía) can be rewarding. At low tide you can walk from the Bahía beach to good snorkeling spots. You can arrange with park rangers to hire a local boatman. The boatmen can take you fishing outside the park, or you can arrange a boat trip from Dominical or Uvita.

The town of Bahía, Ballena National Marine Park headquarters, and the beach are located on a *tombolo*, similar to Punta Catedral in Manuel Antonio. The water here is gentle and at bathtub temperature. There is a natural swimming pool in the rocks during low tide. Playas Ballena and Piñuela to the south are also protected by the park; Piñuela is one of the park's prettiest areas. Camping is not allowed in the park.

UVITA   On the road nearing Uvita, and back in the hills, is a private biological reserve belonging to the Duarte family, **Oro Verde**. Selva Mar (771-4582) can arrange tours that will take you there on horseback. After hiking through their rainforest, you eat lunch at their home and get an overview of how medicinal plants are used in the countryside. Birders will find this trip rewarding, as it covers a wide range of habitats and altitudes. Fees ($10/person for horseback tour, including lunch) help the Duartes preserve their remaining rainforest. Guided walks in the forest cost $10. Humble cabins are available if you wish to stay longer ($10/person, including meals).

Staying at ✪ **Rancho La Merced** is a great way to enter into Costa Rican rural life. David Sequeira, who oversees the ranch, is a dedicated animal observer and protector. He takes guests to the beach on horseback, or hiking to waterfalls in the forested wildlife refuge in the hills above the ranch. Inéz, his wife, cooks wonderful country cuisine, served in their home. Lodging is in a simple *campesino* house in the hills, **El Kurukuzungo** (private bath, cold water, kitchen; $55/person, including meals and a daily tour; 771-4582; e-mail: selvamar@racsa.co.cr). This is quite a good deal. Recommended.

The village of Uvita, a couple of kilometers inland from Bahía and park headquarters, has two simple cabinas owned by friendly local families.

Both families offer horseback rides and hikes through their own and surrounding farms and to a nearby waterfall, and they arrange boat rides at the national park. **Los Laureles** (shared bath, $20-$30; private bath, cold water, table fans; $30-$40; 771-4582) consists of three small concrete houses in a grassy forest clearing—very quiet and peaceful—and some rooms nearer the road. The owners will share family meals with guests, if desired. A bit farther is **El Coco Tico** (private bath, cold water; $20-$30; 771-4582), with a large, clean *soda* on the premises. Some of the rooms are in a row set back from the road, others in a new two-story building next to the *soda*.

BAHÍA   This is the closest village to the park, a couple of kilometers west of the Costanera (when traveling south, make the first or second right after the bridge over the Uvita river). If you're looking for a quiet beach town where you can live as the Ticos do, this might be for you. The nicest place to stay is **Villa Hegalva** (private bath, cold water, table fans; $12-$20; 771-8507), with its clean rooms and covered patio strung with hammocks. They allow camping in their yard for $1.25 per person, and rent tents for $2 per person. The grounds are lovely. Good food is served in their little restaurant. Recommended for budget travelers.

GETTING THERE: By Bus: Buses leave daily at 9 a.m. and 4 p.m. from San Isidro's Empresa Blanco terminal (just off the Interamerican Highway), arriving in Bahia two hours later. From Quepos, follow the directions in the "Getting There" section for Dominical. Travelers from Quepos can intercept the San Isidro–Uvita bus in Dominical around 10 a.m. or 5 p.m. Another option: intercept the San José–Uvita bus as it passes through Quepos at 7 p.m. When leaving the area, there are buses (6 a.m. and 2 p.m.) to San Isidro, and a bus (4:30 a.m. and, on weekends only, 12:30 p.m.) to San José passes through Quepos. Buses to San Isidro stop in Dominical in time to connect with the San Isidro–Quepos bus.

By Car: The Costanera Sur between Dominical and Uvita is paved and in good condition. The drive takes about 15 minutes. To reach Dominical from San Isidro or Quepos follow the directions in the "Getting There" section under Dominical.

FARTHER SOUTH ALONG THE COSTANERA   The recent "completion" of the Costanera has opened up the coast between Uvita and Puerto Cortés. This makes roundtrip circuits through the Southern Zone more reasonable: you can drive one way from San José to Puntarenas or Jacó Beach, south along the coast to Cortés, and then north, inland along the Térraba River, through San Isidro, and over Cerro de la Muerte.

Count on finding a number of beach hotels that we don't mention; they seem to be cropping up daily.

Two kilometers south of Uvita is **Villas Bejuco** (private bath, cold water, natural ventilation, pool; $80-$90; 771-4582), featuring hilltop duplexes with nice gardens, breezes, and views.

A few kilometers south, **Finca Tres Hermanas** (shared bath, solar hot water, natural ventilation; $30-$40/person, including meals for groups of six or more; 771-2465) is a beautiful rain forest reserve and education center next to the ocean. An open classroom with a panoramic view of rainforest and sea is below, and bunk-bed sleeping quarters are above. Baths and dining area are a few steps away. All materials used are natural and display their innate beauty. This would be a great option for those who don't have time to explore Corcovado. Highly recommended.

Kayakers and sightseers will be awed by the tunnels and caves of **Playa Ventanas**, just around the point south from Playa Piñuela. Over millennia, the sea has carved huge arches in the limestone cliffs that form the small bay. Our daredevil captain chugged his fishing boat right through the one on the point. The other tunnels and caves offer plenty of chances for an adrenaline rush to jolt Class IV and V sea kayakers out of their tropical lethargy. Land access is through a private farm: call from the gate to ask the caretaker to let you through. Wading is recommended over swimming, since the waves can be quite rough. During low tide you can walk halfway through the cave at the northern end of the beach; at high tide there is an awesome boom and a cloud of sea vapor as each wave hits the other opening of the cave and the water rushes through. **Kayak Joe** (787-0121), in the Plaza Pacífica in Dominical, does kayak tours to this area.

GETTING THERE: If coming from Dominical, follow directions above for Uvita and continue south.

By Air: You can cut many hours from your trip by flying as far as Palmar Sur (about ten kilometers from Cortés) and taking a bus or taxi the rest of the way. SANSA (221-9414, fax: 255-2176) flies daily at 9:30 a.m. for $50. Travelair (232-7883, 220-3054, fax: 220-0413) flies at 8:45 a.m. via Quepos, leaving Quepos at 9:15 a.m. and returning at 10:40 a.m. with a stop in Quepos at 11:05 a.m. A one-way ticket is $78, and roundtrip it's $127. Osa Tours runs a daily charter flight to Palmar for $55, including refreshments (786-6584, 784-6635).

OSA PENINSULA

The Osa Peninsula reaches out of southwestern Costa Rica into the Pacific Ocean. Historically it has been one of the most remote areas of the country, unknown to most Costa Ricans. Now, nature-loving Ticos and foreign tourists are arriving in large numbers to explore the incredible richness of the peninsula. Its large virgin rainforests receive 160 inches of precipitation a year, and it hosts an incredible variety of tropical flora and fauna. The peninsula has been the site of much ecological destruction by lumbermen, campesino settlers, and gold miners, but the creation of Corcovado National Park in 1975 and the cooperative work of both international and grassroots organizations has served to protect much of the region's natural wealth. Illegal logging is still a serious threat. Most visitors in the 1980s had to go on a hardcore mission to backpack through Corcovado National Park. In the last few years, options have sprung up for softer-core tourists who want to see the rainforest but want their strawberry macadamia nut pancakes for breakfast too.

PALMAR NORTE AND SUR

Palmar Norte and **Palmar Sur**, while not tourist destinations in themselves, are the gateways to Drake Bay, the Osa Peninsula and Golfito to the south. Also, if you have traveled down the Costanera to Cuidad Cortéz, you can turn north in Palmar to visit Boruca and the Dúrika Reserve, or cross the Río Térraba at Paso Real to continue south to the Altamira entrance of Parque Internacional La Amistad and San Vito (see below). You can also fly into the airport in Palmar Sur and continue to the above destinations or head up the Costanera to Uvita and Dominical. If you must stay in Palmar en route to somewhere else, the best place is the **Casa Amarilla** (cold water, table or ceiling fans; with shared bath, under $7; with private bath, $12-$20; 786-6251), next to the Plaza de Deportes in Palmar Norte. The upstairs rooms have balconies. It is often full, so make reservations.

The airport is in Palmar Sur, across the Río Térraba. Taxis are usually around when flights come in.

GETTING THERE: See "Drake Bay" section for air, bus, and car directions to Sierpe and Palmar.

SIERPE

Sierpe used to be a steamy riverside village that you'd just pass through to get to well-known Drake Bay, but recently it has developed a tourism industry of its own. The **Hotel Pargo Rojo** (private bath, hot water, ceiling fans, air-conditioning; $30-$40; 786-7311, fax: 786-7366), located right at the dock, is very clean. They will watch your car for you for a nominal fee while you go to Drake Bay. **Hotel Margarita** (shared bath, cold water; $7-$12; with private bath, $12-$20; 786-7574) is "el cheapo" in Sierpe. It has clean, small rooms with screened windows and is run by friendly local people. It's across the plaza from the discotheque, so you might not want to stay there on weekends. They arrange trips to Poor Man's Paradise, south of Drake Bay. Recommended for budget travelers.

Restaurante Las Vegas, on the river side of the plaza, serves good fish and chicken, and **Rosita's** is popular for *comida típica*. **Sonia's** *pulpería* is the communications center for Sierpe, with telephones, faxes, radios, etc. for public use, plus an incredibly wide variety of items for sale.

Cabinas Tour Gaviotas (private bath, cold water; $12-$20; 786-7591, fax: 786-7579) is owned by the local boat builder and his wife, who makes wonderful breakfasts. They are clean rooms right on the river as you enter town. They offer various tours of the area, including a nighttime crocodile tour.

A unique place in Sierpe is **Veragua River House** (shared bath, $40-$50; private bath, hot water, ceiling fans, $70-$80, including breakfast; 786-7460). Owned and designed by Italian-Austrian artist Benedetto Wallnofer, the main house is run-down but has quirky charm. Our favorite cabina has its own kitchen and screened porch. Other cabins overlook the river, a five-minute walk away. Wallnofer also rents a beach house on Isla Violines, across the mouth of the Sierpe River from Drake Bay. You can reach Veragua by driving or walking across the swinging bridge at the entrance to Sierpe, or by arranging for Ben to pick you up by boat at the main dock.

DRAKE BAY

Drake Bay, purported to be where Sir Francis Drake anchored the *Golden Hinde* and set foot in Costa Rica in 1579, is on the northern coast of the Osa Peninsula, accessible by boat from Sierpe. Scarlet macaws and monkeys are easy to spot there as you hike along the trail above the rocky coves south of the Río Agujitas. The bay is rich in marine life. Four types of whales visit the bay. **Elderhostel** sponsors a whale research expedition based at Drake Bay Wilderness Resort (see below). Delfin Amor will take you on **Wild Dolphin Encounters**. They have established relationships with pods of dolphins in the area, who seem to love to gather around their boat, arcing out of the water and leaping high into the air. You can also spend a fascinating evening with biologist **Tracy the Bug Lady**, who will lead you into the jungle with hand-held night-vision optics devices which cast an eerie green color on everything, but allow you to see clearly in the dark without disturbing the animals. She and her partner teach you how to see the eye-glow from frogs and spiders, and explain the weird mating rituals of leaf-cutter ants and stick insects. You might even see a boa. It's well worth the $35 fee. She supplies you with boots and walking sticks.

Note: It really is smart to bring well-fitting rubber boots to this area. They give much-needed traction on the muddy trails, and can keep you dry through most stream crossings at low tide. Otherwise, sand gets in your wet sandals and rubs your feet—the same happens with wet sneakers. If you bring boots, be sure to bring several pairs of thick socks that extend above the rim of the boots. If you don't, the boots rub your calves.

Fishing is excellent along the coast. All the lodges on Drake Bay offer fishing trips and guided tours to Corcovado National Park and **Isla del Caño**, a small, round, forest-covered island about 20 kilometers off the coast that is thought to be the site of a pre-Columbian cemetery. Stones carved into perfect spheres can be found on the island; their significance is still unknown. Snorkeling is especially good at Isla del Caño, as the water is crystal clear and five coral platforms surround the island. The lodges all lend out snorkeling equipment, unless noted, and most of them have kayaks for rent. Scuba diving is offered by La Paloma, Aguila, and Jinetes de Osa lodges, which specialize in dives off Isla del Caño.

The most common way of getting to Drake Bay involves a 75-minute boat trip down the Sierpe River and across the river mouth to the open sea before you get to the lodges. The San Pedrillo entrance to Corcovado is about half an hour's boat ride beyond Drake Bay, or a four-hour hike. If the beach landing at San Pedrillo looks rough, boats will turn back and go to Playa San Josecito, which is outside the park. It's a 40-minute boat ride from Drake Bay to Isla del Caño.

The lodges listed first are south of the village of Drake Bay. Drake Bay Wilderness Camp, Aguila de Osa, and La Paloma are clustered around the Río Agujitas where the main docks are. The next seven are scattered along isolated beaches between Drake and the border of Corcovado National Park. While these more-remote lodges offer boat transportation, reaching them on foot from the Agujitas area is not impossible at low tide. Just south of Drake Bay are Las Caletas, a series of small coves bordered by rocky outcroppings. The trail goes up above the coves. It's a lovely hike, with plenty of chances to swim and snorkel if you want to. South of Marenco the landscape flattens out and the trail is sometimes on the beach itself.

LODGING   On the north side of the Río Aguijitas is **Aguila de Osa** (private bath, hot water, ceiling fans; $145/person, including meals; suites, $313-$382; discount for children; transfers extra; $795 for three-night package including transfer from Palmar; phone/fax: 232-7722, 296-2190; www.centralamerica. com/cr/hotel/aguila, e-mail: aguila@centralamerica.com; closed in October) with stunning views, sunken bathrooms with even deeper tubs, and good service. The hotel caters to anglers and their families, offering inshore and deep-sea fishing in 24-foot and 31-foot Garretts. Scuba diving is also available.

Across the Río Agujitas is **Drake Bay Wilderness Resort** (solar- and gas-heated water, ceiling fans; $50-$60 in tent-cabins; $70-80 in cabins; both rates per person, including meals; transfers extra; discount for children, four- and seven-day packages available; 284-4107, phone/fax: 770-8012, 221-4948; www.drakebay.com, e-mail: hdrake@amerisol.net) is a family-style camp right at the mouth of the Río Agujitas with good American- and Tico-style food and plenty to do near the lodge. Snorkeling is good both right at the resort and ten minutes away by boat at Punta San Joseçito. They will lend you masks and fins, and canoes for exploring the Río Agujitas, known for its needlefish. You can canoe up the river in search of monkeys, then relax in the giant tidepools at the far end of the property or in their new saltwater swimming pool. There's a butterfly farm you can ride to on horseback, an hour and a half from the lodge. Kayaks are available for rent and sea-kayaking instruction is also offered. A seven-day tour of the area by boat and kayak based at the resort is available through **Gulf Islands Kayaking** (in Canada: 604-539-2442). A four-day package, including transportation to the new Drake airstrip from San José or Quepos, costs $534. Boat transfers can be arranged from Dominical, for groups ($140, two-hour trip). Laundry service is free for guests. You might not grasp what an important service this is unless you have tried to dry your clothes in the tropics. It can take several days. The gas-run dryers seem heaven-sent. This hotel charters a plane that leaves the Pavas Airport in San José every day at 8 a.m. and arrives in Drake at 9:30 a.m. ($160).

Staying in the ranchos at ✪ **La Paloma Lodge** (private bath, solar-heated water, ceiling fans, pool; ranchos, $162/person; rooms, $133/person; meals included; transfers extra; three-night package, $735-$825; phone/fax: 239-0954, 239-2854, fax: 239-2801; www.lapalomalodge.com, e-mail: bahdrake@racsa.co.cr) is like waking up in the jungle. Perched high on a hill, the private, two-story ranchos are surrounded by greenery and birds, with views of Drake Bay and Caño Island beyond. The standard rooms are spacious and have balconies with hammocks. Their tiled swimming pool offers spectacular ocean views. The owners pride themselves on the personalized service to guests. The airy dining room serves delicious food. Kayaks, canoes, boogie boards and snorkeling equipment are available as well as PADI-certified scuba instruction. They use a 36-foot catamaran for their tours. Recommended.

A 15-minute walk south of La Paloma is the Canadian-owned ✪ **Cocalito Lodge** (private bath, solar-heated water, floor fans, mosquito nets, screens; $65/person, including meals; camping, $7/person; tent rentals, $15; three night packages, $275-$325; cell phone: 284-6369, phone/fax in Canada: 519-782-3978; www.costaricanet.net/cocalito, e-mail: berrybend@aol.com). A good swimming beach lies directly in front of its cabins. Its restaurant special-izes in grilled and barbecued seafood served by candlelight. They offer tours, sea kayaks, canoes, fishing, and diving, plus an interesting cultural experi-ence: a one-hour hike inland on forest trails to the small community of Los Planes where they have a three-story rancho-observatory with a view over the bay, great for naturalists and birdwatchers ($50/night, including meals).

A half-hour's hike along the lovely trail above Las Caletas brings you to ✪ **Delfin Amor Eco-Lodge** (shared bath, cold water, no fans; $65/person, including meals; transportation: $60 roundtrip from Palmar; cell phone: 394-2632, fax: 786-7642; www.divinedolphin.com, e-mail delfinamor@divine dolphin.com) whose mission is "enriching the deep connection that humans have with dolphins and whales" and helping protect the sea mammals as well. Delfin Amor's Wild Dolphin Encounters epitomize respect—the animals are never chased or fed, and the choice to interact is always their choice. Guests at the lodge dine family-style, and gather on the stone veranda of the dining room overlooking the sea to watch the sunset. Jerry, the Pirate Chef, dishes out some awesome fare, and will cook up the fish you catch on your way back from communing with the dolphins (dolphins' sonar keeps them away from hooks). Above the dining room is the Marine Education Center, with a library and a giant map of the Osa. Lodging consists of three large tents with two double beds in each, and a shared bath area. Check out the nine-day package ($1250) on their website. Volunteering is a possibility if your skills match their needs. Recommended.

A 15-minute walk south of Delfin Amor brings you to **Marenco Beach and Rainforest Lodge** (private bath, cold water, fans; $717/person for three nights, including meals, tours, and transportation from San José; 258-1919, fax: 255-1346, in the U.S.: 800-278-6223; www.marencolodge.com, e-mail: info@marencolodge.com), one of the original eco-tourism projects in Costa Rica. Cabins, high on a hill with private porches, look out at gardens that attract birds and butterflies, and at Isla del Caño beyond. Researchers are always in residence at Marenco, and double as naturalist guides. Marenco Beach shares the view and a 500-hectare forest reserve with its neighbor, ✪ **Punta Marenco Lodge** (private bath, cold water, no fans, mosquito nets; $87/person, including meals; $495/person for a three-night package includ-ing meals, tours, and roundtrip transportation from San José; 222-3305, 268-9441; www.puntamarenco.com, e-mail: info@puntamarenco.com), individual *ranchos* with one side totally open to the view, owned and operated by Guillermo Miranda, the founder of the reserve, and his family. A half-hour hike from either lodge through a series of lovely rocky coves ends at the Río Claro, where a deep natural pool lends itself to a refreshing swim.

✪ **Poor Man's Paradise** (cell phone at lodge: 383-4209, fax: 786-6150; in the U.S.: 715-588-3950; e-mail: selvamar@racsa.co.cr), is a family-run project on isolated Playa Rincón, a three-hour hike (go at low tide only) or a 20-minute boat ride south of Drake. A little grass-roofed *rancho* on the beach, which serves as an evangelical church for the community, is the only sign you see from the water. In back of it are four immaculate cabins with good mattresses (private bath, cold water, table fans; $50-$60/person, including meals), a common hanging-out area, and a platform with tents (shared bath, cold water; $30-$40/person, including meals; $7/person without meals if you bring your own tent). Farther back is the restaurant where Doña Carmen takes care of her guests as if they were family. Her husband, Don Concho, learned herbal medicine when he lived with the Guaymi Indians. Their son, Pincho, specializes in low-cost sportfishing trips. They offer horseback riding and have a sheltered reef ideal for snorkeling at low tide. This is a unique opportunity to get to know a Costa Rican family in a beautiful setting. Recommended.

✪ **Proyecto Campanario** (shared baths, cold water, no fans; 282-5898; fax: 282-8750; www.campanario.org, e-mail: campanar@racsa.co.cr) is a biological reserve and field station on a beautiful cove about an hour's walk or a short boat ride south of Poor Man's Paradise. It's the brainchild of Nancy Aitken, a high school teacher with a dream to help people understand the rainforest. She has set up tables and benches in the most beautiful parts of the reserve so you can spend time being quiet and listening to the forest. The no-frills field station provides bunkbed accommodations with shared baths downstairs. Large tents on platforms up the hill from the field station are more private. Their three-night package ($297) includes meals and transportation from Sierpe plus guided trips to the reserve and Corcovado. They also offer a six-day Rainforest Conservation camp ($579), a ten-day course in Tropical Biology for students ($820), and a two-week Tropical Biology course for teachers ($1775). The last three include transport from San José. This is a great volunteer opportunity for people willing to do trail maintenance work and help in the kitchen. Visiting Campanario is a friendly, educational, and inexpensive way to see this beautiful area.

✪ **Casa Corcovado** (private baths, hot water, ceiling fans; $140/person, including meals and tours; 256-3181, fax: 256-7409, beeper: 233-3333; www.casa corcovado.com, e-mail: corcovdo@racsa.co.cr; closed September 1 through November 15) is on the border of Corcovado National Park, a half-hour boat ride from Drake Bay. After a beach landing that has to be done at exactly the right gap in the waves, guests are transported straight uphill for a welcome cocktail at a simple but elegant screened bar with a great view of Isla del Caño. The bungalows are set back at the edge of the forest and do not have views. They are private and well designed, with good mattresses and spacious, tiled bathrooms. Another attractive open-air bar is cantilevered over the jungle where chances for birdwatching abound. Also here are a spacious recreation room with videos and a library, and a fresh-water pool surrounded by jungle. Casa Corcovado is known for excellent service. Their three-night package costs $600 including air transport from San José and trips to Corcovado and Caño Island.

Drake Village: North of Río Agujitas, toward the town of Drake (pronounced "Drah-kay" in Spanish), are the budget places. There is also an administered public telephone at the *pulpería* about halfway down the beach. **Albergue Jinetes de Osa** (solar-heated water, ceiling fans, shared or private bath; $70/person, meals included, transfers extra; camping on platforms, $10/person; cell phone: 385-9541, 800-317-0333; e-mail: crventur@costa ricadiving.com) specializes in scuba diving, rents snorkel equipment, and can arrange inexpensive small-craft fishing trips in the bay.

Halfway down the beach, an uphill road next to the *pulpería* leads you to ✪ **Cabinas Jade Mar** (private bath, cold water, table fans; $50/person, including meals; cell phone/fax: 284-6681, beeper: 233-3333, for Marta Perez Mendoza), simple but very clean cabins run by a local woman who has training as a nature guide. You will really get a sense of life in this small beach town by staying with Doña Marta, and though we didn't get to eat there, the tempting aroma of fried fish emanating from her breezy, open-air dining room indicated that she's a very good cook. She can take you to her family's farm, where you can swim in a waterfall-fed lagoon, and she offers group rates to Corcovado and Isla de Caño. Recommended.

At the end of the beach you'll see a road coming from the north and following a river inland. This is the Rincón–Rancho Quemado road which could change the face of Drake forever if it becomes viable year-round. If you wade across the river and scramble up the embankment and over the road, you'll see a steep trail that will bring you to ✪ **Mirador Lodge** (private bath, cold water, natural ventilation; no electricity; $30-$40/person, including meals; cell phone: 387-9138, 770-8051), rustic accommodations with a beautiful view of Drake Bay and nearby rivers and waterfalls. A steep hike uphill from the cabins is a covered camping area ($15/person, including meals) with an even more amazing view. Owner Don Toño and his family are ardent vegetarians and organic gardeners. They cook soymeat specialties on their woodstove. Recommended for budget travelers who like to hike.

Back down the Río Sierpe again, you'll come to ✪ **Río Sierpe Lodge** (private bath, solar-heated water, fans, screens; $60-$70, including meals and transportation from Palmar; cell phone: 284-5595, fax: 786-7366; e-mail: vsftrip@racsa.co.cr), a good place for serious birders, naturalists, and anglers. Owner Mike Stiles is a bird expert with years of experience in the region, and particular knowledge of the birds that frequent the estuarine and primary forest systems near the lodge. Try to get one of the new cabins that has a screened upstairs bedroom ($15 more) and views of the jungle or the river. Mike has a great library of nature books. The lodge offers attractive group rates for eight or more: $295 (even less for students and birders) for four days and three nights, including Corcovado and Isla del Caño tours and transport from Palmar. A six-day mangrove kayaking trip is available, as well as trips to the Panama cloud forest and Bocas del Toro.

We have heard glowing reports about the food, hospitality, and peacefulness of **Sábalo Lodge** (private or shared baths, solar hot water; $50-$60, including meals; 226-0355, 771-4582, phone/fax: 286-2839; www.online.co.cr/ sabalo, e-mail: sabalo@racsa.co.cr). Located on a canal leading off the Río Sierpe, this converted family farm has a rustic, relaxed atmosphere. You can also study Spanish during your stay—Nidia, one of the owners, is an experienced instructor.

GETTING THERE: You should definitely make reservations and travel arrangements before you go to Drake Bay, because crossing the river mouth is best done with the tides. Also many lodges do not have their own docks, and landings need to be coordinated by captains and assistants experienced with each place. For these reasons it is best to let your lodge arrange transportation for you from San José, Palmar, or Sierpe. You can get to Palmar by bus or plane, or drive to Sierpe if you have a car (the Hotel Pargo Rojo, next to the main dock in Sierpe, will watch your car while you are in Drake). Most lodges charge about $25 for a round trip Palmar-Sierpe taxi, and $40 roundtrip for the boat ride. You are met at each step by people from your hotel. If you have a package deal, transportation costs are included.

By Bus: If you want to get there on your own, take a bus to Palmar, which leaves San José (Calle 14, Avenida 5; 222-2160, 222-2666, 223-7685; $4) seven times a day. The trip takes six hours. After you get to Palmar, follow directions for boat travel from Sierpe, below.

By Car to Sierpe: At Palmar Sur on the Interamerican Highway, drive south through a maze of banana plantations to the town of Sierpe. Ask the banana workers directions at every intersection (there are no signs and it's easy to get lost). From Sierpe, follow boat directions below.

By Car to Drake: A new road connects Drake with the eastern Osa Peninsula. This is the road that has been facilitating the massive logging operations north of

Corcovado. It runs from the town of Rincón on the Golfo Dulce to Rancho Quemado and on to Agujitas. It doesn't cross the Agujitas river, so you'd have to leave your car on the village side if you wanted to visit lodges to the south. Jademar will watch your car for you. When we were there in November 1999 it was completely impassible. It can only be driven by a high-clearance vehicle, and only in the dry season. Check with your hotel regarding road conditions and driving times.

By Air to Palmar: You can take a plane to Palmar. SANSA (221-9414, fax: 255-2176; $55 one-way) leaves at 9:30 a.m., returning at 10:30 a.m. Travelair (220-3054, 232-7883, fax: 220-0413; $78 one way, $127 roundtrip) leaves every morning at 8:45 a.m. You can pick up the flight in Quepos if coming from Manuel Antonio, at 9:15 a.m. It returns at 10:40 a.m. with a stop in Quepos at 11:05 a.m. Osa Tours has a daily charter flight to Palmar for $55 including refreshments (786-6534, fax: 786-6635).

By Air to Drake: Now there is an airstrip in Drake Bay. Roundtrip from San José is $160. Coordinate through Drake Bay Wilderness Resort (770-8012, 221-4948; www.drakebay.com). Their plane leaves the Pavas airport daily at 8 a.m. for the 45-minute flight. They give priority to their own guests.

By Boat: You might be able to save money by hiring a local boatman in Sierpe if you are with a group and you only want to go to the main landing in Drake. They charge by the size of the boat. A $70 boat (one way) will hold six people, an $80 boat holds thirteen. Rates change with the price of gasoline, which was going up when we were there.

A more elegant solution is the Temptress cruise ($1875-$2595 for a seven-night cruise; three- and four-day options also available; 800-255-3585; www. temptresscruises.com), which visits Drake Bay, Corcovado, and Isla del Caño.

PUERTO JIMÉNEZ

Puerto Jiménez is the largest town on the Osa Peninsula. People say its first inhabitants were prisoners sent away from the mainland with machetes and a warning never to come back.

Despite, or perhaps as a result of, its tawdry history, Puerto Jiménez is now the gateway to some of the most beautiful and inspiring tourism projects in the country. Because the Osa was considered such a no-man's land, it opened to tourism much later than the rest of Costa Rica. The people who started tourism projects here did not do so to jump on the bandwagon, but because they had a vision that the beauty of the land could be the key to its preservation. The ecotourism projects in this area are principled, and are already seeing the effects of their efforts: scarlet macaws, monkeys, and jaguars are coming back. You can probably see as much wildlife in the private reserves of these lodges, or from their terraces, as you can by going to Corcovado itself. And it has its positive effects on the local community: Don Alfredo Mesén, an employee of one of the lodges, heard that a neighboring campesino was about to cut the trees on his land—virgin forest. Don Alfredo suggested that in one year, his neighbor could make more money by guiding tourists through his forest than he could by cutting it down. The campesino took him up on it, and Señor Mesén sent him a steady supply of tourists from his beach hotel. At the end of one year the farmer was better off economically, and will be for years to come. Now other campesinos are calling the hotel, asking to be supplied with tourists.

We should not paint too rosy a picture, however: trucks piled high with forest giants rumble through the Osa every night. The **Cercropia Foundation** is trying to fight this massive destruction. Stop by their office in Puerto Jiménez, next to Osa Natural (735-5532).

Osa Natural (open Monday through Saturday, 8 a.m. to 5 p.m.; phone/fax: 735-5440; www.ecoturism.co.cr/osanatural, e-mail: osanatur@racsa.co.cr) is a community-based travel agency that will set you up for air, ground, or sea transportation and all hotels, guides, and tours in the area. They are also the official place to make reservations for Corcovado National Park. As you come into "downtown" Puerto Jimenez, they are at the end of the first block, on the left.

You can arrange sea kayak trips or sunset dolphin watches at the downtown **Escondido Trex** office in Restaurant Carolina (phone/fax: 735-5210; e-mail: osatrex@racsa.co.cr). Joel Stewart (735-5569), of El Remanso (see Cabo Matapalo below), helps you climb 180-foot forest giants or rappel down waterfalls. Bosque del Cabo has an observation platform high in the forest canopy that you can slide to on a cable (381-4847). **Osaventures** (735-3541) specializes in bird and wildlife observation. Isabel Esquivel, the well-organized bilingual radio operator at **Osa Tropical** (735-5062, fax: 735-5043; e-mail: osatropi@racsa.co.cr; 50 meters south of the Catholic Church) offers a variety of naturalist expeditions; she can also make reservations for the lodges on the Osa Peninsula (see below). **El Tigre**, just south of La Carolina on the main street, is a general store where you can cash traveler's checks, change money, and stock up on food or camping supplies. They run a collective taxi service to Cabo Matapalo ($2.50) and Carate ($7) that leaves at 6 a.m. and returns at 8:30 a.m. every day but Sunday ($60 per carload at other times). There is a gas station at the southern end of Puerto Jiménez, where you turn right to go to Matapalo and Carate.

LODGING   Cabinas are described in the order you find them when you come off the ferry from Golfito. Right off the pier, with a back wall on the mangrove swamp (big bathroom windows provide almost an aquarium effect at high tide), are the **Cabinas Agua Luna** (private bath, cold water, air conditioning, bathtubs, TV, refrigerator; $45/person; 735-5034, 735-5393).

On the way into town from the dock, **Cabinas Brisas del Mar** (private bath, some with heated water, ceiling fans; $12-$20; 735-5012) have windows facing the gulf. Find out if there is a dance at the nearby El Rancho before staying here. It can be noisy.

Half a block north of El Rancho Bar and Restaurant are **Cabinas Puerto Jiménez** (private bath, table fans, cold water; $12-$20; 735-5090, 735-5152). These simple, clean rooms are right on the water. It is probably worth finding out whether there is a big dance at El Rancho before staying at these cabinas.

If you start at the soccer field and walk along the road out of town toward La Palma just 100 meters, you will come to the only cabinas around with their own pool: **Cabinas Iguana Iguana** (private bath, cold water, table fan; $15/person; 735-5158; e-mail: ziguana@racsa.co.cr) are simple, have friendly management, and are blessedly beyond the decibel range of El Rancho.

The cheapest option we found is **Pensión Quintero** (shared bath, cold water, table fans; under $7; 735-5087, fax: 735-5261), which has small rooms—some without windows. The owners can organize horseback rides ($6/hour) or guide you through Corcovado National Park ($50 for two to four people plus expenses).

Cabinas Marcelina (private bath, table fans; $12-$20; 735-5007), located in town just off the main street, are simple lodgings with a bit of garden out front. The friendly owners can set up horse rides and fishing trips for guests.

A five-minute walk toward the airport are **Cabinas Manglares** (private bath, cold water, table fans; $20-$30; 735-5002, fax: 735-5605). To find Manglares, make a left off the main street before the church, and continue two blocks past Cabinas Marcelina. Make a right, cross a little bridge over the mangrove swamp; Manglares is around the bend.

You can walk or drive to **Doña Leta's Bungalows** (private bath, heated water, ceiling fans, kitchen; $45/person, including breakfast and use of kayaks; $1350/month; phone/fax: 735-5180; e-mail: letabell@sol.racsa.co.cr) either via the airstrip or from the ferry landing. These are comfortable, well-designed houses on a gentle, shallow beach. To accommodate families and groups, the retired North American owners have a volleyball court and horseshoes, and they lend kayaks. There is an inexpensive laundry service as well.

RESTAURANTS   As far as culinary possibilities in Puerto Jiménez: **Agua Luna** is a restaurant formed by a series of ranchitos (round, indigenous-style buildings with pointy, thatched roofs) on the spit between the gulf and the mangrove, right near the dock. Food is good here. The owner runs the cabinas of the same name (see above).

El Ranchito serves breakfast on the southwest corner of the soccer field. **Restaurant La Campesina** serves a good traditional Costa Rican breakfast. **Carolina's** is very popular, and **Josette's** across the street is cheap and also good.

GETTING THERE: By Bus: Take the Empresa Blanco bus from San José at 6 a.m. or noon ($7; Calle 12, Avenidas 7/9; 257-4121, 771-2550). The trip lasts eight hours. The bus passes through San Isidro at 9 a.m. and 3 p.m.—catch it at the same station the Dominical–Uvita bus leaves from, near the Interamerican Highway. The bus returns from Puerto Jiménez at 5 a.m. and 11 a.m. If you are coming from some other point, intercept the Villa Neily–Puerto Jiménez bus at 7 a.m. or 3 p.m. at Chacarita (Piedras Blancas), at the entrance to the Osa Peninsula on the Interamerican Highway. To reach the hotels south of Puerto Jiménez, contact them for pick-up or hire a taxi in town.

By Car: Follow the Interamerican Highway to Piedras Blancas (Chacarita) and turn right. When we drove to Puerto Jimenez in late 1999 it took us three hours to drive the 75 kilometers between Chacarita and Puerto Jimenez. The road, which had been paved the last time we were there, was totally destroyed by the huge lumber trucks that constantly traverse it, and by flooding a month earlier. Rumor has it that the road will be fixed soon, but don't plan to drive here unless you check with your hotel on road conditions and driving times. Be really alert for bicycle riders along the Interamerican Highway. There are a lot of them, especially at dawn and dusk, and they don't have lights.

By Boat: An old launch leaves the municipal *muelle* in Golfito for Puerto Jiménez every day at 11:30 a.m., returning the next morning from Jiménez at 6 a.m. The enjoyable ride across the gulf takes an hour and a half. Dolphins often swim and dive alongside the boat. Zancudo Boat Tours (776-0012) will take you from Zancudo to Puerto Jiménez for $15-$20 per person.

By Air: SANSA offers a daily flight for Puerto Jiménez at 11:30 a.m, returning at 12:40 p.m. ($60 one way; 221-9414, fax: 255-2176). Travelair ($90 one way, $152 roundtrip; 220-3054, fax: 220-0413) flies to Puerto Jiménez daily at 9 a.m. and 1 p.m., returning at 9:55 a.m. via Golfito and 2:05 p.m. via Quepos. See the "Planes" section under "Local Transportation" in Chapter Four for reservation information.

SOUTH OF PUERTO JIMÉNEZ

The following projects are located south of Puerto Jiménez, an area that is not serviced by public electricity. All of them rely on private generators or solar and candle power, so be sure to bring a flashlight. The phone numbers we give are where the lodges pick up their messages, so call for reservations as far ahead of your arrival as possible. Lodges in the area north of Puerto Jimenez are listed after those in Carate.

PLAYA PLATANARES   **Playa Platanares** is a long, peaceful beach on the Golfo Dulce six kilometers south of Puerto Jiménez. Whales can be spotted there in October and November and it's a turtle beach. A local couple, Don Efraín Mesén and his wife, have a homegrown turtle protection project there. Don Efraín patrols the beach nightly from May to November and moves the nests to a protected area. They date the reburied nests, and then help the baby turtles with their trip to the water when they hatch 60 days later. Don Efraín has also built some whimsical driftwood sculptures on the beach. They will gladly show you their project, which is across from Playa PreciOsa Lodge (see below). Donations are gratefully accepted.

Iguana Lodge (private bath, solar hot water, ceiling fans; $55/person including meals; 735-5205; e-mail: lauren@iguanalodge.com) is the first place you come to when you turn left onto the beach road. The spacious cabins are on stilts so that each has an ocean view, and the screened walls are louvered so you can catch the breeze. There are two beds upstairs and two below, so it's a great place for families. Meals, featuring freshly caught seafood and delicious homemade baked goods, are served in a huge two-story *rancho*. The owners are lawyers from Colorado who are homeschooling their kids on the beach.

About 500 meters north, you'll come to ✪ **Playa PreciOsa Nature Lodge** (private bath, cold water, ceiling fans; $50-$60/person; 735-5062, fax: 735-5043; www.playa-preciosa-lodge.de, e-mail: osatropi@racsa.co.cr). The ocean view is lovely from their airy, open, second-floor dining area. Comfortable, cylindrical cabins also have airy sleeping areas upstairs. The German owners have put a lot of work into their nature trail, a one-and-a-half-kilometer loop through secondary growth that provides a corridor for monkeys and macaws on their way to the beach. The owners offer boogieboarding, horseback rides, mountain-bike rentals, tours of the primary forest, and boat and kayak trips. Closed mid-August through October. To get to either lodge, drive to the airstrip in Puerto Jiménez. Take the road around the perimeter, then follow the signs. The road was pretty slow-going when we were there.

CABO MATAPALO   As you head south of Puerto Jiménez, the road becomes more demanding of four-wheel-drive expertise—several rivers to cross that have steep banks on either side. Torrential rains in the fall of 1999 wreaked havoc with the roads here. If you are not a four-wheel-drive wizard, it's better to fly into Jiménez and let your hotel transport you out here. Maybe things will be better by the time you read this.

Buena Esperanza is a new restaurant and bar just after the Río Carbonera on the left, where an enthusiastic California chef turns out "low fat, high flavor" food to go. It's the only restaurant between there and Carate, and might be a lot more interesting than what's available in Puerto Jiménez. **Playa Matapalo** is *the* surfing beach in the Osa, reachable by an unmarked but obviously well-used road on the left as you climb toward Lapa Ríos.

Owned by one of the Osa's original foreign residents, a surfer and former gold miner, **Bahía Esmeralda** (private bath, cold water, table fans, ceiling fans; $110-$120/person, including meals and transportation from Puerto Jiménez; cell phone: 381-8521, 735-5062, fax: 735-5045; www.bahiaesmeralda. com, e-mail: pandulce@racsa.co.cr) has a large, three-story house and three private cabins with distant ocean views and wide balconies. Gourmet meals are served downstairs. There is a spring-fed, nonchlorinated pool in the glen next to the lodge. **Kapú** ($50-$60/person, including meals; http://home.earth link.net/~kapu) is a quirky "retreat" with nice gardens right on the beach. We barely made it through a lake-sized puddle on the way.

✪ **Lapa Ríos** (private bath, cold water, natural ventilation, screens and mosquito nets, pool, wheelchair accessible; $182/person, including meals; children under 10, $80-$90; 735-5130, fax: 735-5179; www.laparios.com, e-mail: laparios@racsa.co.cr) is a luxury resort on a 1000-acre reserve containing primary and secondary rainforest, and reforested pastureland. Thatch-roofed bungalows dot the side of a hill, at the top of which is a spacious restaurant. Up a tall spiral staircase is an observation deck with a beautiful view of the Golfo Dulce. The rooms are tastefully designed with wide private balconies. Each balcony has a shower surrounded by lush foliage, so you can bathe outside while enjoying the view. The Minnesotan owners conceived Lapa Ríos as a model to show the world that a single small hotel can finance the maintenance of a large natural reserve. Guests can roam the reserve's trails or visit the calm beach at the bottom of the hill. They are given the opportunity to plant a tree in the reforested sector. Monkeys, toucans, and macaws are often visible from the elegant restaurant terrace, which hangs over the jungle high above the sea. The resort came in second on Condé Nast's list of the top 15 small hotels in the Caribbean and Latin America. Recommended.

✪ **Bosque del Cabo** (private bath, cold water, natural ventilation, spring-fed pool; $100-$110/person, including meals; children 3 to 12 half-price, under 3 free; cell phone: 381-4847, phone/fax: 735-5206; www.bosquedel-cabo.com, e-mail: boscabo@racsa.co.cr), a few kilometers farther down the road and left down a mile-long driveway through the forest, has a spectacular view of the ocean from above Playa Matapalo at the very southern tip of the Osa Peninsula. You can take a horseback ride down to the beach where there is a beautiful waterfall with macaws nesting above the pool, or slide Tarzan-like on a cable to a wildlife observation platform in the middle of the forest. The individual bungalows are perched at the edge of a semi-circular cliff overlooking the sea. They are spacious, with porches and unique outdoor showers. The restaurant serves good international food. A house is available for a weekly rental of $850 for up to four people, meals not included. With advance notice, they can arrange a taxi from Puerto Jiménez for $25 each way. Recommended.

Just after the entrance to Bosque del Cabo is the long driveway down to ✪ **El Remanso** (private bath, cold water, natural ventilation, spring-fed pool; $105/person, including meals; 735-5569; www.costaricasur.com/remanso, e-mail: jstewart@racsa.co.cr) owned by Belén Momeñe of Spain and Joel Stewart, a North American who runs tree-climbing and waterfall-rappelling adventure tours from their property. They met while working on Greenpeace's boats. The three spacious bungalows are designed for those who like quiet and privacy, and are decorated with delightful murals of angels. They are screened and offer distant water views. The beach is a ten-minute walk downhill. Recommended.

GETTING THERE: It takes about an hour to get from Puerto Jiménez to Cabo Matapalo. Your hotel can arrange taxi transport for about $25 per car. Note that you shouldn't try to drive down Bosque del Cabo's driveway if it starts to look mucky; leave your car by the side of the road and walk the rest of the way.

CARATE   The road gets better after Lapa Ríos, and we continued an hour through pleasant cattle country to the Río Aguas Buenas, which was definitely too deep to cross in the rainy season. You can ask Luis Arias, the local taxi driver, to arrange for horses to meet you at the river if it looks like crossing on foot is impossible. Carate is another eight kilometers after the river.

Just before you get to Carate, you'll see **The Lookout** (private bath, solar hot water; $119/person, including meals; discounts for children; 735-5431; e-mail: wendy@lookout-inn.com). It's beautiful, comfortable, and has a great view and restaurant.

Costa Rica Expeditions' ✪ **Corcovado Lodge and Tent Camp** (shared bath, cold water, natural ventilation; $60-$70/person, including meals; 257-0766, 222-0033, fax: 257-1665; www.crexped.co.cr, e-mail: costaric@expeditions.co.cr) has an enviable setting: off a pristine beach near La Leona entrance to Corcovado National Park. Guests arrive via plane or vehicle from Puerto Jiménez, and stay in ten-by-ten-foot tents on wooden platforms. There is a large *rancho* up the hill that has hammocks for reading and relaxing, and a family camp–style restaurant. A two-day, one-night package including a charter flight to Carate and all meals costs $699 per person. The lodge is very proud of its platform 120 feet off the ground in an *ajo* tree (so named for the garlicky scent of its flowers). You hike about an hour through the forest, ascend via a rope-and-pulley system, and may spend up to two hours on the platform. An experienced guide accompanies you.

GETTING THERE: There is no public bus service south of Jiménez. Your lodge can arrange transportation from Puerto Jiménez, for about $60. Trucks, whose passengers are mostly backpackers going to Carate, leave Puerto Jiménez across from Carolina's, Monday through Saturday mornings at 6 a.m. ($7/person to Carate). If you wish to go later in the day, it costs $60 per truckload to Carate. If the Río Aguas Buenas is too high, the truck only goes to the river, and you have to hike the remaining eight kilometers to Carate. Luis, the truck/taxi driver, can arrange for horses to meet you at the river. Contact him through El Tigre, in Puerto Jiménez. Apparently there is no problem crossing the river in the dry season.

By Car: The gravel road south of Puerto Jiménez was passable only for four-wheel-drive vehicles in the rainy season. It takes about two hours to get to Carate. Check with your hotel about current road conditions and driving times.

By Air: It costs $578 to charter a five-passenger plane from San José to Carate, $95 from Puerto Jiménez to Carate (a seven-minute flight), $190 from Jiménez to Sirena, $194 from Jiménez to Drake Bay. Alfa Romeo Aero Taxi is the company most familiar with the zone. They have offices in near the airport in Puerto Jiménez (735-5178).

NORTH OF PUERTO JIMÉNEZ

Eight bumpy kilometers inland is the village of **Dos Brazos**. ✪ **Bosque del Río Tigre Sanctuary and Lodge** (private or shared bath, cold water, natural ventilation, mosquito nets; $55/person including meals; fax: 735-5045, Jones, Dos Brazos, in the U.S.: 410-438-3774; www.osaadventures.com, e-mail: info @osaadventures.com) is a 31-acre private reserve just beyond Dos Brazos. Owned by a Tico-gringa couple, the rooms are totally open to the jungle, with no windows or screens. A secluded riverside cabin sits surrounded by lush foliage (private bath) and rooms in the main lodge overlook the river (shared bath). The food is "rustic gourmet." Their birdwatching expeditions and hikes are fun, informative and interesting. To get there by car, take a clearly marked turnoff four kilometers north of Puerto Jiménez, and follow the road eight kilometers to Dos Brazos. Make a left at the concrete bridge at the entrance to town. In the rainy season follow signs to a local house where you can leave your car. From there, locals will show you the best place to wade across the Río Tigre (it's about 2 feet deep). In the dry season you can drive across the river to the lodge.

Antonio Garbanzo runs a collective taxi service to Dos Brazos. He leaves Super 96 in Puerto Jiménez at 11 a.m. and 4 p.m. daily.

CORCOVADO NATIONAL PARK

In the 1970s, scientists realized that the Osa Peninsula was one of the richest, most diverse tropical areas on earth. The tremendous rainfall, remote location, and variety of unique habitats (eight in all, ranging from mountain forest to swamp), made protection from development imperative. Fortunately scientists won the battle against lumbermen and other proponents of rainforest destruction, and the 108,022-acre national park was founded in 1975.

Since then, the park has been the site of much scientific research, and biologists have identified at least 500 species of trees, 285 birds, 139 mammals, 116 amphibians and reptiles, and 16 freshwater fishes. The rainforest canopy reaches higher than anywhere else in the country, due to the abundant rainfall and low altitude.

Besides its ecological wealth, the area has an interesting human history as well. Some of the best-known and most notorious inhabitants of the national park have been the *oreros* (gold panners). The *oreros* are independent, solitary types who know the peninsula like the backs of their hands. During their heyday, they sifted for their fortunes in the streams and rivers of Corcovado National Park, camping in crude lean-tos and hunting wild animals for food. They would only venture out to Puerto Jiménez once in a while to sell their gold nuggets to the Banco Central's special gold-buying office there. But in the mid-1980s, due to massive unemployment in the region, the gold panners' numbers grew so large that their activity started causing real destruction. The silt from their panning was filling up the rivers and the lake in the park's basin. In 1986, the park service and the Costa Rican Civil Guard physically removed all of the gold panners, promising them an indemnity for their lost jobs. After a year without payment, the *oreros* camped out in protest in the city parks of San José until the government came through with the checks they had promised. Many *oreros* are back in Osa, panning in the forest reserve that borders Corcovado. Even though their activity is destructive, the park service has decided to let it continue rather than risk the panners retreating into Corcovado.

Although they have not settled the park itself, there has been a constant parade of migrant farmers to the peninsula since the all-weather road connected the peninsula with the mainland in the mid-1980s. Most new arrivals have settled in the traditional way, by burning off all the forest covering their little plot of land and then cultivating or grazing cattle on it. This approach is productive for a very short period of time. Rainforest soil is quite poor when there's no forest covering it: once the trees are gone, the rainforest's self-fertilization by dead leaves, plants, and animals stops, and the soil becomes infertile. When it rains, the soil erodes and silt fills the rivers. Because there is little biomass left to absorb excess moisture, floods become a problem.

Visiting the Osa Peninsula is a good way to learn firsthand about the conflict between the conservation of natural resources that humans need in the long-term, and the short-term options that many people consider their only means of survival. **Oasis Preserve International** (www.oasispi.org), founded by actor Woody Harrelson, "works with local landowners to create ecologically sound land use practices and industries." They have a Reality Tour, in which you can combine a trip to some of the Osa's best ecotourism destinations with a visit to experimental farms and over-logged areas. Recommended.

VISITING CORCOVADO   To visit Corcovado National Park, contact Osa Natural (phone/fax: 735-5440; www.mundilink.com/osa_natural, e-mail: osa natur@racsa.co.cr) as far ahead as possible for a reservation. Give them the desired dates of your trip, where you will want to stay each night (dorm rooms and campsites are available only at La Leona and Sirena), what meals you will require at each station, and your fax number or e-mail address. You can also buy tickets through MINAE in San José. Bunk-bed, dorm-style lodging costs about $6 per person per night (mosquito nets are provided at Sirena, and mosquitos are not a problem in La Leona); camping is $1.50 per person per night. Meals are approximately $20 per day, and are served at certain times only, often corresponding to the tides so that people can leave or arrive safely. The daily entrance fee is $6.

The park needs volunteers. Call MINAE at 257-2239 to see how you could help.

During the dry season you can camp fairly comfortably, but the beaches are infested with *purrujas*, invisible biting insects that leave itchy welts that seem to never go away. Do not plan to just sack out on the beach—bring a tent and always camp at the ranger stations.

Additional things you will need to bring for a comfortable stay include

• a tent with good screens if you are camping

• a lightweight sleeping bag or a sheet or two—bedding is not provided

• at least two types of insect repellent, in case one doesn't work

• sunscreen

• several changes of cotton clothing, with long pants and long sleeves to protect you from sun and bugs

• a wide-brimmed hat and a bandanna

• a rain poncho or umbrella

• a towel

• a flashlight

• candles and matches

• a Swiss Army knife

• a water bottle or two and water treatment tablets. Plan to carry all the water you will need between ranger stations; the river water is salty

• snacks—a generous supply in case you're delayed on your way to one of the park's stations

• binoculars

• one pair of good hiking boots that will stand up to getting wet, and a pair of tennis shoes. Sandals are not recommended because of the danger of snakes. River crossings should be done in hiking boots, and the tennies can be worn when you're between treks

• rubber boots, if you are comfortable in them

• several pairs of long socks

• a clothesline

Following are the main entrances and routes through the park:

CARATE–LA LEONA–SIRENA   This route traces the coast. Trucks leave Puerto Jiménez every morning but Sunday at 6 a.m. ($7/person). If you want to go on Sunday, or at another hour, you must hire a taxi (at El Tigre in Puerto Jiménez), which costs about $60 per trip. If you'd rather walk, it's about an eight-hour trip, with no stores along the way.

At Carate, stop at the *pulpería* for a meal or a refresco. They have a radio and can call for airplanes, taxis, or emergency help.

To get to La Leona park entrance from Carate, turn right and walk along the soft sand beach about 45 minutes to **La Leona** ranger station. You can eat and spend the night here if you make reservations beforehand. (Don't swim —there are sharks and the current is strong.)

The walk from La Leona to Sirena spans 15 kilometers and takes about four or five hours. It is almost entirely along the soft sand beach. You must do it at low tide, because you walk around a couple of rocky points covered at high tide. There is a rusty shipwreck at Punta Chancha, with huge engines scattered around the rocks.

A bit later you reach **Salsipuedes** (Get-out-if-you-can) **Point**, which has a pretty cave hollowed out of the coast. At some of the rock points there are trails that cut inland for a few hundred meters. The best way to find them is to start looking as soon as the coast seems impassable. The Salsipuedes trail gives you a break from the soft sand for a kilometer or two, but lather yourself up with repellent before starting into the jungle.

There are many monkeys along this trail. You will probably see scarlet macaws singing raucously and winging awkwardly through the sky. Pizotes (coatimundis) also come to the coast frequently. If you bring a machete you can take a break along the way to open up a coconut for a refreshing *agua de pipa*. After you cross the Río Claro, cut in either on the Sirena trail or at the airstrip a bit farther down.

Sirena is a 48-bed research station populated by eco-tourists and biological researchers who are mostly from the United States or Europe. Do not bathe in the ocean, as there are sharks, but as long as you look out for crocodiles you can swim in the nearby Río Claro and Río Sirena.

SIRENA–SAN PEDRILLO   If you want to reward yourself after your wet, buggy time in Corcovado, consider spending a night or two in one of the resorts at Drake Bay (see above), half an hour by boat from San Pedrillo, the northwestern entrance station. The resorts will pick you up there.

The walk from Sirena to San Pedrillo is 25 kilometers: 15 along wide, flat, hard beach, seven through rainforest, and three weaving between beach and coastal jungle. The entire walk can take six to seven hours. Make sure you walk the beaches at low tide. The park service does not allow people to do this hike in the rainy season.

One kilometer from the Sirena research station is the Río Sirena, the deepest river (three to four feet) with the strongest current that you'll have to cross on this hike. There is a boat you can use to get across, holding onto a rope; ask the rangers to unlock it for you. If you start out at high tide and use this boat to cross the river, you will arrive at the next rivers at low tide. It is very important to plan your hike to correspond with the tides. After Río Sirena, it's about two hours to the **Río Corcovado**, which has a sandy bottom and is two feet deep at low tide. Two hours later is the **Río Llorona**, comparable to the Corcovado. A couple of hundred meters later is the **Piedra Arco**, a huge rock arch covered with greenery. Continue down the shore, and around the rocky point to find **La Llorona**, a 100-foot waterfall that cascades onto the beach. Don't be fooled by the tiny waterfall that you see immediately after leaving the sandy beach; continue on another 15 minutes to get to La Llorona. Do not attempt this except at low tide.

The trail through the rainforest climbs steeply at first, then rises and descends to creeks along the way. About a kilometer before San Pedrillo is a lovely stream with natural jacuzzis. Much of the trail is level, winding through the jungle. For the most part it is a good, wide path, but watch the ascents and descents, because there the trail is eroded and slippery. A couple of hours later, you descend back to a beach. It's another hour to the Río San Pedrillo. With long legs you can jump it near the mouth; otherwise, test the waters and wade. If you want to keep walking, take the trail that follows the coast to Drake Bay, ten kilometers away. It's not hard to get a ride back to Drake Bay with the tour boats that drop people off at San Pedrillo. The ride costs about $30.

GETTING THERE: By Air: Five-passenger charter planes will fly you directly to the Sirena airstrip. VEASA (232-1010, fax: 232-7943) charges $550 one way from the Pavas airport in San José, and Taxi Alfa Romeo (phone/fax: 735-5335) flies for $190 one way from Puerto Jiménez.

LA PALMA–LOS PATOS–SIRENA   La Palma is a small town about 25 kilometers north of Puerto Jiménez. A bus leaves Puerto Jiménez at 5:30 a.m. for La Palma. It's an hour-long trip.

There are a couple of inexpensive cabinas in La Palma, and a restaurant or two as well. **Cabinas El Tucán** (private bath, cold water; under $7) on the main street has clean rooms.

From La Palma it's a 12-kilometer, three-hour walk to the park's northeastern entrance at **Los Patos**, crossing the Río Rincón 26 times in an ever-narrowing valley. There's a taxi-jeep in town that will take you part of the way; everyone in La Palma knows the driver.

A few kilometers from La Palma is a good place to stop either for a cold refresco or a night's sleep. Try **Cabinas Corcovado** (loft for your own tent or hammock; cabinas with shared or private bath, cold water, restaurant for guests; $7-$12; message at 775-0433). Owner Luis Angulo is a friendly former gold panner who headed the struggles against the authorities charged with moving the *oreros* out of Corcovado—and has bullet wounds to show for it. He also used to work for INBio—the National Biodiversity Institute—as a parataxonomist, collecting specimens from the field for their census of life forms in Costa Rica, and he is now a full-time guide. Luis is articulate in describing the difficulty of making a living and protecting nature. If you visit when he has some time, he can show you around the area or take you to the nearby Guaymí Indian Reserve to buy their fine wood carvings.

The trail in this stretch is a narrow gravel road. When vehicles pass, the drivers often offer rides to hikers. The worst stretches of the whole trip are immediately before and after Los Patos, where the trail can be swampy and slippery, especially in the rainy season.

When the road arrives at the Los Patos trailhead, instead of plunging right into the park, you might wish to visit Cerro de Oro, two kilometers farther down the road from Los Patos entrance. The organization that runs it, ✪ **Coope Unioro**, was once a successful goldmining cooperative. When goldmining was prohibited in the park, most gonzo panners went into the bush. The people who stayed in Cerro de Oro were those who loved the lifestyle and wanted to continue living in this beautiful place. They formed a cooperative on their 50 acres, and now share all resources, striving towards self-sufficiency. They recently received a prestigious national award for "improving the quality of life in Costa Rica."

Coope Unioro has built a lovely rustic lodge (shared bath, screens, cold water; $30-$40/person, including meals; reservations at phone/fax: 286-4203, or leave a message at 775-0033, fax: 755-0433; www.agroecoturismo.net, e-mail: cooprena@racsa.co.cr) for visitors. Their cuisine features dishes made from wild plants growing in the area, and herbal teas. All types of excursions are offered: horseback in the reserve, river treks, trips into the national park. You can drive there with a high-clearance vehicle in the dry season, but in rainy season you must have four-wheel drive. They will arrange transportation on horseback from La Palma (about $15/person) or by tractor. Call before going, if possible.

When you enter the park at Los Patos, there are six kilometers of steep trails through high mountain forests, then 14 kilometers of flat walking in low, dense rainforest to the research station at Sirena. The trail is clearly marked, but at some river crossings you have to check up- or downstream for where the trail takes off again. Some of the rivers can be thigh-deep in the rainy season. Don't do this walk at night. Most snakes are nocturnal, and they like water. Don't cross the rivers in sandals.

You might want to bring a machete, because the trail is narrow and there are overhanging branches. Be careful not to walk into biting spiders, whose webs span the trail; bring repellent and plenty of patience for the horseflies. On the way you might see frogs, morpho butterflies and monkeys, and perhaps the tracks of tapirs and ocelots.

GOLFITO

The port town of Golfito has a gorgeous setting—lush, forested hills surrounding a deep bay on the Golfo Dulce with the misty outline of the Península de Osa in the distance.

The town is stretched along one main road squeezed between the gulf and the mountains. Virgin forest blankets the mountains, which have been made into a wildlife and watershed reserve. There are several trails through the reserve, good for 45-minute to one-and-a-half-hour hikes. Some take you to hilltop vantage points with beautiful views of the Golfo Dulce. Behind the airstrip a botanical garden and experimental bamboo plots are managed by the University of Costa Rica.

The northern part of town is the Zona Americana. United Fruit administrators once lived in this quiet neighborhood in big wooden houses on stilts, surrounded by large lawns and gardens. The southern part of town is called the Pueblo Civil and is a noisy collection of bars, restaurants, and hotels. Buses run along the road the length of the town, passing about every 15 minutes during the day. At the northern end of town, they stop at the airport and the *depósito*. Taxis are plentiful (it's about 75 cents to travel anywhere in town).

Many new hotels have opened due to the influx of Central Valley shoppers, who visit the **Depósito Libre**, a huge outdoor mall with air-conditioned shops filled with *electrodomésticos* (household appliances) and luxury items.

The government established the town as a duty-free port in 1990. Ticos and foreigners alike are allowed to buy $500 worth of merchandise every six months. The imported items are still sold with a hefty tax, which will not make them of much interest to tourists, but does make them cheaper than in San José. Shoppers come mainly on weekends, so during the week Golfito is relatively empty, except before Christmas.

Because there is frequent plane and bus service to Golfito, it is a good jumping-off place for touring the southern part of Costa Rica—Corcovado National Park on the Osa Peninsula, the Wilson Botanical Gardens and Amistad International Park near San Vito, the gentle black-sand beach at Zancudo, the surfer's mecca at Pavones, and the small, isolated, and interesting ecotourism projects around the Golfo Dulce area.

For a good orientation to the Zona Sur, pick up a copy of Alexander del Sol's *The Southern Costa Rica Guide*, a very informative booklet that gives complete details about some of the author's favorite places in the area. It's distributed widely in San José and the Zona Sur. You can order it on the internet from www.costaricasur.com.

Land Sea Services (phone/fax: 775-1614, VHF marine radio ch. 16; e-mail: landsea@racsa.co.cr) is a tourist information center next to the Banana Bay Marina on the left as you enter Golfito. They book national and international flights, have a trading library, and rent four-wheel-drive vehicles. They have internet access, send faxes and radio messages, and can help arrange transport for medical emergencies. On top of that, they run a laundry service! Open Monday through Saturday, 8 a.m. to 5 p.m. **Banana Bay Marina**

(775-0838) next door, is a full-fledged marina with a popular restaurant serving gringo food.

We've heard that the best place to change money is with Doña Rosa at the *bomba*—the large gas station to the left of the municipal dock. She also has telephone and fax services. Nearby, at the **Soda Muellecita** or the **Coconut Café** across the street (great cappuccino and internet access), you can ask about transport to Zancudo and Pavones. Traveler's checks must be cashed at the Depósito Libre (closed Monday) or at the new Banco Nacional on the far side of the soccer field.

PLAYA CACAO   Since the beaches in Golfito proper are so polluted, Golfiteños like to visit a cleaner, more peaceful side of the bay at **Playa Cacao**. The cocoa-colored sand tends to be a bit muddy. If you want a tropical-paradise beach experience in this area you'll have to go farther out into the Golfo Dulce—you won't get it in Golfito.

The open-air restaurant at Playa Cacao, **Siete Mares** (open daily, 9 a.m. to 8 p.m.; 775-0322) serves fairly inexpensive *comida típica*. The circular cement-with-thatched-roof **Cabinas Playa Cacao** (private bath, heated water, ceiling fans, kitchens; $30-$40; 221-1169, fax: 256-4850; e-mail: isabel@racsa.co.cr) offers paddleboats and kayaks. Water taxis can bring you here from Golfito ($5 roundtrip). Locals say to tell the boatman what time you want to be picked up, and pay him on the way back.

LODGING AND RESTAURANTS   The following hotels and restaurants are presented in order of appearance south to north—the order you'll come across them if you drive or take the bus to Golfito. The order is the opposite if you fly there; the airstrip is at the extreme north point of town.

Seven kilometers before the entrance to town, in a grassy orchard with cabins and camping spots, is **La Purruja Lodge** (private bath, cold water, ceiling fans; $12-$20; camping, $2/tent; phone/fax: 775-1054). The rooms are very clean, with separate bathing and laundry facilities for campers, all in a beautiful setting. Breakfast and dinner are served at the lodge, and the owners provide tours to see crocodiles and caves nearby. It's a great place to stay with kids, because it's away from the road with lots of room to run around. Buses to Golfito pass in front every half hour. Recommended.

Two hundred meters more will bring you to **Bar Río de Janeiro** (also known as **Mike's Place**), famous in Golfito for spare ribs. Stuffed peppers and goulash are also on the menu—the owner is a Hungarian-American wed to a Tica. In 800 meters more, you'll come to **Margarita's Rancho Grande** (775-1951), known for *comida típica* cooked over a wood fire, as well as filet mignon and *sopa de mariscos*.

At the entrance to town, **El Gran Ceibo** (private bath, hot water, pool; with ceiling fans, $20-$30; with air conditioning, $30-$40; phone/fax: 775-0403) is clean and friendly. Across the street, on the water's edge, with a dock for visitors' boats, is one of the nicest places in town, **Las Gaviotas**, which had just been acquired by the Barceló hotel chain and was being remodeled when we were there. The town bus makes its last stop at these two hotels.

Hotel Delfina (775-0043), 200 meters south of the dock, is divided in two. If you stay in the cheaper south half (shared bath, cold water; under $7), try to get a room with windows, and be forewarned that almost everyone who stays there wakes up at 4 a.m. to catch a bus. The other half (private bath, cold water; with table fans, $7-$12; with air conditioning, $12-$20) is more modern and probably quieter, but poorly ventilated. They speak English and offer many services for tourists such as private parking, a laundry service, and a well-stocked *pulpería*.

In the heart of the Pueblo Civil are several open-air restaurants overlooking the coastal road: **La Eurekita**, the most popular, has an ice cream parlor. **La Cubana** is also a good choice.

Continuing north along the coastal road, **Samoa del Sur** (private bath, hot water, ceiling fans, phone, cable TV; $40-$50; 775-0264, 775-0237, fax: 775-0573) has spacious rooms, the nicest in Golfito. The thatched open-air restaurant **Le Coquillage** offers a varied international menu at moderate prices and has dart boards, Foosball, and billiards, all contributing to its lively atmosphere.

Dozens of homes in the Zona Americana, near the Depósito Libre, have been converted into guest houses, mostly catering to shoppers. As many beds as possible are crowded into each room. One of the nicest is **Cabinas Casa Blanca** (private bath, cold water, ceiling fans; $7-$12; cabinas, $12-$20; 775-0124), which has rooms on the first floor of the owner's house and a row of cabinas in the yard. Across the street, **El Vivero** (private baths in first-floor rooms, shared baths on second floor, cold water, table fans; $7-$12; 775-0217) is a good bet for budget travelers. The rooms are basic, but the hosts are helpful and know a lot about the area. These two places are about 350 meters south of the Depósito.

Nearby, **Hotel Golfo Azul** (private bath, heated water, ceiling fans, air conditioning; $20-$30; 775-0871, fax: 775-1849) is clean and well run. A block toward the Depósito, on the main road, **La Cazuelita** is one of the Zona Americana's best restaurants.

Hotel Sierra (private bath, hot water, ceiling fans, air conditioning, phone, TV, pools; $30-$50; 775-0666), next to the airstrip, is a large, rather faceless hotel near the Deposito Libre.

GETTING THERE: By Bus: Golfito buses leave the Alfaro–Tracopa station (Calle 14, Avenida 5; 222-2160, 222-2666, 223-7685) at 7 a.m. and 3 p.m., and cost $6.50. They return at 5 a.m. and 1 p.m. It's a seven-hour trip. Or you can take any Zona Sur bus to Río Claro—that's the turnoff to Golfito. Villa Neily–Golfito buses pass through Río Claro hourly. It's a half-hour trip. Buy your return tickets as soon as you get to Golfito.

By Car: Follow the Interamerican Highway from San José to Río Claro and turn right. The trip takes about seven hours. If you want to do the trip in two days, San Isidro de El General or Playa Dominical are good places to stay overnight.

By Air: You can avoid the long, winding (though scenic) bus ride by flying SANSA to Golfito (221-9414, fax: 255-2176; $60 one way) daily at 6 a.m., 9:30 a.m., and 12:30 p.m., returning at 7 a.m., 10:30 a.m., and 1:30 p.m. Make reservations, buy tickets in advance, and be aware that the schedules change often. Travelair leaves San José for Golfito (220-3054, fax: 220-0413; $84 one way, $144 round-trip) daily at 9 a.m. via Puerto Jiménez, returning at 10:10 a.m.

PIEDRAS BLANCAS NATIONAL PARK   In 1991, the President of Costa Rica declared 14,000 hectares in the Esquinas Rainforest, on the eastern side of the Golfo Dulce, a national park. The land is blanketed by lush virgin forest, and is an important corridor for the wildlife protected around the corner in Corcovado National Park. There are many endemic species of plants and animals, especially birds. It is also a refuge for migratory birds. There have been no studies of what wildlife it contains yet, but apparently it is visited by large mammals including jaguars.

✪ **Esquinas Rainforest Lodge** (private bath, heated water, ceiling fans; $70-$80/person, including meals; cell phone: 382-5798, 293-0780, fax: 293-2632; www.regenwald.at, e-mail: verein@regenwald.at) is a cluster of well-appointed duplexes, kept cool because three of the four walls have large, screened windows and there is a layer of insulation between the roof and ceiling. There's a chlorine-free, stream-fed pool, whose outflow feeds a pond with tilapia and caimans. The reception area, library, and restaurant are in a large building topped with a locally woven palm roof; the advantage of this type of roof is clear as soon as you walk inside and feel the cool temperature. All profits from the lodge are used for improvement projects proposed by the people of La Gamba, a village near the park entrance. Recommended.

GETTING THERE: By Car: Drive toward Golfito as far as Villa Briceño, at kilometer marker 37 on the Interamerican Highway. Make a right, and follow signs for five kilometers on a gravel road that has several small wooden bridges without guardrails. If you take the Golfito bus or fly to Golfito, the lodge can pick you up for $10. There is a mountainous back road that will take you from Golfito to Esquinas in about 15 minutes in the dry season.

GOLFO DULCE

North of Golfito, the *costa* is *rica* indeed: lush vegetation; breezy, rocky beaches; deep green waters. There are several ecotourism projects set on the eastern rim of the gulf, which really make the area worth visiting. They are all near (and some of them even own parts of) Piedras Blancas National Park—Esquinas Sector. Because all the lodges are isolated and accessible only by boat, prices are per person including meals and sometimes transportation from Golfito. The best way to contact any of these lodges is through **Osa Tropical** (735-5062; e-mail: osatropi@sol.racsa.co.cr) a Puerto Jiménez travel agency that has radio contact with all the hotels in the area.

○ **Golfo Dulce Lodge** (private bath, solar-heated shower, ceiling fans; $110/person, including meals and transportation from Golfito, minimum two nights; 222-2900, fax: 223-5173; www.golfodulcelodge.com) has roomy cabins set well apart, huge bathrooms with European showers, and hammocks on every porch. Set in a clearing down a path from the stony beach, the cabins do not have views, but they do have a swimming pool. The Swiss owners bought their land with the specific purpose of preserving the rainforest. Their 680-acre reserve is now part of the National Park System. They offer hiking and boating tours in the area.

Dolphin Quest (rustic *ranchos*, shared baths, natural ventilation; with double occupancy: $60/person in private *ranchos*; camping, $20-$30; prices include meals but not transportation; leave messages at 775-1742, fax: 775-0373; www.dolphinquest.com, e-mail: dolphinquest@email.com), located down the beach from Golfo Dulce Lodge, is a laid-back farm where you can explore the jungle, help with gardening, ride horses, kayak, snorkle, or swim with dolphins. It's definitely for people who are comfortable with alternative lifestyles. They are interested in hosting retreats and workshops in their large, open-sided, cement-floored, thatched *rancho*.

Casa Orquideas (radio channel 68 from Golfito; Apdo. 69, Golfito) is a beautifully landscaped private botanical garden overlooking the sea. Long-time residents Ron and Trudy McAllister take you on an hour's tour of the garden, where you can see what the spices and fruits in your kitchen look like on the vine—and taste them if they're in season. You'll see ginger, vanilla, black pepper, cinnamon, cacao, cashew, mango, avocado, and papaya, as well as tons of beautiful orchids and familiar houseplants in their native habitat. Tours begin around 8:15 a.m. Sunday through Thursday, $5 per person, minimum four visitors or $20. They also rent a simple but very pleasant screened cabin (private bath, kitchen; $150/week; $500/month) at the back of the garden. All the nearby lodges plus Zancudo Boat Tours (see below) will take you there, or you can rent a boat in Golfito.

✪ **Caña Blanca** (private bath, cold water, natural ventilation; $145/ person, including gourmet meals, tours, and transportation from Golfito or Puerto Jiménez; minimum three night stay; 735-5062, voice mail: 383-5707; e-mail: canablan@racsa.co.cr), the dream of a couple of gourmet cooks from Seattle, gives you the feeling of being alone on a deserted tropical beach. The three private cabins are totally open to the jungle and to the resident macaw, toucan and parrot, the owners' pets. Located on an isolated cove about 9 miles from Puerto Jimenez and 16 miles from Golfito, the tastefully designed cabins all overlook the gentle waters of the Golfo Dulce. A 750-acre reserve backs the property, with six miles of trails. When you have had your fill of relaxing. the owners can take you hiking into a nearby valley to lunch with a tico family, or kayaking on the peaceful Río Esquinas. Recommended.

GETTING THERE: If your lodge cannot pick you up, take a taxi boat from the *muellecito* in Golfito. A boat taxi to Casa Orquideas for example, costs $50 roundtrip with a two-hour wait. Ask at Land Sea Services for going rates.

ZANCUDO

Playa Zancudo, on a strip between the ocean and the Coto River, is one of the Zona Sur's most popular beaches during the dry season. The fine blacksand beach stretches for miles, and the surf is mostly gentle. This safe beach is ideal for families with children. The southern section of Zancudo (in front of Zancudo Beach Club) offers good surfing, with beach breaks in both directions. Because it is relatively unknown, there is no line-up. Zancudo has earned the prestigious Bandera Azul from the government, indicating that residents work together to keep the beach and water clean.

The mangroves along the Río Coto and the Atrocha canal connecting Zancudo with Golfito serve as a safe nursery for the area's rich fishing grounds. **Zancudo Boat Tours** (776-0012) offers scenic kayak trips along the Río Coto to view birds, crocodiles, monkeys, and otters. Trips to Casa Orquídeas Botanical Garden (see above), and the Osa Peninsula are available as well. It's only $20 per person to go by boat from Zancudo to Puerto Jiménez—a pleasant way to arrive at the gateway to Cocovado. Andrew Robertson, a transplant from the U.K., is ZBT's witty and entertaining captain.

LODGING   Hotels and cabinas are plentiful, and a better value than those at many other Costa Rican beaches. We'll describe them in order from north to south. If you drive (not recommended—it's a long, bumpy trip, possible only with four-wheel drive during rainy season), reverse the order. If your boat lets you off at the public dock, turn right on the main road for Roy's and Río Mar; the rest are to the left.

The northernmost cabinas are **Río Mar** (private bath; with cold water and wall or ceiling fans, some refrigerators; $12-$20; with kitchen and room for six, $40-$50; 776-0056), whose somewhat run-down rooms are well placed between the ocean and river.

Just south is **Roy's Zancudo Lodge** (private bath, heated water, ceiling fans, some with air conditioning or refrigerator, pool, jacuzzi; $50-$60; 776-0008, 284-7759, in the U.S.: 800-515-7697, 813-889-0662, fax: 813-889-9189; e-mail: rroig@golfito.net), a fishing lodge holding over 51 world records. Cabinas are comfortable, and there is a restaurant with satellite TV. They have packages for anglers ($360/person/day), and accommodate others for $75 per day including meals.

In "downtown" Zancudo, left from the dock, is **Soda Katherin** (open every day, all day), a great place to eat. We had baby shrimp there that were perfectly cooked and seasoned. And it's very inexpensive. **Cabinas Tío Froilan** (private bath, cold water, ceiling fans; $7-$12; 776-0103), offers two parallel rows of simple cabinas; the first row blocks the breeze and view for the second. Down the street on the left is the locally acclaimed **Macondo** (open noon to 3 p.m. and 5:30 p.m. to 9:30 p.m.; 776-0157), a second-floor Italian restaurant that overlooks the mangrove estuary. They also rent cabins (shared bath, heated water, ceiling fans; $12-$20) and have a small pool.

Abastecdor El Buen Precio is a good place to stock up on groceries or make telephone calls.

The owners of Zancudo Boat Tours also operate **Cabinas Los Cocos** (private bath, heated water, table fans, kitchens; $40-$50; weekly and monthly rates available; 776-0012; www.zancudo.com, e-mail: loscocos@racsa.co.cr), about two kilometers or a 20-minute walk south of the municipal dock. Los Cocos consists of three individual houses, two of which are reconditioned banana company cabins, with big decks overlooking the ocean. They are quiet, private, and shipshape. Bikes, kayaks, and boogieboards are available for guests. Recommended.

Next door, **Cabinas Sol y Mar** (private bath, heated water, ceiling fans; $30-$40; 776-0014, fax: 776-0015; e-mail: solymar@zancudo.com), with cabinas and a restaurant, is a good place for families, with a horseshoe (tournaments on Sunday) and volleyball court (tournaments on Wednesday and Saturday), and surfboards for rent. The cabins have good air circulation. There's also a house for rent ($40 per day; $550/month).

The last hotel south is the friendly, U.S.-owned **Zancudo Beach Club** (private bath, solar hot water with back-up, fans; $50 for up to three people; 776-0087, fax: 776-0052; www.zancudobeachclub.com, e-mail: zbc@costa

rica.net), right on the beach, with individual elevated cabins and breezy res-
taurant/bar (open 7 a.m. to 9 p.m.) which is becoming a meeting-place for
the gringo community. We happened to arrive on Thanksgiving and had an
excellent turkey dinner with all the trimmings. Quite a feat in Zancudo. The
cabins are well-appointed and very comfortable and come complete with
refrigerators, microwaves, and coffee makers. Surfing is good here. Recommended. **Los Tres Amigos** (775-0123) down the street sells clothes, sandwiches, and familiar U.S. groceries.

GETTING THERE: By Bus: From Golfito, take the Pavones bus that leaves at
5 a.m. and noon every day from the *bomba*. Get off in Conte, where the Pavones
and Zancudo routes converge, and transfer to the Zancudo bus. It might be very
crowded. If you happen to be in Villa Neily (more convenient if you are coming
from San Vito), take the 1:30 p.m. bus to Conte. Bus travel to Zancudo is to be
avoided if possible, because of the bumps and the length of the trip. The boat trip
is faster and more scenic.

By Car: If you have a four-wheel-drive vehicle, driving is usually possible,
and the trip from Golfito takes between one and two hours. Locals say that the
trip can be done in a regular car in the dry season, but it's always best to have a
high clearance. Look for the Rodeo bar at kilometer 14 of the Río Claro–Golfito
road, and turn south. Fifteen minutes later on paved road you come to an old-
fashioned barge that takes about five minutes to ferry you across the Coto River.
The ferry shuts down at 6 p.m., so be sure to get there before dark. In another
half hour you'll get to the place where the road goes south to Pavones and north
to Zancudo. There are signs in most crucial places. It's good to ask directions as
often as possible. When in doubt, turn right.

By Boat: The *Macarela,* a public ferry ($1.50), leaves the municipal *muelle* in
Golfito at around 5 a.m. Monday through Friday only. Since the schedule depends on the tide, the ferry will take either the Atrocha (mangrove canal shortcut,
only possible in high tide) or the ocean route (beach landing; you have to walk
ashore). The trip takes an hour and a half. To charter a boat call Andrew and Susan at Zancudo Boat Tours (776-0012; $20 minimum; more than two passengers,
$10/person extra).

PAVONES

Pavones is highly publicized in surfer magazines for having the longest wave
in the world (www.wavefacts.com). It draws throngs during the rainy season,
when the waves are largest. On peak days, expect rides more than a minute
long, and between 50 and 80 surfers in the water. If you don't surf, try another beach (such as nearby Zancudo). Pavones is crowded and not suited to

body surfing or swimming. The area has recently been the site of some Wild West–like confrontations involving land disputes.

It is a beautiful area, much more lush and green than Zancudo, and there are some delightful places to stay. **Restaurante La Piramide**, on the left as you enter Pavones, is a nice place to eat. It's open all day, every day. Fish would be a good thing to order if you get there at the right time—we saw local fishermen bringing in their catch. They have dances there on weekends.

An international group of surfers has taken over the old cantina, **Esquina del Mar**, in Pavones *centro* and made it into a very happening place, with an open-air restaurant and bar downstairs, a tasteful souvenir shop that sells Boruca handicrafts and has internet access, and four simple upstairs rooms (shared bath, cold water, natural ventilation; $10/person, $50/week; fax: 383-6939; e-mail: nativo@racsa.co.cr) whose unscreened windows open to a blue view of water and sky. This place has been grandfathered in to the Ley Maritimo Terrestre. You would never be able to build so close to the water now. The *pulpería* next to the soccer field also rents a few dark rooms ($12-$20).

Mira Olas (private bath, cold water, fans, mosquito nets, hammocks, kitchens; $20-$40, $140-$190/week; 393-7742; e-mail: nativo@racsa.co.cr) are two private cabins on a hill full of fruit trees. One is rustic, the other is "Jungle Deluxe." The *finca*, owned by a U.S.-German couple, is accessed by a dirt road heading a quarter mile inland from the fishermen's co-op at the entrance to town. It's great for couples or families who like peace and quiet, and is an easy walk to the river or the beach. Recommended.

South from town are several places to stay, described in order of appearance. To get there, go back a quarter mile to the fish co-op and turn inland. Turn right at the school and go another quarter mile to the bridge over the Río Claro.

An attractive, spacious bed and breakfast built on a hill overlooking the sea, **Casa Siempre Domingo** (private bath, heated water; $35/person, including breakfast; 775-0131; www.casa-domingo.com, e-mail: yapada@racsa.

co.cr) is owned by a couple from Cape Cod, and has a fantastic view. You should have a car to stay here.

One and a half kilometers south of town are ☺ **Cabinas La Ponderosa** (private bath, hot water, some with air conditioning, ceiling fans; $40-$50/person, three meals included; $20-$30 without meals; 384-7430, in the U.S.: 954-771-9166; www.ccgnv.net/ponderosa), with well-designed, completely screened-in cabins owned by two friendly Florida brothers, who have put a tremendous amount of love and care into their project. There is a volleyball court and a large, screened game room with satellite TV, ping pong, and hammocks. It's just 50 meters from the ocean. They were planting trees when we were there. Recommended.

Four and a half kilometers south, high on a jungle-covered hillside, is ☺ **Tiskita Lodge** (private bath, cold water, pool; $110/person, double occupancy, including meals; phone/fax: 233-6890, 257-3418; www.crsuntours.com/tiskita, e-mail: tiskita@racsa.co.cr). The rustic but comfortable cabins all have superb ocean views and are cooled by sea breezes. Agronomist Peter Aspinall has planted more than 100 varieties of tropical fruits from around the world here, which attract many birds and monkeys. Guided nature walks are available and trails wind up and down the mountain backdrop in their 400-acre reserve. A 65-foot waterfall and swimmable ponds are close to the cabins. Three-night packages ($535) include charter flights. Package options also include trips to Corcovado and Drake Bay.

GETTING THERE: By Bus: A bus for Pavones leaves at 10 a.m. and 3 p.m. every day from the *bomba* in Golfito. If you happen to be in Villa Neily, catch the bus there at 1:30 p.m. for Conte, where you can transfer to the Golfito–Pavones bus. The bus reaches Pavones *centro* around noon and 4 p.m. A taxi to Pavones costs $40 to $50, depending on how far south you're going.

By Car: It takes a little over an hour to get from Zancudo to Pavones, with gorgeous views on the way. It takes about an hour and a half to get to Pavones from Golfito. As with Zancudo, look for the Rodeo Bar at kilometer 14 of the Río Claro–Golfito road, and turn south. The section up to the Río Coto is paved. Cars cross the river on an interesting ferry contraption ($1.25 for car and driver, 15 cents for each passenger). The ferry shuts down at dark, so don't get stuck there. Roads south of the river to Pavones are gravel or dirt, very bumpy, but almost always passable without four-wheel drive (although it's good to have a high-clearance vehicle). You will probably want to ask directions frequently.

By Boat: The boatmen's cooperative in Golfito provides transportation to Pavones for $60 per boatload, but you might have to swim to shore once you get there since it's usually too rough for the boat to reach land. Pavones boatmen, through their cooperative, charge $25-$30 per boat to Zancudo. We don't recommend taking the boat to Pavones. The bus is much cheaper and just as fast (an hour and a half from Zancudo) and your stuff won't get wet.

SAN VITO

Founded in the early 1950s by immigrants from postwar Italy, **San Vito** is in a high, mountainous valley with an invigorating climate. The town of 40,000 has a strong sense of its roots, with good Italian restaurants and the Dante Aligheri cultural center, which offers Italian films, exhibits, and language classes. **Pizzeria y Restaurante Lilliana** (773-3080), 50 meters west of the park, is a popular place run by an Italian family. Two spurs off the Interamerican Highway lead to San Vito. From the north, cross the Térraba River on the Paso Real bridge, and drive 38 kilometers up the fertile backbone of the Coto Brus. This is the route the bus takes from San José. From the south, take the Villa Neily–San Vito road, built by the United States in 1945 during World War II as a strategic protection point, because the area is due west of the Panama Canal. The road rises so sharply that, in 20 minutes, Villa Neily's sweltering heat is forgotten in the cool misty mountains above San Vito. Views are spectacular, but the road is so winding that you should really pull over to enjoy the vista.

Halfway between San Vito and Wilson Botanical Gardens is the unique **Finca Cántaros** (open 8 a.m. to 4 p.m., closed Monday; 773-3760; admission $1). The *finca* consists of grassy picnic grounds with a pond and panoramic views, a renovated historic farmhouse with a children's reading room, and a gift shop with high-quality, hand-painted ceramics, Boruca and Guaymi woven goods, and delicious orange-guava jam, all at reasonable prices. Proceeds from sales of the handicrafts, both locally produced and brought from other areas of the country, go toward staffing the reading room—the first of its kind in Costa Rica. Recommended.

LODGING   **Hotel El Ceibo** (private bath, hot water, some with TV; $20-$30; phone/fax: 773-3025) is very clean and by far the most comfortable. It is behind the Municipalidad, right in the center of town. The rooms in the back have views.

Albergue Firenze (private bath, heated water; $7-$12; 773-3741) is a small, basic place, down a road to the left after the gas station at the entrance to town on the Paso Real (Río Térraba) route.

WILSON BOTANICAL GARDENS   San Vito's main attraction is undoubtedly ✪ **Las Cruces Biological Station** and **Wilson Botanical Gardens**, 5.4 kilometers uphill from town on the Villa Neily road. This floral wonder-

land is fascinating for lay visitors and the botanically inclined alike. Its aston-
ishingly diverse collection was gathered from around the world and designed
by the original owners, Robert and Catherine Wilson, with help from the great
Brazilian horticulturist Roberto Burle-Marx. The garden is now owned by the
Organization of Tropical Studies, a consortium of U.S., Latin American, and
Australian universities. Much important botanical and agro-ecological research takes place on the grounds and in the laboratories.

One could spend days on the self-guided tours through the garden's 25
acres of cultivated sectors—trails are dedicated to heliconias, bamboos, orchids, lilies, gingers, palms, and ferns, to name a few. Nine kilometers of
trails in the 632-acre forest reserve offer mountain vistas, overlooks of the
rainforest canopy, and hikes to the lovely, rocky pools of the Río Java. The
gardens' bird list of 330 species includes some aquatic species of the nearby
San Joaquín marsh.

Day visits cost $6 ($16 including a hearty lunch); children 12 and under
free. Lodging is in comfortable cabins with balconies (private bath, heated
water; $70-$80/person, including meals). Some units are wheelchair accessible. There is library and video room for rainy afternoons. You must make
reservations before you visit: contact the San José office of the Organization for Tropical Studies (240-6696, fax: 240-6783; www.ots.ac.cr, e-mail:
reservas@ots.ac.cr). Recommended.

GETTING THERE: By Air: You can charter a five-passenger plane to San Vito,
or fly to Coto 47 with SANSA (221-9414, fax: 255-2176; $60 one way) and take
a taxi ($40) to the botanical gardens.

By Bus: A direct bus to San Vito leaves San José at 5:45 a.m. and 8:15 a.m.
from Empresa Alfaro (Calle 14, Avenida 5; 222-2750; $6.65). It's a five-hour trip.
Buy tickets in advance. Most of these buses pass the botanical gardens after a stop
in San Vito. Check with the driver. The bus that returns to San Jose at 5 a.m. passes
by Wilson Gardens on its way to San Vito at 4:10 a.m. The Alfaro office in San
Vito is around the curve from the Municipalidad (city hall). San Isidro–San Vito
buses leave at 5:30 a.m. and 2 p.m., returning at 6:30 a.m. and 1:30 p.m.

You can take the San Vito–Villa Neily bus to the garden at 7 a.m. and 1 p.m.,
or take the Villa Neily–San Vito bus at 6 a.m., 1 p.m., or 3 p.m. A taxi from San
Vito is about $2.50.

By Car: The San José–San Vito trip takes five hours: two and a half hours to
San Isidro, after which the road straightens out a bit, then one and a half hours to
the Rio Térraba bridge, then another hour on the paved but pot-holed road to San
Vito. Be sure not to miss the turnoff to the bridge at Paso Real, 15 kilometers after Buenos Aires. You'll see the river on your left, then you'll pass the bridge
down below before you see a small sign indicating the road to San Vito. Once in

San Vito, turn right onto the main street and follow it 15 minutes more to the botanical gardens.

La Amistad Lodge (shared bath, hot water; $70-$80/person, including meals and tours; 770-8143, fax: 289-7858) is located on a 7000-hectare farm, mostly preserved as virgin forest and partly developed as a coffee plantation bordering La Amistad Biosphere Reserve. A Swiss-style chalet towers over the *beneficio*, the processing plant that now produces one of Costa Rica's only organic brands of coffee. Lance-tailed manikins, birds native to the Chiriquí province of Panama, are as sought out by birders in this region as are quetzals in the cloud forest, and are frequently seen here. If you are staying in the San Vito area, day tours are available. During the coffee-picking season, September to January, the last 22 kilometers to the lodge is the worst road we have been on in our many travels all over Costa Rica. We do not recommend going there during that time.

GETTING THERE: By Car: From the main intersection in San Vito, head to Sabalito. Turn left at the gas station, and drive over gravel roads an hour and a half to Las Mellizas. The road is extremely muddy and slippery in the rainy season. A taxi from San Vito costs about $30.

PARQUE INTERNACIONAL LA AMISTAD

Parque Internacional La Amistad extends over the Talamanca mountains from the southern border of Chirripó National Park down into Panama. It is the largest park in the country (474,240 acres), and its Panamanian counterpart is more than three times larger. Comprising eight life zones, La Amistad is one of the richest ecological biospheres in Central America. The United Nations has declared the park and its neighboring reserves and protected zones a World Heritage site and has given it the status of Biosphere.

Preliminary surveys indicate that two-thirds of the country's vertebrate species are found in this park. It is an extremely important refuge for animals that require large areas in order to hunt, forage, and reproduce, like the jaguar, margay, and puma. Some of these animals are not protected anywhere else in Costa Rica.

The official gateway to La Amistad is the **Altamira** entrance. You'll see signs for it about halfway down the Paso Real–San Vito road. The signs are confusing, but it's a 20 kilometer (one hour) drive up a gravel road from the turnoff. On the way you'll pass through the village of **El Carmen**, where you can rent rooms, buy food supplies or eat at the **Soda y Hospedaje La Amistad** (shared bath, cold water; $7-12; 773-8153). Once you get to Altamira there are beautiful views, a campground with tiled bathrooms, and a covered cooking area with picnic tables. The park guards will lend you a gas stove. You can buy fresh organic vegetables from Olivier Cortez, who has his farm near the entrance. **Sendero los Gigantes del Bosque** is a circular four-kilometer hike. You can also hike to the 8000-foot **Valle del Silencio** from here in about eight hours. There is a shelter to stay in after about two hours of hiking.

No matter how adventurous you feel, don't undertake the trip without a guide. It's very easy to get lost, and hikers have died from hypothermia and falls in the slippery, precipitous terrain. Camping in this area is most enjoyable in the dry season (January through April).

To plan your trip, call or visit the office of La Amistad Conservation Area in San Isidro de El General (150 meters west and 50 meters south of Central Park; 771-5116, phone/fax: 771-3155) at least two weeks in advance, so that guides and porters can be contracted. Dúrika, below, will guide you into La Amistad as well, or call Selvamar (771-4582), the Southern Zone trekking specialists.

GETTING THERE: See description, above.

Above the cow town of Potrero Grande is an establishment whose picturesque site, friendly owners, and good cooking we greatly enjoyed: ✪ **Albergue Monte Amuo** (private bath, heated water; $55/person, including meals; 265-6149). Several kilometers of trails pass through their beautiful forest reserve, just across the Río Mosca from Parque Internacional La Amistad. Recommended.

GETTING THERE: By Car: Follow the Paso Real route toward San Vito, but leave the main road at the turnoff for Potrero Grande, just a few kilometers south of the Río Térraba bridge. In town ask directions for the road to the lodge. It is 14 kilometers (one hour) from town on a dirt/gravel road. Four-wheel drive is best, but we did make it in rainy season in a high-centered pickup with front-wheel drive. Signs mark the way.

By Bus: Take the San Vito bus from San José (Calle 14, Avenida 5; 5:45 a.m. or 8:15 a.m.; 222-2160, 222-2666, 223-7685; $6.50) and get off at the turnoff for Potrero Grande. The owners will pick you up, with advance notice. If you are already in the area, you can catch a bus to Potrero Grande from the market in Buenos Aires at 10 a.m. or 2 p.m.

DÚRIKA BIOLOGICAL RESERVE   High in the Talamanca mountains above Buenos Aires is ✪ **Dúrika Biological Reserve** (730-0657, fax: 730-0003; www.gema.com/durika, e-mail: durika@racsa.co.cr), operated by a self-sufficient agricultural community. The private reserve is a buffer zone for this section of La Amistad International Biosphere Reserve. Biologists visiting the

Dúrika reserve have identified over 350 species of birds native to this micro-region and, in informal collecting expeditions, have discovered several new species of insects. The community's resident naturalist can lead hikes of one to five days through Reserva Biológica Dúrika and La Amistad, including a three-day trek up Cerro Dúrika, a peak of over 11,000 feet, and a six-day trek across the Talamanca mountains to the Atlantic coast (which is only done in May and October; $1000). He or the other guides will also take visitors to nearby indigenous and campesino villages, with whose inhabitants the community trades for fruits and vegetables. You can even hike to a *trapiche* where *tapa dulce*, the traditional hard brown sugar, is made.

With the money it earns from tourism, the community hopes to buy adjoining farms. They will form an important biological corridor for local wildlife, which needs to migrate altitudinally according to the season. The community itself offers classes ($5) in vegetarian cooking, bread-baking, gardening, relaxation, and meditation techniques. Members of the community are professional Costa Ricans and a few foreigners, who wanted a healthier life for themselves and their families than urban existence could offer.

Even if you can't visit the *finca*, it's worth stopping by their office in Buenos Aires to buy some of their healthy cookies and pastries (730-0657).

Accommodations (private or shared bath, solar-heated water; $30-$40/person, students $25/person, volunteers $15/person) in the guest cabins are rustic but cozy. Prices include three delicious vegetarian meals per day.

GETTING THERE: Call the reserve as far ahead as possible so they can prepare for your visit. Take a Tracopa–Alfaro bus to Buenos Aires (8:30 a.m. and 2:30 p.m.; Calle 14, Avenida 5; 222-2160, 222-2666, 223-7685; $3). Once you are in Buenos Aires, they will arrange for a taxi to pick you up and take you to the community ($30 for up to seven people). Their office is near the entrance to town. As you enter Buenos Aires you will see a sign on the right that says "Clinica." Turn right one street before that, go one block, and then a quarter block to the right.

By Car: It takes about 90 minutes to get to Dúrika from Buenos Aires. The last three and a half kilometers are on very bad road. Try to get to Buenos Aires no later than 4 p.m. so you can reach the reserve in daylight.

BORUCA

Boruca is a small town cradled in a green valley in the southwestern part of Costa Rica. The surrounding countryside is beautiful—you can walk up the red dirt trails for views across mountains, valleys, and rivers.

The Borucas offer a glimpse into the traditions of Costa Rica's indigenous peoples. For instance, they traditionally celebrate the New Year with the Fiesta de los Diablitos, a dramatic reenactment of the war between the Spanish conquistadores and the local native people, in which the locals win. (Native peoples throughout the Americas share the Diablitos tradition, though usually their drama represents a war between the Spanish and the Moors.) The Diablitos are men disguised as devils. One man is the bull. The Diablitos taunt the bull with sticks, and the bull prances around and chases them. Costumes are fashioned from burlap sacks and balsa-wood masks carved by Boruca artisans.

The group, accompanied by a drummer and a flute player, meets on a hill the night of December 30. At midnight, a conch shell sounds, and they run down the hill into town. They spend the whole night going from house to house, giving a short performance at each, then relaxing to enjoy the *chicha* (homebrew) and tamales they are offered. The group visits most houses in town that night and during the next three days. On the third day of the fiesta, the Diablitos symbolically kill the bull. A huge bonfire reduces the bull to ashes.

The Borucas are known for their fine handicrafts. Men carve expressive balsa-wood masks. Both women and men etch elaborate scenes onto large, hollow *jícaras* (gourds). Boruca women are especially known for their weavings, done with yarn spun from species of cotton that grow only in Boruca. The cotton is dyed with natural tints, including a purple extracted from a terrestrial mollusk that lives on cliffs near the Terraba River delta. The men make periodic trips to gather this dye. To obtain it, they scale the cliffs, locate the now-scarce shells, remove them from the rock wall, blow on the animals so they will spray their dye, and then replace them on the cliff for their next visit. That's true sustainability.

You can buy the Borucas' handicrafts from families all over Boruca. Local ladies Marina Lazaro and Igenia Gonzalez (771-2533) do a demonstration of Borucan weaving and dying techniques at the **Museo Comunitario**. Call them in advance if you would like them to set up a demonstration for you. If you don't have time to visit Boruca, you can buy the handicrafts at the cooperative stands in Rey Curré, an indigenous village along the Interamerican Highway between the Paso Real turnoff for San Vito and Palmar Norte. They are also sold at many hotels throughout the Zona Sur.

Doña Mildred Pereira, an anthropologist and legislative advisor on indigenous issues, leads occasional educational tours to Boruca and other nearby indigenous communities. She works with community leaders on designing tourism projects that allow the indigenous people to attract visitors who respect their culture. For more information, call her at 253-9935.

We know of no formal hotels here, but you can probably arrange to stay with a local family or camp if you ask around.

Note: You might want to combine a stop in Boruca with a visit to the Dúrika Biological Reserve, which borders La Amistad Biosphere Reserve above Buenos Aires.

GETTING THERE: By Bus: A bus leaves Buenos Aires at 11:30 a.m. and arrives in Boruca (18 kilometers up and down a mountainous dirt road) at 1 p.m. Or you can get off the Zona Sur bus at the Entrada de Boruca, about 30 minutes past the entrance to Buenos Aires, and walk eight kilometers up the path that takes off to the right of the highway. The hike takes about two hours.

By Car: Look for the Térraba turnoff from the Interamerican Highway about 12 kilometers south of the entrance to Buenos Aires and just after the Brujo gas station. Boruca is about 18 kilometers from there. Your car should have high clearance and a powerful engine.

ISLA DEL COCO

Isla del Coco (Coco Island), 500 kilometers off the Pacific Coast, boasts 200 dramatic waterfalls, many of which fall directly into the sea. Because the island is uninhabited, animals there are not afraid of humans. The fairy terns find humans so interesting that they hover about them curiously.

Although its geological origin remains a mystery, scientists believe Isla del Coco is a volcanic hot spot at the center of the Cocos tectonic plates. The Coco Island finch is a subspecies of the finch endemic to the Galapagos Islands that prompted Darwin's questions about evolution. Several species of birds, lizards, and freshwater fish found on the island have not been seen anywhere else on earth. Whereas on mainland Costa Rica there are so many species that the behavior of each is highly specialized, on Isla del Coco individual birds of the same species will have different feeding habits—very interesting from an evolutionary standpoint. Some 77 nonendemic species, mainly seabirds, can also be observed.

European sailors probably first discovered the island in the 1500s. Many early visitors were pirates who rested and restocked fresh water there during expeditions. They named the island after its many coconut palms, but apparently enjoyed the coconuts so much that there are almost none left today. Passing boats installed pigs, deer, and goats on the island to provide meat for return voyages. With no predators, these animals now constitute the majority of the wildlife there.

There are tales of buried treasure on the island. The Portuguese Benito Bonito, "The One of the Bloody Sword," is said to have buried his fabulous treasure there. Also during the early 19th century, at the time of Peru's wars of independence from Spain, the aristocracy and clergy entrusted their gold and jewels to Captain James Thompson, who promised to transport their riches to a safe port. Thompson disappeared with the loot and is supposed to have hidden it on Isla del Coco. Although many treasure hunters have searched the island, no one has found anything yet.

Hunting for gold doubloons might not be rewarding at Isla del Coco, but scuba divers find it rich in natural treasures. The ship **Okeanos** (289-3333, in the U.S.: 800-348-2628; www.agressor.com, e-mail: seascape@okeanos.net) takes divers to the island for ten days of heavy-duty diving ($2995/person from San José). Several sailboat companies in Guanacaste offer trips to Coco. See the Tamarindo, Flamingo, and Playa del Coco sections.

THIRTEEN

Staying Longer

OPTIONS FOR RESIDENCY

Tourists may own vehicles, property, and businesses in Costa Rica, and may generate income from self-employment, but they have to leave the country for three days every three months. Securing permanent residency in Costa Rica is a complicated and increasingly difficult process. *Temporary residency* can be obtained by students in registered university or language school programs, by volunteers with the U.S. Peace Corps (or its Canadian, European, or Japanese equivalents), by employees who have proven that they are not displacing Costa Rican workers, and by members of church-affiliated service groups.

To live here on a permanent basis you must either have a lot of money to invest in starting your own company—*inversionista* (investor) status—or apply for *pensionado* or *rentista* status. You could also marry a Costa Rican. *Inversionistas* must invest $50,000 in an export or tourism project, $100,000 in reforestation, or $150,000 in any other business proposition. *Pensionados* must receive at least $600 per month from Social Security or from a qualified pension or retirement plan. *Rentistas* must prove that they have investments guaranteeing them a monthly income of $1000, or deposit $60,000 in a Costa Rican bank. Both *pensionados* and *rentistas* must be able to prove that they live in Costa Rica at least four months per year.

If only one spouse has a pension or investment income, the other spouse is considered a dependent, and does not need to meet the income requirements.

You may apply for *pensionado* or *rentista* status while in Costa Rica, but you will need to supply the following documents: birth certificates for you and your dependents; all marriage and divorce certificates; naturalization certificates (if applicable); copies of any academic degrees or certificates; and a letter from your home police department certifying that you, your spouse, and dependents of ages 18 to 25 have no criminal record. The police report must be no more than six months old, and must be complete up to the date of issuance. Let it be the last thing you get, so that it won't expire while you are waiting for the other documents.

Pensionados will need to obtain a letter from Social Security or their pension or retirement plan verifying that the pension is for life and that the stated monthly amount will be paid out in Costa Rica. The pension plan must have been in existence for at least 20 years and the company must provide a statement of incorporation and economic solvency, certified by a CPA, which in turn must be authenticated by a Costa Rican consul. References from two banks with which the pension plan deals must also be provided.

Rentistas are required to submit a letter from their bank or recognized investment company stating that the investment is tied up for a minimum of five years; the amount of monthly income received from investments is stable, permanent, and irrevocable; and income from these will be paid out in Costa Rica. The company providing the income must have existed for more than three years and must supply statements of incorporation and economic solvency, as well as bank references, the same as with the pension plans mentioned above.

Signatures on all foreign documents have to be notarized. The Costa Rican consul nearest to the place where the documents were issued will authenticate the commissioner's signature. This costs $40 per document. All documents must be translated into Spanish by a translator approved by the Costa Rican Ministry of Foreign Relations. To find the consulate nearest you, see www.rree.go.cr.

In addition, all candidates for permanent residency must submit two certified copies of their passport, one copy of each dependent's passport, and 20 passport-size photographs (thirteen front and seven profile) for each adult involved, 16 for minors (nine front and seven profile).

Pensionados and *rentistas* must provide fingerprints and photographs before they can receive residency permits, so that their identities can be checked by Interpol. This is done in an effort to exclude criminals, who may present falsified police documents.

Both *pensionados* and *rentistas* can set up their own businesses, but they cannot replace a Costa Rican worker in an employment situation. Each month, their $600 or $1000 must be converted into *colones* at approved banks, or twelve months–worth can be presented at the beginning of the year. These residents are not required to spend it all or to keep it in the bank—they just have to show that they have it. Receipts for currency exchange must be presented yearly. At one time this entitled *pensionados* and *rentistas* to import their belongings into the country duty-free, but that privilege no longer exists. Now taxes of up to 15 to 100 percent must be paid on shipments of household furniture, appliances, and vehicles—the same taxes Costa Ricans would pay on imported items.

Once you get your residency, your *carnet* must be renewed every two years, at a cost of $100-$200/card. After two years in Costa Rica as a *pensionado* or *rentista,* you may apply for permanent residency, which means you can be employed.

If all of this sounds complicated, expensive, and frustrating, it is. However, it's just the tip of the iceberg if you want to live or do business in Costa Rica. Do not plan to make your residency application yourself unless you have plenty of patience to deal with lines, national holidays, lunch breaks, misunderstandings, offices that have moved from where they were a month ago, impossible-to-find phone numbers, and so on. If you've got comfortable shoes and love to meditate or read novels while waiting in line, you'll find *trámites* (bureaucratic machinations) just your cup of tea. If you are nervous and impatient or have fallen arches, you will suffer.

Presently, there are about 5000 bona fide *pensionado* and *rentista* families living in Costa Rica. Potential residents will want to visit the **Asociación de Residentes de Costa Rica** (Avenida 4, Calle 40, San José; 233-8068, 221-2053, fax: 233-1152; www.casacanada.net/arcr, e-mail: arcr@casa canada.net). The association provides a number of services for its members, including help with various residency *trámites*; help with shipping and customs; mail and courier service; property title searches; discounted home, car, and medical insurance; professional references; and social events. They work to protect privileges and rights of foreign residents through lobbying and by filing lawsuits when necessary. For $735-$1000 per filer, plus $265 for spouse and $105 per child (private lawyers charge $1500 and up), the association's contracted specialists will see potential residents through the lengthy approval process for *pensionado* or *rentista* status. They will not obtain your personal documents for you, nor will they handle translation or authentication by Costa Rican consulates; you should gather your documents before leaving home. Contact them, or visit their website before leaving home for an up-to-date list of what you will need.

Christopher Howard of **Relocational and Retirement Consultants** (www.liveincostarica.com) offers similar services, but provides more personalized help.

WAYS TO WORK

The Costa Rican government doesn't want foreigners to take jobs from Costa Ricans. Therefore, most foreigners are not allowed to work unless they are performing a task that Ticos cannot do. But with some thought, you might be able to discover a skill you have that will help you establish temporary residency (*residencia temporal*). Qualified teachers are needed at the English-, French-, Japanese-, and German-speaking schools in San José. English teachers are often needed by the various language institutes. The National Symphony needs musicians; *The Tico Times* needs reporters. You would be surprised at how many gorgeous, isolated eco-tourism projects need bilingual people with managerial experience—many educated Ticos are not willing to live so far from "civilization."

Doctors, lawyers, architects, and engineers are plentiful here and are protected by powerful professional associations that make entry difficult for foreigners.

Retired businessmen can join the **International Executive Service Corps**, a private, nonprofit firm that helps local businesses and institutions upgrade technologies, productivity, and management skills. Volunteers must apply at the skills bank in the U.S. (P.O. Box 10005, Stamford, CT 06904; 203-967-6000, fax: 203-324-2531; www.iesc.org, e-mail: asantiago@mail. iesc.org). The office in San José cannot process volunteers; you must apply before arriving in Costa Rica. Volunteers are paid living expenses and transportation only. Contact the U.S. office of IESC for addresses of similar organizations worldwide.

LEGAL ADVICE

If you live here and have a business or buy land, sooner or later you will need to hire a lawyer. Here are our guidelines for choosing one in Costa Rica:

Shop around. There is usually no charge for meeting and consulting with a lawyer. Find someone you respect and can communicate with easily. Often your paperwork will be handled by law students working in the lawyer's office, and they will be the ones you end up having to communicate with, so be sure to meet them, too. Probably the most important person to have a trusting relationship with is the secretary. Some lawyers are always "not there" or "in a meeting" according to their secretaries. You can call for *weeks* and never get to talk to them.

Get recommendations from other residents, including the Residents Association, above. Find a lawyer in the field you are interested in with whom people have had positive experiences. Licenciado X may be a terrific international lawyer, but you can bet his specialty isn't residencies, so don't expect him to be good at it.

Legal fees vary greatly. Some very good lawyers charge more because they know that what they do is far superior to the run of the mill. If you have the money, it is worth every penny to have a good lawyer here. Of course, just because a lawyer charges more does not mean he is good. Some very reliable lawyers are not all that expensive.

Most legal work does not get done unless you keep tabs on your lawyer. Educate yourself on rules and regulations. Do not sit back and expect that everything is humming along now that Licenciado X has your affairs in his capable hands. Check and double-check; ask to see receipts; ask to see your *expediente* (file). Watch out if the lawyer tells you *"Tranquilo. No hay problema. No se preocupe."* ("Relax. No problem. Don't worry.") This is Costa Rican for "Don't make me think about it."

Whether you have a good lawyer or a mediocre one, things take a long time to get done here. So, as long as you know that things are *en trámite*, enjoy the relaxed pace and take a couple of long weekends yourself.

The Legal Guide to Costa Rica ($25 including postage from Centro Legal R & M, S.A., Interlink 553, P.O. Box 025635, Miami, FL 33152; 256-6395, fax: 233-2507; e-mail: crlaws@racsa.co.cr) offers translations of laws governing immigration, wills, intellectual property, social security, marriage, the environment, and taxes. The updated second edition includes chapters on landlord/tenant laws and tourism incentives, as well as regulations governing establishment of new businesses and powers of attorney. Updates to the book appear at www.costaricalaw.com.

REAL ESTATE AND INVESTMENTS

According to an article in *The Tico Times,* ". . . the potential investor in Costa Rica should beware of *all* glib, 'fact-filled,' English-speaking promoters flogging *anything*, whether it's gold mines, beach property, condominiums, agribusiness, or mutual funds. Costa Rica has long been a haven for con artists whose favorite targets are trusting newcomers. This doesn't mean, however, that legitimate investment opportunities don't exist, in agribusiness as well as in other areas. Investors here, like everywhere else, are advised simply to move cautiously, ask lots of questions, and check with well-established, reputable companies before parting with any money. That way, investors can be confident of making a good choice."

Know that any land within 200 meters of the high tide line on the beach is public and cannot be legally owned. You can "buy" it and build on it only after meeting a series of prerequisites and dealing with the local municipality, often a hotbed of corruption and greed.

Owning land and houses anywhere in Costa Rica can transform it from paradise into living hell unless you follow a few rules of thumb: Hire a lawyer you trust before undertaking any transaction. Always place deposit money in an escrow account; never give it to the seller or the seller's attorney. Beware of being an absentee landlord or business-owner. It doesn't work.

For real estate and business opportunities, you might subscribe to *The Tico Times* (see below).

The **American Chamber of Commerce of Costa Rica** (open 8 a.m. to 5 p.m.; Sabana Norte, 300 meters to the northeast of ICE; 220-2200, fax: 220-2300; www.amcham.co.cr, e-mail: chamber@amcham.co.cr) publishes *Guide to Investing and Doing Business in Costa Rica* ($22), which contains information on taxation, infrastructure, insurance, the stock exchange, banking, immigration, real estate, investments, free-trade zones, and retirement.

RENTING

Houses and apartments in San José rent from about $300 per month and up. The less expensive places are on the eastern side of San José, near the University, while rents in the upscale western neighborhoods of Rohrmoser and Escazú can range from $1000 to $5000 per month. "Unfurnished" usually means without stove or refrigerator as well as without furniture. Many houses and apartments have telephones, but if they don't, you will have to pay a hefty installation fee, and wait sometimes weeks for the phone to be installed. It's smart to consider the aparthotels listed in our San José hotel section. They are completely furnished (even with dishes), secure, and quite reasonably priced.

As you will see from the cagelike appearance of most houses, Costa Ricans do not trust each other very much, and you shouldn't either. Most people do not leave their homes unoccupied at all. That means you have to pay a maid or housesitter if you want to go away for an evening or a weekend, unless your house is very secure. Currently, $1.25 to $1.50 per hour is considered good pay for maids and housesitters. Neighbors can tell you what the incidence of robberies is in your area, and having a good neighbor who will watch out for you is invaluable. You might want to ask the landlord to change the lock before you move in. Gated communities are becoming popular among foreigners and Tico professionals. Most of them are being built in the towns of San Antonio de Belén, La Garita, Santa Ana, and Ciudad Colón in the western Central Valley.

Beach rentals are around $1200 a week or $3600 a month for a three-bedroom house in Tamarindo or Flamingo; slightly more if there is a pool. Many internet realtors handle rentals as well. More inexpensive rentals (sometimes as little as $250/week) can be found on the Caribbean coast. See **www. greencoast.com.**

DRIVER'S LICENSE

After three months in Costa Rica, your home country's driver's license expires. To get a Tico license, visit the MOPT license bureau at Avenida 18, Calle 7 in San José. Bring your passport and residence permit, your license, and a copy of the license. When you get to the neighborhood, visit one of the seedy-looking "doctor's offices," where you have to obtain a *dictamen médico,* a form confirming that you are physically fit to drive. After a five-minute exam, the doctor will sign it and take your $9. Once you get to the bureau, it should take you another $9 and two to three hours to negotiate the multiple lines and counters. If you speak basic Spanish and aren't afraid to ask directions about what to do next, you probably don't need to pay one of the "guides" who fish for customers at the entrance.

SCHOOLS

Costa Rica has free public education, but few foreigners are content to send their children to public schools. Like most government institutions, the schools are understaffed. Teachers are underpaid, classrooms are crowded, infrastructure is lacking, and there is an emphasis on boring, repetitive, rote learning. Even parents who feel their children might be "enriched" by the experience of being in a completely Spanish-speaking classroom usually end up at English-speaking or bilingual private schools after a few weeks. Ticos who can afford it also send their kids to private schools, where students are of many races and nationalities. According to Mavis Biesanz's book *The Ticos,* one in five Costa Rican students attends private school.

Many parents want their children to come away from Costa Rica speaking Spanish. Spanish lessons from native speakers are included in the curriculum at English-speaking schools. Children are also often motivated to learn Spanish by the friendships they make at school or in their neighborhood. In other words, they will learn some Spanish without having to be subjected to the public school system.

The English-language private schools are excellent, and many parents feel their children are more academically stimulated here than in the public schools at home. These schools follow the U.S. academic year and prepare students for acceptance in foreign as well as Costa Rican universities. The European School and Lincoln School are members of the International Baccalaureate Program. Students earning an IBP diploma may be awarded up to a year of university credit in the U.S.

The American International School in Costa Rica. Prekinder through grade 12. West of Cariari Country Club, Alajuela; 293-2567, fax: 239-0625; www.cra.ed.cr, e-mail: aiscr@cra.ed.cr

Country Day School. Prekinder through grade 12. Escazú; 289-8406, fax: 228-2076; www.cds.ed.cr. This large school with many extracurricular activities is about to open a branch in Playa Flamingo

The European School. Prekinder through grade 12. Emphasis on humanities, literature-based curriculum, International Baccalaureate Degree. Heredia; 261-0717, fax: 261-0718; e-mail: eurschool@cafebritt.com

International Christian School. Prekinder through grade 12. San Miguel de Santo Domingo de Heredia; 236-7879

Kiwi Learning Center. For children 18 months to seven years. Santa Ana; 282-6512; www.edenia.com/kiwi, e-mail: kiwi@edenia.com

Marian Baker School. Preparatory through grade 12. San Ramón de Trés Ríos, east of San José; 273-3426, fax: 273-4609; e-mail: mbschool@racsa.co.cr

Monteverde Friends School. Prekinder through high school. Monteverde; 645-5302; e-mail: mfschool@racsa.co.cr

Bilingual private schools are usually less expensive; they also prepare students for U.S. college acceptance. They follow the Costa Rican academic year, which begins in March and ends in November, unless otherwise indicated.

Anglo-American School. Primary and secondary. Barrio Escalante; Apdo. 3188, 1000 San José; 225-1729, 225-1723, fax: 234-7813

Blue Valley School. Primary through grade 8. Escazú; Apdo. 1745-2050, San Pedro Montes de Oca; phone/fax: 228-0551

Centro de Educación Creativa. Prekinder through 8th grade. Ecology-based curriculum (see "Monteverde" section) Apdo. 23-5655, Monteverde, Puntarenas; phone/fax: 645-5161; www.iac.net/~cecclc, e-mail: cecclc@racsa.co.cr. Runs year-round, with one-week breaks every six weeks, and six-week vacations in June–July and December–January

Colegio Humboldt. Prekinder through grade 12. Classes in German, English, and Spanish. Pavas; 232-1455, fax: 232-0093; www.infoweb.co.cr/humboldt

Colegio Británica (The British School). Kinder through grade 12. Pavas; Apdo. 3184, 1000 San José; 220-0131, 220-0719, fax: 232-7833; e-mail: britsch@racsa.co.cr

Lincoln School. Prekinder through grade 12. Montessori used in early childhood education, International Baccalaureate Degree. Moravia; 236-7733; www.lincoln.ed.cr, e-mail: director@ns.lincoln.ed.cr

The School of Rasur. Preschool through elementary holistic education in San Rafael de Escazú; 228-5475

LABOR RELATIONS FOR DOMESTIC HELP

All domestic employees have the right to social security benefits from the Caja Costarricense de Seguro Social, maternity benefits set by the Ministry of Labor, a workplace risk policy from the Instituto Nacional de Seguros, a Christmas bonus, and severance pay.

Whether live-in or not, a domestic employee is entitled to the minimum wage set by the Ministry of Labor (257-8211). However, this wage is disastrously low—about $125 per month at current rates of exchange. Ask around for the going rate in your neighborhood. Domestic help can be required to work not more than 8 hours a day. The employee has a day off each week, a 15-day paid vacation after 50 weeks of continual service, and paid days off on January 1, Holy Thursday, Good Friday, April 11 (Juan Santamaría Day), May 1 (Labor Day), July 25 (Annexation of Guanacaste Day), September 15 (Independence Day), and December 25. If an employee works these days, then double time must be paid. Days off should be previously scheduled.

New employees must be registered with the Caja, in the fifth-floor Department of Inspections (Avenida 2, Calles 5/7; 223-9890). The employer (or an authorized representative) must bring identification, such as a passport or residency *cédula*, a photocopy of the employee's *cédula*, an old electric bill to verify the address, and the facts about the job and wages. The employer then receives a monthly bill, which is used to make the payments to the Caja (22 percent of the monthly wages). Employees receive a paper giving them the right to the Caja's services (health care, maternity care, pensions). The monthly payment may be made by a messenger. If you lack a messenger, lines at the Caja seem shortest between 10:45 and 11:15 a.m.

A pregnant employee is entitled to one month off before the baby's birth and three months afterwards, with half of her monthly wage and *caja* payment. Pregnancy is not a legal reason for dismissal.

The *aguinaldo* (Christmas bonus) is paid to all employees. If an employee has worked all year, the *aguinaldo* is equivalent to one-and-a-half month's salary. If the employee has worked more than one month but less than a year, add up the total earned between December 1 and November 30, divide by 12, then multiply by 1.5. The result will be the *aguinaldo* you owe to your employee. Employees who have worked less than three months are not legally entitled to an *aguinaldo*. Most employers pay the *aguinaldo* early in December.

If the employer has cause to dismiss an employee, the employee must be paid unused vacation time, the proportionate *aguinaldo*, and all wages due. The employer must also document the dismissal with the *Caja*. If the employer must lay off help for reasons other than performance (i.e., leaving the country), employees must be given prior notice, unused vacation pay, the *aguinaldo*, and wages due, plus severance pay (one month's pay for every year of work). Should an employee decide to leave, the employer is not obligated to pay severance pay.

HEALTH CARE

The Social Security system makes low-cost medical care available to those who need it, but its clients must deal with long lines, short appointments, and delays lasting months between referral and delivery for x-rays, ultrasounds, operations, and other diagnostic treatment services. Doctors also have their private practices in the afternoons. A gynecological exam including Pap test costs around $30; a sonogram costs about $30; a complete cardiac stress exam runs about $70. Dental care is also considerably less expensive here. All of the above services are available to foreigners. Facelifts and other plastic surgeries cost a fraction of what they do elsewhere, and postoperative care is also a lot cheaper. Consult *The Tico Times* for advertisements or check out www.cocori.com/healthtourcr on the web.

Well-qualified alternative medicine practitioners such as acupuncturists, homeopaths, chiropractors, and massage therapists are also available in Costa Rica and charge less than their northern counterparts. Check *The Tico Times*. Homeopaths are listed in the phone directory.

There are several English-speaking chapters of AA, CODA, and NA in Costa Rica. They list meetings in "Weekend" section of *The Tico Times*.

One thing that few retirees take into consideration is that in Costa Rica it is illegal to refuse life-supporting devices such as respirators.

RESOURCES

There are several books written especially for *extranjeros* trying to forge a new life in Costa Rica: *The Golden Door to Retirement and Living in Costa*

Rica by Chris Howard is a handbook with good everyday tips. Look for it in most hotel bookshops, at www.liveincostarica.com and www.costaricabooks. com, or send $17.95 plus $3 postage to Costa Rica Books, Suite 1SJO981, P.O. Box 025216, Miami, FL 33102. *Choose Costa Rica* by John Howells is available in U.S. and Costa Rican bookstores or through www.discovery press.com.

See our guide to Costa Rica on the Internet at the beginning of the Planning Your Trip Chapter.

RECOMMENDED READING

BOOKS

Abrams, Harry. *Between Continents, Between Seas: Precolumbian Art of Costa Rica*. New York: Detroit Institute of Arts, 1981. A coffee-table book.

Baker, Bill. *The Essential Road Guide for Costa Rica*. Florida: International Marketing Partners, 1994. (Order for 19.80 from International Marketing Partners, 104 Half Moon Circle, Suite H-3, Hypoluxo, FL 33462; 800-881-8607.) A comprehensive, detail-oriented guide for drivers.

Barrientos, Zaidett, and J. Monge Nájera. *The Biodiversity of Costa Rica*. San José: INBio, 1995. (Available in San José bookstores, or contact INBio at Apdo. 22-3100, Santo Domingo de Heredia, fax: 244-2816; www.inbio. ac.cr.) This small, bilingual paperback has lots of photos and entertaining anecdotes about Costa Rica's flora and fauna.

Bell, John. *Crisis in Costa Rica: The 1948 Revolution*. Austin: The University of Texas Press, 1971. History of the 1948 civil war.

Biesanz, Mavis, Richard, and Karen. *The Costa Ricans*. Prospect Heights, IL: Waveland Press, Inc., 1988. A sympathetic portrayal of traditional Costa Rican culture.

Biesanz, Mavis and Richard. *The Ticos: Culture and Social Change in Costa Rica*. Lynne Rienner, 1998. A new and fun-to-read look at Costa Rican culture from Doña Mavis, who has been observing Ticos since the 1940s. Available by calling 228-1811, fax: 228-6184, or through www.biesanz. com/book.

Boza, Mario. *Costa Rica National Parks*. San José: Editorial Heliconia, 1992. Beautiful photographs of the national parks in hardbound and softbound Spanish and English editions.

Carr, Archie. *The Windward Road: Adventures of a Naturalist on Remote Caribbean Shores*. Gainesville, FL: University Press of Florida, 1979. The book that inspired the worldwide turtle conservation movement.

Chavarría-Aguilar, O.L. *A Bite of Costa Rica.* San José: Gallo Pinto Press, 1994. Recipes for *comida típica*, including tamales, empanadas, and *sopa negra.*

Cornelius, Stephen E. *The Sea Turtles of Santa Rosa National Park.* San José: Fundación de Parques Nacionales, 1985. Pictures and notes on turtle research.

Costa Rican–American Chamber of Commerce. *The Guide to Investing and Doing Business in Costa Rica.* San José: Costa Rican–American Chamber of Commerce. (Order from the publisher: Apdo. 4946-1000, San José, Costa Rica; 220-2200, fax: 220-2300; e-mail: chamber@amcham.co.cr.) A useful book for anyone considering investing in Costa Rica.

DeVries, Philip. *The Butterflies of Costa Rica and Their Natural History.* Princeton University Press, 1997. A color-filled volume about butterflies.

The Ecotourism Society. *Ecotourism Guidelines for Nature Tour Operators.* Vermont: The Ecotourism Society, 1993. (Order from The Ecotourism Society, P.O. Box 755, North Bennington, VT 05257; www.ecotourism. org.) An international standard of ethics and practices for nature tour operators, established by the industry's most prominent experts.

Edelman, Marc, and Joanne Kenen, eds. *The Costa Rica Reader.* New York: Grove Atlantic, 1989. A collection of essays by Costa Rican experts.

Gallo, Rafael and Michael Mayfield. *The Rivers of Costa Rica: A Canoeing, Kayaking, and Rafting Guide.* Menasha Ridge Press, 1992. Color photographs, maps, hydrographic tables of the Costa Rican rivers.

Gingold, Andy and Avie. *Let's Discover Costa Rica.* (Order from A. Gingold, Apdo. 1-6100 Mora, Ciudad Colón, Costa Rica; 249-1179, fax: 249-1107; e-mail: agingold@racsa.co.cr.) This beautifully done bilingual coloring and activity book tells the story of an English-speaking brother and sister and their Costa Rican friend.

Gómez, Luis Diego. *Vegetación y Clima en Costa Rica.* San José: UNED, 1987. Two volumes of nature study by Costa Rica's top botanist.

Hidalgo, Carmen. *Birds of the Rain Forest: Costa Rica.* San José: Trejos Hermanos Sucesores, S.A., 1996. (Order by fax: 224-1528; $50 plus shipping.) A beautiful coffee-table book.

Howard, Chris. *The Golden Door to Retirement and Living in Costa Rica.* California: Costa Rica Books, 1999. Order from www.costaricabooks.com, or send $17.95 plus $3 postage to Costa Rica Books, Suite 1SJO981, P.O. Box 025216, Miami, FL 33102. An informative guide for potential retirees.

Janzen, Daniel, ed. *Costa Rican Natural History.* Chicago: University of Chicago Press, 1983. The undisputed bible of Costa Rican ecology, with 174 biologist contributors covering almost everything there is to know about the subject. Entertaining and well-written. Also published in Spanish.

LeFever, Harry G. *Turtle Bogue: Afro-Caribbean Life and Culture in a Costa Rican Village.* New Jersey: Susquehanna University Press, 1992. An oral history and description of life in Tortuguero.

Lindberg, Kreg, and Donald Hawkins. *Ecotourism: A Guide for Planners and Managers.* Vermont: The Ecotourism Society, 1993. A collection of well-written essays and papers on how to best plan ecotourism projects so they fulfill their mandate to protect the environment and benefit local people.

Miller, Kenton, and Laura Tangley. *Trees of Life: Saving Tropical Forests and Their Biological Wealth.* Boston: Beacon Press, 1991.

Moser, Don. *Central American Jungles.* New York: Time Life Books, 1975. Beautiful photos by Co Rentmeester and interesting poetic, anecdotal descriptions of many Central American habitats.

Norman, David. *Costa Rican Wildlife Natural History and Conservation, A Set of Educational Pamphlets.* Well-written, illustrated pamphlets on species like quetzals, leatherback turtles, agoutis, etc., available inexpensively in Costa Rican bookstores or from the author at Apdo. 387-3000, Heredia. Also available is *An Educational Coloring Book of Costa Rican Wildlife.*

Palmer, Paula. *What Happen: A Folk-History of Costa Rica's Talamanca Coast.* San José: Publications in English, 1993. Distributed by Zona Tropical, 256-8251, e-mail: marroca@racsa.co.cr. A revised edition of the classic oral history of the Afro-Caribbean Talamancans.

Palmer, Sanchez, Mayorga. *Taking Care of Sibö's Gifts, an Environmental Treatise.* San José: Asociación de Desarrollo Integral de la Reserva Indígena Cocles/Kéködi, 1991. Distributed by Zona Tropical (see above). The Kéködi tribe writes about their stewardship of nature.

Perry, Donald. *Life Above the Jungle Floor.* San José: Don Perro Press, 1991. Account of this biologist's quest for the canopy, including a number of well-explained new theories of evolution. Fifty-two color photographs; well-written and accessible to lay readers.

Pritchard, Ray. *Driving the Panamerican Highway to Mexico and Central America.* Thousand Oaks, CA: Costa Rica Books (www.costaricabooks.com), 1996. Provides routing and preparation information for a U.S.–Costa Rica road trip.

Ras, Barbara. *Costa Rica: A Traveler's Literary Companion.* San Francisco: Whereabouts Press, 1994. An excellent English translation of short stories by Costa Rica's best writers.

Skutch, Alexander. *Trogons, Laughing Flacons, and Other Neotropical Birds.* Texas A&M University Press, 1999. Now 95 years old, Costa Rica's master birder, author of 25 other books, describes the behavior of the trogon family, which includes the resplendent quetzal.

Stiles, Gary F., and Alexander Skutch. *A Guide to the Birds of Costa Rica*. Ithaca, NY: Cornell University Press, 1990. *The* birder's guide to Costa Rica. Illustrated by Dana Gardner. See companion audiotape, below.

Vilchez, Ricardo. *All Costa Rica*. Barcelona: Escudo de Oro, 1999. A collection of 179 photographs illustrating Costa Rica's history, archaeology, geography, architecture, beaches, parks, and more.

PERIODICALS

Costa Rica Outdoors. A full-color monthly devoted to fishing and outdoor adventure. Edited and published by Jerry Ruhlow, long-term resident and fishing expert. 800-308-3394, phone/fax: 282-6743; www.costaricaoutdoors. com, e-mail: jruhlow@racsa.co.cr.

Mesoamérica. Published monthly by the Institute for Central American Studies, Apdo. 300, 1002 San José, Costa Rica; phone/fax: 234-7682; www. amerisol.com/costarica/edu, e-mail: mesoamer@racsa.co.cr.

The Tico Times. The best way to keep up with what is happening in Costa Rica. Apdo. 4632, San José. 258-1558, fax: 233-6378; www.ticotimes.co.cr.

AUDIO FIELD GUIDES FOR BIRDERS
AND NATURALISTS

The Cornell Laboratory of Ornithology's Library of Natural Sounds has several audiotapes that can help you identify birds and animals in the wild:

Costa Rican Bird Song Sampler has the songs of 180 bird species arranged by habitat. A booklet provides the page and plate numbers for the species as they are found in *A Guide to the Birds of Costa Rica* by Stiles, Skutch and Gardner (see "Books," above).

Voices of Costa Rican Birds: Caribbean Slope, a two-CD set containing 225 species, the largest compilation available.

Voices of the Cloud Forest, a CD of sounds from a day in the Monteverde Cloud Forest Preserve. Sounds of cloud forest denizens are identified at the end.

Sounds of Neotropical Rainforest Mammals is an audio companion to the book *Neotropical Rainforest Mammals* by Louise H. Emmons. Disc One features primates, Disc Two has all other mammals.

You can get copies of these recordings through www.clarityconnect.com/webpages3/dross or through the Cornell Lab of Ornithology's **Wild Birds Unlimited** store (607-266-7425; http://birds.cornell.edu/lns).

VIDEOS

Costa Rica Unica! A comprehensive and intelligent look at Costa Rican culture and tourist destinations like Manuel Antonio, Monteverde, Talamanca, Guayabo, Sarchí, and Guanacaste: one hour, Mentor Productions, P.O. Box 1148, San Clemente, CA 92674, or order through Costa Rica Books, 800-365-2342; www.costaricabooks.com.

Index

Lodging Index

LODGING SERVICES

Dining Index

Notes from the Publisher

An alert, adventurous reader is as important as a travel writer in keeping a guidebook up-to-date and accurate. So if you happen upon a great restaurant, discover a hidden locale, or (heaven forbid) find an error in the text, we'd appreciate hearing from you. Just write to:

Ulysses Press
P.O. Box 3440
Berkeley, CA 94703
www.ulyssespress.com
e-mail: readermail@ulyssespress.com

It is our desire as publishers to create guidebooks that are responsible as well as informative. We hope that our guidebooks treat the people, country, and land we visit with respect. We ask that our readers do the same. The hiker's motto, "Walk softly on the Earth," applies to travelers everywhere . . . in the desert, on the beach, and in town.

We Need Your Help!

We have done the best we could to evaluate "eco-tourism" projects that agreed to participate in our sustainable eco-tourism survey. But we need your help to monitor those on our list, add new lodgings, and check on those that have made improvements since our last visit. As you travel through Costa Rica, keep your eyes open for positive and negative environmental, cultural, and economic impacts of the eco-tourism-oriented hotels you visit. Hotel owners may be more open with you. You might catch things that we couldn't in our brief interview.

Please fill out this form or write to us. We promise to follow up on your tips, and if you request, we will be happy to write back to you and let you know what we have done with your suggestions. Your comments will help us determine the lodging facilities that are truly making extra-special efforts to have a positive effect on the environment and culture of Costa Rica, and thus deserve to be recognized in The New Key.

POSSIBLE ADDITION TO THE SUSTAINABLE TOURISM LIST:

Name of hotel: _____

Location: _____

Phone/fax (if there is one): _____

What environmental, sociocultural, and/or economic practices made you feel the lodging facility should be recognized?

POSSIBLE DELETION FROM THE SUSTAINABLE TOURISM LIST:

Name of hotel: _____

Location: _____

Phone/fax (if there is one): _____

What environmental, sociocultural, and/or economic practices made you feel this lodging facility should not be on our list?

Mail to: Publications in English, Apdo. 7-1230, 1000 San José, CR

You're already helping!

Simply by purchasing *The New Key to Costa Rica*,
you have helped preserve Costa Rica's environment

Would you like to do more?

At Ulysses Press, we believe that eco-tourism can have a positive impact
on a region's environment and can actually help preserve its natural state.
In line with this philosophy, we donate a percentage of the sales from all New
Key guides to conservation organizations working in the destination country—in Costa Rica, our environmental partner is the Resource Foundation.

The Resource Foundation, a nonprofit membership organization founded
in 1987, is working through its Costa Rican affiliate, Arbofilia (Asociación
Protectora de Árboles), to improve agricultural productivity and assist low-
income rural families, while at the same time protecting natural resources
and promoting conservation.

The target area is near Carara Biological Reserve, in the central part of
Costa Rica, on the west coast near the Pacific Ocean. From an ecological
standpoint, the area lies between the northern limits of the South American
tropical rainforests and the beginnings of the dry forests of Mesoamerica. It
has a number of major rivers that supply water for many important communities in the Central Pacific region.

Ulysses Press encourages you to further support this organization. For
more information, or to make a donation, contact:

The Resource Foundation
P.O. Box 3006
Larchmont, NY 10538
phone/fax: 914-834-5810
e-mail: resourcefnd@msn.com

HIDDEN GUIDES

Adventure travel or a relaxing vacation?—"Hidden" guidebooks are the only travel books in the business to provide detailed information on both. Aimed at environmentally aware travelers, our motto is "Adventure Travel Plus." These books combine details on unique hotels, restaurants and sightseeing with information on camping, sports and hiking for the outdoor enthusiast.

THE NEW KEY GUIDES

Based on the concept of eco-tourism, The New Key Guides are dedicated to the preservation of Central America's rare and endangered species, architecture and archaeology. Filled with helpful tips, they give travelers everything they need to know about these exotic destinations.

Order Form

HIDDEN GUIDEBOOKS

____ Hidden Arizona, $14.95

____ Hidden Bahamas, $14.95

____ Hidden Baja, $14.95

____ Hidden Belize, $15.95

____ Hidden Boston and Cape Cod, $13.95

____ Hidden British Columbia, $17.95

____ Hidden Cancún & the Yucatán, $16.95

____ Hidden Carolinas, $17.95

____ Hidden Coast of California, $17.95

____ Hidden Colorado, $14.95

____ Hidden Disneyland, $13.95

____ Hidden Florida, $17.95

____ Hidden Florida Keys & Everglades, $12.95

____ Hidden Georgia, $16.95

____ Hidden Guatemala, $16.95

____ Hidden Hawaii, $18.95

____ Hidden Idaho, $14.95

____ Hidden Maui, $13.95

____ Hidden Montana, $14.95

____ Hidden New England, $18.95

____ Hidden New Mexico, $14.95

____ Hidden Oahu, $13.95

____ Hidden Oregon, $14.95

____ Hidden Pacific Northwest, $18.95

____ Hidden San Francisco & Northern California, $18.95

____ Hidden Southern California, $17.95

____ Hidden Southwest, $18.95

____ Hidden Tahiti, $17.95

____ Hidden Tennessee, $15.95

____ Hidden Utah, $16.95

____ Hidden Walt Disney World, $13.95

____ Hidden Washington, $14.95

____ Hidden Wine Country, $13.95

____ Hidden Wyoming, $14.95

THE NEW KEY GUIDEBOOKS

____ The New Key to Costa Rica, $17.95

____ The New Key to Ecuador and the Galápagos, $16.95

Mark the book(s) you're ordering and enter total here ⟹ [____]

California residents add 8% sales tax here ⟹ [____]

Shipping: Check box for preferred method and enter cost here ⟹ [____]

❏ Book Rate   **FREE! FREE! FREE!**

❏ Priority Mail $3.20 first book, $1.00/each additional book

❏ UPS 2-Day Air $7.00 first book, $1.00/each additional book

[____]

Billing: Enter total amount due here and check method of payment ⟹

❏ Check   ❏ Money Order

❏ VISA/MasterCard _____ Exp. Date_____

Name_____Phone _____

Address_____

_____

City _____ State _____ Zip_____

Money-back guarantee on direct orders placed through Ulysses Press.

ABOUT THE AUTHORS

Beatrice Blake lived in Costa Rica for 12 years. In 1985 she rewrote *The New Key to Costa Rica*, which her late mother Jean Wallace had originally published in 1978, and has updated it yearly since then. Beatrice now resides in East Blue Hill, Maine, with her husband Dennis Moran, and children Danny and Elizabeth.

Anne Becher is a freelance journalist and translator (M.A., Hispanic Linguistics). In addition to co-authoring *The New Key to Costa Rica*, she co-edits a bilingual literary magazine, *Selvática*, and writes reference books for publisher ABC-Clio. She has traveled the full length of the Americas by land; she now lives in Boulder, Colorado with her husband and their two children.

ABOUT THE PHOTOGRAPHER

For more than 25 years British-born photographer Nik Wheeler has documented the world from Vietnam to the Seychelles. His many books include *Return to the Marshes of Iraq*, *Cloud Dwellers of the Himalayas*, and *This is China*. He is a regular contributor to leading travel magazines such as *Islands*, *Gourmet*, and *Travel Holiday*. He currently lives in Montecito with his wife and three sons.

ABOUT THE ILLUSTRATOR

Deidre Hyde is an illustrator working out of Costa Rica. A graduate of the University of Reading, England, with a degree in Fine Arts and Philosophy, her work has taken her throughout Central and South America, West Africa, and Spain. Her main focus is on conservation themes and she works closely with conservation groups such as World Wildlife Fund. Hyde is painting for conservation.